AN OUTLINE OF

PSYCHOANALYSIS

AN OUTLINE OF
PSYCHOANALYSIS

REVISED EDITION

EDITED BY Clara Thompson, M.D.,

Milton Mazer, M.D. AND Earl Witenberg, M.D.

THE MODERN LIBRARY · NEW YORK

LIBRARY OF CONGRESS CATALOG CARD NUMBER: 55-6392

Random House IS THE PUBLISHER OF The Modern Library
BENNETT A. CERF   DONALD S. KLOPFER   ROBERT K. HAAS
Manufactured in the United States of America
By H. Wolff

CONTENTS

I THEORY

Freud's Formulations

The Study of the Ego

Anxiety

Dreams

Childhood

The Study of Character

Contents

II THERAPY

Goals of Therapy

Transference and Countertransference

The Psychoanalytic Process

FOREWORD

In 1924 the Modern Library published a collection of important psychoanalytic contributions entitled *Outline of Psychoanalysis* edited by J. S. van Teslaar. At that time psychoanalysis was just beginning to be a subject of interest to the informed layman. The book was timely and represented well the theoretical and practical contributions of psychoanalysis up to that point. But psychoanalysis has continued to grow and change since that time. It has entered new fields of study of the human personality and a vast literature has accumulated. In 1924 in the United States only one psychoanalytic journal existed, while today at least five journals published quarterly are devoted to the field of psychoanalysis. In addition, two psychiatric journals also publish psychoanalytic articles from time to time. There are many new books presenting the subject both for those in the professional field and for the informed layman. The task of collecting an anthology is therefore much more arduous than it was in 1924, and, although it has not been possible to include writings from all the outstanding contributors to present-day psychoanalysis, an attempt has been made to make the volume truly representative of psychoanalytic thinking today.

An anthology serves a special purpose. By presenting the views of many authors it gives the reader an opportunity to see and evaluate for himself the many approaches which go to make up a science such as psychoanalysis. In this anthology we attempt to bring the reader up to date. We have especially emphasized the changes in theory and therapeutic goals which have developed in the last thirty years.

INTRODUCTION

The Development of Psychoanalysis

If psychiatry was once called the stepchild of medicine, psychoanalysis was certainly the stepchild of psychiatry. One of Freud's bitter disappointments in the early years of his work was the lack of interest and often open hostility for his theories on the part of his medical colleagues. Today this has disappeared in most informed medical circles. Instruction in psychoanalytic theory has become a part of the curricula of many medical schools as well as of other graduate departments of universities. Its principles are used by social workers, teachers, lawyers and ministers as well as by psychologists and psychiatrists. Psychoanalysis has gained the attention of the public. It has achieved a position not only of popularity but of respect and status. At the same time it has continued to be a growing expanding science. There have been far-reaching changes in its theory, therapeutic techniques and goals of treatment. Its various stages have developed out of the preceding ones as knowledge of the dynamics of the human personality has grown.

It is now nearly seventy years since Freud first started his study of the causes and cure of the neuroses. In 1885, after making important contributions to organic neurology, Freud became interested in the functional neuroses. After brief study with Charcot, the outstanding hypnotist of his time, he became associated with Breuer in Vienna and continued his efforts to cure functional neuroses by hypnosis. The two men came to the conclusion that neurotic symptoms were produced by the repression of unpleasant or painful memories or affects. These repressed experiences, seemingly forgotten, remained unconscious, influencing the personality until they were brought back into consciousness and re-experienced under the influence of hypnosis.

In many cases this caused the symptoms to disappear. However, it sometimes happened that a patient could not be hypnotized. In the course of trying to help such a person Freud and the patient made the discovery of the psychoanalytic method of *free association* which remains one of the chief tools of psycho-analytic inquiry, although more active techniques have also been developed. In free association the patient reports without censor-ship whatever goes through his mind. No exceptions are to be made; it matters not whether the thoughts are painful, em-barrassing, inconsequential or important. All must be said. If this is done results similar to those achieved under hypnosis are obtained. It soon became apparent that free association was a very difficult thing to persuade a patient to do. Interruptions of the flow of associations repeatedly occurred. Freud soon recog-nized these as *resistances* and concluded that resistance was pro-duced by the same sort of attitude which had caused the patient to put the experience out of his mind in the first place. Thus shame, guilt, fear of disapproval seemed especially potent mo-tives for forgetting and/or blocking the attempt to recall. Freud concluded from his cases that repression of early sexual experi-ence could always be shown to be the cause of the neurosis. At first he thought that the sexual traumata reported by his patients were genuine, but about 1900 he began to doubt this; at least it was apparent that not all people suffering from neurosis had been exposed to actual sexual traumata.

This led him to an investigation of the sexual life of the child and to his discoveries of the erotic component in the pregenital activities of children which have had a far-reaching effect on the understanding and education of children. However, when the pregenital sex life of the patient becomes the main focus of therapy it tends to concentrate his attention on reconstructing his past at the expense of understanding his disturbed present. Neither the past nor the present should be the main interest of the psychoanalyst. The terms themselves imply a dichotomy that does not exist, for personality is an evolving continuum.

Freud gradually succeeded in interesting some fertile minds in his theories. Among them were Abraham, Adler, Ferenczi, Jones, and Jung, to mention only a few. But Adler and Jung were skeptical of some of Freud's theories, especially his theory of the sexual etiology of the neuroses. By 1910 their disagreements were becoming more obvious. Freud himself was beginning to turn his attention to an aspect of the personality which he had neglected until this time, the self-preservation (or ego) drive. From this point on psychoanalysis concerned itself less with symptoms and more with understanding the total personality. Adler made a significant contribution to this although his approach was oversimplified. He was the first pupil of Freud to disagree with him so extensively that they could no longer work together. He left the Freudian group in 1911 and established his own school. Adler differed with Freud in two main respects: he denied the importance of sex in the etiology of the neuroses and in its place he saw the "will to power" as the great neurosis-producing drive in man. He thought that the goals that the individual was seeking were more potent sources of difficulty than traumatic experiences in the past. Thus he placed relatively little emphasis on the recall of early childhood experiences and a great deal of emphasis on the current motivations. In a sense he was the first person to suggest a method of character analysis. Jung's disagreement with Freud also centered around denial of the sexual etiology of the neuroses. He saw libido as a vital force not necessarily sexual in origin. He felt that Freud had not sufficiently stressed the "higher" nature of man and he believed that many difficulties were due to inability to achieve "self-realization." He recognized the importance of early childhood but did not see the early ties to the parents as primarily sexual. Rather he saw the early dependency on the mother as based on her food-providing role. During the first years of his association with Freud he made contributions to Freudian theory but by 1913 his thinking differed so widely from Freud's that he left the Freudian group and eventually established his own school.

In the course of his study of the total personality, Freud began to note aspects of behavior which were not readily explained by his theory that man is dominated by the pleasure principle, namely, that he seeks constantly to free himself from tension and to achieve satisfaction. He also began to question whether repressed libido was the sole source of neurotic difficulties. He noted that not all cases of hostile and aggressive behavior could be explained as sadistic expression of the libido. He also observed that there was a tendency for people to get into the same types of difficulty repeatedly, that there seemed to be a tendency in man to repeat earlier experiences automatically irrespective of whether the experience was pleasant or painful. This drive seemed to be a stronger force than the pleasure principle. Freud named it the *repetition compulsion*. By 1920 his ideas of a new theory of the instincts became crystallized and were described in a book, *Beyond the Pleasure Principle*. In it he presented for the first time the idea of a death instinct which he saw as existing side by side with the life instinct. He postulated that these two forces are active from birth. The death instinct, which was a new idea, he saw as primarily a self-destructive force which could be prevented from destroying the individual in two ways. It might be turned outwards toward others in the form of hostility or aggression or it might unite with the life (sexual) instinct and become sadism or masochism. By thus erotizing the destructive force it lost some of its destructive power, he thought. Whether the theoretical explanation is correct or not, the scope of psychoanalytic investigation was greatly increased by bringing into prominence the importance of repressed aggression. The concept of the repetition compulsion proved to be another theory which was very useful therapeutically. At about the same time Freud clarified the function of the ego and divided the human personality into three parts, the ego, superego and id. The chapters in this book on Freud's basic formulations will further explain these changes.

Still another contribution of Freud's in the 1920's was a new theory of anxiety which is summarized in this volume by Rollo May. This theory stated clearly for the first time that the attempt to escape anxiety was at the root of every neurosis. Freud had noted earlier that anxiety was often present in neurosis but the theory of the dynamic interaction with neurotic symptoms was first presented in 1926. This discovery has formed the basis for later contributions to theory. The theory, expressed in very condensed form, is that anxiety tends to appear when the instinctual forces within a person threaten his relation to the outside world, that is, when he is threatened with loss of love, punishment (*castration* is the term used in classical Freudian literature) or social ostracism. In these situations the ego develops a defense against the anxiety, a defense designed to prevent the forbidden impulse from expressing itself. The protection may be a character trait or symptom.

It is seen, then, that in the 1920's Freud made several important new theoretical formulations which have helped to guide psychoanalytic research into new channels. The important new theories pertained to the function of the ego, the role of anxiety in character and symptom formation, the importance of repressed aggression in emotional disorder and the observation that people in general tend to repeat earlier patterns in their lives even when they are unpleasant or painful (the repetition compulsion).

Changes in therapeutic technique began to develop at about the same time, partly no doubt as a result of the changes in theory. A more active method than free association, first stated specifically by Reich, later somewhat modified and elaborated by Anna Freud, Sullivan and many others, was devised for the analysis of character. *Free association* was not discarded, but was seen as one of several possible tools of psychoanalytic treatment.

Another important change concerned the therapeutic use of transference. Freud started his work as a hypnotist. One of the basic necessities for successful hypnosis is that there should be no questioning of the authority of the therapist. The patient gets well because he is urged to improve. This attitude was taken over in the early days of psychoanalysis in the form of utilizing the positive transference of the patient to encourage him toward mental health. That is, the patient developed an exaggerated confidence in the doctor, making him a benevolent father figure; the doctor used this authority to lead the patient to "insight." Only when the patient became hostile, that is, had negative transference, was there an attempt to point out the irrationality of the attitude. The analyst utilized the patient's dependency as a means of helping him. This did not always produce the desired results and it often fostered dependencies which were difficult to resolve. In order to maintain his neutrality the analyst was advised to remain as nearly as possible a mirror, that is, to avoid any personal involvement, give no information about himself and sit behind the patient so that there were few clues to any reactions he might have. Ferenczi and Rank, in about 1925, were the first to point out, each in somewhat different ways, that the therapeutic results of analysis were comparatively unsatisfactory because analysis under these conditions was not a vital emotional experience. Rank pointed out the authoritarian nature of the method. He believed the cure lay in the direction of encouraging the patient to rebel against the analyst, to assert his counter will. By being able to struggle against the father authority (or mother authority), the patient would gain his independence.

Ferenczi also felt that the destruction of the infallible authoritarian position of the analyst was important. He suggested, as a means of bringing this about and making the analytic situation a more genuine emotional experience, greater frankness on the part of the analyst about himself and his attitudes. He should be more ready to admit any mistakes he might make and he should not try to work with a patient toward whom he could not feel a genuinely friendly attitude of acceptance. Among the contributions in this book those of Balint come closest to representing Ferenczi's approach. Ferenczi himself published almost nothing about the work of his later years.

Although there was considerable resistance among analysts to both Rank's and Ferenczi's ideas of the role of the therapist, the attitude toward the patient has been gradually shifting in the direction of their views. At least it has changed to the extent that the patient's dependency and transference are dealt with earlier in treatment and the analyst seeks to avoid and certainly does not encourage an authoritarian type of relationship. In the course of developing his "will" theory, Rank turned away from Freud's instinct theories and in 1925 left the Freudian group. In time he developed his own school.

By 1930 the findings of anthropologists in the study of comparative cultures began to interest a few psychoanalysts. Freud himself, in the latter part of the 1920's, had become interested in making some application of psychoanalysis to the study of society. Other analysts became interested in using the understanding of different cultures to examine the validity of Freudian theory. It became apparent to this group that some of man's behavior which Freud had thought biologically determined, that is, a part of innate human nature, is in fact a product of the Western culture and is not present in all societies. For example the latency period and the Oedipus complex found very frequently in our society are believed by most authorities not to be universal. The discovery that society is a constantly changing organization made by the people in it and at the same time molding their lives has led to increased interest in the interaction of people with each other. Sullivan's theory of interpersonal relations stresses this.

In the last twenty-five years much greater emphasis in therapy has been placed on understanding and altering the defensive behavior than on recalling memories of traumatic experiences of early childhood. There has been less stress on understanding the instinct life and more on understanding the defensive system than was the case in early psychoanalytic work. What is today recognized as the defense system of the ego was called *resistance* in the early years. Effort was exerted to overcome it either through suggestion or reassurance. Today understanding the dynamic function of the resistance is used as a means of studying the ego, observing how character is formed and how it can be changed. The changes in technique which accompany this new field of interest are less reliance on free association as a means of making conscious the unconscious, greater activity in pointing out the ways in which the patients defend themselves, and greater concern on the part of therapists about the impact of their own personalities in the analyst-patient relationship. This last area of research, the study of the importance of the *countertransference,* is currently a subject of great interest. It is the topic about which Ferenczi was talking in 1930. At that time openly discussing it with a patient was considered a dangerous and revolutionary practice. Today we have come to see that the analytic situation is an interpersonal one in which the impact of the analyst's personality can not and should not be ignored. In fact, his reactions have a positive role in curing the patient.

In this book we have attempted to present characteristic contributions not only of the classical Freudian school but of all other schools which have developed out of a Freudian background. The papers have been grouped under the important topics of psychoanalysis. With the exception of a few papers of great historical importance, the majority of the articles have been written in the last thirty years. In other words, this book is a presentation of psychoanalysis today. Thus under the heading "Freud's Formulations" we have Freud's own review of his life work as he looked back on it just before his death. The papers on "The Study of the Ego" are all relatively recent, Reich's being the oldest. This is the first formulation of a technique for understanding ego defenses. Under "Anxiety" we have included two contemporary writers who together cover the writings on the subject, stressing Freud's second theory of anxiety, the foundation on which later theories have been developed.

The most comprehensive and classical work on the interpretation of dreams is Freud's famous book, written in the 1890's. Ella Sharpe presents the present standard Freudian view but Jung's contribution has seemed to the editors also noteworthy. The papers on "Childhood" are all of very recent origin. Anna Freud was one of the first contributors in this field, as was Melanie Klein. Their contributions have influenced the writers represented.

"The Study of Character" is in a sense but an extension of "The Study of Ego." Under this heading are presented conclusions drawn from clinical material while the earlier topic considered theories about the structure and function of the ego. The first paper in this section goes back to 1908, presenting Freud's first formulation of the subject. Adler's contribution as well as Abraham's also antedates the modern era of intensive ego psychology.

As I have already pointed out, the goals of psychoanalytic treatment have varied in the course of seventy years. Under the topic "Goals" in this book only the modern approach is emphasized since the earlier views on the subject are chiefly of historical interest.

"Transference and Countertransference" presents the two topics of great interest in psychoanalysis at the present time. The papers in this section explore these phenomena in their contemporary setting, at the same time pointing out their dynamic roots in the past.

Finally, in "The Psychoanalytic Process" we have attempted to present papers which will add to the understanding of the analytic process as a method of therapy.

The tremendous literature of psychoanalysis makes it impossible for any one volume to provide a complete and comprehensive account of the field. What this volume does present, we trust, is a coherent selection of contributions which will engage the interest of the reader and whet his appetite for further explorations.

I

THEORY

Freud's Formulations

The discovery of the essential building stones of psychoanalysis —psychic determinism, the unconscious, the significance of dreams, the importance of infancy and early childhood in personality development, and the transference and countertransference phenomena—is due to the genius of Sigmund Freud. These cardinal clinically observable facts are the bases of any theory of psychoanalysis. They are universally accepted.

The theoretical framework within which Freud has incorporated these concepts is the libido theory. Depending on their interpretation of the term "libido," this theory has been utilized by many analysts in many ways; some have continued to accept it in its original form and have added minor concepts which for them explain additional observations; others have emphasized its foundation in nineteenth-century physics and have proposed theoretical formulations more in accord with the conceptions of contemporary physics. Still others have objected to the formulation of the instincts as the sole source of energy and have proposed another source, namely the ego.

Influenced by research in sociology and anthropology, some workers have abandoned the libido concept entirely and have attempted to formulate systems which can be tested operationally.

The first presentation is taken from the last book written by Freud—these chapters give a concise and readable statement of the libido theory, a definition of the term "sexual," and his approach to mental phenomena.

1

SIGMUND FREUD

The Theory of the Instincts*

The power of the id expresses the true purpose of the individual
organism's life. This consists in the satisfaction of its innate
needs. No such purpose as that of keeping itself alive or of protecting itself from dangers by means of anxiety can be attributed
to the id. That is the business of the ego, which is also concerned
with discovering the most favorable and least perilous method
of obtaining satisfaction, taking the external world into account.
The superego may bring fresh needs to the fore, but its chief
function remains the *limitation* of satisfactions.

The forces which we assume to exist behind the tensions
caused by the needs of the id are called *instincts*. They represent
the somatic demands upon mental life. Though they are the
ultimate cause of all activity, they are by nature conservative;
the state, whatever it may be, which a living thing has reached,
gives rise to a tendency to re-establish that state so soon as it has
been abandoned. It is possible to distinguish an indeterminate
number of instincts and in common practice this is in fact done.
For us, however, the important question arises whether we may
not be able to derive all of these various instincts from a few
fundamental ones. We have found that instincts can change their
aim (by displacement) and also that they can replace one another—the energy of one instinct passing over to another. This
latter process is still insufficiently understood. After long doubts

* Reprinted from *An Outline of Psychoanalysis* by Sigmund Freud, by per-
mission of W. W. Norton & Company, Inc. and The Hogarth Press, Ltd.
Copyright 1949 by W. W. Norton & Company, Inc. Translated by James
Strachey.

and vacillations we have decided to assume the existence of only two basic instincts, *Eros* and *the destructive instinct*. (The contrast between the instincts of self-preservation and of the preservation of the species, as well as the contrast between ego-love and object-love, fall within the bounds of Eros.) The aim of the first of these basic instincts is to establish ever greater unities and to preserve them thus—in short, to bind together; the aim of the second, on the contrary, is to undo connections and so to destroy things. We may suppose that the final aim of the destructive instinct is to reduce living things to an inorganic state. For this reason we also call it the *death instinct*. If we suppose that living things appeared later than inanimate ones and arose out of them, then the death instinct agrees with the formula that we have stated, to the effect that instincts tend toward a return to an earlier state. We are unable to apply the formula to Eros (the love instinct). That would be to imply that living substance had once been a unity but had subsequently been torn apart and was now tending toward re-union.[1]

In biological functions the two basic instincts work against each other or combine with each other. Thus, the act of eating is a destruction of the object with the final aim of incorporating it, and the sexual act is an act of aggression having as its purpose the most intimate union. This interaction of the two basic instincts with and against each other gives rise to the whole variegation of the phenomena of life. The analogy of our two basic instincts extends from the region of animate things to the pair of opposing forces—attraction and repulsion—which rule in the inorganic world.[2]

Modifications in the proportions of the fusion between the instincts have the most noticeable results. A surplus of sexual aggressiveness will change a lover into a sexual murderer, while a sharp diminution in the aggressive factor will lead to shyness or impotence.

There can be no question of restricting one or the other of the

---

[1] Something of the sort has been imagined by poets, but nothing like it is known to us from the actual history of living substance.

[2] This picture of the basic forces or instincts, which still arouses much opposition among analysts, was already a familiar one to the philosopher Empedocles of Acragas.

basic instincts to a single region of the mind. They are necessarily present everywhere. We may picture an initial state of things by supposing that the whole available energy of Eros, to which we shall henceforward give the name of *libido,* is present in the as yet undifferentiated ego-id and serves to neutralize the destructive impulses which are simultaneously present. (There is no term analogous to "libido" for describing the energy of the destructive instinct.) It becomes relatively easy for us to follow the later vicissitudes of the libido; but this is more difficult with the destructive instinct.

So long as that instinct operates internally, as a death instinct, it remains silent; we only come across it after it has become diverted outward as an instinct of destruction. That that diversion should occur seems essential for the preservation of the individual; the musculature is employed for the purpose. When the superego begins to be formed, considerable amounts of the aggressive instinct become fixated within the ego and operate there in a self-destructive fashion. This is one of the dangers to health to which mankind become subject on the path to cultural development. The holding back of aggressiveness is in general unhealthy and leads to illness. A person in a fit of rage often demonstrates how the transition from restrained aggressiveness to self-destructiveness is effected, by turning his aggressiveness against himself: he tears his hair or beats his face with his fists— treatment which he would evidently have preferred to apply to someone else. Some portion of self-destructiveness remains permanently within, until it at length succeeds in doing the individual to death, not, perhaps, until his libido has been used up or has become fixated in some disadvantageous way. Thus it may in general be suspected that the *individual* dies of his internal conflicts but that the *species* dies of its unsuccessful struggle against the external world, when the latter undergoes changes of a kind that cannot be dealt with by the adaptations which the species has acquired.

It is difficult to say anything of the behavior of the libido in the id and in the superego. Everything that we know about it relates to the ego, in which the whole available amount of libido is at first stored up. We call this state of things absolute, primary *narcissism.* It continues until the ego begins to cathect[3] the presentations of objects with libido—to change narcissistic libido into *object libido.* Throughout life the ego remains the great reservoir from which libidinal cathexes[3] are sent out on to objects and into which they are also once more withdrawn, like the pseudopodia of a body of protoplasm. It is only when someone is completely in love that the main quantity of libido is transferred on to the object and the object to some extent takes the place of the ego. A characteristic of libido which is important in life is its *mobility,* the ease with which it passes from one object to another. This must be contrasted with the *fixation* of libido to particular objects, which often persists through life.

There can be no question that the libido has somatic sources, that it streams into the ego from various organs and parts of the body. This is most clearly seen in the case of the portion of the libido which, from its instinctual aim, is known as sexual excitation. The most prominent of the parts of the body from which this libido arises are described by the name of *erotogenic zones,* though strictly speaking the whole body is an erotogenic zone. The greater part of what we know about Eros—that is, about its exponent, the libido—has been gained from the study of the sexual function, which, indeed, in the popular view, if not in our theory, coincides with Eros. We have been able to form a picture of the way in which the sexual impulse, which is destined to exercise a decisive influence on our life, gradually develops out of successive contributions from a number of component instincts, which represent particular erotogenic zones.

---

[3] [The words "cathexis" and "to cathect" are used as renderings of the German "*Besetzung*" and "*besetzen.*" These are the terms with which Freud expresses the idea of psychical energy being lodged in or attaching itself to mental structures or processes, somewhat on the analogy of an electric charge. —Trans.]

2

SIGMUND FREUD

The Development of the
Sexual Function*

According to the popular view, human sexual life consists essentially in the impulse to bring one's own genitals into contact with those of someone of the opposite sex. With this are associated, as accessory phenomena and introductory acts, kissing this extraneous body, looking at and touching it. This impulse is supposed to make its appearance at puberty, that is, at the age of sexual maturity, and to serve the purposes of reproduction. Nevertheless, certain facts have always been known that fail to fit into the narrow framework of this view. (1) It is a remarkable fact that there are people who are only attracted by the persons and genitals of members of their own sex. (2) It is equally remarkable that there are people whose desires behave in every way like sexual ones, but who at the same time entirely disregard the sexual organs or their normal use; people of this kind are known as "perverts." (3) And finally it is striking that many children (who are on that account regarded as degenerates) take a very early interest in their genitals and show signs of excitation in them.

It may well be believed that psychoanalysis provoked astonishment and denials when, partly upon the basis of these three neglected facts, it contradicted all the popular opinions upon sexuality. Its principal findings are as follows:

* Reprinted from *An Outline of Psychoanalysis* by Sigmund Freud, by permission of W. W. Norton & Company, Inc. and The Hogarth Press, Ltd. Copyright 1949 by W. W. Norton & Company, Inc.

(*a*) Sexual life does not begin only at puberty, but starts with clear manifestations soon after birth.

(*b*) It is necessary to distinguish sharply between the concepts of "sexual" and "genital." The former is the wider concept and includes many activities that have nothing to do with the genitals.

(*c*) Sexual life comprises the function of obtaining pleasure from zones of the body—a function which is subsequently brought into the service of that of reproduction. The two functions often fail to coincide completely.

The chief interest is naturally focused upon the first of these assertions, the most unexpected of all. It has been found that in early childhood there are signs of bodily activity to which only ancient prejudice could deny the name of sexual, and which are connected with mental phenomena that we come across later in adult love, such as fixation to a particular object, jealousy, and so on. It is further found that these phenomena which emerge in early childhood form part of a regular process of development, that they undergo a steady increase and reach a climax toward the end of the fifth year, after which there follows a lull. During this lull, progress is at a standstill and much is unlearned and undone. After the end of this period of latency, as it is called, sexual life is resumed with puberty, or, as we might say, it has a second efflorescence. Here we come upon the fact that the onset of sexual life is *diphasic,* that it occurs in two waves; this is unknown except in man and evidently has an important bearing upon his genesis.[1] It is not a matter of indifference that, with few exceptions, the events of the early period of sexuality fall a victim to *infantile amnesia.* Our understanding of the etiology of the neuroses and the technique of analytic therapy are derived from these views; and the tracing of the process of development in this early period has also provided evidence for yet other conclusions.

---

[1] Cf. the hypothesis that man is descended from a mammal which reached sexual maturity at the age of five, but that some great external influence was brought to bear upon the species and interrupted the straight line of development of sexuality. This may also have been related to some other transformations in the sexual life of man as compared with that of animals, such as the suppression of the periodicity of the libido and the exploitation of the part played by menstruation in the relation between the sexes.

The first organ to make its appearance as an erotogenic zone and to make libidinal demands upon the mind is, from the time of birth onward, the mouth. To begin with, all mental activity is centered upon the task of providing satisfaction for the needs of that zone. In the first instance, of course, the latter serves the purposes of self-preservation by means of nourishment; but physiology should not be confused with psychology. The baby's obstinate persistence in sucking gives evidence at an early stage of a need for satisfaction which, although it originates from and is stimulated by the taking of nourishment, nevertheless seeks to obtain pleasure independently of nourishment and for that reason may and should be described as "sexual."

Sadistic impulses already begin to occur sporadically during the oral phase along with the appearance of the teeth. Their extent increases greatly during the second phase, which we describe as the sadistic-anal phase, because satisfaction is then sought in aggression and in the excretory function. We justify our inclusion of aggressive impulses in the libido by supposing that sadism is an instinctual fusion of purely libidinal and purely destructive impulses, a fusion which thenceforward persists without interruption.[2]

The third phase is the so-called phallic one, which is, as it were, a forerunner of the final shape of sexual life, and already greatly resembles it. It is to be noted that what comes in question at this stage is not the genitals of both sexes but only those of the male (the phallus). The female genitals long remain unknown: in the child's attempt at understanding sexual processes, he pays homage to the venerable cloacal theory—a theory which has a genetic justification.[3]

With the phallic phase and in the course of it the sexuality of early childhood reaches its height and approaches its decline.

---

[2] The question arises whether satisfaction of purely destructive instinctual impulses can be felt as pleasure, whether pure destructiveness without any libidinal component occurs. Satisfaction of what remains in the ego of the death instinct seems not to produce feelings of pleasure, although masochism represents a fusion which is precisely analogous to sadism.

[3] The occurrence of early vaginal excitations is often asserted. But it is most probably a question of excitations in the clitoris, that is, in an organ analogous to the penis, so that this fact would not preclude us from describing the phase as phallic.

Thenceforward boys and girls have different histories. To begin with, both place their intellectual activity at the service of sexual research; both start off from the presumption of the universal presence of the penis. But now the paths of the sexes divide. The boy enters the Œdipus phase; he begins to manipulate his penis, and simultaneously has phantasies of carrying out some sort of activity with it in relation to his mother; but at last, owing to the combined effect of a threat of castration and the spectacle of women's lack of a penis, he experiences the greatest trauma of his life, and this introduces the period of latency with all its attendant consequences. The girl, after vainly attempting to do the same as the boy, comes to recognize her lack of a penis or rather the inferiority of her clitoris, with permanent effects upon the development of her character; and, as a result of this first disappointment in rivalry, she often turns away altogether from sexual life.

It would be a mistake to suppose that these three phases succeed one another in a clear-cut fashion: one of them may appear in addition to another, they may overlap one another, they may be present simultaneously.

In the earlier phases the separate component instincts set about their pursuit of pleasure independently of one another; in the phallic phase there are the first signs of an organization which subordinates the other trends to the primacy of the genitals and signifies the beginning of a co-ordination of the general pursuit of pleasure into the sexual function. The complete organization is not attained until puberty, in a fourth, or genital, phase. A state of affairs is then established in which (1) many earlier libidinal cathexes are retained, (2) others are included in the sexual function as preparatory or auxiliary acts, their satisfaction producing what is known as fore-pleasure, and (3) other tendencies are excluded from the organization, and are either entirely suppressed (repressed) or are employed in the ego in some other way, forming character-traits or undergoing sublimation with a displacement of their aims.

This process is not always carried out perfectly. Inhibitions in the course of its development manifest themselves as the various disturbances of sexual life. Fixations of the libido to conditions at earlier phases are then found, the trend of which, moving independently of the normal sexual aim, is described as *perversion*. One example of an inhibition in development of this kind is homosexuality, if it is manifest. Analysis shows that in every case a homosexual attachment to an object has at one time been present and in most cases has persisted in a latent condition. The situation is complicated by the fact that the processes necessary for bringing about a normal outcome are not for the most part either completely present or completely absent; they are as a rule *partially* present, so that the final result remains dependent upon *quantitative* relations. Thus genital organization will be attained, but will be weakened in respect of those portions of the libido which have not proceeded so far but have remained fixated to pregenital objects and aims. Such weakening shows itself in a tendency, if there is an absence of genital satisfaction or if there are difficulties in the real world, for the libido to return to its earlier pregenital cathexes (*i.e.* to *regress*).

During the study of the sexual functions it has been possible to gain a first, preliminary conviction, or rather suspicion, of two p▮▮▮ knowledge which will later be found to be important o▮ the whole of our field. Firstly, the normal and abnormal phenomena that we observe (that is, the phenomenology of the subject) require to be described from the point of view of dynamics and of economics (*i.e.,* in this connection, from the point of view of the quantitative distribution of the libido). And secondly, the etiology of the disturbances which we are studying is to be found in the developmental history of the individual, that is to say, in the early part of his life.

3

SIGMUND FREUD

Mental Qualities*

We have described the structure of the psychical apparatus and
the energies or forces which are active in it, and we have followed
in a striking example the way in which those energies (and
principally the libido) organize themselves into a physiological
function which serves the purpose of the preservation of the
species. There was nothing in all this to exemplify the quite
peculiar character of what is mental, apart, of course, from the
empirical fact that this apparatus and these energies underlie the
functions which we call our mental life. We will now
something which is a unique characteristic of what is mental, and
which, in fact, according to a widely held opinion, actually coincides with it to the exclusion of all else.

The starting point for this investigation is provided by a fact
without parallel, which defies all explanation or description—the
fact of consciousness. Nevertheless, if anyone speaks of consciousness, we know immediately and from our own most personal experience what is meant by it.[1] Many people, both inside
and outside the science of psychology, are satisfied with the
assumption that consciousness alone is mental, and nothing then
remains for psychology but to discriminate in the phenomenology
of the mind between perceptions, feelings, intellective processes

---

* Reprinted from An Outline of Psychoanalysis by Sigmund Freud, by permission of W. W. Norton & Company, Inc. and The Hogarth Press, Ltd.
Copyright 1949 by W. W. Norton & Company, Inc.
[1] Extreme lines of thought, such as the American doctrine of behaviorism,
think it possible to construct a psychology which disregards this fundamental
fact.

14

and volitions. It is generally agreed, however, that these conscious processes do not form unbroken series which are complete in themselves; so that there is no alternative to assuming that there are physical or somatic processes which accompany the mental ones and which must admittedly be more complete than the mental series, since some of them have conscious processes parallel to them but others have not. It thus seems natural to lay the stress in psychology upon these somatic processes, to see in *them* the true essence of what is mental and to try to arrive at some other assessment of the conscious processes. The majority of philosophers, however, as well as many other people, dispute this position and declare that the notion of a mental thing being unconscious is self-contradictory.

But it is precisely this that psychoanalysis is obliged to assert, and this is its second fundamental hypothesis. It explains the supposed somatic accessory processes as being what is essentially mental and disregards for the moment the quality of consciousness. It does not stand alone in this opinion. Many thinkers (such as Theodor Lipps, for instance) have made the same assertion in the same words. And the general dissatisfaction with the usual view of what is mental has resulted in an ever more urgent demand for the inclusion in psychological thought of a concept of the unconscious, though the demand has been of such an indefinite and vague nature that it could have no influence upon science.

Now it might appear as though this dispute between psychoanalysis and philosophy was only concerned with a trifling matter of definition—the question whether the name "mental" should be applied to one or another series of phenomena. Actually, however, this step has been of the greatest importance. Whereas the psychology of consciousness never went beyond this broken sequence of events which was obviously dependent upon something else, the other view, which held that what is mental is in itself unconscious, enabled psychology to take its place as a natural science like any other. The processes with which it is concerned are in themselves just as unknowable as those dealt with by the other sciences, by chemistry or physics, for example; but it is possible to establish the laws which those processes obey and to follow over long and unbroken stretches their mutual relations and interdependences—in short, to gain what is known as an "understanding" of the sphere of natural phenomena in question. This cannot be effected without framing fresh hypotheses and creating fresh concepts; but these are not to be despised as evidence of our embarrassment but must on the contrary be valued as enriching science. We can claim for them the same value as approximations as belongs to the corresponding intellectual scaffolding found in other natural sciences, and we look forward to their being modified, corrected and more precisely determined as more experience is accumulated and sifted. So too it will be entirely in accordance with our expectations if the basic concepts and principles of the new science (instinct, nervous energy, etc.) remain for a considerable time no less indeterminate than those of the older sciences (force, mass, attraction, etc.).

Every science is based upon observations and experiences arrived at through the medium of our psychical apparatus. But since *our* science has as its subject that apparatus itself, the analogy ends here. We make our observations through the medium of the same perceptual apparatus, precisely by the help of the breaks in the series of [conscious] mental events, since we fill in the omissions by plausible inferences and translate them into conscious material. In this way we construct, as it were, a series of conscious events complementary to the unconscious mental processes. The relative certainty of our mental science rests upon the binding force of these inferences. Anyone who goes deeply into the subject will find that our technique holds its ground against every criticism.

In the course of our work the distinctions which we denote as *mental qualities* force themselves on our attention. There is no need to characterize what we call *conscious:* it is the same as the consciousness of philosophers and of everyday opinion. Everything else that is mental is in our view *unconscious*. We are soon led to make an important division in this unconscious. Some processes become conscious easily; they may then cease to be conscious, but can become conscious once more without any trouble: as people say, they can be reproduced or remembered. This reminds us that consciousness is in general a very highly fugitive condition. What is conscious is conscious only for a moment. If our perceptions do not confirm this, the contradiction is merely an apparent one. It is explained by the fact that the stimuli of perception can persist for some time, so that in the course of it the perception of them can be repeated. The whole position can be clearly seen from the conscious perception of our intellective processes; it is true that these may persist, but they may just as easily pass in a flash. Everything unconscious that behaves in this way, that can easily exchange the unconscious condition for the conscious one, is therefore better described as "capable of entering consciousness," or as *preconscious*. Experience has taught us that there are hardly any mental processes, even of the most complicated kind, which cannot on occasion remain preconscious, although as a rule they press forward, as we say, into consciousness. There are other mental processes or mental material which have no such easy access to consciousness, but which must be inferred, discovered, and translated into conscious form in the manner that has been described. It is for such material that we reserve the name of the unconscious proper.

Thus we have attributed three qualities to mental processes: they are either conscious, preconscious, or unconscious. The division between the three classes of material which have these qualities is neither absolute nor permanent. What is preconscious becomes conscious, as we have seen, without any activity on our part; what is unconscious can, as a result of our efforts, be made conscious, though in the process we may have an impression that we are overcoming what are often very strong resistances. When we make an attempt of this kind upon someone else, we ought not to forget that the conscious filling up of the breaks in his perceptions—the construction which we are offering him—does not so far mean that we have made conscious in him the unconscious material in question. All that is so far true is that the material is present in his mind in two versions, first in the conscious reconstruction that he has just received and secondly in its original unconscious condition. By persistent efforts we usually succeed in bringing it about that this unconscious material too becomes conscious to him, as a result of which the two versions come to coincide. The amount of effort needed, by which we estimate the resistance against the material becoming conscious, varies in magnitude in each individual case. For instance, what comes about in an analytic treatment as the result of our efforts can also occur spontaneously: material which is ordinarily unconscious can transform itself into preconscious and then into conscious material—a thing that happens upon a large scale in psychotic states. From this we may infer that the maintenance of certain internal resistances is a *sine qua non* of normality. A lowering of resistances of this sort, with a consequent pressing forward of unconscious material, takes place regularly in the state of sleep and thus brings about a necessary precondition for the formation of dreams. On the other hand, preconscious material can become temporarily inaccessible and cut off by resistances, as on occasions of passing forgetfulness, or a preconscious thought can actually be temporarily pushed back into the unconscious condition, as seems to be necessary in the case of jokes. We shall see that a similar reversion of preconscious material or processes to the unconscious condition plays a great part in the causation of neurotic disorders.

The theory of the three qualities of mental events, as described in this generalized and simplified manner, seems likely to be a source of endless confusion rather than a help to clarification. But it must not be forgotten that it is properly not a theory at all, but a first attempt at a stock-taking of the facts of our observation, that it keeps as close as possible to those facts and does not seek to explain them. The complications which it reveals may bring into relief the peculiar difficulties with which our investigation has to contend. It seems likely however that we shall learn more about the subject if we follow out the relations between the mental qualities and the provinces or agencies which we have postulated in the mental apparatus—though these relations too are far from being simple.

The process of a thing becoming conscious is above all linked with the perceptions which our sense organs receive from the external world. From the topographical point of view, therefore, it is a phenomenon which occurs in the outermost cortex of the ego. It is true that we also receive conscious information from the inside of the body—the feelings, which actually exercise a more peremptory influence upon our mental life than external perceptions; moreover, in certain circumstances the sense organs themselves transmit feelings, sensations of pain, in addition to the perceptions which are specific to them. Since, however, these feelings (as we call them, in contrast to conscious perceptions) also emanate from the terminal organs, and since we regard all of those organs as prolongations or offshoots of the cortex, it is still possible to maintain the assertion made at the beginning of this paragraph. It need only be said by way of distinction that, as regards the terminal organs of *feeling,* the body itself takes the place of the external world.

Conscious processes on the periphery of the ego and everything else in the ego unconscious—such would be the simplest state of affairs that we might picture. And such may in fact be the conditions prevailing in animals. But in men there is an added complication owing to which internal processes in the ego may also acquire the quality of consciousness. This complication is produced by the function of speech, which brings the material in the ego into a firm connection with the memory-traces of visual and more particularly of auditory perceptions. Thenceforward the perceptual periphery of the cortex of the ego can be stimulated to a much greater extent from inside as well; internal events such as sequences of ideas and intellective processes can become conscious; and a special apparatus becomes necessary in order to distinguish between the two possibilities—that is, what is known as *reality-testing*. The equation "perception = reality (external world)" no longer holds. Errors, which can now easily arise and do in fact habitually arise in dreams, are called *hallucinations*.

The inside of the ego, which comprises above all the intellective processes, has the quality of being preconscious. This is characteristic of the ego and belongs to it alone. It would not be right, however, to assert that a connection with the memory-traces of speech is a prerequisite of the preconscious condition. On the contrary, that condition does not depend upon any such prerequisite, although the presence of speech gives a safe clue to the preconscious nature of a process. The preconscious condition, which is characterized on the one hand by having access to consciousness and on the other hand by being linked with the verbal residues, is nevertheless something peculiar, the nature of which is not exhausted by these two characteristics. The proof of this is that large portions of the ego, and in particular of the superego, which cannot be denied the characteristic of being preconscious, none the less remain for the most part unconscious in the phenomenological sense of the word. We do not know why this must be so. We shall attempt later on to attack the problem of the true nature of the preconscious.

The sole quality that rules in the id is that of being unconscious. Id and unconscious are as intimately united as ego and preconscious; indeed, the former connection is even more exclusive. If we look back at the developmental history of the individual and of his psychical apparatus, we shall be able to make an important distinction in the id. Originally, of course, everything was id; the ego was developed out of the id by the continual influence of the external world. In the course of this slow development certain material in the id was transformed into the preconscious condition and was thus taken into the ego. Other material remained unaltered in the id, as its hardly accessible nucleus. But during this development the young and feeble ego dropped and pushed back into the unconscious condition certain material which it had already taken in, and behaved similarly in regard to many new impressions which it *might* have taken in, so that these were rejected and were able to leave traces in the id only. In consideration of its origin, we term this portion of the id *the repressed*. It is of little importance that we are not always able to draw a sharp distinction between these two categories of material in the id. They coincide approximately with the division between what was originally present and what was acquired during the development of the ego.

Having now decided upon the topographical division of the mental apparatus into an ego and an id, with which the difference in quality between preconscious and unconscious runs parallel, and having agreed that this quality is only an *indication* of the distinction and does not constitute its essence, we are faced by a further question. What is the true nature of the condition which is disclosed in the case of the id by the quality of being unconscious and in the case of the ego by that of being preconscious, and in what does the distinction between them consist?

But of this we know nothing; and the profound obscurity of our ignorance is scarcely illuminated by a glimmer or two of light. For here we have approached the still shrouded secret of the nature of what is mental. We assume, as the other natural sciences have taught us to expect, that in mental life some kind of energy is at work; but we have no data which enable us to come nearer to a knowledge of it by an analogy with other forms of energy. We seem to recognize that nervous or psychical energy exists in two forms, one freely mobile and the other, by contrast, bound; we speak of cathexes and hypercathexes of the material of the mind and even venture to suppose that a hypercathexis brings about a sort of synthesis of different processes—a synthesis in the course of which free energy is transformed into bound energy. Further than this we have been unable to go. Nevertheless, we hold firmly to the view that the distinction between the unconscious and the preconscious condition also lies in dynamic relations of this same kind, which would explain how it is that, whether spontaneously or with our assistance, the one can be changed into the other.

But behind all of these uncertainties there lies one new fact, the discovery of which we owe to psychoanalytic research. We have learned that processes in the unconscious or in the id obey different laws from those in the preconscious ego. We name these laws in their totality the *primary process,* in contrast to the *secondary process* which regulates events in the preconscious or ego. Thus the study of mental qualities has after all proved not unfruitful in the end.

The Study of the Ego

The first great clinical and theoretical advances in psychoanalysis were in the study of the "id," the area that interested Freud primarily. It remains a tribute to his genius that the libidinal factors and their vicissitudes have been so thoroughly studied.

Both Glover and Alexander were among the first to describe neuroses in terms of character traits rather than symptoms and applied the term character neuroses to them. At the same time, it was realized that when psychoanalysis limited itself to making unconscious phenomena conscious it was a very inadequate therapeutic instrument.

As an inevitable development from Freud's work, the ego properly became the major field of study for analysts. Wilhelm Reich was the first to describe the importance of the defensive aspects of the ego in any systematic approach to therapy, while Anna Freud has added the same concepts to the theoretical framework of psychoanalysis. The study of the ego has remained a major preoccupation of many psychoanalysts. Hartmann, Kris, and Loewenstein are among the more notable contributors. Hartmann and Silverberg have suggested that the ego is autonomous as well as being dependent on the id—and French has in addition emphasized its integrative function.

Whatever the present state of the psychoanalytic theory of the ego, it is a pragmatic fact that analyses make progress only insofar as they clarify the defenses and resistances of the ego.

4

WILHELM REICH

On the Technique of Character-Analysis*

1. Introductory Review

Our therapeutic method is determined by the following basic theoretical concepts. The *topical* standpoint determines the technical principle that the unconscious has to be made conscious. The *dynamic* standpoint determines the rule that this has to take place not directly but by way of resistance analysis. The *economic* standpoint and the psychological structure determine the rule that the resistance analysis has to be carried out in a certain order according to the individual patient.

As long as the topical process, the making conscious of the unconscious, was considered the only task of analytic technique, the formula that the unconscious manifestations should be interpreted *in the sequence in which they appeared* was correct. The dynamics of the analysis, that is, whether or not the making conscious also released the corresponding affect, whether the analysis influenced the patient beyond a merely intellectual understanding, that was more or less left to chance. The inclusion of the dynamic element, that is, the demand that the patient should not only remember things but also experience them, already complicated the simple formula that one had to "make the unconscious conscious." However, the dynamics of the analytic affect do not depend on the contents but on the resistances which the patient

* First presented at the X. International Psychoanalytic Congress, Innsbruck, 1927. Reprinted by permission from *Character Analysis* (3d edition, New York, 1949). Copyright, 1949, Orgone Institute Press, Inc.

puts up against them and on the emotional experience in overcoming them. This makes the analytic task a vastly different one.
From the topical standpoint, it is sufficient to bring into the patient's consciousness, one after the other, the manifest·elements
of the unconscious; in other words, the guiding line is the *content* of the material. If one also considers the dynamic factor one
has to relinquish this guiding line in favor of another which comprehends the content of the material as well as the affects: that of
the *successive resistances*. In doing so we meet, in most patients,
with a difficulty which we have not yet mentioned.

2. Character Armor and Character Resistance

a) *The inability to follow the fundamental rule.*

Rarely are our patients immediately accessible to analysis,
capable of following the fundamental rule and of really opening
up to the analyst. They cannot immediately have full confidence
in a strange person; more importantly, years of illness, constant
influencing by a neurotic milieu, bad experiences with physicians,
in brief, the whole secondary warping of the personality have
created a situation unfavorable to analysis. The elimination of
this difficulty would not be so hard were it not supported by the
character of the patient which is part and parcel of his neurosis.
It is a difficulty which has been termed "narcissistic barrier."
There are, in principle, two ways of meeting this difficulty, in
especial, the rebellion against the fundamental rule.

One, which seems the usual one, is a direct education to analysis by information, reassurance, admonition, talking-to, etc. That
is, one attempts to educate the patient to analytic candor by the
establishment of some sort of positive transference. This corresponds to the technique proposed by Nunberg. Experience shows,
however, that this pedagogical method is very uncertain; it lacks
the basis of analytic clarity and is exposed to the constant variations in the transference situation.

The other way is more complicated and as yet not applicable
in all patients, but far more certain. It is that of *replacing the*

pedagogical measures by analytic interpretations. Instead of inducing the patient into analysis by advice, admonitions and transference manoeuvres, one focuses one's attention on the actual behavior of the patient and its meaning: *why* he doubts, or is late, or talks in a haughty or confused fashion, or communicates only every other or third thought, why he criticizes the analysis or produces exceptionally much material or material from exceptional depths. If, for example, a patient talks in a haughty manner, in technical terms, one may try to convince him that this is not good for the progress of the analysis, that he better give it up and behave less haughtily, for the sake of the analysis. Or, one may relinquish all attempts at persuasion and wait until one understands why the patient behaves in this and no other way. One may then find that his behavior is an attempt to compensate his feeling of inferiority toward the analyst and may influence him by consistent interpretation of the meaning of his behavior. This procedure, in contrast to the first-mentioned, is in full accord with the principle of analysis.

This attempt to replace pedagogical and similar active measures seemingly necessitated by the characteristic behavior of the patient, by purely analytic interpretations led unexpectedly to the analysis of the *character*.

Certain clinical experiences make it necessary to distinguish, among the various resistances we meet, a certain group as *character resistances.* They get their specific stamp not from their content but from the patient's specific way of acting and reacting. The compulsive character develops specifically different resistances than does the hysterical character; the latter different resistances from the impulsive or neurasthenic character. The *form* of the typical reactions which differ from character to character—though the contents may be the same—*is determined by infantile experiences just like the content of the symptoms or phantasies.*

b) Whence the character resistances?

Quite some time ago, Glover worked on the problem of differentiating character neuroses from symptom neuroses. Alexander also operated on the basis of this distinction. In my earlier writings, 1 also followed it. More exact comparison of the cases showed, however, that this distinction makes sense only insofar as there are neuroses with circumscribed symptoms and others without them; the former were called "symptom neuroses," the latter, "character neuroses." In the former, understandably, the symptoms are more obvious, in the latter the neurotic character traits. But, we must ask, are there symptoms without a neurotic reaction basis, in other words, without a neurotic character? The difference between the character neuroses and the symptom neuroses is only that in the latter the neurotic character also produced symptoms, that it became concentrated in them, as it were. If one recognizes the fact that the basis of a symptom neurosis is always a neurotic character, then it is clear that we shall have to deal with character-neurotic resistances in *every* analysis, that every analysis must be a character-analysis.

Another distinction which becomes immaterial from the standpoint of character-analysis is that between chronic neuroses, that is, neuroses which developed in childhood, and acute neuroses, which developed late. For the important thing is not whether the symptoms have made their appearance early or late. The important thing is that the neurotic character, the reaction basis for the symptom neurosis, was, in its essential traits, already formed at the period of the Oedipus phase. It is an old clinical experience that the boundary line which the patient draws between health and the outbreak of the disease becomes always obliterated during the analysis.

Since symptom formation does not serve as a distinguishing criterion we shall have to look for others. There is, first of all, insight into illness, and rationalization.

The lack of insight into illness is not an absolutely reliable but an essential sign of the character neurosis. The neurotic symptom is experienced as a foreign body and creates a feeling of being ill. The neurotic character trait, on the other hand, such as the exaggerated orderliness of the compulsive character or the anxious shyness of the hysterical character, are organically built into the personality. One may complain about being shy but does not feel ill for this reason. It is not until the characterological shyness turns into pathological blushing or the compulsion-neurotic orderliness into a compulsive ceremonial, that is, not until the neurotic character exacerbates symptomatically, that the person feels ill.

True enough, there are also symptoms for which there is no or only slight insight, things that are taken by the patient as bad habits or just peculiarities (chronic constipation, mild ejaculatio praecox, etc.). On the other hand, many character traits are often felt as illness, such as violent outbreaks of rage, tendency to lie, drink, waste money, etc. In spite of this, generally speaking, insight characterizes the neurotic symptom and its lack the neurotic character trait.

The second difference is that the symptom is never as thoroughly rationalized as the character. Neither a hysterical vomiting nor compulsive counting can be rationalized. The symptom appears meaningless, while the neurotic character is sufficiently rationalized not to appear meaningless or pathological. A reason is often given for neurotic character traits which would immediately be rejected as absurd if it were given for symptoms: "he just is that way." That implies that the individual was born that way, that this "happens to be" his character. Analysis shows this interpretation to be wrong; it shows that the character, for definite reasons, had to become that way and no different; that, in principle, it can be analyzed like the symptom and is alterable.

Occasionally, symptoms become part of the personality to such an extent that they resemble character traits. For example, a counting compulsion may appear only as part of general orderliness or a compulsive system only in terms of a compulsive work arrangement. Such modes of behavior are then considered as peculiarities rather than as signs of illness. So we can readily see that the concept of disease is an entirely fluid one, that there are all kinds of transitions from the symptom as an isolated foreign body over the neurotic character and the "bad habit" to rational action.

In comparison to the character trait, the symptom has a very simple construction with regard to its meaning and origin. True, the symptom also has a multiple determination; but the more deeply we penetrate into its determinations, the more we leave the realm of symptoms and the clearer becomes the characterological reaction basis. Thus one can arrive—theoretically—at the characterological reaction basis from any symptom. The symptom has its immediate determination in only a limited number of unconscious attitudes; hysterical vomiting, say, is based on a repressed fellatio phantasy or an oral wish for a child. Either expresses itself also characterologically, in a certain infantilism and maternal attitude. But the hysterical character which forms the basis of the symptom is determined by many—partly antagonistic—strivings and is expressed in a specific attitude or *way of being.* This is not as easy to dissect as the symptom; nevertheless, in principle it is, like the symptom, to be reduced to and understood from infantile strivings and experiences. While the symptom corresponds essentially to a single experience or striving, the character represents the specific way of being of an individual, an expression of his total past. For this reason, a symptom may develop suddenly while each individual character trait takes years to develop. In saying this we should not forget the fact that the symptom also could not have developed suddenly unless its characterological neurotic reaction basis had already been present.

The totality of the neurotic character traits makes itself felt in the analysis as a compact *defense mechanism* against our therapeutic endeavors. Analytic exploration of the development of this character "armor" shows that it also serves a definite economic purpose: on the one hand, it serves as a protection against the stimuli from the outer world, on the other hand against the inner libidinous strivings. The character armor can perform this task because libidinous and sadistic energies are consumed in the neurotic reaction formations, compensations and other neurotic attitudes. In the processes which form and maintain this armor, anxiety is constantly being bound up, in the same way as it is, according to Freud's description, in, say, compulsive symptoms. We shall have to say more later about the economy of character formation.

Since the neurotic character, in its economic function of a protecting armor, has established a certain *equilibrium,* albeit a neurotic one, the analysis presents a danger to this equilibrium. This is why the resistances which give the analysis of the individual case its specific imprint originate from this narcissistic protection mechanism. As we have seen, the mode of behavior is the result of the total development and as such can be analyzed and altered;

thus it can also be the starting point for evolving the technique of character-analysis.

c) The technique of analyzing the character resistance.

Apart from the dreams, associations, slips and other communications of the patients, their attitude, that is, *the manner* in which they relate their dreams, commit slips, produce their associations and make their communications, deserves special attention.[1] A patient who follows the fundamental rule from the beginning is a rare exception; it takes months of character-analytic work to make the patient halfway sufficiently honest in his communications. The manner in which the patient talks, in which he greets the analyst or looks at him, the way he lies on the couch, the inflection of the voice, the degree of conventional politeness, all these things are valuable criteria for judging the latent resistances against the fundamental rule, and understanding them makes it possible to alter or eliminate them by interpretation. The *how* of saying things is as important "material" for interpretation as is *what* the patient says. One often hears analysts complain that the analysis does not go well, that the patient does not produce any "material." By that is usually meant the content of associations and communications. But the manner in which the patient, say, keeps quiet, or his sterile repetitions, are also "material" which can and must be put to use. There is hardly any situation in which the patient brings "no material"; it is our fault if we are unable to utilize the patient's behavior as "material."

That the behavior and the form of the communications have analytic significance is nothing new. What I am going to talk about is the fact that these things present an avenue of approach to the analysis of the character in a very definite and almost perfect manner. Past failures with many cases of neurotic characters have taught us that in these cases the form of the communications is, at least in the beginning, always more important than

---

[1] *Footnote, 1945:* The *form* of expression is far more important than the *ideational content.* Today, in penetrating to the decisively important infantile experiences, we make use of the form of expression *exclusively.* Not the ideational contents but the form of expression is what leads us to the biological reactions which form the basis of the psychic manifestations.

their content. One only has to remember the latent resistances of the affect-lame, the "good," over-polite and ever-correct patients; those who always present a deceptive positive transference or who violently and stereotypically ask for love; those who make a game of the analysis; those who are always "armored," who smile inwardly about everything and everyone. One could continue this enumeration indefinitely; it is easy to see that a great deal of painstaking work will have to be done to master the innumerable individual technical problems.

For the purpose of orientation and of sketching the essential differences between character-analysis and symptom-analysis, let us assume two pairs of patients for comparison. Let us assume we have under treatment at the same time two men suffering from premature ejaculation; one is a passive-feminine, the other a phallic-aggressive character. Also, two women with an eating disturbance; one is a compulsive character, the other a hysteric.

Let us assume further that the premature ejaculation of both men has the same unconscious meaning: the fear of the paternal penis in the woman's vagina. In the analysis, both patients, on the basis of their castration anxiety which is the basis of the symptom, produce a negative father transference. Both hate the analyst (the father) because they see in him the enemy who frustrates their pleasure; both have the unconscious wish to do away with him. In this situation, the phallic-sadistic character will ward off the danger of castration by insults, depreciation and threats, while the passive-feminine character, in the same case, will become steadily more passive, submissive and friendly. In both patients, the character has become a resistance: one fends off the danger aggressively, the other tries to avoid it by a deceptive submission. It goes without saying that the character resistance of the passive-feminine patient is more dangerous because he works with hidden means: he produces a wealth of material, he remembers all kinds of infantile experiences, in short, he seems to cooperate splendidly. Actually, however, he camouflages a secret spitefulness and hatred; as long as he maintains this attitude he does not have the courage to show his real self. If, now, one enters only upon *what* he produces, without paying attention to his way of behavior, then no analytic endeavor will change his condition. He may even remember the hatred of his father, but he will not *experience* it unless one interprets consistently the meaning of his deceptive attitude *before* beginning to interpret the deep meaning of his hatred of the father.

In the case of the second pair, let us assume that an acute positive transference has developed. The central content of this positive transference is, in either patient, the same as that of the symptom, namely, an oral fellatio phantasy. But although the positive transference has the same content in either case, the form of the transference resistance will be quite different: the hysterical patient will, say, show an *anxious* silence and a shy behavior; the compulsive character a *spiteful* silence or a cold, haughty behavior. In one case the positive transference is warded off by aggression, in the other by anxiety. And the form of this defense will always be the same in the same patient: the hysterical patient will always defend herself anxiously, the compulsive patient aggressively, no matter what unconscious content is on the point of breaking through. That is, *in one and the same patient, the character resistance remains always the same and only disappears with the very roots of the neurosis.*

In the character armor, the *narcissistic defense* finds its concrete chronic expression. In addition to the known resistances which are mobilized against every new piece of unconscious material, we have to recognize a constant factor of a *formal* nature which originates from the patient's character. Because of this origin, we call the constant formal resistance factor "character resistance."

In summary, the most important aspects of the character resistance are the following:

The character resistance expresses itself not in the content of the material, but in the formal aspects of the general behavior, the manner of talking, of the gait, facial expression and typical attitudes such as smiling, deriding, haughtiness, over-correctness, the *manner* of the politeness or of the aggression, etc.

What is specific of the character resistance is not *what* the patient says or does, but *how* he talks and acts, not *what* he gives away in a dream but *how* he censors, distorts, etc.

The character resistance remains the same in one and the same patient no matter what the material is against which it is directed. Different characters present the same material in a different manner. For example, a hysteric patient will ward off the positive father transference in an anxious manner, the compulsive woman in an aggressive manner.

The character resistance, which expresses itself formally, can be understood as to its content and can be reduced to infantile experiences and instinctual drives just like the neurotic symptom.[2]

During analysis, the character of a patient soon becomes a resistance. That is, in ordinary life, the character plays the same role as in analysis: that of a psychic protection mechanism. The individual is "characterologically armored" against the outer world and against his unconscious drives.

Study of character formation reveals the fact that the character armor was formed in infancy for the same reasons and purposes which the character resistance serves in the analytic situation. The appearance in the analysis of the character as resistance reflects its infantile genesis. The situations which make the character resistance appear in the analysis are exact duplicates of those situations in infancy which set character formation into motion. For this reason, we find in the character resistance both a defensive function and a transference of infantile relationships with the outer world.

Economically speaking, the character in ordinary life and the character resistance in the analysis serve the same function, that of avoiding unpleasure, of establishing and maintaining a psychic equilibrium—neurotic though it may be—and finally, that of absorbing repressed energies. One of its cardinal functions is that of binding "free-floating" anxiety, or, in other words, that of absorbing dammed-up energy. Just as the historical, infantile element is present and active in the neurotic symptoms, so it is in the character. This is why a consistent dissolving of character resistances provides an infallible and immediate avenue of approach to the central infantile conflict.

What, then, follows from these facts for the technique of char-

---

[2] By the realization of this fact, the formal element becomes included in the sphere of psychoanalysis which, hitherto, was centered primarily on the content.

acter-analysis? Are there essential differences between character-analysis and ordinary resistance analysis? There are. They are related to

a) the selection of the sequence in which the material is interpreted;

b) the technique of resistance interpretation itself.

As to a): If we speak of "selection of material," we have to expect an important objection: some will say that any selection is at variance with basic psychoanalytic principles, that one should let oneself be guided by the patient, that with any kind of selection one runs the danger of following one's personal inclinations. To this we have to say that in this kind of selection it is not a matter of neglecting analytic material; it is merely a matter of *safeguarding a logical sequence* of interpretation which corresponds to the structure of the individual neurosis. All the material is finally interpreted; only, in any given situation this or that detail is more important than another. Incidentally, the analyst always makes selections anyhow, for he has already made a selection when he does not interpret a dream in the sequence in which it is presented but selects this or that detail for interpretation. One also has made a selection if one pays attention only to the content of the communications but not to their form. In other words, the very fact that the patient presents material of the most diverse kinds forces one to make a selection; what matters is only that one select *correctly* with regard to the given analytic situation.

In patients who, for character reasons, consistently fail to follow the fundamental rule, and generally where one deals with a character resistance, one will be forced *constantly to lift the character resistance out of the total material* and to dissolve it by the interpretation of its meaning. That does not mean, of course, that one neglects the rest of the material; on the contrary, every bit of material is valuable which gives us information about the meaning and origin of the disturbing character trait; one merely postpones the interpretation of what material does not have an immediate connection with the transference resistance until such time as the character resistance is understood and overcome at least in its essential features. I have already tried to show (*cf.* Chapter III) what are the dangers of giving deep-reaching interpretations in the presence of undissolved character resistances.

As to b): We shall now turn to some special problems of character-analytic technique. First of all, we must point out a possible misunderstanding. We said that character-analysis begins with the emphasis on and the consistent analysis of the character resistance. It should be well understood that this does not mean that one asks the patient, say, not to be aggressive, not to deceive, not to talk in a confused manner, etc. Such procedure would be not only un-analytic but altogether sterile. The fact has to be emphasized again and again that what is described here as character-analysis has nothing to do with education, admonition, trying to make the patient behave differently, etc. In character-analysis, we ask ourself *why* the patient deceives, talks in a confused manner, why he is affect-blocked, etc.; we try to arouse the patient's interest in his character traits in order to be able, with his help, to explore analytically their origin and meaning. All we do is to lift the character trait which presents the cardinal resistance out of the level of the personality and to show the patient, if possible, the superficial connections between character and symptoms; it is left to him whether or not he will utilize his knowledge for an alteration of his character. In principle, the procedure is not different from the analysis of a symptom. What is added in character-analysis is merely that we isolate the character trait and confront the patient with it repeatedly until he begins to look at it objectively and to experience it like a painful symptom; thus, the character trait begins to be experienced as a foreign body which the patient wants to get rid of.

Surprisingly, this process brings about a change—although only a temporary one—in the personality. With progressing character-analysis, that impulse or trait automatically comes to the fore which had given rise to the character resistance in the transference. To go back to the illustration of the passive-feminine character: the more the patient achieves an objective attitude toward his tendency to passive submission, the more aggressive does he become. This is so because his passive-feminine attitude was essentially a reaction to repressed aggressive impulses. But with the aggression we also have a return of the infantile castration anxiety which in infancy had caused the change from aggressive to passive-feminine behavior. In this way the analysis of the character resistance leads directly to the center of the neurosis, the Oedipus complex.

One should not have any illusions, however. The isolation of such a character resistance and its analytic working-through usually takes many months of sustained effort and patient persistence. Once the breakthrough has succeeded, though, the analysis usually proceeds rapidly, with *emotionally* charged analytical experiences. If, on the other hand, one neglects such character resistances and instead simply follows the line of the material, interpreting everything in it, such resistances form a ballast which it is difficult if not impossible to remove. In that case, one gains more and more the impression that every interpretation of meaning was wasted, that the patient continues to doubt everything or only pretends to accept things, or that he meets everything with an inward smile. If the elimination of these resistances was not begun right in the beginning, they confront one with an insuperable obstacle in the later stages of the analysis, at a time when the most important interpretations of the Oedipus complex have already been given.

I have already tried to refute the objection that it is impossible to tackle resistances before one knows their *infantile* determination. The essential thing is first to see through the *present-day* meaning of the character resistance; this is usually possible without the infantile material. The latter is needed for the *dissolution* of the resistance. If at first one does no more than to show the patient the resistance and to interpret its present-day meaning, then the corresponding infantile material with the aid of which we can eliminate the resistance soon makes its appearance.

If we put so much emphasis on the analysis of the *mode* of behavior, this does not imply a neglect of the contents. We only add something that hitherto has been neglected. Experience shows that the analysis of character resistances has to assume first rank. This does not mean, of course, that one would only analyze character resistances up to a certain date and then begin with the interpretation of contents. The two phases—resistance analysis and analysis of early infantile experiences—overlap essentially; only in the beginning, we have a preponderance of character-analysis, that is, "education to analysis *by* analysis," while in the later stages the emphasis is on the contents and the infantile. This is, of course, no rigid rule but depends on the attitudes of the individual patient. In one patient, the interpretation of the infantile material will be begun earlier, in another later. It is a basic rule, however, not to give any deep-reaching interpretations—no matter how clear-cut the material—as long as the patient is not ready to assimilate them. Again, this is nothing new, but it seems that differences in analytic technique are largely determined by what one or the other analyst means by "ready for analytic interpretation." We also have to distinguish those contents which are part and parcel of the character resistance and others which belong to other spheres of experiencing. As a rule, the patient is in the beginning ready to take cognizance of the former, but not of the latter. Generally speaking, our character-analytic endeavors are nothing but an attempt to achieve the greatest possible security in the introduction of the analysis and in the interpretation of the infantile material. This leads us to the important task of studying and systematically describing the various forms of characterological transference resistances. If we understand them, the technique derives automatically from their structure.

d) *Derivation of the situational technique from the structure of the character resistance (interpretation technique of the defense).*

We now turn to the problem of how the situational technique of character-analysis can be derived from the structure of the character resistance in a patient who develops his resistances right in the beginning, the structure of which is, however, completely unintelligible at first. In some cases the character resistance has a very complicated structure; there are a great many coexistent and overlapping determinations. There are reasons for beginning the interpretation work with one aspect of the resistance and not with any other. A consistent and logical interpretation of the defenses and of the mechanisms of the "armor" leads directly into the central infantile conflicts.

5

ERNEST JONES

The Genesis of the Superego[*]

In a paper[1] published some twenty years ago I laid stress on
the tentative nature of the contribution I was offering to what
was then an entirely new concept, one of the most important
that Freud ever made. There is no reason for surprise, therefore,
that the experience since gained makes me welcome the opportunity for revising some of those tentative conclusions or
extending them in the light of further knowledge. Most of what I
wrote concerning the functions and structure of the superego
still stands, though very much could be added to it, so I propose
to confine myself here to the more obscure problem of its genesis.

There can be no more fascinating problem than this in the
whole of psychology or anthropology, and that for two reasons.
We have good grounds for supposing that to the activity of the
superego we are mainly beholden for the imposing structure of
morality, conscience, ethics, aesthetics, religion—in short to the
whole spiritual aspiration of man that sunders him most strikingly from the beast. The well-nigh universal belief that man is
qualitatively different from other animals in possessing a divine
and immortal soul itself emanates from this source. Anything,
therefore, that can throw light on such a remarkable, and indeed
unique, aspect of humanity must needs prove of the highest
interest to the student of man and his institutions.

In the second place the superego possesses a further and

* Reprinted from *Samiksa*, Vol. I, No. 1, 1947, pp. 3-12.
[1] "The Origin and Structure of the Superego," *International Journal of
Psychoanalysis*, 1926. Reprinted as Chapter VII in the Fourth Edition of my
Papers on Psychoanalysis.

equally important claim on our interest. There is a darker side
to it. The superego is man's foe as well as his friend. It is not
only concerned with promoting man's spiritual welfare, but is
also responsible for much of his spiritual distress and even for
the infernal activities that so deface the nature of man and cause
this distress. In the obscure depths of the unconscious the superego plays a vital part in the conflicts and turmoil characteristic
of that region. It is no exaggeration to say that man's mental
life is essentially composed of struggling efforts either to escape
from or to support the claims of the superego. Superficially regarded our life appears to consist of a small section concerned
with more or less abstract speculations and reflections and a far
larger one concerned with more directly material interests and
activities. The subjective element in the former is not very hard
to perceive, although it is often denied. But it is seldom understood that even with the latter subjective, and more usually irrational, elements play a very large part also. Were our reason free
to function it would probably be not very difficult to arrange our
lives and our institutions so as to provide a vast increase of
happiness, achievement and security. But the inexorable claims
of the superego, irrational as they mostly are, are more urgent
than our real interests, which are commonly subordinated to
them. And so we have to suffer.

Before coming closer to our problem it is necessary to be
clear on one or two prelusive matters. The superego has several
conscious derivations, for instance, conscience, ego ideal, etc., but
it itself has to be carefully distinguished from them. Thus the
essential superego is an institution of the unconscious, so much
so that to make a patient aware of its activities is often an extremely difficult task.

Then we have to be specially careful when we use the word
"morality," for it is just with the early genesis of this conception
that we are concerned. The conscience is plainly the guardian of
morality in the fully developed sense of that term: what is socially right (according to the *mores*) and ethically laudable. Now
the superego is certainly not moral in that sense in extreme cases;
for example, it may even dictate an act of murder as both desirable and commendable—and yet it possesses one important

attribute that closely mimics it. That is the sense of urgent "ought-ness," a categorical imperative. Actually this "oughtness" in the superego may get attached to attitudes that are either moral or immoral as judged by our reason and conscience, although in both cases it is at least as strong and compelling as any corresponding dictate of the conscience. If, therefore, it is to be called moral it can only be in an extended-irrational sense of the word. Furthermore I have been able to trace this pseudo-moral feeling of "oughtness" to an earlier stage in development that antedates any sense of right or wrong, one to which I have given the name of "prenefarious inhibition." It would seem to be in this dark region that we have to search for the beginnings of what later becomes a moral attitude.

A paradox that must be faced is that we are able to describe the superego only by using two apparently incompatible terminologies, one static, and the other dynamic. There is an analogy to this in the dilemma of modern physics which has to describe its ultimates both as particles and as waves, neither alone being able to comprehend all the data. Presumably with psychology as with physics it indicates the imperfection of our knowledge. On the one hand it seems necessary to describe the superego as an object, an introjected object, an entity which can be offered to the id to love or hate or fear, in place of an external object, originally a parent. And on the other hand, we know that this internalized object has no corporeal existence but emanates from a process of fantasy which is itself the expression of some instinctual drive: here, therefore, we can describe the superego only in the dynamic terms of a *process*, a trend with sexual, aggressive or "moral" aims. If it is a thing it is a very living thing, full of activity: watching, warning, guarding, threatening, punishing, prohibiting, ordaining, encouraging, and so on.

The attention paid in the last twenty years by a number of London analysts, notably Melanie Klein, to the processes of introjection and projection in infancy has led to a deeper insight into the origins of the superego. In the light of this experience Freud's formulations concerning it now seem to me to call for an important modification in one respect and important extensions in two others.

The first of these points relates to Freud's picture of the superego as the resolution of the oedipus complex. The child, faced with the hopelessness of his oedipus wishes, both because of the inexorable privation and because of the fear of punishment, effects a renunciation of them on condition that he permanently incorporates something of the parents within himself. This image of love and dread, derived from both parents, though more especially from the one of the same sex, then constitutes the superego, which continues to exercise its function of watching, threatening and if necessary punishing the ego when there is any likelihood of its listening to the now forbidden and repressed oedipus wishes of the id. Freud thus termed the superego the heir of the oedipus complex: its derivative and substitute. Now if all this refers to the fully developed and finished product, the superego as it will on the whole remain through life, and also if one reserves the term superego exclusively to this finished product, then Freud's formula still stands. But if it means that nothing of the superego is to be discerned until the oedipus wishes are renounced—according to Freud at about the age of four or five—then the conclusions based on later experience widely depart from it. It is partly a matter of nomenclature, though only partly. Freud would restrict the term superego to what I have called the finished product, and he would attach the greatest importance in its genesis to the oedipus conflicts between the ages of three and five. But he would certainly have also agreed that there is some further prehistory both to the oedipus complex itself (pregenital difficulties, etc.) and perhaps even to the anxieties and fear of punishment antedating the classical oedipus situation and preparing the ground for the guilt attributes of the superego.

Before taking up the modern modification one is impelled to make to this formula of Freud I will briefly mention the two other points alluded to above. One concerns the dating of the whole matter. We have now much reason to think that both the oedipus complex itself, with all its characteristic features (carnal desire for the mother, jealousy and hatred of the father, fear of castration, etc.) and the superego in a sufficiently developed form to be clearly recognizable long antedate the period in which Freud envisaged them and reach back certainly to the second, and perhaps even the first, year of life. Secondly, the fear of punishment and also other sources of anxiety which play such an essential part in the genesis of the superego do not by any means all emanate from the oedipus situation itself, but have still deeper origins. To put it plainly, the boy has other reasons for anxiety besides the dread of punishment at the hands of his paternal rival; they spring more directly from the relation to his mother alone.

As was mentioned above, the reasons for these extensions and modifications of Freud's formula come from closer study of the processes of introjection and projection. Thanks mainly to the work of Melanie Klein, we have become familiar, not merely with the early age at which they operate, but with the extraordinary and quite continuous interplay between them at every moment of the infant's experiences of life. The introjections are what constitute the superego, but—and this is a most essential point— they are far from simple incorporations of external realities, but are to a greater extent incorporations of the infant's projections as well. Once this point is grasped one understands that the infant's own contribution to its future superego is more important than those made by the outer world (essentially the parents), a conclusion to which Freud would perhaps have demurred.

We may now return to Freud's view concerning the relationship of the oedipus complex to the superego. He would undoubtedly have agreed that the child's picture of the prohibiting and threatening parent is an exaggerated or distorted one. Though fathers may kill or castrate their boy children they very seldom do: nevertheless every boy feels these eventualities to be likely ones and is in consequence terrified of them. When, therefore, Freud says that the superego gains its power of affecting the ego from its representing reality demands,[2] one certainly has to add "and unreality demands as well": more accurately, the demands of psychical reality as well as those of physical reality. In my opinion these additions made by the child's imagination to the picture of the parent are more important and have a longer

---

[2] Freud: *Collected Papers*, Vol. II, pp. 251-253.

and more complicated history than Freud believed likely. And, as I pointed out many years ago,[3] the earliest fantasies and conflicts exercise a decisive importance on the form taken by the oedipus complex, its course and outcome.

It is, however, agreed on all sides that these additions exist, so at once we are presented with the problem of their origin. Rather to our surprise we find to start with that the child has a motive in magnifying external dangers, *i.e.*, in picturing the parent as stricter and more dangerous than he or she actually is. The child can find in this way relief from its fears of internal dangers, which are more intolerable and are less assuaged by the reassurance given by the knowledge that the external object (parent) after all has some love and that there are limits to his anger. It achieves this, of course, by the familiar mechanism of projection. The matter, however, is not so simple as this, since the child oscillates in his estimate of internal versus external dangers, especially when the latter includes the projected ones. The external bogey may become so fearsome that the child, evidently with the aim of securing better control over it, introjects it (into its superego). Once inside, however, it again becomes intolerably dangerous and the child is compelled to look around for a suitable object in the outer world on whom it can once more project it. This double process is continually and perhaps endlessly repeated in the endeavor to procure some relief from the anxiety. These desperate expedients show that the child has within itself extremely formidable sources of anxiety, for which the formation of the superego is one attempted mode of salvation. This defensive function of the superego is the main theme of the present paper.

Whence come all these fearsome bogies and with them the need for such desperate defenses? The superego is certainly, among other things, a cruelly persecuting agency which the ego has good reason to dread. But, after all, the superego is only in small part thrust on to the growing child by outer prohibitions and condemnations. It is in a larger part its own creation. Why does it have to create such a very unpleasant institution inside itself?

---

[3] Papers on *Psychoanalysis*, Fourth Edition, Chapter XXI, p. 457.

There must be a good reason for its doing so strange a thing. Or, put more objectively, the superego must fulfill some highly important function of value to compensate for its obvious disadvantages.

There can be little doubt that the sense of "oughtness" characteristic of the superego, the source of what later will be a moral attitude, is derived from an earlier sense of "mustness." Put in other words, the superego's threat to the ego: "You ought not to do that and I will punish you if you do" is a replacement of an earlier: "You must not do that for it is harmful (or dangerous)." How is this transformation effected from fear into the earliest traces of morality, and what is the nature of the fear in question? The earliest fears of the child are on the material rather than the spiritual plane: they are fears of damage to its interests (privation, deprivation, bodily injury, and so on). But in the first year of life love and the need for love begin to play an increasingly important part. This brings with it a new possibility, the fear of losing love by offending or injuring the loved and loving object —partially the mother. And it is this extension of its needs from the bodily to the spiritual plane that effects the transformation from mustness to "oughtness." To provoke the risk of castration is still a non-moral situation: to run the risk of offending the mother and losing her love becomes a "wrong" thing to do. And in time, as the relationship with the parents becomes more complex, it becomes quite as important to abstain from doing wrong things as to avoid doing dangerous ones. Perhaps the most important region in which this takes place is that of sphincter control, the earliest "moral" training of the infant and one which takes place long before, according to Freud, the oedipus complex is in action, or at all events when it is only in the stage of inception. Ferenczi, with the intuition of genius, spoke of "sphincter morality," sensing that here was to be found the dawn of moral attitudes. But he had little comprehension of the rich meanings the infant can attach to its excretory activities. They are not simply physical needs, though they derive much of their compulsive nature from this fact, nor simply important components of the sexual instinct (urethral and anal erotism). They are also vehicles of aggressive and destructive impulses, and are still further connected with the cannibalistic incorporations of the parents that precede or accompany them. When to soil the bed signifies to defile, poison or destroy the mother and at the same time to reveal that one has swallowed and killed the father then one begins to understand in what weighty terms the nurse's "normal" training can be conceived.

The superego may profitably be regarded both as a barrier against those forbidden and harmful impulses and also as an indirect vent for them. Traces of all the sexual components can be found in its activities even if they are imperfectly desexualized. The scopophilic impulse reveals itself in the alert watching and guarding attitude of the superego; the anal-erotic component reactively in the need for orderliness and most important in the sense of duty; while the sadistic one is all too obvious in the cruel torturing the superego can inflict on the ego. The reaction to the more developed genital impulse is shown later in the moral condemnation of incest, but besides this is the more positive love towards the parental substitute (ego ideal, etc.).

We have now traced the superego back to premoral stage, one which I have previously termed a stage of prenefarious inhibition, where its main function would seem to be that of a simple barrier against the id impulses or rather against the intolerable anxiety that these produce in the ego. At this point it becomes merely one defense among others, though one with peculiar history. Its special features are due to its formation through introjection of parental objects. We may inquire further into the nature of the anxiety in question and of the danger arising from the id impulses. These are problems I have discussed at some length elsewhere,[4] but I will summarize the main conclusions I have reached concerning them.

Whether there is a separate aggressive instinct in man or not, it is certain that the sexual one is, especially in its primordial stage, essentially aggressive in its nature, far more so than psychoanalysts originally thought. So far as I can judge, there appears to be no satisfactory evidence of aggression occurring apart from some libidinal impulse, which would seem to be always the

---

[4] *Op. cit.*

starting point. There is good reason to suppose that these aggressive components are felt by the infant to be in themselves harmful or dangerous, quite directly so and apart from any effects on either the infant or the loved object. The response to them is anxiety, and at first what may be called pre-ideational anxiety, *i.e.,* without any sense of the nature of the danger. It is we who have to construct from various clues what this danger is. We know that physiologically and psychologically the result of sustained tension from the absence of relief or gratification leads to exhaustion. Some parents take advantage of this knowledge to leave an angry baby alone "to cry itself out," in my opinion a very harmful procedure at that age. The dread of this total exhaustion of the libido I have termed the fear of aphanisis, and it is in my opinion the important starting point of the anxiety against which the superego, as well as other defenses, is instituted.

6

WILLIAM V. SILVERBERG

Toward a Theory of Personality and Neurosis*

Those who read detailed accounts of the trials of criminal cases are often puzzled and baffled by the rule of evidence which restrains a witness from stating conclusions based upon what he has perceived and confines him to reporting his perceptions only. The witness is expected to tell what he saw and what he heard, but his conclusions as to the meanings of these things or as to the intentions of the persons concerned in his testimony are subject to being ruled out of evidence either by the objection of opposing counsel or by the trial judge himself. The layman often finds such procedure difficult to understand, since all of us are forever coming to conclusions as to another person's intentions when we see him act or hear him speak. But, nevertheless, there is wisdom in this rule of evidence: such conclusions are, after all, merely the opinions of those who make them and in the final analysis only the person who acted or spoke can say what his intentions were. This reasoning, arrived at long ago, does not, of course, take unconscious mental functioning into account; but the witness is no more competent to assay the unconscious motivations of another person than that person himself, and a psychoanalysis of every person involved in criminal proceedings whose unconscious intentions are in question would be cumbersome indeed. Ultimately the jurymen must decide this matter of

---

* Reprinted by permission from *Childhood Experience and Personal Destiny* (New York, 1952). Copyright, 1952, Springer Publishing Company, Inc.

intentions, and while their conclusions may be just as unfounded as those of a witness, it is felt that, since somebody must decide, the defendant's interests are better served by leaving such decisions to the unanimous opinion of twelve people, supposedly personally disinterested, than to the perhaps biased opinion of one witness. The point here is that it is a precarious thing to come to a conclusion about what is or was in another person's mind, conscious or unconscious, unless the other person is able to confirm it by his own words.

The foregoing statement has great pertinence when we attempt to say anything at all about what goes on in the mind of a newborn infant or of any child up to the time when he has attained a sufficient proficiency in the use of language. The infant is, in etymological terms, the unspeaking, and he cannot tell us what goes on in his mind. Fond parents, for instance, will often suppose that their two month old infant is showing unmistakable signs of sociability by smiling at them; the pediatrician, on the other hand, tells us that this infant's facial gesture is no smile, but a grimace occasioned by gas pains in the abdomen. I have no way of saying which interpretation of the infant's behavior is right, since only the baby is in a position to know, and he is an "unspeaking," an infant. Whatever is stated about the nature of consciousness in infancy is necessarily the result of conjecture or of reconstruction, reasoning after the fact, and can never be definitively proved.

It is ofen felt by psychologists that we are on safe ground in supposing that the fetus exists in a state of complete and effortless satisfaction. This supposition is based upon a consideration of the physiologic circumstances of intrauterine life; physiologically speaking, the fetus is living under optimal conditions. It exists enveloped in a warm fluid in which temperature change (if any) has an infinitesimal range: its skin cannot feel too cold or too hot. It needs to engage in no exertion whatsoever; it does not even have to breathe, as all the oxygen it requires is supplied to it by the mother's bloodstream, which flows through the fetus via the placenta and the umbilical cord. It does not need to digest, as the food-substances, already prepared by the mother's physiologic processes for assimilation, come to it by the same means as its oxygen. It does not need to evacuate waste materials, as the same flow of blood carries metabolic products from its body to the mother's, whose physiologic processes dispose of them. It does not need to adjust to changing intensities of light, since the womb is a place of perpetual darkness. All this is true if the mother is in good health and well fed; if she is not, there may be some vicissitudes of fetal life. However, under ordinary conditions, a consideration of these physiologic matters would seem to justify the conclusion that, psychologically speaking, the fetus exists in a state of uninterrupted and effortless satisfaction: in other words, a state of physiologic and psychic homeostasis is maintained up to the beginning of labor.

There arise, however, certain questions in connection with even this apparently simple and justifiable conclusion. We need not, perhaps, question the physiologic facts. But when, at what point in fetal development, may we begin to speak of *psychic* homeostasis? When, if at any time, does or *can* awareness begin in fetal life? Do we have to conclude that in the fetus physiologic homeostasis is identical with psychic homeostasis? If so, does that identity change, once the fetus is born, and when, and how, and why? In cases where the mother is ill and the physiologic homeostasis of the fetus is disturbed, does it have awareness of this? Can it experience anxiety? Does the fetus experience anything psychically when it is headed for intrauterine death? Such questions cannot be answered except by conjecture. The supposition that the fetus in the process of birth experiences anxiety, is merely a supposition and leaves unanswered the question, When does the fetus begin to have the capacity for feeling anxiety?

Another question involves the meaning of fetal movements, which after the fourth month of fetal life can be felt tactilely and can often be seen in their impact upon the mother's abdominal wall. Do the movements signify interruptions of physiologic homeostasis, and are they attempts to restore it? If so, is there any fetal awareness of such interruptions, and how are they felt? This query cannot be answered, but the fact that it can be asked makes us immediately question the absoluteness of the supposed unbroken and effortless satisfaction of fetal life. By asking it, we have implied that even the fetus may upon occasion have a sense of "something is the matter." Perhaps this implication contains a tentative answer to the question, When does the fetal psyche originate? Possibly it begins as soon as the fetus is capable of having a sense of "something is the matter," which comes about ordinarily during the fifth month of its life.

In any case, we are cautioned by this line of thought to regard the concept of unbroken, effortless satisfaction during fetal life as a relative one, and to be skeptical about the contention that the so-called trauma of birth marks the *first* experience of anxiety in the life of the human organism. It has been pointed out by Freud [10, pp. 96 ff., and especially p. 101] that the most common somatic manifestations of anxiety—acceleration of the respiratory rate and of the heart beat—have a utility and an expediency in the situation of birth that they do not have in later situations of anxiety: they aid the organism in performing the transition from the placental type of oxygenation and circulatory flow to the autonomous one in which oxygenation depends upon the organism's own respiratory efforts and circulatory flow depends upon the organism's own cardiac action.

Freud [10, p. 97] likewise pointed out in the same connection that anxiety is characterized not only by such somatic phenomena but also by a sensation whose "unpleasurable quality seems to have a character of its own." Disturbed physiologic homeostasis in the fetus could perhaps cause the fetus to experience this unpleasurable sensation, which would thus become the most rudimentary manifestation of anxiety, that portion of the psychosomatic complex of anxiety which may be present even in fetal life, and without the presence of which we should be skeptical about a diagnosis of anxiety. Clinically, we often encounter anxiety that has no perceptible somatic manifestations. On the other hand, we are accustomed to diagnose anxiety from the presence of one or more somatic manifestations (sweating of the palms, for instance) even when the unpleasurable subjective sensation is denied. Perhaps we should be more skeptical about this than we are: either the subject of our diagnosis serves a purpose of his own in denying the subjective sensation (for example, maintaining face by denying he is afraid or uncomfortable in the given situation), or, if the subjective sensation is actually absent, the somatic manifestation may have a quite different significance. Again we are confronted with the difficulty of knowing what goes on in the mind of another without verbal confirmation from him. Ultimately such confirmation may be forthcoming, but meanwhile we do well to maintain a question in our own minds. Possibly the fetus feels only *discomfort;* anxiety, as Freud conceived it, perhaps occurs in a full and complete form only after the experience of birth. We may regard the homeostatic state of the fetus as one in which satisfaction is only relatively uninterrupted and effortless—relatively, that is, as compared with postnatal life.

The newborn infant, now literally cut off from his fetal connection with his mother's physiologic processes, is utterly helpless to survive without the care given by the mother or a surrogate for her. His newly acquired respiration and cardiac action fulfill his metabolic needs for tissue oxygenation and for exchange within the tissues of food-substances for metabolic products; his digestive system now begins the lifelong tasks of assimilation of food and elimination of wastes. He is, physiologically speaking, a competent, functioning organism. But there his competence ends. He cannot procure for himself the food which, once it is in his mouth, he is now competent to handle. He cannot keep himself warm, nor protect himself from any of the myriad dangers which beset his intactness and his life. Needs he has and feels, for he cries when he is hungry or cold or when he experiences pain or other discomfort; but fulfill his needs he cannot. If his cry brings no one to divine his need and to satisfy it, he is at the end of his resources.

How the infant *feels* in this situation of relative helplessness —relative because, while the cry is his only resource, it is a resource—is what we should like to know, but can only speculate about. Two workers, Sandor Ferenczi and Trigant Burrow, have engaged in what seem to be useful speculations about this matter. Even though there is evidence that seems to give support to their speculations, it cannot be too strongly emphasized that their hypotheses cannot ever be more than provisionally accepted, since the unspeakingness of the infant will always limit our thinking about the nature of his consciousness to conjecture and reconstruction.

Ferenczi [4] conjectured that the newborn infant, with his intrauterine history of unvarying physiologic homeostasis, regarded himself as omnipotent; that, having never known frustration, the infant supposed this freedom from frustration to be the result of his own powers. Ferenczi based this idea on Freud's findings [6] in cases of obsessional neurosis and his own clinical confirmation of these. The infant's notion of his own omnipotence, according to Ferenczi, becomes modified, as time goes on, in response to two factors: (1) the introduction of more and more frustration, producing more frequent and longer delays between the incidence of a need and its fulfillment, and more frequent and more prolonged disturbances of psychic homeostasis; (2) the emergence, through growth, of new functioning —better muscular coordination and the rudiments of speech. Thus, while at the start of extrauterine life the infant's subjective omnipotence operates in a hallucinatory manner (he hallucinates fulfillment of his need and it is fulfilled), later on it operates by gestures, and still later by words and by thoughts. Ferenczi appears to have omitted the cry from this series, but Sullivan [21, p. 7] has pointed out that the cry is an instrumentality much used by the infant in his effort to live by the use of power. Infantile omnipotence is ultimately renounced, according to Ferenczi, because increasing frustration, resulting from the gradual withdrawal of the mother or her surrogate from the role of constant watchful helper, demonstrates to the child that he does not possess omnipotence, reconciles him to the need to take into account factors of external reality, and induces in him the endeavor to manipulate them toward his ends. Thus the sense of omnipotence is replaced by the sense of reality [20, pp. 387 ff.].

This replacement is never complete; it is made only to the extent that it has a pragmatic value for the child and not because the child perceives any moral value or other virtue in adherence to his newly acquired sense of reality. In so far as functioning in terms of a sense of reality gets him more, in so far as it increases the effectiveness of his activity, he is for it; if it fails him, if this effectiveness is not increased by it or is perchance lowered by it, he will abandon the sense of reality and will attempt to function in terms of a sense of supposed omnipotence. This we see clearly and often in the case of adults, and we may therefore postulate it a fortiori in the case of the child. Furthermore, it should here be remarked that when we speak of omnipotence in the psychic sense, we do not give the word precisely the same meaning as we do when we use it in a metaphysical or in a theological context. In the latter we mean literally *all-power,* power over everything conceivable, as when we speak of God's omnipotence. The omnipotence of the human being, the omnipotence that he sometimes strives for, is more limited in its application: he seeks all-power only over those things which are of direct concern to him. While the child might desire all-power over the movements and activity of the mother or other person significant to him, he would not be interested in power over the Argentinians, for example, or over the Paris subway system. When we use the concept of omnipotence in human psychology, we must confine its application to those factors of the individual's world which are of direct and immediate significance to him.

The speculations of Burrow [3] on the nature of the infantile psyche are perhaps implied in Ferenczi's hypotheses, just described, and were certainly assumed by Freud, apparently without the awareness that Burrow had explicitly formulated them. Burrow supposed that psychically the newborn infant exists in a "primary subjective phase" of consciousness. By this he meant that the infant makes no distinction between self and nonself, that he conceives his existence as an unbroken continuum of himself and all the perceived world about him, both persons and things. Thus the mother's nipple in his mouth as he sucks milk and derives a sensory thrill as well as nourishment from it is regarded by him as belonging to his own self, as a part of his own body-image, and not as something nonself, belonging to another person and able to be used and enjoyed only so long as the other person, to whom it belongs, permits. It will be seen that this wide, extended concept of self resembles the "oceanic feeling" mentioned by Freud in *Civilization and Its Discontents* [11], where it is related to early states of consciousness.

The increasing frequency and prolongation of disturbances in psychic homeostasis—experiences of intensifying frustration —and the gradual lessening of the mother's or her surrogate's constant and alert attention to the infant's comfort and well-being, teach the infant that his needs or wishes can often not be fulfilled by any efforts of his own; he learns that the satisfaction of his wants requires the mediation of another person, one who is not always available to him and who, even if available, does not always attend to his needs or wishes. Such experience produces a gradual disintegration of the primary subjective phase and results eventually in the awareness that a sharp distinction exists between what is self and what is other, or nonself. Here, too, as in Ferenczi's hypothesis of an infantile sense of omnipotence, experiences of frustration play a dominant part in the transition to a sense of reality in the developing infant. He learns that all the world is not encompassed in his own body, that his oceanic feeling is illusory and untenable, and that he does not possess all-power over all those things which are of significance and concern to his comfort and well-being. These lessons are but tentatively learned.

For the infant the sense of reality has no virtue in itself; the value of the distinctions he learns to make lies in the fact that his disillusionment enables him to adapt himself to the world about him in such a way that he can sometimes manipulate its various factors to achieve wish-fulfillment more readily than he could before he learned the lessons of reality. Bernard S. Robbins [15] has shown that this pragmatic attitude toward the sense of reality exists in adult life.

We must assume, for we see the clearest evidences of it not only in adult human beings but in the behavior of animals as well, that it is inherent in all living organisms to strive toward the fulfillment of needs and wishes which have a biologic provenance and which may or may not have psychic representation. By the latter I mean simply that such needs and wishes may be felt or they may not be felt. The fact that in acculturated human beings and in some animals capable of training, the efforts toward such fulfillment of needs and wishes may be temporarily or "permanently" inhibited does not vitiate the general statement: we suppose that the tendency to fulfillment exists even when behavior fails to give testimony that it is in operation. The man who offers his seat in a crowded bus to a woman would prefer to remain seated but chooses to discommode himself either in the interest of considering himself or of being considered a "gentleman" or in the interest of some other form of altruism. The man who covets his neighbor's wife would try to take her if he could square it with his acculturated set of moral scruples or if he did not fear the humiliation of being rejected by her or the anger of her husband. Inhibiting factors merely complicate the general principle that we set the greatest store by the fulfillment of all that we may wish or need.

We do well to try to maintain this distinction between wish and need, although it is not always easy to distinguish them. A need may be defined as that which is necessary to health and to survival (for instance, the need for sufficient food to maintain health and life). All else desired may be regarded as wish, regardless of the intensity with which it is desired. The fulfillment of sexual desire, while often felt with great intensity, is never necessary to survival, though we often postulate that it is essential to psychic or physiologic health. Many instances could be cited in which sexual abstinence is maintained for long periods without apparent detriment to health. However this may be, whether sexual fulfillment in general is to be considered a need or a wish, it is true that the fulfillment of sexual desire with a specific partner is a wish rather than a need, even though the chooser may insist that it is a need.

It happens often enough that people will make certain conditions, the fulfillment of which is represented as needs, and then bully or otherwise coerce others into fulfilling these conditions. A mother, for example, will get it established that she has an attack of cardiac failure whenever her grown up son disobeys her. Thus her wish to dominate her son is represented as a need. A child who intensely wants a particular toy may attempt to coerce the parents by saying with great feeling, "I *need* it, I NEED it." Subjectively, one often does not take the trouble to distinguish between an intense wish and a need, and often enough one is quite sincere in the feeling or statement of need where merely a strong wish is involved. Under such circumstances, whether that which is desired might be objectively defined as a wish or as a need, the individual puts into operation whatever procedures he is capable of for bringing about its achievement. The degree of success attendant upon these efforts comes under the heading of what I have termed *effective aggression*.[1] In this sense, effective aggression represents the success with which the ego functions in the carrying out of impulses. The impulse may be purely biologic in origin or, arising from biologic sources, may become greatly modified by experiences of acculturation. The impulse to evacuate the rectum when it contains feces is purely biologic (physiologic) in origin. Toilet-training temporarily inhibits this impulse until culturally suitable conditions can be found for its release.

Effective aggression refers to the executive function of the ego. The ego, as Freud saw it, was that part of the psyche in closest contact with the external world. Through it, perceptions of internal and external reality are received and given meaning. The ego also controls the innervations which can produce or inhibit muscular action and therefore motility. An impulse arising from the id, the great reservoir of that energy which Freud called *libido*, can of itself produce no muscular activity, no motility toward its goal, unless the ego acquiesces and sets in operation the necessary muscular innervations. Thus no aggression, effective or otherwise, can occur, unless initiated by the ego. The theoretic difficulty mentioned in the Introduction in connection with Freud's instinct-theories now becomes painfully apparent. In his conception of the ego, Freud set up an executive agency of determining importance: one of its functions is to decide whether or not a given impulse shall receive motor expression or be inhibited. Yet the energy wherewith the ego operates in carrying out this function is not specifically its own: the energy is borrowed from precisely the same source from which the impulse, now submitted to the ego's decision, arises.

---

[1] This phrase was introduced in my paper "On the Origin of Neurosis" [17]. The interested reader will there find the formulation of this concept (pp. 116 ff.), as well as remarks on the drawbacks involved in the phrase. In the latter connection it should be noted that the key-word is *effective*; the term *aggression* might be replaced by *action*, *activity*, *behavior*, or the like.

We are confronted with a dilemma: either we are dealing with a single, unitary kind of energy, in itself undifferentiated and nonspecific in its aims, upon which any psychic agency, whether impulse or ego, may draw in its attempts to function; or we are dealing with different types of energy, each specific to the type of psychic agency concerned. In a sense, Freud attempted to encompass both horns of this dilemma. In terms of his earlier instinct-theory, libido was a single, unitary type of energy, and yet it had a specifically sexual character: it was uniformly pleasure-seeking. Freud [7, pp. 460 ff.] objected to Jung's attempt [12, pp. 77 ff.] to define libido as nonspecific, as not specifically sexual, and, therefore, as a general, undifferentiated energy (somewhat equivalent to Bergson's *élan vital*) upon which any psychic agency might draw. Freud ascribed to the ego no other source of energy but the libido; furthermore in so far as the ego might oppose a libidinal impulse, it had to compete with that impulse for enough energy (libido) to make good its opposition.

Freud's concept of primary narcissism carried the implication that ego and id had originally been one, without differentiation, and that libido was originally at the disposal of this undifferentiated id-ego, or primitive self. Once the differentiation of id and ego occurred, in response to situations threatening the intactness of the whole organism (in psychic terms, this id-ego), id and ego had to compete for quanta of libido. Freud now spoke of ego-libido and object-libido; withdrawal of libido from objects resulted in a proportionate accretion of libido to the ego. But what psychic agency determined the withdrawal of libido from an object, unless it was the ego itself? If libido is to be withdrawn from an object, ego-libido would have to be stronger than id-libido—object-libido can be nothing other than the id's investment of an object with desire for pleasure by means of that object—and the crucial question arises, What factor has produced the ascendancy of ego-libido over id-libido?

The difficulty here is entirely a theoretic one and results from the untenability of the hypothesis of libido as both a single, unitary energy and a specific pleasure-seeking energy. If, whatever their original state, ego and id are seen to be often in opposition one to the other, it is simpler to suppose that their obviously different aims are based upon different types of drive or energy. The fact that ego and id are often enough not in a state of mutual antagonism and that they often operate synergistically does not vitiate this hypothesis of their operating upon the basis of specifically different drives. Just as different people may function, now in antagonism, now in cooperation, so different psychic agencies within the same person may function. Indeed, effective aggression may be seen as an attempt to achieve synergism of id and ego, the goal of total effective aggression or omnipotence being an ideal restoration of the primitive id-ego. If the ego never opposed or modified an id-impulse, or, putting the matter somewhat differently, if every impulse were unquestioningly and successfully put into effect by the ego, something like omnipotence would have been achieved, something resembling the intrauterine state of effortless satisfaction would have been restored, neurosis would no longer exist, and books such as the present one would not be written.

Freud's later instinct-theory does not alter the situation greatly. This theory did introduce a new energic principle, that of Thanatos, thus destroying the conception of libido as a single, unitary energy and requiring it to share the field with another energy having a specifically different *quality*. Freud seemed thereby to resolve the aforementioned dilemma, by abandoning the first horn of it. But he did not adopt the second horn of this dilemma: Thanatos and Eros were equally energies of the id, and the ego was still left to borrow one or the other from the id or to bring about a variety of fusions and defusions of them, by means of what additional energy was not stated. As a matter of fact, neither Thanatos nor Eros, as Freud defined them, was well adapted to become specifically an ego-drive, since survival was given a subordinate role in the theory. Thanatos received the major role; it was the death instinct and drove toward non-survival in its primary position (directed "inward") and toward destructiveness in its secondary position (directed "outward"). Eros was regarded as opposed to the death instinct and drove toward growth, union with others, and what in general one might term constructiveness. To Eros was bequeathed the libido, but, since Freud assigned it the minor role, its operations were seen as mere temporizings, as detours from the highroad of death, as delays and interim arrangements in the major process that had as its goal the decay and disintegration of the living, organic substances of the body into nonliving, chemically inorganic substances. The psyche desired passionately the death of its own soma and the destruction of the soma of others; survival meant little to it in comparison to the peace of biologic nothingness.

This metapsychologic picture seems greatly at odds with human nature—and, in fact, with general organic nature—as it is observed. Freud [9, chap. 6] himself attempted to deal critically with it when he first presented it to the world. He raised the questions whether instinctual death is not merely characteristic of the metazoa (many-celled animals) as compared with the protozoa (single-celled animals), and whether instinctual death occurs in the somatic cells of the human body but not in the germ-plasm (the sperm and ova), which consists of single-celled entities like the protozoa. He showed very clearly that death "from natural causes" occurs among the protozoa only when external conditions are unfavorable to life—in stagnant water or in a test tube, where the protozoon is killed by its own unremoved metabolic products; or when amphimixis (nonreproductive, rejuvenating conjugation between protozoa) is prevented from occurring. Freud used these examples to demonstrate his point about instinctual death even among the protozoa, but what he actually showed by the evidence he adduced is that protozoan death occurs only under extraordinary external circumstances—in confined, stagnant water or in the absence of the opportunity for conjugation. This is not death "from natural causes" or endogenous death. It is either accidental death or murder.

Freud must be credited with having presented his new instinct theory with a tentativeness disarmingly frank. He wrote [9, p. 76], "I might be asked whether I am myself convinced of the views here set forward, and if so how far. My answer would be that I am neither convinced myself, nor am I seeking to arouse conviction in others. More accurately: I do not know how far I believe in them." Or again [9, p. 77], "People unfortunately are seldom impartial where they are concerned with ultimate things. . . . There everyone is under the sway of preferences deeply rooted within, into the hands of which he unwittingly plays as he pursues his speculation." In his later work [11] he assumed the validity of his speculation and was never again so critical of it.

I would contend that a metapsychology is useful and valid only in so far as it is able to account for observed phenomena, and that the metapsychology above described fails to account for the drive of all organic life toward survival, which appears empirically to take precedence over all other drives, and for the executive function of the ego. These are serious deficiencies, and Freud's particular "preferences" seem to have relegated the ego to the position of stepchild of psychoanalysis. The historical reasons for this are well known, but whether they were inherent in the material that confronted Freud in his early work and as he went along, or whether they were inherent in his preferences, is a debatable question. There can be little doubt that it is to the advantage of psychology that Freud elected to pursue first the study of libidinal factors and their vicissitudes, as these needed for their elucidation precisely those unique qualities of observation, intuition, and formulation, which he brought to the work. Ego psychology is much more obvious and superficial, and much easier to study and describe. It does not require the genius which was uniquely Freud's. It is perhaps unduly demanding to have expected Freud to do the thorough job with ego factors that he did with libidinal ones. But it seems to me that the legitimate task of his successors is to restore to the ego its full and proper significance and to assign to it its proportionate role in the affairs of the human psyche.

The task demands, I believe, that the ego be given a theoretic basis for its functioning; in other words, to postulate for it a specific kind of drive or energy which has survival of the total organism as its chief goal and which operates by the medium of effective aggression. An advantage of the latter concept is that it permits us to see the ego as concerned with matters not accounted for if we regard it as actuated solely, or even mainly, by motivations of defense. It is an operational concept which accounts for the ego's efforts in the direction of *achievement* as well as of defense.

The psychologists—including Freud, Sullivan (with his anxiety-based self-system), and Horney (with her concept of basic anxiety)—who base the ego's functioning solely or even mainly upon the organism's defensive needs, appear to have overlooked one of the outstanding facts in the observable behavior of the young child: his obvious tendency to *do* something, a something which is neither defense against nor avoidance of danger, but merely wish-fulfilling. Certainly, as we observe the infant and the young child, we see that defense is not his only concern and that his resources for defense are mobilized and utilized only when he senses danger. In the absence of a sense of danger —which is usually the case during the greater part of each twenty-four hours—the child is apt to engage in behavior we would have to describe as *doing* something rather than *avoiding* something. The infant of eight or nine months does not ordinarily spend his waking hours in perceiving dangers and devising means of circumventing them; he sits on the floor or in his play-pen and manipulates in some fashion that appears satisfying to him whatever objects come to his hand: he shakes his rattle, he puts the foot or hand of his rag doll into his mouth, he vocalizes with apparent joy and enthusiasm, and he does such things repeatedly and tirelessly and with obvious pleasure. The somewhat older child who has achieved locomotion has a correspondingly wider repertory of doing. To a vast extent the activity of the young child is not defensive but is simply pleasurable doing, a patent fact not hitherto adequately taken into account in formulating theories of personality and neurosis. Freud was able to show in one instance [9, pp. 11 ff.] that a child's game did have defensive significance, but it may be doubted that this is universally, or even most frequently, the case (nor did Freud claim that it was).

It seems reasonable enough to accept Freud's conclusion that for reasons of defense the ego becomes differentiated from the primitive ego-id continuum and that its origin serves a defensive purpose. But it is likewise reasonable to suppose that one of the outcomes of this differentiation—and therefore perhaps one of the considerations motivating it—is that the organism as a whole is thus placed in a better position to achieve fulfillment of its positive needs and wishes. The reasoning here is much like that of Freud in one of his early metapsychologic papers [8]: experience teaches one the expediency of denying immediate fulfillment to some of one's wishes, which is counter to the dictates of the pleasure principle; the delay in fulfillment is often dictated by the reality principle in order that the ultimate fulfillment of the wish may be assured. Thus it is seen that the reality principle does not differ essentially from the pleasure principle; the former is merely a modification of the latter and is adopted to make more certain the operation of the pleasure principle in its original form. So the differentiation into ego and id, while undertaken for defensive reasons and while sacrificing the homogeneity, the oneness, of the primitive self, results in a condition superior to the original one—the world and its frustrations being what they are—for the achievement of pleasure-goals.

Indeed, the ego throughout life is characterized by its tendency to compromise and to make sacrifices in order to maintain life and to achieve, even though in delayed and partial and substitutive fashion, goals signalized by id-impulses. The ego's major aim, however, is survival, and in this sense, defense may be said to be its cornerstone. Just as a trapped animal will sacrifice a paw or a leg if this enables it to escape from the trap, so the ego will sacrifice any id-impulse which, if carried out, seems to threaten survival. (Certain "heroic" exceptions to the foregoing statement are discussed in the following chapter.) Survival is thus the main concern of the ego, and its energic force may thus be defined as whatever in the organism drives toward survival. But if survival seems assured or is not threatened, then the ego's other task, the achieving of pleasure-goals, becomes paramount. The drive for survival must be regarded as primarily irrational and as not requiring any rational basis: it merely exists. In so far as this drive might be rationalized, the continued opportunity to achieve pleasure-goals, to *do,* would constitute its rationale. I mention this in order to place these two drives in proper perspective: the drive for survival cannot be reasoned with; when survival is at stake, the ego drops everything else and concentrates its adaptative powers upon it.

Survival is usually striven for even if every potentiality for *doing* is lost. Suicide (or suicidal impulses or thoughts) in such circumstances may seem to contradict the primacy of the drive for survival and thus to give the drive to *do* the major role. This is true only if suicide is taken at its face value and if the fact, clinically demonstrable, is ignored that suicide is essentially an act of vengeance and murder, an act calculated to torture, through a perpetual bad conscience, the someone else (in some instances, perhaps, God) held responsible for one's woes. The act of suicide seems postulated upon a conviction of survival in some form, a contention supported by many of the popular superstitions about death and the dead, particularly, in this instance, the beliefs concerning the possibility of the dead returning and haunting their enemies. Relevant here is the common unconscious conviction that though dead one remains in a sense alive. Frazer [5, chap. 18] deals with such beliefs among primitive peoples.

In any case, the concept of effective aggression can encompass both the defensive function of the ego (its concern with survival) and its function of *doing,* of achieving the pleasure-goals to which the id impels it.

Thus far I have dealt with effective aggression descriptively, endeavoring to define its quality. It is clear, however, that it has also a *quantitative* aspect, which is perhaps the more important one for our purpose. For we have to be concerned not only with the kind of effort made by the ego in its operations, but more importantly with how effective the effort is. To what extent is the ego's effort successful? Does the ego achieve what it attempts to perform in exactly the manner contemplated in its intention at the start of its maneuver? Has it, along the way had to compromise? If so, how much less than its original intention has it had to settle for, or has it had to abandon its original goal entirely? If it has had to compromise or abandon its goal, what are the causes of this change? Has the ego met with obstacles which it may regard as insuperable in the nature of things or merely insuperable to it? Is the compromise or failure due to deficiencies of the particular ego and its capacities, or was the goal to be achieved an impossible one? If the latter alternative obtains, could the difficulty have been foreseen, or was the impossibility not predictable and only discoverable in the course of the attempt? All these questions and many similar ones indicate the quantitative aspects of effective aggression and suggest how these may be linked to self-esteem.

Self-esteem may be regarded as the psychic counterpart to somatic survival. Totally and continuously effective aggression, if such a thing were possible, would result in an indestructible self-esteem. On the other hand, failures in effectiveness of aggression produce a lowering or loss of self-esteem. In the early weeks and months of extrauterine life the relative helplessness of the infant ordinarily evokes in the mother an alert attention to his needs and their fulfillment. But if, in accordance with Burrow's hypothesis, the infant, being in the primary subjective phase, does not distinguish between himself and his mother, this alert behavior of the latter will produce in him the impression that *he* has brought about the desired restoration of homeostasis and that his own *doing* (whether by hallucination, gesture, cry, word, or thought) is responsible for the fulfillment of his need or wish. The difficulty of expressing what *may* go on in the mind of the infant still in the primary subjective phase is well illustrated by the foregoing sentence. The entire structure of language seems predicated upon the distinction between "self" and "other," a distinction which we assume the infant has not yet made. A more accurate version of the sentence referred to would probably be: "This alert behavior on the part of the mother will produce in the infant the impression that the desired restoration of homeostasis *has been brought about* and that a certain action performed (whether hallucination, etc.) is relevant to the outcome (restored homeostasis)."

Thus the infant's doing or aggression is felt by him as effective to the extent to which the mother fulfills his needs. The more alert the mother, the briefer and less frequent will be the periods of disturbed homeostasis, and in accord with his subjective bias, the more effective and powerful the infant will feel himself to be. It would seem that such a sense of adequacy and competence, despite its objective inaccuracy, must be basic to self-esteem and must form the foundation of the healthy ego.

Loretta Bender has pointed out [2] that where such alert care by maternal agencies is inadequate (as in foundling institutions, for example) the outcome in later childhood and adult life is an incurable psychopathy—a marked retardation and flatness, emotionally and intellectually. Such infants are given no basis for the illusion of effective aggression, which the mother's alert attention grants to more fortunate ones, and are therefore unable to establish that degree of self-esteem upon which healthy ego-functioning is based. The work of Bender would suggest that a constitutional factor is here operative, for the very frustrations and delays which, when they occur somewhat later in the infant's life, favor the healthy establishment of a sense of reality, operate with permanently damaging effect when they occur in the earliest weeks and months. It would seem that too much disturbance of homeostasis too soon in life cannot be tolerated by the psychosomatic constitution as it then exists.

One is reminded here of Freud's concept (in *Beyond the Pleasure Principle* [9]) of a *Reizschutz* or protective barrier against excessive stimuli arising both from the external world and from within the organism itself. He likened this to a hard rind developing from the surface membrane of an organism of vesicular shape, as if the originally delicate surface layer had become toughened through continuously repeated contacts with environmental substances and objects. It is as if, in the situation mentioned above, this psychic *Reizschutz* had not yet had time to develop, so that such stimuli, assailing the organism prematurely, break through the surface and do damage to the interior substance. The same stimuli, if they can be held off until after the *Reizschutz* has developed, will be fended off by the latter without damaging effect to inner substance.

This is a perfectly comprehensible concept, but it is difficult to translate it into psychic or somatic or psychosomatic terms. It may be conjectured that this difficulty exists because of our present ignorance of certain factors whose discovery and elucidation may not be too far off. The work of Selye [16] and others upon the physiologic effects of stress and the manner in which the organism meets them and attempts to ward them off or to compensate for them would seem to offer the possibility of giving substance, not too far off in the future, to Freud's conception of a *Reizschutz* and to my attempt to explain the constitutional nature of the damage, clinically described by Bender, which results from too great frustration too early in life.

In the ordinary case, where the incidence of frustration is more gradual and not so drastic, the sense of reality supervenes as an acceptance of a distinction between self and other and as a realization of limits to one's own power. As has already been said, this acceptance and this realization may be unwilling and tentative, but by the end of the first year of life they are established in large degree. This change to a sense of reality would have to be accompanied by some reduction in effectiveness of aggression and some corresponding reduction in self-esteem. These effects are, however, counteracted to some extent by the emergence of new capacities—greatly increased muscular coordination (with the concomitant power of locomotion) and the acquisition of the rudiments of language. Such factors not only increase the child's resourcefulness, making him thereby less helpless than he was at birth, but often produce in his parents enthusiastic and affectionate approval. Much of what is lost in self-esteem by the reduction in an illusory type of effective aggression is made up for by these accretions to real effectiveness of aggression and by the pleasing sense of being approved of and having the favor of these important people, the parents. The self-esteem of the one year old is not so absolute or indestructible as it was in infancy; it is more relative and more precarious, but it exists on the more realistic basis of the actual capacities of the child and has the additional support of parental approval.

Throughout life self-esteem has these two sources: an inner source, the degree of effectiveness of one's own aggression; and an external source, the opinions of others about oneself. Both are important, but the former is the steadier and more dependable one; the latter is always more uncertain. Unhappy and insecure is the man who, lacking an adequate inner source for self-esteem, must depend for this almost wholly upon external sources. It is the condition seen by the psychotherapist almost universally among his patients.

In the child, threats to self-esteem are of two kinds: threatened failures of the effectiveness of his aggression and threatened withdrawal of parental (mainly maternal) love and approval. Such threats constitute the psychic counterpart of threats to somatic intactness and survival. In later childhood, threatened loss of parental approval may readily equate, in certain instances, with threats to somatic survival, since parental love and approval may become to the child the guarantee of such survival. The relation of this to self-esteem will be discussed in the following chapter. In the presence of actual danger to such intactness or survival, *fear* is the emotion felt; and the perception of such a danger immediately impending, though not yet present, arouses *anxiety*. Actual injury to self-esteem produces the emotion of *humiliation,* the intensity of which corresponds to the extent of the injury. The perception of an impending blow to self-esteem produces anxiety, as in the case of apprehended somatic danger.

Fear and humiliation produce on-the-spot and usually quite random measures for dealing with the situations that evoke them. One is immediately confronted with a threatening situation and must improvise a defense. Such improvisations may or may not be successful in avoiding the danger or in mitigating its effects; the defense responses may be partially successful, which means also partially unsuccessful.

Anxiety, as differentiated above from both fear and humiliation, produces somewhat different results. Since, in the case of anxiety, the danger is not yet actually present, but only impending or threatening to be present, there may yet be time to plan an effective means of coping with the threat. Forewarned is forearmed, and anxiety has the advantage of a forewarning.

Because the faculty of perception is involved in such foresight of dangerous situations, and because perception is one of the ego's functions, Freud regarded the ego as the seat and point of origin of anxiety. He therefore supposed that measures to avert foreseen danger emanate from the ego. Repression is one such measure: the ego, aware of an impulse arising from the id, perceives from its watchtower overlooking the environment that danger from the outside will attack the total organism if an attempt is made to carry out the impulse. Such a perception arouses anxiety in the ego, and its obvious way of averting the danger is to quell the impulse, if it can. The stronger the impulse —in the ego's own terms, the stronger the temptation to perform the act implied by the impulse—the greater the anxiety, because of the greater likelihood of the ego's initiating the motor actions appropriate to expressing the impulse. The ego's best plan, then, is to quell the impulse by disowning it, by "forgetting" it, by repressing it.

The ego has other devices for dealing with id-impulses that threaten to upset the harmony and safety which the ego has been at pains to establish and maintain in the organism's relations with the outside world. Prominent among these is reaction-formation, in which the ego manifests an impulse precisely opposite to the one actually aroused in the id by the external situation. The impulse manifested in the device of reaction-formation is, as Sullivan once pointed out,[2] the appropriate id-syntonic impulse with a *not* prefixed to it. If the original impulse is to *kill,* reaction-formation transforms it into *to not-kill,* which may come to mean *to take care of.* It must be added, however, that reaction-formation is not simply a matter of grammar and semantics. If the opposite impulse, the one expressed by the prefixed *not,* does not exist *in its own right* as a psychic potentiality, it cannot be used for purposes of reaction-formation. Suppose that the example given arises in a situation of sibling hostility: the original impulse, then, is to kill the sibling, but owing to the process above described it becomes transformed by reaction-formation into the not-kill, take-care-of impulse. This transformation will the more readily take place if the child has already evolved some tendency to want a baby of his own to take care of, in whatever specific terms he conceives this. In other words, reaction-formation involves of necessity some positive quality in the not-impulse; the negativity of the not-impulse, taken alone, is an insufficient basis for its adoption even as an anxiety-solving device. It seems to me likely that where the appropriate not-

---

[2] In a lecture in Washington, D. C., in 1935, so far as I know unpublished.

impulse lacks positive value, the ego will be constrained to choose a different defensive device, such as repression, for example.

Regression, another of the ego's defensive devices, handles the danger-provoking impulse by expressing it in an earlier form, one which has proved in the past to be safe. For example, if one's impulse takes the form of seeking pleasure through exhibiting the penis to the mother in an attempt to seduce her into touching it (as in the case of Little Hans [6, pp. 162, 163, 166]) and the ego senses danger, emanating from mother or father or both, as a likely outcome of such an act, the ego may try to avoid the danger and yet to achieve the pleasure by altering the new impulse into an old version. Thus, sitting on mother's lap and being embraced by her is a way of being pleasurably touched which one has found safe by previous experience, or inducing her to give one a bath requires that she legitimately wash and dry—hence touch—one's genitals.

It is this device of regression which doubtless gave Freud the strong impression that libido is an energy whose manifestations develop in stages or levels, since old manifestations become replaced by new ones and since the tendency toward new manifestations can give place to recurrences of older manifestations when difficulties arise. Certainly he was here correctly observing a general psychic principle to the effect that when new behavior is attempted and for whatever reason fails or seems destined to fail of its purposed goal, it is wise to have recourse to something tried and true. Folk wisdom expresses the conflict in two antithetic proverbs: "If at first you don't succeed, try, try again," and "Let sleeping dogs lie."

A study of the antitheses frequently observed in folk wisdom has still to be made and would probably prove both interesting and profitable. Proverbs, which are the vehicles of folk wisdom, often exist in opposites, such as the pair just mentioned, and indicate the existence of frequent conflict with respect to many proposed modes of behavior. Another antithesis: "Make hay while the sun shines"—do it now; "Don't cross the bridge until you come to it"—put it off until tomorrow. From the viewpoint of common sense, the fact that mutually contradictory proverbs often occur has no very profound meaning beyond the idea that no form of adaptative behavior has universal application and that people have learned to fit their behavior to different situations as they apperceive them. From the viewpoint, however, of unconscious psychic functioning, which often, as we have learned, transcends common sense, these antitheses of folk proverbs may have a significance similar to that of word-pairs which have antithetic meaning but derive from the same etymologic roots [1]. This significance is the existence of profound unconscious conflict with reference to all potential modes of behavior in important matters: it indicates the deep uncertainty with which individuals approach meaningful situations. With reference to the ego's defensive device of regression, the conflict lies between doing something new which may be dangerous and doing something old which is known to be safe. If the uncertainty is resolved by adopting the latter behavior, the ego has altered the impulse by regression.

Whether the general principle which is implied by the antithetic proverbs and word-pairs supports the idea that, because libidinal manifestations show the possibility of regression, they therefore normally "develop" in a series of stages, is quite another matter, depending upon what is postulated concerning the libido and its manifestations.

The devices of the ego thus far mentioned have the common quality of being *autoplastic*. They are *self-molding* devices and attempt to adapt to the environment and its potential dangers by producing alterations in the organism's own impulses. The impulses may be disowned or postponed (repression in varying degrees), or they may be replaced by opposite impulses if such exist in their own right (reaction-formation), or they may be replaced by older and safer forms of the original impulses (regression).

One may also speak of another group of ego-devices which differ from those just enumerated by being *alloplastic,* or *other-molding.* These seek to alter the environment rather than the self and they comprise, doubtless among others, the three maneuvers that I have elsewhere described in detail [18, 19, 20]. I shall here merely name them as the schizoid, the magical, and the transference maneuvers. To classify the two groups of devices as autoplastic and alloplastic is convenient and is accurate in a general sense. But it must be realized that the autoplastic devices are also alloplastic in that their ultimate aim is to change the environment from a dangerous to a safe one, and that the alloplastic devices cannot be engaged in without producing certain alterations in the self.

The autoplastic and alloplastic devices may be further distinguished roughly in that the former are in the main oriented toward defense, while the latter are oriented toward achievement of pleasure-goals. I characterize this as a rough distinction because both types of devices have ultimately a pleasure-goal in view and because the alloplastic devices are often motivated by concern with security and survival, and particularly with self-esteem (which is the psychic version of security and survival). In the most common instances, the autoplastic devices are adopted because the ego senses that the organism is not safe constituted as it is and that inner modifications are essential, whereas the alloplastic devices, which are modes of attempting to alter factors external to the organism itself, may operate with no immediate purpose of producing inner modifications. The former devices might be summed up in the sentence: "I am not safe as I am; I'd better change myself"; while the latter might be expressed: "I am all right as I am; but I have to change him, her, them, or it." Both are adopted in order that aggression may be the more effective and therefore that self-esteem may be maintained at the highest possible level. The ego's own survival (self-esteem) corresponds to the survival of the total organism, when the latter is at stake. When it is not, when somatic survival is not involved in the organism's *doing,* then what is involved is homeostasis, whether described as psychic, somatic, or psychosomatic. When not confronted with emergencies that threaten life, the ego's chief concern is to maintain a high level of competence and thus to avoid illness, whether this takes the form of low self-esteem or a bodily deficiency that impairs competence in *doing.*

Psychic illness, then, implies illness of the ego—low self-esteem primarily occasioned by a diminution in the effectiveness of aggression. All of the ego's defensive devices, which are originally used to promote and improve this effectiveness, indicate that the ego does not feel itself strong enough or safe enough to pursue the organism's aim directly; hence, the devices emerge in an indirection which not only signalizes a relatively weak ego, but which in itself further weakens the ego. The strength of the ego lies in the degree to which it is at one with the remainder of its own organism. Freud [10, p. 141] pointed out that the differentiation into ego and id signifies a defect in the human psyche, by which he meant that the human psyche functions poorly in so far as it is at war with itself, and that this differentiation would not have occurred had not the psyche at an early stage of its existence fallen into inner conflict. Since this differentiation never fails to occur even in the healthiest human being, a certain inner psychic disunity seems inevitable in everyone. If the very existence of an ego implies some degree of psychic disunity, the strength of the ego must always be seen as a relative strength: it is *more or less* at one with the remainder of its organism.

Whether an ego may rightly be considered as inherently or constitutionally strong or weak, is a problem about which we are in such profound ignorance that we cannot even propound the question in a form that might evoke responses, nor have we any idea what factors such constitutional strength or weakness might relate to. Our ignorance is here so complete that any statement concerning the constitutional strength or weakness of the ego would be begging the question and would necessarily reflect, not truth, but one's *Weltanschauung*. The very question may in itself be a species of *non sequitur* since, from a strictly biologic point of view, the ego *should* not even exist (if the emergence of the ego is to be regarded as a psychobiologic defect).

It is best to leave untouched this question of a constitutional, inherent quality of the ego. We can only know that, regardless of such a factor, the specific experiences of the organism in its specific environment appear closely related to the ego's necessity to adopt devices of indirection, to the extent to which these are adopted in general, and to the specific nature of these devices in a given case. Likewise related to specific experiences is the matter of whether a given device is temporarily adopted, to be later abandoned, or whether it becomes permanently characteristic of the given ego. We may say, then, that the ego *becomes* weak or strong (perhaps we should say *weaker* or *stronger,* supposing constitutional factors to exist) as a result of what its organism specifically experiences. It grows to be less at one with the remainder of the psyche (more conflicted) or more at one (less conflicted), depending upon its life-situation, which, in early life, is mainly the situation presented by the human environment (the biologic family, in our society).

It is unnecessary to labor here the factor of cultural relativity. It is by now well known from Sullivan's postulates on interpersonal relations, and from the pioneering work of A. Kardiner [13, 14] that different societies (geographically as well as temporally different) evolve markedly varied forms and that each society attempts to mold its denizens to its own specific form. Kardiner's concept of *basic personality* implies that what is "normal" or well-adapted personality in one culture is "pathologic" or maladapted personality in another.

In the consideration of the kind of experience that favors growth or diminution of ego-strength—equivalent, respectively, to psychic health or psychic illness (neurosis)—I shall be concerned solely with our own culture. By "our own culture" I mean specifically the American culture. This may be at times extended to include the contemporary culture of western civilization as a whole, or it may at times be narrowed down to the form of culture extant along the northern Atlantic seaboard of this country. It is not always possible to be aware when one is being excessively general in one's cultural assumptions and when one is being too provincial.

References

[1] ABEL, KARL: *Ueber den Gegensinn der Orworte.* Reviewed by S. Freud in *Jahrb. f. Psychoanalytische Forschungen* 4:349-352, 1910.

[2] BENDER, LORETTA: *An observation nursery; a study of 250 pre-school children on the psychiatric division of Bellevue Hospital. Am. J. Psychiat.* 97:1158-1172, 1941. Infants reared in institutions permanently handicapped. *Child Welfare League of America Bulletin* 24:1-4, 1945. There is no substitute for family life. *Child Study* (April) 1946.

Psychopathic Behavior Disorders in Children. In LINDER AND SELIGER: *Handbook of Correctional Psychology*. New York, Philosophical Library, 1947.
Anxiety in Disturbed Children. In HOCH, P. H., and ZUBIN, J.: *Anxiety*, New York, Grune & Stratton, 1950.

[3] BURROW, TRIGANT: Cited in MacCurdy, J. T.: *Problems of Dynamic Psychology*. New York, The Macmillan Company, 1923, pp. 188 ff.

[4] FERENCZI, SANDOR: Entwicklungsstufen des Wirklichkeitssinnes (1913). In *Bausteine zur Psychoanalyse*. Vienna, Internationaler Psychoanalytischer Verlag, 1927, vol. 1.

[5] FRAZER, SIR JAMES GEORGE: *The Golden Bough*. New York, The Macmillan Company, 1951, abridged ed.

[6] FREUD, SIGMUND: Analysis of a Phobia in a Five-year-old Boy (1909). *Collected Papers*, Volume 3, 1925.

[7] ———: Notes upon an Autobiographical Account of a Case of Paranoia (Dementia Paranoides) (1911). *Collected Papers*, Volume 3, 1925.

[8] ———: Formulations Regarding the Two Principles of Mental Functioning (1911). *Collected Papers*, Volume 4 (1925).

[9] ———: *Beyond the Pleasure Principle*. Transl. by C. J. M. Hubback New York, Boni & Liveright, 1922.

[10] ———: *Inhibitions, Symptoms and Anxiety*. Transl. by A. Strachey. London, The Hogarth Press, 1936.

[11] ———: *Civilization and Its Discontents*. Transl. by J. Riviere. London, The Hogarth Press, 1946.

[12] JUNG, C. G.: *The Psychology of the Unconscious*. Transl. by Beatrice Hinkle. London, Kegan Paul, Trench, Trubner & Company, Ltd., 1922.

[13] KARDINER, A.: *The Individual and His Society*. New York, Columbia University Press, 1939.

[14] ———: with the collaboration of Ralph Linton, Cora Du Bois, and James West: *The Psychological Frontiers of Society*. New York, Columbia University Press, 1945.

[15] ROBBINS, BERNARD S.: Escape into reality. *Psychoanalyt. Quart.* 6:353-364, 1937.

[16] SELYE, HANS: *Stress*. Montreal, Acta, Inc., 1950.

[17] SILVERBERG, WILLIAM V.: On the origin of neurosis. *Psychiatry* 7:111, 120, 1944.

[18] ————: The schizoid maneuver. *Psychiatry* 10:383-393, 1947.

[19] ————: The concept of transference. *Psychoanalyt. Quart.* 17:303-321, 1948.

[20] ————: The factor of omnipotence in neurosis. *Psychiatry* 12:387-398, 1949.

[21] SULLIVAN, HARRY STACK: *Conceptions of Modern Psychiatry.* Washington, The William Alanson White Psychiatric Foundation, 1947. First published in *Psychiatry* 3:1-117, 1940.

7

ERNST KRIS

Ego Psychology and Interpretation in Psychoanalytic Therapy*

While during half a century of its history the development of psychoanalysis has been comparatively little influenced by simultaneous discoveries in other fields of science, the various applications of psychoanalysis have almost continuously influenced each other. It is in this sense that the history of psychoanalysis can be viewed as a progressive integration of hypotheses. The clearest interrelationship exists between clinical observations and the development of both psychoanalytic technique and theory [23, 24]. The development of the structural point of view in psychoanalysis, i.e., the development of psychoanalytic ego psychology, can profitably be traced in terms of such an interdependence. Freud was at one point influenced by his collaborators in Zürich who impelled him to an intensified interest in the psychoses. This led him to formulate the concept of narcissism and thus to approach the ego not as a series of isolated functions but as a psychic organization. The second group of clinical impressions that favored the development of a structural psychology was the observation by Freud of individuals motivated by an unconscious sense of guilt, and of patients whose response to treatment was a negative therapeutic reaction. These types of behavior reinforced his conception of the unconscious

* Presented at the panel on Technical Implications of Ego Psychology at the midwinter meeting of the American Psychoanalytic Association, New York, December 1948. Reprinted by permission from the *Psychoanalytic Quarterly*, Vol. 20, No. 1, 1951. Copyright, 1951, by The Psychoanalytic Quarterly, Inc.

nature of self-reproaches and autopunitive tendencies, and thus contributed to the recognition of important characteristics of the superego. There is little doubt that other clinical impressions to which Freud referred during these years were derived from what we would today describe as "character neuroses"— cases in whose analyses the unconscious nature of resistance and defense became particularly clear and which, therefore, facilitated formulations of unconscious and preconscious functions of the ego.

However, these events were not fortuitous. Nobody can believe that the clinical impressions of which we speak reached Freud accidentally. Surely Freud did not turn to the study of psychoses merely to engage in polemics with Jung, or in response to suggestions of Abraham; nor can it be assumed that his interest in character neuroses was due only to an increase in the incidence of character neuroses among his patients during the early 1920's, and hence to a "psychosocial" event [17]—though it is probable that such a change of frequency distribution occurred. It is obviously more sensible to assume that a readiness in the observer and a change in the objects observed were interacting.

Freud's readiness for new formulations is perhaps best attested by the fact that the principles of ego psychology had been anticipated in his Papers On Technique[1] [18]. Most of these papers were written contemporaneously with his first and never completed attempt at a reformulation of theory, which was to be achieved in the Papers On Metapsychology.[2] The precedence of technical over theoretical formulations extended throughout Freud's development. It was evident during the 1890's when in the Studies in Hysteria[3] Freud reserved for himself the section on therapy and not that on theory. Several years later, when his interest in dreams and neuroses was synthetized, and the importance of infantile sexuality gained ascendancy, he was first concerned with a modification of therapeutic procedure: the "concentration technique" was replaced by the technique

---

[1] Freud: Coll. Papers, II.
[2] Freud: Coll. Papers, IV.
[3] Freud (with Breuer): *Studies in Hysteria*. Translated by A. A. Brill. New York: Nervous and Mental Disease Monographs, 1936.

of free association [22]. Similarly, Freud's papers on technique during the second decade of the century anticipate by implication what a few years later he was to formulate in terms of ego psychology. His advice that analysis should start from the surface, and that resistance be analyzed before interpreting content implies principles basic in ego psychology. This accounts for the status of Freud's papers on technique in psychoanalytic literature: they have retained a pivotal position and most treatises on technique have illustrated or confirmed rather than modified his rare fundamental precepts. If one rereads Freud's address to the Psychoanalytic Congress in Budapest in 1918 [11], one becomes aware of the fact that many current problems concerning the variation of technical precepts in certain types of cases, as well as the whole trend of the development that at present tries to link psychoanalytic therapy to psychotherapy in the broader sense, were accurately predicted by Freud. The development which he predicted became possible, however, through the new vistas that ego psychology opened to the earliest and probably best systematized modifications of psychoanalytic techniques, the development of child analysis by Anna Freud, the psychoanalysis of delinquents by Aichhorn, and later to some of the various modifications of technique in the psychoanalytic treatment of borderline cases and psychoses.

Not only did ego psychology extensively enlarge the scope of psychoanalytic therapy, but the technique of psychoanalysis of the neuroses underwent definite changes under its impact. These changes are part of the slow and at times almost imperceptible process of development of psychoanalytic technique. Isolated changes which constitute this development are difficult to study because what one may describe as *change* can also be viewed as *difference*, and differences in technique among analysts who share approximately the same fundamental views may be due to many factors; however, if we study the trends of changing attitudes, we are in a more favorable position.

Neither all nor most of the changes in psychoanalytic technique are consequences of the development of some aspect of psychoanalytic theory. If we reread Freud's older case histories, we find, for example, that the conspicuous intellectual indoctrination of the Rat Man was soon replaced by a greater emphasis on reliving in the transference, a shift which has no apparent direct relation to definite theoretical views. Similarly, better understanding and management of transference was probably not initially connected with any new theoretical insight. It was a process of increasing skill, of improved ability, in which Freud and his early collaborators shared,[4] not dissimilar to that process of a gradual acquisition of assurance in therapy which characterizes the formative decade in every analyst's development. But other changes in psychoanalytic therapy can, I believe, clearly be traced to the influence of theoretical insight.[5] Every new discovery in psychoanalysis is bound to influence to some extent therapeutic procedure. The value of clinical presentations is that in listening to them we are stimulated to review our own clinical experiences, revise our methods, and to profit—in what we may have overlooked or underrated—from the experience of others. To assess this influence of ego psychology it is necessary to recall the ideas which developed synchronously with or subsequent to the new structural orientation: the psychoanalytic theory of instinctual drives was extended to include aggression, and the series of ontogenetic experiences studied included in ever greater detail preœdipal conflicts deriving from the uniqueness of the mother-child relation. A historical survey of the psychoanalytic literature would, I believe, confirm that these new insights were having reverberations in therapy, influencing, however, mainly the content of interpretation and not the technique of therapy in a narrower sense. A gradual transformation of technique came about largely through better understanding and improvement in the handling of resistances. In interpreting resistance we not only refer to its existence and determine its cause, but seek also its method of operation which is then

---

[4] Such a view is not uncontested. In describing her own development as an analyst Ella Sharpe stresses the fact that only familiarity with the structural concept, particularly the superego, enabled her to handle transference problems adequately [31, p. 74]. For a similar report of his early technical vicissitudes see also Abraham [1].

[5] This naturally does not apply to all individuals. The relation of theoretical insight to therapeutic procedure varies from analyst to analyst, and there is no evidence upon which to base an opinion as to which type of relation is optimal.

reviewed in the context of other similar types of behavior as part of the defensive activities of the ego. Resistance is no longer simply an "obstacle" to analysis, but part of the "psychic surface" which has to be explored.[6] The term resistance then loses the unpleasant connotation of a patient who "resists" a physician who is angry at the patient's opposition. This was the manifestation of a change in what may be described as the "climate" of analysis.

In one of his last papers Freud [12] defended analytic interpretations against the reproach of arbitrariness especially in dealing with resistance; he discussed in detail the criteria according to which, by the patient's subsequent reaction, correctness of the interpretations can be verified. In doing so he stresses an area of coöperation between analyst and patient and implicitly warns against dictatorially imposed interpretations.[7] That does not mean that it is possible or desirable always to avoid opposition of the patient to any interpretation, but it means that through the development of ego psychology a number of changes in the technique of interpretation have come about— not "random" changes, characteristic of the work of some analysts and not of others, but changes that constitute a set of adjustments of psychoanalytic technique to psychoanalytic theory.

Illustrations

To clarify issues, I cite first a simplified version of an incident in the analysis of a six-year-old boy reported by Anna Freud [6, p. 119]. The visit to the dentist had been painful. During his analytic interview the little boy displayed a significant set of symptomatic actions related to this experience. He damaged or

---

[6] These or similar formulations of the analysis of resistance were achieved in two steps, in the writings of Wilhelm Reich [27, 28], and of Anna Freud [6]. The difference between them is significant. Reich regards the problem predominantly as one of technical "skill"; formulations tend to be oversimplified or exaggerated. They lead to the rigorous "resistance" or layer analysis, the shortcomings of which have been criticized by Hartmann [18]. By Anna Freud, resistance is fully seen as part of the defensive function of the ego.

[7] Waelder [33] has further elaborated this point.

destroyed various objects belonging to the analyst, and finally
repeatedly broke off the points and resharpened a set of pencils.
How is this type of behavior to be interpreted?

The interpretation may point to retaliatory castration, may
stress the turning of a passive experience into an active one, or
may demonstrate that the little boy was identifying himself with
the dentist and his aggression. All three interpretations can
naturally be related to the anxiety which he had experienced.
The choice between these and other possible interpretations will
clearly depend on the phase of the analysis. The first interpretation, an "id interpretation," is directly aimed at the castration
complex. The second and the third aim at mechanisms of
defense. The second emphasizes that passivity is difficult to
bear and that in assuming the active role danger is being mastered. The third interpretation implements the second by pointing
out that identification can serve as a mechanism of defense. It
might well prove to be a very general mechanism in the little
boy's life. It may influence him not only to react aggressively,[8]
but to achieve many goals, and may be the motivation of many
aspects of his behavior. The interpretation that stresses the
mechanism of identification is, therefore, not only the broadest,
but it may also open up the largest number of new avenues, and
be the one interpretation which the little boy can most easily
apply in his self-observation. He might learn to experience certain of his own reactions as "not belonging" (i.e., as symptoms)
and thus be led an important step on the way toward readiness
for further psychoanalytic work.

We did not choose this example to demonstrate the potentialities of an interpretation aimed at making the use of a mechanism of defense conscious, but rather in order to demonstrate
that the situation allows for and ultimately requires all three
interpretations. A relevant problem in technique consists in
establishing the best way of communicating the full set of
meanings to the patient. The attempt to restrict the interpretation to the id aspect only represents the older procedure, the one

---

[8] This is probably what Anna Freud means when she says that the child was
not identifying himself "with the person of the aggressor but with his aggression."

which we believe has on the whole been modified by the change of which we speak. To restrict interpretation to the defense mechanism only may be justifiable by the assumption that the patient is not yet ready—a valuable piece of caution, though it seems that there is a tendency among some analysts to exaggerate such caution at times. It may also happen that though we carefully restrict the range of interpretation the patient reacts as if we had not done so. While our interpretation points to the mechanism by which he wards off danger (e.g., identification), the next set of associations causes the patient to react as if we had interpreted his femininity. A sequence of this kind indicates normal progress: the interpretation concerns the warding-off device, the reaction reveals the impulse warded off.[9]

No truly experimental conditions can be achieved in which the effects of alternative interpretations can be studied. Comparisons of "similar cases" or comparisons of patients' reactions to "similar situations" help us to reach some useful generalizations. The occasional situation under which somewhat more precise comparisons can be made is the study of patients who have a second period of analysis with a different analyst. The need for a second analysis is no disparagement of the first analyst, nor does it imply that the first course of treatment was unsuccessful. In several instances of reanalysis in which I functioned as second analyst, the first analysis had been undertaken at a time when the problems of ego psychology had not yet influenced analytic technique, or by a colleague who (at the time) did not appreciate its importance. The initial treatment had produced considerable improvements, but the very same problems appeared in a new light, or new relationships, when interpretations of a different kind, "closer to the surface," were "inserted." In a few of the cases in which these conditions existed, a published record of the first analysis was available and furnished some reliable comparison.

At the time of his second analysis a patient, who was a young

---

[9] Another apparent discontinuity or "jump" in reaction, no less frequent and no less important, is designated by what Hartmann calls "the principle of multiple appeal" in interpretations [18]. Examples of this kind make the idea of interpretation proceeding in layers, advocated by Wilhelm Reich, highly doubtful [27, 28]; see also in this connection Nunberg [26] and Alexander [2].

scientist in his early thirties, successfully filled a respected academic position without being able to advance to higher rank because he was unable to publish any of his extensive researches. This, his chief complaint, led him to seek further analysis. He remembered with gratitude the previous treatment which had improved his potency, diminished social inhibitions, producing a marked change in his life, and he was anxious that his resumption of analysis should not come to the notice of his previous analyst (a woman) lest she feel in any way hurt by his not returning to her; but he was convinced that after a lapse of years he should now be analyzed by a man.

He had learned in his first analysis that fear and guilt prevented him from being productive, that he "always wanted to take, to steal, as he had done in puberty." He was under constant pressure of an impulse to use somebody else's ideas—frequently those of a distinguished young scholar, his intimate friend, whose office was adjacent to his own and with whom he engaged daily in long conversations.

Soon, a concrete plan for work and publication was about to materialize, when one day the patient reported he had just discovered in the library a treatise published years ago in which the same basic idea was developed. It was a treatise with which he had been familiar, since he had glanced at it some time ago. His paradoxical tone of satisfaction and excitement led me to inquire in very great detail about the text he was afraid to plagiarize. In a process of extended scrutiny it turned out that the old publication contained useful support of his thesis but no hint of the thesis itself. The patient had made the author say what he wanted to say himself. Once this clue was secured the whole problem of plagiarism appeared in a new light. The eminent colleague, it transpired, had repeatedly taken the patient's ideas, embellished and repeated them without acknowledgment. The patient was under the impression he was hearing for the first time a productive idea without which he could not hope to master his own subject, an idea which he felt he could not use because it was his colleague's property.

Among the factors determining the patient's inhibitions in his work, identification with his father played an important part.

Unlike the grandfather, a distinguished scientist, the father had failed to leave his mark in his field of endeavor. The patient's striving to find sponsors, to borrow ideas, only to find that they were either unsuitable or could only be plagiarized, reproduced conflicts of his earlier relationship with his father. The projection of ideas to paternal figures was in part determined by the wish for a great and successful father (a *grand*father). In a dream the œdipal conflict with the father was represented as a battle in which books were weapons and conquered books were swallowed during combat. This was interpreted as the wish to incorporate the father's penis. It could be related to a definite phase of infancy when, aged four and five, the little boy was first taken as father's companion on fishing trips. "The wish for the bigger fish," the memory of exchanging and comparing fishes, was recalled with many details. The tendency to take, to bite, to steal was traced through many ramifications and disguises during latency and adolescence until it could be pointed out one day that the decisive displacement was to ideas. Only the ideas of others were truly interesting, only ideas one could take; hence the taking had to be engineered. At this point of the interpretation I was waiting for the patient's reaction. The patient was silent and the very length of the silence had a special significance. Then, as if reporting a sudden insight, he said: "Every noon, when I leave here, before luncheon, and before returning to my office, I walk through X Street [a street well known for its small but attractive restaurants] and I look at the menus in the windows. In one of the restaurants I usually find my preferred dish—fresh brains."

It is now possible to compare the two types of analytic approach. In his first analysis the connection between oral aggressiveness and the inhibition in his work had been recognized: "A patient who during puberty had occasionally stolen, mainly sweets or books, retained later a certain inclination to plagiarism. Since to him activity was connected with stealing, scientific endeavor with plagiarism, he could escape from these reprehensible impulses through a far-reaching inhibition of his activity and his intellectual ventures" [30]. The point which the second analysis clarified concerned the mechanism used in inhibiting activity. The second set of interpretations, therefore, implemented the first by its greater concreteness, by the fact that it covered a large number of details of behavior and therefore opened the way to linking present and past, adult symptomatology and infantile fantasy. The crucial point, however, was the "exploration of the surface." The problem was to establish how the feeling, "I am in danger of plagiarizing," comes about.

The procedure did not aim at direct or rapid access to the id through interpretation; there was rather an initial exploratory period, during which various aspects of behavior were carefully studied. This study started on a descriptive level and proceeded gradually to establish typical patterns of behavior, present and past.[10] Noted first were his critical and admiring attitudes of other people's ideas; then the relation of these to the patient's own ideas and intuitions. At this point the comparison between the patient's own productivity and that of others had to be traced in great detail; then the part that such comparisons had played in his earlier development could be clarified. Finally, the distortion of imputing to others his own ideas could be analyzed and the mechanism of "give and take" made conscious. The exploratory description is aimed, therefore, mainly at uncovering a defense mechanism and not at an id content. The most potent interpretative weapon is naturally the link between this defense and the patient's resistance in analysis, an aspect which in the present context will not be discussed in any detail. The exploratory steps in this analysis resemble those which

---

[10] The value of similar attempts at starting from careful descriptions has been repeatedly discussed by Edward Bibring. I quote his views from a brief report given by Waelder [32, p. 471]. "Bibring speaks of 'singling out' a patient's present patterns of behavior and arriving, by way of a large number of intermediate patterns, at the original infantile pattern. The present pattern embodies the instinctual impulses and anxieties now operative, as well as the ego's present methods of elaboration (some of which are stereotyped responses to impulses and anxieties which have ceased to exist). Only by means of the most careful phenomenology and by taking into consideration all the ego mechanisms now operative can the present pattern of behavior be properly isolated out. If this is done imperfectly . . . or if all the earlier patterns are not equally clearly isolated, there is a danger that we shall never arrive at a correct knowledge of the infantile pattern and the result may well be an inexact interpretation of infantile material."

Helene Deutsch [3] describes in a strikingly similar case, in which the unconscious tendency to plagiarize ideas of an admired friend led to so severe a memory disturbance that the psychoanalytic method was used to eliminate fully the diagnosis of neurological disease. Had it been possible to obtain material from the childhood of Helene Deutsch's patient, we might have been able to link similarities and dissimilarities in the early history of both men to the later differences in the structure of their defenses and their symptomatology.[11] The mechanism described and made conscious in our patient's analysis, the id impulse, the impulse to devour, emerged into consciousness and further steps of interpretation led without constraint into the area which the first analysis had effectively analyzed. It is naturally not claimed that such procedures were altogether new at the time. There surely always have been analysts who approach a problem of interpretation approximately as outlined here. This type of approach has to some extent been systematized by the support and guidance of ego psychology. It seems that many more analysts now proceed similarly and that they have gained the impression that such a shift in emphasis is therapeutically rewarding.[12]

Planning and Intuition

One difference between older and newer methods of analyzing defense mechanisms and linking "surface" and "depth" of psychoanalytic findings to each other deserves a more detailed discussion. The advance in theory has made the interrelations of various steps in analytic work clearer and has thus facilitated communication about these problems. We can now teach more

---

[11] When analyzing the patient here discussed I was familiar with Deutsch's paper. Without being consciously aware of it, I followed her example when entering into the detailed examination of the patient's intellectual pursuits.

[12] In the case here discussed the analysis was interrupted by the Second World War. During its course the patient published at least one of the contributions he had for a long time planned to publish. He intended to resume analysis after the end of the war but contact with him could not be re-established at the time. I have since heard that he has found satisfaction in his home life and in his career.

accurately both the "hierarchy" and the "timing" of interpretations, and the "strategy" and "tactics" of therapy [25]. We are, however, gradually becoming aware of many uncertainties in this area. In speaking of hierarchy and timing of interpretations, and of strategy or tactics in technique, do we not refer to a plan of treatment, either to its general outline or to one adapted to the specific type of case and the specific prognosis? How general or specific are the plans of treatment which individual analysts form? At what point of the contact with the patient do the first elements of such plans suggest themselves, and at what point do they tend to merge? Under what conditions are we compelled to modify such impressions and plans; when do they have to be abandoned or reshaped? These are some of the questions on which a good deal of our teaching in psychoanalysis rests, and which are inadequately represented in the literature.[13] The subject is of considerable importance because in using checks and controls on prediction we could satisfy ourselves as to the validity and reliability of tentative forecasts of those operations on which analytic technique *partly* depends.[14]

The tendency to discuss "planning" and "intuition" as alternatives in analytic technique permeates psychoanalytic writings though it has repeatedly been shown that such an antithesis is unwarranted.[15] Theodor Reik's and Wilhelm Reich's unprofitable polemics against each other are liberally quoted in such discussions. In my opinion not only this controversy but the problem which it attempted to clarify is spurious. It is merely

---

[13] See Fenichel [4], Glover [14, 15], Sharpe [31] and particularly Lorand [23] who discuss some of these problems. A group of colleagues has started a highly promising method of investigation. Long after graduation from supervised work, they continue regularly to consult with several others on some of their cases over periods of years in order to make comparisons of the analytic "style" among the consultants. It is to be hoped that this comparison will include the problem of prediction in analytic discussions.

[14] The idea of small teams working over a number of years (with or without institutional backing) seems rapidly to be gaining ground among analysts. The comparison of technique in general and specifically the study of planning and predicting might well be ideally suited to stimulate team work, which, if adequately recorded, might prove to be of considerable documentary value.

[15] See Fenichel [4], and particularly Herold [19] and Grotjahn [16], who make similar points.

to be determined at what point preconscious thought processes in the analyst "take over" and determine his reaction, a question which touches upon every analyst's personal experience. There are some who are inhibited if they attempt consciously to formulate the steps to be taken, with whom full awareness acts as inhibition or distraction. There are those who at least from time to time wish to think over what they are doing or have done in a particular case, and others who almost incessantly wish to know "where they are." No optimal standard can be established. The idea, however, that the preconscious reactions of the analyst are necessarily opposed to "planning" seems, in the present stage of our knowledge about preconscious thought processes, to say the least, outdated [21].

Once we assume that the optimal distance from full awareness is part of the "personal equation" of the analyst, the contribution of preconscious processes gains considerable importance.[16] For one thing, it guarantees the spontaneity that prompts an analyst to say to a patient who showed considerable apprehension on the eve of a holiday interruption of analysis: "Don't trouble, I shall be all right." Many may at first feel that Ella Sharpe [31, p. 65], who reported this instance, had taken a daring step, and that her unpremeditated short cut went too far. But on second thought we may conclude that, provided the patient had been suitably prepared for the appearance of aggressive impulses within the transference, the wit of the interpretation may have struck home and created insight. Whether or not one approves of such surprise effects—and I confess my own hesitation—it is obvious that conscious premeditation could hardly bring them about. But even those of us who do not share the ebullient mastery of Ella Sharpe have reason to believe in the constructive contribution of intuition. Let me briefly refer to a patient who had been analyzed as a child, and whom I saw fifteen years after his first analytic experience had been interrupted through the influence of a truly seductive mother who could no longer bear to share the child with the child analyst. I was familiar with some of the aspects of the earlier analysis. Some of the symp-

---

[16] See Freud's description of these relationships in various passages of his early papers [13, p. 334].

toms had remained unchanged, some had returned, particularly prolonged states of sexual excitement, interrupted but hardly alleviated by compulsive masturbation or its equivalents, which in some cases led to disguised impulses toward exhibitionism. Long stretches of the analysis were at first devoted to the details of these states of excitement. It became clear that they regularly were initiated and concluded by certain eating and drinking habits. The total condition was designated by the patient and myself as "greed." In a subsequent phase phallic fantasies about the seductive mother were gradually translated into oral terms; the violent demand for love became a key that opened up many repressed memories which had not been revealed during the child's analysis. At one point, however, the process began to stagnate, the analysis became sluggish, when suddenly a change occurred. During one interview the patient manifested vivid emotions; he left the interview considerably moved and reported the next day that "this time it had hit home." He now understood. And as evidence he quoted that when his wife had jokingly and mildly criticized him he had started to cry and, greatly relieved, had continued to cry for many hours. What had happened? In repeating the interpretation I had without conscious premeditation used different terms. I did not speak of his *demand for love,* but of his *need for love* or expressions with a connotation which stressed not the aggressive but the passive craving in his oral wishes. Intuition had appropriately modified what conscious understanding had failed to grasp or, to be kinder to myself, had not yet grasped. This instance may serve to illustrate the necessary and regular interaction of planning and intuition, of conscious and preconscious stages of understanding psychoanalytic material. It is my impression that all advances in psychoanalysis have come about by such interactions, which have later become more or less codified in rules of technique.

Whenever we speak of the intuition of the analyst, we are touching upon a problem which tends to be treated in the psychoanalytic literature under various headings. We refer to the psychic equilibrium or the state of mind of the analyst. One part of this problem, however, is directly linked to the process of interpretation. Many times a brief glance in the direction of self-analysis is part and parcel of the analyst's intervention. The interconnection between attention, intuition, and self-analysis in the process of interpretation has been masterfully described by Ferenczi [5]:

"One allows oneself to be influenced by the free associations of the patient; simultaneously one permits one's own imagination to play on these associations; intermittently one compares new connections that appear with previous products of the analysis without, for a moment, losing sight of, regard for, and criticism of one's own biases.

"Essentially, one might speak of an endless process of oscillation between empathy, self-observation, and judgment. This last, wholly spontaneously, declares itself intermittently as a signal that one naturally immediately evaluates for what it is; only on the basis of further evidence may one ultimately decide to make an interpretation."

References

[1] ABRAHAM, KARL: (1919) A Particular Form of Neurotic Resistance Against the Psychoanalytic Method. In: *Selected Papers on Psychoanalysis.* London: Hogarth Press, 1942. Second Edition.

[2] ALEXANDER, FRANZ: *The Problem of Psychoanalytic Technique.* Psychoanalytic Quarterly, IV, 1935.

[3] DEUTSCH, HELENE: *Über bestimmte Widerstandsformen.* Int. Ztschr. f. Psa. u. Imago, XXIV, 1939.

[4] FENICHEL, OTTO: *Problems of Psychoanalytic Technique.* Albany: The Psychoanalytic Quarterly, Inc., 1941.

[5] FERENCZI, SANDOR: (1927) Die Elastizität der psychoanalytischen Technik. In: *Bausteine zur Psychoanalyse*, III. Bern: Hans Huber Verlag, 1939.

[6] FREUD, ANNA: (1936) *The Ego and the Mechanisms of Defense.* New York: International Universities Press, 1946.

[7] FREUD, SIGMUND: (1910) *The Future Prospects of Psychoanalytic Therapy.* Coll. Papers, II.

[8] ———: (1912) The Dynamics of the Transference. Coll. Papers, II.

[9] ———: (1912) Recommendations for Physicians on the Psychoanalytic Method of Treatment. Coll. Papers, II.

[10] ———: (1913) Further Recommendations on the Technique of Psychoanalysis. Coll. Papers, II.

[11] ———: (1918) Turnings in the Ways of Psychoanalytic Therapy. Coll. Papers, II.

[12] ———: (1937) Constructions in Analysis. Coll. Papers, V.

[13] ———: Aus den Anfängen der Psychoanalyse. London: Imago Publishing Co., Ltd., 1950.

[14] GLOVER, EDWARD: Lectures on Technique in Psychoanalysis. Int. J. Psa., VIII and IX, 1927 and 1928.

[15] ———: An Investigation of the Technique of Psychoanalysis. Research Supplement No. 4 to the Int. J. Psa., 1940.

[16] GROTJAHN, MARTIN: About the Third Ear in Psychoanalysis. Psa. Rev., XXXVII, 1950.

[17] HALLIDAY, JAMES L.: Psychosocial Medicine. New York: W. W. Norton & Co., Inc., 1948.

[18] HARTMANN, HEINZ: Technical Implications of Ego Psychology. Psychoanalytic Quarterly, XX, 1951.

[19] HEROLD, CARL M.: A Controversy About Technique. Psychoanalytic Quarterly, VIII, 1939.

[20] KRIS, ERNST: On Inspiration. Int. J. Psa., XX, 1939.

[21] ———: On Preconscious Mental Processes. Psychoanalytic Quarterly, XIX, 1950.

[22] ———: Introduction to Freud: Aus den Anfängen der Psychoanalyse.

[23] LORAND, SANDOR: Technique of Psychoanalytic Therapy. New York: International Universities Press, 1946.

[24] ———: Comments on Correlation of Theory and Technique. Psychoanalytic Quarterly, XVII, 1948.

[25] LOEWENSTEIN, RUDOLPH M.: The Problem of Interpretation. Psychoanalytic Quarterly, XX, 1951.

[26] NUNBERG, HERMAN: On the Theory of Therapeutic Results of Psychoanalysis. Int. J. Psa., XVIII, 1937.

[27] REICH, WILHELM: (1928) On Character Analysis. In: *The Psychoanalytic Reader*. Edited by Robert Fliess. New York: International Universities Press, 1948.

[28] ————: (1933) *Character Analysis*. New York: Orgone Institute Press, 1945.

[29] REIK, THEODOR: *Surprise and the Psychoanalyst*. New York: E. P. Dutton & Co., 1937.

[30] SCHMIDEBERG, MELITTA: *Intellektuelle Hemmung und Ess-störung*. Ztschr. f. psa. Päd., VIII, 1934.

[31] SHARPE, ELLA F.: (1930) The Technique of Psychoanalysis. In: *Collected Papers on Psychoanalysis*. London: Hogarth Press, 1950.

[32] WAELDER, ROBERT: *The Problem of the Genesis of Psychical Conflict in Earliest Infancy*. Int. J. Psa., XVIII, 1937.

[33] ————: *Kriterien der Deutung*. Int. Ztschr. f. Psa. u. Imago, XXIV, 1939.

Anxiety

Freud was the first to identify anxiety as the central problem in neurosis. A study of the changes in our understanding of the nature and significance of anxiety demonstrates the developing trends in psychoanalytic thinking. The paper by May describes the changes through which Freud's observations passed, from the original formulation on a solely physiological basis to the later conception of anxiety as a response to the danger from significant figures as a result of libidinal desires. The danger from the significant persons was the threat of castration (in the male); later the danger was internalized as fear of the individual's own conscience, or social anxiety. The paper by Fromm-Reichmann elaborates on the role of anxiety in interpersonal relatedness, and its place in the fabric of our social structure.

8

ROLLO MAY

Freud's Evolving Theories
of Anxiety*

Though others, like Kierkegaard, had preceded Freud in recognizing the crucial importance of the problem of anxiety in
understanding human behavior, Freud was the first in the
scientific tradition to see the fundamental significance of the
problem.[1] More specifically, he directed attention to anxiety as
the basic question for the understanding of emotional and psy-

---

* Reprinted by permission from *The Meaning of Anxiety* (New York,
1950). Copyright 1950 by The Ronald Press Company.

[1] Freud stands in the line of those explorers of human nature of the
nineteenth century—including Kierkegaard, Nietzsche, Schopenhauer—who rediscovered the significance of the irrational, dynamic, "unconscious" elements
in personality. (Cf. Thomas Mann, *Freud, Goethe, Wagner* [New York,
1937].) These aspects of personality had tended to be overlooked—and in
many ways suppressed—by the rationalistic preoccupations of most Western
thinking since the Renaissance. Though Kierkegaard, Nietzsche, and Freud
attacked the rationalism of the nineteenth century for different reasons, they
had in common the conviction that the traditional modes of thought omitted
elements vital for the understanding of personality. The so-called irrational
springs of human behavior had been left outside the accepted area of scientific
investigation or lumped under the so-called instincts. Freud's reaction against
the endeavors of academic medicine of his day to explain anxiety by "describing the nerve-pathways by which the excitations travel" and his conviction
that the methods of academic psychology of his day yielded little or no help
in the dynamic understanding of human behavior which he sought can be
understood, it seems to this writer, in this light. At the same time, Freud felt
himself to be an enthusiastic champion of science in his avowed intention
of making the "irrational" elements in behavior explicable in terms of his
broader concept of scientific method. That he carried over into his work some
of the presuppositions of the nineteenth century traditional (physical) science
is illustrated in his libido theory, which will be commented on below.

chological disorders; anxiety, he notes in his later essay devoted to this topic, is the "fundamental phenomenon and the central problem of neurosis." [2]

Students of dynamic psychology would no doubt agree that Freud is the pre-eminent explorer of the psychology of anxiety, that he both showed the way and gave many of the most efficacious techniques for the understanding of the problem, and that therefore his work is of classic importance even though it is now widely believed that many of his conclusions must be qualified and reinterpreted. To study Freud on anxiety is to become aware that his thinking on the topic was in process of *evolution* throughout his life. His theories of anxiety underwent many minor changes as well as one revolutionary change. Since anxiety is so fundamental a question, it cannot be given any simple answers; and Freud significantly confesses in his last writings that he is still presenting hypotheses rather than a "final solution" to the problem.[3] Therefore we shall endeavor in this survey not only to present Freud's central insights and his innumerable observations into the mechanics of anxiety, but also to plot the *directions* in which his concept of anxiety was evolving.

To begin with, Freud makes the customary distinction between fear and anxiety which we have already noted in the work of Goldstein and others. Freud holds that in fear the attention is directed to the object, whereas anxiety refers to the condition of the individual and "ignores the object." [4] To him the more

---

[2] *The problem of anxiety*, trans. H. A. Bunker (American ed.; New York, 1936), p. 111.

[3] *New introductory lectures in psychoanalysis* (New York, 1933), p. 113.

[4] *General introduction to psychoanalysis*, p. 343. Beyond this brief distinction, Freud does not—either in the chapter on anxiety in the *General introduction to psychoanalysis* or in his later *Problem of anxiety*—throw much illumination on the problem of fear as such. He treats Stanley Hall's list of allegedly innate fears, such as fear of darkness, fear of bodies of water, of thunder, etc., as phobias, which are by definition expressions of neurotic anxiety. In a summary of Freud's views in W. Healy, A. F. Bronner, and A. M. Bowers, *The structure and meaning of psychoanalysis* (New York, 1930), p. 366, a distinction between real fear and neurotic fear is made which is parallel to Freud's distinction between real and neurotic anxiety. Real fear, it is stated, is the reaction to an objective danger, whereas neurotic fear is the "fear of an impulse claim." Freud is interpreted as holding that "three practically universal childhood fears"—fear of being alone, fear of darkness, and the fear of strangers—arise out of the "unconscious Ego's fear of loss of

significant distinction is between objective (what we would term "normal") and neurotic anxiety. The former, "real" anxiety, is the reaction to an external danger; he conceives it as a natural, rational, and useful function. This objective anxiety is an expression of the "instincts of self-preservation." "The occasions of it, i.e., the objects or situations about which anxiety is felt, will obviously depend to a great extent upon the state of the person's knowledge and feeling of power regarding the outer world." [5] This "anxious readiness," as Freud terms objective anxiety, is an expedient function, since it protects the individual from being surprised by sudden threats (frights) for which he is unprepared. Objective anxiety does not in itself constitute a clinical problem. But any development of anxiety beyond the initial prompting to survey the danger and make the best preparation for flight is inexpedient: it paralyzes action. "The *anxious readiness* therefore seems to me the expedient element, and the *development* of anxiety the inexpedient element, in what we call anxiety or dread." [6] It is, of course, this development of anxiety in amounts out of proportion to the actual danger, or even in situations where no ostensible external danger exists, which constitutes the problem of neurotic anxiety.

Freud's First Theory: Anxiety as Repressed Libido.[7] How is it possible, Freud asks in his early writing, to bring the phenomenon of neurotic anxiety into logical relationship with objective anxiety? In the endeavor to answer this question he cites his observations in clinical work. He had noticed that patients who exhibit inhibitions or symptoms of various sorts are often remarkably free from overt anxiety. In phobias, for example, the patient exhibits an intense concentration of anxiety on one point in his environment—namely, the object of his phobia—but he is free from anxiety at other points in his en-

the protecting object, namely, the mother"—*Ibid.* This is synonymous with his definition of the source of anxiety in similar situations; apparently the terms "fear" and "anxiety" are here used interchangeably, the former being the term for the emergence of anxiety in specific form.

[5] *General introduction to psychoanalysis,* p. 342.

[6] *Ibid.,* p. 343.

[7] The first and second theories have to do with the mechanics, as contrasted with the *origins,* of anxiety.

vironment. In obsessional acts, likewise, the patient seems to be free of anxiety so long as he is permitted to carry out his act in unmolested fashion, but as soon as he is prevented from performing the obsessional act, intense anxiety appears. So, Freud reasoned understandably, some substitutive process must be occurring, i.e., the symptom must in some way be taking the place of the anxiety. He observed at the same time that his patients who experienced continual sexual excitation which was ungratified—he cites cases of coitus interruptus, for one example —also exhibited a good deal of anxiety. Hence, he concluded, the substitutive process occurring must be the interchange of anxiety, or anxiety-equivalents in the form of symptoms, for unexpressed libido. He writes, "libidinal excitation disappears and anxiety appears in place of it, both in the form of expectant dread and in that of anxiety attacks and anxiety-equivalents." [8] Looking back from a later date on the observations which led to this theory, Freud remarks, "I found that certain sexual practices, such as coitus interruptus, frustrated excitement, enforced abstinence, give rise to outbreaks of anxiety and a general predisposition to anxiety—which may be induced whenever, therefore, sexual excitation is inhibited, frustrated, or diverted in the course of its discharge in gratification. Since sexual excitement is the expression of libidinal instinctual impulses, it did not seem rash to suppose that through the influence of such disturbances the libido became converted into anxiety." [9]

The first theory, therefore, states that when libido is repressed, it becomes transformed into anxiety, and then reappears as free-floating anxiety or as an anxiety-equivalent (symptom). "Anxiety is thus general current coin for which all the affects are exchanged, or can be exchanged, when the corresponding ideational content is under repression." [10] When an affect is repressed, its fate is "to be converted into anxiety, no matter what quality of affect it would otherwise have been had it run a normal course." [11] The source of the child's anxiety at missing his

---

[8] *General introduction to psychoanalysis*, p. 348.
[9] *The problem of anxiety* (American ed.; New York, 1936), pp. 51-52.
[10] *General introduction to psychoanalysis*, p. 350.
[11] *Ibid.*, p. 355.

mother, or at the appearance of strange people (which represents the same danger situation as missing the mother, since the presence of the strange people signifies the mother's absence), lies in the fact that the child cannot then expend his libido towards the mother, and the libido is "discharged through being converted into anxiety." [12]

Recalling that objective anxiety is a flight-reaction to external danger, Freud asks what the individual is afraid of in neurotic anxiety. The latter, he answers, represents a flight from the demands of one's own libido. In neurotic anxiety "the ego is attempting a flight from the demands of its libido, and is treating this internal danger as if it were an external one." "Repression is an attempt at flight on the part of the ego from libido which it feels to be dangerous: the phobia (for example) may be compared to a fortification against the outer danger which now stands for the dreaded libido." [13] To summarize Freud's first theory of neurotic anxiety: the individual experiences libidinal impulses which he interprets as dangerous, the libidinal impulses are repressed, they become automatically converted into anxiety, and they find their expression as free-floating anxiety or as symptoms which are anxiety-equivalents.

This first endeavor of Freud's to formulate a theory of anxiety is undeniably based initially on observable clinical phenomena: everyone has noticed that when strong and persistent desires are held in check or repressed, the individual will often exhibit chronic restlessness or various forms of anxiety. But this is a phenomenological description, which is a quite different thing from a *causal explanation* of anxiety—as Freud himself was later to acknowledge. Furthermore, the phenomenon of sexual repression resulting in anxiety is by no means consistent; the "frank libertine," as Mowrer puts it, may be a very anxious person, and many well-clarified persons may bear a great deal of sexual abstinence without anxiety. On the positive side, this first theory does have the value of emphasizing the intrapsychic locus of neurotic anxiety. But the suggested mechanism of automatic conversion of libido—an attractive concept, perhaps chiefly

---

[12] *Ibid.*, p. 353.
[13] *Ibid.*, p. 355.

because it fits chemical-physiological analogies so handily—is highly dubious, as Freud himself was later to see. Some of the inadequacies of the first theory can best be seen by following the clinical observations and reasoning which led Freud to reject it.

Freud's Second Theory: Anxiety as the Cause of Repressions. On later analysis of patients with phobias and other anxiety symptoms, Freud found that a quite different process with respect to anxiety was occurring. A new theory was made necessary, too, by his increasing emphasis on the role of the ego, which had played only an auxiliary part in the first theory.[14]

He demonstrates the analysis which led to the new theory with the case of Hans, the five-year-old boy who refused to go out into the street (the inhibition) because of his phobia of horses (the symptom). Hans had considerable ambivalence toward his father, which Freud explains in classical Oedipus fashion. The little boy felt strong desires for the love of his mother and consequent jealousy and hatred of his father. But at the same time he was devoted to his father in so far as his mother did not enter the picture as a cause of dissension. Because of the father's strength, the aggressive impulses in Hans would cue off anxiety. The hostility carries with it frightening possibilities of retaliation, and it also involves the boy in continuous ambivalence toward a father to whom he is at the same time devoted; hence the hostility and related anxiety undergo repression. These affects are then displaced upon horses. Without going into detail about the mechanism of phobia formation, we wish only to make Freud's point that the phobia of horses is a symptomatic representation of Hans's fears of his father. Freud interprets this fear in typical castration terms: the fear of the bite of the horse is fear of having the penis bitten off. "This substitute formation [i.e., the phobia] has two patent advantages: first, that it avoids the conflict due to ambivalence, for the father is an object who is at the same time loved; and secondly,

---

[14] "The division of the mental personality into a super-ego, ego and id . . . has forced us to take up a new position with regard to the problem of anxiety."—*New introductory lectures*, p. 118.

that it allows the ego to prevent any further development of anxiety." [15]

The crucial point in this analysis is that the *ego perceives the danger*. This perception arouses anxiety (Freud speaks of the "ego" arousing anxiety), and as an endeavor to avoid the anxiety the ego effects the repression of the impulses and desires which would lead the person into danger. "It is not the repression that creates the anxiety," Freud now remarks against his first theory, "but the anxiety is there first and creates the repression!" [16] The same process holds true for other symptoms and inhibitions: the ego perceives the danger signal, and the symptoms and inhibitions are then created in the endeavor to avoid the anxiety. We may now, writes Freud, take the new view that the "ego is the real locus of anxiety, and reject the earlier conception that the cathectic energy of the repressed impulse automatically becomes converted into anxiety." [17]

A qualification is now also made by Freud in his earlier statement that the danger feared in neurotic anxiety is that simply of inner instinctual impulses. Speaking of Hans, he writes, "But what sort of anxiety can it be? It can only be fear of a threatening external danger; that is to say, objective anxiety. It is true that the boy is afraid of the demands of his libido, in this case of his love for his mother; so that this is really an instance of neurotic anxiety. But this being in love seems to him to be an internal danger, which he must avoid by renouncing his object, only because it involves an external danger-situation [retaliation, castration]." Though this interrelationship of external and internal factors was found by Freud in every case he investigated during this later period, he confesses "that we were not prepared to find that the internal instinctual danger was only a half-way house to an external and real danger-situation." [18]

---

[15] *The problem of anxiety*, p. 80.

[16] *New introductory lectures*, p. 119.

[17] *The problem of anxiety*, p. 22.

[18] *New introductory lectures*, p. 120. This interrelationship between internal and external factors, in Freud's viewpoint, can be demonstrated in terms of conditioned-response psychology. If Hans were merely afraid of his father's punishment (as an external danger), Freud would not call his anxiety neurotic. The neurotic element enters because of the ego's perception of the danger inherent in the internal instinctual promptings (Hans's hostility toward

Many students of anxiety feel that this second theory, with its emphasis on the ego function, makes possible a more adequate description of the mechanics of anxiety. Symonds points out that the second theory is more compatible with other psychological approaches to the problem.[19] In similar vein, Horney holds that whereas the first theory was essentially "physiochemical," the second is "more psychological." In any case, the second hypothesis evidences some clear and significant trends in Freud's understanding of anxiety, which will be discussed below.

Origins of Anxiety. Freud states that the capacity for anxiety is innate in the organism, that it is part of the self-preservation instinct, and that it is phylogenetically inherited. In his words, "we ascribe to the child a strong tendency to objective anxiety and should regard it as only practical if this apprehensiveness had been transmitted by inheritance." [20] Specific anxieties, however, are taught: of genuine "objective anxieties"—by which Freud means fear of climbing on window sills, fear of fire, etc.— "the child seems to bring very little into the world." And "it is entirely due to training that real anxiety does eventually awake in him." [21] We take this to mean that in Freud's viewpoint the tendency to, or capacity for, anxiety is part of the individual's

his father, for example). Now it is well known that inner promptings in the individual's experience can come easily to stand for external, objective dangers. If hostility toward the parent is met by retaliation, the child will soon be conditioned to experience anxiety whenever the hostile promptings arise intra-psychically.

It is questionable whether one ever encounters purely "internal" or "external" factors in a given organism's behavior and whether, therefore, some falsification is not involved in the use of these terms. This query will be dealt with more fully below.

[19] Symonds, *The dynamics of human adjustment, op. cit.*

[20] *General introduction to psychoanalysis*, p. 353. Whether capacities or traits can logically be said to be "phylogenetically inherited" is, of course, questionable. See Goldstein in Chapter 3 of this book [*The Meaning of Anxiety*, pp. 48-57]. It is doubtful to the present writer whether the phylogenetic concept is useful except in terms of transmission via culture.

[21] *Ibid.* Freud takes maturation into account: "A certain predisposition to anxiety on the part of the infant is indubitable. It is not at its maximum immediately after birth, to diminish gradually thereafter, but first makes its appearance later on with the progress of psychic development, and persists over a certain period of childhood."—*The problem of anxiety*, p. 98.

innate capacity, whereas the specific forms this anxiety will take are due to learning.

Beyond the above general statement, Freud finds the origin of anxiety in the *birth trauma* and *fear of castration*. These two concepts are interwoven and progressively reinterpreted in his writings. The *affect* which comes with anxiety, Freud holds in his early lectures, is a reproduction and repetition of some particular very significant previous experience. This he believed to be the birth experience—"an experience which involves just such a concatenation of painful feelings, of discharges and excitation, and of bodily sensations, as to have become a prototype for all occasions on which life is endangered, ever after to be reproduced again in us as the dread or 'anxiety' condition." He adds, foreshadowing his later broadening of the birth concept, "It is very suggestive too that the first anxiety state arose on the occasion of the separation from the mother." [22] The child's having anxiety at the appearance of strange people and its fears of darkness and loneliness (which he terms the first phobias of the child) have their origin in dread lest the child be separated from his mother.

It is an important question, in reviewing Freud's later writings, how far he was considering the birth experience as a literal source of anxiety, to be cued off by later danger situations, and how far he regarded it as a prototype in a symbolic sense, i.e., symbolic for separation from the loved object. Since he places great emphasis on castration as the specific source of anxiety underlying many neuroses, he is at pains to explain how castration and the birth experience are interrelated. We shall, therefore, now investigate how he progressively reinterprets and interrelates castration and the birth experience page by page in his chief essay on anxiety.[23] Speaking of the danger underlying the development of phobias, conversion hysteria, and compulsion neuroses, he notes, "in all these, we assume castration anxiety as the motive force behind the struggles of the ego." [24] Even fear

---

[22] *General introduction to psychoanalysis*, p. 344.
[23] *The problem of anxiety.*
[24] *Ibid.*, p. 75.

of death is an analogue of castration, since no one has actually experienced death but everyone has experienced a castration-like experience in the loss of the mother's breast in weaning. He then speaks of the danger of castration "as a reaction to a loss, to a separation," of which the prototype is the birth experience. But he is critical of Rank's too specific deduction of anxiety and consequent neurosis from the severity of the birth trauma. In reaction against Rank, he holds that the danger situation in birth is "the loss of the loved (longed for) person," and the "most basic anxiety of all, the 'primal anxiety' of birth, arises in connection with separation from the mother." [25] Castration he now relates to the loss of the mother by Ferenczi's reasoning: the loss of the genital deprives the individual of the means of later reunion with the mother (or mother substitute). Fear of castration later develops into dread of conscience, i.e., social anxiety; now the ego is afraid of the anger, punishment, loss of love of the superego. The final transformation of this fear of the superego consists of death anxiety.[26]

Thus we are presented with a hierarchy: fear of loss of the mother at birth, loss of the penis in the phallic period, loss of the approval of the superego (social and moral approval) in the latency period, and finally loss of life, all of which go back to the prototype, the separation from the mother. All later anxiety occasions "signify in some sense a separation from the mother," [27] which must mean that castration stands for the loss of a prized object of value, in the same sense as birth stands for the loss of the mother. Another datum which impelled him to interpret castration in a nonliteral fashion was the fact that the female sex, "certainly more predisposed to neurosis," as he remarks, cannot suffer literal castration because of the absence of a penis to begin with. In the case of women, he states that anxiety arises over fear of the loss of the love of the object (mother, husband) rather than loss of the penis.

Though one cannot be certain as to how far Freud was regarding the birth experience and castration literally and how

[25] *Ibid.*, pp. 99-100.
[26] *Ibid.*, p. 105.
[27] *Ibid.*, p. 123.

far symbolically, we submit that the *trend* in Freud's reasoning cited above is toward an increasingly symbolic interpretation. To the present writer this is a positive trend. With respect to castration, there may legitimately be considerable question as to whether literal castration is a source of anxiety on any wide scale. We suggest that castration is a culturally determined symbol around which neurotic anxiety may cluster.[28]

With respect to the birth trauma, we regard Freud's increasingly symbolic interpretation also as a positive trend. It is still an open question in experimental and clinical psychology how far the severity of the birth experience is a literal source of later anxiety.[29] But even if the actual birth experience cannot be accepted as the source of anxiety in literal fashion, it would certainly be widely agreed that the infant's early relations with its mother, which so intimately condition both its biological and psychological development, are of the greatest significance for later anxiety patterns. Hence the present writer wishes to emphasize that facet of Freud's thought which holds that *anxiety has its source, as far as a primal source is reactivated in later neurotic anxiety, in the fear of premature loss of or separation*

---

[28] Since castration and other aspects of the Oedipus situation are so important in Freudian discussions of anxiety, another question may be raised. Does not neurotic anxiety arise around castration or the Oedipus situation only when there are prior disturbances in the relationship between parents and child? To illustrate in the case of Hans, are not the boy's jealousy and consequent hatred of his father themselves the product of anxiety? Apparently Hans had exclusive needs for his mother, needs which her loving the father would threaten. Are not such needs (which may fairly be termed excessive) in themselves an outgrowth of anxiety? It may well be true that the conflict and anxiety leading to the particular phobic construction which Freud analyzes are specifically related to ambivalence and hostility toward the father. But we submit that this hostility and ambivalence would not have developed except as Hans was already in a disturbed relationship with his mother and father which produced anxiety and led to exclusive demands for his mother. One can understandably hold that every child experiences clashes with its parents in its development of individuality and autonomy (*vide* Kierkegaard, Goldstein, etc.), but in the normal child (defined as the child in a relationship to its parents which is not characterized by pronounced anxiety) such clashes do not produce neurotic defenses and symptoms. It is here suggested, *in fine,* that Oedipus situations and castration fears do not emerge as *problems*—i.e., do not become the foci of neurotic anxiety—unless prior anxieties already exist in the family constellation.

[29] For discussion of the possible relation between birth and anxiety, see Symonds, *op. cit.*

from the mother (or mother's love), and thence fear of the loss of subsequent values. Indeed, in the development and clinical application of Freudian theory, this interpretation is widely made, often in the form of the primal source of anxiety as being rejection by the mother.[30]

Trends in Freud's Theories of Anxiety. Since we are concerned with the evolution of Freud's understanding of anxiety, we shall summarize certain directions in which his thinking was moving from his earlier to his later writings on anxiety.[31] *First, in respect to the role of libido in anxiety.* There is evidenced in Freud a trend toward removing the libido theory from the primary position in his understanding of anxiety to a secondary position. Whereas the earlier theory of anxiety was almost wholly a description of what happened to libido (it was an "exclusively economic interpretation," Freud remarks), in his later writing he states that he is now not so much interested in the fate of the libido. His second theory still presupposes the libido concept, however: the energy which becomes anxiety is still libido withdrawn from the cathexis of repressed libido, the ego performs its repressive functions by means of "desexualized" libido, and the danger faced (to which anxiety is the reaction) is the "economic disturbance brought about by an increase in stimuli demanding some disposition be made of them." [32]

---

[30] Cf. D. M. Levy: "[The] . . . most potent of all influences on social behavior is derived from the primary social experience with the mother."— Maternal over-protection, *Psychiatry*, 1, 561 ff. Grinker and Spiegel, whose viewpoint represents a development of Freudianism, point out in their study of anxiety in combat airmen that fear or anxiety will not develop unless the value or object that is threatened in combat is "something that is loved, highly prized, and held very dear." This may be a person (one's self or a loved one) or a value like an abstract idea.—*Men under stress* (Philadelphia, 1946), p. 120. We here suggest, in line with Freud's discussion above, that the primal form of the prized person is the mother and that the capacity to prize other persons and values is a development from this first prototype.

[31] This approach—plotting the trends in Freud's thinking—is fitting in the respect that Freud's thinking was germinal; it was changing and developing through most of his life. This makes dogmatism about his views of very dubious worth; but the changing nature of his views also makes for ambiguity in his writings. For example, at times Freud writes as though he had completely rejected his first theory, but at other times as though he believed it compatible, in a subsumed position, with the second theory.

[32] *The problem of anxiety*, p. 100.

Though Freud retained the libido concept through all his writings, the trend is *from* a description of anxiety as an automatic conversion of libido *to* a description of the individual perceiving a danger and utilizing libido (energy) in coping with this danger. This trend accounts partially for the fact that Freud's second theory presents a more adequate description of the mechanism of anxiety. But the present writer questions whether the secondary emphasis on the libido theory in Freud's later writings on anxiety does not confuse the problem by its emphasis on the individual as a carrier of instinctual or libidinal needs which must be gratified.[33] The view taken in the present study involves carrying the above trend in Freud's writing further in the respect that libido or energy factors are seen not as given economic quantities which must be expressed, but as functions of the values or goals the individual seeks to attain as he relates himself to his world.

A second trend is seen in Freud's conception of how anxiety symptoms are formed. This trend is shown most vividly in the reversal of his early view that repression causes anxiety to the later view that anxiety causes repression. What this shift implies is that anxiety and its symptoms are seen not as merely the outcome of a simple intrapsychic process, but *as arising out of the individual's endeavor to avoid danger situations in his world of relationships.*

Another trend, with implications similar to that above, is indicated in Freud's endeavor to overcome the *dichotomy between "internal" and "external" factors* in the occasions of anxiety. Whereas in the earlier theory neurotic anxiety was viewed as fear of one's own libidinous impulses, Freud later saw that the libidinous impulses are dangerous because the expression of them would involve an external danger. The external danger was of only minor importance in the first theory when anxiety could be viewed as an automatic intrapsychic transformation of

---

[33] The present writer agrees with those critics of the Freudian libido theory who hold that the theory is a carry-over from nineteenth century physiochemical forms of thought. As an example of this physiochemical form of Freud's thinking, the translator of Freud's latest work makes an analogy between libido and an "electric charge." (*An outline of psychoanalysis,* trans. J. Strachey [New York, 1949], p. 23.)

libido, but it became a pressing problem to him in the cases he was analyzing in his later periods when he saw that the internal danger—danger from one's own impulses—arose from the fact that the individual was struggling against an "external and real danger-situation." This same trend toward seeing the anxious individual in a struggle with his environment (past or present) is indicated in the increasing prominence in Freud's later writings of the phrase "danger situation" rather than merely "danger." In his early writings we are informed that the symptom is developed to protect the individual from the demands of his own libido. But in developing his second theory he writes, "One might say, then, that symptoms are created in order to avoid the development of anxiety, but such a formulation does not go below the surface. It is more accurate to say that symptoms are created in order to avoid the *danger situation* of which anxiety sounds the alarm." [34] Later in this same essay he notes, "We have become convinced also that instinctual demands often become an (internal) danger only because of the fact that their gratification would bring about an external danger—because, therefore, this internal danger represents an external one." [35] Therefore the symptom is not merely a protection against inner impulses: "For our point of view the relationships between anxiety and symptom prove to be less close than was supposed, the result of our having interposed between the two the factor of the danger situation." [36] It may seem at first blush that we are laboring a minor point in emphasizing this shift from "danger" to "danger situation," but we believe that it is by no means an unimportant issue or a mere question of terminology. *It involves the whole difference between seeing anxiety as a more or less exclusively intrapsychic process, on the one hand, and*

---

[34] *The problem of anxiety*, p. 86. This is the point the present writer makes with respect to the function of symptoms (see Chapters 3 and 8).

[35] *Ibid.*, p. 152.

[36] *Ibid.*, p. 112. In some interpretations of Freudian theory the first emphasis of Freud is still made. Cf. Healy, Bronner, and Bowers: "Symptom-formation . . . is now regarded as a defense against or a flight from anxiety" (*The structure and meaning of psychoanalysis*, p. 411). Cf. the view advanced in Chapter 3 above, that the symptom is a protection from the anxiety-creating situation.

the view that anxiety arises out of the individual's endeavor to relate himself to his environment, on the other. In this second view intrapsychic processes are significant because they are reactions to, and means of coping with, the difficulties in the interpersonal world. The trend in Freud is toward a more organismic view—*organismic* being here defined as connoting a view of the person in his constellation of relationships. But it is well known that Freud never developed this trend to its logical conclusions in terms of a consistent organismic and cultural viewpoint. We believe he was prevented from doing so by both his libido theory and his topological concept of personality.

A final trend in Freud's thinking on anxiety is shown in his increased emphasis on the *topology of the psyche,* arising out of his division of the personality into superego, ego, and id. This makes it possible for him to center more of his attention on anxiety as being a function of the way the individual, via the ego, *perceives and interprets the danger situation.* He remarks that the phrase he employed in his earlier theory, "anxiety of the id," is infelicitous since neither id nor superego can be said to perceive anxiety. While this trend, like the others mentioned above, makes Freud's later concepts of anxiety more adequate and more understandable psychologically, we raise the question as to whether this topology, when employed in any strict sense, does not confuse the problem of anxiety. For example, Freud speaks in his later writing of the ego "creating" repression after it perceives the danger situation. Does not repression involve unconscious ("id," in topological terms) functions as well? Indeed, any symptom formation which is effective must involve elements which are excluded from awareness, as Freud himself, despite his topology, would be the first to admit. We suggest that repressions and symptoms can best be viewed as the organism's means of adjusting to a danger situation. While it is helpful and necessary to see in given cases that certain elements are in awareness and others are excluded from awareness, the strict application of the topology makes not only for inconsistencies in the theory but also shifts the attention away from the real locus of the problem, namely the organism and its danger situation.[37]

Another application of his topology made by Freud which reveals this problem is seen in his discussion of helplessness in anxiety. He holds that in neurotic anxiety the ego is made helpless by its conflict with the id and superego. While the present writer would agree that in all neurotic anxiety the individual is engaged in intrapsychic conflict, a question arises as to whether this conflict, rather than being a lack of accord among ego, superego, and id, is not really a conflict between contradictory values and goals the individual seeks to attain in relating himself to his interpersonal world. It is to be granted that certain poles of these conflicts will be in awareness and others will be repressed, and it is also to be granted that in neurotic anxiety previous conflicts in the individual's life-history are reactivated. But to our mind *both the present and the previous conflicts are to be seen not as between different "parts" of the personality but as between mutually exclusive goals made necessary by the individual's endeavor to adapt to a danger situation.*

It is unnecessary to labor the point of Freud's far-reaching contributions to the understanding of anxiety. For the purposes of the present discussion, these contributions consist chiefly in the many-sided illumination he shed upon symptom formation, in his emergent concern with the primal source of anxiety in the separation of the child from its mother, and in his emphasis on the subjective and intrapsychic aspects of neurotic anxiety.

---

[37] The confusing implications of Freud's topology are seen in his tendencies to think of the ego and the id as literally geographical regions in the personality. In his last writing, *Outline of psychoanalysis* (New York, 1949), he refers to his "topographical" viewpoint, speaks of the ego as "developed out of the cortical layer of the id" (p. 110), and uses such phrases as "mental regions" (p. 15) and "the outermost cortex of the ego" (p. 41). The present author believes that the equating of neurological areas with psychological functions can be done only very loosely; the two are never literally equivalent. The tendency to locate the "ego function" geographically reminds the present author of the endeavors of Descartes and others of the seventeenth century to locate man's "soul" in the pineal gland at the base of the brain! Again, we can do no better than to quote Freud himself; the essential thing is to grasp psychological facts psychologically.

9

FRIEDA FROMM-REICHMANN

Psychiatric Aspects of Anxiety*

The most unpleasant and at the same time the most universal experience, except loneliness, is anxiety. We observe both healthy and mentally disturbed people doing everything possible to ward off anxiety or to keep it from awareness.

Mentally disturbed people try to dispel anxiety by developing mental symptoms. In fact as first stated by Freud, mental symptoms are at the same time both the expression of unbearable anxiety and the means of warding it off. [9] In other words mental symptoms and mental illness can be understood simultaneously as the outcome of anxiety and as a defense against it. Mental illness can be understood as a person's response to unbearable anxiety. Therefore, anxiety constitutes an essential problem in psychotherapy.

This holds true even though we consider anxiety to be an experience by no means limited to the mentally disturbed. As initially stated, we realize that anxiety in its milder forms is a universal human phenomenon. Philosophers and psychologists have known and advanced this knowledge for a long time. In their eagerness to be great helpers and healers, psychiatrists have been and are still partly inclined to overlook the difference between what may be called the normal anxieties of the emotionally healthy and the neurotic or psychotic excess anxiety which should be subject to psychotherapy. For a long time, psychiatrists and psychotherapists have also overlooked the fact that

* This paper is part of the author's forthcoming publication on "The Philosophy of Psychotherapy" to be published by Grune & Stratton with whose permission it is preprinted here.

113

anxiety not only has negative, disintegrative facets but also some positive, constructive ones. As we set out to clarify the philosophy of psychotherapy regarding neurotic and psychotic anxieties, we must keep these two aspects of anxiety clearly in mind.

Anxiety, as we know, shows in a great variety of ways. Subjectively it may be experienced as a most unpleasant interference with thinking processes and concentration, as a diffuse, vague and frequently objectless feeling of apprehension or as a discomforting feeling of uncertainty and helplessness. As it arises in its milder forms, it may show objectively by a shift in tone of voice, and/or tempo of speech, by a change of posture, gesture and motion, also by the anxious person's intellectual or emotional preoccupation or blocking of communication. In people who are even more anxious, anxiety manifests itself psychologically in more or less marked degrees of paralysis of thought and action. The well known physical manifestations that may be caused by anxiety are symptoms of a hyperactive sympathetic system such as change of turgor, perspiration, tremor, sensation of a lump in the throat, sinking abdominal sensations, diarrhea, vomiting, changes in pupillary reactions, in heart beat, pulse rate and respiration. If anxiety-states become so severe that the anxiety-stricken person cannot handle them, mental symptoms and mental illness are the final outcome.

In the rare cases when anxiety is so severe that all these expressions of it and all defenses against it fail to bring relief, panic or terror may be the outcome. Panic, as defined by H. S. Sullivan, is an extreme concentration of attention and the direction of all available energy toward only one goal—escape, swift flight from internal dangers which are poorly envisaged, and in the case of failure to escape, by a temporary disintegration of personality with random destructive tendencies against oneself and others. Also according to Sullivan, terror is anxiety of a cosmic quality in the face of a primitively conceived threat of danger. The terror-stricken person feels himself to be alone among deadly menaces, more or less blindly fighting for his survival against dreadful odds. [29, 30] Fortunately, terror and panic are short lived. The organism produces quick defenses against the devastating influence which panic or terror of prolonged duration would exert. John Vassos' empathic pictorial work on Phobia (which, incidentally, is dedicated to H. S. Sullivan) should be mentioned here as an impressive contribution to the understanding of terror and panic. [34]

In contrast to these various forms of anxiety, fear is a useful, rational kind of fright elicited by realistic external dangers. To be described presently, and in contrast to fear, are the dangers from within, which elicit anxiety.

What is anxiety in terms of its conceptions in dynamic psychiatry? Freud says in "The Problems of Anxiety," that anxiety is felt by a person at the realization of formerly repressed inacceptable drives and wishes; his anxiety is with regard to loss of love and punishment, i.e. along the lines of Freud's libidinal concepts, castration-fear. [9]

We need not go into the discussion of Freud's older explanation of anxiety as the result of repressed sexual desires, [5] because he rejected it himself in "The Problems of Anxiety."

Sullivan shares with Freud the concept of the anxiety-arousing power of inacceptable thoughts, feelings, drives, wishes and actions. But in the framework of his interpersonal conceptions he sees these forbidden inner experiences as interpersonal ones, not as instinctual drives per se; also the expected punishment is not seen as castration-fear. Rather, it is experienced by the anxious person as the anticipated disapproval, i.e. loss of love, from the significant people of his early life, from whom he has originally learned to discriminate between acceptable and inacceptable drives, attitudes, and actions. Later on this fear of disapproval may be transferred from the original significant people who trained and educated the anxious person to their emotional successors. Guilt feelings, separately described by other authors, are obviously inherent in Sullivan's conception of anxiety. [29, 30, 31, 32]

This disapproval by the significant people of one's early life, to which both Freud and Sullivan refer, is vital enough to account for severe anxieties because the infant and the young child are dependent upon the early important people for fulfillment of their basic needs. The infant's survival depends upon the loving care he is given by the mothering ones of his infancy.

Nearly all psychological concepts of anxiety have, in common with Freud and Sullivan, this one basic conception: that anxiety is tied up with the inner danger of inacceptable thoughts, feelings, wishes or drives which elicit the expectation of loss of love and approval or of punishment. No matter how much these conceptions may differ in their explanatory details and regardless of whether or not this aspect of anxiety is explicitly mentioned in these conceptions, it is a viewpoint now commonly shared.

Let me quote a few outstanding representatives of various psychiatric schools of thinking. Rank speaks of separation anxiety which people first experience at birth and subsequently throughout their lives, present at all phases of personality-development and individuation, from weaning, i.e. separation from mother's breast, to separation from one's fellowmen, by death. [26]

Adler uses his concept of inferiority feelings where other authors speak of anxiety. He asserts that these inferiority feelings can be overcome by people only in affirmation and strengthening of their social bonds with society, by enforcing the sense of belonging to a social group. [1]

Horney emphasizes the central significance of the interrelatedness between anxiety and hostility—anticipated in others and sensed in the anxious person himself; here again anxiety is seen as being tied up with the fear of disruption of one's interpersonal relationships. [19]

Fromm, Berdyaev, Halmos, Kardiner, Riesman and other social psychologists find the source of man's anxiety in his psychological isolation, his alienation from his own self and from his fellowmen. They consider this the common fate of man in modern society, irrespective of his state of emotional health. [3, 10, 18, 22, 27] A poetic version of this viewpoint may be found in Auden's "Age of Anxiety." [2]

Goldstein's conception of anxiety as being the subjective experience of a danger to existence in the face of failure may also imply anxiety regarding loss of love and recognition by those who recognize the anxious person's failure. [15, 16]

The same holds true for Rollo May's definition of anxiety as "the apprehension set off by a threat to some value which the

individual holds essential to his existence as a personality." [1] [23]
Again this concept implies the fear of losing interpersonal recognition or acceptance since this could be tied up with the loss of
essential values in the life of the individual. I will return later
to the discussion of some other aspects of the conceptions
of these authors. At this point I am primarily interested in
demonstrating the ubiquitously implied acceptance of the concept that anxiety is connected with anticipated fear of punishment and disapproval, withdrawal of love, disruption of interpersonal relationships, isolation or separation.

This conception of anxiety as the expression of the anticipated
loss of love and approval, or separation, social isolation, or
disruption of one's interpersonal relationships implies its close
psychological affinity to loneliness. In fact, I believe that many
of the emotional states to which psychiatrists refer as anxiety
actually are states of loneliness or fear of loneliness. [2]

Now I wish to return to the discussion of the psychodynamics
of anxiety. According to Sullivan, the infant and child's need
for love and approval and the anxiety connected with rejection
and disapproval are utilized by the significant adults in handling
the necessary early processes which are designed to train the
infant and child for his interpersonal adjustment, his socialization
and acculturalization. Out of this educative process evolves the
part of human personality which Sullivan has called "self-
system." This self-system operates in the service of people to
obtain satisfaction without incurring too much anxiety. In the
process of establishing the self-system certain infantile trends
must be barred from awareness, dissociated. If they break into
awareness anxiety will reappear because the structure of the
self-system, the nature of which tends toward rigid maintenance
of its protective status quo, is threatened with change. This
defensiveness against change makes for the danger of personal

---

[1] Rollo May's book is most stimulating as a monograph in its own right,
but also as an excellent survey of the theories of anxiety. The proceedings of
the 39th Annual Meeting of the American Psychopathological Association,
1949; Grune & Stratton, 1950; edited by Hoch & Zubin ought to be quoted
as another useful compendium on the subject.

[2] I will elaborate on this topic in my forthcoming publication "Philosophy
of Psychotherapy." (See footnote on page 113.)

rigidity, which in turn increases the potentialities for further anxiety. [29, 30] This anxiety connected with change is eternally in conflict with man's general innate tendencies toward growth, toward the change which is implied and particularly with the innate motivation of mental patients toward health. One of the great responsibilities of the psychotherapist is to help patients face and overcome this conflict constructively. [12]

I would like to offer an additional explanatory concept about the factors which make people expect punishment, disapproval and loss of love and which has helped me to understand better than I did previously the psychological significance of the anxieties of people in general and of mental patients in particular. Let us ask again: what do people disapprove of most gravely in themselves, i.e. which trends in themselves do they expect will bring the most severe disapproval on the part of the significant people in their lives? Are there other significant causes for the anxiety-arousing anticipation of disapproval and isolation in addition to those we have quoted? Let me offer the following hypothetical answer.

It is a well-known psychological fact that a person will misvalue the significant people of his childhood to the extent to which his early interpersonal tie-ups remain unresolved. If these early interpersonal patterns stand uncorrected, people will distort the image of various people whom they meet in the course of their lives. They may or may not dimly sense that they do so, but they will not recognize the interpersonal misconceptions of their early childhood as the root of the distortions of their interpersonal relationships.

An adult person who finds himself compulsively appraising other people inadequately, incorrectly evaluating their reactions, acting upon and responding to them in line with these misconceptions in terms of early patterns of living, may many times become semi-aware of his erroneous judgment and behavior. However, he may feel inadequate and helpless in his dim wish or attempt to change and correct his judgment and his emotional reactions because he is unaware of their unconscious roots, the unmodified fixations to the patterns of interpersonal relationships which he acquired in his early years. This helplessness in the face of the need to change anachronistic, distorted patterns of interpersonal relationships meets with self-disapproval and discontent; it interferes with the innate tendency to self-realization; it produces deep insecurity in people and meets with the anticipated disapproval of others; thus, it is the expression of anxiety and it produces further anxiety. Goldstein could demonstrate this type of anxiety in his brain-injured patients. When they were faced with a simple task which they could not accomplish for reasons unknown to them, stemming from their neurological brain injury, they became the prey of an abject feeling of helplessness, of nothingness, or a "catastrophic reaction," as Goldstein has called it. [15, 16]

The hypothesis is offered that mentally disturbed people frequently develop a "catastrophic reaction," anxiety, in response to their compulsively determined inability to change their distorted, immature patterns of interpersonal relationships. This task may be set by the demands of their own conscience or by the actual or assumed demands of their elders or friends. This helplessness in the presence of the need to envision and to relate oneself adequately to other people, i.e. in accordance with one's chronological age and with one's psychological reality without full awareness of its causes, is most frightening, for more than one reason. It elicits a general feeling of helplessness and paralysis. It means that the person concerned is living in an unreal psychological world and that he feels he is in danger of pulling the people of his environment actually or in fantasy into the same threatening abyss of unreality. Being unable to successfully avail himself of the possibility of using new means of evaluating people and of relating himself meaningfully to them amounts to being blocked in the utilization of learning processes which serve growth and change. This absence of growth and change is tantamount to psychological stagnation and emotional sterility, i.e. psychological death. [14] In other words, the repetition-compulsion to follow early patterns of interpersonal evaluation and relatedness and the inability to learn to replace them by new patterns, deprives a person of the freedom to live and move about in the world of psychological reality which should be his, deprives him of the freedom for self-realization and conveys feelings of stagnation and sterility, hence the fear of psychological death, of Tillich's "not being," or Goldstein's "nothingness." [15, 16, 33]

By "self-realization" I mean (to repeat a definition I have previously given [12]) a person's use of his talents, skills and powers to his satisfaction within the realm of his own freely established realistic set of values. Furthermore, I mean the uninhibited ability of patients to reach out for and to find fulfillment of their needs for satisfaction and security, as far as it can be obtained, without interfering with the laws and customs which protect the needs of their fellowmen. Goldstein's "self-actualization," Fromm's "productive character," Whitehorn's "mature personality" and the "self-affirmation" of the existentialists are formulations of the same concept. [10, 15, 35] In the classical psychoanalytic literature insufficient attention has been given so far to the concept of self-realization as a great source, if not the greatest source, of human fulfillment. Freud has referred to it in his teachings on secondary narcissism and ego-ideal formation, but he has dealt more with the investigation of the origin of the phenomenon than with the elaboration on the psychological significance of the end-product, mature self-realization. [7, 8]

The lack of freedom for self-realization and the feeling of stagnation and "nothingness" that goes with it, this sense of psychological death, seems to me to be at the root of many people's anxiety. To repeat, they cling to infantile interpersonal patterns, and as a result feel helpless without really knowing why. They are unable to grow emotionally, to develop or change. They are not able to think, feel and act according to their chronological age. They live anachronously in a deadening emotional rut where they compulsively continue to distort their interpersonal images of new people whom they meet, and to misvalue the interpersonal reactions and behavior of these people along the line of the conceptions gained in their unresolved interpersonal childhood contacts.

Example: A young woman, Anna, went to see her older friend and confidant, Mr. N., whom she trusted unequivocally. Anna asked him to contact certain significant people in her family and explain to them some facts about her life which she felt would be of immeasurable value for them and for her in the general family picture. Mr. N. assured Anna of his complete willingness to do this and when Anna left him she was confident that Mr. N. would take care of the situation with understanding and skill. For valid rational reasons, which are beside the point of our discussion, Mr. N. decided later not to meet the members of the family and have a talk with them along the lines suggested by Anna. He did not have an opportunity to discuss this with her. When Anna found out about it a few days later, she felt deep resentment against Mr. N. and developed a spell of severe anxiety. Why? She felt that her friend had not accepted here appraisal of the total situation nor given it serious consideration. She also felt he had treated her the same way her parents had always done; to judge everything the little girl suggested or offered for consideration as not being worthy of serious thought on their part, "little girls are too emotional." Anna realized though, that her resentment against Mr. N., whom she felt had betrayed her and had not taken her suggestion seriously was, somehow, unfounded and sensed dimly that he might well have fallen down on their agreement for valid, rational reasons. However, she felt completely incapable of overcoming her resentment and her severe spell of anxiety lasted for hours. The semi-awareness she had about the irrationality of her anxiety and resentment did not help any until, by psychoanalytic investigation, she finally discovered the reasons, of which she had been unaware. Then she recognized that her resentment was due to a distortion of the present situation between her and Mr. N., in the light of the unresolved interpersonal pattern of living with the parents of her childhood. ("little girl"—"too emotional"—judgment and suggestions deserve no consideration.)

Jurgen Ruesch's interesting new concept of anxiety which he gained from observation and investigation of people under stress, fits into this context. He says that anxiety arises as a result of overstimulation which cannot be discharged by action. [28] The anxious people who have been described are barred from discharging tension by action, from converting anxiety into euphoria because they live in a state of "not-being," or "nothingness."

The anxiety producing aspects of people's unresolved early tie-ups and involvements, of which they are only partially aware, receive additional reinforcement because so many of these anxiety producing aspects are experienced as forbidden and elicit anxiety connected guilt feelings. Love for the parent of the opposite sex and competitive hatred of the parent of the same sex should be mentioned here as the most outstanding example of such anxiety and guilt evoking psychological constellations.

The resolution of such early tie-ups with the parents of one's childhood, which I have implicitly recommended as a preventive against anxiety, should not be confused with manifestations of a child's outwardly breaking away from his parents. Children who succeed in breaking away from their parents early may experience increased anxiety, since this emerging independence of a child meets with a sense of loss on the part of the parents, hence frequently with their disapproval of the child.

The psychology of masturbation is illustrative of our last statement. There has been much discussion about the following question: Why are there so many children who never have been exposed to any warning against masturbation and many adults who intellectually do not consider masturbation forbidden or dangerous and yet there are practically no people who masturbate without feeling guilty and anxious about it? How can we explain this fact? I believe that guilt eliciting masturbatory fantasies are only partly, if at all, responsible. Many cases of masturbatory feelings of guilt and anxiety seem to be connected with the fact that masturbation represents a child's first act of independence from his parents or others who have raised and mothered him. He needs his elders for the fulfillment of all his basic needs; getting food and fresh air and for being kept clean and getting fresh clothes and bedding. Masturbation is the only pleasure he can obtain without their help. As such, it constitutes an act of breaking away from one's parents, for which the child feels guilty and anxious regardless of the permissive or non-permissive attitude of the elders towards the act of masturbation per se.

It has been stated that practically no one in this culture gets ideally rid of his early interpersonal tie-ups and the resulting interpersonal problems. In other words, almost no one is entirely prepared to face the anxiety provoking dangers of his present life, fully undistorted by interpersonal entanglements with the "ghosts of his past" and with full command of his adult emotional equipment. As Grinker puts it, in his research on "Anxiety and Psychosomatic Transactions": "The stimulus" (which arouses anxiety) "must be perceived in the light of inner expectation originating at an early and particularly helpless time in the organism's history, to be dangerous to its protective attachments and hence to his existence," i.e. to have the power to produce anxiety. [17]

People's fear of nothingness, of helplessness in the face of "psychological death," as it has been postulated here as being a central cause of human anxiety, has a factual correlate in the practically universal experience of anxiety with regard to actual death as a general phenomenon. The fact that life ends with death remains to most people an inconceivable experience of ultimate psychobiological separation. To others, the fact that time and cause of death are unpredictable conveys a painful sense of ultimate powerlessness. This fear and anxiety of death gains reinforcement from the fact that it does not stand only for itself but is also an expression and a symbol of other unknown and unpredictable forces which govern human existence. "It is this fact of our being in a finite and limited time, the awareness of (our) mortality and uncertainty of the future," which renders us helpless and anxious, as Podolsky puts it. [25] That is, people seem to feel the same helplessness and anxiety in the face of the phenomenon of actual death as they do in the face of the above defined personal experience of "psychological death."

There are various ways in which people may try to counteract the anxiety and the narcissistic hurt inflicted on them when they are faced with the necessity of accepting the reality of death. The powerfulness of these defenses is a measuring rod for the intenseness of the anxiety which people try to fight off with them.

The religious concept of the Hereafter is the greatest attempt to counteract the inconceivable separation experience which is death.

The well known phenomenon of people's guilt feelings after the death of a close person is, in my judgment, caused not only by the ambivalence toward the deceased, but also and more so by people's anxiety about the uncertainty and unpredictability which go with the very nature of life and death. Feeling guilty about someone's death means assuming part of the responsibility. If we are partly responsible, the inconceivable, unpredictable character of death is mitigated; it is put into some more acceptable context with that which man can influence—or fails to influence—by virtue of his own skills and powers.

A more pathological way of counteracting the anxiety connected with death is used by certain emotionally disturbed people to whom its uncertainty is so anxiety provoking and unbearable that they evade its acceptance, or at least find satisfaction in fantasying that they can evade it, by committing suicide. To these people, suicide means doing away with the unpredictability of the end of their lives. As if, by their own determination, they take the power of decision out of the hands of the Lord, of fate or of nature, as their conceptions may be. [36, 37]

These examples show that the defenses people feel the need to erect against the anxieties connected with actual death are just as powerful as the symptoms with which mental patients try to protect themselves against the anxiety connected with "psychological death."

Some psychoanalysts may ask at this point, how this concept of anxiety in the face of psychological and factual death ties up with the classical psychoanalytic concept of the death instinct? Freud postulated, in his metapsychological treatise, "Beyond the Pleasure Principle," that man is born with aggressive and destructive impulses against himself and others. [6] Man's death instinct, according to Freud, operates throughout his life as the expression of these self-destructive tendencies against himself.

Other psychoanalysts in writing about this topic have tried to prove the existence of the death instinct in terms of what, in their judgment, are self-destructive operations which we can observe in most people, such as their neglect in seeking medical help for obviously harmful pathological processes. [24] I believe this seemingly self-destructive behavior can be better understood as the outcome of man's fear of death than as the response to his death-instinct. He does not consult the doctor lest he be faced with a fatal prognosis of his ailment which might increase his fear of death.

I find myself in agreement with Sullivan, Fromm and several other dynamic psychiatrists and psychoanalysts who do not find any evidence of primary in-born hostile and destructive tendencies in the human mind, but who deduct from their psychiatric experience that the rise of hostile and destructive tendencies is the outcome of and the response to the adversities of people's interpersonal experiences throughout their lives. Consequently, these authors do not see any evidence of the original existence of self-destructive tendencies, of a death instinct, as a given ubiquitous phenomenon. [11, 29]

Irrespective of the controversial issue of Freud's concept of the death instinct, we agree with his conceptions that man must have some kind of an inner awareness, or sense some kind of reflection of the changes of the organism which take place daily and hourly in the direction of its final dissolution and death. I believe that man's inner awareness of these changes of the organism on its gradual way from birth to death contribute to his fear of death and to his anxiety of the unknown which is connected with the facts of death, rather than their being an expression of his death instinct.

So much about the anxiety connected with what I have called "psychological death" and about the anxiety connected with the psychological facts of actual death as a general human phenomenon. Our data corroborates our introductory statement about there being almost no one permanently free from anxiety. Yet, healthy people learn to handle their anxieties without converting them into symptoms. They may even be able to turn them into assets, a topic on which I have elaborated elsewhere. [13]

In the same context, let me also quote Horney who states that both types of anxiety, that of the mentally healthy and of mentally disturbed people, render them helpless and this helplessness in turn produces more anxiety, "secondary" anxiety. However, Horney says that anxiety in the face of actual death and of the other powers of nature must be accepted and does not call for the development of the defense mechanism and of the hostility and destructiveness which people develop in response to other—neurotic or psychotic—forms of helplessness and anxiety. The contrary may even be true. [19] Grinker corroborates this viewpoint when he states: "If anxiety is mild, it is stimulating and facilitates increased and efficient action or thought." [16]

As Fromm pointed out, anxiety in the face of the overwhelming and unpredictable powers of nature, which is the common fate of all of us, may be used as a motivation for increasing the common bonds between human beings.

Freud, and also Adler, have emphasized the viewpoint that human efforts to allay anxiety have led to the development of civilization. Jung and Adler also emphasize the positive powers of constructive defense which may be aroused in people for the sake of counteracting their anxiety. [1, 6, 21]

The existentialists, including one of the outstanding psychiatrists among them, Binswanger, stress the constructive aspects of anxiety even more. They consider it the equivalent of the tension aroused in a person who is able to face the universe and the task which is set to men, to conquer the emanations of the universe by action. [4, 35]

States of anxiety which are severe enough to call for expression and defense by mental symptoms, i.e. the states of excess anxiety of which neurotic and psychotic patients suffer, are, of course, not constructive except for the times when they are reduced to milder degrees.

It should not be overlooked though, that the anxiety of mental patients under treatment can be psychotherapeutically utilized as a signpost indicating underlying conflicts and as a challenge to solve them. This holds true for neurotic patients as well as for psychotics. In fact, it may be generally stated that mild degrees of anxiety, discomforting as they may be, can be useful danger signals to mentally healthy and to mentally disturbed people. [9, 35]

Some readers may be surprised that I suggest psychotherapeutic intervention not only with excess anxiety in neurotic patients but also in psychotics. Clinical experience during the last 25 or 30 years has taught dynamic psychiatrists that both neurotic and psychotic excess anxieties can be successfully treated with psychoanalysis or psychoanalytically oriented dynamic psychotherapy. Time and space permitting, I could corroborate this statement with many examples from my own experience and that of many other psychiatrists who work with both types of patients. We cannot enter into a discussion of the psychotherapeutic techniques which dynamic psychiatrists use in the treatment of anxiety. If our initial statement is correct, that anxiety is at the root of every mental disturbance, then it is also true that any discussion of psychotherapeutic methods in the treatment of neurotic and psychotic anxieties would amount to writing a paper on psychotherapy at large.

I will restrict myself, therefore, to the following brief comments: We have seen that people who suffer from anxiety are at best only semi-aware of its causes. Therefore, the focal point of all psychotherapeutic guidance or treatment of anxiety states is to help the anxious person uncover and understand the unconscious reasons for his helplessness and anxiety. Beyond that it follows from our distinction between mild degrees of anxiety and their predominantly constructive aspects and severe degrees of anxiety with their predominantly disjunctive aspects, that the specific psychotherapeutic usefulness of dynamic psychiatrists in helping anxious patients, encompasses three central therapeutic tasks. One therapeutic goal should be to guide people in understanding and then accepting and learning to live with and to utilize mild degrees of anxiety. In the case of more intensive states of anxiety, the psychotherapeutic goal should be to help people (patients), for preventive reasons, uncover, resolve and integrate the causes of these anxieties, lest they lead up to an expression by mental symptoms which simultaneously are used as defenses against the awareness of these anxiety states. In cases where a person's anxiety is severe enough to express itself in mental symptomatology and mental illness, the psychotherapeutic goal should be to help the mental patient with the methods of intensive psychoanalytically oriented dynamic psychotherapy to gain insight into the emotional roots of his anxiety and of his symptomatology, to understand the psychodynamic linkage between anxiety and symptomatology and to face, work through and eventually vanquish his excess anxiety. Caution is indicated regarding the timing and the dosage of therapeutic intervention and enlightenment, lest a patient be made to face more dynamic insight into his anxiety and greater amounts of open anxiety than he can accept at a given time.

The discussion of the psychotherapeutic aspects of anxiety would be more than incomplete if its focus were not extended to the problem of anxiety in psychotherapists. If it is true that there is practically no one who is permanently free from anxiety, and/or none in whom anxiety cannot be temporarily aroused by all kinds of adverse experiences, then this fact, of course, holds true for psychotherapists as well. In their case, we are especially interested in the feelings of anxiety which may, sometimes, be brought forth in them by their patients.

A psychotherapist who does not know and integrate this fact, who dreams about his non-vulnerability to anxiety, be it aroused in his exchange with patients or other persons, a psychotherapist who dreams about "complete emotional security" as an unreal goal for his own inner life, cannot guide his mental patients to wholesome, constructive testing and evaluation of their anxieties and to a constructive adjustment to the facts and data of their internal and external reality. Awareness of his anxiety, not freedom from or denial of it and sufficient emotional security to accept and handle it is the philosophical attitude toward anxiety to be expected of a competent, mature psychiatrist. Incidentally, there was a time when it was my belief that a well-analyzed psychotherapist should be altogether free from anxiety and emotional insecurity. As a matter of fact, my printed elaborations on such utopianism can still be read in my book "Principles of Intensive Psychotherapy." [12] To repeat, I now believe, or better still, I know that a state of mind permanently free of anxiety is utopianism for the psychotherapist by the same token that it is for anyone else.

There are many pitfalls in the psychiatrist's interaction with patients and for that matter, in the interaction of other people engaged in responsible interpersonal guidance of their fellowmen, if they are not willing and able to accept the awareness of a certain amount of anxiety and emotional insecurity within themselves. Conversely, there is a great and constructive source of help for psychotherapeutic effectiveness in the psychiatrist's awareness and creative acceptance of his own anxieties whenever they are elicited. The therapist's anxiety is frequently indicative of emotional experiences in patients which arouse anxiety in him. Thus the psychiatrists' anxiety becomes an important divining rod for the discovery of many emotional experiences of patients, which might otherwise remain undiscovered and hidden for a long time, as in the case of a psychiatrist who would not feel free to use his own anxiety as a guide to anxiety provoking emotional experiences in patients.

A therapist's denial of his own anxieties may cause him to overlook the possibility of his contaminating patients with them, a danger which in extreme cases may only be eliminated or corrected by its free discussion between patient and doctor, or for that matter between any other two participants in such an experience. Furthermore, in a therapist, denial of anxiety may arouse all kinds of defenses in him which will interfere with his therapeutic usefulness. That is, he may feel he must reassure himself against the onslaught of anxiety aroused in him by a patient by giving the patient uncalled for reassurance. Or, he may try to propitiate his patient by assuming, for his own defense, all types of roles in the therapeutic process (e.g. the "better" parent, the "great" doctor), instead of operating for the benefit of the patient. A psychotherapist (like any other person participating in an interpersonal exchange) is only able to listen with unimpaired alertness, perceptiveness and creative responsiveness, i.e. he is only able to operate effectively, to the extent to which there is no interference from defense against his own recognized anxiety.

At present, I am engaged along with several colleagues at Chestnut Lodge, in a research project on the intuitive elements in the doctor's therapeutic approach to schizophrenics. There, we have ample opportunity to observe clearly the marked interference with free utilization of intuitive abilities stemming from our anxiety, with regard to our patients, as well as with regard to our colleagues in the research group, as long as this anxiety operates unrecognized.

There is one more important psychotherapeutic issue which is in danger of being obscured in cases of psychiatrists' unrecognized anxiety. A therapist who fails to recognize and to accept his own anxieties will also fail to differentiate correctly between the type and the degree of pathological excess anxiety in mental patients, which is subject to treatment, and the general human experience of non-pathological anxieties which everyone may suffer and utilize as part of the business of living. To put the same thought differently: psychotherapists are not Gods who can change man's fate, which includes everyone, at times, being submitted to states of anxiety. In their role as individual psychiatrists, they cannot alter, except very slowly and imperceptively, the structure of a culture and a society which may elicit anxiety in its members. However, psychiatrists can and should be useful in man's fight against his individual, irrational excess anxieties, and in encouraging people to accept and integrate constructively and without psychotherapeutic help the milder degrees of anxiety which we may loosely call "normal" anxiety.

Summary

Anxiety is seen as a universal emotional experience. The reader's attention is directed toward the realization that milder degrees of anxiety have both disintegrative and constructive aspects.

Severe degrees of anxiety are described as leading up to the development of mental illness, mental symptoms being simultaneously an expression of severe anxiety and a defense against it.

The existing genetic theories on anxiety are briefly reviewed and the fear of anticipated disapproval, withdrawal of love, and separation from significant environmental figures is discussed as a factor, about the genetic significance of which most authors agree.

The hypothesis is offered that the genesis of anxiety may also be understood as a result of unresolved early emotional tie-ups with significant persons of one's early environment. People are stuck with these early interpersonal patterns and with their early interpersonal evaluation which remain uncorrected. These fixations, of which people are only partially aware, if at all, render them psychologically helpless, interfere with their ability to change, with their growth, maturation and self-realization, and with their correct evaluation of their own and other peoples' interpersonal interactions. The result is "psychological death," which elicits anxiety. This anxiety is compared to the anxiety which is called forth in most people by factual death and similar phenomena which are beyond human control and, therefore, arouse helplessness and anxiety.

A distinction is proposed between psychotherapeutic guidance in cases of milder forms of anxiety and psychotherapeutic intervention in cases of severe forms of anxiety, which lead to neurotic or psychotic symptom-formation and mental illness.

Finally, the anxieties which may be elicited in psychotherapists during the treatment situation are discussed in their constructive and in their disintegrative aspects.

References

[1] ADLER, ALFRED: *The Neurotic Constitution.* Translated by Bernard Glueck. New York: Moffat, Yard & Co., 1917.

[2] AUDEN, W. H.: *The Age of Anxiety.* New York: Random House, 1946.

[3] BERDYAEV, NICHOLAS: *Solitude and Society.* London: 1938.

[4] BINSWANGER, LUDWIG: *Grundformen und Erkenntnis Menschlichen Daseins.* Zurich: Max Niehans Verlag, 1942.

[5] FREUD, SIGMUND: *A General Introduction to Psychoanalysis.* New York: Liveright, 1935; Garden City Publ. Co., 1943. (Chapter on Anxiety)

[6] ———: *Beyond the Pleasure Principle.* London: Hogarth Press, 1942.

[7] ———: "On Narcissism: An Introduction." In: *Collected Papers* 4:30-59. London: Hogarth Press, 1946.

[8] ———: *The Ego and the Id*. London: Hogarth Press, 1935.

[9] ———: *Problems of Anxiety*. New York: Norton, 1936.

[10] FROMM, ERICH: *Man for Himself*. New York: Rinehart, 1947.

[11] ———: "Selfishness and Self-love." *Psychiatry*, 2:507-23 (1939).

[12] FROMM-REICHMANN, FRIEDA: *Principles of Intensive Psychotherapy*. Chicago: Univ. of Chicago Press, 1950.

[13] ———: "Remarks on the Philosophy of Mental Disorders." *Psychiatry*, 9:293-308 (1946).

[14] ———: "Psychoanalysis and Dynamic Psychotherapy. Similarities and Differences." *Journal Am. Ps. An. Assn.*, 2:711-721 (1954).

[15] GOLDSTEIN, KURT: *Human Nature in the Light of Psychopathology*. Cambridge: Harvard Univ. Press, 1940.

[16] ———: *The Organism*. New York: American Book Co., 1939.

[17] GRINKER, ROY R.: *Psychosomatic Research*. New York: Norton, 1953.

[18] HALMOS, PAUL: *Solitude and Privacy*. New York: Philosophical Library, 1953.

[19] HORNEY, KAREN: *New Ways in Psychoanalysis*. New York: Norton, 1939.

[20] ———: *The Neurotic Personality of Our Time*. New York: Norton, 1937.

[21] JUNG, C. G.: *Collected Papers on Analytical Psychology*. Translated by C. E. Long; London: Baillere, Tindall & Cox, 1920.

[22] KARDINER, ABRAM: *The Psychological Frontiers of Society*. New York: Columbia Univ. Press, 1945.

[23] MAY, ROLLO: *The Meaning of Anxiety*. New York: Ronald Press, 1951.

[24] MENNINGER, KARL: *Man Against Himself*. New York: Harcourt, Brace, 1938.

[25] PODOLSKY: "The Meaning of Anxiety"; *Diseases of the Nervous System*. 14:4 (1953).

[26] RANK, OTTO: *Will Therapy and Truth and Reality*. New York: Knopf, 1945.

[27] RIESMAN, DAVID: *The Lonely Crowd*. New Haven, Yale Univ. Press, 1950.

[28] RUESCH, JURGEN: "The Interpersonal Communication of Anxiety." *Symposium of Stress*; Walter Reed Army Medical Center, Wash., D.C.: 154-164 (1953).

[29] SULLIVAN, H. S.: *Conceptions of Modern Psychiatry*. Wash., D.C.: The Wm. Alanson White Found., 1947. New Edition, New York: Norton, 1953.

[30] ——: *The Interpersonal Theory of Psychiatry*. New York: Norton, 1953.

[31] ——: "The Meaning of Anxiety in Psychiatry and in Life." *Psychiatry*, 11:1-13 (1948).

[32] ——: "The Theory of Anxiety and the Nature of Psychotherapy." *Psychiatry*, 12:3-12 (1949).

[33] TILLICH, PAUL: *The Courage To Be*. New Haven: Yale Univ. Press, 1952.

[34] VASSOS, JOHN: *Phobia*. New York: Covici-Friede, 1931.

[35] WEIGERT, EDITH: "Existentialism and Its Relation to Psychotherapy." *Psychiatry*, 12, 399-412 (1949).

[36] ZILBOORG, GREGORY: "Considerations on Suicide with Particular Reference to that of the Young." *Am. J. Orthopsychiat.* (1937).

[37] ——: "Suicide Among Civilized and Primitive Races." *Am. J. Psychiat.*, 92:1347-69 (1936).

Dreams

The importance of the study of the dream in the development of psychoanalytic theory and practice is emphasized by Freud's statement that the dream is the "royal road to the unconscious." Freud's work in dream interpretation stands as the first modern scientific endeavor to show that dreams are both understandable and meaningful. Ella Freeman Sharpe is one of the more lucid interpreters of Freud's basic hypotheses; namely, the irrational nature of dreams, their wishful character, and their origin in infantile sexual strivings. There have been objections raised by many observers to one or all of these hypotheses. For example, Jung, one of the first dissenters from Freud, presents a theory that states that dreams may make rational statements about the dreamer, that they may have predictive qualities, and are not necessarily sexual in origin.

The use of dreams in actual practice varies greatly with the theoretical orientation of the analyst and probably even more greatly with his personal style.

Our knowledge of dreams has contributed to our understanding of unconscious phenomena. Freud's untiring delving into his own "night life" gave psychoanalysis the personal stamp it carries today.

10

ELLA FREEMAN SHARPE

Evaluation of Dreams
in Psycho-Analytic Practice*

1. Dream interpretation the corner-stone of psycho-analytic technique.

2. The value of the dream for the analyst.

3. The value of exploration of the preconscious with reference to the work of Freud and Jones.

4. The latent content is the clue to the wish-fulfilment.

5. Convenience dreams.

6. Illustrations of the value of dreams in addition to that of latent content.

Freud's *Interpretation of Dreams* was the first textbook for psycho-analysts. His discovery of the unconscious mind placed in the foreground of interest the significance of dreams. Psycho-analytic technique in the early days of the therapy directed the patient's attention to them during the analytical hour almost to the exclusion of other topics in which the patient might be interested. "Free association" sometimes meant in practice free association to dreams, and a patient who insisted upon dwelling upon other things was at times regarded as showing "resistance" to analysis. The technique of analysis was almost synonymous with

* Reprinted by permission of The Hogarth Press Ltd. from *Dream Analysis* (The International Psycho-Analytical Library No. 29, 1937).

the technique of dream interpretation. Every dream was eagerly exploited as the one and only way into the unconscious mind and a patient who did not dream presented a great problem to the analyst for whom the sole key was the dream.

We know that dreams are not indispensable. We treat all that is said and done during the analytical hour as significant and our problem is to find the precise significance.

One wonders sometimes if the pendulum has swung to the opposite extreme, and if instead of an over-valuation of dreams as a means of analysing a patient we are not in some danger of under-valuation. We may need to take stock again of the value of dreams, and to make an assessment concerning dreams in general.

We must remember that the interpretation of dreams stands as the corner-stone of psycho-analysis, and that mainly by such interpretation psycho-analysis first earned by the cures achieved, adherents to the new therapy. The dream still remains, I believe, an important and almost indispensable means of understanding unconscious psychical conflicts.

I will give first some advantages the analyst himself stands to gain by understanding a patient's dreams. Dreams serve as a kind of reference in analytic work. We can gauge by dreams, if we can interpret them, how true or wide of the mark are our interpretations of the patient's general run of associations, of his gestures or behaviour. We eventually either get corroborations of our interpretations or we find that the patient's dreams indicate that we are not grasping the trend of affairs. I do not mean that we can understand every dream recounted by the patient nor can we follow up clearly the psychical problems from one dream to the next continuously. If we could see the end from the beginning we should be as gods. I mean that at intervals we shall find dreams being told to us that show our analytic interpretations are accurate since they will be followed by dreams that corroborate and pursue and unfold further material of the relevant theme. Here is an example of the process I mean. A patient noticed during an hour's analysis some catkins in a vase. She spoke of the pollen falling from them and then of the prodigality of nature. Her thoughts were "tuned in," so to speak, to one idea, that of profusion and generosity. The people who came to her mind were all of one type, generous with money, with ideas, with affection. The analyst said: "There was surely a time when you thought of your father as a generous giver. You seem to have thought of him as having abundance of good things which he gave generously, so much so he could afford not to care if there was waste." To this the patient replied incredulously, "But my father as long as I can remember only gave me two presents." The analyst replied, "That's as far back as you can remember, but you don't remember earlier than four years of age, do you?" The patient agreed. The next day the patient told a dream in which "running water" was the main element. This evoked associations leading to her memory of the ecstasy she felt on first seeing a waterfall. The inference was drawn that she had first experienced this kind of excitement on seeing her father's penis while he was urinating. During the hour there suddenly came to the patient a vision of hanging fruit, clustered pears she thought, and finally she herself volunteered that this picture must be a representation of her father's genitals seen in infancy when primitive oral desires hallucinate fulfilment from shapes that resemble the breast and nipple. This illustrates the value of the dream from the analyst's point of view, namely as a kind of touchstone of the validity of interpretation. Dreams will tell us whether we are really in touch with the unconscious mind of the patient. There are dreams we can only partially interpret in the light of the material given. We have only a partial understanding of an unfolding situation. There are other dreams which confirm and elaborate the accurate interpretations we have given. From this point of view, for grip of his own work, the dream is invaluable for the analyst.

I will give another type of value we gain from dreams. One needs to re-read at times the dream analyses detailed by Freud and Jones in their expositions of dreams. These analyses are classical examples of the bringing to light of the emotional situations of the current day and present-day stimuli. Beyond certain affective situations Freud thought fit to reveal in connection with his own childhood these dreams do not supply us with a great deal of either memory material nor of deep-seated unconscious phantasy. Neither could we expect it. What Freud has shown in a way unsurpassable is the immense ramification of pre-conscious thoughts, so illustrating the distorting mechanisms of condensation, displacement, symbolization and dramatization, for the purpose of psychic ease in wish-fulfilment.

Freud's actual analyses of dreams give us on the massive scale the value of the associations to a dream as a means of understanding the present-day emotional situations and conflicts in terms of the present-day events. They are examples of searching self-analysis of the pre-conscious, such as a fearless mind can undertake when there is enough self-knowledge to draw inferences from the material. These dreams draw our attention to one value of the dream, namely an investigation by free association of the significant present-day stimuli and the present-day setting of conflict and emotion. Without the present-day setting we do not and cannot comprehend the unity of the psychical life. We may know by interpretation of dream symbolism that a woman unconsciously is punishing herself for the wish to deprive her mother of children, or for the belief that omnipotently she brought about the death of her small brother at the age of two, but it is the exploration of the dream in terms of the pre-conscious and conscious mind that will give us just how this primitive wish, belief and guilt feeling work out in present-day life itself and, during the analysis, in terms of transference to the analyst.

Given a woman of fifty, married, and with grown-up children, the dominance of this unconscious conflict will have resulted in specific present-day situations and present-day thinking. More than half a lifetime of psychical building has been done in connection with this major core of the long past. Not by the mere magic of interpretation alone shall we alter the patient's psychical orientation, an interpretation which was possible for the analyst to make in the case of this woman in the first week of analysis. The analyst must illustrate this past still living in the present, the past that cannot be left behind. We can do this only by seeing people of the present day in the rôles of post imagoes, by seeing what are the present-day equivalents of past situations and realize the dénouements that are forever being reached. So in this particular patient the problem revealed itself in terms of houses first of all. Over a period of years her husband had secured house after house for her, always with the one result that her interest gradually waned, she finally disliked her home and decided they must leave it. She then had a prolonged holiday after which they made a fresh start. One factor alone is quite inadequate to explain this woman's unrest but one factor was undoubtedly the self-punishment of turning herself out of her house to make amends for the wish and the belief that she had turned her brother out. My point at the moment is that the dream is a means of exploring the pre-conscious which together with its correlation with the conscious present-day settings of emotion and conflict will also include the past conflicts brought up to date. By this means, whether in transference or in the wider-flung life of the patient in all activities, we can estimate how far repressed memories and unconscious conflicts are contributing an untoward influence upon present-day life and conduct.

I have found dreams an invaluable clue to a repressed major traumatic situation which an adult patient was compelled continually to re-stage again in terms of his current life in order to bring about magically both the same and a different outcome from the original. Such dramatization in real life is of constant occurrence. It may be innocuous when not of a massive type having no untoward effect on the person's life in reality. For example, I know of a patient who for years never knew the reason why a bath taken during the day-time gave her a sense of well-being that no morning or evening bath afforded her. We found in the course of analysis that as a child of five she had been left to her own devices one afternoon and possessed of a jar of paste for sticking scraps in an album she had not only pasted in the scraps but had then proceeded to cover the furniture in the room and finally herself with the sticky paste. Her father on his return had smacked her hands, the first time he had physically punished her. The escapade was followed not only by a washing of the furniture but she herself was bathed. Clean and tidy once more the child saw her father again, was forgiven and kissed. The afternoon bath for the patient of forty still brought a feeling of absolution that was greater than mere cleanliness. Nor, I may add, did the knowledge she gained of the significance of her unconscious dramatization lessen her satisfaction in an afternoon bath. This is a minor and innocuous example of dramatization. More serious types occur. When such dramatization constitutes in itself the re-enacting of the dissociated traumatic occurrence, dreams can be an important means of the resuscitation of the prototype of the dramatization. Here is such a dream which after a long baffling analysis brought me insight concerning the problem the patient was compelled to dramatize. Although the interpretation brought no direct conviction to the patient and no recovered memory it yet had the effect of making the actual dramatizations that subsequently took place less fraught with serious consequences than former ones. The dream ran thus: *"I said good-bye to G. and sent her away and then I turned to you to embrace you* [i.e. the analyst] *and said good-bye. But I was standing on stilts and my dilemma was that if I let go my hand on the stilts to bend forward to kiss you it would mean my legs would give way and I should fall."* From the associations given I was able to make the interpretation that in the dream the analyst represented the patient when a child and the patient in the dream represented a grandparent. The patient had been told, but had no active memory, of an incident that occurred when she was two years of age. The grandparent was bending down to kiss the child when he collapsed from a seizure from which he died. I cannot enter here into all the fatalistic phantasies that subsequently were inseparable from the love impulses of this child. My purpose is to tell you that this dream gave the first satisfactory clue to the repeated dilemmas the patient unconsciously brought about which were an attempt to deal with the early trauma bound up with the deepest anxieties, for this trauma was a sudden dramatic loss by death of a good object—not a phantasied loss only.

I have spoken of the value of dreams as the touchstone by means of which the analyst can gauge how near he is to following the movements of the unconscious mind; that is, he will get corroboration and further elaboration following his interpretation.

I have spoken of the value of exploring the pre-conscious as giving us the modern setting in which the long past is still played out, the modern persons in the old drama, the modern substitutes in present-day situations moulded on the past, the way in which guilt is assuaged in present-day terms, or in which old rebellions are staged again.

My next evaluation of dreams is in the matter of transference. Again, I think the dream is a touchstone with regard to the accuracy of interpretation of the transference. The analyst, by the help of dreams, can keep in close touch with what actually is being transferred unconsciously on to him and from whom transferred. The analyst needs to preserve objectivity if the patient is to gain it in this matter. Only by the analysis of the transference do we ultimately analyse the past in the present and so ultimately the unconscious conflicts. The dream par excellence with its associations gives us the bridge between the present and the past, just as for the time being the analyst is the person on to whom the problems in the unconscious mind are transferred. It is to this aspect of transference the analyst must adhere, and I know of no corrective like dreams to illuminate the fact that it is the infantile elements of development that are thus worked out in transference on to the analyst. We shall not be tempted to look upon the positive transference to ourselves as the equivalent of the love-life of a full personality, but as the transferred affects of a conflict within the psyche. Patients at various stages will of course equate their feelings for the analyst as being those of the mature adult. But the analyst if he is to deliver over the patient to a real love life must never lose sight of the fact that the remote secluded hour of analysis is part of the total phantasy that is being worked out and understood. The dream is the great help and corrective since in the dream we can see what is being transferred, what situation is being enacted, what rôle is being thrust on to the analyst, what past affective situation is being re-staged.

This leads me directly to what may be called the cardinal rule in dream analysis. There are many exceptions to this rule, but I believe there are more pitfalls for the analyst in neglecting the cardinal rule than there are in neglecting the many exceptions. This cardinal rule is that the meaning of a dream is ascertained by analysing the manifest content into its latent thoughts. The first impulse in connection with any dream is to try to interpret its meaning as it is given in the manifest content, and I believe this impulse has to be checked as much by the analyst in himself as in the patient. The understanding of the dream as a wish-fulfilment is only reached in this way. We, as well as patients, may say of the manifest content of a dream "but this cannot possibly be a wish." To find the wishes that are represented we must know the latent thoughts, and along with those (which may represent opposing wishes) we must include those psychical forces that bring about displacement and seeming congruity. To give the idea that all dreams are simple wish-fulfilments as presented in their manifest content is to give that partial truth which leads as much astray as a lie.

Here is a simple example of an anxiety dream. To say the dream as it stands is a wish-fulfilment is manifestly absurd. *"A man is acting for the screen. He is to recite certain lines of the play. The photographers and voice recorders are there. At the critical moment the actor forgets his lines. Time and again he makes the attempt with no result. Rolls of film must have been spoilt."* The dreamer had great anxiety watching the actor fail at these critical moments.

It is only when one knows the latent content that one realizes the conflict of wishes represented in such a dream. The photographers and voice recorders cannot get the actor to perform although they are all assembled for that purpose. He forgets his lines. The anxiety of the dreamer is, in the manifest content, caused by the fact that he can say nothing when everyone is waiting for him to do so. The actual infantile situation revealed by the associations was that the dreamer was once the onlooker when his parents were "operating" together. The baby was the original photographer and recorder and he stopped the parents in the "act" by noise. The baby did not forget his lines! The original anxiety was connected with an actual doing, not with abstention from activity at the critical moment. It is always helpful to remember that original anxieties regarding our impulse life are concerned with what we did or wished to do, not with our sins of omission. The "return of the repressed" is given in the dream by the element "rolls of film must have been wasted" telling us by the device of metonymy, of a huge amount of fæcal matter the baby was able to pass at that moment.

Illustrated in this dream are some of the profoundest activities of the psyche. We have the recording of sight and sound by the infant and the incorporation by the senses of sight and hearing of the primal scene. We have evidence of this incorporated scene by its projection into the dream dramatization. The modern invention of the screen of the cinema is pressed into service as the appropriate symbol, the screen being the modern external device corresponding to the internal dream picture mechanism.

The original onlooker becomes the active doer, drawing attention to himself, not in articulate words, but by inference from the wasted rolls to the one thing he could do, namely make a mess and a noise that brought the operators to a standstill. Moreover, by displacement of affect, of counter-wish against the original wish, by the dream work which attempts to resolve anxiety there is presented in miniature the conflict of desires.

The cardinal rule is to analyse the manifest dream into its latent elements. One finds in transference dreams particularly that patients will attempt to interpret the dream from its manifest content. There is often a marked resistance to submitting such dreams to analysis, that is of treating the elements separately and unearthing the infantile situation and finding the figure for whom the analyst is a proxy. When a strong positive or negative transference is in full swing a dream may so gather up the infantile longings and so strongly picture them with regard to the analyst that the manifest dream content is taken almost as a reality. The reason for this is often due to the fact that in the dream there is embedded a bit of childhood reality not remembered in consciousness, and unknown to the patient this submerged experience is being relieved. Again the important thing is to find the latent thoughts, and to track down the real experience. In the analysis of transference dreams this is vitally important. A patient will often say: *"Well, I dreamt about you last night, and you were doing so and so, or this and that happened."* I find in such transference dreams the patient is particularly anxious to interpret the dream as a whole, and I am inclined to think that the analyst too may be more often tempted to consider manifest content rather than the latent one in such types of dreams. These above all must be explored for the repressed thoughts, phantasies and memories. Here is an example in illustration of my argument. *"I dreamt you were angry with me and would not forgive me.*" The patient who related this dream could not for a time rid herself of the conviction that the analyst was in reality angry with her. Only by the analyst's close following on of the work of the previous day's analysis did there emerge the memory of putting the paste over the furniture, an incident to which I referred in illustrating dramatization. The fact was that the child was angry with her father. In the analysis the affective projection on the analyst came first. "You are angry with me and won't forgive me." The psychical truth was "I am angry with you and won't forgive you," which was the real significance of the childhood escapade.

I find that short compact dreams also are apt to be taken at the valuation of the manifest content and interpreted often by the patient off-hand and dismissed with satisfaction. For example, a man patient says, *"I dreamt I was having successful intercourse with X."* He goes on to say: "I told you I met her the other day and how pretty and attractive I thought she was." He comments further, "A very natural dream, and it is easy to see a wish-fulfilment." This is a good example of what I mean by the urge to interpret the manifest content as it stands. The short compact dream of this type is often most difficult to analyse and when it yields to analysis is often the most fruitful. This particular dream led to the most deep-seated phantasies of the dreamer's infantile fears of the inside of the mother's body. These latent thoughts were only accessible through associative material that was available when he thought of women who had characteristics the exact opposite of the woman in the dream.

Having stated the general rule I would now draw your attention to exceptions. There are dreams in which it is possible to read the meaning without the latent content, dreams of a simple type in which the symbolism is straightforward and typical. The dream I quoted in the first chapter in which the dreamer saw music in pictures which passed before her eyes, pictures of mountains and hills softly rounded, is an example. This dream could be evaluated at once, since it was the dream of a patient who had passed through a severe trauma, who was keeping contact with reality but struggling and finding it almost unbearable. The external reality situation of extreme frustration is compensated for by dreams of fulfilment of desire. Here is another dream that can be partly interpreted without latent content. A patient brought me at close intervals *dreams of being wheeled in a perambulator*. This patient was finding the effort to keep in touch with reality almost impossible. A young girl I had some time ago who had had a nervous breakdown brought me *dreams* for some weeks *in which everything had stopped*. Trains, buses, lifts, everything that in reality is only of value if it moves, had in her dreams come to a standstill. These dreams were important in their latent content, but I am illustrating here the fact that the manifest content as a whole can at times convey a meaning to the analyst. Dreams of making circumstances fit our physical requirements in order to prevent disturbance of sleep can be understood from manifest content. Here are some examples:

"I dreamt I got out of bed to urinate." "I dreamt I arrived in time for my early appointment." I dreamt someone picked up the eiderdown from the floor and replaced it on my bed." Such dreams yield up an immediate significance.

I pass next to another type of evaluation to be gained from dreams.

These are dreams in which the latent content may be of significance, but not of such importance as the psychological purpose which the whole dream fulfils. The manifest content of the dream will not necessarily give the purpose of the dream as in the case of the examples I have cited. The dream will yield up its latent meaning through analysis, and yet to direct the analysis to ascertaining the meaning of the different elements is to miss the chief significance of the dream as a whole. Dreams sometimes serve as a means of placating the analyst, and so assuaging anxiety about the phantasies that have been transferred to the analyst. In this situation it is not the analysis of the actual dream that is important, but the analysis of the necessity to placate. A male patient, for example, who is dealing with unconscious aggressive phantasies towards the father figure, and therefore is unconsciously fearful of the analyst's attack, will often produce numbers of dreams which have the total significance of placation. They are a gift to turn away the imagined wrath of the avenger.

In another type of dream one must think of purpose rather

than of latent content, namely when a long dream requires half an hour to recount, or a series of dreams take up the same length of time. Content may be important, but of first importance is the finding out of the unconscious purpose that is being served by the occupation of half an hour in recounting the dreams. I have known ten dreams to be recorded by one patient in this way. Among the purposes thus served I have found: (*a*) Resistance to speaking of present-day occurrences. (*b*) The dreams may represent potency, urethral, anal and sexual. (*c*) They may be symbolic gifts. (*d*) They may represent a gift following a with-holding. When dreams are written out and read by the patient I often find they represent a good fæcal product, which in contrast to a childhood accident is given neatly and confined to the paper.

I remember an occasion upon which a patient said after re-counting a number of dreams, "I am remembering a poem by Yeats, in which he says:

> I, being poor, have only my dreams;
> Tread softly, for you tread on my dreams."

The significance of the dreams was thus immediately clear. They were a love gift to the analyst. Their significance is still more detailed, for the inference is that the dreams are on the floor, and must be trodden on very softly. The child's mess on the floor may as easily mean a gift as an assault, "Tread softly, for you tread on my dreams."

I have spoken of the dream as a whole serving the purpose of placating, but sometimes the actual manifest content will do this. For example, the manifest content will sometimes give in direct form a phantasy that carries on some interpretation the analyst has given the day before. The dream betrays this by the completeness of its confirmation. An astute patient of my own generally recognizes this and says frankly "This dream is to oblige." The "obliging dream" is a placating one. It resembles the obedience of a fearful child. The analyst, when the patient is well versed in the main problems of psycho-analysis, must be on the alert when a dream presents a perfect "complex." The safeguard here lies in the analysis of the associations and the affects of the patient.

On the other hand we have in contrast to the patient who will obligingly tell us we are right and go on and confirm our interpretations the one who must prove we are wrong, and who will follow up an interpretation we have given by a dream which will prove us wrong. In both these types of dreams the analysis must be directed to the purpose of the dream rather than the content.

Another evaluation concerning dreams may be made from the patient's own attitude to them. Not only do patients differ in their attitudes to their own dreams but the same patient will have different attitudes at varying times. Some tend to undervalue dreams and others do the reverse. One finds on the whole that patients who have the greatest difficulty in bringing into the analysis their present-day emotions as they experience them with regard to people and affairs, who in reality find it difficult to express their opinions and criticisms inside and outside analysis, use their dreams as a means of diverting the attention and interest of the analyst from the patient's daily life. One may know much about unconscious phantasies, much of the patient's childhood, and yet fail to see the interrelation between these and the present-day conflicts. Such patients are often distressed if there are no dreams to recount and even feel they are not progressing and cannot progress unless dreams are forthcoming. In such cases, important as the help is that dreams will give, the objective on the part of the analyst must be the present-day stimuli, reality situations present and past, and suppressed transference affects.

Of the opposite type is the patient who clings to reality and resists all attempts to penetrate into the phantasy life. Such patients frequently undervalue dream-material. One patient I know rationalizes even this fact by saying he welcomes dreams when he can get them because then he feels he is truly getting something direct from his unconscious. In his case this means: "My unconscious has produced this and therefore I am not responsible."

In two situations I have learned to surmise an important dream is being held back though it is not invariably so. In anxiety cases where a certain amount of analysis has been done, or in cases where anxiety has been released, I correlate an excessive outburst of anxiety with the following probable conditions:

(*a*) a present-day stimulus is not remembered during the analytical hour.

(*b*) a repressed event or phantasy that this stimulus has
activated is near to consciousness.

(*c*) a dream of the night before has been forgotten or delayed
in the telling.

Again with patients who are intellectualists and whose affects
are difficult to release I find very often that an hour that has been
baffling in that the patient does not seem to be able to do more
than switch from one topic to another has ended with a recall
of the dream of the previous night. In such cases I find that on
the following day the analysis of this dream can proceed and one
gets some light on the reason why the dream was delayed in the
telling. Sometimes this may be because of latent content; at
others the significance will lie in the transference situation and the
fact of retention.

One may have the experience of a baffling analytical hour and
then be told the following day by the patient that he remembered
a dream after he had gone away. Such delayed dreams are mainly
important because of latent content and worth subsequent inquiry.

A common resistance dream is one in which the patient dreams
that he is telling the analyst something of great importance. It
is "only a dream" and that is itself the reassurance. The matter of
great importance need not be hoped for on that day. I remember
a very marked instance of this type of dream in my experience
with a patient who had an actual repressed traumatic sexual
experience at the age of four. Before we really began to get indications of this fact she had many dreams of a young girl with a
great secret which caused her sorrow and she, the patient, in the
dream would plead with this girl to give her her confidence and
reveal what the secret trouble was. The girl would remain obdurate. These dreams were most distressing in affect and baffling in
analysis and yet they were most revealing in the sense that one
was ultimately led to the revelation of an actual trauma.

I will only refer to typical dreams very briefly. A "crowd" in
a dream indicates a secret. The analyst's work is to find the secret.
Examination and train dreams however typical will have their

individual nuances. Train dreams are used for many purposes. I gave one in the second lecture illustrating oral and anal phantasies. Such dreams will at times be accompanied by anxiety, where they are expressing past situations of incontinence of urine, as for example when the dreamer cannot catch the train since he arrives too late. The analyst's task is to discover a present-day emotional situation comparable to a past one in which the physical accompaniment was incontinence of urine. "Train" dreams can express indecision concerning some problem, as for example when the dreamer is actually in time for the train and then at last fails to board it. The analyst has the task of finding out what this symbolized "doubt" really means.

I should like to call your attention to the type of dream that symbolizes bodily functioning and bodily sensations.

In an earlier chapter I said that intuitive knowledge is experienced knowledge, and that the unconscious is a storehouse of experience which we may have forgotten but have never lost. The experiences of the body ego from earliest infancy can be found in dreams if we can understand them. Dreams will sometimes present us with evidence of bodily experiences before the child was articulate and others will give us knowledge of present-day suppressed experiences. An example of a simple dream that gave evidence of present-day suppressed bodily experience is: *"I dreamt I was picking flowers last night."* We can infer from this that masturbation occurred the night of the dream.

A dream of distress concerning the hearing of a mighty wind will often be stimulated by actual flatulence. Such dreams are of frequent occurrence. There are dreams of this type that give us bodily experiences of very early years and no actual memory will ever be forthcoming, but the body remembers and the eye once having seen has stored a picture which a dream can reproduce. For example, *"I was running one way on one side of the railings and a man in shorts was running the opposite way on the other side of the railings."* "I was running" in the dream proved during analysis to be a pictorial representation of bodily experience of urinating. The "opposite way" referred to the observation of her father's "running" which was different from hers. The "railings" were the intervening bars of the cot bed.

Here is another example. A patient described quite vividly a special place on a road, this road being an element in his dream. He knew exactly how many yards he was from this object and that object. Then he said: "But if I can say so accurately just where I was I must have been quite stationary. The place was stationary and yet I told you I was moving." From the content of the hour the interpretation of "stationary and yet moving" was that he was urinating.

I find that on to all kinds of machinery and movable apparatus can be transferred bodily sensations, especially those experienced at an early age. These are a few examples: *"I was in a room and suddenly the door opened and a great flood of water came in."* This is interesting enough as the evidence of an "accident" but it is the one dream that I am bold enough to quote as possibly embodying also a birth experience. It was ascertained that the patient's birth was heralded by an unexpected sudden bursting of the waters. The fact was unknown to the patient at the time of the dream. *"I was in a lift and suddenly it went down flop."* This dream I found to be the representation of an experience of fluid excreta rushing down and flopping on the floor. Here is an assurance in a dream dealing with the same anxiety experience in childhood. The dreamer said: *"I saw a marvellous thing happen. A 'car' went straight up a building on the outside somehow and got safely to a garage, I suppose on the upper storey."* The associations to this dream through references made to the way in which a dentist's chair works up and down brought the memory of the patient's baby's chair that could be made higher and lower. The dreamer had no actual memory of herself in the chair, but the dream undoubtedly dramatized an experience where instead of the "car" (Ka Ka) going up safely into a garage it came down much to the anxiety of the little child. The dream had further significances. On to the mechanism of the chair were transferred the bodily sensations felt while the child was in the chair, and from this dream the inference could be made that the accident occurred in the chair. To another patient I am indebted for this very valuable dream. The patient dreamt he was trying to get rid of fæces in a lavatory pan, and then it filled up with water instead of emptying. The phantasies involved in this dream were of importance, but I think even then their full significance can only be realized by the understanding of an actual happening. Here in this dream we have a representation of what it felt like first to try to pass a motion and then the subsequent experience of an enema administration.

Here is another dream of the same type. *The dreamer thought he was in a passage with a mop which he was using to swab it out.* During the hour's analysis the patient recounted a conversation of the evening before when someone had said: "Your ears are not set quite alike." After telling me this, the patient covered his ears with his hands. The dream stimulated the patient to give phantasies and associations that had reference both to fæcal matter and hair. The gesture of covering the ears had the significance of both preventing his own hearing and being heard, protecting himself and protecting me. But to understand more fully the significance of the ears and particular inhibitions in connection with hearing and the over-determination of phantasy about ears, other facts have to be taken into account. The patient had an operation on his ear too early for him to retain any conscious memory of it. Underlying all phantasy there is in this dream an inherent body-memory as well: the passage was actually an ear passage that was once swabbed out. In this dream the man is the active doer, not the passive agent. A stimulus for the dream in addition to the reference to ears in the conversation of the evening before was that for a few seconds during his analysis of the previous day the maid was dusting the stairs outside the consulting room. I registered this fact but it was noticeable that the patient made no reference to this at the time.

In the interpretation of dreams the analyst can turn to account the gestures or minor actions performed by the patient during the analytic hour. The technique in this way approximates in adult analysis to the principles of play-technique with children. One has to interpret actions or gestures as either dramatizing the dream in some symbolic way or as a means of dealing with anxiety by correcting the impulse or event in the dream. Here are some illustrations of these different purposes of actual dramatization during analysis.

The patient who dreamt of the eiderdown slipping off the bed and of its being put over her again, suddenly felt cold during the analysis and put her coat over her. The dream gives first an experience of the night before when she really was cold and did not wish to wake up to adjust the eiderdown, and so dreamt it was done for her. This was a convenience dream. The repetition of the situation during the analytical hour, however, needed inquiry, for the room was warm.

Here is an example of dramatization during analysis that must be interpreted alongside the dream material. The purpose served by the dramatization was that the anxiety inherent in the dream was resolved, for the actions were the exact opposite of the repressed memory and wish. The patient, a man, came in and lay down on the couch. A second afterwards he thrust his hands in his pocket. "Hullo," he said, in great surprise. "What's this?" He drew out a crumpled envelope, looked at it and then said: "Oh, it's nothing, waste paper, that's all." He then went on talking in the usual way. A little later he thrust his hand in his pocket again and suddenly got up saying: "I can't stand this any longer, where's your wastepaper basket? I must get this into the wastepaper basket." Still later in the hour when talking about a MS. he was at work upon he said: "Look here, I must just see if I made those corrections," and he jumped up again and went to his attaché case, looked at his MS., and came back with a sigh of relief, "Yes, it's all right, I corrected the errors."

His dream was: *"There were two visitors and I was bothered as to where they would sleep. I put one of them in a bed I knew was to spare. I gave the other visitor my bed, but then I had nowhere to sleep myself."*

The relevant associations during the hour taken in conjunction with the actions I have recorded proved that we were dealing with a repressed incident in early life when the rubbish was not deposited in the wastepaper basket, since it occurred at an early age when he could not correct his errors and as a consequence his parents were turned out of their bed because of the small visitor.

Conversation dreams often prove difficult of analysis. I have learned to recognize the following types. The persons conversing will often represent different aspects of the dreamer's psyche under the guise of different people. In some dreams the conversation will contain words or phrases that have been incorporated because of their own significance or because of the importance of the person who uttered them. Sometimes such an incorporated phrase of the present day may overlay a phrase used by someone in the patient's past. In the "cockatoo" dream I quoted in the last lecture one has an example of two people conversing who represent different parts of the psyche, while the word "cockatoo" itself was an element worth investigating on its own account.

Dreams containing numbers are often difficult to analyse and they do not always repay the inquiry. If one can evoke from the patient something concrete associated with the specific number, it will often lead to a valuable interpretation. One must always remember the term "figure" means shape as well as number. One patient of mine has always maintained that "four" is a feminine number. We have had many symbolical interpretations of the number four which are easy to supply. I never felt convinced about the significance of "four" in this instance until the patient recalled a bedroom scene and said: "You know I remember watching my mother undress when I was a tiny boy. She always plaited her hair in four long tails." "Four" thus became a feminine number for him and the satisfaction in the fact was that the tails were an assurance of masculinity. The number five often ultimately refers to the five fingers and hence to infantile masturbation. A man dreamt that *a husband and wife were together for five days.* The subtle nuance of this dream was to be found through a reference he made to the book of Genesis. He recalled that it was on the sixth day that God made man and on the seventh day he called his whole creation very good. In the dream husband and wife were together five days only.

A patient of mine had an appointment for the first time at the Clinic. He did not arrive at the appointed time, for he tried to find the clinic at number "sixty-three." A dream revealed that "sixty-three" was the number of a house in a certain district where he had once been told prostitutes were to be found.

A dream of the number 180 was interpreted for me during an analytical session as meaning "I ate nothing."

Colours in dreams are very important for one of my patients. I always ask for more details concerning any colour, and in addition, if the colour is pertaining to material, I ask for details concerning the type of material. I have proved conclusively through this patient my surmise that both creative imagination and artistic appreciation are firmly rooted in the earliest reality experiences of taste, touch and sound. For this patient an oatmeal-coloured material had a "crunchy" feeling and the "crunchy" feeling in her fingers always brought sensation in her teeth.

A cherry coloured silk will make her mouth water and she longs to put her cheeks gently on its surface. The range of colours for this patient are in terms of cream, butter, lemon, orange, cherry, peach, damson, wine, plum, nut brown, chestnut brown. Materials can be crunchy like biscuits, soft like beaten white of eggs, thick like cake. Threads can be coarse like the grain of wholemeal bread, shine like the skin of satin. I do not let any reference to colour or material or to dress escape me in the dreams this patient brings.

Another interesting mechanism one patient unconsciously employs made it possible for me to deduce from a dream what reality situation stimulated it. The mechanism throws a light upon the complicated problem of the different methods by which stability of the psyche is achieved, a problem I believe of such immense complexity that we know little of it. We realize only the grosser mechanisms and nothing of the wheels within wheels that work together in the unity of a psyche more subtly than all the physiological forces that work together in the bodily organism. With this patient I only get a really definite dream of hostility to mother, father, brothers and sisters in certain conditions. Many dreams have shown veiled hostile wishes, but a plain uncamouflaged dream of hostility, of actual death wishes, is forthcoming only if in reality there has been the direct stimulus of hearing actual appreciation of the person who afterwards figures in the dream as the object of hostile wishes. If the patient hears unexpectedly words of praise concerning any relative she dreams of that relative in a hostile manner. So marked has this been that I can guess the reality stimulus of an open hostile dream. The explanation is not as simple as it appears. It is only to be understood by appreciating the problem of how and in what manner the psyche maintains its equilibrium of forces. Some people attain this by a much greater interplay with actual people in their environment; their lives so to speak are more psychically interwoven and played out with other people.

The patient of whom I speak had a fairly stable environment until the age of five and no external difficulty of a major type within that period. This meant a degree of genital development. An actual rival to the mother came into the household when the patient was five. This rival who won the father's affection was openly hostile to the mother. The consequence of this was a profound repression of the Œdipus situation in the patient. The hostile feelings to the mother were intolerable. They were embodied by one who was a real obstacle to the mother's happiness and not a phantasied one. The lasting influence of this real situation is given in the special mechanism by which dreams that express the original hostility felt towards her mother and the other children can be expressed. When someone real in the present-day environment is spontaneously appreciative of them then there comes a relaxation within the patient's psyche. We reach then in such dreams the original hostility felt before the trauma at the age of five years. This is the goal of the analysis in order that there may ensue attainment of an inner equilibrium rather than one that is dependent upon the environment. The importance of the time-factor in analysis is brought home to us since in a mechanism of this type the patient's contacts with reality, the dramatizations of the psychic life in these real situations have all to be explored with infinite patience.

I will summarize briefly the different evaluations of dreams.

Dream interpretation is a corner-stone of psycho-analytic technique. The analyst can gauge by dreams how closely he is keeping in touch with the patient's unconscious problem. They help him to understand the transference affects in terms of those same problems.

Dreams are a means of exploring present-day stimuli and current conflicts through the elaboration of pre-conscious thoughts. To understand the unity of psychical life, the interrelation of the pre-conscious with the unconscious must be known.

The latent content of the dream is arrived at by the method of free association to the different elements of the dream. This is dream analysis.

Dreams may prove of value apart from or in addition to the significance of the latent content. They may be used as a means of unconsciously placating the analyst, as symbolic of power, of control over fæcal product, as proof of control over the analyst. The dream may represent a love gift.

The patient's over-valuation or under-estimation of dreams is itself an aid to understanding the psychical problem.

Dreams often reveal both present-day bodily experiences and forgotten ones of childhood. The correlation of such bodily sensations with phantasy is the object of the analyst.

Characteristic gesture and behaviour needs to be correlated with the patient's associations in arriving at the meaning of a dream.

The interpretation of gesture and characteristic actions approximates to the play-technique in the analysis of children.

The key to the dramatization in real life of a major repressed traumatic situation may often be found through a dream.

The clue to the significance of conversation, numbers and colours in dreams can often be reached through the patient's associations to some specific person or specific object.

11

C. G. JUNG

Dream Analysis in Its Practical Application*

The use of dream-analysis in psychotherapy is still a much debated question. Many practitioners find it indispensable in the treatment of neuroses, and ascribe as much importance to the psychic activity manifested in dreams as to consciousness itself. Others, on the contrary, dispute the value of dream-analysis, and regard dreams as a negligible by-product of the psyche.

Obviously, if a person holds the view that the unconscious plays a leading rôle in the formation of neuroses, he will attribute practical significance to dreams as direct expressions of the unconscious. If, on the other hand, he denies the unconscious or thinks that it has no part in the development of neuroses, he will minimize the importance of dream-analysis. It is regrettable that in this year of grace 1931, more than half a century since Carus formulated the concept of the unconscious, over a century since Kant spoke of the "immeasurable . . . field of obscure ideas," and nearly two hundred years since Leibniz postulated an unconscious psychic activity, not to mention the achievements of Janet, Flournoy and Freud—that after all this, the actuality of the unconscious should still be a matter for controversy. Since it is my intention to deal exclusively with questions of practical treatment, I will not attempt in this place a defence of the hypothesis of the unconscious, though it is obvious enough that dream-analysis

* Reprinted by permission of Harcourt, Brace and Company and Routledge and Kegan Paul, Ltd., from *Modern Man in Search of a Soul* by C. G. Jung.

stands or falls with this hypothesis. Without it the dream appears to be merely a freak of nature, a meaningless conglomerate of memory-fragments left over from the happenings of the day. Were the dream nothing more than this, there would be no excuse for the present discussion. We must recognize the unconscious if we are to treat of dream-analysis at all, for we do not resort to it as a mere exercise of the wits, but as a method for uncovering hitherto unconscious psychic contents which are causally related to the neurosis and therefore of importance in its treatment. Anyone who deems this hypothesis unacceptable must simply rule out the question of the practicability of dream-analysis.

But since, according to our hypothesis, the unconscious plays a causal part in the neurosis, and since dreams are the direct expression of unconscious psychic activity, the attempt to analyse and interpret dreams is entirely justified from a scientific standpoint. Quite apart from therapeutic results, we may expect this line of endeavour to give us scientific insight into psychic causality. For the practitioner, however, scientific discoveries can at most be a gratifying by-product of his efforts in the field of therapy. He will not feel called upon to apply dream-analysis to his patients on the chance that it may throw light upon the problem of psychic causality. He may believe, of course, that the insight so gained is of therapeutic value—in which case he will regard dream-analysis as one of his professional duties. It is well known that the Freudian school is of the opinion that important therapeutic effects are achieved by throwing light upon the unconscious causal factors—that is, by explaining them to the patient and thus making him conscious of the sources of his trouble.

If we assume, for the time being, that this expectation is borne out by the facts, we can restrict ourselves to the questions whether or not dream-analysis enables us to discover the unconscious causes of the neurosis, and whether it can do this unaided, or must be used in conjunction with other methods. The Freudian answer, I may assume, is common knowledge. My own experience confirms this view inasmuch as I have found that dreams not infrequently bring to light in an unmistakable way the unconscious contents that are causal factors in a neurosis. Most often it is the initial dreams that do this—I mean, those dreams that a patient reports at the very outset of a treatment. An illustration will perhaps be helpful.

I was consulted by a man who held a prominent position in the world. He was afflicted with a sense of anxiety and insecurity, and complained of dizziness sometimes resulting in nausea, of a heavy head and difficulty in breathing—this being an exact description of the symptoms of mountain-sickness. He had had an unusually successful career, and had risen, with the help of ambition, industry and native talent, from a humble origin as the son of a poor peasant. Step by step he had climbed, attaining at last an important post that offered him every opportunity for further social advancement. He had actually reached a place in life from which he could have begun his ascent into the upper regions, when suddenly his neurosis intervened. At this point of his story the patient could not refrain from that stereotyped exclamation which begins with the familiar words: "And just now, when I . . ." The fact that he had all the symptoms of mountain-sickness was highly appropriate to the peculiar situation in which he found himself. He had brought with him to the consultation two dreams of the preceding night.

The first dream was as follows: "I am once more in the small village where I was born. Some peasant boys who went to school with me are standing together in the street. I walk past them, pretending not to know them. I hear one of them, who is pointing at me, say: 'He doesn't often come back to our village.'" No tricks of interpretation are needed to recognize and to understand the allusion to the humble beginnings of the dreamer's career. The dream says quite clearly: "You forget how far down you began."

Here is the second dream: "I am in a great hurry because I am going on a journey. I hunt up my baggage, but cannot find it. Time flies, and the train will soon be leaving. Finally I succeed in getting all my things together. I hurry along the street, discover that I have forgotten a brief-case containing important papers, dash breathlessly back again, find it at last, and then run towards the station, but make hardly any headway. With a final effort I rush on to the platform only to find the train steaming out into the yards. It is very long, and runs in a curious S-shaped curve. It occurs to me that if the driver is not careful, and puts on full steam when he comes to the straight stretch, the rear coaches will still be on the curve and will be thrown over by the speed of the train. As a matter of fact the driver opens the throttle as I try to shout. The rear coaches rock frightfully, and are actually thrown off the rails. There is a terrible catastrophe. I awake in terror."

Here, too, we can understand without much difficulty the situation represented by the dream. It pictures the patient's frantic haste to advance himself still further. Since the driver at the front of the train goes thoughtlessly ahead, the coaches behind him rock and finally overturn—that is, a neurosis is developed. It is clear that, at this period of life, the patient had reached the highest point of his career—that the effort of the long ascent from his lowly origin had exhausted his strength. He should have contented himself with his achievements, but instead he is driven by his ambition to attempt to scale heights of success for which he is not fitted. The neurosis came upon him as a warning. Circumstances prevented my treating the patient, and my view of his case did not satisfy him. The upshot was that events ran their course in the way indicated by the dream. He tried to exploit the professional openings that tempted his ambition and ran so violently off the track that the train-wreck was realized in actual life. The patient's anamnesis permitted the inference that the mountain-sickness pointed to his inability to climb any further. The inference is confirmed by his dreams which present this inability as a fact.

We here come upon a characteristic of dreams that must take first place in any discussion of the applicability of dream-analysis to the treatment of neuroses. The dream gives a true picture of the subjective state, while the conscious mind denies that this state exists, or recognizes it only grudgingly. The patient's conscious ego could see no reason why he should not go steadily forward; he continued his struggle for advancement, refusing to admit the fact which subsequent events made all too plain—that he was actually at the end of his tether. When, in such cases, we listen to the dictates of the conscious mind, we are always in doubt. We can draw opposite conclusions from the patient's anamnesis. After all, the private soldier may carry a marshal's baton in his knapsack, and many a son of poor parents has achieved the highest success. Why should it not be so in my patient's case? Since my judgement is fallible, why should my own conjecture be more dependable than his? At this point the dream comes in as the expression of an involuntary psychic process not controlled by the conscious outlook. It presents the subjective state as it really is. It has no respect for my conjectures or for the patient's views as to how things should be, but simply tells how the matter stands. I have therefore made it a rule to put dreams on a plane with physiological fact. If sugar appears in the urine, then the urine contains sugar, and not albumen or urobilin or something else that I may have been led to expect. This is to say that I take dreams as facts that are invaluable for diagnosis.

It is the way of dreams to give us more than we ask, and this is true of those I have just cited as illustrations. They not only allowed us an insight into the causes of the neurosis, but afforded a prognosis as well. What is more, they showed us at what point the treatment should begin. The patient must be prevented from going full steam ahead. This is precisely what he tells himself in the dream.

For the time being we will content ourselves with this hint, and return to the question whether dreams enable us to explain the causes of a neurosis. I have cited two dreams that actually do this. But I could equally well cite any number of initial dreams which do nothing of the kind, although they are perfectly transparent. I do not wish for the present to consider dreams which call for searching analysis and interpretation.

The point is that there are neuroses whose actual origins we discover only at the very end of an analysis, and there are also cases in which it is of no benefit to have discovered the origin of the neurosis. This brings me back to the Freudian view, mentioned above, that for the purposes of therapy it is necessary for the patient to become conscious of the causal factors in his disturbance—a view that is little more than a survival of the old theory of the trauma. I do not, of course, deny that many neuroses have a traumatic origin; I simply contest the notion that all neuroses are of this nature and arise without exception from some crucial experience of childhood. This view of the question results in a causalistic approach. The doctor must give his whole atten-

tion to the patient's past; he must always ask: "Why?" and neglect
the equally pertinent question: "What for?" This is frequently
very harmful to the patient, for he is forced to search in his
memory—perhaps over a course of years—for a hypothetical
event in his childhood, while things of immediate importance are
grossly neglected. A purely causalistic approach is too narrow to
do justice to the true significance, either of the dream, or of the
neurosis. A person is biassed who turns to dreams for the sole
purpose of discovering the hidden cause of the neurosis, for he
leaves aside the larger part of the dream's actual contribution.
The dreams I have cited unmistakably present the ætiological
factors in the neurosis; but it is clear that they also offer a prognosis or anticipation of the future and a suggestion as to the
course of treatment as well. We must furthermore bear in mind
that a great many dreams do not touch upon the causes of the
neurosis, but treat of quite different matters—among others, of
the patient's attitude to the doctor. I should like to illustrate this
by recounting three dreams of the same patient. She consulted
three different analysts in turn, and at the beginning of each treatment she had one of these dreams.

Here is the first: "I must cross the frontier into the next country, but no one can tell me where the boundary lies, and I cannot find it." The treatment which followed this dream was
unsuccessful, and was soon broken off.

The second dream is as follows: "I must cross the frontier.
It is a black night, and I cannot find the customhouse. After a
long search I notice a small light far away and suppose that the
frontier lies over there. But in order to reach it, I must cross a
valley and pass through a dark wood, in which I lose my sense
of direction. Then I notice that someone is with me. This person suddenly clings to me like a madman and I awake in terror."
That treatment also was discontinued after a few weeks, the
reason being that the patient was completely disoriented by the
analyst's unconscious identification with her.

The third dream took place when the patient came into my
hands. It runs: "I must cross a frontier, or rather, I have already
crossed it, and find myself in a Swiss customhouse. I have only a
handbag with me, and believe that I have nothing to declare. But

the customs official dives into my bag and, to my astonishment, pulls out two full-sized mattresses." The patient married during the course of her treatment with me, but not without a violent resistance to this step. The cause of her neurotic resistance came to light only after many months, and there is not a hint of it anywhere in these dreams. They are without exception anticipations of the difficulties she is to have with the analysts to whom she has come for treatment.

I could cite many other dreams to the same effect, but these may suffice to show that dreams can be anticipatory and, in that case, must lose their particular meaning if they are treated in a purely causalistic way. These three dreams give clear information about the analytical situation, and it is extremely important for the purposes of therapy that this be rightly understood. The first doctor understood the situation and sent the patient to the second. Here she drew her own conclusions from her dream, and decided to leave. My interpretation of her third dream disappointed her greatly, but she was distinctly encouraged to go on in spite of all difficulties by the fact that it reported the frontier already crossed.

Initial dreams are often amazingly transparent and clear-cut. But as the work of analysis progresses, the dreams in a little while cease to be clear. If they should prove exceptional, and keep their clarity, we can be sure that the analysis has as yet not touched some important part of the personality. As a rule, the dreams become less transparent, and more blurred, shortly after the beginning of the treatment. It becomes increasingly difficult to interpret them, a further reason for this being that a point may soon be reached where the doctor is unable, if the truth be told, to understand the situation as a whole. This is how the matter really stands, for to say that the dreams are unintelligible is a mere reflection of the doctor's subjective opinion. Nothing is unclear to the understanding; it is only when we fail to understand that things appear unintelligible and confused. In themselves, dreams are clear—that is, they are just as they must be under the given conditions. If we look back at these "unintelligible" dreams from a later stage of the treatment or from a distance of some years, we are often astounded at our own blindness. It is a fact that, as an analysis progresses, we come upon dreams that are strikingly obscure in comparison with the initial dreams. But the doctor should not be too sure that the later dreams are really confused, or be too hasty in accusing the patient of deliberate resistance. He would do better to take the fact as an indication of his own growing inability to understand the situation. The psychiatrist likewise is prone to call a patient "confused" when he would do well to recognize the projection and admit his own confusion, for it is really his understanding that grows confused in face of the patient's strange behaviour. For the purposes of therapy, moreover, it is highly important for the analyst to admit his lack of understanding from time to time, for nothing is more unbearable for the patient than to be always understood. The latter in any case relies too much upon the mysterious insight of the doctor, and, by appealing to his professional vanity, lays a dangerous trap for him. By taking refuge in the doctor's self-confidence and "profound" understanding, the patient loses all sense of reality, falls into a stubborn transference, and retards the cure.

Understanding is clearly a subjective process. It may be very one-sided, in that the physician understands while the patient does not. In such a case the doctor sometimes feels it his duty to convince the patient, and if the latter will not allow himself to be convinced, the doctor accuses him of resistance. When the understanding is all on my side, I find it advisable to stress my lack of understanding. It is relatively unimportant whether the doctor understands or not, but everything hangs on the patient's doing so. What is really needed is a mutual agreement which is the fruit of joint reflection. It is one-sided, and therefore dangerous, understanding for the doctor to prejudge the dream from the standpoint of a certain doctrine and to make a pronouncement which may be theoretically sound, but does not win the patient's assent. In so far as the pronouncement fails in this respect, it is incorrect in the practical sense; and it may also be incorrect in the sense that it anticipates and thereby cripples the actual development of the patient. We appeal only to the patient's brain if we try to inculcate a truth; but if we help him to grow up to this truth in the course of his own development, we have reached his heart, and this appeal goes deeper and acts with greater force.

When the doctor's interpretation is based merely upon a one-sided theory or a preconceived opinion, his chances of convincing the patient or of achieving any therapeutic results depend chiefly upon suggestion. And let no one deceive himself as to the effects of suggestion. In itself suggestion is not to be despised, but it has serious limitations, and reacts upon the patient's independence of character in a very undesirable way. A practising analyst may be supposed to believe in the significance and value of the widening of consciousness—I mean by this the procedure of bringing to light the parts of the personality which were previously unconscious and subjecting them to conscious discrimination and criticism. It is an undertaking which requires the patient to face his problems, and taxes his powers of conscious judgment and decision. It is nothing less than a challenge to the ethical sense, a call to arms that must be answered by the whole personality. Therefore, with respect to personal development, the analytical approach is of a higher order than methods of treatment based upon suggestion. This is a kind of magic that works in the dark and makes no ethical demands upon the personality. Methods of treatment based upon suggestion are deceptive make-shifts; they are incompatible with the principles of analytical therapy, and should be avoided. But suggestion can of course be avoided only when the doctor is aware of the many doors through which it can enter. There remains in the best of circumstances enough—and more than enough—unconscious suggestion.

The analyst who wishes to rule out conscious suggestion must consider any dream interpretation invalid that does not win the assent of the patient, and he must search until he finds a formulation that does. This is a rule which, I believe, must always be observed, especially in dealing with those dreams whose obscurity is evidence of lack of understanding on the part of the doctor as well as of the patient. The doctor should regard every dream as a new departure—as a source of information about unknown conditions concerning which he has as much to learn as the patient. It goes without saying that he should hold no preconceived opinions based upon a particular theory, but stand ready in every single case to construct a totally new theory of dreams. There is still a boundless opportunity for pioneer-work in this field.

The view that dreams are merely imaginary fulfilments of suppressed wishes has long ago been superseded. It is certainly true that there are dreams which embody suppressed wishes and fears, but what is there which the dream cannot on occasion embody? Dreams may give expression to ineluctable truths, to philosophical pronouncements, illusions, wild fantasies, memories, plans, anticipations, irrational experiences, even telepathic visions, and heaven knows what besides. One thing we ought never to forget: almost the half of our lives is passed in a more or less unconscious state. The dream is specifically the utterance of the unconscious. We may call consciousness the daylight realm of the human psyche, and contrast it with the nocturnal realm of unconscious psychic activity which we apprehend as dreamlike fantasy. It is certain that consciousness consists not only of wishes and fears, but of vastly more than these, and it is highly probable that the unconscious psyche contains a wealth of contents and living forms equal to or even greater than does consciousness, which is characterized by concentration, limitation and exclusion.

This being the state of affairs, it is imperative that we should not pare down the meaning of a dream to fit some narrow doctrine. We must remember that there are not a few patients who imitate the technical or theoretical jargon of the doctor, and do this even in their dreams. No language exists that cannot be misused. It is hard to realize how badly we are fooled by the abuse of ideas; it even seems as if the unconscious had a way of strangling the physician in the coils of his own theory. All this being so, I leave theory aside as much as possible in analysing dreams. We cannot, of course, dispense with theory entirely, for it is needed to make things intelligible. It is on the basis of theory, for instance, that I expect dreams to have a meaning. I cannot prove in every case that dreams are meaningful, for there are dreams that neither doctor nor patient understands. But I must regard them as hypothetically meaningful in order to find courage to deal with them at all. To say that dreams contribute in an important way to conscious knowledge, and that a dream which fails to do so is a dream which has not been properly interpreted --this, too, is a theoretical statement. But I must adopt this hypothesis in order to make it clear to myself why I analyse dreams. On the other hand, every hypothesis about the nature of the dream, its function and structure, is merely a rule of thumb and must be subject to constant modifications. We must never forget in dream-analysis, even for a moment, that we move on treacherous ground where nothing is certain but uncertainty. A suitable warning to the dream-interpreter—if only it were not so paradoxical—would be: "Do anything you like, only don't try to understand!"

When we take up an obscure dream, our first task is not to understand and interpret it, but to establish the context with minute care. What I have in mind is not a boundless sweep of "free associations" starting from any and every image in the dream, but a careful and conscious illumination of the chains of association that are directly connected with particular images. Many patients have first to be educated to this task, for they resemble the doctor in their urgent desire to understand and to interpret offhand. This is particularly the case when they have already been educated—or rather, miseducated—by their reading or by a previous analysis that went wrong. They give associations in accordance with a theory; that is, they try to understand and interpret, and thus they nearly always get stuck. Like the doctor, they wish at once to get behind the dream in the false belief that it is a mere façade concealing the true meaning. Perhaps we may call the dream a façade, but we must remember that the fronts of most houses by no means trick or deceive us, but, on the contrary, follow the plan of the building and often betray its inner arrangement. The "manifest" dream-picture is the dream itself, and contains the "latent" meaning. If I find sugar in the urine, it is sugar, and not a façade that conceals albumen. When Freud speaks of the "dream-façade," he is really speaking, not of the dream itself, but of its obscurity, and in so doing is projecting upon the dream his own lack of understanding. We say that the dream has a false front only because we fail to see into it. We would do better to say that we are dealing with something like a text that is unintelligible, not because it has a façade, but simply because we cannot read it. We do not have to get behind such a text in the first place, but must learn to read it.

We shall best succeed in reading dreams by establishing their context, as already remarked. We shall not succeed with the help of free associations, any more than we could use that means to decipher a Hittite inscription. Free associations will help me to uncover all my own complexes, but for this purpose I need not start from the dream—I might as well take a sentence in a newspaper or a "Keep out" sign. If we associate freely to a dream, our complexes will turn up right enough, but we shall hardly ever discover the meaning of the dream. To do this, we must keep as close as possible to the dream-images themselves. When a person has dreamed of a deal table, little is accomplished by his associating it with his writing-desk which is not made of deal. The dream refers expressly to a deal table. If at this point nothing occurs to the dreamer his hesitation signifies that a particular darkness surrounds the dream-image, and this is suspicious. We would expect him to have dozens of associations to a deal table, and when he cannot find a single one, this must have a meaning. In such cases we should return again and again to the image. I say to my patients: "Suppose I had no idea what the words 'deal table' mean. Describe this object and give me its history in such a way that I cannot fail to understand what sort of thing it is." We succeed in this way in establishing a good part of the context of that particular dream-image. When we have done this for all the images in the dream, we are ready for the venture of interpretation.

Every interpretation is hypothetical, for it is a mere attempt to read an unfamiliar text. An obscure dream, taken by itself, can rarely be interpreted with any certainty, so that I attach little importance to the interpretation of single dreams. With a series of dreams we can have more confidence in our interpretations, for the later dreams correct the mistakes we have made in handling those that went before. We are also better able, in a dream series, to recognize the important contents and basic themes, and I therefore urge my patients to make a careful record of their dreams and the interpretations given them. I also show them how to work up their dreams in the way I have just indicated, so that they can bring me in writing the dream and the material that forms the context of the dream. In later stages of analysis I let them work out the interpretations as well. The patient learns in this way how to consult the unconscious without the doctor's help.

If dreams did nothing more than inform us about the causal factors in a neurosis, we could safely let the doctor handle them alone. My way of dealing with them, moreover, would be quite superfluous if all that we could expect of them were a collection of hints and insights helpful to the doctor. But since it is probable, as I have shown in a few examples, that dreams contain more than practical helps for the doctor, dream-analysis deserves very special consideration. Sometimes, indeed, it is a matter of life and death.

Among many cases of this sort, I have been especially impressed with one that concerned a colleague of mine in Zürich. He was a man somewhat older than myself whom I saw from time to time, and who always teased me on these occasions about my interest in dream-interpretation. I met him one day in the street, and he called out to me: "How are things going? Are you still interpreting dreams? By the way, I've had another idiotic dream. Does it mean something too?" He had dreamed as follows: "I am climbing a high mountain over steep, snow-covered slopes. I mount higher and higher—it is marvellous weather. The higher I climb, the better I feel. I think: 'If only I could go on climbing like this for ever!' When I reach the summit, my happiness and elation are so strong that I feel I could mount right up into space. And I discover that I actually can do this. I go on climbing on empty air. I awake in a real ecstasy." When he had told me his dream, I said: "My dear man, I know you can't give up mountaineering, but let me implore you not to go alone from now on. When you go, take two guides, and you must promise on your word of honour to follow their directions." "Incorrigible!" he replied laughing, and said good-bye. I never saw him again. Two months later came the first blow. When out alone, he was buried by an avalanche, but was dug out in the nick of time by a military patrol which happened to come along. Three months after this the end came. He went on a climb accompanied by a younger friend, but without guides. An alpinist standing below saw him literally step out into the air as he was letting himself down a rock wall. He fell on to the head of his friend, who was waiting beneath him, and both were dashed to pieces far below. That was *ecstasis* in the full meaning of the word.

No amount of scepticism and critical reserve has ever enabled me to regard dreams as negligible occurrences. Often enough they appear senseless, but it is obviously we who lack the sense and the ingenuity to read the enigmatical message from the nocturnal realm of the psyche. When we see that at least a half of man's life is passed in this realm, that consciousness has its roots there, and that the unconscious operates in and out of waking existence, it would seem incumbent upon medical psychology to sharpen its perceptions by a systematic study of dreams. No one doubts the importance of conscious experience; why then should we question the importance of unconscious happenings? They also belong to human life, and they are sometimes more truly a part of it for weal or woe than any events of the day.

Dreams give information about the secrets of the inner life and reveal to the dreamer hidden factors of his personality. As long as these are undiscovered, they disturb his waking life and betray themselves only in the form of symptoms. This means that we cannot effectively treat the patient from the side of consciousness alone, but must bring about a change in and through the unconscious. As far as present knowledge goes, there is only one way of doing this: there must be a thoroughgoing, conscious assimilation of unconscious contents. By "assimilation," I mean a mutual interpenetration of conscious and unconscious contents, and not—as is too commonly thought—a one-sided valuation, interpretation and deformation of unconscious contents by the conscious mind. As to the value and significance of unconscious contents in general, very mistaken views are abroad. It is well known that the Freudian school presents the unconscious in a thoroughly depreciatory light, just as also it looks on primitive man as little better than a wild beast.

Its nursery-tales about the terrible old man of the tribe and its teachings about the "infantile-perverse-criminal" unconscious have led people to make a dangerous monster out of the unconscious, that really very natural thing. As if all that is good, reasonable, beautiful and worth living for had taken up its abode in consciousness! Have the horrors of the World War really not opened our eyes? Are we still unable to see that man's conscious mind is even more devilish and perverse than the unconscious?

I was recently reproached with the charge that my teaching about the assimilation of the unconscious, were it accepted, would undermine culture and exalt primitivity at the cost of our highest values. Such an opinion can have no foundation other than the erroneous belief that the unconscious is a monster. Such a view arises from fear of nature and of life as it actually is. Freud has invented the idea of sublimation to save us from the imaginary claws of the unconscious. But what actually exists cannot be alchemistically sublimated, and if anything is apparently sublimated, it never was what a false interpretation took it to be.

The unconscious is not a demonic monster, but a thing of nature that is perfectly neutral as far as moral sense, æsthetic taste and intellectual judgement go. It is dangerous only when our conscious attitude towards it becomes hopelessly false. And this danger grows in the measure that we practise repressions. But as soon as the patient begins to assimilate the contents that were previously unconscious, the danger from the side of the unconscious diminishes. As the process of assimilation goes on, it puts an end to the dissociation of the personality and to the anxiety that attends and inspires the separation of the two realms of the psyche. That which my critic feared—I mean the overwhelming of consciousness by the unconscious—is most likely to occur when the unconscious is excluded from life by repressions, or is misunderstood and depreciated.

A fundamental mistake, and one which is commonly made, is this: it is supposed that the contents of the unconscious are unequivocal and are marked with plus or minus signs that are immutable. As I see the question, this view is too naïve. The psyche is a self-regulating system that maintains itself in equilibrium as the body does. Every process that goes too far immediately and inevitably calls forth a compensatory activity. Without such adjustments a normal metabolism would not exist, nor would the normal psyche. We can take the idea of compensation, so understood, as a law of psychic happening. Too little on one side results in too much on the other. The relation between conscious and unconscious is compensatory. This fact, which is easily verifiable, affords a rule for dream interpretation. It is always helpful, when we set out to interpret a dream, to ask: What conscious attitude does it compensate?

Although compensation may take the form of imaginary wish-fulfilment, it generally presents itself as an actuality which becomes the more strikingly actual the more we try to repress it. We know that we do not conquer thirst by repressing it. The dream-content is to be taken in all seriousness as something that has actually happened to us; it should be treated as a contributory factor in framing our conscious outlook. If we do not do this, we shall keep that one-sided, conscious attitude which evoked the unconscious compensation in the first place. But this way holds little hope of our ever judging ourselves correctly or finding any balance in life.

If anyone should set out to replace his conscious outlook by the dictates of the unconscious—and this is the prospect which my critics find so alarming—he would only succeed in repressing the former, and it would reappear as an unconscious compensation. The unconscious would thus have changed its face and completely reversed its position. It would have become timidly reasonable, in striking contrast to its former tone. It is not generally believed that the unconscious operates in this way, yet such reversals constantly take place and constitute its essential function. This is why every dream is a source of information and a means of self-regulation, and why dreams are our most effective aids in the task of building up the personality.

The unconscious itself does not harbour explosive materials, but it may become explosive owing to the repressions exercised by a self-sufficient, or cowardly, conscious outlook. All the more reason, then, for giving heed to that side! It should now be clear why I have made it a practical rule always to ask, before trying to interpret a dream: What conscious attitude does it compensate? As may be seen, I thus bring the dream into the closest possible connection with the conscious state. I even maintain that it is impossible to interpret a dream with any degree of certainty unless we know what the conscious situation is. For it is only in the light of this knowledge that we can make out whether the unconscious content carries a plus or minus sign. The dream is not an isolated psychic event completely cut off from daily life. If it seems so to us, that is only an illusion that arises from our lack of understanding. In reality, the relation between consciousness and the dream is strictly causal, and they interact in the subtlest of ways.

I should like to show with the help of an illustration how important it is to find the true value of unconscious contents. A young man brought me the following dream: "My father is driving away from the house in his new car. He drives very clumsily, and I get very excited about his apparent stupidity. He goes this way and that, forward and backward, repeatedly getting the car into a tight place. Finally he runs into a wall and badly damages the car. I shout at him in a perfect rage, telling him he ought to behave himself. My father only laughs, and then I see that he is dead drunk." There is no foundation in fact for the dream. The dreamer is convinced that his father would never behave in that way, even if he were drunk. The dreamer himself is used to cars; he is a careful driver, and very moderate in the use of alcohol, especially when he has to drive. Bad driving, and even slight injuries to the car, irritate him greatly. The son's relation to his father is good. He admires him for being an unusually successful man. We can say, without any attempt at interpretation, that the dream presents a very unfavorable picture of the father. What, then, should we take its meaning to be as far as the son is concerned? Is his relation to his father good only in appearance, and does it really consist of over-compensated resistances? If this is so we should attribute a plus sign to the dream-content; we should have to tell the young man: "This is your actual relation to your father." But since I could find nothing equivocal or neurotic in the facts about the son's relation to his father, I had no warrant for disturbing the young man's feelings with such a destructive pronouncement. To do so would have prejudiced the outcome of the treatment.

But if his relation to his father is really excellent, why must the dream manufacture such an improbable story to discredit the father? The dreamer's unconscious must have a distinct tendency to produce such a dream. Has the young man resistances to his father, after all, which are perhaps fed by jealousy or a certain sense of inferiority? But before we go out of our way to burden his conscience—and with sensitive young people there is always the risk that we do this too lightly—we had better, for once, drop the question of why he had this dream, and ask ourselves instead: What for? The answer, in this case, would be that his unconscious clearly tries to depreciate his father. If we take this as a compensation, we are forced to the conclusion that his relation to his father is not only good, but even too good. The younger man actually deserves the French sobriquet of *fils à papa*. His father is still too much the guarantor of his existence, and he is still living what I call a provisional life. He runs the risk of failing to realize himself because there is too much "father" on every side. This is why the unconscious manufactures a kind of blasphemy: it seeks to lower the father and to elevate the son. "An immoral business," we may be tempted to say. Every father who lacks insight would be on his guard here. And yet this compensation is entirely to the point. It forces the son to contrast himself with his father, and that is the only way in which he can become aware of himself.

The interpretation just outlined was apparently the correct one, for it struck home. It won the spontaneous assent of the young man, and did no violence to his feeling for his father, or to the father's feeling for him. But this interpretation was only possible when the father-son relation had been studied in the light of all the facts that were accessible to consciousness. Without a knowledge of the conscious situation the true meaning of the dream would have remained in doubt.

It is of the first importance for the assimilation of dream-contents that no violence be done to the real values of the conscious personality. If the conscious personality is destroyed, or even crippled, there is no one left to do the assimilating. When we recognize the importance of the unconscious we are not embarking upon a Bolshevist experiment which puts the lowest on top. This would only bring about a return of the situation we are trying to correct. We must see to it that the conscious personality remains intact, for we can only turn the unconscious compensations to good account when the conscious personality co-operates in the venture. When it comes to the assimilation of a content it is never a question of "this *or* that," but of "this *and* that."

Just as the interpretation of dreams requires exact knowledge of the conscious *status quo,* so the treatment of dream symbolism demands that we take into account the dreamer's philosophical, religious and moral convictions. It is far wiser in practice not to regard the dream-symbols as signs or symptoms of a fixed character. We should rather take them as true symbols—that is to say, as expressions of something not yet consciously recognized or conceptually formulated. In addition to this, they must be considered in relation to the dreamer's immediate state of consciousness. I emphasize that this way of treating the dream-symbols is advisable in practice because theoretically there do exist relatively fixed symbols whose meaning must on no account be referred to anything whose content is known, or to anything that can be formulated in concepts. If there were no relatively fixed symbols, it would be impossible to determine the structure of the unconscious. There would be nothing in it which could be in any way laid hold of or described.

It may seem strange that I should attribute an indefinite content to the relatively fixed symbols. But it is the indefinite content that marks the symbol as against the mere sign or symptom. It is well known that the Freudian school operates with hard and fast sexual "symbols"; but these are just what I should call signs, for they are made to stand for sexuality, and this is supposed to be something definitive. As a matter of fact, Freud's concept of sexuality is thoroughly elastic, and so vague that it can be made to include almost anything. The word itself is familiar, but what it denotes amounts to an indeterminable or variable *x* that stands for the physiological activity of the glands at one extreme and the highest reaches of the spirit at the other. Instead of taking a dogmatic stand that rests upon the illusion that we know something because we have a familiar word for it, I prefer to regard the symbol as the announcement of something unknown, hard to recognize and not to be fully determined. Take, for instance, the so-called phallic symbols, which are supposed to stand for the *membrum virile* and nothing more. Psychologically speaking, the *membrum* is itself—as Kranefeldt has recently pointed out—a symbolic image whose wider content cannot easily be determined. As was customary throughout antiquity, primitive people today make a free use of phallic symbols, yet it never occurs to them to confuse the phallus, as a ritualistic symbol, with the penis. They always take the phallus to mean the creative *mana*, the power of healing and fertility, "that which is unusually potent," to use Lehmann's expression. Its equivalents in mythology and in dreams are the bull, the ass, the pomegranate, the *yoni*, the he-goat, the lightning, the horse's hoof, the dance, the magical cohabitation in the furrow, and the menstrual fluid, to mention only a few of many. That which underlies all of these images—and sexuality itself—is an archetypal content that is hard to grasp, and that finds its best psychological expression in the primitive *mana* symbol. In each of the images given above we can see a relatively fixed symbol—*i.e.* the *mana* symbol—but we cannot for all that be certain that when they occur in dreams they have no other meaning.

The practical need may call for quite another interpretation. To be sure, if we had to interpret dreams in an exhaustive way according to scientific principles, we should have to refer every such symbol to an archetype. But, in practice, this kind of interpretation might be a grave blunder, for the patient's psychological state may require anything rather than the giving of attention to a theory of dreams. It is therefore advisable, for the purposes of therapy, to look for the meaning of symbols as they relate to the conscious situation—in other words, to treat them as if they were not fixed. This is as much as to say that we must renounce all preconceived opinions, however knowing they make us feel, and try to discover the meaning of things for the patient. If we do this, our interpretations will obviously not go very far towards satisfying a theory of dreams; in fact, they may fall very short in this respect. But if the practitioner operates too much with fixed symbols, there is danger of his falling into mere routine and dogmatism, thus failing to meet the patient's need. It is unfortunate that, to illustrate the above, I should have to go into greater detail than space here permits, but I have elsewhere published illustrative material that amply supports my statements.

As already remarked, it frequently happens at the very beginning of a treatment that a dream reveals to the doctor, in a wide perspective, the general direction in which the unconscious is moving. But, for practical reasons, it may not be feasible to make clear to the patient, at this early stage, the deeper meaning of his dream. The demands of therapy are binding upon us in this way also. When the doctor gains such a far-reaching insight, it is thanks to his experience in the matter of relatively fixed symbols. Such insight can be of the very greatest value in diagnosis and in prognosis as well. I was once consulted in the case of a seventeen-year-old girl. One specialist had suggested that she might be in the first stages of progressive atrophy of the muscles, while another thought that she was a hysteric. Because of this second opinion, I was called in. The clinical picture made me suspect an organic disease, but the girl showed traits of hysteria as well. I asked for dreams. The patient answered at once: "Yes, I have terrible dreams. Just recently I dreamed I was coming home at night. Everything is as quiet as death. The door into the living-room is half open, and I see my mother hanging from the chandelier and swinging to and fro in a cold wind that blows in through the open windows. At another time I dreamed that a terrible noise breaks out in the house at night. I go to see what has happened, and find that a frightened horse is tearing through the rooms. At last it finds the door into the hall, and jumps through the hall window from the fourth floor down into the street. I was terrified to see it lying below, all mangled."

The way in which these dreams allude to death is enough to give one pause. But many persons have anxiety dreams now and then. We must therefore look more closely into the meaning of the outstanding symbols, "mother" and "horse." These figures must be equivalent one to the other, for they both do the same thing: they commit suicide. The mother symbol is archetypal and refers to a place of origin, to nature, that which passively creates, hence to substance and matter, to material nature, the lower body (womb) and the vegetative functions. It connotes also the unconscious, natural and instinctive life, the physiological realm, the body in which we dwell or are contained, for the "mother" is also a vessel, the hollow form (*uterus*) that carries and nourishes, and it thus stands for the foundations of consciousness. Being within something or contained in something suggests darkness, the nocturnal—a state of anxiety. With these allusions I am presenting the idea of the mother in many of its mythological and etymological transformations; I am also giving an important part of the *yin* concept of Chinese philosophy. All this is dream-content, but it is not something which the seventeen-year-old girl has acquired in her individual existence; it is rather a bequest from the past. On the one hand it has been kept alive by the language, and on the other hand it is inherited with the structure of the psyche and is therefore to be found in all times and among all peoples.

The familiar word "mother" refers apparently to the best-known of mothers in particular—to "my mother." But the mother symbol points to a darker meaning which eludes conceptual formulation and can only be vaguely apprehended as the hidden, nature-bound life of the body. Yet even this expression is too narrow, and excludes too many pertinent side-meanings. The psychic reality which underlies this symbol is so inconceivably complex that we can only discern it from afar off, and then but very dimly. It is such realities that call for symbolic expression.

If we apply our findings to the dream, its meaning will be: the unconscious life destroys itself. That is the dream's message to the conscious mind of the dreamer and to everyone who has ears to hear.

"Horse" is an archetype that is widely current in mythology and folk-lore. As an animal it represents the non-human psyche, the sub-human, animal side, and therefore the unconscious. This is why the horse in folk-lore sometimes sees visions, hears voices, and speaks. As a beast of burden it is closely related to the mother-archetype; the Valkyries bear the dead hero to Valhalla and the Trojan horse encloses the Greeks. As an animal lower than man it represents the lower part of the body and the animal drives that take their rise from there. The horse is dynamic power and a means of locomotion; it carries one away like a surge of instinct. It is subject to panics like all instinctive creatures who lack higher consciousness. Also it has to do with sorcery and magical spells—especially the black, night horse which heralds death.

It is evident, then, that "horse" is the equivalent of "mother" with a slight shift of meaning. The mother stands for life at its origin, and the horse for the merely animal life of the body. If we apply this meaning to the dream, it says: the animal life destroys itself.

The two dreams make nearly the same assertion, but, as is usually the case, the second is more specific. The peculiar subtlety of the dream is brought out in both instances: there is no mention of the death of the individual. It is notorious that one often dreams of one's own death, but that is no serious matter. When it is really a question of death, the dream speaks another language. Both of these dreams, then, point to a serious, and even fatal, organic disease. The prognosis was shortly after borne out in fact.

As for the relatively fixed symbols, this example gives a fair idea of their general nature. There are a great many of them, and they may differ in individual cases by subtle shifts of meaning. It is only through comparative studies in mythology, folk-lore, religion and language that we can determine these symbols in a scientific way. The evolutionary stages through which the human psyche has passed are more clearly discernible in the dream than in consciousness. The dream speaks in images, and gives expression to instincts, that are derived from the most primitive levels of nature. Consciousness all too easily departs from the law of nature; but it can be brought again into harmony with the latter by the assimilation of unconscious contents. By fostering this process we lead the patient to the rediscovery of the law of his own being.

I have not been able, in so short a space, to deal with anything but the elements of the subject. I could not put together before your eyes, stone by stone, the edifice that is reared in every analysis from the materials of the unconscious and finds its completion in the restoration of the total personality. The way of successive assimilations reaches far beyond the curative results that specifically concern the doctor. It leads in the end to that distant goal (which may perhaps have been the first urge to life), the bringing into reality of the whole human being —that is, individuation. We physicians are without doubt the first scientific observers of these obscure processes of nature. As a rule we see only a pathological phase of the development, and lose sight of the patient as soon as he is cured. But it is only when the cure has been effected that we are in a position to study the normal process of change, itself a matter of years or decades. If we had some knowledge of the ends towards which unconscious, psychic growth is tending, and if our psychological insight were not drawn exclusively from the pathological phase, we should have a less confused idea of the processes revealed by dreams and a clearer recognition of what it is that the symbols point to. In my opinion, every doctor should be aware of the fact that psychotherapy in general, and analysis in particular, is a procedure that breaks into a purposeful and continuous development, now here and now there, and thus singles out particular phases which may seem to follow opposing courses. Since every analysis by itself shows only one part or aspect of the deeper course of development, nothing but hopeless confusion can result from casuistic comparisons. For this reason I have preferred to confine myself to the rudiments of the subject and to practical considerations. It is only in actual contact with the facts as they occur that we can come to anything like a satisfactory agreement.

Childhood

One of the most far-reaching consequences of Freud's work has been to focus attention on the psychic forces in the development of the child and to modify the nature of child rearing. His conclusions concerning childhood sexuality and the role the parents play in its normal or aberrant development were revolutionary. However, he provided what many feel to be a rather limited view of parent-child relationships. He saw parent-child difficulties as arising through conflicts centered about libidinal development and hence did not take into account sufficiently the myriad of other influences in the parent-child relationship, notably the presence or absence of love and anxiety in the parent. That the mother-child relationship is one of dynamic interaction is shown in the paper by Benedek, who also shows the correlation between the emotional and hormonal states of the mother.

Freud believed that the amnesia for childhood experiences arose because of the need to repress the memory of early sexual impulses. The paper by Schachtel suggests another theory, one which much more plausibly explains why the amnesia is not limited to sexual material. But whichever theory one uses to explain the infantile amnesia, it is clear that retrospective reconstruction from adult material has great possibilities for error, as Freud discovered, since it may be difficult to differentiate between fantasy and fact. As a consequence of these difficulties, observation of child play as though it were free association has been developed as a fruitful method for gathering data and is widely used in child therapy. The paper by Erikson concerns itself with this subject.

On the basis of the libido theory, Freud concluded that the crucial period in the child-parent relationship was the first five to eight years, and that little of determining significance was likely to occur after that period. On the basis of an interpersonal theory in which sex is held to be only one factor, though an

*important one, in childhood development, Sullivan emphasizes
two vital conceptions: the effects of the whole field of interpersonal relatedness and the malleability of the personality both for
constructive and non-constructive development through adolescence.*

12

THERESE BENEDEK

The Psychosomatic Implications of the Primary Unit: Mother-Child*

In the recent literature, several observations have been published demonstrating that the child, by some not clearly defined psychic process, incorporates the emotional attitudes of the mother, embodies her anxiety, and develops symptoms which the mother used to have or might have had.[1] The motivations which play a role in the presenting symptom of the child also exist in the mother and can be elicited by analysis. The dynamics of such preconscious or unconscious communication between mother and child may be clarified by a better understanding of the psychobiological factors which motivate motherhood and motherliness.

This discussion deals with the *psychodynamics of the symbiosis* which exists during pregnancy, is interrupted at birth, but remains a functioning force, directing and motivating the mental and somatic interaction between mother and child.

As long as gratification of the emotional need for motherhood was fulfilled without interference by human controls, one rarely

---

* Reprinted by permission from *Psychosexual Functions in Women* (New York, 1952). Copyright 1952 The Ronald Press Company. Originally published in the *American Journal of Orthopsychiatry*, Vol. 19, 1949.

[1] Beata Rank [1] and her collaborators observed such psychic transmission of conflict constellations to children who became feeding problems. Betty Joseph [2] has shown the same in infants of five to seven months who developed biting symptoms and anxiety. Margaret Fries [3] investigated the interaction between mother and infant during the lying-in period, and Dr. René Spitz [4] demonstrated the infant's reactions to the mother's depression.

had opportunity to study the primary psychobiological factors in childbearing. The behavior manifestations which are usually accessible to psychoanalysis reveal that the woman's identification with her mother motivates her attitude toward motherhood and determines her behavior toward her children. While such psychoanalytic observations elucidate how emotionally determined attitudes may be carried over from generation to generation, they do not answer the question whether there is a genuine, primary psychological need (instinct, in Freud's sense) which directs the woman's desire for conception and motherhood and motivates her motherliness.

The study of the sexual cycle in women [5]—a detailed analysis of the emotional processes as they unfold in correlation with the hormonal cycle of the ovaries—has thrown new light upon the female psychosexual organization.

A complete discussion of the sexual cycle is beyond the scope of this presentation. In order to elucidate the psychology of motherhood, however, I shall discuss one phase of the cycle, the postovulative, progestin phase. After ovulation, the wall of the ruptured follicle, from which the ovum has escaped, undergoes a process of luteinization and produces a hormone called lutein or progestin. The function of this hormone is to prepare the mucous membrane of the uterus to receive the impregnated ovum and to help to maintain pregnancy if conception occurs. If conception does not occur, the progestin production declines after four to six days, the uterine mucosa breaks down, and the uterus is prepared for menstruation. The emotional state which develops in correlation with the progestin phase can be compared with the "quiet period" in lower mammals. The psychic apparatus seems to register the somatic preparation for the pregnancy by a change of emotional attitude: the woman's interest shifts from extraverted activities to her body and its welfare. Expressed in psychodynamic terms: the libido is withdrawn from external, heterosexual objects, becomes concentrated upon the self. This is the phase of the cycle during which the woman's desire for pregnancy, or her defense against it, dominates the psychoanalytic material. At the same time, or some days later in the cycle, the analytic material may show preoccupation with care of the child.[2] However, as if mother and child were identical or interchangeable, the tendencies toward child care may be expressed at one time *actively,* as a wish to nurse, to feed, to take care of the baby; and at other times the same woman may express the same tendencies *passively,* as a desire to be fed, to be taken care of.

Helene Deutsch [6] found that a *deep-rooted passivity* and a *specific tendency toward introversion* are characteristic qualities of the female psyche. Our study of the sexual cycle reveals that these propensities of female psychology are repeated in cyclic intervals, in correspondence with the specifically female gonad hormone, *progestin,* during the postovulative phase of the ovarian cycle. On the basis of such observations, we assume that the emotional manifestations of the specific passive-receptive and narcissistic-retentive tendencies represent the psychodynamic correlates of the biological need for motherhood.

The *psychology of pregnancy* is easily understood in the light of the psychodynamic processes which accompany the progestin phase of the cycle. Just as the monthly repetition of the physiological processes represents a somatic preparation for pregnancy, so the corresponding monthly repetition of the emotional attitudes represents a preparation for that introversion of psychic energies which motivates the emotional attitudes of the pregnant woman.

The interaction between mother and child—*the symbiosis*—begins after conception. The enhanced hormonal and general metabolic processes which are necessary to maintain normal pregnancy produce an increase of vital energies. The pregnant woman in her placid vegetative calmness enjoys her pregnant body, which is like a reservoir replenished with libidinous feelings. While such feelings enhance the mother's well-being, they also become the source of her motherliness: they increase her pleasure in bearing the child and her patience in regard to some of the discomforts of her pregnancy. Primary narcissism—the

---

[2] We could not determine whether this occurs in correlation with progestin alone or in correlation with prolactin production in these women who are neither pregnant nor lactating.

result of surplus energy [7] produced by active metabolic balance
—is the reservoir which supplies with libido the various emotional
tasks of living. As the hormonal processes of pregnancy replenish
the primary narcissism of the woman, this becomes the source of
her motherliness. The general behavior and the emotional state
during pregnancy may appear "regressive" if we compare them
with the usual level of ego integration of the same woman; yet
the condition which appears regressive on the ego level represents
a growth of the integrative span of the personality on the biological level. While the mother feels her growing capacity to love and
to take care of the child, she actually experiences a general improvement in her emotional balance. We have observed that many
neurotic women, who suffered severe anxiety states before, have
become free from anxiety during pregnancy. Others become
free from depression and from desperate mood changes. Many
women, despite the discomforts of nausea or morning sickness,
feel emotionally stable and have the "best time" during pregnancy. This does not mean we are forgetting that some women
become severely panic-stricken and/or depressed during pregnancy. (Usually, this happens in the latter part of pregnancy or
after delivery.) If the woman's developmental disturbance is
such that her ego is unable to master the productive task of
childbearing, a dissociation of the functions (physiological and
mental) may occur during the pregnancy. In this paper, however, we are discussing the emotional course of the normal pregnancy, which enriches the somatic and psychic energies of the
woman to a degree that she becomes able to master emotional
conflicts which were disturbing to her at other times. The force
which maintains pregnancy is responsible for the characteristic
attitude of withdrawal which sometimes becomes intensified to
such a degree that nothing else, no other reality, counts for the
pregnant woman, and she lives as in a daze.[3]

Another aspect of the psychology of pregnancy is expressed
by an increase in the *receptive tendencies*. This is a manifesta-

---

[3] This is the reason that some women, even if they have to hide the
pregnancy—for example, unmarried mothers—do not realize the actual difficulties they have to face, but forget about them until the delivery creates a
different emotional situation.

tion of the biological process of growth which it serves. The voraciousness and the bizarre appetite of the pregnant woman are well known. "She eats for two" expresses permission, especially when gratification of such needs is not limited by medical control. The pregnant woman thrives on the sympathy and solicitude of her environment. If, however, her passive receptive needs are unfulfilled, if her husband or her family are not adequately attentive, the sense of frustration may set in action a regressive process which may increase her receptive needs to an exaggerated degree. The resulting anger may destroy the primary narcissistic state of pregnancy, and thus it may interfere with the development of motherliness.

The difference between primary and secondary narcissism in the development of motherliness can easily be seen when we contrast the vital libidinal energy (produced by the metabolic processes maintaining the pregnancy) and the secondary ego gratifications which the pregnant woman may expect in connection with her pregnancy and her child. The need for ego gratification may change the fantasies of the mother from the unqualified desire for a child to definite wishes and ambitions which she hopes and intends to fulfill through the child. Thus the child becomes a means for gratification of individually determined goals, even before it is born. A mother may worry during the pregnancy lest her child will not be all that is desired, i.e., a son for one reason or a daughter for another. Many other conflicts, arising from the secondary narcissistic goals of the personality, may disturb the development of genuine motherliness.[4]

The important role that hormonal stimulation plays in development and performance of motherliness has been well studied in animals. In the human one is inclined to overlook the role of hormonal stimulation, since motherliness, an idealized attitude of

---

[4] There are other factors in the psychology of pregnancy which may interfere with the development of motherliness, such as the fear of death at childbirth, exaggerated fear of labor pains, etc. These are, however, symptoms motivated by developmental conflicts of the woman and are, therefore, secondary. Here the discussion is limited to those aspects of the psychology of motherhood which are related directly to the hormonal processes. However, the hormonal processes may be influenced by environmental factors which motivate the psychosexual development *in toto*, such as the girl's identification with the mother [5].

highest value, is considered as the fulfillment of ethical aspects of the personality rather than of "animalistic" biological functions. Yet motherliness is a function of a specific—biological and psychic—maturation; its completion, as many observations prove, is only rarely reached at and about the birth of the first child.

While *the trauma of birth*—the interruption of the fetal symbiosis—in recent years has been studied often from the point of view of the infant, its significance for the mother has been relatively neglected. I do not refer here to the massive obstetrical traumata and the resulting pathology. I rather want to point out that when the newborn leaves the womb and has to become active in securing the basic needs for living, the mother's organism has to become reorganized also. In some sense, this may be considered as a trauma for the mother. The hormonal and metabolic changes which induce parturition, the labor pains, and the excitement of delivery, even without intensive use of narcotics, interrupt the continuity of the mother-child unity. After delivery, when the organism as a whole is preparing for the next function of motherhood—*lactation*—mothers, especially primiparas, may experience an "emotional lag." For the nine months of the pregnancy, they were preparing to love the baby. After delivery, they may be surprised by a *lack of feeling* for the child.[5] Usually love for the newborn wells up in the mother as she first hears the cry of her baby. The sensation of love reassures the mother about the continuity of her oneness with the child and she may relax and wait serenely to receive her child on her breast. It is different if the mother, instead of love, feels a sense of loss and emptiness; if she has the feeling of a distance between herself and the infant; views the baby as an outsider, an object; and she asks herself with estrangement, "Is this what I had in me?" Mothers having such a disquieting experience usually muster all their self-control to suppress this feeling and try to summon their previous fantasies to establish an emotional relationship with the infant. Such mothers, disappointed in themselves by the lack of love, feel

---

[5] This occurs more often if delivery was performed under complete anesthesia, so that the mother has no memory of the experience.

guilty, become anxious; and with this the insecurity toward the child begins.[6]

The further development of the mother-child relationship depends on the total personality of the mother; she may develop a depression and withdraw from the child; she may turn against the child who exposed her failure in loving and reject it completely; or she may overcompensate the fear of not being able to love and may become overindulgent and protective. This early post-partum *emotional lag* is a critical period during which the husband's relationship to his wife, his readiness for gratifying his wife's dependent needs, is of great importance. The post-partum woman, for many reasons, including physiological motivations, has a regressive tendency, and therefore has a great desire to be mothered. Through the love which she passively receives, she may be able to overcome the depression and give love to her child.

Whether the mother, through the feeling of love, is able to maintain the sense of unity with her child, or whether she has to miss this most significant gratification, the organism of the mother is not ready to give up the symbiosis after parturition. The need for its continuation exists in the mother, whose hormonal household is preparing to continue the symbiosis by *lactation*.

The psychosomatic correlations during normal lactation have not been studied closely because lactation is a contented period in the woman's life. The hormonal function—related to *prolactin* production—which stimulates milk secretion, usually suppresses the gonad function and induces an emotional attitude which is similar to that of the progestin phase of the cycle. As is now known, during the monthly preparation for pregnancy, the intention toward motherliness is expressed by active and passive receptive tendencies. During lactation, both the active and passive receptive tendencies gain in intensity; they become the axis around

---

[6] Whether the post-partum metabolic processes have such a generally depressing effect on the mother that she is unable to feel love, and consequently becomes afraid of the tasks of motherhood, or whether the lack of motherly emotions is the result of the immaturity of those psychic and somatic processes which result in motherliness, deserves further study and probably needs to be established in each case.

which the activities of motherliness center. The woman's desire to nurse the baby, to be close to it bodily, represents the continuation of the original symbiosis, not only for the infant, but for the mother as well. While the infant incorporates the breast, the mother feels united with the baby. The identification with the baby permits the mother to "regress," to repeat and satisfy her own passive, dependent, receptive needs. The emotional experiences of lactation, while they permit a process of identification between mother and child, afford a slow, step-by-step integration of normal motherliness.

What have our present methods of child care done with the woman's ability and readiness to nurse the baby? It would lead us away from the primarily psychosomatic frame of this presentation if I went into a discussion of the sociological and anthropological factors which, in our culture, interfere with the continuation of the symbiosis between mother and infant during lactation. The result of the suppression of the natural process of motherliness is, however, very serious. Possibly the baby's "formula" can improve on nature as far as chemistry is concerned; possibly it can regulate the metabolic needs of the infant better than breast feeding does; but it cannot develop motherliness through the bottle, even if the mother is permitted to hold her baby in her arms while she feeds him, as present-day nursing care encourages.

One example of incipient disturbance of motherliness I observed recently: this young woman was very anxious to have a second baby and was very happy when she became pregnant. Her moodiness, which often led to suicidal ideas, disappeared and she felt serene during the pregnancy. While the delivery of the first baby in a military hospital during the war had been a frightening experience, this fear was now overcome since everything could be arranged according to her wishes. She had a normal delivery with anesthesia only at the end. To the great surprise of the nurses, she wanted her baby rooming-in with her. She felt happy and contented, watching her infant and nursing him, concentrating on him completely. Then she developed a slight infection and the baby was taken away from her. When she went home, a nurse took over the care of the baby. As the nurse watched her feeding the baby, she felt her milk being dissipated. The nurse was eager to give the baby the bottle. The mother became uncomfortable and depressed. Although she felt that she was losing what she wanted so much, her friends began to tell her that it was time for her to go out, to enjoy her freedom while she had the nurse. She became moody. "I spend time fantasying about being sick and in the hospital again," she confessed. She complained that she was superfluous to the baby, yet she did not dare to send the nurse away and take full responsibility, for she was not certain that she could enjoy at home the same concentration upon the infant as she had felt in the hospital. "That would be unfair to the older child," she protested, and it would also seem silly to some of her friends. Thus, five weeks after delivery—in old times, she would still be "in confinement"—she was in the psychiatrist's office complaining about two things: (a) that she loved the baby in the hospital, but now did not know how to love him; and (b) that the baby, who was so quiet and gained weight so well, had become fussy, was crying a great deal, and had even vomited once or twice, and this frightened her.

No single example can completely illustrate the point which I want to make: namely, that not only the infant has the need for the mother's readiness to nurse, to take care of him; not the baby alone thrives on the closeness of the mother, by her warmth and tenderness; but the mother also has an instinctual need to fulfill the physiological and emotional preparedness for her motherliness. If this process of the mother's development is suppressed, the enforced changes in the hormonal function may disturb that psychosomatic balance which is the source of motherliness. The vulnerability of the integration of motherliness can be explained by a summary of the psychosomatic processes of the puerperium[7] and lactation.

1. When one compares the psychosexual integration of the personality during the puerperium with that of the "highest" integration of the personality, the lactating or puerperal mother appears *regressed* to an oral level.

2. While this psychosexual state accounts for the (uncon-

---

[7] Puerperium is the period from termination of labor to the completion of the involution of the uterus—usually six weeks.

scious) communication—identification between mother and infant—it also accounts for the depressive reactions of the mother.[8] Thus the mother becomes oversensitive in regard to her capacity for fulfilling the function of motherhood.

Every indication of her failure increases the mother's sense of inferiority and creates anxious tension and depression. Just as the suppression of lactation interferes with the development of motherliness, so failure of motherliness, originating in other sources of the personality, may interfere with lactation. In old times, one used to say that the emotional disturbance of the mother "goes on the milk," and it was assumed that the emotional disturbance influenced not only the quantity, but also the quality of the milk, so that the baby received milk which was "difficult to digest" and caused colic and other suffering. For many years, one shrugged scientific shoulders over such "superstition." Today, we accept it as fact, although we admit that we do not know the pathways by which the emotional tensions of the mother are transmitted to the infant.

In an earlier paper, I examined the interaction between mother and infant in regard to the development of the adaptive capacity of the ego [8]. It is pertinent to summarize here the main conclusions of that study.

According to our hypothesis, the symbiosis between mother and child continues on a different scale during the neonatal period. The sleeping infant is in a condition closely resembling that of intrauterine life. The arising physiological needs disturb the sleep, and then the course of gratification is as follows: crying —gratification—sleep. This process evolves; as far as the newborn is concerned, *within the self,* without realization of the external environment. The mother's genuine motherliness, her desire and ability to supply the infant with the sensations of "protectedness," reduce the frequency of disturbing stimuli and diminish the intensity and length of the crying fits. Through the rhythmic repetition of the gratification of his physiological needs, the infant develops to the perception that the source of the need (hunger, pain,

---

[8] That the intensification of the oral receptive tendencies represents the psychodynamic conditions for the development of depression is a well-established concept of psychoanalysis.

discomfort) is *within,* and the source of gratification is *outside* the self.

By the same routinely returning process of gratifications, the infant acquires a *sense of confidence* that the mother will gratify his needs. It is difficult to describe the phenomenology of this early emotional state, although mothers will recognize its manifestations—in the baby's way of turning his head, following with his eyes, ceasing to cry for a short while when the mother is near, etc. This indicates that confidence plays an important role in the economy of the psychic apparatus during infancy: it preserves the mother-child unity; it helps to decrease the intensity of the outer stimuli and thus averts anxiety. Lack of confidence stimulates tension which may grow into discomfort and anxiety. This emotional shelter—confidence—and the positive, dependent relationship to the mother which is its consequence, facilitates learning in the normal infant. The ego, strengthened by the libidinal relationship to the mother on the one hand and by the absence of anxiety on the other, develops an adequate capacity to perceive the objects of the outer world; such an ego is able to accept new and unexpected situations (always in a degree which corresponds to the developmental level of the child) and masters them by trust in the mother.[9]

Quite different from this ego structure is the ego of those infants whose development was not guided by the confident relationship to the mother. *Hospitalism* [10] is a severe state of inhibition which develops in infants raised in institutions, where routine substitutes for love. Without the loving stimulation of one individual, children with such dependent needs do not turn to any person with confidence. Such children do not watch the person, but rather the bottle, or some other phase of the routine. It was observed that such children refused the bottle when it was

---

[9] The concept of *confidence* can be compared with the concept of *hope* [9]. French shows how "hope" facilitates the mental processes necessary for achieving a goal. We believe that *hope* develops as a mental habit on the basis of *confidence.* Through confidence in the forthcoming passive gratifications and in the forthcoming help and support in attempts at active mastery, the ego develops to a stage in which it is able to project the expectations for gratification in the future. Hope, like confidence, diminishes the sense of frustration and already in early childhood enables the individual to *wait* for gratification without a sudden increase in the psychic tension.

offered from the side of the bed other than they were used to. Such children adapt to the routine gratification of their needs with conditioned reflexes.

Conditioned reflexes represent a significant part of primary learning in normal children also. Yet there is an important difference between the learning of the healthy infant and that of the infant developing various degrees of hospitalism. Conditioning is an adaptive mechanism, which serves as protection against anxiety. Anxiety has several sources. One of them is the body itself, which generates pain by the sensation of unsatisfied physiologic needs; the other source of anxiety is the danger in which the weak ego finds itself when alone and isolated. Infants raised by loveless routine are exposed to anxiety-producing situations more often than those whose needs are met with loving care. The ego, beset by anxiety too often, and for too long a time, remains fixated to the level of primitive conditioning. Such reflex adaptation saves the child from further increase of tension, and the child remains calm as long as every step of the routine is followed without a change. Every new situation, even a slight change in the routine, will, however, be experienced as a danger; the child responds with anxiety, i.e., with crying. If the environmental situation cannot be improved, the inhibition increases; the child, in order to avoid anxiety, finally refuses to respond and does not accept any new situation. If only the bare physiologic needs of a child are supplied, he may grow up to become a deeply inhibited person. For such an individual, every new situation will reactivate a part of that anxiety which he experienced as an infant. The individual who did not learn to love during the first year of life will be threatened whenever he shall develop a new object relationship.

I have presented two extremes. In the one environment, the processes of growth appear to be ideally regulated by the infant's own needs, the mother responding to them in a way which all but repeats the symbiosis, permitting the infant to develop to independence at his own pace. In the other environment, the symbiosis was interrupted, the nursing care did not supply enough gratification to enable the infant to develop emotional—interpersonalized and intrapsychic—defenses against anxiety. These extremes illustrate that the ego's capacity to learn to master the object world goes hand in hand with the development of object-libidinal relationship. The ego structure developing through the buffer of confidence has a greater span and flexibility in adaptation to reality. In contrast, if the psychic economy is not relieved by a sense of security in the relationship with the mother, but has to concentrate upon mastering and avoiding anxiety, it will produce an ego structure fixated to rigidly conditioned adaptation. Such ego structure may break down at any time when a new adaptive task emerges.

The interaction between mother and infant, however, can be studied in even more detail in the large majority of instances ranging between these extremes.

The activity pattern of the newborn depends upon the irritability of his nervous system, on the one hand, and upon the degree of protection against the disturbing stimuli on the other. In the light of our discussion, we may say that the infant born with a nervous system of greater sensitivity would need a longer, better-functioning substitute for the intrauterine symbiosis.[10] However, experience shows that the mothers of the "nervous" babies are usually less able to provide their infants with an environment of fewer stimulations. The mature, normal newborn calms down under the influence of normal nursing care to this rhythm: need —crying—gratification—sleep. It takes usually four weeks, i.e., the neonatal period, to advance in physiological adjustment to a degree which assures smoother vegetative functioning.

It is observed that a large proportion of babies, instead of becoming "happier" at about the age of four weeks, show a new type of crying. Gesell and Ilg [11] state: "The baby shows a tendency to cry prior to sleep." This "wakefulness crying" tends to occur in the afternoon and the evening. It loses its prominence at about ten or twelve weeks.

What is the cause of this irritability? In the light of our assump-

---

[10] First-born infants, on account of lesser maturation, or on account of greater birth trauma, represent a more difficult task to a mother who has also less maturity in handling the child. Thus, the first-born infant's activity pattern is more fitful; it takes longer for him to quiet down than for subsequent children of the same parent. This statement must be checked, however, in regard to the many factors which may influence mother and child.

tion that the mother as well as the baby has a need for continuation of the symbiosis, we may speculate on the significance of the baby's increased demand on the mother at a time when she begins to turn away from the baby and becomes more active in the other areas of her existence. Do infants then demand more intensely the re-establishment of the symbiosis? Or do they respond to the increased tenseness of the mother? Be that as it may, the infant has no means other than his crying fit for discharging tension. It is fortunate that the infant has no memory of the amount of discomfort and pain which his crying fit would indicate. The unreadiness of his nervous system, the lack of internal barriers (*Reiz-Schutz*), accounts for the spreading of the tension which may increase to a veritable "storm of excitation" and may invade the viscera [12]. It will depend on the degree of maturity of the vegetative nervous system and the gastrointestinal tract whether such excitation becomes bound to definite parts of the gastrointestinal system and its functioning. Thus, symptoms like pyloric spasm, as well as colic, can be explained as steps in the mastery of the general excitation of the nervous system. Generally, the intensity and frequency of such disturbances during the first three months measure the pace of interaction between mother and child.

Melanie Klein [13] assumes that infants, struggling with a breast which does not feed or which overflows, infants suffering from pain of hunger, colic, or other bodily discomfort, acquire the concepts of "good" and "bad" within themselves. Even if we do not follow Klein's complex psychologic elaborations, we may accept, on the basis of observation, that anxiety and pain (any sort of discomfort may cause anxiety in the infant) increase the urge to re-establish security by being close to the mother. The crying, grasping infant bites the nipple with force and suckles with greed; the sick infant, too, gasping with opening and closing of the mouth, wants to incorporate the mother, to re-establish the symbiosis which once supplied all needs without pain. If such intensification of the incorporative needs leads to gratification, the interaction between mother and child improves. If, however, the mother does not succeed in pacifying the infant, his physiological tension increases and the need for incorporation becomes more and more charged with motor energy. We speak of "hostile incorporation" although the psychic representation of hostility can hardly exist so early. But its model is formed. The *hostile incorporation* augments the internal tension of the infant; at the same time, it alienates the helpless mother who feels rejected by her child. Thus while a vicious circle develops between mother and infant, another vicious circle within the infant becomes intensified. The infant, after his attempts at incorporation which have failed to satisfy his needs, is helpless and exhausted. Rado and Fenichel [14] pointed out that the first regulator of self-esteem (*Selbstgefühl*) is the satisfaction acquired by all the processes connected with feeding; they assume that the early disappointments, anxiety, helplessness, which some infants experience in connection with feeding and digestion, may cause a sense of helplessness, of inferiority, of worthlessness; as if "badness" were existing within the self.

It is beyond the scope of this paper to elaborate how the primary self-esteem becomes the basis of ego development. Secure and stable, it is the core of a strong adaptable ego; helpless and insecure, it gives rise to a rigid ego structure which, under the strain of adaptive tasks arising later in life, may regress to the basic insecurity of early childhood. The regressive processes may then bring to the fore psychosomatic conditions which were determined by the developmental processes of infancy.

Summary

The psychosomatic (hormonal) aspects of motherliness were discussed to demonstrate the mother's biological need for continuation of symbiosis in the puerperium and during the child's infancy. This instinctual tendency toward motherliness corresponds to the helplessness of the newborn; it is gratified by sundry intimate functions of motherhood which supply both mother and infant with the gratification of their dependent needs. Motherliness, developing through sublimation of instinctual impulses, enlarges the span of the mother's personality; it encompasses her child.

The physiologic and mental apparatus of the infant represents a system which communicates broadly and fluently with the system of the mother—with all aspects of the mother's personality: with her id, her ego, and her superego. Through the processes of identification with the mother, the infant develops from the undifferentiated state of the newborn to an individual with structuralized mental apparatus which is in control of psychic and somatic processes.[11]

Discussion

JULES V. COLEMAN, M.D.[12] Dr. Benedek presents an interesting and again a classical discussion of a problem of intense practical importance. Motherliness as the central core of the experience of personality development in the infant is shown to be related to the mother's identification with her own mother, to the hormonal-personality interaction, and to a specific psychodynamic system.

I was particularly interested in the discussion of the frequent reaction of early post-partum *emotional lag,* which I suppose may be related psychologically to a kind of separation anxiety, to a lack of tolerance for the sudden shift from a high level of narcissistic possessive enjoyment of the intrauterine child to a sense of detachment and even of loss. The more narcissistic woman for whom the incorporative possession of the child has special value may have difficulty in believing in the reality of the child outside herself, and may develop panic feelings arising out of the ambivalent conflict precipitated by the separation.

Here, then, at any rate, in this early post-partum period, is one of the important crossroad experiences of motherhood, since it is here that the biological and psychological readiness patterns

[11] It would be a mistake to conclude that breast feeding holds the answer to all problems and that by itself it assures a conflictless evolution of the child-mother relationship. Long-term observations are necessary to evaluate the significance of breast feeding and the variations in its techniques for specific developmental conflicts.

[12] University of Colorado Medical Center, Denver.

may be thrown out of gear or entirely displaced, leaving indifference or hatred behind. Regardless of special psychological difficulties in the particular mother, there is always present this psychosomatic push for the preservation, continuation, and development of the symbiotic relationship, which, if not interfered with, does make the mother the final authority in child rearing, at least the rearing of her own child.

One of our pediatricians in Denver insists that his mothers of premature babies visit the hospital on a regular schedule at least once a day, more often if possible, so that their breasts may be pumped to provide breast milk for the infant. Even if the milk is not used for the child, he feels that for the mother it is an essential experience of participation.

It seems to me that in the work of pediatricians and other physicians caring for babies, as well as in the well-baby clinics, a primary concern should be the preservation of the biologically based and psychologically necessary symbiosis. It is not a matter of method of child care but of helping the mother to find and to develop confidence in her own psychosomatic resources for this wholeness of shared experience in the symbiotic relationship.

References

[1] RANK, BEATA, MARIAN C. PUTNAM, and GREGORY ROCHLIN. The Significance of the "Emotional Climate" in Early Feeding Difficulties. Psychosomatic Med., 10:279-283, 1948.

[2] JOSEPH, BETTY. A Technical Problem in the Treatment of the Infant Patient. Internat. J. Psa., 29:58-59, 1948.

[3] FRIES, MARGARET E. Psychosomatic Relationships Between Mother and Infant. Psychosomatic Med., 6:159-162, 1944.

[4] SPITZ, RENÉ A. "Anaclitic Depression: An Inquiry into the Genesis of Psychiatric Conditions in Early Childhood." In The Psychoanalytic Study of the Child, Vol. II, pp. 313-342. Internat. Univ. Press, New York, 1947.

[5] BENEDEK, THERESE, and BORIS B. RUBENSTEIN. The Sexual Cycle in Women: The Relation Between Ovarian Function and Psychodynamic Processes. Psychosomatic Med. Monogs., Vol. III, Nos. 1 and 2. National Research Council, Washington, D. C., 1942.

[6] DEUTSCH, HELENE. The Psychology of Women: A Psychoanalytic Interpretation, Vols. I and II. Grune & Stratton, New York, 1944, 1945.

[7] ALEXANDER, FRANZ. Psychoanalysis Revised. Psa. Quart., 9:1, 1940.

[8] BENEDEK, THERESE. Adaptation to Reality in Early Infancy. Ibid., 7:200-215, 1938.

[9] FRENCH, THOMAS M. The Integration of Social Behavior. Ibid., 14:159-165, 1945.

[10] SPITZ, RENÉ A. "Hospitalism: An Inquiry into the Genesis of Psychiatric Conditions in Early Childhood." In The Psychoanalytic Study of the Child, Vol. I, 1945, pp. 113-117.
———. "Hospitalism: A Follow-up Report." Ibid., Vol. II, 1947, pp. 53-74.

[11] GESELL, ARNOLD, and FRANCES M. ILG. Infant and Child in the Culture of Today. Harper, New York, 1943.

[12] PEIPER, ALBRECHT. Die Krampfbereitschaft des Saüglings. Jahrbuch fuer Kinderheilkunde, 125:194, 1929.

[13] KLEIN, MELANIE. The Psycho-Analysis of Children. Norton, New York, 1932.

[14] RADO, SANDOR. The Psychical Effects of Intoxification: Attempt at a Psychoanalytical Theory of Drug-Addiction. Internat. J. Psa., 9:301-317, 1928.
FENICHEL, OTTO. Fruehe Entwicklungsstadien des Ichs. Imago, 23:243-269, 1937.

13

ERNEST G. SCHACHTEL

On Memory and Childhood Amnesia*

Greek mythology celebrates Mnemosyne, the goddess of memory, as the mother of all art. She bore the nine muses to Zeus.[1] Centuries after the origin of this myth Plato banned poetry, the child of memory, from his ideal state as being idle and seductive. While lawmakers, generals, and inventors were useful for the common good, the fact that Homer was nothing but a wandering minstrel without a home and without a following proved how useless he was.[2] In the Odyssey the voices of the Sirens tempt Ulysses.

> *For never yet hath any man rowed past*
> *This isle in his black ship, till he hath heard*
> *The honeyed music of our lips, and goes*
> *His way delighted and a wiser man.*
> *For see, we know the whole tale of the travail*
> *That Greeks and Trojans suffered in wide Troy-lana*
> *By Heaven's behest; yea, and all things we know*
> *That come to pass upon the fruitful earth.*

* Reprinted by special permission of The William Alanson White Psychiatric Foundation, Inc., and Patrick Mullahy, from *A Study of Interpersonal Relations*, edited by Patrick Mullahy, and published by Hermitage House, Inc., New York. Copyright, 1949, by Hermitage Press, Inc. (Originally published in *Psychiatry*, 1947, 10:1-26; and, in abridged form, in *Politics*, Spring 1948).

[1] The words "muse" and "mnemosyne" derive from the same root: "men" or "man." Preller, Ludwig, *Griechische Mythologie*; Berlin 1872; vol. 1, p. 399, footnote 1. In German, too, the words "Gedächtnis" (memory) and "Dichtung" (poetry) derive from the same root "denken" (think); compare also "gedenken" (remember).

[2] Plato, *Republic*, 599, 600.

Their irresistible song, in evoking the past, promises a delight which will allow no future and will be the end of Ulysses' plans to return to an active life and to resume the rule of Ithaca. He prevents his shipmates from listening to the alluring voices by plugging their ears with wax, and he, too curious to renounce the pleasure, has himself chained to the ship's mast so that he will not be able to yield to their song and abandon the future.

This ambivalent attitude toward memory, especially toward its most potent form as embodied in the song, the epic, the tale, in poetry, music, fiction, and in all art, has accompanied the history of man. The modern, popular attitude, so widespread in the United States, the country of the most advanced industrial and technological civilization—that all art and poetry is "sissy"—is the latter-day implementation of the Platonic taboo. But with this difference: the contemporaries of Plato, and before them the shipmates of Ulysses, were susceptible to the promise of happiness that the song of the Sirens and of the muses contains, so that Ulysses and Plato, concerned with planning and not with the past, had to prevent their listening forcefully. Today the masses have internalized the ancient fear and prohibition of this alluring song and, in their contempt for it, express and repress both their longing for and their fear of the unknown vistas to which it might open the doors.

The profound fascination of memory of past experience and the double aspect of this fascination—its irresistible lure into the past with its promise of happiness and pleasure, and its threat to the kind of activity, planning, and purposeful thought and behavior encouraged by modern western civilization—have attracted the thought of two men in recent times who have made the most significant modern contribution to the ancient questions posed by the Greek myth: Sigmund Freud and Marcel Proust.

Both are aware of the antagonism inherent in memory, the conflict between reviving the past and actively participating in the present life of society. Both illuminate the nature of this conflict from different angles. Proust, the poet of memory, is ready to renounce all that people usually consider as active life, to renounce activity, enjoyment of the present moment, concern with the future, friendship, social intercourse, for the sublime happiness and profound truth recaptured in the most elusive of all treasures that man has hunted for, the "Remembrance of Things Past." He pursues this conflict between activity and memory into its most subtle manifestations. He knows that, as the awakening dreamer may lose the memory of his dream when he moves his limbs, opens his eyes, changes the position of his body, so the slightest motion may endanger and dispel the deep pleasure of the vision of the time in Combray, recaptured by the flavor of the *madeleine,* or the image of Venice conjured up by the sensation and the posture which the unevenness of the pavement in the court of the Guermantes town house brought to him as the unevenness of the pavement of San Marco had years ago. He does not dare to stir, for fear that the exhilarating vision may disappear. Bodily movement is the basic and simplest form of all activity endangering memory. Action itself, the attitude of activity, even the activity of enjoying the immediate present are seen by Proust as the antagonists, the incompatible alternative of memory. From here it is only one step to the insight that the memory which reveals the true vision of something past, the memory celebrated by Proust, is very different from the voluntary, everyday memory, the useful instrument needed by man every hour and every minute to recall a word, a figure, a date, to recognize a person or an object, to think of his plans, tasks, intentions, the eminently utilitarian memory characterized by the very fact that it serves the purposes of active and conventionally organized life in society. Proust speaks of the artificiality and untruth of the pictures that this memory furnishes, of its flat and uniform quality which cannot do justice to the unique flavor and the true qualities of anything remembered.

While for Proust the antagonism between society and memory of the significant past can be resolved only by renouncing either one or the other, Goethe seeks to reconcile the two. When, at a party, a toast was proposed to memory he objected vehemently with these words: "I do not recognize memory in the sense in which you mean it. Whatever we encounter that is great, beautiful, significant, need not be remembered from outside, need not be hunted up and laid hold of as it were. Rather, from the beginning, it must be woven into the fabric of our inmost self, must become one with it, create a new and better self in us and thus live and become a productive force in ourselves. There is no past that one is allowed to long for. There is only the eternally new, growing from the enlarged elements of the past; and genuine longing always must be productive, must create something new and better." [3]

Freud, not unlike Proust, approaches the problem of memory not from wondering what, or how well, or how much man remembers, but how hard it is to remember, how much is forgotten and not to be recovered at all or only with the greatest difficulty, and how the period richest in experience, the period of early childhood, is the one which usually is forgotten entirely save for a few apparently meaningless memory fragments. He finds this surprising since "we are informed that during those years which have left nothing but a few incomprehensible memory fragments, we have vividly reacted to impressions, that we have manifested human pain and pleasure and that we have expressed love, jealousy and other passions as they then affected us." [4] The few incomprehensible memory fragments left over from childhood, he considers as "concealing memories" (Deckerinnerungen),[5] and his painstaking work to decipher their language bears more than a superficial resemblance to Proust's attempt to decipher the hieroglyphic characters of the images of a cloud, a triangle, a belfry, a flower, a pebble—a most difficult undertaking, but the only way to the true memories enclosed in these signs which seemed to be only indifferent material objects or sensations. It was Freud who made the discovery that a conflict, leading to repression, is responsible for the difficulty of remembering the past. His well-known explanation of infantile amnesia is that the forgetting of childhood experiences is due to progressive repression of infantile sexuality, which reaches the

---

[3] Author's translation from *Goethe's Gespräche*; Herausgegeben von Flodoard Freiherr von Biedermann; Vol. 3, Leipzig 1910, p. 37 (November 4th, 1823). Compare with this Proust's "*Les vrais paradis sont les paradis qu'on a perdus.*"
[4] Sigmund Freud, Three Contributions to the Theory of Sex. In *The Basic Writings of Sigmund Freud*; Random House, New York 1938; p. 581.
[5] Sigmund Freud, Psychopathology of Everyday Life; *Basic Writings*, pp. 62-65.

peak of its manifestations in the third and fourth years of life. This repression is brought about by the "psychic forces of loathing, shame, and moral and esthetic ideal demands." [6] These forces have the sanction of society, they are the product of society, they are part and serve the purposes of the same conventionally organized life of society which moulds the functions of all social activity and of that "uniform" memory in which Proust saw the irreconcilable antagonists of the true remembrance of things past.

It is the purpose of this essay to explore further the dynamics of this conflict in memory which leads to the striking phenomenon of childhood amnesia as well as to the difficulty, encountered by Proust though more hidden to the average eye, of recovering *any* true picture of past experience. To speak of a conflict in memory is a convenient abbreviation. Formulated more explicitly and accurately, the intention of this presentation is to shed light on some of the factors and conflicts in man and his society which make it difficult if not impossible for him really to remember his past and especially his early childhood.

No greater change in the needs of man occurs than that which takes place between early childhood and adulthood. Into this change have gone all the decisive formative influences of the culture transmitted by the parents, laying the fundament of the transformation into the grown-up, "useful" member of society from the little heathen, who is helpless but as yet sees nothing wrong with following the pleasure principle completely and immediately and who has an insatiable curiosity and capacity for

---

[6]*Ibid.*, p. 583. Freud asserts that the development of these forces during the latency period is organically determined and that it "can occasionally be produced without the help of education." It is surprising that the man who discovered, explored, described, and emphasized over and over again the conflict between culture, society, and sexual instinct should have ascribed the ontogenetic origin of sexual inhibitions to organic factors as though he wanted to explain as natural those inhibitions which a culture, hostile to pleasure and to sex, has created, deepened, and strengthened in every imaginable way. The only explanation for such a strange and questionable hypothesis lies, to my mind, in Freud's and every great discoverer's tragic conflict between a powerful and lucid mind searching for truth and the person who never can entirely extricate himself from the thousand threads with which he is captured and tied to the prejudices, ideologies, falsehoods, and conventions of his time and society.

experience. An explanation of childhood amnesia that takes into account these changes leads to the following tentative hypothesis:

The categories (or schemata) of adult memory are not suitable receptacles for early childhood experiences and therefore not fit to preserve these experiences and enable their recall. The functional capacity of the conscious, adult memory is usually limited to those types of experience which the adult consciously makes and is capable of making.

It is not merely the repression of a specific content, such as early sexual experiences, that accounts for the general childhood amnesia; the biologically, culturally, and socially influenced process of memory organization results in the formation of categories (schemata) of memory which are not suitable vehicles to receive and reproduce experiences of the quality and intensity typical of early childhood. The world of modern western civilization has no use for this type of experience. In fact, it cannot permit itself to have any use for it; it cannot permit the memory of it, because such memory, if universal, would explode the restrictive social order of this civilization. No doubt the hostility of western civilization to pleasure, and to sexual pleasure as the strongest of all, is a most important factor operative in the transformation and education of the child into an adult who will be able to fulfill the role and the functions he has to take over in society and will be satisfied by them. Freud has not only called attention to the phenomenon of childhood amnesia but has also singled out a decisive factor in its genesis. I believe, however, that two points are important for a more adequate understanding of the phenomenon. First, it is not sufficiently clear why a repression of sexual experience should lead to a repression of all experience in early childhood. For this reason the assumption seems more likely that there must be something in the general quality of childhood experience which leads to the forgetting of that experience. Second, the phenomenon of childhood amnesia leads to a problem regarding the nature of repression, especially repression of childhood material. The term and concept of repression suggest that material which *per se* could be recalled is excluded from recall because of its traumatic nature. If the traumatic factor can be clarified and dissolved, the material is again accessible to recall. But even the most profound and prolonged psychoanalysis does not lead to a recovery of childhood memory; at best it unearths some incidents and feelings that had been forgotten. Childhood amnesia, then, may be due to a formation of the memory functions which makes them unsuitable to accommodate childhood experience, rather than exclusively to a censor repressing objectionable material which, without such repression, could and would be remembered. The adult is usually not capable of experiencing what the child experiences; more often than not he is not even capable of imagining what the child experiences. It would not be surprising, then, that he should be incapable of recalling his own childhood experiences since his whole mode of experiencing has changed. The person who remembers is the present person, a person who has changed considerably, whose interests, needs, fears, capacity for experience and emotion have changed. The two mechanisms of forgetting suggested here shade gradually and imperceptibly into one another. They are neither alternatives nor opposites, but rather the two ends of a continuous scale.

Both Freud and Proust speak of the autobiographical memory, and it is only with regard to this memory that the striking phenomenon of childhood amnesia and the less obvious difficulty of recovering any past experience may be observed. There is no specific childhood amnesia as far as the remembrance of words learned or objects and persons recognized is concerned. This type of material is remembered because, in contrast to the autobiographical past, it is constantly re-experienced and used and because it is essential for the orientation and adaptation of the growing child to his environment.

The autobiographical memory shows indeed in most persons, if not in all, the amnesia for their early childhood from birth to approximately the fifth or sixth years. Of course, there are gaps in the memory of many people for later periods of their lives also, probably more so for the period before than after puberty; but these gaps vary individually to a much greater extent than does the ubiquitous early childhood amnesia. If one believes Proust, life after childhood is not remembered either, save for the elusive flashes of a vision given only to the most sensitive and differentiated mind as the rare grace of a fortunate moment, which then the poet, with passionate devotion and patient labor, may try to transcribe and communicate.

Freud contrasts the presumable riches of childhood experience, the child's great capacity for impressions and experience, with the poverty or total lack of memory of such rich experience. If one looks closely at the average adult's memory of the periods of his life after childhood, such memory, it is true, usually shows no great temporal gaps. It is fairly continuous. But its formal continuity in time is offset by barrenness in content, by an incapacity to reproduce anything that resembles a really rich, full, rounded, and alive experience. Even the most "exciting" events are remembered as milestones rather than as moments filled with the concrete abundance of life. Adult memory reflects life as a road with occasional signposts and milestones rather than as the landscape through which this road has led. The milestones are the measurements of time, the months and years, the empty count of time gone by, so many years spent here, so many years spent there, moving from one place to another, so many birthdays, and so forth. The signposts represent the outstanding events to which they point—entering college, the first job, marriage, birth of children, buying a house, a family celebration, a trip. But it is not the events that are remembered as they really happened and were experienced at the time. What is remembered is usually, more or less, only the fact that such an event took place. The signpost is remembered, not the place, the thing, the situation to which it points. And even these signposts themselves do not usually indicate the really significant moments in a person's life; rather they point to the events that are conventionally supposed to be significant, to the clichés which society has come to consider as the main stations of life. Thus the memories of the majority of people come to resemble increasingly the stereotyped answers to a questionnaire, in which life consists of time and place of birth, religious denomination, residence, educational degrees, job, marriage, number and birthdates of children, income, sickness and death. The average traveler, asked about his trip, will tell you how many miles he has made (how many years he has lived); how fast he went (how successful he was); what places he has visited—usually only the well known ones, often he visits only those that one "simply must have seen"—(the jobs he has held, the prestige he has gained). He can tell you whether the driving was smooth or rough, or whether somebody bumped his fender, but he will be quite unable to give you any real idea of the country through which he went. So the average traveler through life remembers chiefly what the road map or the guide book says, what he is supposed to remember because it is exactly what everybody else remembers too.

In the course of later childhood, adolescence, and adult life, perception and experience themselves develop increasingly into the rubber stamps of conventional clichés. The capacity to see and feel what is there gives way to the tendency to see and feel what one expects to see and feel, which, in turn, is what one is expected to see and feel because everybody else does.[7] Experience increasingly assumes the form of the cliché under which it will be recalled because this cliché is what conventionally is remembered by others. This is not the remembered situation itself, but the words which are customarily used to indicate this situation and the reactions which it is supposed to evoke. While this ubiquitous and powerful tendency toward pseudo-experience in terms of conventional clichés usually takes place unnoticed, it is quite articulate in some people and is used widely in advertising. There are people who experience a party, a visit to the movies, a play, a concert, a trip in the very words in which they are going to tell their friends about it; in fact, quite often, they anticipate such experience in these words. The experience is predigested, as it were, even before they have tasted of it. Like the unfortunate Midas, whose touch turned everything into gold so that he could not eat or drink, these people turn the potential nourishment of the anticipated experience into the sterile currency of the

---

[7] Tolstoi gives a masterful description of how, in an adolescent girl during a visit to the opera, the experience of what happens on the stage changes from a genuine, naive, and fresh view to the conventional "appreciation" of the opera habitué. His account of her initial perceptions, by the way, is a surrealist description of opera more than half a century before surrealism. Tolstoi, *War and Peace*, part 8, chapters 9 and 10.

conventional phrase which exhausts their experience because they have seen, heard, felt nothing but this phrase with which later they will report to their friends the "exciting time" they have had. The advertising business seems to be quite aware of this. It does not have to promise a good book, a well-written and well-performed play, an entertaining or amusing movie. It suffices to say that the book, the play, the movie will be the talk of the town, of the next party, of one's friends. To have been there, to be able to say that one has been present at the performance, to have read the book even when one is unable to have the slightest personal reaction to it, is quite sufficient. But while Midas suffered tortures of starvation, the people under whose eyes every experience turns into a barren cliché do not know that they starve. Their starvation manifests itself merely in boredom or in restless activity and incapacity of any real enjoyment.

Memory is even more governed by conventional patterns than perception and experience are. One might say that, while all human experience, perception, and thought are eminently social —that is, determined by the socially prevailing ways of experiencing, perceiving, and thinking—memory is even more socialized, to an even higher degree dependent on the commonly accepted categories of what and how one remembers. "Rationalization," as psycho-analytic theory knows it, is but one type of such transformation of actual experience into individually and socially acceptable clichés. One important reason why memory is even more susceptible than experience and perception to such conventionalization is that experience and perception always are in *some*, however flimsy, immediate relation to the situation experienced, the object perceived, while memory is distant from it in time and space. The object of memory has less chance than the objects of experience and perception have to penetrate and do away with part of that glass, colored and ground by the social mores and viewpoints, through which man sees everything or fails to see it. Memory is a distance sense, as it were, and—to an even greater degree than the two other distance senses, vision and hearing— less immediately related to its objects than the proximity senses of smell, taste, and touch, and more influenced and moulded by the categories of the mind. Also like sight and hearing, only more so, memory is a phylogenetically and ontogenetically more differentiated, later, and more "spiritual" development than smell, taste, and touch. All this predestines memory to lose contact with actual experience and to substitute preformed, conventional patterns of thought for it. And, as will be seen later, it has significant bearing especially on the problem of early childhood amnesia.

It is safe to assume that early childhood is the period of human life which is richest in experience. Everything is new to the newborn child. His gradual grasp of his environment and of the world around him are discoveries which, in experiential scope and quality, go far beyond any discovery that the most adventurous and daring explorer will ever make in his adult life. No Columbus, no Marco Polo has ever seen stranger and more fascinating and thoroughly absorbing sights than the child that learns to perceive, to taste, to smell, to touch, to hear and see, and to use his body, his senses, and his mind. No wonder that the child shows an insatiable curiosity. He has the whole world to discover. Education and learning, while on the one hand furthering this process of discovery, on the other hand gradually brake and finally stop it completely. There are relatively few adults who are fortunate enough to have retained something of the child's curiosity, his capacity for questioning and for wondering. The average adult "knows all the answers," which is exactly why he will never know even a single answer. He has ceased to wonder, to discover. He knows his way around, and it is indeed a way around and around the same conventional pattern, in which everything is familiar and nothing cause for wonder. It is this adult who answers the child's questions and, in answering, fails to answer them but instead acquaints the child with the conventional patterns of his civilization, which effectively close up the asking mouth and shut the wondering eye. Franz Kafka once formulated this aspect of education by saying that "probably all education is but two things, first, parrying of the ignorant children's impetuous assault on the truth and, second, gentle, imperceptible, step-by-step initiation of the humiliated children into the lie."

Most children go through a period of endless questioning.

While at first they desire an answer, gradually their search turns into an almost automatic repetition of the same seemingly senseless question or into the related ritual of countering every answer with a new question. It is as though the child no longer really expected or perhaps wanted to obtain information by this type of questioning, but expressed only the last stubborn assault against the unbroken wall of adult "answers." The child has already almost forgotten what he wanted to know, but he still knows *that* he wanted to know and did not receive an answer. The automatic questioning may have the unconscious purpose of driving this point home to the adult. It is chiefly during the period of early childhood that the quality of the world around him changes for the growing child from a place where everything is new and to be explored—to be tasted, smelled, touched and handled, wondered about and marveled at—to a place where everything either has received a name and a label or is potentially capable of being "explained" by such a label, a process which will be pursued systematically in school. No experience, no object perceived with the quality of freshness, newness, of something wonder-full, can be preserved and recalled by the conventional concept of that object as designated in its conventional name in language. Even if, in modern western civilization, the capacity for such fresh experience has largely been deadened, most people, unless they have become complete automatons, have had glimpses of the exhilarating quality that makes fresh experience, unlabeled, so unique, concrete, and filled with life. They can realize, if their attention is called to it, the great difference between such experience and one which merely registers the label of things seen, the furniture of the room, the familiar faces, the houses on the street. Yet this difference is small when compared with the difference that separates the young child's fresh experience and discoveries from the adult's recognition of the familiar clichés into which the automatic labeling of perception and language has transformed the objects around him. Since adult memory functions predominantly in terms of recalling clichés, the conventional schemata of things and experiences rather than the things and experiences themselves, it becomes apparent how ill-equipped, in fact incapable, such conventionalized memory is to recall the experiences of early childhood in their freshness, in the real significance which they had at that time. The age of discovery, early childhood, is buried deep under the age of routine familiarity, adulthood.

The process of schematization and conventionalization and its effect on the raw material of experience, especially childhood experience, can be well observed in two of its specific developments which take place as the child learns to make use of his senses and to speak. Language, in its articulating and its obscuring function, may be considered first since the adult, too, encounters the problem of the incompatibility of experience with language and the consequent forgetting of experience or its distortion by the cliché of language. The fact that language is adult language, the language of an adult civilization, and that the infant and small child is moulded only very gradually from its natural existence into a member of the civilization into which it is born makes the discrepancy between his precivilized, unschematized experience and the categories of civilized, conventional language much greater. Yet between this discrepancy and that existing between the adult's experience and his language, there is a difference of degree rather than of kind. Everyone who has honestly tried to describe some genuine experience exactly, however small and insignificant it may have seemed, knows how difficult if not impossible that is. One might well say that the greatest problem of the writer or the poet is the temptation of language. At every step a word beckons, it seems so convenient, so suitable, one has heard or read it so often in a similar context, it sounds so well, it makes the phrase flow so smoothly. If he follows the temptation of this word, he will perhaps describe something that many people recognize at once, that they already know, that follows a familiar pattern; but he will have missed the nuance that distinguishes his experience from others, that makes it his own. If he wants to communicate that elusive nuance which in some way, however small, will be his contribution, a widening or opening of the scope of articulate human experience at some point, he has to fight constantly against the easy flow of words that offer themselves. Like the search for truth, which never reaches its goal yet never can be abandoned, the endeavor to articulate, express, and

communicate an experience can never succeed completely. It consists of an approach, step by step, toward that distant vantage
point, that bend of the road from which one hopes to see the
real experience in its entirety and from where it will become visible to others—a point which is never reached. The lag, the discrepancy between experience and word is a productive force in
man as long as he remains aware of it, as long as he knows and
feels that his experience was in some way more than and different from what his concepts and words articulate. The awareness
of this unexplored margin of experience, which may be its essential part, can turn into that productive energy which enables man
to go one step closer to understanding and communicating his
experience, and thus add to the scope of human insight. It is this
awareness and the struggle and the ability to narrow the gap
between experience and words which make the writer and the
poet.

Two major trends operate in the direction of the eventual outcome of early childhood amnesia. First, the schemata for articulate experience and for recall of such experience are relatively
slow and late in developing. They are entirely lacking in the
earliest period of life and one could say generally that as they
develop, experience gradually loses its character of newness and
acquires the quality of familiarity and recognition. The tremendous amount of experience which the small child undergoes does
not, therefore, find a proportionate variety of suitable vessels
(schemata) for its preservation. Second, the quality of early
childhood experience does not fit into the developing schemata
of experience, thought, and memory since these are fashioned by
the adult culture and all its biases, emphases, and taboos.

Both these trends become even more apparent if one considers
them in connection with the development of the *senses* in the
child. Such a consideration also shows how closely biological and
cultural factors are interwoven in the causation of early childhood amnesia and how difficult, if not impossible, it is to draw a
clear borderline between the two. What might have been a cultural factor in man's prehistory may well seem to the present
observer like a biological development. Phylogenetically as well
as ontogenetically the distance senses, sight and hearing, attain

their full development later than the proximity senses, smell, taste, and touch. Sight and hearing are more highly differentiated and more closely linked up with the human mind than smell, taste, and touch. The latter senses, especially smell and taste, are neglected and to a considerable extent even tabooed by western civilization. They are the animalistic senses *par excellence*. Man, who has been engaged for thousands of years in a battle for control and mastery of nature outside and inside himself, especially western man, does not want to be reminded that he is not only man but also nature, also animal. Because of the cultural taboo on smell and taste—smell even more than taste, but the two are inseparable—it is even possible for the adult to realize clearly the effect which the discrepancy between experience on the one hand, and language and memory schemata, on the other hand, has on the capacity for recall, especially voluntary recall. English vocabulary, and equally the vocabulary of the other western languages, is conspicuously poor in words for the description of smells and tastes. Even when it comes to the flavor of wine or of a dish, in spite of the great material and historical role of drinking and eating, language is quite incapable of expressing any but the crudest differences, in taste. A wine is said to be dry, sweet, robust, fine, full and so on, but none of these words enables one to imagine the flavor and bouquet of the wine. Compared with this poverty of words, the vocabulary for the description of the visible world and its forms and colors is much richer. Even poetry has never succeeded in conjuring the flavor of a smell or taste, although it sometimes enables the imagination to evoke a visual image. For these reasons, the experience schemata for smell and taste sensations are relatively undeveloped. This is true even more of the memory schemata. A taste or a smell is usually remembered only involuntarily; that is, the former experience may be recognized by renewed encounter with the same stimulus. But it is difficult or impossible for most people to recall voluntarily the taste of a particular wine or the smell of a particular flower, animal, or person. In fact, most people are hardly aware of the differences in smell of different people.

Both pleasure and disgust are more intimately linked with the proximity senses than with the distance senses. The pleasure which a perfume, a taste, or a texture can give is much more of a bodily, physical one, hence also more akin to sexual pleasure, than is the more sublime pleasure aroused by sound and the least bodily of all pleasures, the sight of something beautiful. No other sense produces the emotion of disgust more easily and violently and provokes reactions of nausea and vomiting more readily than the olfactory sense. The infant is not disgusted by his feces; he quite likes their smell. Very many, if not most adults do not have the reaction of disgust to the smell of their own excretions; many do not show it with regard to the body odor or the excretions of a beloved person. As everybody knows, animals, especially dogs, are best able to tell one person from another and one dog from another by body and excretion smell. The infant, long before he knows and remembers how his mother looks, knows how she smells and tastes. Very likely, angry or frightened mother tastes and smells rather different from good or comfortable mother to the infant, just as she will look very different to him as he grows older.[8] In his growing experience of the world around him, the proximity senses at first have primacy over the distance senses. He tastes and sniffs and touches earlier and better than he perceives with eye and ear. In order to get really acquainted with something or somebody, he has to touch it and to put it in his mouth as he first did with his mother's nipple. Only very gradually and slowly does the emphasis shift from the proximity to the distance senses. This partly biological and phylogenetically determined shift is helped along powerfully and the development of taste and smell discouraged by the stringent taboos of the significant adults, who do not want baby to take everything in his mouth and who drastically and persistently in cleanliness education show their disgust with the most important objects of smell, those of the body and its excretions, so that the child cannot but feel that he has to refrain not only from the pleasure given by body and excretion odors but even from the

---

[8] Groddeck, speaking about the paramount importance of the sense of smell in infancy and early childhood, asserts that, even more than the dog, the child judges people and objects largely by their smell and, since the child is small or is being held on the lap, this means chiefly the smell of legs, lap, sexual and excretory organs. Groddeck, G., *The World of Man*; The C. W. Daniel Company, London 1934; p. 132.

discriminating perception of them. The proximity senses, which play such a great role in relations between animals and, if not repressed, in the sexual relations of man, are otherwise tabooed in interpersonal relations the more a culture or a group tends to isolate people, to put distance between them, and to prevent spontaneous relationships and the "natural" animal-like expressions of such relations. The emphasis on distance and the taboo on smell in modern society is more outspoken in the ruling than in the laboring class, distance being also a means of domination and of imposing authority. Disgust arises where the repression has not succeeded completely and a powerful deterrent is needed in order to bolster it.[9]

In one other area of life, namely in the realm of *dreams*, one finds a general amnesia, although it is not quite so pervasive as that pertaining to early childhood. A closer study of the recall of dreams and especially of the period of awakening from a dream, when quite often one can observe its disappearance from memory or its transformation or fragmentation, may therefore add to, disprove, or corroborate the hypotheses developed so far. It is probable that the majority of dreams are not remembered at all. A great many others are recalled in fragments only. Of those that are still remembered at the time of awakening, very many are forgotten in the course of the day, quite often in the first few minutes or the first hour of beginning the daily activities of rising, getting dressed, and so on. The relatively small proportion of dreams surviving in memory undergo a rapid transformation and fragmentation and usually they, too, are forgotten after a few days. If they are not forgotten, they lose increasingly their peculiar dream quality, and the peculiar language of the dream changes in the direction of conventionalization and rationalization. The dreams that make such a profound impression on the dreamer that they survive all these obstacles, although not without some damage, are rare indeed. Thus the question arises: What are the causes of this usual, general *dream-amnesia*? Why does

---

[9] Something of the importance of the deeply rooted taboo on smell in western man comes to the surface in the vituperative and hateful use that is made of body odor in interracial conflicts.

one forget by far the greater part of his mental life going on during sleep, a life that in most people, judging from the fragments recalled, seems to be far more original, interesting, spontaneous, and creative than their waking life? It shares these latter qualities with early childhood which, from all one can observe, seems to be the most fascinating, spontaneous, original, and creative period in the life of most or perhaps of all people. Is it because of these qualities that the conventionalized memory schemata cannot reproduce the great majority of dreams and their real character?

Freud devotes a whole section of *The Interpretation of Dreams* to the problem of the forgetting of dreams. His purpose in this section is to defend the validity of dream interpretation against the objection that one does not really know his dreams because he either forgets or distorts them. Freud's answer to the problem is that the "forgetting of dreams depends far more on the resistance [to the dream thought] than on the mutually alien character of the waking and sleeping states" and that the distortion of the dream in recalling or recounting it is "the secondary and often misunderstanding elaboration of the dream by the agency of normal thinking" and thus "no more than a part of the elaboration to which dream thoughts are constantly subjected as a result of the dream-censorship." I think that the question should be raised whether "resistance" and "mutually alien character of the waking and sleeping states" are really, as Freud seems to assume, mutually exclusive and contradictory explanations of dream amnesia and dream distortion by waking thought. Or whether, as I believe, "resistance" is operative in the awake person, not only against the dream thought but against the whole quality and language of the dream, a resistance, to be sure, of a somewhat different character, yet fundamentally related to that which represses and censors those dream thoughts which are intolerable for consciousness.

In sleep and dream, man's activity in the outer world is suspended, especially his motor activity. Attention and perception are withdrawn from outer reality. The necessity to cope with the environment is interrupted for the duration of sleep. The stringent rules of logic and reason subside—rules which during waking life are geared to useful, rational, adaptive, conventional control of behavior and thought. The psyche receives leave, for the period of sleep, from the demands of active life in society. As Freud expresses it, endopsychic censorship is reduced. And the psyche makes good use of this short leave from the demands of reality. Its productions, seen from the usual, realistic viewpoint, seem utterly useless. It is true that other, older civilizations did not always share this viewpoint, but attributed considerable importance to dreams, sometimes greater importance than to waking thought. But measured with the yardstick of modern western civilization with its emphasis on useful, efficient production and work, dreams are really quite useless.

During sleep motor activity, most essential for dealing with the outer reality of objects and people, is reduced to a minimum. The dream is a mental production without any conscious effort and one in which the dreamer passively gives in to the images evoked by his phantasy. In that sense the dream is the opposite of *work* as it is known to western civilization, the opposite of efficiency. When awakening, it is often possible to catch hold of a dream [as Rorschach has pointed out] if one lies perfectly still and does not open his eyes. But the first movement, especially an active one like jumping out of bed, will very often chase the dream into oblivion. In other words, the return to the outer world through motor activity and reshifting of attention and perception to the environment leads to forgetting of the dream. This process is a quite general one and, as far as I have been able to observe, bears no relation to specific dream content. Therefore it seems to stem from the incompatibility of the extroversive attitude of waking with the introversive attitude of dreaming, rather than from resistance to specific strivings which are expressed in the dream thoughts. The antagonism between motor activity and dream recall brings to mind Proust's words, that he could recapture his former being only "dehors de l'action, de la jouissance immédiate" and that in such a moment he did not dare to budge lest he lose the refound memory of the past.

But even without the described effect of the resumption of motor activity on the voluntary recall of dreams, it seems obvious that the experience and memory schemata developed and formed by man's life in his society are much less suitable to preserve the phantastic world of the dream than to recall conventional waking experience. The awakening mind has to cope again with outer reality, and to this end has to remobilize all the patterns and schemata useful for, and developed by, the conventional social forms of life and work. Attention has to be paid to the environment. And the attitude of attention is to the mind what purposeful motor activity is to the body.

In the forgetting and distortion of dreams during waking life it is important to distinguish between that which is due to the resistance to and repression of a specific dream thought or dream content and that which is due to the incapacity of the conventional memory schemata to retain the phantastic general quality and the strange language of dreams. The distortion of a dream thought which resistance wants to keep from awareness has to be distinguished from the process of conventionalization which, more or less, *all* dream elements undergo because the medium of the dream language is incompatible with the medium of the conventional world of waking life. In the degree of this incompatibility there are, of course, considerable variations between different people and, even more so, between different cultures. But modern western civilization with its streamlined efficiency, uniform mass culture, and emphasis on usefulness in terms of profitable, material production is particularly and strikingly at the opposite pole from the world of dreams.

The hidden quality of lost memories, their separation from the rest of life, their inaccessibility, and their incompatibility with voluntary memory and with conventional, purposeful, daily activity are described lucidly by Proust. He compares the recesses of the lost memories to a thousand vases distributed on the various altitudes of the past years of one's life, filled with the particular atmosphere of that period of his life, and containing sometimes a gesture, a word, an insignificant act which, however, may be the key to the recapturing of the lost experiences, the lost past of his life. According to him, the very fact that the experience, the past time, has been forgotten and thus has remained isolated as at the bottom of a valley or on the peak of a summit, gives it an incomparable air of freshness and aliveness when it is recovered, *because it has not been able to form any link with the present.* In other words, it has not been distorted by the memory schemata, by the needs and fears of the present, by the routine of daily life. Proust's view, here, is almost identical with that of Freud, whose theory of memory postulates that *only* that which is unconscious can leave a permanent memory trace and that "becoming conscious and leaving behind a memory trace are processes incompatible with each other in the same system." [10]

In Proust's work the recovery of the forgotten past is characterized as the supreme satisfaction, carrying with it a sense of exhilarating happiness and constituting the very core of the work of art. This is not the place to discuss the profound meaning of his evaluation which, three thousand years after the Greek myth, again celebrates memory as the mother of art and poetry. Be it sufficient to say that in the conflict of modern society between efficient adaptation and activity, on the one hand, and the preservation and recovery of the total personality, which to him seems possible only by the fullest awareness of the individual past, Proust sides against his society and with the "lost paradises" of his own past. And it is true that each genuine recovery of forgotten experience and, with it, something of the person that one was when having the experience carries with it an element of enrichment, adds to the light of consciousness, and thus widens the conscious scope of one's life.

Cultures vary in the degree to which they impose clichés on experience and memory. The more a society develops in the direction of mass conformism, whether such development be achieved by a totalitarian pattern or within a democratic framework by means of the employment market, education, the patterns of social life, advertising, press, radio, movies, best-sellers, and so on, the more stringent becomes the rule of the conventional experience and memory schemata in the lives of the members of that society. In the history of the last hundred years of western civilization the conventional schematization of experi-

---

[10] Freud, *Beyond the Pleasure Principle*; The International Psycho-analytical Press, London 1922; p. 28. See also, *The Interpretation of Dreams*, *Basic Writings*, pp. 488-491.

ence and memory has become increasingly prevalent at an accelerating pace.

Mankind's belief in a lost paradise is repeated in the belief held by most people, in the individual myth of their happy childhood. Like most myths this one contains elements of both truth and illusion, is woven out of wishes, hopes, remembrance and sorrow, and hence has more than one meaning. One finds this belief even in people who have undergone cruel experiences as children and who had, without being or remaining aware of it, a childhood with hardly any love and affection from their parents. No doubt, one reason for the myth of happy childhood is that it bolsters parental authority and maintains a conventional prop of the authority of the family by asserting that one's parents were good and benevolent people who did everything for the good of their children, however much they may have done against it. And disappointed and suffering people, people without hope, want to believe that at least once there was a time in their life when they were happy. But the myth of happy childhood reflects also the truth that as in the myth of paradise lost, there was a time before animalistic innocence was lost, before pleasure-seeking nature and pleasure-forbidding culture clashed in the battle called education, a battle in which the child always is the loser. At no time is life so exclusively and directly governed by the pleasure principle as it is in early infancy; at no other time is man, especially civilized man, capable of abandoning himself so completely to pleasure and satisfaction. The myth of happy childhood takes the place of the lost memory of the actual riches, spontaneity, freshness of childhood experience, an experience which has been forgotten because there is no place for it in the adult memory schemata.

Childhood amnesia covers those aspects and experiences of the former personality which are incompatible with the culture. If they were remembered, man would demand that society affirm and accept the total personality with all its potentialities. In a society based on partial suppression of the personality such a demand, even the mere existence of a really free personality, would constitute a threat to the society. Hence it becomes necessary for the society that the remembrance of a time in which the potentialities of a fuller, freer, and more spontaneous life were strongly present and alive be extinguished. In memory's service of this purpose one may distinguish two processes which overlap and shade into one another. One process leaves the culturally unacceptable or unusable experiences and the memory thereof to starvation by the expedient of providing no linguistic, conceptual, and memory schemata for them and by channeling later experience into the experience schemata of the culture. As the person, in the process of education, gradually comes to live more and more exclusively within the framework of the culturally and conventionally provided experience schemata, there is less and less to remind him of the possibility of trans-schematic experience.

Compared with this process, the dynamism of the taboo and of repression of individually or culturally tabooed experience and strivings is like the nightstick of the policeman compared with the gradual, slow, insinuating process of education in which some things are just not mentioned and others said to be for the best of the child. But the dynamism active in normal amnesia is even more subtle than what is usually called education. It is an education of which the educators are not aware and of which the child is too helpless and too inarticulate to have more than the vaguest feeling that something is happening to him. On the other hand, those strivings, qualities, and potentialities of the child which are too strong to be left behind to die by the side of the road of education and which endanger the current social and cultural pattern have to be battled by the more drastic means of taboo and repression. In this sphere sexuality and the conflict with parental authority play central roles. One might say that taboo and repression are the psychological cannons of society against the child and against man, whereas in normal amnesia society uses the method of blockade and slow starvation against those experiences and memories which do not fit into the cultural pattern and which do not equip man for his role in the social process. The two methods of warfare supplement each other and, in the siege conducted by society against the human potentialities and inclinations which transcend the cultural pattern, the cannon helps to maintain the blockade, and the blockade and ensuing starvation make it less necessary to use the cannon.

Hesiod tells us that Lethe (Forgetting) is the daughter of Eris (Strife).[11] Amnesia, normal and pathological, is indeed the daughter of conflict, the conflict between nature and society and the conflict in society, the conflict between society and man and the conflict within man. Lethe is the stream of the underworld, of forgetting, the stream which constantly flows and never retains. In the realm of Lethe dwell the Danaïdes, who are condemned eternally to pour water into a leaking vessel. Plato interprets this as the punishment of those unwise souls who leak, who cannot remember and are therefore always empty.[12]

But Mnemosyne is an older and more powerful goddess than Lethe. According to Hesiod she was one of the six Titanesses from whom all gods stem. And it was one of the world-founding deeds of Zeus that he begot the muses on her. Memory cannot be entirely extinguished in man, his capacity for experience cannot be entirely suppressed by schematization. It is in those experiences which transcend the cultural schemata, in those memories of experience which transcend the conventional memory schemata, that every new insight and every true work of art have their origin, and that the hope of progress, of a widening of the scope of human endeavor and human life, is founded.

---

[11] Hesiod, *Theogony*, 227.
[12] Plato, *Gorgias*, 493 c 2. For the mythology of Mnemosyne and Lethe, see Kerényi, Karl, Mnemosyne-Lesmosyne, in *Die Geburt der Helena*; Rhein Verlag, Zuerich 1945.

14

ERIK H. ERIKSON

Toys and Reasons*

I would look at a play act as, vaguely speaking, a function of
the ego, an attempt to bring into synchronization the bodily and
the social processes of which one is a part even while one is a
self. . . . To hallucinate ego mastery is the purpose of play—
but play, as we shall see presently, is the undisputed master of
only a very slim margin of existence. What is play—and what
is it not? Let us consult language, and then return to children. . . .

When man plays he must intermingle with the laws of things
and people in a similarly uninvolved and light fashion. He must
do something which he has chosen to do without being compelled by urgent interests or impelled by strong passion; he must
feel entertained and free of any fear or hope of serious consequences. He is on vacation from reality—or, as is most commonly
emphasized: he *does not work*. It is this opposition to work
which gives play a number of connotations. One of these is
"mere fun"—whether it is hard to do or not. As Mark Twain
commented, "constructing artificial flowers . . . is work, while
climbing the Mont Blanc is only amusement." In Puritan times
and places, however, mere fun always connoted sin; the Quak-
ers warned that you must "gather the flowers of pleasure
in the fields of duty." Men of equally puritan mind could permit
play only because they believed that to find "relief from moral
activity is in itself a moral necessity." Poets, however, place the

---

* Reprinted from *Childhood and Society* by Erik H. Erikson, by permission
of W. W. Norton & Company, Inc. Copyright 1950 by W. W. Norton &
Company, Inc.

emphasis elsewhere: "Man is perfectly human only when he plays," said Schiller. Thus play is a borderline phenomenon to a number of human activities and, in its own playful way, it tries to elude definition.

It is true that even the most strenuous and dangerous play is by definition not work, i.e., does not produce commodities. Where it does, it "goes professional." But this fact, from the start, makes the comparison of adult and child's play somewhat senseless; for the adult is a commodity-producing and commodity-exchanging animal, whereas the child is only preparing to become one. To the working adult, play is re-creation. It permits a periodical stepping out from those forms of defined limitation which are his reality. . . .

The playing child, then, poses a problem: whoever does not work shall not play. Therefore, to be tolerant of the child's play the adult must invent theories which show either that childhood play is really work—or that it does not count. The most popular theory and the easiest on the observer is that the child is *nobody yet*, and that the nonsense of his play reflects it. Scientists have tried to find other explanation for the freaks of childish play by considering them representative of the fact that childhood is neither here nor there. According to Spencer, play uses up *surplus energy* in the young of a number of mammalians who do not need to feed or protect themselves because their parents do it for them. However, Spencer noticed that wherever circumstances permit play, tendencies are "simulated" which are "unusually ready to act, unusually ready to have their correlative feelings aroused." Early psychoanalysis added to this the "cathartic" theory, according to which play has a definite function in the growing being in that it permits him to work off past emotions and to find imaginary relief for past frustrations.

In order to evaluate these theories, let us turn to the game of another, a younger boy. He lived near another mighty river, the Danube, and his play was recorded by another great psychologist, Sigmund Freud, who wrote: [1]

---

[1] Sigmund Freud, *A General Selection*, edited by John Rickman, The Hogarth Press and the Institute of Psycho-Analysis, London, 1937.

Without the intention of making a comprehensive study of these phenomena, I availed myself of an opportunity which offered of elucidating the first game invented by himself of a boy eighteen months old. It was more than a casual observation, for I lived for some weeks under the same roof as the child and his parents, and it was a considerable time before the meaning of his puzzling and continually repeated performance became clear to me.

The child was in no respect forward in his intellectual development; . . . but he made himself understood by his parents and the maidservant, and had a good reputation for behaving "properly." He did not disturb his parents at night; he scrupulously obeyed orders about not touching various objects and not going into certain rooms; and above all he never cried when his mother went out and left him for hours together, although the tie to his mother was a very close one: she had not only nourished him herself, but had cared for him and brought him up without any outside help. Occasionally, however, this well-behaved child evinced the troublesome habit of flinging into the corner of the room or under the bed all the little things he could lay his hands on, so that to gather up his toys was often no light task. He accompanied this by an expression of interest and gratification, emitting a loud, long-drawn-out "O-o-o-oh" which in the judgment of the mother (one that coincided with my own) was not an interjection but meant "go away" [*fort*]. I saw at last that this was a game, and that the child used all his toys only to play "being gone" [*fort sein*] with them. One day I made an observation that confirmed my view. The child had a wooden reel with a piece of string wound round it. It never occurred to him, for example, to drag this after him on the floor and so play horse and cart with it, but he kept throwing it with considerable skill, held by the string, over the side of his little draped cot, so that the reel disappeared into it, then said his significant "O-o-o-oh" and drew the reel by the string out of the cot again, greeting its reappearance with a joyful *"Da"* [there]. This was therefore the complete game, disappearance and return, the first act being the only one generally observed by the onlookers, and the one untiringly repeated by the child as a game for its own sake, although the greater pleasure unquestionably attached to the second act. . . . This interpretation was fully established by a further observation. One day when the mother had been out for some hours she was greeted on her return by the information "Baby o-o-o-oh" which at first remained unintelligible. It soon proved that during his long lonely hours he had found a method of bringing about his own disappearance. He had discovered his reflection in the long mirror which nearly reached to the ground and had then crouched down in front of it, so that the reflection was *fort*.

To understand what Freud saw in this game we must note that at the time he was interested in (and, in fact, writing about) the strange phenomenon of the "repetition compulsion"—i.e., the need to re-enact painful experiences in words or acts. . . .

As Freud was writing about this, he became aware of the solitary play described and of the fact that the frequency of the main theme (something or somebody disappears and comes back) corresponded to the intensity of the life experience reflected—namely, the mother's leaving in the morning and her return at night.

This dramatization takes place in the play sphere. Utilizing his mastery over objects, the child can arrange them in such a way that they permit him to imagine that he is master of his life predicament as well. For when the mother had left him, she had removed herself from the sphere of his cries and demands; and she had come back only when it happened to suit her. In his game, however, the little boy has the mother by a string. He makes her go away, even throws her away, and then makes her come back at his pleasure. He has, as Freud put it, *turned passivity into activity;* he plays at doing something that was in reality done to him.

Freud mentions three items which may guide us in a further social evaluation of this game. First, the child threw the object away. Freud sees in this a possible expression of revenge—"If you don't want to stay with me, I don't want you"—and thus an additional gain in active mastery by an apparent growth of emotional autonomy. In his second play act, however, the child goes further. He abandons the object altogether and, with the use of a full-length mirror, plays "going away" from himself and returning to himself. He is now both the person who is being left and the person who leaves. He has become master by incorporating not only the person who, in life, is beyond his control, but the whole situation, with *both* its partners. . . .

But does the child's play—so a frequent question goes—always "mean" something personal and sinister? What if ten children, in horse-and-buggy days, begin to play with reels on strings, pulling them behind themselves and playing horsie? Must it mean anything to one of them over and beyond what it seems to mean to all?

As we have said already, children, if traumatized, choose for their dramatizations play material which is available in their culture and manageable at their age. What is available depends on the cultural circumstances and is therefore common to all children who share these circumstances. Boys today do not play steamboat but use bicycles as more tangible objects of co-ordination—which does not prevent them from imagining, on the way to school or the grocery, that they are flying through the air and machine-gunning the enemy; or that they are the Lone Ranger himself on a glorious Silver. What is manageable, however, depends on the child's powers of co-ordination, and therefore is shared only by those who have reached a certain level of maturation. What has a *common meaning* to all the children in a community (i.e., the idea of having a reel and string represent a living thing on a leash) may have a *special meaning* to some (i.e., all those who have just learned to manipulate reel and string and may thus be ready to enter a new sphere of participation and communal symbolization). Yet all of this may have, in addition, a *unique meaning* to individual children who have lost a person or an animal and therefore endow the game with a particular significance. What these children "have by the string" is not just any animal—it is the personification of a particular, a significant, and a lost animal—or person. To evaluate play the observer must, of course, have an idea of what all the children of a given age in a given community are apt to play. Only thus can he decide whether or not the unique meaning transcends the common meaning. To understand the unique meaning itself requires careful observation, not only of the play's content and form, but also of accompanying words and visible affects, especially those which lead to what we shall describe in the next chapter as "play disruption."

In order to approach the problem of anxiety in play, let us consider the activity of building and destroying a tower. Many a mother thinks that her little son is in a "destructive stage" or even has a "destructive personality" because, after building a big, big tower, the boy cannot follow her advice to leave the tower for Daddy to see, but instead *must* kick it and make it collapse. The almost manic pleasure with which children watch the collapse in a second of the product of long play labor has puzzled many, especially since the child does not appreciate it at all if his tower falls by accident or by a helpful uncle's hand. He, the builder, must destroy it himself. This game, I should think, arises from the not so distant experience of sudden falls at the very time when standing upright on wobbly legs afforded a new and fascinating perspective on existence. The child who consequently learns to *make* a tower "stand up" enjoys causing the same tower to waver and collapse: in addition to the active mastery over a previously passive event, it makes one feel stronger to know that there is somebody weaker—and towers, unlike little sisters, can't cry and call Mummy. But since it is the child's still precarious mastery over space which is thus to be demonstrated, it is understandable that watching somebody else kick one's tower may make the child see himself in the tower rather than in the kicker: all fun evaporates. Circus clowns later take over when they obligingly fall all over the place from mere ineptness, and yet continue to challenge gravity and causality with ever renewed innocence: there are, then, even big people who are funnier, dumber, and wobblier. Some children, however, who find themselves too much identified with the clown cannot stand his downfalls: to them they are "not funny." This example throws light on the beginning of many an anxiety in childhood, where anxiety around the child's attempt at ego mastery finds unwelcome "support" from adults who treat him roughly or amuse him with exercises which he likes only if and when he himself has initiated them.

The child's play begins with and centers on his own body. This we shall call *autocosmic play*. It begins before we notice it as play, and consists at first in the exploration by repetition of sensual perceptions, of kinesthetic sensations, of vocalizations, etc. Next, the child plays with available persons and things. He may playfully cry to see what wave length would serve best to make the mother reappear, or he may indulge in experimental excursions on her body and on the protrusions and orifices of her face. This is the child's first geography, and the basic maps acquired in such interplay with the mother no doubt remain guides for the ego's first orientation in the "world." . . .

The *microsphere*—i.e., the small world of manageable toys—is a harbor which the child establishes, to return to when he needs to overhaul his ego. But the thing-world has its own laws: it may resist reconstruction, or it may simply break to pieces; it may prove to belong to somebody else and be subject to confiscation by superiors. Often the microsphere seduces the child into an unguarded expression of dangerous themes and attitudes which arouse anxiety and lead to sudden play disruption. This is the counterpart in waking life of the anxiety dream; it can keep children from trying to play just as the fear of night terror can keep them from going to sleep. If thus frightened or disappointed in the microsphere, the child may regress into the autosphere, day-dreaming, thumb-sucking, masturbating. On the other hand, if the first use of the thing-world is successful and is guided properly, the pleasure of mastering toy things becomes associated with the mastery of the traumata which were projected on them, and with the prestige gained through such mastery.

Finally, at nursery-school age playfulness reaches into the *macrosphere,* the world shared with others. First these others are treated as things, are inspected, run into, or forced to "be horsie." Learning is necessary in order to discover what potential play content can be admitted only to fantasy or only to autocosmic play; what content can be successfully represented only in the microcosmic world of toys and things; and what content can be shared with others and forced upon them.

As this is learned, each sphere is endowed with its own sense of reality and mastery. For quite a while, then, solitary play remains an indispensable harbor for the overhauling of shattered emotions after periods of rough going in the social seas. This, and the fact that a child can be counted upon to bring into the solitary play arranged for him whatever aspect of his ego has been ruffled most, form the fundamental condition for our diagnostic reliance on "play therapy," which will be discussed next.

What is infantile play, then? We saw that it is not the equivalent of adult play, that it is not recreation. The playing adult steps sideward into another reality; the playing child advances forward to new stages of mastery. I propose the theory that the child's play is the infantile form of the human ability to deal with experience by creating model situations and to master reality by experiment and planning. It is in certain phases of his work that the adult projects past experience into dimensions which seem manageable. In the laboratory, on the stage, and on the drawing board, he relives the past and thus relieves leftover affects; in reconstructing the model situation, he redeems his failures and strengthens his hopes. He anticipates the future from the point of view of a corrected and shared past.

No thinker can do more and no playing child less. As William Blake puts it: "The child's toys and the old man's reasons are the fruits of the two seasons."

Play and Cure

Modern play therapy is based on the observation that a child made insecure by a secret hate against or fear of the natural protectors of his play in family and neighborhood seems able to use the protective sanction of an understanding adult to regain some play peace. Grandmothers and favorite aunts may have played that role in the past; its professional elaboration of today is the play therapist. The most obvious condition is that the child has the toys and the adult for himself, and that sibling rivalry, parental nagging, or any kind of sudden interruption does not disturb the unfolding of his play intentions, whatever they may be. For to "play it out" is the most natural self-healing measure childhood affords.

Let us remember here the simple, if often embarrassing, fact that adults, when traumatized, tend to solve their tension by "talking it out." They are compelled, repeatedly, to describe the painful event: it seems to make them "feel better." Systems designed to cure the soul or the mind make ritual use of this tendency by providing, at regular intervals, an ordained or otherwise sanctioned listener who gives his undivided attention, is sworn not to censure arbitrarily or to betray, and bestows absolution by explaining how the individual's problem makes sense in some larger context, be it sin, conflict, or disease. The method finds its limitations where this "clinical" situation loses the detachment in which life can be reflected, and itself becomes a passionate conflict of dependence and hostility. In psychoanalytic terms, the limitation is set by the tendency (especially strong in neurotics) to transfer basic conflicts from their original infantile setting into every new situation, including the therapeutic one. This is what Freud meant when he said that the treatment itself, at first, becomes a "transference neurosis." . . .

This phenomenon of *transference* in the playing child, as well as in the verbalizing adult, marks the point where simple measures fail—namely, when an emotion becomes so intense that it defeats playfulness, forcing an immediate discharge into the play and into the relationship with the play observer. The failure is characterized by what is to be described here as *play disruption* —i.e., the sudden and complete or diffused and slowly spreading inability to play. We saw such play disruption occur, on my provocation, in Ann's case, when she had to leave me and my tempting toys in order to rejoin her mother. Similarly, we saw Sam trapped by his overpowering emotions in the middle of a game. In both cases we used play as an incidental diagnostic tool. I shall now introduce a little girl who, although she came for diagnostic purposes only, led me through a full cycle of play disruption and play triumph, and thus offered a good example of the way in which the ego, flooded by fear, regains through transference its synthesizing power.

Our patient is Mary. She is just three years old. She is a somewhat pale brunette, but looks (and is) intelligent, pretty, and quite feminine. She is said to be stubborn, babyish, and shut-in when disturbed. Recently she has enriched her inventory of expression by nightmares and by violent anxiety attacks in the play group which she has recently joined. All that the play group teachers can say is that Mary has a queer way of lifting things and has a rigid posture: and that her tension seems to increase in connection with the routines of resting and going to the toilet. With this information at hand we invite Mary to our office.

Maybe a word should be said here about the thoroughly difficult situation which ensues when a mother brings a child for observation. The child has not chosen to come. He often does not feel sick at all in the sense that he has a symptom which he wishes to get rid of. On the contrary, all he knows is that certain things and, most of all, certain people make him feel uncomfortable and he wishes that we would do something about these things and people—not about him. Often he feels that something is wrong with his parents, and mostly he is right. But he has no words for this and, even if he did have, he has no reason to trust us with such weighty information. On the other hand, he does not know what the parents have told us about him—while God only knows what they have told the child about us. For the parents, helpful as they may wish to be and necessary as they are as initial informants, cannot be trusted in these matters: the initial history given is often distorted by the wish to justify (or secretly punish) themselves or to punish (and unconsciously justify) somebody else, perhaps the grandparents who "told you so."

In this case, my office was in a hospital. Mary had been told that she was coming to discuss her nightmares with me—a man whom she had never seen before. Her mother had consulted a pediatrician regarding these nightmares and Mary had heard the mother and the doctor argue over the possible indication for a tonsillectomy. I had hoped, therefore, that she would notice that the appointments of my office indicated a strictly non-medical affair and that she would give me a chance in simple and straightforward terms to acknowledge the purpose of her visit, to tell her that I was not a doctor and then to make clear that we were going to play together in order to get acquainted. Such explanations do not quite settle a child's doubts, but they may permit him to turn to the toys and do something. The moment he does something we can observe what he selects and repudiates in our standard inventory of toys. Our next step, then, will be guided by the meaning thus revealed.

Mary holds on to her mother as she enters my office. When

she offers me her hand it is both rigid and cold. She gives me a brief smile, then turns to her mother, puts her arms around her, and holds her close to the still open door. She buries her head in her mother's skirt as if she wanted to hide in it, and responds to my advances only by turning her head to me—with tightly closed eyes. Yet she *had* for a split moment looked at me with a smile that seemed to convey an interest—as if she wanted to see whether or not the new adult was going to understand fun. This makes her flight to her mother seem somewhat dramatic. The mother tries to encourage her to look at the toys, but Mary again hides her face in her mother's skirt and repeats in a dramatically babyish voice, "Mommy, mommy, mommy!" A dramatic young lady: I am not even quite sure that she is not hiding a smile. I decide to wait.

Now Mary does make a decision. Still holding on to her mother, she points to a (girl) doll and says several times quickly and babyishly, "What that, what that?" After the mother has patiently explained that it is a dolly, Mary repeats "Dolly, dolly, dolly," and suggests in words not understandable to me that the mother take off the dolly's shoes. The mother tries to make her perform this act herself, but Mary simply repeats her demand. Her voice becomes quite anxious, and it is clear that we may have tears in a moment.

Now the mother asks if it is not time for her to leave the room and wait outside as she has told Mary she would. I ask Mary whether we can let her mother go now and she, unexpectedly, makes no objection, not even when she suddenly finds herself without anybody to lean on. I try to start a conversation about the doll, which the mother has left in Mary's hand. Mary grasps it firmly around the legs and suddenly, smiling mischievously, she begins to touch various things in the room with the doll's head. When a toy falls from the shelf, she looks at me to see whether she has gone too far; when she sees me smile permissively she laughs and begins to push smaller toys, always with the doll's head, in such a way that they fall too. Her excitement increases. With special glee she pushes with the doll's head a toy train which is on the floor in the middle of the room. She overturns all the cars, apparently having some exciting kind of fun. But as the engine overturns she suddenly stops and becomes pale. She leans with her back against the sofa, holds the doll over her lower abdominal region, and drops it on the floor. She picks it up again, holds it over the same region, and drops it again. While repeating this several times, she begins first to whine and then to yell, "Mommy, mommy, mommy."

The mother re-enters, sure that communication has failed, and asks Mary whether she wants to go. I tell Mary that she may go if she wishes but that I hope she will be back in a few days. Quickly calmed, she leaves with her mother, saying good-by to the secretary outside as if she had had a pleasant visit.

Strangely enough, I too felt that the child had made a successful communication. With children, words are not always necessary at the beginning. I had felt that the play was leading up to a conversation. The fact of the mother's anxious interruption was, of course, as significant as the child's play disruption. Together, they probably explain the child's babyish anxiety. But what had she communicated with this emotional somersault, this sudden hilarity and flushed aggressiveness, and this equally sudden inhibition and pale anxiety?

The discernible mode content had been *pushing* things, not with her hand but with the doll as an extension of her hand; and then *dropping* the same doll from the genital region.

The doll as an extension of the hand has been, as it were, a pushing tool. This suggests that she may not dare to touch or push things with her bare hand—just as according to observation in her play group she seemed to touch or lift things in her own special way. This, together with the general rigidity in her extremities, suggests that Mary may be worried about her hands, maybe as aggressive tools.

The transfer of the doll to the lower abdominal region leads to the suggestion that she was dramatizing the loss from that region of an aggressive tool, a pushing instrument. The attack-like state which overcame her at this point reminds me of something which I learned long ago: severe hysterical attacks in adult women have been interpreted as dramatizations representing both partners in an imagined scene. Thus, one hand in tearing off the patient's dress may dramatize an aggressor's approach, while the other, in clutching it, may represent the victim's attempt to protect herself. Mary's attack impressed me as being of such a nature: by dropping the doll several times, panicky and yet as if obsessed, she seemed to be inexorably driven to dramatize both the robbed and the robber.

But what was to be stolen from her? Here we would have to know which meaning is more relevant, the doll's use as an aggressive tool—or the doll as representing a baby. In the play school, toilet situations were prominent among those which led to similar outbreaks of anxiety. In this play hour the dropped doll had first been the prolongation of an extremity and a tool of (pushing) aggression, and then something lost in the lower abdominal region under circumstances of extreme anxiety. Does Mary consider a penis such an aggressive weapon, and does she dramatize the fact that she does not have one? From the mother's account it is entirely probable that on entering the nursery school Mary was given her first opportunity to go to the toilet in the presence of boys.

I am thinking of the mother when she raps on the door. She has left the child, now quite composed, outside to come back and tell me that Mary was born with a sixth finger which was removed when she was approximately six months old. Just prior to the outbreak of her anxiety attacks, Mary had repeatedly and urgently asked about the scar on her hand ("What that, what that?") and had received the routine answer that it was "just a mosquito bite." The mother admits that the child when somewhat younger could easily have been present when her congenital anomaly was mentioned. Mary, the mother adds, has recently been equally insistent in her sexual curiosity.

We can now understand the fact that Mary feels uneasy about the aggressive use of her hand, which has been robbed of a finger. But why did she put the hand extension over the genital region only to dramatize its loss from there? Is there some association between the lost finger and the absent penis? Such an association would bring into juxtaposition the observation of sex differences in the play school and the immediate question of an operation.

Before Mary's second visit, her mother offered this further

information: Mary's sexual curiosity had recently received a specific blow when her father, irritable because of a regional increase in unemployment which threatened his means of livelihood, had shown impatience with her during her usual morning visit to him in the bathroom. In fact, he had shoved her out of the room. As he told me later, he had angrily repeated the words, "You stay out of here!" She had liked to watch the shaving process and had also on recent occasions (to his slight annoyance) asked about his genitals. A strict adherence to a routine in which she could do, say, and ask the same thing over and over again had always been a necessary condition for Mary's inner security. She was "heartbroken" over the consequent exclusion from the father's toilet.

We also discussed the fact (which I have already mentioned) that Mary's disturbed sleep and foul breath had been attributed by a pediatrician to a bad condition of the tonsils, and that the mother and the physician had engaged in a discussion in front of Mary as to whether she needed an immediate operation or not. *Operation*, then, and *separation* are seen to be the common denominators: the actual operation on the finger, the anticipated operation of the tonsils, and the mythical operation by which boys become girls; the separation from her mother during playschool hours, and the estrangement from her father. At the end of the first hour of play observation, then, this was the closest we could come to meanings on which all of the play elements and biographic data seemed to converge.

The antithesis of play disruption is play satiation, play from which a child emerges refreshed as a sleeper from a dreamless sleep. Both disruption and satiation are very marked and very clear only in rare cases. More often they are diffused and must be ascertained by detailed study. But not so in Mary's case. During her second appointment she obliged me with as dramatic a specimen of play satiation as she had previously demonstrated of play disruption.

At first Mary again smiles bashfully at me. Again she turns her head away, holding on to her mother's hand and insisting that the mother come with her into the room. Once in the room, however, she lets her mother's hand go and, forgetting about the mother's and my presence, she begins to play animatedly and with obvious determination and goal-mindedness. I quickly close the door and motion the mother to sit down, because I do not want to disturb the play.

Mary goes to the corner where the blocks are on the floor. She selects two blocks and arranges them in such a way that she can stand on them each time she comes to the corner to pick up more blocks. Thus, play begins again with an extension of extremities, this time her feet. She now makes a collection of blocks in the middle of the room, moving to the corner and back without hesitation. Then she kneels on the floor and builds a small house for a toy cow. For about a quarter of an hour she is completely absorbed in the task of arranging the house so that it is strictly rectangular and at the same time fits tightly about the cow. She then adds five blocks to one long side of the house and experiments with a sixth block until its position satisfies her (see Figure 1).

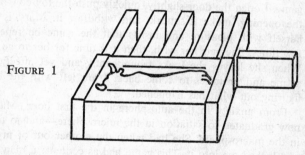

FIGURE 1

This time, then, the dominant emotional note is peaceful play concentration with a certain maternal quality of care and order. There is no climax of excitement, and the play ends on a note of satiation; she has built something, she likes it, now the play is over. She gets up with a radiant smile—which suddenly gives place to a mischievous twinkle. Before I realize the mischief I am about to fall victim to, I note that the close-fitting stable looks like a hand—with a sixth finger. At the same time it expresses the "inclusive" mode, a female-protective configuration, corresponding to the baskets and boxes and cradles arranged by little and big girls to give comfort to small things. Thus we see two restorations in one: The configuration puts the finger back on the hand and the happily feminine pattern belies the "loss from the genital region" previously dramatized. The second hour's play thus accomplishes an expression of restoration and safety—and this concerning the same body parts (hand, genital region) which in the play disruption of the first hour had appeared endangered.

But, as I said, Mary suddenly looks teasingly at me, laughs, takes her mother's hand and pulls her out of the room, saying with determination, "Mommy, come out." I wait for a while, then look out into the waiting room. A loud and triumphant, "Thtay in there!" greets me. I strategically withdraw, whereupon Mary closes the door with a bang. Two further attempts on my part to leave my room are greeted in the same gay way. She has me cornered.

There is nothing to do but to enter into the spirit of the game. I open the door slightly, quickly push the toy cow through the opening, make it squeak, and withdraw it. Mary is beside herself with pleasure and insists that the game be repeated a few times. She gets her wish, then it is time for her to go home. When she leaves she looks triumphantly and yet affectionately at me and promises to come back. I am left with the task of figuring out what has happened.

From anxiety in the autosphere in the first hour, Mary had now graduated to satiation in the microsphere—and to triumph in the macrosphere. She had taken the mother out of my space and locked me into it. This game had as content: a man is teasingly locked into his room. It is only in connection with this playful superiority that Mary had decided to talk to me, and this in no uncertain terms. "Thtay in there!" were the first words she had ever addressed to me! They were said clearly and in a loud voice, as if something in her had waited for the moment when she would be free enough to say them. What does that mean?

I think we have here an episode of "father transference." It will be remembered that from the moment Mary came into my room at the beginning of the first contact she showed a somewhat coquettish and bashful interest in me. Since it can be expected that she would transfer to me (the man with toys) a conflict which disturbed her usually playful relationship with her father, it seems more than probable that in this game she is repeating with active mastery ("Thtay in there") and with some reversal of vectors (out-in) the situation of exclusion of which she has been a passive victim at home ("Stay out of here").

To some this may seem like a lot of complicated and devious transformations for such a little girl. But here it is well to realize that these matters are difficult for rational thinking only. It would indeed be difficult to think up such a play trick. It is even difficult to recognize and analyze it. But it happens, of course, unconsciously and automatically: here, never underestimate the power of the ego—even of such a little girl.

This episode is presented to illustrate the self-curative trend in spontaneous play; for play therapy and play diagnosis must make systematic use of such self-curative processes. They may help the child to help himself—and they may help us to advise the parents. Where this fails, more complicated methods of treatment (child psychoanalysis)[2] must be initiated—methods which have not been discussed in this chapter. With advancing age, prolonged conversation would take the place of play. Here, however, it was my purpose to demonstrate that a few play hours can serve to inform us of matters which the child could never verbalize. Trained observers, in the possession of numerous data, can see from a few play contacts which of these data are subjectively relevant to the child, and why. In Mary's case, her play disruption and her play satiation, if seen in the framework of all the known circumstances, strongly suggests that a variety of contemporaneous events had been incorporated into a system of mutually aggravating items. In her play she restored her finger, reassured herself, reaffirmed her femininity—and told the big man off. Such play peace gained must, however, be sustained by the parents.

Mary's parents accepted (and partly themselves suggested) the following recommendations. Mary's curiosity in regard to

[2] Anna Freud, *Psycho-Analytical Treatment of Children*, Imago Publishing Co., London, 1946.

both her scar and her genitals required a truthful attitude. She needed to have other children, especially boys, visit her for play at her home. The matter of the tonsils called for the decision of a specialist, which could be candidly communicated to the child. It did not seem wise to awaken and to restrain her during her nightmares; perhaps she needed to fight her dreams out, and there would be opportunity to hold her lightly and to comfort her when she awoke spontaneously. The child needed much activity; playful instruction in rhythmic motion might relax some of the rigidity in her extremities, which, whatever the initial cause, may have been at least aggravated by fearful anticipation since hearing for the first time about the secret amputation of her finger.

When Mary, somewhat later, paid me a short visit, she was entirely at home and asked me in a clear, loud voice about the color of the train I had taken on my vacation. It will be remembered that she overturned a toy engine on the occasion of her first visit: now she could talk about engines. A tonsillectomy had proved unnecessary; the nightmares had ceased; Mary was making free and extensive use of the new play companions provided in and near her home. There was a revived play relationship with her father. He had intuitively made the most of Mary's sudden enraptured admiration for shining locomotives. He took her for regular walks to the railroad yards where together they watched the mighty engines.

Here the symbolism which has pervaded this clinical episode gains a new dimension. In the despair of play disruption, the toy engine apparently had a destructive meaning in some context with phallic-locomotor anxiety: when Mary pushed it over, she apparently had that awesome "Adam, where art thou" experience which we first observed in Ann. At the time, Mary's play relationship to her father had been disrupted, and this (as she could not know or understand) because of his worries over a possible disruption of his work status. This she seems to have interpreted entirely in terms of her maturational state and of her changes in status: and yet her reaction was not unrelated to the unconscious meaning implied in the father's actions. For threatened loss of status, threatened marginality, often result in an unconscious attempt by more stringent self-control and by purified standards to regain the ground lost or at least to keep from slipping any further. This, I believe, made the father react in a less tolerant way to the little girl's exploration, thus offending and frightening her in the general area which was already disturbed. It was, then, this area which appeared in her play in a condensed form, while she attempted, from the frightfulness of isolation, to work her way back to playful mutuality.

Neither Mary's play nor the insight it provided could change the father's economic worries. But the moment he recognized the impact of his anxieties on his daughter's development, he realized that from a long-range point of view her anxieties mattered much more than the threatened change of his work status. In fact, actual developments did not confirm his apprehensions.

The father's idea of taking walks to the engine yards was felicitous. For now the real engines became symbols of power shared by father and daughter alike and sustained by the whole imagery of the machine culture in which this child is destined to become a woman.

Thus at the end of any therapeutic encounter the parent must sustain in a child what the adult patient must gain for himself: a realignment with the images and the forces governing the cultural development of his day, and from it an increased sense of identity.

But here, at last, we must try to come to a better description and definition of what we mean by identity.

The Beginnings of Identity

A. Play and milieu

A child who has just found himself able to walk, more or less coaxed or ignored by those around him, seems driven to repeat the act for the pure enjoyment of functioning, and out of the need to master and perfect a newly initiated function. But he also acts under the immediate awareness of the new status and stature of "one who can walk," with whatever connotation this happens to have in the co-ordinates of his culture's space-time—be it "one who will go far," "one who will be able to stand on his own feet," "one who will be upright," or "one who must be watched because he might go too far." The incorporation of a particular version of "one who can walk" into the ego is one of the many steps in child development which (through the coincident experience of physical mastery and of cultural meaning, of functional pleasure and of social prestige) contribute to a more realistic self-esteem. This self-esteem grows to be a conviction that the ego is learning effective steps toward a tangible collective future, that it is developing into a defined ego within a social reality. The growing child must, at every step, derive a vitalizing sense of reality from the awareness that his individual way of mastering experience (his ego synthesis) is a successful variant of a group identity and is in accord with its space-time and life plan.

In this children cannot be fooled by empty praise and condescending encouragement. They may have to accept artificial bolstering of their self-esteem in lieu of something better, but their ego identity gains real strength only from wholehearted and consistent recognition of real accomplishment—i.e., of achievement that has meaning in the culture. . . .

The study of contemporary neuroses, however, points to the significance of this lag between child training and social reality. Neuroses contain, so we find, unconscious and futile attempts to adjust to the heterogeneous present with the magic concepts of a more homogeneous past, fragments of which are still transmitted through child training. But mechanisms of adjustment which once made for evolutionary adaptation, tribal integration, caste coherence, national uniformity, etc., are at loose ends in an industrial civilization.

No wonder, then, that some of our troubled children constantly break out of their play into some damaging activity in which they seem to us to "interfere" with our world; while analysis reveals that they only wish to demonstrate their right to find an identity in it. They refuse to become a specialty called "child," who must play at being big because he is not given an opportunity to be a small partner in a big world. . . .

A child has quite a number of opportunities to identify himself, more or less experimentally, with habits, traits, occupations, and ideas of real or fictitious people of either sex. Certain crises force him to make radical selections. However, the historical era in which he lives offers only a limited number of socially meaningful models for workable combinations of identification fragments. Their usefulness depends on the way in which they simultaneously meet the requirements of the organism's maturational stage and the ego's habits of synthesis. . . .

The desperate intensity of many a symptom, then, may be the defense of a step in ego identity which to the child promises to integrate the rapid changes taking place in all areas of his life. What to the observer looks like an especially powerful manifestation of naked instinct is often only a desperate plea for the permission to synthesize and sublimate in the only way possible. We can therefore expect our young patients to respond only to therapeutic measures which will help them to acquire the prerequisites for the successful completion of their ego identity. Therapy and guidance may attempt to substitute more desirable for less desirable items, but the total configuration of the ego identity remains unalterable. It follows that therapy and guidance by professionals are doomed to failure where the culture (through the mother) refuses to provide an early basis for an ego identity and where opportunities for appropriate later adjustments are missing.

15

HARRY STACK SULLIVAN

Preadolescence*

Need for Interpersonal Intimacy

Just as the juvenile era was marked by a significant change—
the development of the need for compeers, for playmates rather
like oneself—the beginning of preadolescence is equally spectacularly marked, in my scheme of development, by the appearance of
a new type of interest in another person. These changes are the
result of maturation and development, or experience. This new
interest in the preadolescent era is not as general as the use of
language toward others was in childhood, or the need of similar
people as playmates was in the juvenile era. Instead, it is a specific
new type of interest in a *particular* member of the same sex
who becomes a chum or a close friend. This change represents
the beginning of something very like full-blown, psychiatrically
defined *love*. In other words, the other fellow takes on a perfectly
novel relationship with the person concerned: he becomes of
practically equal importance in all fields of value. Nothing remotely like that has ever appeared before. All of you who have
children are sure that your children love you; when you say that,
you are expressing a pleasant illusion. But if you will look very
closely at one of your children when he finally finds a chum—
somewhere between eight-and-a-half and ten—you will discover
something very different in the relationship—namely, that your

* Reprinted by permission of the William Alanson White Psychiatric
Foundation and W. W. Norton & Co. from *The Interpersonal Theory of
Psychiatry* by Harry Stack Sullivan, edited by Helen Swick Perry and Mary
Ladd Gawel. Copyright, 1953, by The William Alanson White Psychiatric
Foundation, Inc.

child begins to develop a real sensitivity to what matters to another person. And this is not in the sense of "what should I do to get what I want," but instead "what should I do to contribute to the happiness or to support the prestige and feeling of worth-whileness of my chum." So far as I have ever been able to discover, nothing remotely like this appears before the age of, say, eight-and-a-half, and sometimes it appears decidedly later.

Thus the developmental epoch of preadolescence is marked by the coming of the integrating tendencies which, when they are completely developed, we call love, or, to say it another way, by the manifestation of the need for interpersonal intimacy. Now even at this late stage in my formulation of these ideas, I still find that some people imagine that intimacy is only a matter of approximating genitals one to another. And so I trust that you will finally and forever grasp that interpersonal intimacy can really consist of a great many things without genital contact; that intimacy in this sense means, just as it always has meant, closeness, without specifying that which is close other than the persons. Intimacy is that type of situation involving two people which permits validation of all components of personal worth. Validation of personal worth requires a type of relationship which I call collaboration, by which I mean clearly formulated adjustments of one's behavior to the expressed needs of the other person in the pursuit of increasingly identical—that is, more and more nearly mutual—satisfactions, and in the maintenance of increasingly similar security operations.[1] Now this preadolescent collaboration is distinctly different from the acquisition, in the juvenile era, of habits of competition, cooperation, and compromise. In preadolescence not only do people occupy themselves in moving toward a common, more-or-less impersonal objective, such as the success of "our team," or the discomfiture

---

[1] [Editors' note: Sullivan's use of the terms "collaboration" and "cooperation" should be kept in mind throughout this section. By cooperation, he means the usual give-and-take of the juvenile era; by collaboration, he means the feeling of sensitivity to another person which appears in preadolescence. "Collaboration . . . is a great step forward from cooperation—*I* play according to the rules of the game, to preserve *my* prestige and feeling of superiority and merit. When we collaborate, it is a matter of *we*." (*Conceptions of Modern Psychiatry*, p. 55.)]

of "our teacher," as they might have done in the juvenile era, but they also, specifically and increasingly, move toward supplying each other with satisfactions and taking on each other's successes in the maintenance of prestige, status, and all the things which represent freedom from anxiety, or the diminution of anxiety.[2]

Psychotherapeutic Possibilities in Preadolescence

Because of the rapidly developing capacity to revise one's personifications of another person on the basis of great interest in observation and analysis of one's experience with him, it comes about that the preadolescent phase of personality development can have and often does have very great inherent psychotherapeutic possibilities. I believe I have said earlier that it is at the developmental thresholds that the chance for notable favorable change tends to segregate itself. Although the structure of the self-system is such that its development in general is rather powerfully directed along the lines it has already taken, it is much more subject to influence through new experience, either fortunate or unfortunate, at each of the developmental thresholds. The fact that the self-system can undergo distinct change early in each of the developmental stages is of very real significance. For it is the self-system—the vast organization of experience which is concerned with protecting our self-esteem—which is involved in all inadequate and inappropriate living and is quite central to the whole problem of personality disorder and its remedy. And it is this capacity for distinct change in the self-system which begins to be almost fantastically important in preadolescence.

During the juvenile era a number of influences of vicious family life may be attenuated or corrected. But in the Western world a great deal of the activity of juveniles is along the lines

---

[2] [Editors' note: Up to this point, this chapter is taken from 1944-1945 lectures, rather than from the series on which this book is primarily based, since this portion is missing in the latter series because of failures of recording equipment. The material corresponds, however, to the outline in Sullivan's Notebook.]

of our ideals of intensely competitive, invidious society; only recently—and, I fear, still quite insularly—has there been any marked social pressure toward developing the other aspects of the same thing, the capacity to compromise and cooperate. Because of the competitive element, and also because of the juvenile's relative insensitivity to the importance of other people, it is possible that one can maintain throughout the juvenile era remarkably fantastic ideas about oneself, that one can have a very significantly distorted personification of the self, and keep it under cover. To have a very fantastic personification of oneself is, actually, to be very definitely handicapped. In other words, it is a misfortune in development.

Because one draws so close to another, because one is newly capable of seeing oneself through the other's eyes, the preadolescent phase of personality development is especially significant in correcting autistic, fantastic ideas about oneself or others. I would like to stress—at the risk of using superlatives which sometimes get very tedious—that development of this phase of personality is of incredible importance in saving a good many rather seriously handicapped people from otherwise inevitable serious mental disorder.

I may perhaps digress to the extent of saying that for some years I have had no negative instance to the following generalization: As a psychiatrist and a supervising psychiatrist, I have had occasion to hear about many male patients who find all relationships with other men occasions for considerable tenseness and vigilance, and who are uncomfortable in all their business, social, or other dealings with other men; of this group, I have found without exception that each one has lacked anything like good opportunities for preadolescent socialization. (I am confining my remarks to male patients here because the female picture is more complicated and I have less material on it.) These male patients may have what they call very close friends of the same sex, may even be overt and promiscuous homosexuals; but they are not at ease with strange men, they have much more trouble doing business with other men than seems to be justified by the factual aspects of the difficulty, and they are particularly uncertain as to what members of their own sex think of them. In other words, I am practically convinced that capacity for ease, for maximum profit from experience, in carrying on the conventional businesses of life with members of one's own sex requires that one should have been fortunate in entering into and profiting from relations with a chum in the preadolescent phase of personality development.

It is self-evident, I suppose, that I am conspicuously taking exception to the all-too-prevalent idea that things are pretty well fixed in the Jesuitical first seven years. This idea has constituted one of the greatest problems for some anthropologists who have tried to translate psychiatric thought into anthropologically useful ideas. The anthropologists have noised at them from all sides the enormous importance of infantile experience—meaning experience certainly under the age of eight. Yet one of the most conspicuous observations of an anthropologist working anywhere is that children of the privileged, who are raised by servants, do not grow up to be like the servants. That is a little bit difficult for an anthropologist to reconcile with the tremendous emphasis on very early experience. My work has shown me very clearly that, while early experience does a great many things—as I have been trying to suggest thus far—the development of capacity for interpersonal relations is by no means a matter which is completed at some point, say, in the juvenile era. Very far from it. And even preadolescence, which is a very, very important phase of personality development, is not the last phase.

Preadolescent Society

Except in certain rural communities, there occurs in preadolescence the development of at least an approach to what has long been called by sociologists "the gang." I am again speaking rather exclusively of male preadolescents, because by this time the deviations prescribed by the culture make it pretty hard to make a long series of statements which are equally obviously valid for the two sexes. The preadolescent interpersonal relation is primarily, and vastly importantly, a two-group; but these two-groups tend to interlock. In other words, let us say that persons

A and *B* are chums. Person *A* also finds much that is admirable about person *C*, and person *B* finds much that is admirable about person *D*. And persons *C* and *D* each has his chum, so that there is a certain linkage of interest among all of these two-groups. Quite often there will be one particular preadolescent who is, thanks to his having been fortunate in earlier phases, the sort of person that many of these preadolescent people find useful as a model; and he will be the third member, you might say, of many three-groups, composed of any one of a number of two-groups and himself. At the same time, he may have a particular chum just as everybody in this society may have. Thus these close two-groups, which are extremely useful in correcting earlier deviations, tend at the same time to interlock through one person or a few people who are, in a very significant sense, leaders. And incidentally, let me say that many of us are apt to think of leadership in political terms, in terms of "influence" and the "influential." We overlook the fact that influence is exerted by the influential in certain conspicuous areas other than that of getting people to do what the leader wants done. The fact is that a very important field of leadership phenomena—and one that begins to be outstandingly important in preadolescence—is opinion leadership; and understanding this and developing techniques for integrating it might be one of the few great hopes for the future.

Thus some few people tend to come out in leadership positions in preadolescent society. Some of them are the people who can get the others to collaborate, to work with understanding and appreciation of one another toward common objectives or aims, which sometimes may be crimes, or what not. And others are the leaders whose views gradually come to be the views of a large number in the group, which is opinion leadership. This kind of leadership has certain fairly measurable and perhaps some imponderable aspects. One of its reasonably measurable aspects is that people whose development, combined with their intellectual abilities, has given them the ability to separate facts and opinions, tend to be considered by the others as well informed, right in their thinking about things of interest at that particular stage, and thus tend to do the thinking for a good many of the others because of the latter's unfortunate personality warp. And the time when these leaders in opinion do the thinking almost exclusively is when there are serious problems confronting the members of the group. The level of general insecurity about the human future is high at this stage of development, and in any case probably increases when serious problems arise, whether they occur in the preadolescent gang or in society as a whole. It is at those times that perhaps far more than half of the statistical population— handicapped by lack of information, by lack of training, and by various difficulties in personal life which call out a good deal of anxiety, which in turn interferes with practically everything useful—has to look to opinion leadership for anything like reassuring views or capable foresight. Thus an important part of the preadolescent phase of personality development is the developing patterning of leadership-led relationships, which are so vital in any social organization and which are, theoretically at least, of very great importance in relatively democratic organizations of society.

I have suggested that an important aspect of the preadolescent phase is that, practically for the first time, there is consensual validation of personal worth. Now it is true that some children are fortunate, indeed; through the influences to which they have been subjected in the home and school, they are about as sure as they can be that they are worth while in certain respects. But very many people arrive in preadolescence in the sad state which an adult would describe as "getting away with murder." In other words, they have had to develop such remarkable capacities for deceiving and misleading others that they never had a chance to discover what they were really good for. But in this intimate interchange in preadolescence—some preadolescents even have mutual daydreams, spend hours and hours carrying on a sort of spontaneous mythology in which both participate—in this new necessity for thinking of the other fellow as right and for being thought of as right by the other fellow, much of this uncertainty as to the real worth of the personality, and many self-deceptive skills at deceiving others which exist in the juvenile era, may be rectified by the improving communication of the chums and, to a

In a given person, the beginning of adolescence, as far as personality development is concerned, takes place at an indefinite time; that is, although it does not take place overnight, it is observable at the end of a matter of months, instead of years. Early adolescence, in my scheme of development, is ushered in by the beginning of the array of things called the puberty change, by the frank appearance of the lust dynamism. And the frank appearance of the lust dynamism is, in a great many instances, manifested by the intrusion, into fantasy or the sleeplife, of experience of a piece with the sexual orgasm; in other instances, where there has been preliminary genital play, and so on, it is manifested by the occurrence of orgasm in certain play. Lust is the last to mature of the important integrating tendencies, or needs for satisfaction, which characterize the underlying human animal now well advanced to being a person.

In our society, the age when early adolescence appears varies within three or four years, I think. This remarkable developmental discrepancy which is possible among different people of the same chronological age—a vastly greater discrepancy than occurs in the maturing of any of the previously discussed needs—is one of the important factors which makes adolescence such a time of stress. And incidentally, only by studying a different social organization from ours could one see how much less a time of stress the period of adolescence might be. In certain other societies, where the culture provides a great deal more real preparation for adolescence than ours does, the extraordinarily stressful aspect of adolescence is not nearly so conspicuous. There are, however, certain elements of the puberty change and its associated adolescent phase of personality organization that are not to be overlooked in any social order; those are the ones associated with the remarkable speeding up of certain growth factors which, for example, makes people clumsy and awkward who were previously quite skillful and dexterous. Thus there are always, or almost always, some stresses concerned with this very rapid maturation of the somatic organization which is ushered in by the puberty change. But so far as the psychological stresses are concerned, they are more apt to result from disasters in timing than from anything else.

The Experience of Loneliness[3]

Before going on, I would like to discuss the developmental history of that motivational system which underlies the experience of loneliness.

Now loneliness is possibly most distinguished, among the experiences of human beings, by the toneless quality of the things which are said about it. While I have tried to impress upon you the extreme undesirability of the experience of anxiety, I, in common apparently with all denizens of the English-speaking world, feel inadequate to communicate a really clear impression of the experience of loneliness in its quintessential force. But I think I can give you some idea of why it is a terribly important component of personality, by tracing the various motivational systems by developmental epochs that enter into the experience of loneliness. Of the components which culminate in the experience of real loneliness, the first, so far as I know, appears in infancy as the need for contact. This is unquestionably composed of the elaborate group of dependencies which characterize infancy, and which can be collected under the need for tenderness. This kind of need extends into childhood. And in childhood we see components of what will ultimately be experienced as loneliness appearing in the need for adult participation in activities. These activities start out perhaps in the form of expressive play in which the very young child has to learn how to express emotions by successes and failures in escaping anxiety or in increasing euphoria; in various kinds of manual play in which one learns coordination, and so on; and finally in verbal play—the pleasure-giving use of the components of verbal speech which gradually move over into the consensual validation of speech. In the juvenile era we see components of what will eventually be loneliness in the need for

[3] [*Editors' note:* Several times, in the series of lectures which has been used as the basis for this book, Sullivan has made reference to a later discussion of loneliness. Yet this discussion does not appear in this particular series, probably through an oversight. We have therefore included here a discussion of loneliness from a 1945 lecture.]

compeers; and in the later phases of the juvenile era, we see it in what I have not previously mentioned by this name, but what you can all recognize from your remembered past, as the need for acceptance. To put it another way, most of you have had, in the juvenile era, an exceedingly bitter experience with your compeers to which the term "fear of ostracism" might be justifiably applied—the fear of being accepted by no one of those whom one must have as models for learning how to be human.

And in preadolescence we come to the final component of the really intimidating experience of loneliness—the need for intimate exchange with a fellow being, whom we may describe or identify as a chum, a friend, or a loved one—that is, the need for the most intimate type of exchange with respect to satisfactions and security.

Loneliness, as an experience which has been so terrible that it practically baffles clear recall, is a phenomenon ordinarily encountered only in preadolescence and afterward. But by giving this very crude outline of the components that enter into this driving impulsion, I hope I have made it clear why, under continued privation, the driving force of this system may integrate interpersonal situations despite really severe anxiety. Although we have not previously, in the course of this outline of the theory of personality, touched on anything which can brush aside the activity of the self-system, we have now come to it: Under loneliness, people seek companionship even though intensely anxious in the performance. When, because of deprivations of companionship, one does integrate a situation in spite of more or less intense anxiety, one often shows, in the situation, evidences of a serious defect of personal orientation. And remember that I am speaking of orientation in living, not orientation in time and space, as the traditional psychiatrists discuss it. I have already given my conception of orientation in living in discussing the juvenile era. Now this defective orientation may be due, for instance, to a primary lack of experience which is needed for the correct appraisal of the situation with respect to its significance, aside from its significance as a relief of loneliness. There are a good many situations in which lonely people literally lack any experience with things which they encounter. . . .

Loneliness reaches its full significance in the preadolescent era, and goes on relatively unchanged from thenceforth throughout life. Anyone who has experienced loneliness is glad to discuss some vague abstract of this previous experience of loneliness. But it is a very difficult therapeutic performance to get anyone to remember clearly how he felt and what he did when he was horribly lonely. In other words, the fact that loneliness will lead to integrations in the face of severe anxiety automatically means that loneliness in itself is more terrible than anxiety. While we show from the very beginning a curiously clear capacity for fearing that which might be fatally injurious, and from very early in life an incredible sensitivity to significant people, only as we reach the preadolescent stage of development does our profound need for dealings with others reach such proportion that fear and anxiety actually do not have the power to stop the stumbling out of restlessness into situations which constitute, in some measure, a relief from loneliness. This is not manifest in anything like driving force until we arrive at the preadolescent era.

16

HARRY STACK SULLIVAN

Early Adolescence*

The earlier phase of adolescence as a period of personality development is defined as extending from the eruption of true genital interest, felt as lust, to the patterning of sexual behavior which is the beginning of the last phase of adolescence. There are very significant differences, in the physiological substrate connected with the beginning of adolescence, between men and women; but in either case there is a rather abrupt change, relatively unparalleled in development, by which a zone of interaction with the environment which had been concerned with excreting waste becomes newly and rapidly significant as a zone of interaction in physical interpersonal intimacy. In other words, what had been, from the somatic viewpoint, the more external tissues of the urinary-excretory zone now become the more external part of the genital zone as well. The change, from the psychological standpoint, pertains to new needs which have their culmination in the experience of sexual orgasm; the felt tensions associated with this need are traditionally and quite properly identified as *lust*. In other words, lust is the felt component of integrating tendencies pertaining to the genital zone of interaction, seeking the satisfaction of cumulatively augmented sentience culminating in orgasm.

There is, so far as I know, no necessarily close relationship between lust, as an integrating tendency, and the need for intimacy, which we have previously discussed, except that they both char-

* Reprinted by permission of The William Alanson White Psychiatric Foundation and W. W. Norton & Co. from *The Interpersonal Theory of Psychiatry* by Harry Stack Sullivan, edited by Helen Swick Perry and Mary Ladd Gawel. Copyright, 1953, by The William Alanson White Psychiatric Foundation, Inc.

acterize people at a certain stage in development. The two are
strikingly distinct. In fact, making very much sense of the com-
plexities and difficulties which are experienced in adolescence and
subsequent phases of life, depends, in considerable measure, on
the clarity with which one distinguishes three needs, which are
often very intricately combined and at the same time contradictory. These are the need for personal security—that is, for
freedom from anxiety; the need for intimacy—that is, for collaboration with at least one other person; and the need for lustful
satisfaction, which is connected with genital activity in pursuit of
the orgasm.

The Shift in the Intimacy Need

As adolescence is ushered in, there is, in people who are not too
much warped for such a development, a change in the so-called
object of the need for intimacy. And the change is from what I
shall presently be discussing as an isophilic choice to what may be
called a heterophilic choice—that is, it is a change from the seeking of someone quite like oneself to the seeking of someone who
is in a very significant sense very different from oneself. This
change in choice is naturally influenced by the concomitant appearance of the genital drive. Thus, other things being equal and
no very serious warp or privation intervening, the change from
preadolescence to adolescence appears as a growing interest in
the possibilities of achieving some measure of intimacy with a
member of the other sex, rather after the pattern of the intimacy
that one has in preadolescence enjoyed with a member of one's
own sex.

The degree to which the need for intimacy is satisfied in this
heterophilic sense in the present-day American scene leaves very
much to be desired. The reason is not that the shift of interest
toward the other sex in itself makes intimacy difficult, but that
the cultural influences which are borne in upon each person include very little which prepares members of different sexes for
a fully human, simple, personal relationship together. A great
many of the barriers to heterophilic intimacy go back to the

very beginnings of the Western world. Just to give a hint of what I am talking about, I might mention the so-called double standard of morality and the legal status which surrounds illegitimate birth. One can get an idea of the important influence of cultural organization and cultural institutions on the possibilities of relationships in adolescence which are easy and, in terms of personality development, successful, by studying a culture very significantly different from our own in this respect. For some years I have recommended in this connection Hortense Powdermaker's *Life in Lesu*.[1] There, the institutions bearing on the distinction between the sexes are very significantly different from ours, and the contrast between our institutions and theirs perhaps sheds some light in itself on unfortunate aspects of the Western world.

But to return to our culture: The change in the need for intimacy—the new awakening of curiosity in the boy as to how he could get to be on as friendly terms with a girl as he has been on with his chum—is usually ushered in by a change of covert process. Fantasy undergoes a rather striking modification—a modification almost as abrupt and striking as the sudden acceleration of somatic growth which begins with the puberty change and leads, for instance, to the awkwardness which I have mentioned. And there may also be a change of content in overt communicative processes, both in the two-group and in the gang. That is, if the preadolescents are successfully progressing toward maturation and uniformly free from personality warp, this interest in members of the other sex also spreads into the area of communication between the chums, even though the one chum may not be quite up to the other and may be somewhat opposed to this new preoccupation with girls. In the more fortunate circumstances, this is presently a gang-wise change, and those who are approximately ready for it profit considerably from this last great topic of preadolescent collaboration—the topic of who's who and what's what in the so-called heterosexual world. If the group includes some members whose development is delayed, the social pressure in the group, in the gang, is extremely hard on their self-esteem and may lead to very serious disturbances of personality

---

[1] [Hortense Powdermaker, *Life in Lesu: The Study of a Melanesian Society in New Ireland*; New York: W. W. Norton & Co., Inc., 1933.]

indeed. As I have previously hinted, it is not uncommon for the preadolescent phase to fade imperceptibly into the early adolescent phase, and for gang-wise genital activity to become part of the pattern of the very last stage of preadolescence or the verge of adolescence. Thus one not uncommonly finds at this point that the lust dynamism is actually functioning and governing a good part of group activity, but this is very definitely oriented to that which is to follow with members of the other sex.

In this change from preadolescence to adolescence, there has to be a great deal of trial-and-error learning by human example. A considerable number of those at the very beginning of adolescence have some advantage in this learning by virtue of having already acquired data from their observation of and experience with a sibling of the other sex not very far removed from them in developmental age; these data which had been previously unimportant are now rapidly activated.

I believe that according to conventional, statistical experience, women undergo the puberty change somewhat in advance of men; in a great many instances, this leads to a peculiar sort of stutter in developmental progress between the boys and the girls in an age community so that by the time most of the boys have gotten really around to interest in girls, most of the girls are already fairly well wound up in their problems about boys. From the standpoint of personality development, it would be convenient if these things were timed slightly better; but I suppose that in the beginning when everything was arranged—I've never had any private information on the subject, by the way—procreation was fully as important as a feeling of self-esteem is now in a highly developed civilization. And so women get ready for procreation quite early; in fact one of the important problems of adolescence is how to avoid the accident of procreation.

Various Collisions of Lust, Security, and the Intimacy Need

After lust gets under way, it is extremely powerful. In fact, if one overlooks his experience with loneliness, he may well think that lust is the most powerful dynamism in interpersonal relations. Since our culture provides us with singular handicaps for lustful activity rather than with facilitation, lust promptly collides with a whole variety of powerful dynamisms in personality. The most ubiquitous collision is naturally *the collision between one's lust and one's security;* and by security I mean one's feeling of self-esteem and personal worth. Thus a great many people in early adolescence suffer a lot of anxiety in connection with their new-found motivation to sexual or genital activity—and I use those words interchangeably. Besides the puzzlement, embarrassment, and so on, which the culture practically makes certain, there are lamentably too many instances of people who already have a rather profound warp with respect to the general area of the body which is concerned. I have called this the primary genital phobia, which is not entirely to be interpreted on the basis of the usual ideas about phobia. By primary genital phobia I refer to an enduring warp of personality which is often inculcated in late infancy and early childhood and practically converts that area of the body into something not quite of the body. In discussing the excretory function and the exploratory power of the hand, I have commented on the incredible efforts made by certain parents to keep the young child from handling the genitals, from exploring and getting sensations from them. In cases in which this is successful, that area of the body becomes distinctly related to that area of personality to which I long since referred as the not-me. It is almost impossible for the adolescent who has this type of warp to arrive at any simple and, shall I say, conventional type of learning of what to do with lust. Therefore, as that person becomes lustful, he has the energy of the genital dynamism added to loneliness and other causes for restlessness; thus his activity with others becomes comparatively pointless, which almost certainly is humiliating and is not a contribution to his self-esteem. Or he may actually have some fairly serious disturbance of personality because of the outstanding power of the lust dynamism and the comparative hopelessness of learning how he, in particular, can do anything about it. Thus a person in this era may know a good deal about what other people do, but if he finds he can't do it himself, he doesn't feel quite up to the average.

Not only does lust collide with the need for security, but *the shift in the intimacy need may also collide with the need for security*. In early adolescence, the need for intimacy, for collaboration with some very special other person, reaches out toward, and tends to settle on, a member of the other sex. Now the ways in which this may collide with self-esteem are numerous, but there are a few particular instances that I want to bring to your attention. Quite often we discover that the young reach adolescence very much to the discontent of their elders in the home. In those situations it is not uncommon to find that there has been no serious taboo by the family group against the development of a chum relationship or even against membership in a gang; but now as the interest begins to move toward members of the other sex, there does begin to be strong repressive influence brought to bear on the adolescent by the family group.

One of the most potent instruments used in this particular is ridicule; many an adolescent has been ridiculed practically into very severe anxiety by parents who just do not want him to become, as they think of it, an adult interested in such things as sex, which may get him diseased or what not, or may result in marriage and his leaving home. Ridicule from parents and other elders is among the worst tools that are used on early adolescents. Sometimes a modification of ridicule is used by parents who are either too decent to use ridicule or are unaware of its remarkable power; and this modification takes the form of interfering with, objecting to, criticizing, and otherwise getting in the way of any detectable movement of their child toward a member of the other sex. This can go to the point of being a pathological performance which we call jealousy, in which the parent literally gets incredibly wrapped up in the rudimentary two-group that the adolescent is trying to establish with some member of the opposite sex. We will touch on jealousy again when we get around to discussing the particular group of difficulties in living which are called paranoid states. It should merely be noted at this point that jealousy is invariably a matter of more than two people, and that very often everyone concerned in jealousy is pretty fantastic —that is, there are a great many parataxic processes mixed up in it. Sometimes the third person concerned is purely a parataxic delusion on the part of the jealous person. So much for merely a few high spots on the type of collisions between the feeling of personal worth and the change in the direction of the need for intimacy.

There are also *collisions between the intimacy need and lust.* In establishing collaborative intimacy with someone, four varieties of awkwardnesses are common, of which the first three—embarrassment, diffidences, and excessive precautions—make up one group. The fourth represents one of our magic tricks of swinging to the other extreme to get away from something that doesn't work, which I call the *not* technique. In other words, you know what an apple is, and if you were under pressure enough you could produce an imaginary truth, *not apple,* made up entirely of the absence-of-apple characteristics. Thus, one of the ways of attempting to solve this collision between the intimacy need and lust is by something which is about the opposite of diffidence— namely, the development of a very bold approach in the pursuit of the genital objective. But the approach is so poorly addressed to the sensitivities and insecurities of the object that the object is in turn embarrassed and made diffident; and so it overreaches and has the effect of making the integration of real intimacy quite improbable.

A much more common evidence of the collision of these two powerful motivational systems is seen among adolescents in this culture as the segregation of object persons, which is in itself an extremely unfortunate way of growing up. By this I refer to the creating of distinctions between people toward whom lustful motivations can apply, and people who will be sought for the relief of loneliness—that is, for collaborative intimacy, for friendship. The classical instance is the old one of the prostitute and the good girl. The prostitute is the only woman who is to be thought of for genital contact; the good girl is never to be thought of in that connection, but only for friendship and for a somewhat nebulous future state referred to as marriage. When this segregation has been quite striking, this nebulous state takes on a purely fantastic character. Nowadays, the far more prevalent distinction is between sexy girls and good girls, rather than this gross division into bad and good women. But no matter how it comes about that the other sex is cut into two groups—one of which can satisfy a person's loneliness and spare him anxiety, while the other satisfies his lust—the trouble with this is that lust is a part of personality, and no one can get very far at completing his personality development in this way. Thus satisfying one's lust must be at considerable expense to one's self-esteem, since the bad girls are unworthy and not really people in the sense that good girls are. So wherever you find a person who makes this sharp separation of members of the other sex into those who are, you might say, lustful and those who are nonlustful, you may assume that this person has quite a cleavage with respect to his genital behavior, so that he is not really capable of integrating it into his life, simply and with self-respect.

These sundry collisions that come along at this stage may be the principal motives for preadolescents or very early adolescents getting into "homosexual" play, with some remarkable variations. But a much more common outcome of these various collisions—these difficulties in developing activity to suit one's needs—is the breaking out of a great deal of autosexual behavior, in which one satisfies one's own lust as best one can; this behavior appears because of the way in which preadolescent society breaks up, and because of the various inhibitions which have been inculcated on the subject of freedom regarding the genitals. Now this activity, commonly called masturbation, has in general been rather severely condemned in every culture that generally imposes marked restrictions on freedom of sexual development. That's very neat, you see; it means that adolescence is going to be hell whatever you do, unless you have wonderful preparation for being different from everyone else—in which case you may get into trouble for being different.

Incidentally, problems of masturbation are sufficiently common, even among the wise, so that a word might be said here regarding what seems to be a sound psychiatric view of the matter. The question sometimes arises as to whether masturbation is good or bad. Now whenever a psychiatrist is confronted by such a question, he may well take it under advisement to see whether he can reformulate it into a question that he can, as a psychiatrist, deal with; psychiatrists don't dispense these absolute qualifications of good or bad. The nearest we can approach such values is to decide whether a thing is better or worse in terms of the interpersonal present and near future. From this approach, one can note that in this culture the developmental progress in connection with the adolescent change is handicapped by both lack of preparation and absolute taboos on certain freedoms; but lust *combined with* the need for intimacy frequently does drive the victim toward correcting certain warps in personality and toward developing certain facilities, certain abilities, in interpersonal relations. There is no way that I know of by which one can, all by oneself, satisfy the need for intimacy, cut off the full driving power of loneliness, although loneliness can be manipulated or reduced to a certain extent. But through autosexual performance one can prevent lust from reaching tension sufficient to break down one's barriers. For that reason, the entirely exclusive use of autoerotic procedures can contribute to the prolongation of warp, which in turn contributes to the continued handicap for life of the person concerned. It is from this viewpoint alone that I would consider that masturbation, as the *only* solution for the sundry collisions that lust enters into, is worse than almost anything else that is not definitely malevolent. Needless to say, such an argument becomes meaningless if, as is so often the case in genital behavior, the autoerotic performance is not fixed and exclusive but is incidental or occasional. Arguments against masturbation based on anything other than this particular reason seem to me to smack more of unanalyzed prejudice on the part of the arguer than of good sense.

Fortune and Misfortune in Heterosexual Experimentation

My next topic is the rather important one of the fortune and misfortune which the early adolescent has in his experimentation toward reaching a heterosexual type of experience. In the olden days when I was distinctly more reckless than now, I thought that a good many of the people I saw as mental patients would have been luckier in their adolescence had they carried on their preliminary heterosexual experimentation with a good-natured prostitute—that is, this would have been fortunate in comparison to what actually had happened to them. Not that I regard prostitutes as highly developed personalities of the other sex; but if they happen to be in the business of living off their participation in genital sport and are friendly, they at least will know a good deal about the problems in this field that earlier adolescents encounter, and will treat them with sympathy, understanding, and encouragement; but unfortunately, a great many of these experiments are conducted with people who are themselves badly, though differently, warped. The number of wretched experiences connected with adolescents' first heterosexual attempts is legion, and the experiences are sometimes very expensive to further maturation of personality. If there has been a lively lustful fantasy and little or no overt behavior with respect to the genitals—which incidentally will tend very strongly to characterize everyone who has this primary genital phobia I have spoken of—then it is almost certain that on the verge of an actual genital contact, precocious orgasm will occur in the man; and this precocious orgasm suddenly wipes out the integration and just leaves two people in a practically meaningless situation although they had previously made immense sense to each other. Such an occurrence reflects very severely on the self-esteem of the man concerned and thereby initiates a still more unfortunate process which is apt to appear as impotence. The recollection of so disastrous an occurrence, which has been in terms of anxiety pretty costly, is quite apt to result in either of two outcomes: there may be an overweening conviction that that's the way it's going to go, that one just hasn't any "virility," that one's manhood is deficient; or there may be frantic attempts to prove otherwise, which, if they were kept up long enough, would work. Unless there has been some genital activity, or unless the woman is quite expert in reducing the anxiety of the male, or even his sexual excitement, this precocious orgasm is very apt to be a man's introduction to heterosexual life. Needless to say, it has about as much true significance as drinking a glass of water—that is, if one could accept it in perfectly calm and rational fashion, it would prove absolutely nothing except that it had occurred once, and one could subsequently see whether it was going to be typical behavior or whether it was an accident. It usually isn't typical unless its effects are disastrous, in which case it can be stamped in as a sort of morbid way of handling one's incapacity to integrate true lust-ful situations, or as a channel for various other things which I shall discuss presently.

In other instances in which there is a lack of experience and considerable warp in the personalities concerned, lust may carry things through to orgasm, usually of only one partner; but im-mediately upon the satisfaction of the lust dynamism and the disintegration of the situation as a lustful situation, the persons concerned may become the prey of guilt, shame, aversion, or revulsion for each other, or at least this may be true for one of the people concerned. And this experience is not a particularly fortu-nate addition to one's learning how to live in the world as it is. A much less usual, but also unfortunate, event in this initial experimentation in genital activity is that if it has gone pretty well it may become a high-grade preoccupation. This is usually to be understood on the general theory of preoccupation and is just as morbid as any other preoccupation. Since lust has a peculiarly strong biological basis, and, in some people, may be an ever re-current and very driving force in early adolescence, this preoccu-pation with lust can lead to serious deterioration of self-respect because of the unpleasant situations one is driven into, because of the disapproval one encounters, and because this type of pre-occupation literally interferes with almost any commonplace way of protecting one's self-esteem. A great many people whose self-esteem has been somewhat uncertain, depending on scholarship only, find their standing as students rapidly declining as they become completely preoccupied with the pursuit of lust objects. Thus they become the prey of severe anxiety, since their only distinction is now being knocked in half.

With truly distressing frequency, these sundry problems con-nected with early adolescence cause the persons concerned to turn to alcohol, one of the great mental-hygiene props in the cul-ture, with unfortunate results. I sometimes think alcohol is, more than any other human invention, the basis for the duration and growth of the Western world. I am quite certain that no such complex, wonderful, and troublesome organization of society

could have lasted long enough to become conspicuous if a great
number of its unhappy denizens did not have this remarkable
chemical compound with which to get relief from intolerable
problems of anxiety. But its capacity for dealing with those problems naturally makes it a menace under certain circumstances,
as I scarcely think I need argue. Like a good many other props
which temporarily remedy but do not in any sense favorably
alter cultural impossibilities, it is costly, not to all, but to too
many. A peculiarity of alcohol is that it interferes very promptly
with complex, refined referential operations, particularly those
that are recent—that have not been deeply and extensively
involved in the whole business of living—while it does not particularly disturb the older and more essential dynamisms of personality. It definitely poisons the self-system progressively, beginning with the most recent and most complex of the self-system's
functions. So personality under alcohol is less competent at protecting itself from anxiety, but practically all the anxiety is experienced later, retrospectively. Since the self-function, which is, of
course, very intimately connected with the occurrence of anxiety,
is inhibited and disturbed by alcohol, but one's later recall is not,
one experiences the anxiety in retrospect, you see. And the problems that get one all too dependent on alcohol are, I think, the
problems of sexual adjustment, which hit hardest in early adolescence.

The Separation of Lust from Intimacy

I want next to discuss misfortunes of development in early
adolescence in which there is, as the outstanding characteristic,
a separation of those interpersonal relations motivated by lust
from those based on the need for intimacy—that is, motivated by
loneliness. This sharp division is merely a very much more extensive and enduring deviation of personality than the kind of classification of heterophilic objects—for example, into good women
and bad women—which I previously mentioned. The need for intimacy has been gradually developing along its own lines from
very ancient roots, while lust has only recently and vividly

appeared. The complex outcomes of these developmental inter-personal relations which are scarcely parallel and are actually divergent are a very rich source for problems which concern the psychiatrist. Some people are unfortunate enough to sublimate, as we still have to call it, their lust—that is, to partially satisfy it while connecting it with socially acceptable goals. This is, as I would again like to remind you, an extremely dangerous over-loading of possibilities, which is very apt to collapse in a lament-able way. I am postponing a discussion of what happens to lust under these circumstances. But the intimacy need sometimes shows itself as follows: A member of the other sex who is in a good many ways like the parent of that sex may become invested with full-fledged "love" and devotion. Another, not so striking instance, is the pseudo-sibling relation. There are, of course, many jokes in the culture about the girl who is willing to be a sister to you. But I wonder if you realize how many unfortunate early adolescents get by with the appearance of personality de-velopment by striking up one of these pseudo-sibling relation-ships, which can be mistaken by others for a satisfactory move toward developing a solution for the problems of lust and loneli-ness. Another change of this kind is, we might say, a prolonga-tion and refinement of the separation of good and bad girls: All women are good—too good; they are noble, and one cannot approach them for anything so something-or-other as genital satisfaction. And there is the alternative of that, in which all women are regarded as extremely unattractive, unsuited to any-thing but a particular kind of hateful entanglement which be-comes practically official business.

In the process of trying to separate one's need for intimacy from one's need for genital integration, certain peculiarities of personality appear which we will later discuss as *dissociation*. Among the people with these peculiarities of personality pertain-ing to the need for intimacy, there is the one who feels pursued by the other sex and actually spends a lot of time in trying to avoid being hounded by the other sex. There is also the true woman-hater—that is, the man who literally feels the most strenu-ous antipathy to any but the most superficial relation with mem-bers of the other sex. When lust is dissociated—and components in lust are quite frequently dissociated—such things occur, even from early adolescence, as the celibate way of life, in some cases with accessible lustful fantasies, and in other cases with no representation of lustful needs in awareness. This latter can go so far that actually there are no recollections of any content connected with what must have been the satisfaction of lust in sleep; in other words, there are nocturnal orgasms, but there is never any recollectable content at all. When one encounters that sort of thing, one thinks immediately that something has gone very radically wrong with the personality. Another manifestation in this field is what I call, in terms of a man's viewpoint, horror of the female genitals; even though the man considers that women are all right, and in fact, in many instances, may make a very good approach to them, the actual attempt at a physical intergenital situation causes the man to be overcome with a feeling which is literally uncanny, which is quite paralyzing. As I have already hinted, all these uncanny feelings refer to the not-me, and are, by this stage of personality, practically always signs that there is serious dissociation somewhere in personality. Another solution of this kind is to fall into a homosexual way of getting rid of lust; this is accompanied either by liking, by indifference, or by aversion toward the partner, or by revulsion or by fascination for the whole type of situation.

In this special group of disturbances of development, there are also the instances in which the genital drive is discharged with infrahuman or nearly infrahuman participation—that is, some of the lower animals are used as genital partners, or people are used whom the person has so much prejudice against that he scarcely considers them to be human. Very occasionally human ingenuity leads people who suffer from primitive genital phobia to invent what are called masturbating machines. This is a phenomenon that gets a good deal of attention, more than it deserves, and is, supposedly, very interestingly connected with paranoid states. As a matter of fact, it does coincide more than occasionally with later paranoid states, but this relation has been vastly overaccentuated.

Character

The study of character is the contemporary successor to the study of symptoms in Freud's time. It was soon realized that symptoms were more than discrete examples of aberrant behavior; they were the results of the failure to maintain the organization of the relatively fixed modes of reaction which we call character.

Freud was the first to point out character traits. He categorized them as "unchanged perpetuations of instinctual impulses, reactions against them, or sublimations of them." The implication that there is a direct relationship between infantile experience and adult character according to one or all of the three mechanisms quoted above persists in Freudian theory. Adler, one of the early deviants, emphasizes the importance of drives directed toward goals in the development of character.

The contemporary selections given in this section demonstrate what some of the leading thinkers in the field consider important in the development of character types, without minimizing the importance of infancy and early childhood. These workers do not agree with the mechanisms postulated by Freud. In their views, the individual achieves this relatively fixed constellation of character traits on the basis of his adaptation to all of life's experiences, rather than on the way in which he handled conflicts arising at one or another libidinal state.

17

SIGMUND FREUD

Character and Anal Erotism*

Among those whom one tries to help by means of psycho-analytic treatment, one very often meets with a type of character in which certain traits are strongly marked, while at the same time one's attention is arrested by the behaviour of these persons in regard to a certain bodily function and of the organ connected with it during their childhood. I can no longer say on what precise occasions I first received the impression that a systematic relationship exists between this type of character and the activities of this organ, but I can assure the reader that no theoretical anticipations of mine played any part in its production.

My belief in such a relationship has been so much strengthened by accumulated experience that I venture to make it the subject of a communication.

The persons whom I am about to describe are remarkable for a regular combination of the three following peculiarities: they are exceptionally *orderly*, *parsimonious*, and *obstinate*. Each of these words really covers a small group or series of traits which are related to one another. "Orderly" comprises both bodily cleanliness and reliability and conscientiousness in the performance of petty duties: the opposite of it would be "untidy" and "negligent." "Parsimony" may be exaggerated up to the point of avarice; and obstinacy may amount to defiance, with which irascibility and vindictiveness may easily be associated. The two latter

* First published in the *Psychiatrisch-Neurologische Wochenschrift*, Bd. IX., 1908; reprinted in *Sammlung, Zweite Folge*. Reprinted here by permission of The Hogarth Press Ltd. from Freud's *Collected Papers*, Volume 2 (The International Psycho-Analytical Library, No. 8). Translated by R. C. McWatters.

qualities—parsimony and obstinacy—hang together more closely than the third, orderliness; they are, too, the more constant element in the whole complex. It seems to me, however, incontestable that all three in some way belong together.

From the history of the early childhood of these persons one easily learns that they took a long time to overcome the infantile *incontinentia alvi,* and that even in later childhood they had to complain of isolated accidents relating to this function. As infants they seem to have been among those who refuse to empty the bowel when placed on the chamber, because they derive an incidental pleasure from the act of defæcation;[1] for they assert that even in somewhat later years they have found a pleasure in holding back their stools, and they remember, though more readily of their brothers and sisters than of themselves, all sorts of unseemly performances with the stools when passed. From these indications we infer that the erotogenic significance of the anal zone is intensified in the innate sexual constitution of these persons; but since none of these weaknesses and peculiarities are to be found in them once childhood has been passed, we must conclude that the anal zone has lost its erotogenic significance in the course of their development, and that the constant appearance of this triad of peculiarities in their character may be brought into relation with the disappearance of their anal erotism.

I know that no one feels inclined to accept a proposition which appears unintelligible, and for which no explanation can be offered, but we can find the basis of such an explanation in the postulates I have formulated in my *Drei Abhandlungen zur Sexualtheorie.* I there attempt to show that the sexual instinct of man is very complex and is made up of contributions from numerous components and partial impulses. The peripheral stimulation of certain specialized parts (genitals, mouth, anus, urethra), which may be called erotogenic zones, furnishes important contributions to the production of sexual excitation, but the fate of the stimuli arising in these areas varies according to their source and according to the age of the person concerned. Generally speaking, only a part of them finds a place in the sexual life; another part is deflected from a sexual aim and is directed to

---

[1] Cf. Freud, *Drei Abhandlungen zur Sexualtheorie,* 1905.

other purposes, a process which may be called sublimation. During the period of life which may be distinguished as the "sexual latency period," *i.e.* from the end of the fourth year to the first manifestations of puberty at about eleven, reaction-formations, such as shame, disgust, and morality, are formed in the mental economy at the expense of the excitations proceeding from the erotogenic zones, and these reaction-formations erect themselves as barriers against the later activity of the sexual instinct. Now anal erotism is one of those components of the instinct which in the course of evolution and in accordance with our present civilizing education has become useless for sexual aims: it would therefore be no very surprising result if these traits of orderliness, parsimony, and obstinacy, which are so prominent in persons who were formerly anal erotics, turned out to be the first and most constant results of the sublimation of anal erotism.[2]

---

[2] Since it is just these remarks about the anal erotism of infants in my three contributions to the sexual theory that have most scandalized uncomprehending readers, I venture to insert here an observation which I owe to a very intelligent patient. "An acquaintance of mine who has read the *Drei Abhandlungen zur Sexualtheorie* was talking about the book and said he fully accepted it, but one passage—though naturally he also accepts and understands it—appeared to him so grotesque and comic that he sat down and laughed over it for a quarter of an hour. This passage runs: 'It is one of the best signs of later eccentricity or nervousness if an infant obstinately refuses to empty its bowel when placed on the chamber, that is, when the nurse wishes, but withholds this function at his own pleasure. Naturally it does not matter to the child if he soils his bed; his only concern is not to lose the pleasure incidental to the act of defæcation.' The picture of this infant sitting on the chamber and deliberating whether he should allow such a limitation of his personal independence, and of his anxiety not to lose the pleasure of defæcation, caused my friend the greatest merriment. Some twenty minutes later, as we were sitting at tea, my acquaintance suddenly remarked without any preliminary, 'Do you know, there just occurs to me, as I see the cocoa in front of me, an idea that I always had as a child. I then always pretended to myself that I was the cocoa manufacturer Van Houten' (he pronounced it 'Van Hauten'), 'that I possessed a great secret for the preparation of this cocoa, and that all the world was trying to get this valuable secret from me, but that I carefully kept it to myself. Why it was Van Houten that I hit upon I do not know. Probably it was that his advertisements made the greatest impression on me.' Laughing, and without thinking much about the meaning of my words, I replied, '*Wann haut'n* (Van Houten) *die Mutter?*' [When do mothers smack?] It was only later that I realized that my pun really contained the key to the whole of his sudden recollection from childhood, which I now recognized as a striking example of a screen-phantasy, setting at rest the sense of guilt by means of a complete reversal of the value of its memory content, while it retained its reference to

The inherent necessity of this relationship is naturally not clear even to myself, but I can make some suggestions which help towards an understanding of it. The cleanliness, orderliness, and reliability give exactly the impression of a reaction-formation against an interest in things that are unclean and intrusive and ought not to be on the body ("Dirt is matter in the wrong place"). To bring obstinacy into relation with interest in defæcation seems no easy task, but it should be remembered that infants can very early behave with great self-will about parting with their stools (see above), and that painful stimuli to the skin of the buttocks (which is connected with the anal erotogenic zone) are an instrument in the education of the child designed to break his self-will and make him submissive. As an expression of defiance or of defiant mockery, a challenge referring to a caress on this part of the body is used even at the present day, as in former times—that is, it represents a tender feeling which has undergone repression. An exposure of the buttocks corresponds to the reduction of this speech to a gesture; in Goethe's *Götz von Berlichingen* we find both speech and gesture introduced most appropriately as expression of defiance.

The connections which exist between the two complexes of interest in money and of defæcation, which seem so dissimilar, appear to be the most far-reaching. It is well known to every physician who has used psycho-analysis that the most refractory and obdurate cases of so-called chronic constipation in neurotics can be cured by this means. This is less surprising if we remember that this function has shown itself equally amenable to hypnotic suggestion. But in psycho-analysis one only attains this result when one deals with the money complex of the persons con-

---

actual experience (the nutritional process) and was supported by a phonetic association: 'cocoa'—'Wann haut'n' (Van Houten). (Displacement from behind forwards; excrement becomes aliment; the shameful substance which has to be concealed turns into a secret which enriches the world.) It was interesting to me how in this case, after a defense-reaction, which to be sure took the comparatively mild form of a merely formal objection, the most striking evidence was supplied from the subject's own unconscious after a quarter of an hour without any effort on his part.'

[Besides the pun on the word Van Houten, there is probably a further association between the German for cocoa (*Kakao*) and for the nursery term for fæces in that language, *Kakis*. Compare also the English *caca* for fæces.— Trans.]

cerned, and induces them to bring it into consciousness with all its connections. One might suppose that the neurosis is here only following a hint from common speech which calls a person who keeps too careful a hold on his money "dirty" or "filthy," but this would be far too superficial an explanation. In reality, wherever archaic modes of thought predominate or have persisted—in ancient civilizations, in myth, fairy-tale and superstition, in unconscious thoughts and dreams, and in the neuroses—money comes into the closest relation with excrement. We know how the money which the devil gives his paramours turns to excrement after his departure, and the devil is most certainly nothing more than a personification of the unconscious instinctual forces.[3] The superstition, too, which associates the finding of treasure with defæcation is well known, and everyone is familiar with the figure of the "excretor of ducats" (*Dukatenscheisser*).[4] Even in the early Babylon cult gold is "the excrement of Hell," Mammon = ilu manman.[5] Thus in following common speech, the neurosis, here as elsewhere, takes the words in their original most significant sense, and wherever it appears to express a word figuratively it usually only reproduces its original meaning.

It is possible that the contrast between the most precious substance known to man and the most worthless, which he rejects as "something thrown out," has contributed to this identification of gold with fæces.

Yet another circumstance facilitates this equivalence in the mental processes involved in neurosis. The original erotic interest in defæcation is, as we know, destined to be extinguished in later years; it is in these years that the interest in money is making its appearance as something new which was unknown in childhood. This makes it easier for the earlier impulse, which is in process of relinquishing its aim, to be carried over to the new one.

---

[3] Compare hysterical possession and demoniac epidemics.

[4] [Unfamiliar to English readers, but compare "the goose which lays golden eggs."—Trans.]

[5] Jeremias, *Das Alte Testament im Lichte des alten Orients*, 1906, p. 216, and *Babylonisches im Neuen Testament*, 1906, p. 96. "Mammon is Babylonian 'Manman,' another name of Nergal, the god of the underworld. According to an Oriental myth which has passed over into sagas and folk-tales, gold is the excrement of hell; see *Monotheistische Strömungen innerhalb der babylonischen Religion*, S. 16, Anmk. i."

If there is any reality in the relation described here between anal erotism and this triad of character-traits, one may expect to find but little of the "anal character" in persons who have retained the erotogenic quality of the anal zone into adult life, as for example certain homosexuals. Unless I am greatly mistaken experience on the whole is fully in accord with this anticipation.

One ought to consider whether other types of character do not also show a connection with the excitability of particular erotogenic zones. As yet I am aware only of the intense, "burning" ambition of those who formerly suffered from enuresis. At any rate, one can give a formula for the formation of the ultimate character from the constituent character-traits: the permanent character-traits are either unchanged perpetuations of the original impulses, sublimations of them, or reaction-formations against them.

18

ALFRED ADLER

Individual Psychology, Its Assumptions and Its Results*

A survey of the views and theories of most psychologists indicates a peculiar limitation both in the nature of their field of investigation and in their methods of inquiry. They act as if experience and knowledge of mankind were, with conscious intent, to be excluded from our investigations and all value and importance denied to artistic and creative vision as well as to intuition itself. While the experimental psychologists collect and devise phenomena in order to determine types of reaction—that is, are concerned with the physiology of the psychical life properly speaking —other psychologists arrange all forms of expression and manifestations in old customary, or at best slightly altered, systems. By this procedure they naturally rediscover the interdependence and connection in individual expressions, implied from the very beginning in their schematic attitude toward the psyche.

Either the foregoing method is employed or an attempt is made by means of small, if possible measurable individual phenomena of a physiological nature, to construct psychical states and thought by means of an equation. The fact that all subjective thinking and subjective immersion on the part of the investigator are excluded—although in reality they dominate the very nature of these connections—is from this viewpoint regarded as an advantage.

* Reprinted from *The Practice and Theory of Individual Psychology* by permission of Routledge and Kegan Paul Ltd. and the Humanities Press Inc.

The method employed, and the very importance it seems to possess as a preparation for the human mind, reminds us of the type of natural science completely antiquated to-day, with its rigid systems, replaced everywhere now by views that attempt to grasp living phenomena and their variations as connected wholes, biologically, philosophically, and psychologically. This is also the purpose of that movement in psychology that I have called *"comparative individual-psychology."* By starting with the assumption of the *unity of the individual,* an attempt is made to obtain a picture of this unified personality regarded as a variant of individual life-manifestations and forms of expression. The individual traits are then compared with one another, brought into a common plane, and finally fused together to form a composite portrait that is, in turn, individualized.[1]

It may have been noticed that this method of looking upon man's psychic life is by no means either unusual or even particularly daring. This type of approach is particularly noticeable in the study of child-psychology, in spite of other lines of inquiry also used there. It is the essence and the nature above all of the work of the artist, be he painter, sculptor, musician, or particularly poet, so to present the minute traits of his creations that the observer is able to obtain from them the general principles of personality. He is thus in a position to reconstruct those very things that the artist when thinking of his *finale* had previously hidden therein. Since life in any given society, life without any of the preconceptions of science, has always been under the ban of the question "whither?", we are warranted in definitely stating that, scientific views to the contrary notwithstanding, no man has ever made a judgment about an event without endeavouring to strain toward the point which seems to bind together all the psychic manifestations of an individual; even to an *imagined goal* if necessary.

When I hurry home, I am certain to exhibit to any observer the carriage, expression, the gait, and the gestures that are to be expected of a person returning home. My reflexes indeed might be different from those anticipated, the causes might vary. The

---

[1] William Stern has come to the same conclusions starting from a different method of approach.

essential point to be grasped psychologically and the one which interests us exclusively and practically and psychologically more than all others, *is the path followed.*

Let me observe that if I know the goal of a person I know in a general way what will happen. I am in a position to bring into their proper order each of the successive movements made, to view them in their connections, to correct them and to make, where necessary, the required adaptations for my approximate psychological knowledge of these associations. If I am acquainted only with the causes, know only the reflexes, the reaction-times, the ability to repeat and such facts, I am aware of nothing that actually takes place in the soul of the man.

We must remember that the person under observation would not know what to do with himself were he not orientated toward some goal. As long as we are not acquainted with the objective which determines his "life-line," the whole system of his recognized reflexes, together with all their causal conditions, can give us no certainty as to his next series of movements. They might be brought into harmony with practically any psychic resultant. This deficiency is most clearly felt in association-tests. I would never expect a man suffering from some great disappointment to associate "tree" with "rope." The moment I knew his objective, however, namely suicide, then I might very well expect that particular sequence of thoughts—expect it with such certainty that I would remove knives, poison, and weapons from his immediate vicinity.

If we look at the matter more closely, we shall find the following law holding in the development of all psychic happenings: *we cannot think, feel, will, or act without the perception of some goal.* For all the causalities in the world would not suffice to conquer the chaos of the future nor obviate the planlessness to which we would be bound to fall a victim. All activity would persist in the stage of uncontrolled gropings; the economy visible in our psychic life unattained; we should be unintegrated and in every aspect of our physiognomy, in every personal touch, similar to organisms of the rank of the amœba.

No one will deny that by assuming an objective for our psychic life we accommodate ourselves better to reality. This can be easily demonstrated. For its truth in individual examples, where phenomena are torn from their proper connections, no doubt exists. Only watch, from this point of view, the attempts at walking made by a small child or a woman recovering from a confinement. Naturally he who approaches this whole matter without any theory is likely to find its deeper significance escape him. Yet it is a fact that before the first step has been taken the objective of the person's movement has already been determined.

In the same way it can be demonstrated that all psychic activities are given a direction by means of a previously determined goal. All the temporary and partially visible objectives, after the short period of psychic development of childhood, are under the domination of an imagined terminal goal, of a final point felt and conceived of as definitely fixed. In other words the psychic life of man is made to fit into the fifth act like a character drawn by a good dramatist.

The conclusion thus to be drawn from the unbiased study of any personality viewed from the standpoint of individual-psychology leads us to the following important proposition: *every psychic phenomenon, if it is to give us any understanding of a person, can only be grasped and understood if regarded as a preparation for some goal.*

To what an extent this conception promotes our psychological understanding, is clearly apparent as soon as we become aware of the *multiplicity of meaning of those psychical processes that have been torn from their proper context.* Take for example the case of a man with a "bad memory." Assume that he is quite conscious of this fact and that an examination discloses an inferior capacity for the repetition of meaningless syllables. According to present usage in psychology, which we might more properly call an abuse, we would have to make the following inference: the man is suffering, from hereditary or pathological causes, from a deficient capacity for repetition. Incidentally, let me add, that in this type of investigation we generally find the inference already stated in different words in the premises. In this case *e.g.* we have the following proposition: if a man has a bad memory, or if he only remembers a few words—then he has an inferior capacity for repetition.

The procedure in individual-psychology is completely different.

After excluding the possibility of all organic causes, we would ask ourselves what is the objective of this weakness of memory? This we could only determine if we were in possession of an intimate knowledge of the whole individual, so that an understanding of one part becomes possible only after we have understood the whole. And we should probably find the following to hold true in a large number of cases: this man is attempting to prove to himself and to others that for certain reasons of a fundamental nature, that are either not to be named or have remained unconscious, *but which can most effectively be represented by poorness of memory,* he must not permit himself to perform some particular act or to come to a given decision (change of profession, studies, examination, marriage). We should then have unmasked this weakness of memory as tendentious and could understand its importance as a weapon against a contemplated undertaking. In every test of ability to repeat we should then expect to find the deficiency due to the secret life-plan of an individual. The question then to be asked is how such deficiencies or evils arise. They may be simply "arranged" by purposely underlining general physiological weaknesses and interpreting them as personal sufferings. Others may succeed either by subjective absorption into an abnormal condition or by pre-occupation with dangerous pessimistic anticipations, in so weakening their faith in their own capacities, that their strength, attention or will-power are only partially at their disposal.

A similar observation may be made in the case of affects. To give one more example, take the case of a woman subject to outbreaks of anxiety recurring at certain intervals. As long as nothing of greater significance than this was discernible, the assumption of some hereditary degeneration, some disease of the vaso-motor system, of the vagus nerve, etc., sufficed. It is also possible that we might have regarded ourselves as having arrived at a fuller understanding of the case, if we had discovered in the previous history of the patient, some frightful experience, or traumatic condition and attributed the disease to it. As soon, however, as we examined the personality of this individual and inquired into her directive-lines we discovered an excess of will-to-power, with which anxiety as a weapon of aggression had associated itself, an anxiety which was to become operative as soon as the force of the will-power had abated and the desired resonance was absent, a situation occurring, for example, when the patient's husband left the house without her consent.

Our science demands a markedly individualizing procedure and is consequently not much given to generalizations. For general guidance I would like to propound the following rule: *as soon as the goal of a psychic movement or its life-plan has been recognized, then we are to assume that all the movements of its constituent parts will coincide with both the goal and the life-plan.*

This formulation, with some minor provisos, is to be maintained in the widest sense. It retains its value even if inverted: *the properly understood part-movements must when combined, give the picture of an integrated life-plan and final goal.* Consequently we insist that, without worrying about the *tendencies, milieu and experiences,* all psychical powers are under the control of a directive idea and all expressions of emotion, feeling, thinking, willing, acting, dreaming as well as psycho-pathological phenomena, are permeated by one unified life-plan. Let me, by a slight suggestion, prove and yet soften down these heretical propositions: more important than tendencies, objective experience and milieu is *the subjective evaluation,* an evaluation which stands furthermore in a certain, often strange, relation to realities. Out of this evaluation, however, which generally results in the development of a permanent mood *of the nature of a feeling of inferiority* there arises, depending upon the unconscious technique of our thought-apparatus, an imagined goal, an attempt at a planned final compensation and a life-plan.

I have so far spoken a good deal of men who have "grasped the situation." My discussion has been as irritating as that of the theorists of the "psychology of understanding" or of the psychology of personality, who always break off just when they are about to show us what exactly it is they have understood, as for instance, Jaspers. The danger of discussing briefly this aspect of our investigations, namely, *the results of individual-psychology,* is sufficiently great. To do so we should be compelled to force the dynamics of life into static words and pictures, overlook differences in order to obtain unified formulas, and have, in short, in our description to make that very mistake that in practice is strictly prohibited: of approaching the psychic life of the individual with a dry formula, as the Freudian school attempt.

This then being my assumption, I shall in the following present to you the most important results of our study of psychic life. Let me emphasize the fact that the dynamics of psychic life that I am about to describe hold equally for healthy and diseased. What distinguishes the nervous from the healthy individual is the stronger safeguarding tendency with which the former's life-plan is filled. With regard to the "positing of a goal" and the life-plan adjusted to it there are no fundamental differences.

I shall consequently speak of a general goal of man. A thorough-going study has taught us that we can best understand the manifold and diverse movements of the psyche as soon as our *most general pre-supposition,* that the psyche has as its objective the *goal of superiority,* is recognized. Great thinkers have given expression to much of this; in part everyone knows it, but in the main it is hidden in mysterious darkness and comes definitely to the front only in insanity or in ecstatic conditions. Whether a person desires to be an artist, the first in his profession, or a tyrant in his home, to hold converse with God or humiliate other people; whether he regards his suffering as the most important thing in the world to which everyone must show obeisance, whether he is chasing after unattainable ideas or old deities, over-stepping all limits and norms, at every part of his way he is guided and spurred on by his longing for superiority, the thought of his godlikeness, the belief in his special magical power. In his love he desires to experience his power over his partner. In his purely optional choice of profession the goal floating before his mind manifests itself in all sorts of exaggerated anticipations and fears, and thirsting for revenge, he experiences in suicide a triumph over all obstacles. In order to gain control over an object or over a person, he is capable of proceeding along a straight line, bravely, proudly, overbearing, obstinate, cruel; or he may on the other hand prefer, forced by experience, to resort to by-paths and circuitous routes, to gain his victory by obedience, submission, mildness and modesty. Nor have traits of character an independent existence, for they are also adjusted to the individual life-plan, really representing the most important preparations for conflict possessed by the latter.

This goal of complete superiority, with its strange appearance at times, does not come from the world of reality. Inherently we must place it under "fictions" and "imaginations." Of these Vaihinger (*The Philosophy of "As If"*) rightly says that their importance lies in the fact that whereas in themselves without meaning, they nevertheless possess in practice the greatest importance. For our case this coincides to such an extent that we may say *that this fiction of a goal of superiority so ridiculous from the view-point of reality, has become the principal conditioning factor of our life as hitherto known.* It is this that teaches us to differentiate, gives us poise and security, moulds and guides our deeds and activities and forces our spirit to look ahead and to perfect itself. There is of course also an obverse side, for *this goal introduces into our life a hostile and fighting tendency,* robs us of the simplicity of our feelings and is always the cause for an estrangement from reality since it puts near to our hearts the idea of attempting to over-power reality. Whoever takes this goal of godlikeness seriously or literally, will soon be compelled to flee from real life and compromise, by seeking a life within life; if fortunate in art, but more generally in pietism, neurosis or crime.[2]

I cannot give you particulars here. A clear indication of this super-mundane goal is to be found in every individual. Sometimes this is to be gathered from a man's carriage, sometimes it is disclosed only in his demands and expectations. Occasionally one comes upon its track in obscure memories, phantasies and dreams. If purposely sought it is rarely obtained. However, every bodily or mental attitude indicates clearly its origin in a striving for power and carries within itself the ideal of a kind of perfection and infallibility. In those cases that lie on the confines of neurosis there is always to be discovered a reinforced pitting of oneself against the environment, against the dead or heroes of the past.

A test of the correctness of our interpretation can be easily made. If everyone possesses within himself an ideal of superiority,

---

[2] Cf. also "The Problem of Distance," in this volume [pp. 100-108 of *The Practice and Theory of Individual Psychology*].

such as we find to an exaggerated degree among the nervous, then we ought to encounter phenomena whose purpose is the oppression, the minimizing and undervaluation of others. Traits of character such as intolerance, dogmatism, envy, pleasure at the misfortune of others, conceit, boastfulness, mistrust, avarice,— in short all those attitudes that are the substitutes for a struggle, force their way through to a far greater extent, in fact, than self-preservation demands.

Similarly, either simultaneously or interchangingly, depending upon the zeal and the self-confidence with which the final goal is sought, we see emerging indications of pride, emulation, courage, the attitudes of saving, bestowing and directing. A psychological investigation demands so much objectivity that a moral evaluation will not disturb the survey. In fact *the different levels of character-traits* actually neutralize our good-will and our disapproval. Finally we must remember that these hostile traits, particularly in the case of the nervous, are often so concealed that their possessor is justifiably astonished and irritated when attention is drawn to them. For example, the elder of two children can create quite an uncomfortable situation in trying to arrogate to himself through defiance and obstinacy, all authority in the family. The younger child pursues a wiser course, poses as a model of obedience and succeeds in this manner in becoming the idol of the family and in having all wishes gratified. As ambition spurs him on, all willingness to obey becomes destroyed and pathological-compulsion phenomena develop, by means of which every parental order is nullified even when the parents notice that the child is making efforts to remain obedient. Thus we have an act of obedience immediately nullified by means of a compulsion-thought. We get an idea of the circuitous path taken here in order to arrive at the same objective as that of the other child.

The whole weight of the personal striving for power and superiority passes, at a very early age in the case of the child, into the form and the content of its striving, its thought being able to absorb for the time being only so much as the eternal, real and physiologically rooted *community-feeling* permits. Out of the latter are developed tenderness, love of neighbour, friendship and love, the desire for power unfolding itself in a veiled manner and

seeking secretly to push its way along the path of group consciousness.

At this place let me go out of my way to endorse an old fundamental conception of all who know human nature. Every marked
attitude of a man can be traced back to an origin in childhood.
In the nursery are formed and prepared all of man's future attitudes. Fundamental changes are produced only by means of an
exceedingly high degree of introspection or among neurotics by
means of the physician's individual psychological analysis.

Let me, on the basis of another case, one which must have
happened innumerable times, discuss in even greater detail the
positing of goals by nervous people. A remarkably gifted man
who by his amiability and refined behaviour had gained the love
of a girl of high character, became engaged to her. He then
forced upon her his ideal of education which made severe demands upon her. For a time she endured these unbearable orders
but finally put an end to all further ordeals by breaking off relations. The man then broke down and became a prey to nervous
attacks. The individual-psychological examination of the case
showed that the superiority-goal in the case of this patient—as
his domineering demands upon his bride indicated—had long ago
pushed from his mind all thought of marriage, and that his object
really was to secretly work toward a break, secretly because he
did not feel himself equal to the open struggle in which he
imagined marriage to consist. *This disbelief in himself* itself
dated from his earliest childhood, to a time during which he, an
only son, lived with an early widowed mother somewhat cut off
from the world. During this period, spent in continuous family
quarrels he had received the ineradicable impression, one he had
never openly admitted to himself, that he was not sufficiently
virile, and would never be able to cope with a woman. These
psychical attitudes are comparable to a permanent inferiority-
feeling and it is easily understood how they had decisively interfered in his life and compelled him to obtain prestige along other
lines than those obtainable through the fulfilment of the demands
of reality.

It is clear that the patient attained just what his concealed preparations for bachelordom aimed at, and what his fear of a life-partner, with the quarrels and restless relationship this implied, had awakened in him. Nor can it be denied that he took the same attitude toward both his bride and his mother, namely the wish to conquer. This attitude induced by a longing for victory has been magnificently misinterpreted by the Freudian school as the permanently incestuous condition of being enamoured of the mother. As a matter of fact this reinforced childhood-feeling of inferiority occasioned by the patient's painful relation to his mother, spurred this man on to prevent any struggle in later life with a wife by providing himself with all kinds of safeguards. Whatever it is we understand by love, in this particular case it is simply *a means to an end* and that end is the final securing of a triumph over some suitable woman. Here we have the reason for the continual tests and orders and for the cancelling of the engagement. This solution had not just "happened," but had on the contrary been artistically prepared and arranged with the old weapons of experience employed previously in the case of his mother. A defeat in marriage was out of the question because marriage was prevented.

Although we consequently realize nothing puzzling in the behaviour of this man and should recognize in his domineering attitude simply aggression *posing as love,* some words of explanation are necessary to clear up the less intelligible nervous breakdown. We are here entering upon the real domain of the psychology of neuroses. As in the nursery so here our patient has been worsted by a woman. The neurotic individual is led in such cases to strengthen his protections and to retire to a fairly great distance from danger.[3] Our patient is utilizing his break-down in order to feed an evil reminiscence, to bring up the question of guilt again, to solve it in an unfavourable sense for the woman, so that in future he may either proceed with even greater caution or take final leave of love and matrimony! This man is thirty years old now. Let us assume that he is going to carry his pain along with him for another ten or twenty years and that he is

---

[3] Cf. "The Problem of Distance" in this volume. [*The Practice and Theory of Individual Psychology,* pp. 100-108]

going to mourn for his lost ideal for the same length of time. He has thereby protected himself against every love-affair and permanently saved himself from new defeat.

He interprets his nervous break-down by means of old, now strengthened, weapons of experience, just as he had as a child refused to eat, sleep or to do anything and played the rôle of a dying person. His fortunes ebb and *his beloved carries all the stigma,* he himself rises superior to her in both culture and character, and lo and behold: he has attained that for which he longed, for he is the superior person, becomes the better man and his partner like all girls is the guilty one. Girls cannot cope with the man in him. In this manner he has consummated what as a child he had already felt, the duty of demonstrating his superiority over the female sex.

We can now understand that this nervous reaction can never be sufficiently definite or adequate. *He is to wander through the world as a living reproach against women.*[4]

Were he aware of his secret plans he would realize how ill-natured and evil-intentioned all his actions have been. However he would, in that case, not succeed in attaining his object of elevating himself above women. He would see himself just as we see him, falsifying the weights and how everything he has done has only led to a goal previously set. His success could not be described as due to "fate" nor assuredly would it represent any increased prestige. But his goal, his life-plan and his life-falsehood demand this prestige! In consequence it so "happens" that the *life-plan remains in the unconscious,* so that the patient may believe that an *implacable fate* and not a long prepared and long meditated plan for which he alone is responsible, is at work.

I cannot go into a detailed description of what I call the "distance" that the neurotic individual places between himself and the final issue, which in this case is marriage. The discussion of the manner in which he accomplishes it I must also postpone to my chapter on nervous "arrangements." I should like to point out here however that the "distance" expresses itself clearly in the

---

[4] The paranoidal trait is recognizable. Cf. "Life-lie and Responsibility in Neurosis and Psychosis," in this volume. [*The Practice and Theory of Individual Psychology,* pp. 235-245.]

"hesitating attitudes," the principles, the point of view and the life-falsehood. In its evolution neurosis and psychosis play leading rôles. The appropriation for this purpose of perversions and every type of impotence arising from the latter is quite frequent. Such a man concludes his account and reconciles himself with life by constructing one or a number of "if-clauses." "If conditions had been different. . . ."

The importance of the educational questions that arise and upon which our school lays the greatest stress (*Heilen und Bilden,* Munich, 1913) follows from what has been discussed.

From the method of presentation of the present work it is to be inferred that as in the case of a psychotherapeutic cure, our analysis proceeds backwards; examining first the *superiority-goal,* explaining by means of it the type of *conflict-attitude*[5] adopted particularly by nervous patients and only then attempting to investigate the sources of the vital psychic mechanism. One of the bases of the psychical dynamics we have already mentioned, the presumably unavoidable artistic trait of the psychical apparatus which, by means of the *artistic artifice of the creation of a fiction and the setting of a goal,* adjusts itself to and extends itself into the world of possible reality. I shall now proceed to explain briefly how the goal of godlikeness transforms the relation of the individual to his environment into hostility and how the struggle drives an individual towards a goal either along a direct path such as aggressiveness or along by-ways suggested by precaution. If we trace the history of this aggressive attitude back to childhood we always come upon the outstanding fact that *throughout the whole period of development, the child possesses a feeling of inferiority in its relations both to parents and the world at large.* Because of the immaturity of his organs, his uncertainty and lack of independence, because of his need for dependence upon stronger natures and his frequent and painful feeling of subordination to others, a sensation of inadequacy develops that betrays itself throughout life. This feeling of inferiority is the cause of his continual restlessness as a child, his craving for action, his playing of rôles, the pitting of his strength

---

[5] The "struggle for existence," the "struggle of all against all," etc., are merely other perspectives of the same kind.

against that of others, his anticipatory pictures of the future and his physical as well as mental preparations. The whole potential educability of the child depends upon this feeling of insufficiency. In this way the future becomes transformed into the land that will bring him compensations. His conflict-attitude is again reflected in his feeling of inferiority; and only conflict does he regard as a compensation which will do away permanently with his present inadequate condition and will enable him to picture himself as elevated above others. Thus the child arrives at the positing of a goal, an imagined goal of superiority, whereby his poverty is transformed into wealth, his subordination into domination, his suffering into happiness and pleasure, his ignorance into omniscience and his incapacity into artistic creation. The longer and more definitely the child feels his insecurity, the more he suffers either from physical or marked mental weakness, the more he is aware of life's neglect, the higher will this goal be placed and the more faithfully will it be adhered to. He who wishes to recognize the nature of this goal, should watch a child at play, at optionally selected occupations or when phantasying about his future profession. The apparent change in these phenomena is purely external for in every new goal the child imagines a predetermined triumph. A variant of this weaving of plans, one frequently found among weakly aggressive children, among girls and sickly individuals, might be mentioned here. This consists of so misusing their frailties that they compel others to become subordinate to them. They will later on pursue the same method until their life-plan and life-falsehood have been clearly unmasked.

The attentive observer will find the nature of the *compensatory dynamics* presenting a quite extraordinary aspect as soon as he permits the sexual rôle to be relegated to one of minor importance and realizes that it is the former that is impelling the individual toward superhuman goals. In our present civilization both the girl and the youth will feel themselves forced to extraordinary exertions and manœuvres. A large number of these are admittedly of a distinctively progressive nature. To preserve this progressive nature but to ferret out those by-paths that lead us astray and cause illness, to make these harmless, that is our object and one that takes us far beyond the limits of medical art. It is to this aspect of our subject that society, child-education and folk-education may look for germs of a far-reaching kind. *For the aim of this point-of-view is to gain a reinforced sense of reality, the development of a feeling of responsibility and a substitution for latent hatred of a feeling of mutual goodwill, all of which can be gained only by the conscious evolution of a feeling for the common weal and the conscious destruction of the will-to-power.*

He who is looking for the power-phantasies of the child will find them drawn with a master hand by Dostoevsky in his novel entitled *A Raw Youth*. I found them blatantly apparent in one of my patients. In the dreams and thoughts of this individual the following wish recurred repeatedly: others should die so that he might have enough room in which to live, others should suffer privations so that he might obtain more favourable opportunities. This attitude reminds one of the inconsiderateness and heartlessness of many men who trace all evil back to the fact that there are already too many people in the world; impulses that have unquestionably made the world-war more palatable. The feeling of certainty, in fictions of this kind, has been taken over in the above-mentioned case from the basic facts of capitalistic trade, where admittedly, the better the condition of one individual the worse that of another. "I want to be a grave-digger," said a four-year-old boy to me; "I want to be the person who digs graves for others."

19

KARL ABRAHAM

Contributions to the Theory
of the Anal Character*

The wide field which is open to the science of psycho-analysis at the present time offers an abundance of instances of the rapid increase of psychological knowledge along the lines of purely inductive investigation. Perhaps the most remarkable and instructive of these is the development of the theory of the anal character. In 1908, about fifteen years after the appearance of his first contributions to the psychology of the neuroses, Freud published a short paper entitled "Character and Anal Erotism." It occupied only three pages of a journal, and was a model of condensed statement and of cautious and clear summing up. The gradually increasing number of his co-workers, among whom may be mentioned Sadger, Ferenczi, and Jones, has helped to extend the range of ascertained knowledge. The theory concerning the products of the transformation of anal erotism gained unsuspected significance when in 1913, following on Jones' important investigation on "Hate and Anal Erotism in the Obsessional Neurosis," Freud formulated an early "pregenital" organization of the libido. He considered that the symptoms of the obsessional neurosis were the result of a regression of libido to this stage of development, which is characterized by a preponderance of the anal and sadistic component instincts. This threw a new light both on the symptomatology of the obsessional neurosis and on the charac-

* Reprinted from the Selected Papers of Karl Abraham, M.D. (International Psycho-Analytical Library, No. 13) by permission of The Hogarth Press Ltd., and Basic Books, Inc.

terological peculiarities of the person suffering from it—on the so-called "obsessional character." I might add, anticipating a future publication, that very similar anomalies of character are found in those people who tend to melancholic or manic states of mind. And the strictest possible study of the sadistic-anal character-traits is necessary before we can proceed to investigate those last mentioned diseases which are still so enigmatical to us. The present study is mainly concerned with the anal contributions to the formation of character. Jones' [1] last great work on this subject presents an abundance of valuable material, but it does not exhaust it. For the work of a single person cannot do justice to the multiplicity and complexity of the phenomena; each analyst who possesses data of his own should publish them, and so help to contribute to the body of psycho-analytical knowledge. In the same way the purpose of the following remarks is to extend the theory of the anal character-traits in certain directions. Another problem of great theoretical importance will be very frequently alluded to in this study. Up to the present we understand only very incompletely the particular psychological connections that exist between the two impulses of sadism and anal erotism which we always mention in close association with each other, almost as a matter of habit. And I shall attempt the solution of this question in a later paper.

In his first description of the anal character Freud has said that certain neurotics present three particularly pronounced character-traits, namely, a love of orderliness which often develops into pedantry, a parsimony which easily turns to miserliness, and an obstinacy which may become an angry defiance. He established the fact that the primary pleasure in emptying the bowels and in its products was particularly emphasized in these persons; and also that after successful repression their coprophilia either becomes sublimated into pleasure in painting, modelling, and similar activities, or proceeds along the path of reaction-formation to a special love of cleanliness. Finally he pointed out the unconscious equivalence of fæces and money or other valuables. Among other observations Sadger[2] has remarked that per-

[1] "Anal-erotic Character Traits" (1918).
[2] "Analerotik und Analcharakter" (1910).

sons with a pronounced anal character are usually convinced that they can do everything better than other people. He also speaks of a contradiction in their character, namely, great perseverance side by side with the tendency to put off doing everything till the last moment.

I will pass over isolated remarks in psycho-analytic literature by other authors and turn to Jones' very thorough and comprehensive study on this subject. I might remark in advance that I do not differ from this author on any points, but that nevertheless I feel that his statements need amplification and completion in certain respects.

Jones quite rightly distinguishes two different acts in the process we usually designate as the education of the child in cleanly habits. The child has not only to be taught not to soil its body and surroundings with excreta, but it has also to be educated to perform its excretory functions at regular times. In other words, it has to give up both its coprophilia and its pleasure in the process of excretion. This double process of limitation of infantile impulses together with its consequences in the psychical sphere requires further investigation.

The child's primitive method of evacuation brings the entire surface of its buttocks and lower extremities in contact with urine and fæces. This contact seems unpleasant, even repulsive, to adults, whose repressions have removed them from the infantile reaction to these processes. They cannot appreciate the sources of pleasure on which the libido of the infant can draw, in whom the stream of warm urine on the skin and contact with the warm mass of fæces produce pleasurable feelings. The child only begins to give signs of discomfort when the excreted products grow cold against its body. It is the same pleasure which the child seeks when it handles its fæces at a somewhat later period. Ferenczi [3] has traced the further development of this infantile tendency. It must not be forgotten, moreover, that pleasure in the sight and smell of fæces is associated with these feelings.

The special pleasure in the *act* of excretion, which we must differentiate from pleasure in the *products* of the excretory process, comprises besides physical sensations a psychical grati-

[3] "On the Ontogenesis of an Interest in Money" (1916).

fication which is based on the *achievement* of that act. Now in that the child's training demands strict regularity in its excretions as well as cleanliness it exposes the child's narcissism to a first severe test. The majority of children adapt themselves sooner or later to these demands. In favourable cases the child succeeds in making a virtue out of necessity, as it were; in other words, in identifying itself with the requirements of its educators and being proud of its attainment. The primary injury to its narcissism is thus compensated, and its original feeling of self-satisfaction is replaced by gratification in its achievement, in "being good," in its parents' praise.

All children are not equally successful in this respect. Particular attention should be drawn here to the fact that there are certain over-compensations behind which is hidden that obstinate holding fast to the primitive right of self-determination which occasionally breaks out violently later. I have in mind those children (and of course adults also) who are remarkable for their "goodness," polite manners, and obedience, but who base their underlying rebellious impulses on the grounds that they have been forced into submission since infancy. These cases have their own developmental history. In one of my patients I could trace back the course of events to her earliest infancy, in regard to which, it is true, previous statements of her mother were of assistance.

The patient was the middle one of three sisters. She showed unusually clearly and completely the traits characteristic of a "middle" child, which Hug-Hellmuth[4] has recently described in such an illuminating way. But her refractoriness, which was associated in the clearest manner with her assertion of the infantile right of self-determination in the sense mentioned above, went back, in the last instance, to a particular circumstance of her childhood.

When she was born her elder sister had been still under a year old. Her mother had not quite succeeded in educating the elder child to habits of cleanliness when the newcomer had imposed on her a double amount of washing, both of clothes and body. When the patient was a few months old her mother

[4] "Vom 'mittlerem' Kinde" (1921).

had become pregnant for the third time, and had determined to hasten the education of her second child in cleanly habits, so that she should not still be too much taken up with her when the third child was born. She had demanded obedience on its part regarding the carrying out of its needs earlier than is usual, and had reinforced the effect of her words by smacking it. These measures had produced a very welcome result for the harassed mother. The child had become a model of cleanliness abnormally early, and had grown surprisingly submissive. When she was grown up, the patient was in a constant conflict between a conscious attitude of submissiveness, resignation and willingness to sacrifice herself on the one hand, and an unconscious desire for vengeance on the other.

This brief account illustrates in an instructive manner the effect of early injuries to infantile narcissism, especially if these injuries are of a persistent and systematic nature, and force a habit prematurely upon the child before it is psychically ready for it. This psychical preparedness only appears when the child begins to transfer on to objects (its mother, etc.) the feelings which are originally bound narcissistically. Once the child has acquired this capacity it will become cleanly "for the sake of" this person. If cleanliness is demanded too soon, it will acquire the habit through fear. Its inner resistance will remain and its libido will continue in a tenacious narcissistic fixation, and a permanent disturbance of the capacity to love will result.

The full significance of such an experience for the psycho-sexual development of the child only becomes apparent if we examine in detail the course of narcissistic pleasure. Jones lays stress on the connection between the child's high self-esteem and its excretory acts. In a short paper[5] I have brought forward some examples to show that the child's idea of the omnipotence of its wishes and thoughts can proceed from a stage in which it ascribed an omnipotence of this kind to its excretions. Further experience has since convinced me that this is a regular and typical process. The patient about whose childhood I have spoken had doubtless been disturbed in the enjoyment of a narcissistic

---

[5] "The Narcissistic Evaluation of Excretory Processes in Dreams and Neurosis" (1920).

pleasure of this sort. The severe and painful feelings of insufficiency with which she was later afflicted very probably went back in the last instance to this premature destruction of her infantile "megalomania."

This view of the excretions as a sign of enormous power is foreign to the consciousness of normal adults. That it persists in the unconscious, however, is shown in many everyday expressions, mostly of a jocular nature; for example, the seat of the closet is often denoted as the "throne." It is not to be wondered at that children who grow up in a strong anal-erotic environment incorporate these kinds of comparisons which they so frequently hear, in the fixed body of their recollections and make use of them in their later neurotic phantasies. One of my patients had a compulsion to read a meaning of this kind into the German national anthem. By transposing himself in his phantasies of greatness into the Kaiser's place he pictured to himself "the high delight" of "bathing in the glory of the throne," *i.e.* of touching his own excreta.

Once again language gives us characteristic instances of this over-estimation of defæcation. In Spanish, the common expression for it, *"regir el vientre"* ("to rule the belly"), which is used quite seriously, clearly indicates the pride taken by the person in the functioning of his bowels.

If we recognize in the child's pride in evacuation a primitive feeling of power we can understand the peculiar feeling of helplessness we so often find in neurotically constipated patients. Their libido has been displaced from the genital to the anal zone, and they deplore the inhibition of the bowel function just as though it were a genital impotence. In thinking of the person who is hypochondriacal about his motions one is tempted to speak of an *intestinal* impotence.

Closely connected with this pride is the idea of many neurotics, which was first described by Sadger, that they must do everything themselves because no one else can do it as well. According to my experience this conviction is often exaggerated until the patient believes that he is a unique person. He will become pretentious and arrogant and will tend to under-estimate everyone else. One patient expressed this as follows: "Everything that is not me is dirt." These neurotics only take pleasure in possessing a thing that no one else has, and will despise any activity which they have to share with other people.

The sensitiveness of the person with an anal character to external encroachments of every kind on the actual or supposed field of his power is well known. It is quite evident that psycho-analysis must evoke the most violent resistance in such persons, who regard it as an unheard-of interference with their way of life. "Psycho-analysis pokes about in my affairs," one patient said, thereby indicating unconsciously his passive-homosexual and anal attitude towards his analyst.

Jones emphasizes the fact that many neurotics of this class hold fast obstinately to their own system of doing things. They refuse altogether to accommodate themselves to any arrange-ment imposed from without, but expect compliance from other people as soon as they have worked out a definite arrangement of their own. As an example, I might mention the introduction of strict regulations for use in the office, or possibly the writing of a book which contains binding rules or recommendations for the organization of all offices of a certain kind.

The following is a glaring example of this kind. A mother drew up a written programme in which she arranged her daugh-ter's day in the most minute manner. The orders for the early morning were set out as follows: (1) Get up. (2) Use the chamber. (3) Wash, etc. In the morning she would knock from time to time at her daughter's door, and ask, "How far have you got now?" The girl would then have to reply, "9" or "15," as the case might be. In this way the mother kept a strict watch over the execution of her plan.

It might be mentioned here that all such systems not only testify to an obsession for order in its inventor, but also to his love of power which is of sadistic origin. I intend later to deal with the combination of anal and sadistic impulses in detail.

Allusion may be made here to the pleasure these neurotics take in indexing and registering everything, in making up tabu-lar summaries, and in dealing with statistics of every kind.

They furthermore show the same self-will in regard to any demand or request made to them by some other person. We are reminded of the conduct of those children who become constipated when defæcation is demanded of them, but afterwards yield to the need at a time that is agreeable to themselves. Such children rebel equally against the "shall" (being told to empty their bowels) as against the "must" (a child's expression for the need to defæcate); their desire to postpone evacuation is a protection against both imperatives.

The surrender of excrement is the earliest form in which the child "gives" or "presents" a thing; and the neurotic often shows the self-will we have described in the matter of giving. Accordingly in many cases he will refuse a demand or request made to him, but will of his own *free choice* make a person a handsome present. The important thing to him is to preserve his right of decision. We frequently find in our psycho-analyses that a husband opposes any expenditure proposed by his wife, while he afterwards hands her of his "own free will" more than what she first asked for. These men delight in keeping their wives permanently dependent on them financially. Assigning money in portions which they themselves determine is a source of pleasure to them. We come across similar behaviour in some neurotics regarding defæcation, which they only allow to take place *in refracta dosi*. One special tendency these men and women have is to distribute food in portions according as they think best, and this habit occasionally assumes grotesque forms. For instance, there was a case of a stingy old man who fed his goat by giving it each blade of grass separately. Such people like to arouse desire and expectation in others and then to give them gratification in small and insufficient amounts.

In those instances where they have to yield to the demand of another person some of these neurotics endeavour to maintain a semblance of making a personal decision. An example of this is the tendency to pay even the smallest amounts by cheque; in this way the person avoids using current notes and coin, but creates his "own money" in each case. The displeasure of paying out is thereby diminished by just as much as it would be increased if payment were made in coin. I should like to make it quite clear, however, that other motives are also operative here.

Neurotics who wish to introduce their own system into everything are inclined to be exaggerated in their criticism of others, and this easily degenerates into mere carping. In social life they constitute the main body of malcontents. The original anal characteristic of self-will can, however, develop in two different directions, as Jones has convincingly shown. In some cases we meet with inaccessibility and stubbornness, that is, with characteristics that are unsocial and unproductive. In others we find perseverance and thoroughness, *i.e.* characteristics of social value as long as they are not pushed to extremes. We must here once more draw attention to the existence of other instinctual sources besides anal erotism which go to reinforce these tendencies.

The opposite type has received very little consideration in psycho-analytical literature. There are certain neurotics who avoid taking any kind of initiative. In ordinary life they want a kind father or attentive mother to be constantly at hand to remove every difficulty out of their way. In psycho-analysis they resent having to give free associations. They would like to lie quite still and let the physician do all the analytical work, or to be questioned by him. The similarity of the facts disclosed by the analysis of these cases enables me to state that these patients used in childhood to resist the act of defæcation demanded of them, and that then they used to be spared this trouble by being given frequent enemas or purges by their mother or father. To them free association is a psychical evacuation, and—just as with bodily evacuation—they dislike being asked to perform it. They are continually expecting that the work should be made easier or done for them altogether. I may recall a reverse form of this resistance, which I have likewise traced back to anal erotic sources in an earlier paper.[6] It concerns those patients who wish to do everything themselves according to their own method in their psycho-analysis, and for this reason refuse to carry out the prescribed free association.

In this paper I do not intend so much to discuss the neurotic symptom-formations arising from repressed anal erotism, as its characterological manifestations. I shall therefore only touch

---

[6] "The Narcissistic Evaluation of Excretory Processes in Dreams and Neurosis" (1920).

upon the various forms of neurotic inhibition which obviously have to do with a displacement of libido to the anal zone. The fact that avoidance of effort is a frequent feature of the anal character needs further discussion; and we must briefly consider what the state of affairs is in the person with a so-called "obsessional character."

If the libido of the male person does not advance in full measure to the stage of genital organization, or if it regresses from the genital to the anal developmental phase, there invariably results a diminution of male activity in every sense of the word. His physiological productiveness is bound up with the genital zone. If his libido regresses to the sadistic-anal phase he loses his productive power, and not only in the purely generative sense. His genital libido should give the first impulse to the procreative act, and therewith to the creation of a new being. If the initiative necessary for this reproductive act is lacking, we invariably find a lack of productivity and initiative in other respects in his behaviour. But the effects go even beyond this.

Together with the man's genital activity there goes a positive feeling-attitude towards his love-object, and this attitude extends to his behaviour towards other objects and is expressed in his capacity for social adaptation, his devotion to certain interests and ideas, etc. In all these respects the character-formation of the sadistic-anal stage is inferior to that of the genital phase. The sadistic element, which in a normal man's emotional life is of great importance once it has undergone appropriate transformation through sublimation, appears with particular strength in the obsessional character, but becomes more or less crippled in consequence of the ambivalence in the instinctual life of such persons. It also contains destructive tendencies hostile to the object, and on account of this cannot become sublimated to a real capacity for devotion to a love-object. For the reaction-formation of too great yieldingness and gentleness which is frequently observed in such people must not be confused with a real transference-love. Those cases in which object-love and genital libido-organization have been attained to a fair extent are more favourable. If the character-trait of over-kindness mentioned above is combined with a partial object-love of this kind, a socially useful "variety" is produced, which in essential respects is, nevertheless, inferior to full object-love.

In individuals with more or less impaired genitality we regularly find an unconscious tendency to regard the anal function as the productive activity, and to make it appear as if the genital activity were unessential and the anal one far more important. The social behaviour of these persons is accordingly strongly bound up with money. They like to make presents of money or its equivalent, and tend to become patrons of the arts or benefactors of some kind. But their libido remains more or less detached from objects, and so the work they do remains unproductive in the essential sense. They are by no means lacking in perseverance—a frequent mark of the anal character—but their perseverance is largely used in unproductive ways. They expend it, for instance, in the pedantic observance of fixed forms, so that in unfavourable cases their preoccupation with the external form outweighs their interest in the reality of the thing. In considering the various ways in which the anal character impairs male activity we must not forget the tendency, often a very obstinate one, of postponing every action. We are well acquainted with the origin of this tendency. There is often associated with it a tendency to interrupt every activity that has been begun; so that in many cases as soon as a person begins doing anything it can already be predicted that an interruption will occur very soon.

More rarely I have found the reverse conduct. For instance, one of my patients was prevented from writing his doctor's thesis through a long-standing resistance. After several motives for his resistance had come to light we found the following one: he declared that he shrank from beginning his work because when he had once begun he could not leave off again. We are reminded of the behaviour of certain neurotics in regard to their excretions. They retain the contents of the bowel or bladder as long as they possibly can. When finally they yield to the need that has become too strong for them there is no further holding back, and they evacuate the entire contents. A fact to be particularly noted here is that there is a double pleasure, that of holding back the excreta, and that of evacuating it. The essential difference between the two forms of pleasure lies in the protracted nature of the process in the one case, and in its rapid course in the other. As regards the patient just mentioned the long-deferred beginning of the work signified a turning from pleasure in retention to pleasure in evacuation.[7]

A detail from the history of the same patient will show the degree to which a preponderance of anal over genital erotism makes the neurotic inactive and unproductive. During his analysis as well he remained wholly inactive for a long period, and by means of this resistance prevented any alteration taking place in his condition and circumstances. As is often the case in obsessional patients, his sole method of dealing with his external and internal difficulties was to swear violently. These expressions of affect were accompanied by very significant behaviour. Instead of thinking about the success of his work, he used to ponder over the question of what would happen to his curses—whether they reached God or the devil, and what was the fate of sound-waves in general. His intellectual activity was thus replaced by neurotic brooding. It appeared from his associations that the brooding question about the place where noise finally got to referred also to smell, and was in the last instance of anal erotic origin (flatus).

Generally speaking, it may be said that the more male activity and productivity is hindered in neurotics, the more pronounced their interest in possession becomes, and this in a way which departs widely from the normal. In marked cases of anal character-formation almost all relationships in life are brought into the category of having (holding fast) and giving,

---

[7] The tendency to retain the fæces represents a special form of adherence to fore-pleasure, and seems to me to merit special consideration. I will only mention one point concerning it in this place. Recently frequent attempts have been made to set up two opposite "psychological types" and to bring all individuals into one or other category. We may recall in this connection Jung's "extraverted" and "introverted" types. The patient whom I mentioned above was undoubtedly turned in upon himself in the highest degree, but he gave up this attitude of hostility to objects more and more in the course of his analysis. This and many similar experiences go to prove that "introversion" in Jung's sense is an infantile clinging to the pleasure in retention. We are therefore dealing with an attitude that can be acquired or given up, and not with a manifestation of a rigid psychological type.

i.e. of proprietorship. It is as though the motto of many of these people were: "Whoever gives me something is my friend; whoever desires something from me is my enemy." One patient said that he could not have any friendly feelings towards me during his treatment, and added in explanation: "So long as I have to pay anybody anything I cannot be friendly towards him." We find the exact reverse of this behaviour in other neurotics; their friendly feeling towards a person increases in proportion to the help he needs and asks for.

In the first and larger group envy stands out clearly as the main character-trait. The envious person, however, shows not only a desire for the possessions of others, but connects with that desire spiteful impulses against the privileged proprietor. But we will only make a passing reference to the sadistic and anal roots of envy, since both are of minor and auxiliary significance in the production of that character-trait, which originates in the earlier, oral phase of libido-development. One example will suffice to illustrate the connection of envy with anal ideas of possession, and that is the frequent envy of his analyst on the part of the patient. He envies him the position of a "superior," and continually compares himself with him. A patient once said that the distribution of the rôles in psycho-analysis was too unjust, for it was he who had to make all the sacrifices; he had to visit the physician, produce his associations, and to pay the money into the bargain. The same patient also had the habit of calculating the income of everyone he knew.

We have now come very close to one of the classical traits of the person with an anal character, namely, his special attitude to money, which is usually one of parsimony or avarice. Often as this characteristic has been confirmed in psycho-analytical literature, there are yet a number of features connected with it which have not received much notice, and which I shall therefore proceed to deal with.

There are cases in which the connection between intentional retention of fæces and systematic parsimony is perfectly clear. I may mention the example of a rich banker who again and again impressed on his children that they should retain the contents of the bowels as long as possible, in order to get the benefit of every bit of the expensive food they ate.

Some neurotics limit their parsimony or their avarice to certain kinds of expenditure, while in other respects they spend money with surprising liberality. There is a class of patient who avoids spending any money on "passing" things. A concert, a journey, a visit to an exhibition, involves expense and nothing permanent is got in return. I knew a person who avoided going to the opera for this reason; nevertheless he bought piano scores of the operas which he had not heard, because in this way he obtained something "lasting." Some of these neurotics avoid spending money on food, because it is not retained as a permanent possession. It is significant that there is another type of patient who readily incurs expense for food in which he has an overgreat interest. These are the neurotics who are always anxiously watching their bodies, testing their weight, etc. Their interest is concerned with the question of what remains of the material introduced into their body as a lasting possession. It is evident that they identify the content of the body with money.

In other cases we find that the neurotic carries his parsimony into every part of his life; and on certain points he goes to extremes without effecting any appreciable economy. I might mention an eccentric miser who used to go about in his house with the front of his trousers unbuttoned, in order that the buttonholes should not wear out too quickly. It is easy to guess that in this instance other impulses were also operative. Nevertheless it is characteristic that these could be concealed behind the anal erotic tendency to save money, and that this motive should be so much emphasized. In some patients we find a parsimony in the special instance of using toilet paper. In this a dislike of soiling a clean thing co-operates as a determining factor.

The displacement of avarice from money or the value of money to time may be observed quite frequently. Time, it may be remembered, is likened to money in a familiar saying. Many neurotics are continually worrying over waste of time. It is only the time which they spend alone or at their work that seems to them well employed. Any disturbance in their work irritates them exceedingly. They hate inactivity, pleasures, etc. These are the people who tend to exhibit the "Sunday neuroses" described by Ferenczi,[8] *i.e.* who cannot endure an interruption of their work. Just as every neurotically exaggerated purpose often fails to achieve its object, so is this the case here. The patients often save time on a small scale and waste it on a great one.

Such patients frequently undertake two occupations at once in order to save time. They like, for example, to learn, read, or accomplish other tasks during defæcation.[9] I have repeatedly come across people who in order to save time used to put on or take off their coat and waistcoat together, or on going to bed would leave their pants in their trousers in order to put on both garments in one movement in the morning. Examples of this kind could easily be multiplied.

The forms in which pleasure in possession can express itself are very numerous. The stamp-collector who deeply feels the gap in his set of stamps is not so far removed from the miser who, according to popular notion, counts and gloats over his gold pieces. But Jones' work concerning the impulse to collect is so informative that I can add nothing of importance to it.

On the other hand, it seems to me necessary to make a brief allusion to a phenomenon which is closely related to the subject's pleasure in looking at his own possessions. I refer to the pleasure in looking at one's own mental creations, letters, manuscripts, etc., or completed works of all kinds. The prototype of this tendency is looking at one's own fæces, which is an ever-new source of pleasure to many people, and is in some neurotics a form of psychical compulsion.

This fact of a libidinal over-emphasis of possession explains the difficulty our patients have in separating themselves from objects of all kinds, when these have neither practical use nor monetary value. Such people often collect all sorts of broken objects in the attics under the pretext that they might need them later. Then on some occasion or other they will get rid of the

---

[8] "Sunday Neurosis" (1919).

[9] For these neurotics the w.c. is the true place of "production," to which its solitude is an assistance. One patient who showed violent resistance against giving free associations during the analytic hours produced them at home in the w.c., and brought them ready made to the analysis.

whole lot of rubbish at once. Their pleasure in having a mass of material stored up entirely corresponds to pleasure in the retention of fæces. We find in this case that the removal (evacuation) of the material is delayed as long as possible. The same persons collect bits of paper, old envelopes, worn-out pens and similar things, and cannot get rid of these possessions for long periods of time, and then at rare intervals they make a general clearance, which is likewise associated with pleasure. Among business men and clerks I have sometimes come across a particular tendency to preserve carefully quite soiled and torn blotting-paper. In the unconscious of these neurotics the spots of ink are equivalent to the stain of fæces. I might mention that I knew a senile and weak-minded woman with a strong regression of libido to the anal stage who used to put the toilet paper she had used in her pocket and carry it about with her.

The following peculiar habit of a woman who also exhibited unusually pronounced anal traits in other respects shows clearly that throwing away objects is equivalent in the unconscious to evacuating fæces. This woman was unable to throw away objects that had become useless. Nevertheless, she sometimes felt impelled to throw some object of this kind away, and so she had invented a method of tricking herself, as it were. She would go from her house into a neighbouring wood with the object to be removed—perhaps some old clothes—fixed to her back by one corner tucked under her apron-string. On her way through the wood she would "lose" it and return home another way so that she should not catch sight of the "lost" object. In order to give up possession of an object, therefore, she had to let it fall from the back part of her body.

People who do not like to get rid of worn-out objects do not as a rule readily take to new ones. They buy new clothes, but do not wear them; they "keep" them for the future, and only take a real pleasure in them so long as they hang unused in the cupboard.

The disinclination to throw away worn-out or worthless objects frequently leads to a compulsive tendency to make use of even the most trifling thing. A rich man used to cut his empty match-boxes into small strips and give them to his servants to light the fires with. A similar tendency appears in women in the period of involution.

In many cases the person's interest in making use of remnants undergoes an incomplete kind of sublimation; as, for instance, when a neurotic has as his favourite day-dream the utilization of the refuse of a whole town, though no practical result of his reflections may appear. We shall deal later with day-dreams of this nature.

We find a tendency to extravagance less frequent than parsimony in our patients. In an observation communicated to the Berlin Psycho-Analytical Society, Simmel made the parallel between extravagance and neurotic diarrhœa just as evident as that between avarice and constipation, which has long been clear to us. I can confirm the correctness of his view from my own experience, and indeed I drew attention some years ago to the fact that spending money can represent an equivalent for a longed-for but neurotically inhibited release of libido.[10] I might mention here the inclination some women have to throw away money. It expresses hostility towards the husband, whose "means" [11] are taken from him in this way; it concerns, therefore—if we leave out other determinants—an expression of the female castration complex in the sense of a revenge on the man. We see here again sadistic motives co-operating with those of anal-erotic origin.

We can quite understand, from their contradictory attitude towards defæcation, the meanness many neurotics show in saving small sums of money while they will spend largely and generously from time to time. These persons postpone emptying the bowels as long as possible—often giving lack of time as a reason—and when they do go to the w.c. only evacuate a small quantity of fæces. But every now and then they have an evacuation on a grand scale.

We occasionally come across persons with pronounced anal character whose libido has turned quite exclusively to the possession of money. A patient told me that as a boy he did not play

---

[10] "The Spending of Money in Anxiety States" (1917).

[11] [The German word "Vermögen" = "means," "wealth"; also = "sexual capacity."—Trans.]

at battles with lead soldiers like other children, but with pieces of money. He got people to give him copper coins, and these represented ordinary soldiers. Nickel ones were non-commissioned officers of various rank, and silver ones were officers. A silver five-mark piece was the field-marshal. This officer was secured from all attack in a special building "behind the front." One side took "prisoners" from the other in the battle and added them to its own army. In this manner one side increased its possession of money until the other had nothing left. It is quite obvious that the "struggle" in the patient's unconscious was against his "rich" father. It is worth noting, however, that money entirely replaced human beings. And indeed when this patient came to me for treatment he took no personal interest in other people whatever; only the possession of money and money values attracted him.

The conduct of our patients with regard to order and cleanliness is just as contradictory as it is in spending money. This fact is so familiar to every psycho-analyst that a general reference to it should not be necessary; but certain particulars in this connection deserve special consideration.

Pleasure in indexing and classifying, in compiling lists and statistical summaries, in drawing up programmes and regulating work by time-sheets, is well known to be an expression of the anal character. This tendency is so marked in many people that the fore-pleasure they get in working out a plan is stronger than their gratification in its execution, so that they often leave it undone. I have known a number of patients with a long-standing inhibition in their work who would draw up a plan of work, say, every Sunday for the coming week, and would then fail utterly to put it into practice. It is to be noted that they included not only undecided people but obstinate ones who in their self-opinionated way rejected the proved methods of others and wanted to act according to their own.

Many neurotics remain during life in a particular attitude of ambivalency towards order and cleanliness. There are people who are very well groomed as far as their exterior goes. But whereas their visible costume and linen is irreproachable, their under-clothing and the covered parts of their body are exceedingly dirty.[12] These same people tend to preserve scrupulous order in their houses. On the writing table, for instance, every object will have its special place, and the books are placed with great care and regularity in the book-case where they are visible. In the drawers, however, complete disorder reigns, a disorder which is only corrected by a thorough clearance on rare occasions, and then only in a temporary way.

I might mention here that in the unconscious of these neurotics a disordered room, disarranged drawers, etc., represent the bowel filled with fæces. I have repeatedly had occasion to analyse dreams which allude to the bowel in this way. One of my patients brought me a dream in which he climbed up a ladder after his mother in order to get into a lumber-room in the attics. It was an incest-dream with an anal coitus-phantasy in which the anus was represented symbolically as a narrow ladder and the bowel as a lumber-room.

Character-traits connected with orderliness, as, for example, thoroughness and accuracy, are often closely associated with the opposite characteristic. These traits are particularly dealt with in Jones' investigations, and I need not go into them, but I may mention the craving for symmetry and "fairness" which is often represented in the anal character.

Just as some neurotics count their steps in order to reach their destination with an even number of paces, so they tolerate no asymmetry in other matters. They arrange all their objects symmetrically. They divide everything with minute exactness. A husband will draw up calculations to show his wife that there is no equality between their respective expenditure on clothes, etc.; he will constantly be working out what the one has spent and what the other is therefore entitled to spend to make things even. During the food shortage in the Great War two unmarried brothers kept house together. When the rationed meat for both was put on the table they divided it by weighing each portion on a pair of letter scales. Both were anxious lest the other should

---

[12] There is a saying in Berlin regarding such people: *Oben hui, unten pfui!* ["On top all spry, below, oh fie!"]. In Bavaria they say more coarsely, *Oben beglissen* [= "shining"], *unten beschissen* [= "beshat"]. The contradictions in some people in this respect is a matter, therefore, of common knowledge.

go short or feel himself unfairly treated. The perpetual desire to be "quits" with other people, *i.e.* to be under no obligation, however trifling, is also significant. That other people with pronounced anal character have a tendency to forget their debts (particularly when they are for small sums) may be taken as a symptom of unsublimated anal erotism.

Finally, a discovery of Jones must be discussed which he only mentions by the way, but which obviously is the condensed result of wide experience.

A most interesting result of anal erotism, he writes, "is the tendency to be occupied with the reverse side of various things and situations. This may manifest itself in many different ways; in marked curiosity about the opposite or back side of objects and places—*e.g.* in the desire to live on the other side of a hill because it has its back turned to a given place; in the proneness to make numerous mistakes as to right and left, east and west; to reverse words and letters in writing; and so on."

I could support Jones' view with numerous examples from my own experience. They are of far-reaching importance for understanding certain neurotic symptoms and character-traits. There is no doubt that the displacement of libido from the genital to the anal zone is the prototype of all these "reversals." In this connection the conduct of many people who are considered eccentric may be mentioned. Their nature is built up for the most part on anal character-traits. They tend to act in great and small things in a manner opposite to that of other people. They wear clothes that are as dissimilar as possible from the prevailing fashion. They work when others play. If they do work at which others sit, they stand. When others ride, they go on foot; or run while others walk. If people wear warm clothing, they do the opposite. The food they enjoy is opposed to the general taste. The connection between this and the familiar character-trait of obstinacy is unmistakable.

During my student days I knew a young man who was noticeable for his peculiar habits. He lived unsocially, resisted the fashion of the time in an ostentatious manner, and would not conform to the customs of the rest of the students. As I was having a mid-day meal with him one day in a restaurant I noticed

that he took the menu in the reverse order, *i.e.* he commenced
with the sweet and ended with the soup. Some years later I was
asked by his relatives to see him professionally. I found that
he had already developed definite paranoic delusions. If we bear
in mind the great significance of anal erotism in the psychogenesis of paranoia, a significance which Ferenczi has pointed
out, we can understand this man's eccentric behaviour as an
anal character-formation, and therefore as a precursor of paranoia.

Certain cases of neuroses in women, in which an unusually
strong castration complex is expressed, reveal to us best the
deeper meaning of such a tendency to reversal. We find in them
that it springs from two main motives—a displacement of libido
from "in front" to "behind," and the wish for a change of sex.
I hope to have something to say concerning this condition of
mind in another connection.

I should like to conclude these remarks on anal character-
traits with an observation the truth of which I should like others
to test. This is that the anal character sometimes seems to stamp
itself on the physiognomy of its possessor. It seems particularly
to show itself in a morose expression. Persons who are deprived
of normal genital gratification tend to surliness[13] as a rule. A
constant tension of the line of the nostril together with a slight
lifting of the upper lip seem to me significant facial characteristics
of such people. In some cases this gives the impression that they
are constantly sniffing at something. Probably this feature is
traceable to their coprophilic pleasure in smell. In the case of
a man who had this kind of facial expression I once remarked
that he looked as though he were constantly smelling himself.
Someone who knew him quite well said that he really did have
the habit of smelling his hands and every object he picked up.
I might add that he exhibited the typical anal character-traits in
a pronounced form.

I do not claim to have dealt exhaustively with the subject
of anal character-traits in this paper. On the contrary, I am
conscious how little justice I have done to the richness and

---

[13] Some, it is true, have at their command plentiful narcissistic sources of
pleasure, and live in a state of smiling self-satisfaction.

variety of the material. In reality I have had in view another object, namely, to increase our knowledge of the pregenital phases of the development of the libido by making some additions to the investigation of the anal character. As I have said at the beginning, this paper is intended to be followed by a study of the manic-depressive states, for the understanding of which a knowledge of the pregenital stages of development is essential.

20

ERICH FROMM

Selfishness, Self-Love, and Self-Interest*

Thou shalt love thy neighbour as thyself.
                                                    BIBLE

Modern culture is pervaded by a tabu on selfishness. We are taught that to be selfish is sinful and that to love others is virtuous. To be sure, this doctrine is in flagrant contradiction to the practice of modern society, which holds the doctrine that the most powerful and legitimate drive in man is selfishness and that by following this imperative drive the individual makes his best contribution to the common good. But the doctrine which declares selfishness to be the arch evil and love for others to be the greatest virtue is still powerful. Selfishness is used here almost synonymously with self-love. The alternative is to love others, which is a virtue, or to love oneself, which is a sin.

This principle has found its classic expression in Calvin's theology, according to which man is essentially evil and powerless. Man can achieve absolutely nothing that is good on the basis of his own strength or merit. "We are not our own," says Calvin. "Therefore neither our reason nor our will should predominate in our deliberations and actions. We are not our own; therefore let us not propose it as our end to seek what may be expedient for us according to the flesh. We are not our own; therefore, let

* From *Man for Himself: An Inquiry into the Psychology of Ethics*, by Erich Fromm. Copyright 1947 by Erich Fromm, reprinted by permission of Rinehart & Co., Inc. and Routledge & Kegan Paul Ltd.

us, as far as possible, forget ourselves and all things that are ours. On the contrary, we are God's; for Him, therefore, let us live and die. For, as it is the most devastating pestilence which ruins people if they obey themselves, it is the only haven of salvation not to know or to want anything by oneself but to be guided by God Who walks before us." [1] Man should have not only the conviction of his absolute nothingness but he should do everything to humiliate himself. "For I do not call it humility if you suppose that we have anything left . . . . we cannot think of ourselves as we ought to think without utterly despising everything that may be supposed an excellence in us. This humility is unfeigned submission of a mind overwhelmed with a weighty sense of its own misery and poverty; for such is the uniform description of it in the word of God." [2]

This emphasis on the nothingness and wickedness of the individual implies that there is nothing he should like and respect about himself. The doctrine is rooted in self-contempt and self-hatred. Calvin makes this point very clear: he speaks of self-love as "a pest." [3] If the individual finds something "on the strength of which he finds pleasure in himself," he betrays this sinful self-love. This fondness for himself will make him sit in judgment over others and despise them. Therefore, to be fond of oneself or to like anything in oneself is one of the greatest sins. It is supposed to exclude love for others[4] and to be identical with selfishness.[5]

The view of man held by Calvin and Luther has been of

---

[1] Johannes Calvin, *Institutes of the Christian Religion*, trans. by John Allen (Philadelphia: Presbyterian Board of Christian Education, 1928), in particular Book III, Chap. 7, p. 619. From "For, as it is . . . ." the translation is mine from the Latin original (Johannes Calvini, *Institutio Christianae Religionis. Editionem curavit*, A. Tholuk, Berolini, 1935, par. 1, p. 445).

[2] *Ibid.*, Chap. 12, par. 6, p. 681.

[3] *Ibid.*, Chap. 7, par. 4, p. 622.

[4] It should be noted, however, that even love for one's neighbor, while it is one of the fundamental doctrines of the New Testament, has not been given a corresponding weight by Calvin. In blatant contradiction to the New Testament, Calvin says: "For what the schoolmen advance concerning the priority of charity to faith and hope, is a mere reverie of a distempered imagination . . . ."—Chap. 24, par. 1, p. 531.

[5] Despite Luther's emphasis on the spiritual freedom of the individual, his theology, different as it is in many ways from Calvin's, is pervaded by the same conviction of man's basic powerlessness and nothingness.

tremendous influence on the development of modern Western society. They laid the foundations for an attitude in which man's own happiness was not considered to be the aim of life but where he became a means, an adjunct, to ends beyond him, of an all-powerful God, or of the not less powerful secularized authorities and norms, the state, business, success. Kant, who, with regard to the idea that man should be an end in himself and never a means only, was perhaps the most influential ethical thinker of the Enlightenment period, nevertheless had the same condemnation for self-love. According to him, it is a virtue to want happiness for others, but to want one's own happiness is ethically indifferent, since it is something for which the nature of man is striving, and since a natural striving cannot have a positive ethical value.[6] Kant admits that one must not give up one's claims to happiness; under certain circumstances it may even be a duty to be concerned with it, partly because health, wealth, and the like may be means necessary for the fulfillment of one's duty, partly because the lack of happiness—poverty—can prevent one from fulfilling his duty.[7] But love for oneself, striving for one's own happiness, can never be a *virtue*. As an ethical principle, the striving for one's own happiness "is the most objectionable one, not merely because it is false . . . . but because the springs it provides for morality are such as rather to undermine it and destroy its sublimity . . . ."[8]

Kant differentiates egotism, self-love, *philautia*—a benevolence for oneself—and arrogance, the pleasure in oneself. But even "rational self-love" must be restricted by ethical principles, the pleasure in oneself must be battered down, and the individual must come to feel humiliated in comparing himself with the sanctity of moral laws.[9] The individual should find supreme happiness in the fulfillment of his duty. The realization of the moral principle—and, therefore, of the individual's happiness—is only

---

[6] Compare Immanuel Kant, *Kant's Critique of Practical Reason and Other Works on the Theory of Ethics*, trans. by Thomas Kingsmill Abbott (New York: Longmans, Green & Co., 1909), Part I, Book I, Chap. I, par. VIII, Remark II, p. 126.

[7] *Ibid.*, in particular Part I, Book I, Chap. III, p. 186.

[8] *Loc. cit.*, Fundamental Principles of the Metaphysics of Morals; second section, p. 61.

[9] *Loc. cit.*, Part I, Book I, Ch. III, p. 165.

possible in the general whole, the nation, the state. But "the welfare of the state"—and *salus rei publicae suprema lex est*— is not identical with the welfare of the citizens and their happiness.[10]

In spite of the fact that Kant shows a greater respect for the integrity of the individual than did Calvin or Luther, he denies the individual's right to rebel even under the most tyrannical government; the rebel must be punished with no less than death if he threatens the sovereign.[11] Kant emphasizes the native propensity for evil in the nature of man,[12] for the suppression of which the moral law, the categorical imperative, is essential lest man should become a beast and human society end in wild anarchy.

In the philosophy of the Enlightenment period the individual's claims to happiness have been emphasized much more strongly by others than by Kant, for instance, by Helvetius. This trend in modern philosophy has found its most radical expression in Stirner and Nietzsche.[13] But while they take the opposite position to that of Calvin and Kant with regard to the value of selfishness, they agree with them in the assumption that love for others and love for oneself are alternatives. They denounce love for others as weakness and self-sacrifice and postulate egotism, selfishness, and self-love—they too confuse the issue by not clearly differentiating between these last—as virtue. Thus Stirner says: "Here, egoism, selfishness must decide, not the principle of love, not love motives like mercy, gentleness, good-nature, or even justice and equity—for *iustitia* too is a phenomenon of love, a product of love; love knows only sacrifice and demands self-sacrifice." [14]

---

[10] Immanuel Kant, *Immanuel Kant's Werke* (Berlin: Cassierer), in particular "Der Rechtslehre Zweiter Teil" I. Abschnitt, par. 49, p. 124. I translate from the German text, since this part is omitted in the English translation of *The Metaphysics of Ethics* by I. W. Semple (Edinburgh: 1871).

[11] *Ibid.*, p. 126.

[12] Compare Immanuel Kant, *Religion within the Limits of Reason Alone*, trans. by T. M. Greene and H. H. Hudson (Chicago: Open Court, 1934), Book I.

[13] In order not to make this chapter too long I discuss only the modern philosophical development. The student of philosophy will know that Aristotle's and Spinoza's ethics consider self-love a virtue, not a vice, in striking contrast to Calvin's standpoint.

[14] Max Stirner, *The Ego and His Own*, trans. by S. T. Byington (London: A. C. Fifield, 1912), p. 339.

The kind of love denounced by Stirner is the masochistic dependence by which the individual makes himself a means for achieving the purposes of somebody or something outside himself. Opposing this concept of love, he did not avoid a formulation, which, highly polemical, overstates the point. The positive principle with which Stirner was concerned [15] was opposed to an attitude which had been that of Christian theology for centuries —and which was vivid in the German idealism prevalent in his time; namely, to bend the individual so that he submits to, and finds his center in, a power and a principle outside himself. Stirner was not a philosopher of the stature of Kant or Hegel, but he had the courage to rebel radically against that side of idealistic philosophy which negated the concrete individual and thus helped the absolute state to retain its oppressive power over him.

In spite of many differences between *Nietzsche* and *Stirner*, their ideas in this respect are very much the same. Nietzsche too denounces love and altruism as expressions of weakness and self-negation. For Nietzsche, the quest for love is typical of slaves unable to fight for what they want and who therefore try to get it through love. Altruism and love for mankind thus have become a sign of degeneration.[16] For Nietzsche it is the essence of a good and healthy aristocracy that it is ready to sacrifice countless people for its interests without having a guilty conscience. Society should be a "foundation and scaffolding by means of which a select class of beings may be able to elevate themselves to their higher duties, and in general to a higher existence." [17]

---

[15] One of his positive formulations, for example, is: "But how does one use life? In using it up like the candle one burns. . . . Enjoyment of life is using life up." F. Engels has clearly seen the one-sidedness of Stirner's formulations and has attempted to overcome the false alternative between love for oneself and love for others. In a letter to Marx in which he discusses Stirner's book, Engels writes: "If, however, the concrete and real individual is the true basis for our 'human' man, it is self-evident that egotism—of course not only Stirner's egotism of reason, but also the egotism of the heart—is the basis for our love of man."—*Marx-Engels Gesamtausgabe* (Berlin: Marx-Engels Verlag, 1929), p. 6.

[16] Friedrich Nietzsche, *The Will to Power*, trans. by Anthony M. Ludovici (Edinburgh and London: T. N. Foulis, 1910), stanzas 246, 326, 369, 373, and 728.

[17] Friedrich Nietzsche, *Beyond Good and Evil*, trans. by Helen Zimmer (New York: The Macmillan Company, 1907), stanza 258.

Many quotations could be added to document this spirit of contempt and egotism. These ideas have often been understood as *the* philosophy of Nietzsche. However, they do not represent the true core of his philosophy.[18]

There are various reasons why Nietzsche expressed himself in the sense noted above. First of all, as with Stirner, his philosophy is a reaction—a rebellion—against the philosophical tradition of subordinating the empirical individual to powers and principles outside himself. His tendency to overstatement shows this reactive quality. Second, there were, in Nietzsche's personality, feelings of insecurity and anxiety that made him emphasize the "strong man" as a reaction formation. Finally, Nietzsche was impressed by the theory of evolution and its emphasis on the "survival of the fittest." This interpretation does not alter the fact that Nietzsche believed that there is a contradiction between love for others and love for oneself; yet his views contain the nucleus from which this false dichotomy can be overcome. The "love" which he attacks is rooted not in one's own strength, but in one's own weakness. "Your neighbor-love is your bad love of yourselves. Ye flee unto your neighbor from yourselves and would fain make a virtue thereof! But I fathom your 'unselfishness.' " He states explicitly, "You cannot stand yourselves and you do not love yourselves sufficiently." [19] For Nietzsche the individual has "an enormously great significance." [20] The "strong" individual is the one who has "true kindness, nobility, greatness of soul, which does not give in order to take, which does not want to excel by being kind;—'waste' as type of true kindness, wealth of the person as a premise." [21] He expresses the same thought also in *Thus Spake Zarathustra:* "The one goeth to his neighbor because he seeketh himself, and the other because he would fain lose himself." [22]

The essence of this view is this: Love is a phenomenon of

---

[18] Cf. G. A. Morgan, *What Nietzsche Means* (Cambridge: Harvard University Press, 1943).

[19] Friedrich Nietzsche, *Thus Spake Zarathustra,* trans. by Thomas Common (New York: Modern Library), p. 75.

[20] *The Will to Power,* stanza 785.

[21] *Ibid.,* stanza 935.

[22] *Thus Spake Zarathustra,* p. 76.

abundance; its premise is the strength of the individual who can give. Love is affirmation and productiveness, "It seeketh to create what is loved!" [23] To love another person is only a virtue if it springs from this inner strength, but it is a vice if it is the expression of the basic inability to be oneself.[24] However, the fact remains that Nietzsche left the problem of the relationship between self-love and love for others as an unsolved antinomy.

The doctrine that selfishness is the arch-evil and that to love oneself excludes loving others is by no means restricted to theology and philosophy, but it became one of the stock ideas promulgated in home, school, motion pictures, books; indeed in all instruments of social suggestion as well. "Don't be selfish" is a sentence which has been impressed upon millions of children, generation after generation. Its meaning is somewhat vague. Most people would say that it means not to be egotistical, inconsiderate, without any concern for others. Actually, it generally means more than that. Not to be selfish implies not to do what one wishes, to give up one's own wishes for the sake of those in authority. "Don't be selfish," in the last analysis, has the same ambiguity that it has in Calvinism. Aside from its obvious implication, it means, "don't love yourself," "don't be yourself," but submit yourself to something more important than yourself, to an outside power or its internalization, "duty." "Don't be selfish" becomes one of the most powerful ideological tools in suppressing spontaneity and the free development of personality. Under the pressure of this slogan one is asked for every sacrifice and for complete submission: only those acts are "unselfish" which do not serve the individual but somebody or something outside himself.

This picture, we must repeat, is in a certain sense one-sided. For besides the doctrine that one should not be selfish, the opposite is also propagandized in modern society: keep your own advantage in mind, act according to what is best for you; by so doing you will also be acting for the greatest advantage of all

---

[23] *Ibid.*, p. 102.

[24] See Friedrich Nietzsche, *The Twilight of Idols*, trans. by A. M. Ludovici (Edinburgh: T. N. Foulis, 1911), stanza 35; *Ecce Homo*, trans. by A. M. Ludovici (New York: The Macmillan Company, 1911), stanza 2; *Nachlass. Nietzsches Werke* (Leipzig: A. Kroener), pp. 63-64.

others. As a matter of fact, the idea that egotism is the basis of the general welfare is the principle on which competitive society has been built. It is puzzling that two such seemingly contradictory principles could be taught side by side in one culture; of the fact, however, there is no doubt. One result of this contradiction is confusion in the individual. Torn between the two doctrines, he is seriously blocked in the process of integrating his personality. This confusion is one of the most significant sources of the bewilderment and helplessness of modern man.[25]

The doctrine that love for oneself is identical with "self-ishness" and an alternative to love for others has pervaded theology, philosophy, and popular thought; the same doctrine has been rationalized in scientific language in *Freud's* theory of narcissism. Freud's concept presupposes a fixed amount of libido. In the infant, all of the libido has the child's own person as its objective, the stage of "primary narcissism," as Freud calls it. During the individual's development, the libido is shifted from one's own person toward other objects. If a person is blocked in his "object-relationships," the libido is withdrawn from the objects and returned to his own person; this is called "secondary narcissism." According to Freud, the more love I turn toward the outside world the less love is left for myself, and vice versa. He thus describes the phenomenon of love as an impoverishment of one's self-love because all libido is turned to an object outside oneself.

These questions arise: Does psychological observation support the thesis that there is a basic contradiction and a state of alternation between love for oneself and love for others? Is love for oneself the same phenomenon as selfishness, or are they opposites? Furthermore, is the selfishness of modern man really a *concern for himself* as an individual, with all his intellectual, emotional, and sensual potentialities? Has "he" not become an appendage of his socioeconomic role? *Is his selfishness identical with self-love or is it not caused by the very lack of it?*

---

[25] This point has been emphasized by Karen Horney, *The Neurotic Personality of Our Time* (New York: W. W. Norton & Company, 1937), and by Robert S. Lynd, *Knowledge for What?* (Princeton: Princeton University Press, 1939).

Before we start the discussion of the psychological aspect of selfishness and self-love, the logical fallacy in the notion that love for others and love for oneself are mutually exclusive should be stressed. If it is a virtue to love my neighbor as a human being, it must be a virtue—and not a vice—to love myself since I am a human being too. There is no concept of man in which I myself am not included. A doctrine which proclaims such an exclusion proves itself to be intrinsically contradictory. The idea expressed in the Biblical "Love thy neighbor as thyself!" implies that respect for one's own integrity and uniqueness, love for and understanding of one's own self, can not be separated from respect for and love and understanding of another individual. The love for my own self is inseparably connected with the love for any other self.

We have come now to the basic psychological premises on which the conclusions of our argument are built. Generally, these premises are as follows: not only others, but we ourselves are the "object" of our feelings and attitudes; the attitudes toward others and toward ourselves, far from being contradictory, are basically *conjunctive*. With regard to the problem under discussion this means: Love of others and love of ourselves are not alternatives. On the contrary, an attitude of love toward themselves will be found in all those who are capable of loving others. *Love, in principle, is indivisible as far as the connection between "objects" and one's own self is concerned*. Genuine love is an expression of productiveness and implies care, respect, responsibility, and knowledge. It is not an "affect" in the sense of being affected by somebody, but an active striving for the growth and happiness of the loved person, rooted in one's own capacity to love.

To love is an expression of one's power to love, and to love somebody is the actualization and concentration of this power with regard to one person. It is not true, as the idea of romantic love would have it, that there is *only the one* person in the world whom one could love and that it is the great chance of one's life to find that one person. Nor is it true, if that person be found that love for him (or her) results in a withdrawal of love from others. Love which can only be experienced with regard to one person demonstrates by this very fact that it is not love, but a symbiotic attachment. The basic affirmation contained in love is directed toward the beloved person as an incarnation of essentially human qualities. Love of one person implies love of man as such. The kind of "division of labor" as William James calls it, by which one loves one's family but is without feeling for the "stranger," is a sign of a basic inability to love. Love of man is not, as is frequently supposed, an abstraction coming after the love for a specific person, but it is its premise, although, genetically, it is acquired in loving specific individuals.

From this it follows that my own self, in principle, must be as much an object of my love as another person. *The affirmation of one's own life, happiness, growth, freedom, is rooted in one's capacity to love,* i.e., in care, respect, responsibility, and knowledge. If an individual is able to love productively, he loves himself too; if he can love *only* others, he can not love at all.

Granted that love for oneself and for others in principle is conjunctive, how do we explain selfishness, which obviously excludes any genuine concern for others? The *selfish* person is interested only in himself, wants everything for himself, feels no pleasure in giving, but only in taking. The world outside is looked at only from the standpoint of what he can get out of it; he lacks interest in the needs of others, and respect for their dignity and integrity. He can see nothing but himself; he judges everyone and everything from its usefulness to him; he is basically unable to love. Does not this prove that concern for others and concern for oneself are unavoidable alternatives? This would be so if selfishness and self-love were identical. But that assumption is the very fallacy which has led to so many mistaken conclusions concerning our problem. *Selfishness and self-love, far from being identical, are actually opposites.* The selfish person does not love himself too much but too little; in fact he hates himself. This lack of fondness and care for himself, which is only one expression of his lack of productiveness, leaves him empty and frustrated. He is necessarily unhappy and anxiously concerned to snatch from life the satisfactions which he blocks himself from attaining. He seems to care too much for himself but actually he only makes an unsuccessful attempt to cover up and compensate for his failure to care for his real self. Freud holds that the selfish person is narcissistic, as if he had withdrawn his love from others and turned it toward his own person. *It is true that selfish persons are incapable of loving others, but they are not capable of loving themselves either.*

It is easier to understand selfishness by comparing it with greedy concern for others, as we find it, for instance, in an over-solicitous, dominating mother. While she consciously believes that she is particularly fond of her child, she has actually a deeply repressed hostility toward the object of her concern. She is overconcerned not because she loves the child too much, but because she has to compensate for her lack of capacity to love him at all.

This theory of the nature of selfishness is borne out by psycho-analytic experience with neurotic "unselfishness," a symptom of neurosis observed in not a few people who usually are troubled not by this symptom but by others connected with it, like de-pression, tiredness, inability to work, failure in love relationships, and so on. Not only is unselfishness not felt as a "symptom"; it is often the one redeeming character trait on which such people pride themselves. The "unselfish" person "does not want any-thing for himself"; he "lives only for others," is proud that he does not consider himself important. He is puzzled to find that in spite of his unselfishness he is unhappy, and that his relation-ships to those closest to him are unsatisfactory. He wants to have what he considers are his symptoms removed—but not his un-selfishness. Analytic work shows that his unselfishness is not something apart from his other symptoms but one of them; in fact often the most important one; that he is paralyzed in his capacity to love or to enjoy anything; that he is pervaded by hostility against life and that behind the façade of unselfishness a subtle but not less intense self-centeredness is hidden. This person can be cured only if his unselfishness too is interpreted as a symptom along with the others so that his lack of produc-tiveness, which is at the root of both his unselfishness *and* his other troubles, can be corrected.

The nature of unselfishness becomes particularly apparent in its effect on others and most frequently, in our culture, in the effect the "unselfish" mother has on her children. She believes that by her unselfishness her children will experience what it means to be loved and to learn, in turn, what it means to love. The effect of her unselfishness, however, does not at all correspond to her expectations. The children do not show the happiness of persons who are convinced that they are loved; they are anxious, tense, afraid of the mother's disapproval and anxious to live up to her expectations. Usually, they are affected by their mother's hidden hostility against life, which they sense rather than recognize, and eventually become imbued with it themselves. Altogether, the effect of the "unselfish" mother is not too different from that of the selfish one; indeed, it is often worse because the mother's unselfishness prevents the children from criticizing her. They are put under the obligation not to disappoint her; they are taught, under the mask of virtue, dislike for life. If one has a chance to study the effect of a mother with genuine self-love, one can see that there is nothing more conducive to giving a child the experience of what love, joy, and happiness are than being loved by a mother who loves herself.

Having analyzed selfishness and self-love we can now proceed to discuss the concept of *self-interest,* which has become one of the key symbols in modern society. It is even more ambiguous than selfishness or self-love, and this ambiguity can be fully understood only by taking into account the historical development of the concept of self-interest. The problem is what is considered to constitute self-interest and how it can be determined.

There are two fundamentally different approaches to this problem. One is the objectivistic approach most clearly formulated by Spinoza. To him self-interest or the interest "to seek one's profit" is identical with virtue. "The more," he says, "each person strives and is able *to seek his profit,* that is to say, to preserve his being, the more virtue does he possess; on the other hand, in so far as each person neglects his own profit he is impotent." [26] According to this view, the interest of man is to preserve his existence, which is the same as realizing his inherent potentialities. This concept of self-interest is objectivistic inasmuch as "interest" is not conceived in terms of the subjective feeling of

[26] Spinoza, *Ethics,* IV, Prop. 20.

what one's interest is but in terms of what the nature of man is, objectively. Man has only one real interest and that is the full development of his potentialities, of himself as a human being. Just as one has to know another person and his real needs in order to love him, one has to know one's own self in order to understand what the interests of this self are and how they can be served. It follows that man can deceive himself about his real self-interest if he is ignorant of his self and its real needs and that the science of man is the basis for determining what constitutes man's self-interest.

In the last three hundred years the concept of self-interest has increasingly been narrowed until it has assumed almost the opposite meaning which it has in Spinoza's thinking. It has become identical with selfishness, with interest in material gains, power, and success; and instead of its being synonymous with virtue, its conquest has become an ethical commandment.

This deterioration was made possible by the change from the objectivistic into the erroneously subjectivistic approach to self-interest. Self-interest was no longer to be determined by the nature of man and his needs; correspondingly, the notion that one could be mistaken about it was relinquished and replaced by the idea that what a person *felt* represented the interest of his self was necessarily his true self-interest.

The modern concept of self-interest is a strange blend of two contradictory concepts: that of Calvin and Luther on the one hand, and on the other, that of the progressive thinkers since Spinoza. Calvin and Luther had taught that man must suppress his self-interest and consider himself only an instrument for God's purposes. Progressive thinkers, on the contrary, have taught that man ought to be only an end for himself and not a means for any purpose transcending him. What happened was that man has accepted the contents of the Calvinistic doctrine while rejecting its religious formulation. He has made himself an instrument, not of God's will but of the economic machine or the state. He has accepted the role of a tool, not for God but for industrial progress; he has worked and amassed money but essentially not for the pleasure of spending it and of enjoying life but in order to save, to invest, to be successful. Monastic asceticism has been, as Max Weber has pointed out, replaced by an *inner-worldly asceticism* where personal happiness and enjoyment are no longer the real aims of life. But this attitude was increasingly divorced from the one expressed in Calvin's concept and blended with that expressed in the progressive concept of self-interest, which taught that man had the right—and the obligation—to make the pursuit of his self-interest the supreme norm of life. The result is that modern man *lives* according to the principles of self-denial and *thinks* in terms of self-interest. He believes that he is acting in behalf of *his* interest when actually his paramount concern is money and success; he deceives himself about the fact that his most important human potentialities remain unfulfilled and that he loses himself in the process of seeking what is supposed to be best for him.

The deterioration of the meaning of the concept of self-interest is closely related to the change in the concept of self. In the Middle Ages man felt himself to be an intrinsic part of the social and religious community in reference to which he conceived his own self when he as an individual had not yet fully emerged from his group. Since the beginning of the modern era, when man as an individual was faced with the task of experiencing himself as an independent entity, his own identity became a problem. In the eighteenth and nineteenth centuries the concept of self was narrowed down increasingly; the self was felt to be constituted by the property one had. The formula for this concept of self was no longer "I am what I think" but "I am what I have," "what I possess." [27]

---

[27] William James expressed this concept very clearly. "To have," he says, "a self that I can care for, Nature must first present me with some object interesting enough to make me instinctively wish to appropriate it for its own sake. . . . My own body and what ministers to its needs are thus the primitive object, instinctively determined, of my egoistic interests. Other objects may become interesting derivatively, through association with any of these things, either as means or as habitual concomitants; and so, in a thousand ways, the primitive sphere of the egoistic emotions may enlarge and change its boundaries. This sort of interest is really the meaning of the word *mine*. Whatever has it, is, eo ipso, a part of me!"—*Principles of Psychology* (New York: Henry Holt and Company, 2 vols., 1896), I, 319, 324. Elsewhere James writes: "It is clear that between what a man calls *me* and what he simply calls *mine*, the line is difficult to draw. We feel and act about certain things that are ours very much as we feel and act about ourselves. Our fame, our children,

In the last few generations, under the growing influence of the market, the concept of self has shifted from meaning "I am what I possess" to meaning "I am as you desire me." [28] Man, living in a market economy, feels himself to be a commodity. He is divorced from himself, as the seller of a commodity is divorced from what he wants to sell. To be sure, he is interested in himself, immensely interested in his success on the market, but "he" is the manager, the employer, the seller—and the commodity. His self-interest turns out to be the interest of "him" as the subject who employs "himself," as the commodity which should obtain the optimal price on the personality market.

The "fallacy of self-interest" in modern man has never been described better than by Ibsen in *Peer Gynt*. Peer Gynt believes that his whole life is devoted to the attainment of the interests of his *self*. He describes this self as:

> *"The Gyntian Self!*
> *—An army, that, of wishes, appetites, desires!*
> *The Gyntian Self!*
> *It is a sea of fancies, claims and aspirations;*
> *In fact, it's all that swells within my breast*
> *And makes it come about that I am I and live as such."* [29]

At the end of his life he recognizes that he had deceived himself; that while following the principle of "self-interest" he had failed to recognize what the interests of his real self were, and had lost the very self he sought to preserve. He is told that he never had been himself and that therefore he is to be thrown back into the melting pot to be dealt with as raw material. He discovers that he has lived according to the Troll principle: "To

the work of our hands, may be as dear to us as our bodies are, and arouse the same feelings and the same acts of reprisal if attacked. . . . In its widest possible sense, however, a man's Self is the sum-total of all that he can call his, not only his body, and his psychic powers, but his clothes and his house, his wife and children, his ancestors and friends, his reputation and works, his land and horses and yacht and bank account. All these things give him the same emotions. If they wax or prosper, he feels triumphant, if they dwindle and die away, he feels cast down—not necessarily in the same degree for each thing, but in much the same way for all."—*Ibid.*, I, 291-292.

[28] Pirandello in his plays has expressed this concept of self and the self-doubt resulting from it.

[29] *Loc. cit.*, Act V, Scene I.

thyself be enough"—which is the opposite of the human principle: "To thyself be true." He is seized by the horror of nothingness to which he, who has no self, can not help succumbing when the props of pseudo self, success, and possessions are taken away or seriously questioned. He is forced to recognize that in trying to gain all the wealth of the world, in relentlessly pursuing what seemed to be his interest, he had lost his soul—or, as I would rather say, his self.

The deteriorated meaning of the concept of self-interest which pervades modern society has given rise to attacks on democracy from the various types of totalitarian ideologies. These claim that capitalism is *morally* wrong because it is governed by the principle of selfishness, and commend the moral superiority of their own systems by pointing to their principle of the unselfish subordination of the individual to the "higher" purposes of the state, the "race," or the "socialist fatherland." They impress not a few with this criticism because many people feel that there is no happiness in the pursuit of selfish interest, and are imbued with a striving, vague though it may be, for a greater solidarity and mutual responsibility among men.

We need not waste much time arguing against the totalitarian claims. In the first place, they are insincere since they only disguise the extreme selfishness of an "elite" that wishes to conquer and retain power over the majority of the population. Their ideology of unselfishness has the purpose of deceiving those subject to the control of the elite and of facilitating their exploitation and manipulation. Furthermore, the totalitarian ideologies confuse the issue by making it appear that they represent the principle of unselfishness when they apply to the state as a whole the principle of ruthless pursuit of selfishness. Each citizen ought to be devoted to the common welfare, but the state is permitted to pursue its own interest without regard to the welfare of other nations. But quite aside from the fact that the doctrines of totalitarianism are disguises for the most extreme selfishness, they are a revival—in secular language—of the religious idea of intrinsic human powerlessness and impotence and the resulting need for submission, to overcome which was the essence of modern spiritual and political progress. Not only do the authoritarian ideologies threaten the most precious achievement of Western culture, the respect for the uniqueness and dignity of the individual; they also tend to block the way to constructive criticism of modern society, and thereby to necessary changes. The failure of modern culture lies not in its principle of individualism, not in the idea that moral virtue is the same as the pursuit of self-interest, but in the deterioration of the meaning of self-interest; not in the fact that people are *too much concerned with their self-interest,* but that they are *not concerned enough with the interest of their real self; not in the fact that they are too selfish, but that they do not love themselves.*

If the causes for persevering in the pursuit of a fictitious idea of self-interest are as deeply rooted in the contemporary social structure as indicated above, the chances for a change in the meaning of self-interest would seem to be remote indeed, unless one can point to specific factors operating in the direction of change.

Perhaps the most important factor is the inner dissatisfaction of modern man with the results of his pursuit of "self-interest." The religion of success is crumbling and becoming a façade itself. The social "open spaces" grow narrower; the failure of the hopes for a better world after the First World War, the depression at the end of the twenties, the threat of a new and immensely destructive war so shortly after the Second World War, and the boundless insecurity resulting from this threat, shake the faith in the pursuit of this form of self-interest. Aside from these factors, the worship of success itself has failed to satisfy man's ineradicable striving to be himself. Like so many fantasies and day-dreams, this one too fulfilled its function only for a time, as long as it was new, as long as the excitement connected with it was strong enough to keep man from considering it soberly. There is an increasing number of people to whom everything they are doing seems futile. They are still under the spell of the slogans which preach faith in the secular paradise of success and glamour. But doubt, the fertile condition of all progress, has begun to beset them and has made them ready to ask what their real self-interest as human beings is.

This inner disillusionment and the readiness for a revaluation of self-interest could hardly become effective unless the economic conditions of our culture permitted it. I have pointed out that while the canalizing of all human energy into work and the striving for success was one of the indispensable conditions of the enormous achievement of modern capitalism, a stage has been reached where the problem of *production* has been virtually solved and where the problem of the *organization* of social life has become the paramount task of mankind. Man has created such sources of mechanical energy that he has freed himself from the task of putting all his human energy into work in order to produce the material conditions for living. He could spend a considerable part of his energy on the task of living itself.

Only if these two conditions, the subjective dissatisfaction with a culturally patterned aim and the socioeconomic basis for a change, are present, can an indispensable third factor, rational insight, become effective. This holds true as a principle of social and psychological change in general and of the change in the meaning of self-interest in particular. The time has come when the anesthetized striving for the pursuit of man's real interest is coming to life again. Once man knows what his self-interest is, the first, and the most difficult, step to its realization has been taken.

21

ERICH FROMM

Character*

1. The Dynamic Concept of Character

Character traits were and are considered by behavioristically oriented psychologists to be synonymous with behavior traits. From this standpoint character is defined as "the pattern of behavior characteristic for a given individual," [1] while other authors like William McDougall, R. G. Gordon, and Kretschmer have emphasized the conative and dynamic element of character traits.

Freud developed not only the first but also the most consistent and penetrating theory of character as a system of strivings which underlie, but are not identical with, behavior. In order to appreciate Freud's dynamic concept of character, a comparison between behavior traits and character traits will be helpful. Behavior traits are described in terms of actions which are observable by a third person. Thus, for instance, the behavior trait "being courageous" would be defined as behavior which is directed toward reaching a certain goal without being deterred by risks to one's comfort, freedom, or life. Or parsimony as a behavior trait would be defined as behavior which aims at saving money or other material things. However, if we inquire into the motivation and particularly into the unconscious motivation of

---

* From Man for Himself: An Inquiry into the Psychology of Ethics, by Erich Fromm, Copyright 1947 by Erich Fromm, reprinted by permission of Rinehart & Co., Inc. and Routledge & Kegan Paul Ltd.

[1] Leland E. Hinsie and Jacob Shatzky, Psychiatric Dictionary. (New York: Oxford University Press, 1940.)

such behavior traits we find that the behavior trait covers numerous and entirely different character traits. Courageous behavior may be motivated by ambition so that a person will risk his life in certain situations in order to satisfy his craving for being admired; it may be motivated by suicidal impulses which drive a person to seek danger because, consciously or unconsciously, he does not value his life and wants to destroy himself; it may be motivated by sheer lack of imagination so that a person acts courageously because he is not aware of the danger awaiting him; finally, it may be determined by genuine devotion to the idea or aim for which a person acts, a motivation which is conventionally assumed to be the basis of courage. Superficially the behavior in all these instances is the same in spite of the different motivations. I say "superficially" because if one can observe such behavior minutely one finds that the difference in motivation results also in subtle differences in behavior. An officer in battle, for instance, will behave quite differently in different situations if his courage is motivated by devotion to an idea rather than by ambition. In the first case he would not attack in certain situations if the risks are in no proportion to the tactical ends to be gained. If, on the other hand, he is driven by vanity, this passion may make him blind to the dangers threatening him and his soldiers. His behavior trait "courage" in the latter case is obviously a very ambiguous asset. Another illustration is parsimony. A person may be economical because his economic circumstances make it necessary; or he may be parsimonious because he has a stingy character, which makes saving an aim for its own sake regardless of the realistic necessity. Here, too, the motivation would make some difference with regard to behavior itself. In the first case, the person would be very well able to discern a situation where it is wise to save from one in which it is wiser to spend money. In the latter case he will save regardless of the objective need for it. Another factor which is determined by the difference in motivation refers to the prediction of behavior. In the case of a "courageous" soldier motivated by ambition we may predict that he will behave courageously only if his courage can be rewarded. In the case of the soldier who is courageous because of devotion to his cause we can predict that the question of whether or not his courage will find recognition will have little influence on his behavior.

Closely related to Freud's concept of unconscious motivation is his theory of the conative nature of character traits. He recognized something that the great novelists and dramatists had always known: that, as Balzac put it, the study of character deals with "the forces by which man is motivated"; that the way a person acts, feels, and thinks is to a large extent determined by the specificity of his character and is not merely the result of rational responses to realistic situations; that "man's fate is his character." Freud recognized the dynamic quality of character traits and that the character structure of a person represents a particular form in which energy is canalized in the process of living.

Freud tried to account for this dynamic nature of character traits by combining his characterology with his libido theory. In accordance with the type of materialistic thinking prevalent in the natural sciences of the late nineteenth century, which assumed the energy in natural and psychical phenomena to be a substantial not a relational entity, Freud believed that the sexual drive was the source of energy of the character. By a number of complicated and brilliant assumptions he explained different character traits as "sublimations" of, or "reaction formations" against, the various forms of the sexual drive. He interpreted the *dynamic* nature of character traits as an expression of their *libidinous source*.

The progress of psychoanalytic theory led, in line with the progress of the natural and social sciences, to a new concept which was based, not on the idea of a primarily isolated individual, but on the *relationship* of man to others, to nature, and to himself. It was assumed that this very relationship governs and regulates the energy manifest in the passionate strivings of man. H. S. Sullivan, one of the pioneers of this new view, has accordingly defined psychoanalysis as a "study of interpersonal relations."

The theory presented in the following pages follows Freud's characterology in essential points: in the assumption that character traits underlie behavior and must be inferred from it; that they constitute forces which, though powerful, the person may be entirely unconscious of. It follows Freud also in the assumption that the fundamental entity in character is not the single character trait but the total character organization from which a number of single character traits follow. These character traits are to be understood as a syndrome which results from a particular organization or, as I shall call it, orientation of character. I shall deal only with a very limited number of character traits which follow immediately from the underlying orientation. A number of other character traits could be dealt with similarly, and it could be shown that they are also direct outcomes of basic orientations or mixtures of such primary traits of character with those of temperament. However, a great number of others conventionally listed as character traits would be found to be not character traits in our sense but pure temperament or mere behavior traits.

The main difference in theory of character proposed here from that of Freud is that the fundamental basis of character is not seen in various types of libido organization but in specific kinds of a person's relatedness to the world. In the process of living, man relates himself to the world (1) by acquiring and assimilating things, and (2) by relating himself to people (and himself). The former I shall call the process of assimilation; the latter, that of socialization. Both forms of relatedness are "open" and not, as with the animal, instinctively determined. Man can acquire things by receiving or taking them from an outside source or by producing them through his own effort. But he must acquire and assimilate them in some fashion in order to satisfy his needs. Also, man cannot live alone and unrelated to others. He has to associate with others for defense, for work, for sexual satisfaction, for play, for the upbringing of the young, for the transmission of knowledge and material possessions. But beyond that, it is necessary for him to be related to others, one with them, part of a group. Complete isolation is unbearable and incompatible with sanity. Again man can relate himself to others in various ways: he can love or hate, he can compete or cooperate; he can build a social system based on equality or authority, liberty or oppression; but he must be related in some fashion and the particular form of relatedness is expressive of his character.

These orientations, by which the individual relates himself to the world, constitute the core of his character; character can be defined as the (*relatively permanent*) *form in which human energy is canalized in the process of assimilation and socialization*. This canalization of psychic energy has a very significant biological function. Since man's actions are not determined by innate instinctual patterns, life would be precarious, indeed, if he had to make a deliberate decision each time he acted, each time he took a step. On the contrary, many actions must be performed far more quickly than conscious deliberation allows. Furthermore, if all behavior followed from deliberate decision, many more inconsistencies in action would occur than are compatible with proper functioning. According to behavioristic thinking, man learns to react in a semiautomatic fashion by developing habits of action and thought which can be understood in terms of conditioned reflexes. While this view is correct to a certain extent, it ignores the fact that the most deeply rooted habits and opinions which are characteristic of a person and resistant to change grow from his character structure: they are expressive of the particular form in which energy has been canalized in the character structure. The character system can be considered the human substitute for the instinctive apparatus of the animal. Once energy is canalized in a certain way, action takes place "true to character." A particular character may be undesirable ethically, but at least it permits a person to act fairly consistently and to be relieved of the burden of having to make a new and deliberate decision every time. He can arrange his life in a way which is geared to his character and thus create a certain degree of compatibility between the inner and the outer situation. Moreover, character has also a selective function with regard to a person's ideas and values. Since to most people ideas seem to be independent of their emotions and wishes and the result of logical deduction, they feel that their attitude toward the world is confirmed by their ideas and judgments when actually these are as much a result of their character as their actions are. This confirmation in turn tends to stabilize their character structure since it makes the latter appear right and sensible.

Not only has character the function of permitting the individual to act consistently and "reasonably"; it is also the basis for his adjustment to society. The character of the child is molded by the character of its parents in response to whom it develops. The parents and their methods of child training in turn are determined by the social structure of their culture. The average family is the "psychic agency" of society, and by adjusting himself to his family the child acquires the character which later makes him adjusted to the tasks he has to perform in social life. He acquires that character which makes him want to do what he has to do and the core of which he shares with most members of the same social class or culture. The fact that most members of a social class or culture share significant elements of character and that one can speak of a "social character" representing the core of a character structure common to most people of a given culture shows the degree to which character is formed by social and cultural patterns. But from the social character we must differentiate the individual character in which one person differs from another within the same culture. These differences are partly due to the differences of the personalities of the parents and to the differences, psychic and material, of the specific social environment in which the child grows up. But they are also due to the constitutional differences of each individual, particularly those of temperament. Genetically, the formation of individual character is determined by the impact of its life experiences, the individual ones and those which follow from the culture, on temperament and physical constitution. Environment is never the same for two people, for the difference in constitution makes them experience the same environment in a more or less different way. Mere habits of action and thought which develop as the result of an individual's conforming with the cultural pattern and which are not rooted in the character of a person are easily changed under the influence of new social patterns. If, on the other hand, a person's behavior is rooted in his character, it is charged with energy and changeable only if a fundamental change in a person's character takes place.

In the following analysis *nonproductive orientations* are differentiated from the *productive orientation*. It must be noted that these concepts are "ideal-types," not descriptions of the character of a given individual. Furthermore, while, for didactic purposes, they are treated here separately, the character of any given person is usually a blend of all or some of these orientations in which one, however, is dominant. Finally, I want to state here that in the description of the nonproductive orientations only their negative aspects are presented, while their positive aspects are discussed briefly in a later part of this chapter.[2]

2. Types of Character: The Nonproductive Orientations

a) *The receptive orientation*

In the receptive orientation a person feels "the source of all good" to be outside, and he believes that the only way to get what he wants—be it something material, be it affection, love, knowledge, pleasure—is to receive it from that outside source. In this orientation the problem of love is almost exclusively that of "being loved" and not that of loving. Such people tend to be indiscriminate in the choice of their love objects, because being loved by anybody is such an overwhelming experience for them that they "fall for" anybody who gives them love or what looks like love. They are exceedingly sensitive to any withdrawal or rebuff they experience on the part of the loved person. Their orientation is the same in the sphere of thinking: if intelligent, they make the best listeners, since their orientation is one of receiving, not of producing, ideas; left to themselves, they feel paralyzed. It is characteristic of these people that their first thought is to find somebody else to give them needed information rather than to make even the smallest effort of their own. If religious, these persons have a concept of God in which they expect everything from God and nothing from their own activity.

---

[2] See pp. 112 ff. [of *Man for Himself*]. The following description of the non-productive orientations, except that of the marketing, follows the clinical picture of the pregenital character given by Freud and others. The theoretical difference becomes apparent in the discussion of the hoarding character.

If not religious, their relationship to persons or institutions is very much the same; they are always in search of a "magic helper." They show a particular kind of loyalty, at the bottom of which is the gratitude for the hand that feeds them and the fear of ever losing it. Since they need many hands to feel secure, they have to be loyal to numerous people. It is difficult for them to say "no," and they are easily caught between conflicting loyalties and promises. Since they cannot say "no," they love to say "yes" to everything and everybody, and the resulting paralysis of their critical abilities makes them increasingly dependent on others.

They are dependent not only on authorities for knowledge and help but on people in general for any kind of support. They feel lost when alone because they feel that they cannot do anything without help. This helplessness is especially important with regard to those acts which by their very nature can only be done alone —making decisions and taking responsibility. In personal relationships, for instance, they ask advice from the very person with regard to whom they have to make a decision.

This receptive type has great fondness for food and drink. These persons tend to overcome anxiety and depression by eating or drinking. The mouth is an especially prominent feature, often the most expressive one; the lips tend to be open, as if in a state of continuous expectation of being fed. In their dreams, being fed is a frequent symbol of being loved; being starved, an expression of frustration or disappointment.

By and large, the outlook of people of this receptive orientation is optimistic and friendly; they have a certain confidence in life and its gifts, but they become anxious and distraught when their "source of supply" is threatened. They often have a genuine warmth and a wish to help others, but doing things for others also assumes the function of securing their favor.

b) The exploitative orientation

The exploitative orientation, like the receptive, has as its basic premise the feeling that the source of all good is outside, that whatever one wants to get must be sought there, and that one cannot produce anything oneself. The difference between the two, however, is that the exploitative type does not expect to receive things from others as gifts, but to take them away from others by force or cunning. This orientation extends to all spheres of activity.

In the realm of love and affection these people tend to grab and steal. They feel attracted only to people whom they can take away from somebody else. Attractiveness to them is conditioned by a person's attachment to somebody else; they tend not to fall in love with an unattached person.

We find the same attitude with regard to thinking and intellectual pursuits. Such people will tend not to produce ideas but to steal them. This may be done directly in the form of plagiarism or more subtly by repeating in different phraseology the ideas voiced by others and insisting they are new and their own. It is a striking fact that frequently people with great intelligence proceed in this way, although if they relied on their own gifts they might well be able to have ideas of their own. The lack of original ideas or independent production in otherwise gifted people often has its explanation in this character orientation, rather than in any innate lack of originality. The same statement holds true with regard to their orientation to material things. Things which they can take away from others always seem better to them than anything they can produce themselves. They use and exploit anybody and anything from whom or from which they can squeeze something. Their motto is: "Stolen fruits are sweetest." Because they want to use and exploit people, they "love" those who, explicitly or implicitly, are promising objects of exploitation, and get "fed up" with persons whom they have squeezed out. An extreme example is the kleptomaniac who enjoys things only if he can steal them, although he has the money to buy them.

This orientation seems to be symbolized by the biting mouth which is often a prominent feature in such people. It is not a play upon words to point out that they often make "biting" remarks about others. Their attitude is colored by a mixture of hostility and manipulation. Everyone is an object of exploitation and is judged according to his usefulness. Instead of the confidence and optimism which characterizes the receptive type, one finds here suspicion and cynicism, envy and jealousy. Since they are satisfied only with things they can take away from others, they tend to overrate what others have and underrate what is theirs.

c) *The hoarding orientation*

While the receptive and exploitative types are similar inasmuch as both expect to get things from the outside world, the hoarding orientation is essentially different. This orientation makes people have little faith in anything new they might get from the outside world; their security is based upon hoarding and saving, while spending is felt to be a threat. They have surrounded themselves, as it were, by a protective wall, and their main aim is to bring as much as possible into this fortified position and to let as little as possible out of it. Their miserliness refers to money and material things as well as to feelings and thoughts. Love is essentially a possession; they do not give love but try to get it by possessing the "beloved." The hoarding person often shows a particular kind of faithfulness toward people and even toward memories. Their sentimentality makes the past appear as golden; they hold on to it and indulge in the memories of bygone feelings and experiences. They know everything but are sterile and incapable of productive thinking.

One can recognize these people too by facial expressions and gestures. Theirs is the tight-lipped mouth; their gestures are characteristic of their withdrawn attitude. While those of the receptive type are inviting and round, as it were, and the gestures of the exploitative type are aggressive and pointed, those of the hoarding type are angular, as if they wanted to emphasize the frontiers between themselves and the outside world. Another characteristic element in this attitude is pedantic orderliness. The hoarder will be orderly with things, thoughts, or feelings, but again, as with memory, his orderliness is sterile and rigid. He cannot endure things out of place and will automatically rearrange them. To him the outside world threatens to break into his fortified position; orderliness signifies mastering the world outside by putting it, and keeping it, in its proper place in order to avoid the danger of intrusion. His compulsive cleanliness is another expression of his need to undo contact with the outside world. Things beyond his own frontiers are felt to be dangerous and "unclean"; he annuls the menacing contact by compulsive washing, similar to a religious washing ritual prescribed after contact with unclean things or people. Things have to be put not only in their proper place but also into their proper time; obsessive punctuality is characteristic of the hoarding type; it is another form of mastering the outside world. If the outside world is experienced as a threat to one's fortified position, obstinacy is a logical reaction. A constant "no" is the almost automatic defense against intrusion; sitting tight, the answer to the danger of being pushed. These people tend to feel that they possess only a fixed quantity of strength, energy, or mental capacity, and that this stock is diminished or exhausted by use and can never be replenished. They cannot understand the self-replenishing function of all living substance and that activity and the use of one's powers increase strength while stagnation paralyzes; to them, death and destruction have more reality than life and growth. The act of creation is a miracle of which they hear but in which they do not believe. Their highest values are order and security; their motto: "There is nothing new under the sun." In their relationship to others intimacy is a threat; either remoteness or possession of a person means security. The hoarder tends to be suspicious and to have a particular sense of justice which in effect says: "Mine is mine and yours is yours."

d) *The marketing orientation*

The marketing orientation developed as a dominant one only in the modern era. In order to understand its nature one must consider the economic function of the market in modern society as being not only analogous to this character orientation but as the basis and the main condition for its development in modern man.

Barter is one of the oldest economic mechanisms. The traditional local market, however, is essentially different from the market as it has developed in modern capitalism. Bartering on a local market offered an opportunity to meet for the purpose of exchanging commodities. Producers and customers became acquainted; they were relatively small groups; the demand was more or less known, so that the producer could produce for this specific demand.

The modern market[3] is no longer a meeting place but a mechanism characterized by abstract and impersonal demand. One produces for this market, not for a known circle of customers; its verdict is based on laws of supply and demand; and it determines whether the commodity can be sold and at what price. No matter what the *use value* of a pair of shoes may be, for instance, if the supply is greater than the demand, some shoes will be sentenced to economic death; they might as well not have been produced at all. The market day is the "day of judgment" as far as the *exchange value* of commodities is concerned.

The reader may object that this description of the market is oversimplified. The producer does try to judge the demand in advance, and under monopoly conditions even obtains a certain degree of control over it. Nevertheless, the regulatory function of the market has been, and still is, predominant enough to have a profound influence on the character formation of the urban middle class and, through the latter's social and cultural influence, on the whole population. The market concept of value, the emphasis on exchange value rather than on use value, has led to a similar concept of value with regard to people and particularly to oneself. The character orientation which is rooted in the experience of oneself as a commodity and of one's value as exchange value I call the marketing orientation.

In our time the marketing orientation has been growing rapidly, together with the development of a new market that is a phenomenon of the last decades—the "personality market." Clerks and salesmen, business executives and doctors, lawyers and artists all appear on this market. It is true that their legal status and economic positions are different: some are independent, charging

---

[3] Cf., for the study of history and function of the modern market, K. Polanyi's *The Great Transformation* (New York: Rinehart & Company, 1944).

for their services; others are employed, receiving salaries. But all are dependent for their material success on a personal acceptance by those who need their services or who employ them.

The principle of evaluation is the same on both the personality and the commodity market: on the one, personalities are offered for sale; on the other, commodities. Value in both cases is their exchange value, for which use value is a necessary but not a sufficient condition. It is true, our economic system could not function if people were not skilled in the particular work they have to perform and were gifted only with a pleasant personality. Even the best bedside manner and the most beautifully equipped office on Park Avenue would not make a New York doctor successful if he did not have a minimum of medical knowledge and skill. Even the most winning personality would not prevent a secretary from losing her job unless she could type reasonably fast. However, if we ask what the respective weight of skill and personality as a condition for success is, we find that only in exceptional cases is success predominantly the result of skill and of certain other human qualities like honesty, decency, and integrity. Although the proportion between skill and human qualities on the one hand and "personality" on the other hand as prerequisites for success varies, the "personality factor" always plays a decisive role. Success depends largely on how well a person sells himself on the market, how well he gets his personality across, how nice a "package" he is; whether he is "cheerful," "sound," "aggressive," "reliable," "ambitious"; furthermore what his family background is, what clubs he belongs to, and whether he knows the right people. The type of personality required depends to some degree on the special field in which a person works. A stockbroker, a salesman, a secretary, a railroad executive, a college professor, or a hotel manager must each offer different kinds of personality that, regardless of their differences, must fulfill one condition: to be in demand.

The fact that in order to have success it is not sufficient to have the skill and equipment for performing a given task but that one must be able to "put across" one's personality in competition with many others shapes the attitude toward oneself. If it were enough for the purpose of making a living to rely on what one knows and what one can do, one's self-esteem would be in proportion to one's capacities, that is, to one's use value; but since success depends largely on how one sells one's personality, one experiences oneself as a commodity or rather simultaneously as the seller *and* the commodity to be sold. A person is not concerned with his life and happiness, but with becoming salable. This feeling might be compared to that of a commodity, of handbags on a counter, for instance, could they feel and think. Each handbag would try to make itself as "attractive" as possible in order to attract customers and to look as expensive as possible in order to obtain a higher price than its rivals. The handbag sold for the highest price would feel elated, since that would mean it was the most "valuable" one; the one which was not sold would feel sad and convinced of its own worthlessness. This fate might befall a bag which, though excellent in appearance and usefulness, had the bad luck to be out of date because of a change in fashion.

Like the handbag, one has to be in fashion on the personality market, and in order to be in fashion one has to know what kind of personality is most in demand. This knowledge is transmitted in a general way throughout the whole process of education, from kindergarten to college, and implemented by the family. The knowledge acquired at this early stage is not sufficient, however; it emphasizes only certain general qualities like adaptability, ambition, and sensitivity to the changing expectations of other people. The more specific picture of the models for success one gets elsewhere. The pictorial magazines, newspapers, and newsreels show the pictures and life stories of the successful in many variations. Pictorial advertising has a similar function. The successful executive who is pictured in a tailor's advertisement is the image of how one should look and be, if one is to draw down the "big money" on the contemporary personality market.

The most important means of transmitting the desired personality pattern to the average man is the motion picture. The young girl tries to emulate the facial expression, coiffure, gestures of a high-priced star as the most promising way to success. The young man tries to look and be like the model he sees on the screen. While the average citizen has little contact with the life of the most successful people, his relationship with the motion-picture stars is different. It is true that he has no real contact with them either, but he can see them on the screen again and again, can write them and receive their autographed pictures. In contrast to the time when the actor was socially despised but was nevertheless the transmitter of the works of great poets to his audience, our motion-picture stars have no great works or ideas to transmit, but their function is to serve as the link an average person has with the world of the "great." Even if he can not hope to become as successful as they are, he can try to emulate them; they are his saints and because of their success they embody the norms for living.

Since modern man experiences himself both as the seller and as the commodity to be sold on the market, his self-esteem depends on conditions beyond his control. If he is "successful," he is valuable; if he is not, he is worthless. The degree of insecurity which results from this orientation can hardly be overestimated. If one feels that one's own value is not constituted primarily by the human qualities one possesses, but by one's success on a competitive market with ever-changing conditions, one's self-esteem is bound to be shaky and in constant need of confirmation by others. Hence one is driven to strive relentlessly for success, and any setback is a severe threat to one's self-esteem; helplessness, insecurity, and inferiority feelings are the result. If the vicissitudes of the market are the judges of one's value, the sense of dignity and pride is destroyed.

But the problem is not only that of self-evaluation and self-esteem but of one's experience of oneself as an independent entity, of one's *identity with oneself*. As we shall see later, the mature and productive individual derives his feeling of identity from the experience of himself as the agent who is one with his powers; this feeling of self can be briefly expressed as meaning "*I am what I do*." In the marketing orientation man encounters his own powers as commodities alienated from him. He is not one with them but they are masked from him because what matters is not his self-realization in the process of using them but his success in the process of selling them. Both his powers and what they create become estranged, something different from himself, something for others to judge and to use; thus his feeling of identity becomes as shaky as his self-esteem; it is constituted by the sum total of roles one can play: *"I am as you desire me."*

Ibsen has expressed this state of selfhood in Peer Gynt: Peer Gynt tries to discover his self and he finds that he is like an onion—one layer after the other can be peeled off and there is no core to be found. Since man cannot live doubting his identity, he must, in the marketing orientation, find the conviction of identity not in reference to himself and his powers but in the opinion of others about him. His prestige, status, success, the fact that he is known to others as being a certain person are a substitute for the genuine feeling of identity. This situation makes him utterly dependent on the way others look at him and forces him to keep up the role in which he once had become successful. If I and my powers are separated from each other then, indeed, is my self constituted by the price I fetch.

The way one experiences others is not different from the way one experiences oneself.[4] Others are experienced as commodities like oneself; they too do not present *themselves* but their salable part. The difference between people is reduced to a merely quantitative difference of being *more or less* successful, attractive, hence valuable. This process is not different from what happens to commodities on the market. A painting and a pair of shoes can be expressed in, and reduced to, their exchange value, their price; so many pairs of shoes are "equal" to one painting. In the same way the difference between people is reduced to a common element, their price on the market. Their individuality, that which is peculiar and unique in them, is valueless and, in fact, a ballast. The meaning which the word *peculiar* has assumed is quite expressive of this attitude. Instead of denoting the greatest achievement of man—that of having developed his individuality—it has become almost synonymous with *queer*. The word *equality* has also changed its meaning. The idea that all men are created equal implied that all men have the same fundamental right to be considered as ends in themselves and not as means. Today,

---

[4] The fact that relationship to oneself and to others is conjunctive will be explained in Chapter IV [of *Man for Himself*].

equality has become equivalent to *interchangeability,* and is the very negation of individuality. Equality, instead of being the condition for the development of each man's peculiarity, means the extinction of individuality, the "selflessness" characteristic of the marketing orientation. Equality was conjunctive with difference, but it has become synonymous with "in-difference" and, indeed, indifference is what characterizes modern man's relationship to himself and to others.

These conditions necessarily color all human relationships. When the individual self is neglected, the relationships between people must of necessity become superficial, because not they themselves but interchangeable commodities are related. People are not able and cannot afford to be concerned with that which is unique and "peculiar" in each other. However, the market creates a kind of comradeship of its own. Everybody is involved in the same battle of competition, shares the same striving for success; all meet under the same conditions of the market (or at least believe they do). Everyone knows how the others feel because each is in the same boat: alone, afraid to fail, eager to please; no quarter is given or expected in this battle.

The superficial character of human relationships leads many to hope that they can find depth and intensity of feeling in individual love. But love for one person and love for one's neighbor are indivisible; in any given culture, love relationships are only a more intense expression of the relatedness to man prevalent in that culture. Hence it is an illusion to expect that the loneliness of man rooted in the marketing orientation can be cured by individual love.

Thinking as well as feeling is determined by the marketing orientation. Thinking assumes the function of grasping things quickly so as to be able to manipulate them successfully. Furthered by widespread and efficient education, this leads to a high degree of intelligence, but not of reason.[5] For manipulative purposes, all that is necessary to know is the surface features of things, the superficial. The truth, to be uncovered by penetrating to the essence of phenomena, becomes an obsolete

---

[5] The difference between intelligence and reason will be discussed later on, pp. 96 ff. [of *Man for Himself*].

concept—truth not only in the prescientific sense of "absolute" truth, dogmatically maintained without reference to empirical data, but also in the sense of truth attained by man's reason applied to his observations and open to revisions. Most intelligence tests are attuned to this kind of thinking; they measure not so much the capacity for reason and understanding as the capacity for quick mental adaptation to a given situation; "mental adjustment tests" would be the adequate name for them.[6] For this kind of thinking the application of the categories of comparison and of quantitative measurement—rather than a thorough analysis of a given phenomenon and its quality—is essential. All problems are equally "interesting" and there is little sense of the respective differences in their importance. Knowledge itself becomes a commodity. Here, too, man is alienated from his own power; thinking and knowing are experienced as a tool to produce results. Knowledge of man himself, psychology, which in the great tradition of Western thought was held to be the condition for virtue, for right living, for happiness, has degenerated into an instrument to be used for better manipulation of others and oneself, in market research, in political propaganda, in advertising, and so on.

Evidently this type of thinking has a profound effect on our educational system. From grade school to graduate school, the aim of learning is to gather as much information as possible that is mainly useful for the purposes of the market. Students are supposed to learn so many things that they have hardly time and energy left to *think*. Not the interest in the subjects taught or in knowledge and insight as such, but the enhanced exchange value knowledge gives is the main incentive for wanting more and better education. We find today a tremendous enthusiasm for knowledge and education, but at the same time a skeptical or contemptuous attitude toward the allegedly impractical and useless thinking which is concerned "only" with the truth and which has no exchange value on the market.

Although I have presented the marketing orientation as one

---

[6] Cf. Ernest Schachtel, "Zum Begriff und zur Diagnosis der Persoenlichkeit in 'Personality Tests' [On the Concept and Diagnosis of Personality Tests]," *Zeitschrift fuer Sozialforschung* (Jahrgang 6, 1937), pp. 597-624.

of the nonproductive orientations, it is in many ways so different that it belongs in a category of its own. The receptive, exploitative, and hoarding orientations have one thing in common: each is one form of human relatedness which, if dominant in a person, is specific of him and characterizes him. (Later on it will be shown that these four orientations do not necessarily have the negative qualities which have been described so far.[7]) The marketing orientation, however, does not develop something which is potentially in the person (unless we make the absurd assertion that "nothing" is also part of the human equipment); its very nature is that no specific and permanent kind of relatedness is developed, but that the very changeability of attitudes is the only permanent quality of such orientation. In this orientation, those qualities are developed which can best be sold. Not one particular attitude is predominant, but the emptiness which can be filled most quickly with the desired quality. This quality, however, ceases to be one in the proper sense of the word; it is only a role, the pretense of a quality, to be readily exchanged if another one is more desirable. Thus, for instance, respectability is sometimes desirable. The salesmen in certain branches of business ought to impress the public with those qualities of reliability, soberness, and respectability which were genuine in many a businessman of the nineteenth century. Now one looks for a man who instills confidence because he *looks* as if he had these qualities; what this man sells on the personality market is his ability to look the part; what kind of person is behind that role does not matter and is nobody's concern. He himself is not interested in his honesty, but in what it gets for him on the market. The premise of the marketing orientation is emptiness, the lack of any specific quality which could not be subject to change, since any persistent trait of character might conflict some day with the requirements of the market. Some roles would not fit in with the peculiarities of the person; therefore we must do away with them—not with the roles but with the peculiarities. The marketing personality must be free, free of all individuality.

The character orientations which have been described so far are by no means as separate from one another as it may appear

----

[7] [*Man for Himself*], pp. 112 ff.

from this sketch. The receptive orientation, for instance, may be dominant in a person but it is usually blended with any or all of the other orientations. While I shall discuss the various blendings later on in this chapter, I want to stress at this point that all orientations are part of the human equipment, and the dominance of any specific orientation depends to a large extent on the peculiarity of the culture in which the individual lives. Although a more detailed analysis of the relationship between the various orientations and social patterns must be reserved for a study which deals primarily with problems of social psychology, I should like to suggest here a tentative hypothesis as to the social conditions making for the dominance of any of the four non-productive types. It should be noted that the significance of the study of the correlation between character orientation and social structure lies not only in the fact that it helps us understand some of the most significant causes for the formation of character, but also in the fact that specific orientations—inasmuch as they are common to most members of a culture or social class—represent powerful emotional forces the operation of which we must know in order to understand the functioning of society. In view of the current emphasis on the impact of culture on personality, I should like to state that the relationship between society and the individual is not to be understood simply in the sense that cultural patterns and social institutions "influence" the individual. The interaction goes much deeper; the whole personality of the average individual is molded by the way people relate to each other, and it is determined by the socioeconomic and political structure of society to such an extent that, in principle, one can infer from the analysis of one individual the totality of the social structure in which he lives.

The receptive orientation is often to be found in societies in which the right of one group to exploit another is firmly established. Since the exploited group has no power to change, or any idea of changing, its situation, it will tend to look up to its masters as to its providers, as to those from whom one receives everything life can give. No matter how little the slave receives, he feels that by his own effort he could have acquired even less, since the structure of his society impresses him with the fact that he is unable to organize it and to rely on his own activity and reason. As far as contemporary American culture is concerned, it seems at first glance that the receptive attitude is entirely absent. Our whole culture, its ideas, and its practice discourage the receptive orientation and emphasize that each one has to look out, and be responsible, for himself and that he has to use his own initiative if he wants to "get anywhere." However, while the receptive orientation is discouraged, it is by no means absent. The need to conform and to please, which has been discussed in the foregoing pages, leads to the feeling of helplessness, which is the root of subtle receptiveness in modern man. It appears particularly in the attitude toward the "expert" and public opinion. People expect that in every field there is an expert who can tell them how things are and how they ought to be done, and that all they ought to do is listen to him and swallow his ideas. There are experts for science, experts for happiness, and writers become experts in the art of living by the very fact that they are authors of best sellers. This subtle but rather general receptiveness assumes somewhat grotesque forms in modern "folklore," fostered particularly by advertising. While everyone knows that realistically the "get-rich-quick" schemes do not work, there is a widespread daydream of the effortless life. It is partly expressed in connection with the use of gadgets; the car which needs no shifting, the fountain pen which saves the trouble of removing the cap are only random examples of this phantasy. It is particularly prevalent in those schemes which deal with happiness. A very characteristic quotation is the following: "This book," the author says, "tells you how to be twice the man or woman you ever were before—happy, well, brimming with energy, confident, capable and free of care. You are required to follow no laborious mental or physical program; it is much simpler than that. . . . As laid down here the route to that promised profit may appear strange, for few of us can imagine *getting without striving.* . . . Yet that is so, as you will see." [8]

The exploitative character, with its motto "I take what I need," goes back to piratical and feudal ancestors and goes forward

---

[8] Hal Falvey, *Ten Seconds That Will Change Your Life* (Chicago: Wilcox & Follett, 1946).

from there to the robber barons of the nineteenth century who exploited the natural resources of the continent. The "pariah" and "adventure" capitalists, to use Max Weber's terms, roaming the earth for profit, are men of this stamp, men whose aim was to buy cheap and sell dear and who ruthlessly pursued power and wealth. The free market as it operated in the eighteenth and nineteenth centuries under competitive conditions nurtured this type. Our own age has seen a revival of naked exploitativeness in the authoritarian systems which attempted to exploit the natural and human resources, not so much of their own country but of any other country they were powerful enough to invade. They proclaimed the right of might and rationalized it by pointing to the law of nature which makes the stronger survive; love and decency were signs of weakness; thinking was the occupation of cowards and degenerates.

The hoarding orientation existed side by side with the exploitative orientation in the eighteenth and nineteenth centuries. The hoarding type was conservative, less interested in ruthless acquisition than in methodical economic pursuits, based on sound principles and on the preservation of what had been acquired. To him property was a symbol of his self and its protection a supreme value. This orientation gave him a great deal of security; his possession of property and family, protected as they were by the relatively stable conditions of the nineteenth century, constituted a safe and manageable world. Puritan ethics, with the emphasis on work and success as evidence of goodness, supported the feeling of security and tended to give life meaning and a religious sense of fulfillment. This combination of a stable world, stable possessions, and a stable ethic gave the members of the middle class a feeling of belonging, self-confidence, and pride.

The marketing orientation does not come out of the eighteenth or nineteenth centuries; it is definitely a modern product. It is only recently that the package, the label, the brand name have become important, in people as well as in commodities. The gospel of working loses weight and the gospel of selling becomes paramount. In feudal times, social mobility was exceedingly limited and one could not use one's personality to get ahead. In the days of the competitive market, social mobility was relatively great, especially in the United States; if one "delivered the goods" one could get ahead. Today, the opportunities for the lone individual who can make a fortune all by himself are, in comparison with the previous period, greatly diminished. He who wants to get ahead has to fit into large organizations, and his ability to play the expected role is one of his main assets.

The depersonalization, the emptiness, the meaninglessness of life, the automatization of the individual result in a growing dissatisfaction and in a need to search for a more adequate way of living and for norms which could guide man to this end. The productive orientation which I am going to discuss now points to the type of character in whom growth and the development of all his potentialities is the aim to which all other activities are subordinated.

3. The Productive Orientation

a) *General characteristics*

From the time of classic and medieval literature up to the end of the nineteenth century a great deal of effort was expended in describing the vision of what the good man and the good society ought to be. Such ideas were expressed partly in the form of philosophical or theological treatises, partly in the form of utopias. The twentieth century is conspicuous for the absence of such visions. The emphasis is on critical analysis of man and society, in which positive visions of what man ought to be are only implied. While there is no doubt that this criticism is of utmost significance and a condition for any improvement of society, the absence of visions projecting a "better" man and a "better" society has had the effect of paralyzing man's faith in himself and his future (and is at the same time the result of such a paralysis).

Contemporary psychology and particularly psychoanalysis are no exception in this respect. Freud and his followers have given a splended analysis of the neurotic character. Their clinical description of the nonproductive character (in Freud's terms, the pregenital character) is exhaustive and accurate—quite regardless of the fact that the theoretical concepts they used are in need of revision. But the character of the normal, mature, healthy personality has found scarcely any consideration. This character, called the genital character by Freud, has remained a rather vague and abstract concept. It is defined by him as the character structure of a person in whom the oral and anal libido has lost its dominant position and functions under the supremacy of genital sexuality, the aim of which is sexual union with a member of the opposite sex. The description of the genital character does not go far beyond the statement that it is the character structure of an individual who is capable of functioning well sexually and socially.

In discussing the *productive character* I venture beyond critical analysis and inquire into the nature of the fully developed character that is the aim of human development and simultaneously the ideal of humanistic ethics. It may serve as a preliminary approach to the concept of productive orientation to state its connection with Freud's genital character. Indeed, if we do not use Freud's term literally in the context of his libido theory but *symbolically,* it denotes quite accurately the meaning of productiveness. For the stage of sexual maturity is that in which man has the capacity of natural production; by the union of the sperm and the egg new life is produced. While this type of production is common to man and animals, the capacity for material production is specific for man. Man is not only a rational and social animal. He can also be defined as a producing animal, capable of transforming the materials which he finds at hand, using his reason and imagination. Not only *can* he produce, he *must* produce in order to live. Material production, however, is but the most frequent symbol for productiveness as an aspect of character. The "productive orientation" [9] of personality refers to a fundamental attitude, a *mode of relatedness* in all realms of human experience. It covers mental, emotional, and sensory responses to others, to oneself, and to things. Productiveness is man's ability to use his powers and to realize the potentialities

[9] Productiveness as used in this book is meant as an expansion of the concept of spontaneity described in *Escape from Freedom.*

inherent in him. If we say *he* must use *his* powers we imply
that he must be free and not dependent on someone who controls
his powers. We imply, furthermore, that he is guided by reason,
since he can make use of his powers only if he knows what they
are, how to use them, and what to use them for. Productiveness
means that he experiences himself as the embodiment of his
powers and as the "actor"; that he feels himself one with his
powers and at the same time that they are not masked and
alienated from him.

In order to avoid the misunderstandings to which the term
"productiveness" lends itself, it seems appropriate to discuss
briefly what is not meant by productiveness.

Generally the word "productiveness" is associated with creativeness, particularly artistic creativeness. The real artist, indeed,
is the most convincing representative of productiveness. But not
all artists are productive; a conventional painting, e.g., may
exhibit nothing more than the technical skill to reproduce the
likeness of a person in photographic fashion on a canvas. But
a person can experience, see, feel, and think productively without
having the gift to create something visible or communicable.
*Productiveness is an attitude which every human being is capable
of, unless he is mentally and emotionally crippled.*

The term "productive" is also apt to be confused with "active,"
and "productiveness" with "activity." While the two terms can
be synonymous (for instance, in Aristotle's concept of activity),
activity in modern usage frequently indicates the very opposite
of productiveness. Activity is usually defined as behavior which
brings about a change in an existing situation by an expenditure
of energy. In contrast, a person is described as passive if he is
unable to change or overtly influence an existing situation and is
influenced or moved by forces outside himself. This current concept of activity takes into account only the actual expenditure of
energy and the change brought about by it. It does not distinguish
between the underlying psychic conditions governing the activities.

An example, though an extreme one, of nonproductive activity
is the activity of a person under hypnosis. The person in a deep
hypnotic trance may have his eyes open, may walk, talk, and do

things; he "acts." The general definition of activity would apply to him, since energy is spent and some change brought about. But if we consider the particular character and quality of this activity, we find that it is not really the hypnotized person who is the actor, but the hypnotist who, by means of his suggestions, acts through him. While the hypnotic trance is an artificial state, it is an extreme but characteristic example of a situation in which a person can be active and yet not be the true actor, his activity resulting from compelling forces over which he has no control.

A common type of nonproductive activity is the reaction to anxiety, whether acute or chronic, conscious or unconscious, which is frequently at the root of the frantic preoccupations of men today. Different from anxiety-motivated activity, though often blended with it, is the type of activity based on submission to or dependence on an authority. The authority may be feared, admired, or "loved"—usually all three are mixed—but the cause of the activity is the command of the authority, both in a formal way and with regard to its contents. The person is active because the authority wants him to be, and he does what the authority wants him to do. This kind of activity is found in the authoritarian character. To him activity means to act in the name of something higher than his own self. He can act in the name of God, the past, or duty, but not in the name of himself. The authoritarian character receives the impulse to act from a superior power which is neither assailable nor changeable, and is consequently unable to heed spontaneous impulses from within himself.[10]

Resembling submissive activity is automaton activity. Here we do not find dependence on overt authority, but rather on anonymous authority as it is represented by public opinion, culture patterns, common sense, or "science." The person feels or does what he is supposed to feel or do; his activity lacks spontaneity in the sense that it does not originate from his own mental or emotional experience but from an outside source.

---

[10] But the authoritarian character does not only tend to submit but also wishes to dominate others. In fact, both the sadistic and the masochistic sides are always present, and they differ only in degree of their strength and their repression respectively. (See the discussion of the authoritarian character in *Escape from Freedom*, pp. 141 ff.)

Among the most powerful sources of activity are irrational passions. The person who is driven by stinginess, masochism, envy, jealousy, and all other forms of greed is compelled to act; yet his actions are neither free nor rational but in opposition to reason and to his interests as a human being. A person so obsessed repeats himself, becoming more and more inflexible, and more stereotyped. He is active, but he is not productive.

Although the source of these activities is irrational and the acting persons are neither free nor rational, there can be important results, often leading to material success. In the concept of productiveness we are not concerned with activity *necessarily* leading to practical results but with an attitude, with a mode of reaction and orientation toward the world and oneself in the process of living. We are concerned with *man's character, not with his success.*[11]

Productiveness is man's realization of the potentialities characteristic of him, the use of his *powers*. But what is "power"? It is rather ironical that this word denotes two contradictory concepts: *Power of* = capacity and *power over* = domination. This contradiction, however, is of a particular kind. Power = domination results from the paralysis of power = capacity. *"Power over" is the perversion of "power to."* The ability of man to make productive use of his powers is his potency; the inability is his impotence. With his power of reason he can penetrate the surface of phenomena and understand their essence. With his power of love he can break through the wall which separates one person from another. With his power of imagination he can visualize things not yet existing; he can plan and thus begin to create. Where potency is lacking, man's relatedness to the world is perverted into a desire to dominate, to exert power over others as though they were things. Domination is coupled with death,

---

[11] An interesting although incomplete attempt to analyze productive thinking is Max Wertheimer's posthumously published work, *Productive Thinking* (New York: Harper & Brothers, 1945). Some of the aspects of productiveness are dealt with by Munsterberg, Natorp, Bergson, and James; in Brentano's and Husserl's analysis of the psychic "act"; in Dilthey's analysis of artistic production and in O. Schwarz, *Medizinische Anthropologie* (Leipzig: Hirzel, 1929), pp. iii ff. In all these works, however, the problem is not treated in relation to character.

potency with life. Domination springs from impotence and in turn reinforces it, for if an individual can force somebody else to serve him, his own need to be productive is increasingly paralyzed.

How is man related to the world when he uses his powers productively?

The world outside oneself can be experienced in two ways: *reproductively* by perceiving actuality in the same fashion as a film makes a literal record of things photographed (although even mere reproductive perception requires the active participation of the mind); and *generatively* by conceiving it, by enlivening and re-creating this new material through the spontaneous activity of one's own mental and emotional powers. While to a certain extent everyone does react in both ways, the respective weight of each kind of experience differs widely. Sometimes either one of the two is atrophied, and the study of these extreme cases in which the reproductive or the generative mode is almost absent offers the best approach to the understanding of each of these phenomena.

The relative atrophy of the generative capacity is very frequent in our culture. A person may be able to recognize things as they are (or as his culture maintains them to be), but he is unable to enliven his perception from within. Such a person is the perfect "realist," who sees all there is to be seen of the surface features of phenomena but who is quite incapable of penetrating below the surface to the essential, and of visualizing what is not yet apparent. He sees the details but not the whole, the trees but not the forest. Reality to him is only the sum total of what has already materialized. This person is not lacking in imagination, but his is a calculating imagination, combining factors all of which are known and in existence, and inferring their future operation.

On the other hand, the person who has lost the capacity to perceive actuality is insane. The psychotic person builds up an inner world of reality in which he seems to have full confidence; he lives in his own world, and the common factors of reality as perceived by all men are unreal to him. When a person sees objects which do not exist in reality but are entirely the product of his imagination, he has hallucinations; he interprets events in terms of his own feelings, without reference to, or at least without proper acknowledgment of, what goes on in reality. A paranoid person may believe that he is being persecuted, and a chance remark may indicate a plan to humiliate and ruin him. He is convinced that the lack of any more obvious and explicit manifestation of such intention does not prove anything; that, although the remark may appear harmless on the surface, its real meaning becomes clear if one looks "deeper." For the psychotic person actual reality is wiped out and an inner reality has taken its place.

The "realist" sees only the surface features of things; he sees the manifest world, he can reproduce it photographically in his mind, and he can act by manipulating things and people as they appear in this picture. The insane person is incapable of seeing reality as it is; he perceives reality only as a symbol and a reflection of his inner world. Both are sick. The sickness of the psychotic who has lost contact with reality is such that he cannot function socially. The sickness of the "realist" impoverishes him as a human being. While he is not incapacitated in his social functioning, his view of reality is so distorted because of its lack of depth and perspective that he is apt to err when more than manipulation of immediately given data and short-range aims are involved. *"Realism" seems to be the very opposite of insanity and yet it is only its complement.*

The true opposite of both "realism" and insanity is productiveness. The normal human being is capable of relating himself to the world simultaneously by perceiving it as it is and by conceiving it enlivened and enriched by his own powers. If one of the two capacities is atrophied, man is sick; but the normal person has both capacities even though their respective weights differ. The presence of both reproductive and generative capacities is a precondition for productiveness; they are opposite poles whose interaction is the dynamic source of productiveness. With the last statement I want to emphasize that productiveness is not the sum or combination of both capacities but that it is something new which springs from this interaction. . . .

b) *Productive love and thinking*

Human existence is characterized by the fact that man is alone and separated from the world; not being able to stand the separation, he is impelled to seek for relatedness and oneness. There are many ways in which he can realize this need, but only one in which he, as a unique entity, remains intact; only one in which his own powers unfold in the very process of being related. It is the paradox of human existence that man must simultaneously seek for closeness and for independence; for oneness with others and at the same time for the preservation of his uniqueness and particularity.[12] As we have shown, the answer to this paradox—and to the moral problem of man—is *productiveness.*

One can be productively related to the world by acting and by comprehending. Man *produces things,* and in the process of creation he exercises his powers over matter. Man *comprehends the world,* mentally and emotionally, through love and through reason. His power of reason enables him to penetrate through the surface and to grasp the essence of his object by getting into active relation with it. His power of love enables him to break through the wall which separates him from another person and to comprehend him. Although love and reason are only two different forms of comprehending the world and although neither is possible without the other, they are expressions of different powers, that of emotion and that of thinking, and hence must be discussed separately.

The concept of productive love is very different indeed from what is frequently called love. There is hardly any word which is more ambiguous and confusing than the word "love." It is used to denote almost every feeling short of hate and disgust. It comprises everything from the love for ice cream to the love for a symphony, from mild sympathy to the most intense feeling

---

[12] This concept of relatedness as the synthesis of closeness and uniqueness is in many ways similar to the concept of "detached—attachment" in Charles Morris' *Paths of Life* (New York: Harper & Brothers, 1942), one difference being that Morris' frame of reference is that of temperament while mine is that of character.

of closeness. People feel they love if they have "fallen for" some-body. They call their dependence love, and their possessiveness too. They believe, in fact, that nothing is easier than to love, that the difficulty lies only in finding the right object, and that their failure to find happiness in love is due to their bad luck in not finding the right partner. But contrary to all this confused and wishful thinking, love is a very specific feeling; and while every human being has a capacity for love, its realization is one of the most difficult achievements. Genuine love is rooted in produc-tiveness and may properly be called, therefore, "productive love." Its essence is the same whether it is the mother's love for the child, our love for man, or the erotic love between two indi-viduals. (That it is also the same with regard to love for others and love for ourselves we shall discuss later.)[13] Although the objects of love differ and consequently the intensity and quality of love itself differ, certain basic elements may be said to be characteristic of all forms of productive love. These are *care, responsibility, respect,* and *knowledge.*

[13] "Selfishness, Self-Love, and Self-Interest," pp. 320-337.

22

KAREN HORNEY

The Search for Glory*

Whatever the conditions under which a child grows up, he will, if not mentally defective, learn to cope with others in one way or another and he will probably acquire some skills. But there are also forces in him which he cannot acquire or even develop by learning. You need not, and in fact cannot, teach an acorn to grow into an oak tree, but when given a chance, its intrinsic potentialities will develop. Similarly, the human individual, given a chance, tends to develop his particular human potentialities. He will develop then the unique alive forces of his real self: the clarity and depth of his own feelings, thoughts, wishes, interests; the ability to tap his own resources, the strength of his will power; the special capacities or gifts he may have; the faculty to express himself, and to relate himself to others with his spontaneous feelings. All this will in time enable him to find his set of values and his aims in life. In short, he will grow, substantially undiverted, *toward self-realization*. And that is why I speak of the *real self* as that central inner force, common to all human beings and yet unique in each, which is the deep source of growth.[1]

Only the individual himself can develop his given potentialities. But, like any other living organism, the human individuum needs

* Reprinted from *Neurosis and Human Growth* by Karen Horney, by permission of W. W. Norton & Company, Inc. Copyright 1950 by W. W. Norton & Company, Inc.

[1] When in the future a reference is made to growth, it is always meant in the sense presented here—that of free, healthy development in accordance with the potentials of one's generic and individual nature.

favorable conditions for his growth "from acorn into oak tree"; he needs an atmosphere of warmth to give him both a feeling of inner security and the inner freedom enabling him to have his own feelings and thoughts and to express himself. He needs the good will of others, not only to help him in his many needs but to guide and encourage him to become a mature and fulfilled individual. He also needs healthy friction with the wishes and wills of others. If he can thus grow *with* others, in love and in friction, he will also grow in accordance with his real self.

But through a variety of adverse influences, a child may not be permitted to grow according to his individual needs and possibilities. Such unfavorable conditions are too manifold to list here. But, when summarized, they all boil down to the fact that the people in the environment are too wrapped up in their own neuroses to be able to love the child, or even to conceive of him as the particular individual he is; their attitudes toward him are determined by their own neurotic needs and responses.[2] In simple words, they may be dominating, overprotective, intimidating, irritable, overexacting, overindulgent, erratic, partial to other siblings, hypocritical, indifferent, etc. It is never a matter of just a single factor, but always the whole constellation that exerts the untoward influence on a child's growth.

As a result, the child does not develop a feeling of belonging, of "we," but instead a profound insecurity and vague apprehensiveness, for which I use the term *basic anxiety*. It is his feeling of being isolated and helpless in a world conceived as potentially hostile. The cramping pressure of his basic anxiety prevents the child from relating himself to others with the spontaneity of his real feelings, and forces him to find ways to cope with them. He must (unconsciously) deal with them in ways which do not arouse, or increase, but rather allay his basic anxiety. The particular attitudes resulting from such unconscious strategical necessities are determined both by the child's given temperament and by the contingencies of the environment. Briefly, he may try to cling to the most powerful person around him; he may try

---

[2] All the neurotic disturbances in human relations which are summarized in Chapter 12 [*Neurosis and Human Growth*] of this book may operate.

Cf. also Karen Horney, *Our Inner Conflicts*, Chapter 2, The Basic Conflict, and Chapter 6, The Idealized Image.

to rebel and fight; he may try to shut others out of his inner life and withdraw emotionally from them. In principle, this means that he can move toward, against, or away from others. . . .

This first attempt at solving neurotic conflicts is by no means superficial. On the contrary, it has a determining influence upon the further course his neurotic development takes. Nor does it exclusively concern attitudes toward others; inevitably, it entails certain changes in the whole personality. According to his main direction the child also develops certain appropriate needs, sensitivities, inhibitions, and the beginnings of moral values. The predominantly complying child, for instance, tends not only to subordinate himself to others and to lean on them, but also tries to be unselfish and good. Similarly, the aggressive child starts to place value on strength and on the capacity to endure and to fight. . . .

Despite his early attempts at solving his conflicts with others, the individual is still divided and needs a firmer and more comprehensive *integration*.

For many reasons, he has not had the chance to develop real self-confidence: his inner strength has been sapped by his having to be on the defensive, by his being divided, by the way in which his early "solution" initiated a one-sided development, thereby making large areas of his personality unavailable for constructive uses. Hence, he desperately needs self-confidence, or a substitute for it.

He does not feel weakened in a vacuum, but feels specifically less substantial, less well equipped for life than others. If he had a sense of belonging, his feeling inferior to others would not be so serious a handicap. But living in a competitive society, and feeling at bottom—as he does—isolated and hostile, he can only develop an urgent need *to lift himself above others*.

Even more basic than these factors is his beginning alienation from self. Not only is his real self prevented from a straight growth, but in addition his need to evolve artificial, strategic ways to cope with others has forced him to override his genuine feelings, wishes, and thoughts. To the extent that safety has become paramount, his innermost feelings and thoughts have receded in importance—in fact, have had to be silenced and have become indistinct. (It does not matter what he feels, if only he is safe.) His feelings and wishes thus cease to be determining factors; he is no longer, so to speak, the driver, but is driven. Also the division in himself not only weakens him in general, but reinforces the alienation by adding an element of confusion; he no longer knows where he stands, or "who" he is. . . . Hence, most of all, the individual alienated from himself needs—it would be absurd to say a "substitute" for his real self, because there is no such thing—something that will give him a hold, *a feeling of identity*. This could make him meaningful to himself and, despite all the weakness in his structure, give him a feeling of power and significance.

Provided his inner conditions do not change (through fortunate life circumstances), so that he can dispense with the needs I have listed, there is only one way in which he can seem to fulfill them, and seem to fulfill all of them at one stroke: through imagination. Gradually and unconsciously, the imagination sets to work and creates in his mind an *idealized image* of himself. In this process he endows himself with unlimited powers and with exalted faculties; he becomes a hero, a genius, a supreme lover, a saint, a god.

Self-idealization always entails a general self-glorification, and thereby gives the individual the much-needed feeling of significance and of superiority over others. But it is by no means a blind self-aggrandizement. Each person builds up his personal idealized image from the materials of his own special experiences, his earlier fantasies, his particular needs, and also his given faculties. If it were not for the personal character of the image, he would not attain a feeling of identity and unity. He idealizes, to begin with, his particular "solution" of his basic conflict: compliance becomes goodness; love, saintliness; aggressiveness becomes strength, leadership, heroism, omnipotence; aloofness becomes wisdom, self-sufficiency, independence. What—according to his particular solution—appear as shortcomings or flaws are always dimmed out or retouched. . . .

Eventually the individual may come to identify himself with his idealized, integrated image. Then it does not remain a visionary image which he secretly cherishes; imperceptibly he becomes this image: the idealized image becomes an *idealized self*. And this idealized self becomes more real to him than his real self, not primarily because it is more appealing but because it answers all his stringent needs. This transfer of his center of gravity is an entirely inward process; there is no observable or conspicuous outward change in him. The change is in the core of his being, in his feeling about himself. It is a curious and exclusively human process. It would hardly occur to a cocker spaniel that he "really" is an Irish setter. And the transition can occur in a person only because his real self has previously become indistinct. While the healthy course at this phase of development—and at *any* phase—would be a move toward his real self, he now starts to abandon it definitely for the idealized self. The latter begins to represent to him what he "really" is, or potentially is—what he could be, and should be. It becomes the perspective from which he looks at himself, the measuring rod with which he measures himself.

Self-idealization, in its various aspects, is what I suggest calling a *comprehensive neurotic solution*—i.e., a solution not only for a particular conflict but one that implicitly promises to satisfy all the inner needs that have arisen in an individual at a given time. Moreover, it promises not only a riddance from his painful and unbearable feelings (feeling lost, anxious, inferior, and divided), but in addition an ultimately mysterious fulfillment of himself and his life. No wonder, then, that when he believes he has found such a solution he clings to it for dear life. No wonder that, to use a good psychiatric term, it becomes *compulsive*.[3] The regular occurrence of self-idealization in neurosis is the result of the regular occurrence of the compulsive needs bred in a neurosis-prone environment.

We can look at self-idealization from two major vantage points: it is the logical outcome of an early development and it is also the beginning of a new one. It is bound to have far-reaching influence upon the further development because there simply

---

[3] We shall discuss the exact meaning of *compulsiveness* when we have a more complete view of some further steps involved in this solution.

is no more consequential step to be taken than the abandoning of the real self. But the main reason for its revolutionary effect lies in another implication of this step. *The energies driving toward self-realization are shifted to the aim of actualizing the idealized self.* This shift means no more and no less than a change in the course of the individual's whole life and development.

We shall see throughout this book the manifold ways in which this shift in direction exerts a molding influence upon the whole personality. Its more immediate effect is to prevent self-idealization from remaining a purely inward process, and to force it into the total circuit of the individual's life. The individual wants to—or, rather, is driven to—express himself. And this now means that he wants to express his idealized self, to prove it in action. It infiltrates his aspirations, his goals, his conduct of life, and his relations to others. For this reason, self-idealization inevitably grows into a more comprehensive drive which I suggest calling by a name appropriate to its nature and its dimensions: *the search for glory.* Self-idealization remains its nuclear part. The other elements in it, all of them always present, though in varying degrees of strength and awareness in each individual case, are the need for perfection, neurotic ambition, and the need for a vindictive triumph.

Among the drives toward actualizing the idealized self *the need for perfection* is the most radical one. It aims at nothing less than molding the whole personality into the idealized self. Like Pygmalion in Bernard Shaw's version, the neurotic aims not only at retouching but at remodeling himself in his special kind of perfection prescribed by the specific features of his idealized image. He tries to achieve this goal by a complicated system of shoulds and taboos.

The most obvious and the most extrovert among the elements of the search for glory is *neurotic ambition,* the drive toward external success. While this drive toward excelling in actuality is pervasive and tends toward excelling in everything, it is usually most strongly applied to those matters in which excelling is most feasible for the given individual at a given time. Hence the content of ambition may well change several times during a lifetime. At school a person may feel it an intolerable disgrace not to have the very best marks in class. Later on, he may be just as compulsively driven to have the most dates with the most desirable girls. And again, still later, he may be obsessed with making the most money, or being the most prominent in politics. Such changes easily give rise to certain self-deceptions. A person who has at one period been fanatically determined to be the greatest athletic hero, or war hero, may at another period become equally bent on being the greatest saint. He may believe, then, that he has "lost" his ambition. Or he may decide that excelling in athletics or in war was not what he "really" wanted. Thus he may fail to realize that he still sails on the boat of ambition but has merely changed the course. Of course, one must also analyze in detail what made him change his course at that particular time. I emphasize these changes because they point to the fact that people in the clutches of ambition are but little related to the *content* of what they are doing. What counts is the excelling itself. If one did not recognize this unrelatedness, many changes would be incomprehensible. . . .

The picture varies, however, in many ways, according to the nature of the desired success. Roughly, it may belong more in the category of power (direct power, power behind the throne, influence, manipulating), or more in the category of prestige (reputation, acclaim, popularity, admiration, special attention).

These ambitious drives are, comparatively speaking, the most realistic of the expansive drives. At least, this is true in the sense that the people involved put in actual efforts to the end of excelling. These drives also seem more realistic because, with sufficient luck, their possessors may actually acquire the coveted glamor, honors, influence. But, on the other hand, when they do attain more money, more distinction, more power, they also come to feel the whole impact of the futility of their chase. They do not secure any more peace of mind, inner security, or joy of living. The inner distress, to remedy which they started out on the chase for the phantom of glory, is still as great as ever. Since these are not accidental results, happening to this or that individual, but are inexorably bound to occur, one may rightly say that the whole pursuit of success is intrinsically unrealistic. . . .

The last element in the search for glory, more destructive than the others, is the drive *toward a vindictive triumph*. It may be closely linked up with the drive for actual achievement and success but, if so, its chief aim is to put others to shame or defeat them through one's very success; or to attain the power, by rising to prominence, to inflict suffering upon them—mostly of a humiliating kind. On the other hand, the drive for excelling may be relegated to fantasy, and the need for a vindictive triumph then manifests itself mainly in often irresistible, mostly unconscious impulses to frustrate, outwit, or defeat others in personal relations. I call this drive "vindictive" because the motivating force stems from impulses to take revenge for humiliations suffered in childhood—impulses which are reinforced during the later neurotic development. These later accretions probably are responsible for the way in which the need for a vindictive triumph eventually becomes a regular ingredient in the search for glory. Both the degree of its strength and the person's awareness of it vary to a remarkable extent. Most people are either entirely unaware of such a need or cognizant of it only in fleeting moments. Yet it is sometimes out in the open, and then it becomes the barely disguised mainspring of life. Among recent historical figures Hitler is a good illustration of a person who went through humiliating experiences and gave his whole life to a fanatic desire to triumph over an ever-increasing mass of people. In his case vicious circles, constantly increasing the need, are clearly discernible. One of these develops from the fact that he could think only in categories of triumph and defeat. Hence the fear of defeat made further triumphs always necessary. Moreover, the feeling of grandeur, increasing with every triumph, rendered it increasingly intolerable that anybody, or even any nation, should not recognize his grandeur. . . .

Much more frequently the drive toward a vindictive triumph is hidden. Indeed, because of its destructive nature, it is the most hidden element in the search for glory. It may be that only a rather frantic ambition will be apparent. In analysis alone are we able to see that the driving power behind it is the need to defeat and humiliate others by rising above them. The less harmful need for superiority can, as it were, absorb the more destructive compulsion. This allows a person to act out his need, and yet feel righteous about it. . . .

There are various solid proofs that the search for glory is a comprehensive and coherent entity. In the first place, all the individual trends described above regularly occur together in one person. Of course one or another element may so predominate as to make us speak loosely of, say, an ambitious person, or of a dreamer. But that does not mean that the dominance of one element indicates the absence of the others. The ambitious person will have his grandiose image of himself too; the dreamer will want realistic supremacy, even though the latter factor may be apparent only in the way in which his pride is offended by the success of others.[4]

Furthermore, all the individual trends involved are so closely related that the prevailing trend may change during the lifetime of a given person. He may turn from glamorous daydreams to being the perfect father and employer, and again to being the greatest lover of all time.

Lastly, they all have in common *two general characteristics,* both understandable from the genesis and the functions of the whole phenomenon: their compulsive nature and their imaginative character. Both have been mentioned, but it is desirable to have a more complete and succinct picture of their meaning.

The *compulsive nature* stems from the fact that the self-idealization (and the whole search for glory developing as its sequel) is a neurotic solution. When we call a drive compulsive we mean the opposite of spontaneous wishes or strivings. The latter are an expression of the real self; the former are determined by the

---

[4] Because personalities often look different in accordance with the trend which is prevailing, the temptation to regard these trends as separate entities is great. Freud regarded phenomena which are roughly similar to these as separate instinctual drives with separate origins and properties. When I made a first attempt to enumerate compulsive drives in neurosis they appeared to me too as separate "neurotic trends."

inner necessities of the neurotic structure. The individual must abide by them regardless of his real wishes, feelings, or interests lest he incur anxiety, feel torn by conflicts, be overwhelmed by guilt feelings, feel rejected by others, etc. In other words, the difference between spontaneous and compulsive is one between "I want" and "I must in order to avoid some danger." Although the individual may consciously feel his ambition or his standards of perfection to be what he *wants* to attain, he is actually *driven* to attain it. The need for glory has him in its clutches. Since he himself is unaware of the difference between wanting and being driven, we must establish criteria for a distinction between the two. The most decisive one is the fact that he is driven on the road to glory with an utter *disregard for himself, for his best interests.* . . .

Another criterion of the compulsive nature of the drive for glory—as of any other compulsive drive—is its *indiscriminateness.* Since the person's real interest in a pursuit does not matter, he *must* be the center of attention, *must* be the most attractive, the most intelligent, the most original—whether or not the situation calls for it; whether or not, with his given attributes, he *can* be the first. He *must* come out victorious in any argument, regardless of where the truth lies. His thoughts in this matter are the exact opposite of those of Socrates: ". . . for surely we are not now simply contending in order that my view or that of yours may prevail, but I presume that we ought both of us to be fighting for the truth." [5] The compulsiveness of the neurotic person's need for indiscriminate supremacy makes him indifferent to truth, whether concerning himself, others, or facts.

Furthermore, like any other compulsive drive, the search for glory has the quality of *insatiability.* It must operate as long as the unknown (to himself) forces are driving him. There may be a glow of elation over the favorable reception of some work done, over a victory won, over any sign of recognition or admiration—but it does not last. A success may hardly be experienced as such in the first place, or, at the least, must make room for despondency or fear soon after. In any case, the relentless

---

[5] From Philebus, *The Dialogues of Plato*, translated into English by B. Jowett, M.A., Random House, New York.

chase after more prestige, more money, more women, more victories and conquests keeps going, with hardly any satisfaction or respite.

Finally, the compulsive nature of a drive shows in the *reactions to its frustration*. The greater its subjective importance, the more impelling is the need to attain its goal, and hence the more intense the reactions to frustration. These constitute one of the ways in which we can measure the intensity of a drive. Although this is not always plainly visible, the search for glory is a most powerful drive. It can be like a demoniacal obsession, almost like a monster swallowing up the individual who has created it. And so the reactions to frustration must be severe. They are indicated by the terror of doom and disgrace that for many people is spelled in the idea of failure. Reactions of panic, depression, despair, rage at self and others to what is conceived as "failure" are frequent, and entirely out of proportion to the actual importance of the occasion. The phobia of falling from heights is a frequent expression of the dread of falling from the heights of illusory grandeur. Consider the dream of a patient who had a phobia about heights. It occurred at a time when he had begun to doubt his established belief of unquestioned superiority. In the dream he was at the top of a mountain, but in danger of falling, and was clinging desperately to the ridge of the peak. "I cannot get any higher than I am," he said, "so all I have to do in life is to hold on to it." Consciously, he referred to his social status, but in a deeper sense this "I cannot get any higher" also held true for his illusions about himself. He could not get higher than having (in his mind) a godlike omnipotence and cosmic significance!

The second characteristic inherent in all the elements of the search for glory is the great and peculiar role *imagination* plays in them. It is instrumental in the process of self-idealization. But this is so crucial a factor that the whole search for glory is bound to be pervaded by fantastic elements. No matter how much a person prides himself on being realistic, no matter how realistic indeed his march toward success, triumph, perfection, his imagination accompanies him and makes him mistake a mirage for

the real thing. One simply cannot be unrealistic about oneself
and remain entirely realistic in other respects. When the wanderer
in the desert, under the duress of fatigue and thirst, sees a mirage,
he may make actual efforts to reach it, but the mirage—the glory
—which should end his distress is itself a product of imagination.

Actually imagination also permeates all psychic and mental
functions in the healthy person. When we feel the sorrow or the
joy of a friend, it is our imagination that enables us to do so.
When we wish, hope, fear, believe, plan, it is our imagination
showing us possibilities. But imagination may be productive or
unproductive: it can bring us closer to the truth of ourselves—
as it often does in dreams—or carry us far away from it. It can
make our actual experience richer or poorer. And these differences roughly distinguish neurotic and healthy imagination.

When thinking of the grandiose plans so many neurotics
evolve, or the fantastic nature of their self-glorification and their
claims, we may be tempted to believe that they are more richly
endowed than others with the royal gift of imagination—and
that, for that very reason, it can more easily go astray in them.
This notion is not borne out by my experience. The endow-
ment varies among neurotic people, as it does among more
healthy ones. But I find no evidence that the neurotic per se is
by nature more imaginative than others.

Nevertheless the notion is a false conclusion based upon accurate observations. Imagination does in fact play a greater role
in neurosis. However, what accounts for this are not constitutional but functional factors. Imagination operates as it does in
the healthy person, but in addition it takes over functions which
it does not normally have. It is put in the service of neurotic
needs. This is particularly clear in the case of the search for
glory, which, as we know, is prompted by the impact of powerful needs. In psychiatric literature imaginative distortions of
reality are known as "wishful thinking." It is by now a well-
established term, but it is nevertheless incorrect. It is too narrow: an accurate term would encompass not only thinking but
also "wishful" observing, believing, and particularly feeling.
Moreover, it is a thinking—or feeling—that is determined not
by our *wishes* but by our *needs*. And it is the impact of these

needs that lends imagination the tenacity and power it has in neurosis, that makes it prolific—and unconstructive.

The role imagination plays in the search for glory may show unmistakably and directly in daydreams. . . . But daydreams, while important and revealing when they occur, are not the most injurious work of imagination. For a person is mostly aware of the fact that he is daydreaming, i.e., imagining things which have not occurred or are not likely to occur in the way he is experiencing them in fantasy. At least it is not too difficult for him to become aware of the existence and the unrealistic character of the daydreams. The more injurious work of imagination concerns the subtle and comprehensive distortions of reality which he is not aware of fabricating. The idealized self is not completed in a single act of creation: once produced, it needs continuing attention. For its actualization the person must put in an incessant labor by way of falsifying reality. He must turn his needs into virtues or into more than justified expectations. He must turn his intentions to be honest or considerate into the fact of being honest or considerate. The bright ideas he has for a paper make him a great scholar. His potentialities turn into factual achievements. Knowing the "right" moral values makes him a virtuous person—often, indeed, a kind of moral genius. And of course his imagination must work overtime to discard all the disturbing evidence to the contrary.[6]

Imagination also operates in changing the neurotic's beliefs. He needs to believe that others are wonderful or vicious—and lo! there they are in a parade of benevolent or dangerous people. It also changes his feelings. He needs to feel invulnerable—and behold! his imagination has sufficient power to brush off pain and suffering. He needs to have deep feelings—confidence, sympathy, love, suffering: his feelings of sympathy, suffering, and the rest are magnified.

The perception of the distortions of inner and outer reality which imagination can bring about when put to the service of the search for glory leaves us with an uneasy question. Where does the flight of the neurotic's imagination end? He does not

---

[6] *Cf.* the work of the Ministry of Truth in George Orwell's *Nineteen Eighty-Four.*

after all lose his sense of reality altogether; where then is the border line separating him from the psychotic? If there is any border line with respect to feats of imagination, it certainly is hazy. We can only say that the psychotic tends to regard the processes in his mind more exclusively as the only reality that counts, while the neurotic—for whatever reasons—retains a fair interest in the outside world and his place in it and has therefore a fair gross orientation in it.[7] Nevertheless, while he may stay sufficiently on the ground to function in a way not obviously disturbed, there is no limit to the heights to which his imagination can soar. It is in fact the most striking characteristic of the search for glory that it goes into the fantastic, into the realm of *unlimited possibilities*. . . .

This soaring into the unlimited is determined by the power of the needs behind the drive for glory. The needs for the *absolute* and the *ultimate* are so stringent that they override the checks which usually prevent our imagination from detaching itself from actuality. For his well-functioning, man needs both the vision of possibilities, the perspective of infinitude, *and* the realization of limitations, of necessities, of the concrete. If a man's thinking and feeling are primarily focused upon the infinite and the vision of possibilities, he loses his sense for the concrete, for the here and now. He loses his capacity for living in the moment. He is no longer capable of submitting to the necessities in himself, "to what may be called one's limit." He loses sight of what is actually necessary for achieving something. "Every little possibility even would require some time to become actuality." His thinking may become too abstract. His knowledge may become "a kind of inhuman knowing for the production of which man's self is squandered, pretty much as men were squandered for the building of the Pyramids." His feelings for others may evaporate into an "abstract sentimentality for humanity." If, on the other hand, a man does not see beyond the narrow horizon of the concrete, the necessary, the finite, he becomes "narrow-minded and mean-spirited." It is not, then, a question of either-or, but of

---

[7] The reasons for this difference are complicated. It would be worth examining whether crucial among them is a more radical abandoning of the real self (and a more radical shift to the idealized self) on the part of the psychotic.

both, if there is to be growth. The recognition of limitations, laws, and necessities serves as a check against being carried away into the infinite, and against the mere "floundering in possibilities." [8]

The *checks on imagination are malfunctioning* in the search for glory. This does not mean a general incapacity to see necessities and abide by them. A special direction in the further neurotic development may make many people feel safer to restrict their lives, and they may then tend to regard the possibility of being carried away into the fantastic as a danger to be avoided. They may close their minds to anything that to them looks fantastic, be averse to abstract thinking, and overanxiously cling to what is visible, tangible, concrete, or immediately useful. But while the conscious attitude toward these matters varies, every neurotic at bottom is loath to recognize limitations to what he expects of himself and believes it possible to attain. His need to actualize his idealized image is so imperative that he must shove aside the checks as irrelevant or nonexistent. . . .

To be sure, the development is not always so extreme. But every neurotic, even though he may pass superficially for healthy, is averse to checking with evidence when it comes to his particular illusions about himself. And he must be so, because they would collapse if he did. The attitude toward external laws and regulations varies, but he always tends to deny laws operating within himself, refuses to see the inevitability of cause and effect in psychic matters, or of one factor following from the other or reinforcing the other. . . .

It remains to bring into clearer relief the difference between the search for glory and healthy human strivings. On the surface they may look deceptively similar, so much so that differences seem to be variations in degree only. It looks as though the neurotic were merely more ambitious, more concerned with power, prestige, and success than the healthy person; as though his moral standards were merely higher, or more rigid, than ordinary ones; as though he were simply more conceited, or

---

[8] In this philosophical discussion I roughly follow Sören Kierkegaard, *Sickness unto Death,* Princeton University Press, 1941, written in 1844. The quotations in this paragraph are taken from this book.

considered himself more important than people usually do. And, indeed, who will venture to draw a sharp line and say: "This is where the healthy ends, and the neurotic begins"?

Similarities between healthy strivings and the neurotic drives exist because they have a common root in specific human potentialities. Through his mental capacities man has the faculty to reach beyond himself. In contrast to other animals, he can imagine and plan. In many ways he can gradually enlarge his faculties and, as history shows, has actually done so. The same is also true for the life of a single individual. There are no rigidly fixed limits to what he can make out of his life, to what qualities or faculties he can develop, to what he can create. Considering these facts, it seems inevitable that man is uncertain about his limitations and, hence, easily sets his goals either too low or too high. This existing uncertainty is the base without which the search for glory could not possibly develop.

The basic difference between healthy strivings and neurotic drives for glory lies in the forces prompting them. Healthy strivings stem from a propensity, inherent in human beings, to develop given potentialities. The belief in an inherent urge to grow has always been the basic tenet upon which our theoretical and therapeutic approach rests.[9] And this belief has grown ever since with ever-new experiences. The only change is in the direction of more precise formulation. I would say now that the live forces of the real self urge one toward self-realization. . . .

The difference, then, between healthy strivings and neurotic drives for glory is one between spontaneity and compulsion; between recognizing and denying limitations; between a focus upon the vision of a glorious end-product and a feeling for evolution; between seeming and being, fantasy and truth. The difference thus stated is not identical with that between a relatively healthy and a neurotic individual. The former may not be wholeheartedly

---

[9] By "our" I refer to the approach of the whole Association for the Advancement of Psychoanalysis.

In the introduction to *Our Inner Conflicts* I said: "My own belief is that man has the capacity as well as the desire to develop his potentialities. . . ." *Cf.* also Dr. Kurt Goldstein, *Human Nature*, Harvard University Press, 1940. Goldstein, however, does not make the distinction—which is crucial for human beings—between self-realization and the actualization of the idealized self.

engaged in realizing his real self nor is the latter wholly driven to actualize his idealized self. The tendency toward self-realization operates in the neurotic too; we could not in therapy give any help to the patient's growth if this striving were not in him to begin with. But, while the difference between the healthy and the neurotic person in this respect is simply one of degree, the difference between genuine striving and compulsion drives, despite surface similarities, is one of quality and not of quantity.[10]

The most pertinent symbol, to my mind, for the neurotic process initiated by the search for glory is the ideational content of the stories of the devil's pact. The devil, or some other personification of evil, tempts a person who is perplexed by spiritual or material trouble with the offer of unlimited powers. But he can obtain these powers only on the condition of selling his soul or going to hell. The temptation can come to anybody, rich or poor in spirit, because it speaks to two powerful desires: the longing for the infinite and the wish for an easy way out. According to religious tradition, the greatest spiritual leaders of mankind, Buddha and Christ, experienced such temptation. But, because they were firmly grounded in themselves, they recognized it as a temptation and could reject it. Moreover, the conditions stipulated in the pact are an appropriate representation of the price to be paid in the neurotic's development. Speaking in these symbolic terms, the easy way to infinite glory is inevitably also the way to an inner hell of self-contempt and self-torment. By taking this road, the individual is in fact losing his soul—his real self.

---

[10] When I speak of "the neurotic" I mean a person in whom neurotic drives prevail over healthy strivings.

23

VIOLA KLEIN

The Feminine Character*

The Victorian attitude towards sex, which has loomed so large
behind Weininger's philosophy, found another expression in the
doctrine which more than any other ideological factor has contributed to dispel it. There is a peculiar irony in the fact that
the very theory which was chiefly responsible for a more enlight-
ened outlook in matters of sex and for the disappearance of
Victorian morality should have been tinged with its ideology,
particularly in its dealing with women. It is probably fair to
say that no other single scientific theory has so much affected the
outlook of the present generation as psycho-analysis. It has
created what W. H. Auden calls "a whole climate of opinion,"
and, no matter whether we are aware of it or not, the way we
think and the way we feel is coloured by its discoveries. Its
imprint is perceptible in contemporary art, philosophy, literature,
no less than in psychology, psychiatry, anthropology, sociology
and education, and even our every-day commonsense judgments
bear the mark of its influence. If we no longer take people's
feelings and thoughts at their face value; if we ask ourselves what
function certain attitudes fulfil in the life organization of a person;
if we attribute to unconscious drives the motivation of people's
overt behaviour; if we talk in a frank and matter-of-fact way about
sex problems; if we pay attention to early childhood experiences;
or if we generally attempt to apply a rational system of causation

* Reprinted from The Feminine Character by Viola Klein by permission of
International Universities Press, Inc., and Routledge and Kegan Paul Ltd.
Copyright 1948, by International Universities Press, Inc.

to irrational psychic processes, we proceed on a foundation which Freud has built. His technical terms have become part of our common vocabulary, and even if we criticize him we use the tools which he has supplied. But in doing so we shall at once come into conflict with the orthodox school of psycho-analysts. For in the same way as doctrinaire Marxists regard as "ideological superstructures" all social theories except Marxism, Freudians are inclined to take other scientific theories for "rationalizations" of unconscious libidinal forces, but refuse to have their own system analysed with respect to underlying emotional motives and hidden cultural implications.

In the interest, however, not only of consistency but of scientific advance it is necessary to apply an equal measure of scrutiny to psycho-analysis itself and to try, as far as this is possible, to show the extent to which it reflects existing trends of thought, prevailing prejudices and unconscious personal sentiments. Freud's views on feminine psychology (expressed in many places, but expounded most comprehensively in *The Psychology of Women*)[1] seem to give particular proof of these influences.

The tendency to seek in congenital, constitutional factors the clue to what was considered the characteristically feminine personality type, was, as we have seen, common to Freud and his contemporaries. It is mainly due to the vast progress which biological science had made since Darwin and which gave impetus and direction to the scientific interest of the later nineteenth century. It has been reflected in Havelock Ellis's work, and expressed in such books as Lombroso's *La Donna Delinquente, la Prostituta e la Donna Normale*, P. J. Möbius' *Ueber den physiologischen Schwachsinn des Weibes* (On the Physiological Imbecility of Woman) or, more recently, in A. W. Nyemilov's *The Biological Tragedy of Woman* and others. The underlying assumption is summed up in the statement: "Anatomy is destiny." [2] The interpretation Freud gave to the meaning of this anatomical difference is, however, his own personal contribution to the discussion of

---

[1] Chapter XXXIII, "New Introductory Lectures on Psycho-Analysis" (Hogarth Press, London, 1933).

[2] "Some Psychological Consequences of the Anatomical Distinction between the Sexes" (*Internat. Journ. of Ps-An.*, 1927).

feminine psychology, and it is in accordance with his general view on the overruling importance of sexual factors in mental life.

In Freud's view the development of the feminine character is shaped at the outset by one essential anatomical characteristic (typically formulated in negative terms): the lack of a penis. The difference in external genitals is conceived by psycho-analytical theory as a deficiency on the part of women. All feminine character-traits, interests, attitudes, emotions and wishes are reactions, in some form or other, to this basic "defect." Experience with female neurotics has taught Freud that there is among women a widespread, in fact a general dissatisfaction with their sexual rôle. It is expressed in inferiority feelings, in contempt for their own sex, in revolt against their passive rôle, in envy of man's greater freedom, in the ambition to equal man in intellectual or artistic achievements, in strivings for independence, in tendencies to domineer over other people, and in all sorts of devices to make up for the social disadvantage of not being a man. The root of all these grievances and compensatory mechanisms, the key note, so to speak, to which the entire psychology of women is tuned, is, according to Freud, to be found in the early discovery of the girl that she is lacking an essential organ.

As we learn from our psycho-analytic work all women feel that they have been injured in their infancy, and that through no fault of their own they have been slighted and robbed of a part of their body; and the bitterness of many a daughter towards her mother has as its ultimate cause the reproach that the mother has brought her into the world as a woman instead of a man.[3]

The psycho-analytic theory is, in short, this: At an early age the little girl discovers, by the observation of other children, of brothers, or of her father, that there are other human beings who have external genitals whereas she has none. This discovery comes as a shock to her, "which leaves ineradicable traces on her development and character formation, and even in the most favourable instances, is not overcome without a great expenditure

---

[3] *Some Character-Types met with in Psycho-Analysis*, Collected Papers.

of mental energy." [4] Her envy of man, based on an anatomical difference, has an enormous influence on the mental traits of women. It is responsible for the comparatively greater part envy and jealousy play in their mental life and the consequent lack of a sense of justice. It is at the root of the "greater amount of narcissism attributed by psycho-analysis to women." "Their vanity is partly a further effect of penis-envy, for they are driven to rate their physical charms more highly as a belated compensation for their original sexual inferiority" [sic].[5] Feminine beauty and "especially that of a woman's face is a substitute to her for the loss of a penis." [6]

Modesty "which is regarded as *par excellence* a characteristic of women" is, however much modified by civilized conventions, "originally designed to hide the deficiency in their genitals." [7] If women are thought to have "contributed but little to the discoveries and inventions of civilization," they may at least be found inventors of the technical processes of plaiting and weaving —discoveries which owe their origin to the same impulse: to hide their physical deficiency.

The little girl's attachment to her father, the mature woman's desire for a child, the mother's particular satisfaction at the birth of a son, in fact almost all phenomena of feminine psychology, are explained by psycho-analysis as effects of the same basic envy and the endeavour to compensate for an organic inferiority. The woman who comes to the psycho-analyst for treatment is very often, says Freud, driven by the same impulse. "And what she quite reasonably expects to get from analysis, such as the capacity to pursue an intellectual career, can often be recognized as a sublimated modification of this repressed wish." [8]

There are three possible lines of psychological development as a reaction to the basic experience of woman's organic "deficiency." The one leads to "normal femininity," i.e. to recon-

[4] *The Psychology of Women*, p. 160.
[5] Op. cit.
[6] J. Harnik: "The Various Developments Undergone by Narcissism in Men and Women" (*Internat. Journ. of Ps.-An.*, Vol. V, 1925).
[7] S. Freud: *The Psychology of Women*, p. 170.
[8] Ibid., p. 161.

ciliation with the feminine sexual rôle, to acquiescence in the passivity that in Freud's view constitutionally goes with it, and to the desire for a child. In less favourable cases the painful discovery of her "castration" may lead to sexual inhibitions and to neuroses, or else it may result in a "modification of character in the sense of a masculinity complex." [9] The term "masculinity complex" is used in psycho-analytical literature in the widest sense, including all shades from open homosexuality to mere "dreams with male tendencies," or to intellectual interests in normal women. It is conceived so widely that it embraces cases where

the repressed wish to be male is found in a sublimated form, i.e. masculine interests of an intellectual and professional character and other kinds are preferred and accentuated. Femininity, however, is not consciously denied; they (i.e. women with a "masculinity complex") usually proclaim that these interests are just as much feminine as masculine ones. They consider it irrelevant to say that the performances of a human being, especially in the intellectual sphere, belong to the one or the other sex. This type of woman is well represented in the woman's movement of to-day.[10]

According to this description the great majority of women in our day would have failed to develop "normal femininity" but would have acquired a "masculinity complex" instead. Why this should be the case, i.e. why in our time the one pattern should prevail over the other, cannot be answered by psychoanalysis, according to which both patterns are individual psychological reactions to the realization of an organic deficiency. However much Freud was aware of the scope of possible variations he had no doubts about the "norm." The standards of his own culture he took for unalterable laws and he was convinced that the division of labour in force in the middle class of his period was based on innate sexual differences.

Further and very far-reaching consequences for the psychological development of women result from the different conditions

[9] Ibid.
[10] Karl Abraham: "Manifestations of the Female Castration Complex" (*Internat. Journ. of Ps.-An.*, Vol. III, 1922).

under which the Oedipus complex develops in women and in men, according to their different anatomical structure.

In her first infancy—the pre-Oedipal period—the little girl is, like the little boy, intensely attached to her mother. With the discovery of her own "castration" and, later, the realization that her mother, too, lacks a male genital organ, she turns away from her mother and chooses her father as a love object. "This means, therefore, that as a result of the discovery of the absence of a penis, women are as much depreciated in the eyes of the girl as in the eyes of the boy, and later, perhaps, of the man." (Note the matter of fact way in which the contempt of women is taken for granted!) From her father the little girl expects the male organ which her mother has refused her; a wish which is later transformed into the wish for a child by the father.

This development is in striking contrast to that of a boy and is used to explain a characteristic mental difference between the sexes. According to psycho-analytical theory every little boy forms an intense attachment to his mother, the Oedipus complex, "in which he desires his mother and wants to get rid of his father as a rival." [11] Owing, however, to the fear of castration—resulting either from threats or from the observation that there are human beings without external sex organs and the fear lest he may lose his as a punishment—he represses his Oedipus-complex. The result of this repression is the formation of a "super-ego," i.e. a rigid system of moral standards and valuations imparting to the individual a striving for perfection.

As we have seen before, the relation of the two complexes (Castration and Oedipus) is completely different in the two sexes. Whereas in the boy they are antagonistic—the one being used to repress the other—in the girl there is no such conflict. Her "castration" is an accomplished fact and no threat of it therefore exists to counteract her libidinal wishes for her father. She feels no urgent need to overcome her Oedipus-complex and she

remains in the Oedipus situation for an indefinite period; she abandons it only late in life, and then only incompletely. The formation of the super-ego must suffer in these circumstances; it cannot attain the strength and independence which give it its cultural importance, and

[11] *The Psychology of Women*, p. 166.

feminists are not pleased if one points to the way in which this factor affects the development of the average feminine character.[12]

It is due to these circumstances that women have "weaker social interests" than men and that "their capacity for sublimation is less." [13] Although Freud would not go as far as to ascribe to women an inferior intelligence, he prejudices judgments about their intellectual capacity by the rather axiomatic statement that, owing to their libidinal organization, women have only a limited urge for sublimation. Translated into ordinary language this means that women are, by their organic nature, excluded from participation in cultural and creative activities. The old argument about the intellectual faculties of woman has been transferred on to a different plane; clad in a new jargon the traditional view of feminine inferiority is here presented afresh.

There is, according to Freud's theory, still another impedimental factor in the psychological development of woman. In her case the transition from infantile to adult sexuality is particularly difficult—again for organic reasons. Libido, "the motor force of sexual life itself is only one for both sexes and is as much in the service of the male as of the female sexual function. To itself we can assign no sex." [14] In its infantile stage it develops much in the same way in boys and in girls. They both pass through the oral, sadistic-anal, and the phallic phase (so called after the organ which at each stage forms the centre of libidinal satisfaction). They both display the same amount of activity and aggressiveness. Any difference that exists is due to individual variations rather than to sex differences.

The organ which in the little girl is the dominant erotogenic zone and centre of masturbatory activity during the "phallic" phase is her "penis equivalent," the clitoris. In the transition to adult sexuality the girl therefore has to change the centre of sensitivity and to discover, so to speak, a new, hidden organ, the vagina. Thus, with the development of femininity two important changes have to be gone through by the girl to which the boy is not subjected: Change of the love object (the transfer of her

---

[12] Ibid., p. 166.
[13] Ibid., p. 172.
[14] Ibid., p. 169.

attachment from her mother to her father) and, secondly, change of the erotogenic zones. This process is in Freud's view very difficult and complicated and absorbs a great amount of mental energy.

It is our impression that more violence is done to libido when it is forced into the service of the female function; and that—so to speak teleologically—Nature has paid less careful attention to the demands of the female function than to those of masculinity. And —again speaking teleologically—this may be based on the fact that the achievement of the biological aim is entrusted to the aggressiveness of the male, and is to some extent independent of the co-operation of the female.[15]

The peculiar Freudian concept of sexual intercourse as a purely masculine act, viewed in terms more or less similar to rape, which underlies the above statement, can be left till later. At the present moment the main concern is with the psychological consequences resulting, in Freud's view, from the constitutional process of maturing femininity. In contrast to the boy for whom puberty means a stage of new intensification of the libido, for the girl it is a period of increased repressions. It is the masculine part of her being which is repressed, coinciding with the transition of the erotogenic zone from the "masculine" counterpart of her genitals, the clitoris, to her feminine organ, the vagina. This repression and the change of centres of sensitivity account for the greater disposition of women to neurosis and particularly to hysteria[16] which in consequence is a kind of functional disease of woman. The absorption of so much mental energy by the process of developing femininity is, moreover, in part responsible for the diminished power of sublimation in women. And it is, according to Freud, due to this process that the psychological development of woman is arrested at a much earlier age than that of man.

A man of about thirty seems a youthful and, in a sense, an incompletely developed individual of whom we expect that he will be able to make good use of the possibilities of development which analy-

[15] Ibid., p. 169.
[16] "Three Contributions to the Theory of Sex" (*Imago*, London, 1942).

sis lays open to him. But a woman of about the same age frequently staggers us by her psychological rigidity and unchangeability. Her libido has taken up its final positions and seems powerless to leave them for others. There are no paths open for further development; it is as though the whole process had been gone through and remained inaccessible to influences for the future; as though, in fact, the difficult development which leads to femininity had exhausted all possibilities of the individual.[17]

It did not occur to Freud that under the conditions prevalent in his society a woman of thirty had, in fact, not many "paths open for further development" and not many possibilities to make good use of. At thirty her "final positions" must have either been taken up, i.e. she must have been married, or else she could not have any expectations for the future. This lack of opportunities would in itself suffice to explain the "rigidity" and "unchangeability" which Freud observed in his women patients, without having to resort to biological hypotheses.

Summing up, the characteristic mental traits associated with the constitutional structure of women and mentioned so far are: penis-envy, resulting in a general disposition to envy, jealousy and social injustice; a greater amount of narcissism as compared with that of men; a weaker urge and a smaller capacity for sublimation, i.e. for cultural activities. To this may be added a general antagonism to civilization, caused not so much by woman's physiological structure as by the biological purpose which she represents.

Women represent the interests of the family and sexual life; the work of civilization has become more and more men's business; it confronts them with ever harder tasks, compels them to sublimations of instinct which women are not easily able to achieve. Since man has not an unlimited amount of mental energy at his disposal, he must accomplish his tasks by distributing his libido to the best advantage. What he employs for cultural purposes he withdraws to a great extent from women and his sexual life; his constant association with men and his dependence on his relations with them even estrange him from his duties as husband and father. Woman finds herself thus forced

---

[17] The Psychology of Women, p. 173.

into the background by the claims of culture and she adopts an inimical attitude towards it.[18]

The portrait of woman which results if we thus fit together the details expounded in different contexts certainly is far from flattering. It represents an envious, hysterical person with limited intellectual interests and a hostile attitude towards cultural achievements.

The implicit assertion of man's primary superiority, which was in strange contrast to contemporary changes in the cultural rôle of women, has been a stumbling-block to many psychoanalysts and has evoked doubts and divergencies among some of Freud's disciples. Ernest Jones, for instance, said in 1927: "There is a healthy suspicion growing that men analysts have been led to adopt an unduly phallocentric view of the problems in question, the importance of the female organs being correspondingly underestimated." [19]

Karen Horney, too, has taken Freud's interpretation of feminine psychology as a challenge of "masculine narcissism" and opposed it by an assertion of the feminine point of view within psycho-analytical theory. To confront the two views affords an interesting example of the same set of premises, the same method of investigation and the same scientific terminology being used to defend two divergent standpoints. Karen Horney would agree with Freud that the little girl is in fact constitutionally at a disadvantage compared with the little boy. Her organic structure makes the gratification of certain (exhibitionistic and masturbatory) tendencies more difficult for her, and the greater ease with which a boy can satisfy his impulse to investigate by examining his own body may be the basis for greater objectivity and for a greater interest in external objects in the man. But—and here Karen Horney is in striking contrast to Freud—"when she reaches maturity a great part in sexual life (as regards creative power perhaps even a greater part than that of men) devolves upon a

---

[18] *Civilization and Its Discontent*, p. 73, 2nd ed., Hogarth Press, London, 1939.

[19] "Early Development of Female Sexuality" (*Internat. Jour. of Ps.-An.*, 1927).

woman—I mean when she becomes a mother." [20] Her capacity
for motherhood is—so Karen Horney asserts—an "indisputable
superiority" of woman and is the cause of intense envy in boys.
This envy of feminine productivity is a dynamic factor in masculine psychology and "serves as one, if not as the essential, driving
force in the setting up of cultural values." [21] Karen Horney
admits that the cultural productivity has been incomparably
greater in men than in women, but, she asks, "is not the tremendous strength in men of the impulse to creative work in every
field precisely due to the feeling of playing a relatively small part
in the creation of living beings, which constantly impels them
to an over-compensation in achievement?" The penis-envy in
women has not found a corresponding compensatory expression,
"either because it is absolutely less than the envy of men," or
because in normal cases it is transformed into a desire for husband and child and in this way loses its power as an "incentive
to sublimation." If, nevertheless, a "flight from womanhood" can
be observed in women, it is due not to primary instinct but to
the experience of real—physical and social—disadvantages. Her
sense of inferiority is not constitutional but acquired.

Karen Horney's reply to Freud is an almost exact inversion of
his theory. To his masculine claim of superiority she opposes
her claim to feminine biological superiority; his assumption of
penis-envy in women she answers with her assumption of "envy
of motherhood" in men; and Freud's contention that sexual
activity is a masculine prerogative, and that "the achievement of
the biological aim is entrusted to the aggressiveness of the male,"
she contradicts with the statement that the greater part in sexual
life and actual biological creation devolves upon women.

---

[20] Karen Horney: "On the Genesis of the Castration Complex in Women"
(*Internat. Jour. of Ps.-An.*, Vol. V, Jan., 1924).

[21] Karen Horney: "The Flight from Womanhood: The Masculinity Complex
in Women as Viewed by Men and by Women" (*Internat. Jour. of Ps.-An.*,
Vol. VII, 1926).

More recently another psycho-analyst, Gregory Zilboorg, equally "inclined to
think that it is not penis-envy on the part of woman, but woman-envy on the
part of man, that is psychologically older and therefore more fundamental,"
has made a new departure in psycho-analytical theory based on the assumption
of a basic feminine superiority in his study: "Masculine and Feminine. Some
Biological and Cultural Aspects" (*Psychiatry*, Vol. 7, Aug., 1944, No. 3).

The whole argument looks like a bid for supremacy between two highly interested competitors. It certainly shows how hard it is to achieve scientific detachment in matters of personal concern. And it bears witness to the competitive spirit that has animated discussions about feminine traits ever since women voiced their claims to consideration as complete individuals and pretenders to the Rights of Man.

Against the rather obvious accusation of masculine partiality Freud defends his position with a gallant gesture towards women which is quite an amusing example of chivalry entering a scientific argument:

Whenever a comparison was made which seemed to be unfavourable to their sex, the ladies were able to express a suspicion that we, the men analysts, had never overcome certain deep-rooted prejudices against the feminine, and that consequently our investigation suffered from bias. On the other hand, on the basis of bisexuality, we found it easy to avoid any impoliteness. We had only to say: "This does not apply to you. You are an exception, in this respect you are more masculine than feminine." [22]

Freud could not have given away his attitude of masculine superiority more clearly than by this polite bow to the "ladies" and his willingness to distinguish some of them with the order of merit of being "more masculine than feminine."

As the bisexuality referred to in the above quotation is a corner-stone in Freud's libido-theory it still needs closer examination. The bisexuality of all living organisms is one of the more recent discoveries of biological science. We have met with some of its implications for human psychology both in Havelock Ellis's and in Weininger's theories. It means, in short, that every individual has, at least potentially if not actually, the characteristics of both sexes, but normally develops the one set to a greater extent than the other. There is no clear-cut line between absolute masculinity and absolute femininity, but reality presents us with a mixture of both in different proportions which vary considerably with each individual. It is, in Freud's words, "as though the

[22] *The Psychology of Women*, pp. 149-50.

individual were neither man nor woman, but both at the same time, only rather more the one than the other." [23]

In order to determine the proportion of the two elements in a given mixture one has first to reduce these to their fundamental essence as, for instance, Weininger has done with the stipulation of two pure types *M* and *W*. For Freud the contrast masculine-feminine is, ultimately, the contrast between active and passive; or, to be more exact: masculinity implies activity, femininity is characterized by a "preference for passive aims," which is not quite the same as passivity. ("It may require a good deal of activity to achieve a passive end.") [24] In Freud's own words:

> Psychoanalysis has a common basis with biology in that it presupposes an original bisexuality in human beings (as in animals). But psychoanalysis cannot elucidate the intrinsic nature of what in conventional or in biological phraseology is termed "masculine" and "feminine": it simply takes over the two concepts and makes them the foundation of its work. When we attempt to reduce them further we find masculinity vanishing into activity and femininity into passivity and that does not tell us enough. [25]

Now, it is a peculiar and interesting phenomenon that in Freud's interpretation "bisexuality" has a distinctly masculine connotation. The period in human life in which bisexuality is most pronounced is, naturally, early childhood, i.e. the time before adult sexuality, secondary sex characteristics, and psychological corollaries intensify the tendencies towards one sex rather than the other. At that age we find children of both sexes developing the same kind of activity and aggressiveness and a sexuality centered on a "masculine" genital. (In girls it is represented by a corresponding but, so to speak, underdeveloped organ—an "inadequate substitute," as Helene Deutsch calls it [26]—the clitoris.) The auto-eroticism of both boys and girls is masculine in character.

Equally, libido, which as the instinctual source of energy to

---

[23] Ibid., p. 146.

[24] Ibid., p. 148.

[25] "The Psychogenesis of a Case of Homosexuality in a Woman" (*Coll. Papers*, pp. 202-32, London, 1920).

[26] Helene Deutsch: "The Psychology of Women in Relation to the Functions of Reproduction" (*Internat. Jour. of Ps.-An.*, Vol. VI, 1925).

both men and women is understood to be bisexual, actually, if we keep to Freud's definition of masculinity = activity, is a masculine force. Freud himself remarks that "libido could always be called 'masculine,' no matter whether it appears in man or in woman, in the sense that, as an instinct, it is always active, even if directed towards a passive aim." [27]

This identification of the masculine with an absolute norm is a remarkable example of the way in which, in a masculine culture, standards of the one sex are generalized and represented as neutral—here called bisexual—and taken as valid for mankind in general, irrespective of sex. Georg Simmel, the German sociologist, has pointed out[28] that the same is true of all the values of our culture: the historical development has been such that all categories of our thinking, all norms of our ethics, all artistic forms and social institutions are based on this equation of masculine and "objective" which transforms a psychological superiority, resulting from a superior power position, into a logical one. In the same way, says Simmel, every government based on subjective force tries to defend its authority by an objective justification and thus to transform might into right. The psychological mechanism by which this generalization of the masculine norm is performed is described by Simmel in a passage which is worth quoting in full:

To take from two opposite notions, which derive their meaning and value from each other, one, and to raise this one to embrace and dominate once more the whole game of give and take and of balance, this time in an absolute sense, is a thoroughly human tendency, presumably of deep metaphysical origin, which has found an historic paradigm in the fundamental sexual relation of Man.

The fact that the male sex is not only considered relatively superior to the female, but that it is taken as the universal human norm, applied equally to the phenomena of the individual masculine and of the individual feminine—this fact is, in many different ways, based on the power position of the male. If we express the historic relation between the sexes crudely in terms of master and slave, it is part of the master's

[27] S. Freud: "Three Contributions to the Theory of Sex" (*Imago*, London, 1942).

[28] Georg Simmel: "Das Relative und das Absolute im Geschlechterproblem" (*Philosophische Kultur*, Leipzig, 1911).

privileges not to have to think continuously of the fact that he is the master, while the position of the slave carries with it the constant reminder of his being a slave. It cannot be overlooked that the woman forgets far less often the fact of being a woman than the man of being a man. Innumerable times the man seems to think purely objectively, without his masculinity entering his consciousness at all. On the other hand it seems as if the woman would never completely lose the more or less vague feeling of being a woman; this feeling forms the ever-present background underlying all her experiences of life. Because masculinity, as a differential factor, in phantasies and principles, in achievements and emotional complexes, escapes the consciousness of its protagonists more easily than is the case with femininity in the corresponding situation (for within the sphere of his activities man's interest in his relation to the Feminine is not as vital as woman's interest in her relation to the Masculine) expressions of masculinity are easily elevated for us to the realm of a supra-specific, neutral objectivity and validity (to which their specifically masculine connotation, if noticed at all, is subordinated as something individual and casual). This fact is evident in the extremely frequent phenomenon that certain judgments, institutions, aims, or interests which we men, naively so to speak, consider purely objective, are felt by women to be thoroughly and characteristically masculine.

In generalizing the masculine type and making it a universal norm Freud went further than anyone else: for, to him, even being equipped with male sex organs is part of the general standard, to the extent that the "poverty in external genitals" (in K. Abraham's term) is considered to be an organic deficiency, and that woman is supposed to regard her own biological function (i.e. the ability to bear children) as a compensation for her constitutional inadequacy. It seems plausible to Freud and his school that one half of humanity should have *biological* reasons to feel at a disadvantage for not having what the other half possesses (but not vice versa).

The adoption of masculine standards as the absolute norm applicable to mankind as a whole has two equally harmful results for the judgment of women. The one is a mystifying overestimation of woman by virtue of those qualities which cannot be explained by male criteria. The other is contempt for human beings who fail to live up to the norm.

In Freud's writings we find both attitudes represented: on the one hand the wonder at the "enigmatic" woman, the approach to feminine psychology as a "riddle" to be solved, and a theory which views the development of femininity as a particularly "difficult and complicated process"; on the other hand there is the contempt—as we had sufficient occasion to see—for her inferior intellectual capacities, her greater vanity, her weaker sexual instincts, her disposition to neuroses and hysteria, and for her constitutional passivity. The latter is, in Freud's view, associated with masochistic tendencies. There is, he says, in feminine psychology "some secret relationship with masochism."— "The repression of their aggressiveness, which is imposed upon women by their constitution and by society, favours the development of strong masochistic impulses, which have the effect of binding erotically the destructive tendencies which have been turned inward." [29] This contention has been worked out by Helene Deutsch into a theory according to which masochistic wishes to be violated and humiliated—both physically and mentally—are the clue to feminine psychology. Her view of sexual intercourse as a "sadistic act of taking possession" on the part of man, and a "masochistic subjugation" on the part of woman [30] is but the elaboration of an assumption ever recurring in psychoanalytical literature: the view that "sexual activity is essentially associated with the male organ, that the woman is only in the position to excite the man's libido or respond to it, and that otherwise she is compelled to adopt a waiting attitude," [31] that, moreover, the sex instinct in woman is weaker and that she derives only a limited or indirect satisfaction from sexual intercourse. Ferenczi has developed this view into a "Genital Theory" according to which the sexual impulse is ultimately man's wish to return into the mother's womb—a meaning which the sexual act cannot assume for woman, who therefore has no fundamental impulse for, or primary satisfaction from coitus. What pleasure she does derive results partly by way of a "masochistic conversion

[29] *The Psychology of Women*, pp. 148-9.

[30] Helene Deutsch: "The Significance of Masochism in the Mental Life of Women" (*Internat. Jour. of Ps.-An.*, 1930).

[31] K. Abraham: "Manifestations of the Female Castration Complex" (*Inter. Journ. of Ps.-An.*, Vol. III, 1922).

and partly by identification with the child which she may conceive. These, however, are only compensatory devices." The feminine attitude towards sex is, like other traits, considered by psycho-analytical theory to be based on organic constitution and biological function and therefore part of the unchanging "human nature." Evidences to the contrary which are supplied by other cultures are disregarded, although they are numerous. In Hindu books, for instance—such as *Kâmasutrâm* and *Anángaránga*—women's urge of love is reckoned to be "eight times as potent as that of man"; the code of Manu states that "women are by their very nature experts in the seduction of men, hence man should avoid being found even with his nearest kin in lonely places . . ."; Ovid, in his *Ars Amandi,* considers woman's uncontrollable passion "ten times fiercer than ours and full of madness"; in the famous medieval novel *Roman de la Rose* it is said: "A virtuous woman; Nay, I swear by good St. Denis that this is more rare than is a phoenix"; and in a seventeenth-century book by Vendette a passage runs thus: "In love-affairs men are mere children in comparison with women; women have, in such matters, a greater imagination and command more time to dwell on the affairs of the heart; they are more lascivious and love-sick than men." [32]

It thus appears that judgments on the strength or weakness of the sex impulse in women are not based on organic facts but are in accordance with a cultural pattern, and vary with time and milieu. In Western civilization during the nineteenth and at the beginning of the twentieth century it would have been not only scandalous to admit the existence of a strong sex urge in women, but it would have been contrary to all observation. And although the enforcement of rules of conduct and of so many restrictions was deemed prudent in order to keep up the illusion of "innate" feminine virtuousness, it never occurred to our fathers and grandfathers that it was but an illusion and that, had this not been so, the rigorous supervision of their daughters and wives would hardly have been necessary.

---

[32] Examples quoted from *The Riddle of Woman* (op. cit.) by Joseph Tenenbaum, who gives these and more instances in his chapter on "The Sex Urge in Woman."

Even Karen Horney, the "equalitarian" among the psycho-analysts, would not go as far as to oppose to the masculine sex impulse a corresponding primary feminine sex impulse, but would base her claims to feminine equality on woman's capacity for motherhood. It thus seems that in psycho-analytical theory it is understood that there are two different instincts in men and women: a sex instinct which is masculine, and an instinct of procreation which is feminine.

Underlying this assumption, as well as other psycho-analytical ideas, is the Victorian notion that "sexual activity is lawfully masculine" (this is Freud's term), but that for women sexuality is a matrimonial duty they have to put up with. To admit that from her sexual function a woman could derive an equal amount of satisfaction, pleasure, happiness—and, if it comes to it, even sense of power—with man, would have been shocking to Victorian ideology. The same attitude is also at the bottom of Freud's theory of penis-envy; it is the inability to understand that woman no less than man has been equipped by Nature with a sex instinct and the means to gratify it, and that, if she has any reasons for envying man, they are not likely to be of a physiological character.

Alfred Adler, who had made inferiority feelings and the "masculine protest" the central ideas of his Individual Psychology, comes nearer to a sociological interpretation when he asserts that in our competitive culture the dichotomy masculine–feminine has assumed a symbolic value, serving as an analogy to more general ideas of socially "superior" and "inferior," of "above" and "below." In a society based, like ours, on individual competition, Adler finds two unconscious presuppositions underlying the thoughts of both his men and women patients: first, that "human relations in all circumstances represent a struggle," and, secondly, that "the feminine sex is inferior and by its reaction serves as the measure of masculine strength." [33] Therefore the struggle upwards assumes the form of what Adler calls the "masculine protest," i.e. a fight against those qualities in oneself which by tradition and consent usually are associated with the

---

[33] Alfred Adler: *The Practice and Theory of Individual Psychology* (Kegan Paul, London, 1924, p. 35).

feminine sex, such as weakness, timidity, shyness, passivity, prudishness, etc. Adler's "masculine protest" represents all strivings for "strength, greatness, riches, knowledge, victory," and all "coarseness, cruelty, violence, and activity as such." As the child grows up into a hard and competitive world it increasingly wants to get rid of those qualities which hamper its struggle for existence.

The normal craving of the child for nestling, the exaggerated submissiveness of the neurotically-disposed individual, the feeling of weakness, of inferiority protected by hyper-sensitiveness, the realization of actual futility, the sense of being permanently pushed aside and of being at a disadvantage, all these are gathered together into a feeling of femininity. On the contrary, active strivings, both in the case of a girl as of a boy, the pursuit of self-gratification, the stirring up of instincts and passions are thrown challengingly forward as a masculine protest.[34]

The terms "masculine" and "feminine" are clearly used here as symbols of a contrasting pair of values: the one implies all positive, desirable qualities, the other one is associated with all negative, despicable characteristics. This analogy is based, Adler says, on a "false evaluation but one which is extensively nourished by our social life."

Envy of men, refutation of the feminine rôle, attempts to compete with men, or to copy them in order to feel "complete individuals," contempt for their own inferiority—these are the phenomena observed in their women patients both by Freud and by Adler and occupying a central position in their respective theories. But while Psycho-analysis seeks a biological explanation and regards these attitudes as conscious rationalizations designed to cover up an underlying organic deficiency, Individual Psychology views them as the expression of a striving for power, a power which in our society is associated with the male sex.

It is as well to remind ourselves that the beginning of women's emancipation coincided with the height of capitalist expansion and liberal ideology and that both theories originated at this time. The striving for power which Adler took as the primary motive

---

[34] Op. cit. (p. 22).

in human psychology is a typical characteristic of a competitive culture. Women who endeavoured to participate in this culture did so on a competitive basis. Out of their feminine seclusion they came into the open and found all places occupied by men. When they wanted to contend with them on the ground of a philosophy of Human Rights they found themselves classified as *hors concours* because of their sex. No doubt this disqualification was resented by a very great number of them, who reacted to it in different ways: with envy, hatred, revolt, inferiority feelings, increased exertions to make themselves acceptable by adopting as completely as possible the rules of the game (Freud's "masculinity complex") and other reactions listed by Freud under the heading of "penis-envy." The resentment is likely to find a most acute expression in unbalanced personalities, such as the neurotics who are the patients and objects of the psychiatrist's investigation. There is no doubt that the factual observations made by Freud are correct. They are valid, that is to say, for the class of people who made up his objects of observation: the neurotic persons of middle and upper middle-class origin in the Central-European society of his time. They are also valid, most probably with corresponding modifications, in every society with strong patriarchal traditions. For Freud and his orthodox pupils there was no doubt that the patients they analysed, and the people they met, were representatives of "the" human type. Future research will have to concentrate on defining the specific character of the field of observation on the basis of comparative evidence. A modified Freudian theory will have to include such social and cultural factors as particular influences of the environment, the power of prevailing traditions, ideals and historical institutions.

It was in a sense rather fortunate for psycho-analytical theory that, owing to otherwise very fateful political developments in Central Europe, a great number of its supporters had to go abroad. In foreign countries they came into close contact with divergent cultural patterns and different personality types. In consequence there came into existence—mainly in the United States of America—a new type of psycho-analyst who, while preserving the fundamental achievements of the Freudian school, became increasingly culture-conscious and inclined to a more sociological orientation. This new trend has, of course, not affected all exiled psycho-analysts. Helene Deutsch, for instance, has only recently published a *Psychology of Woman*,[35] in which she restates her former orthodox views. But the number of psycho-analysts with a definite leaning to sociology is large enough to be regarded as a new psycho-analytical "school." Among these are Karen Horney, Erich Fromm, Clara Thompson and others. (Paul Bousfield has, in this country, expressed similar tendencies.) These people are supported not only by their own experience but by anthropology and sociology—two sciences of a fairly recent development—in their conviction that there is no "universal man" or "universal woman," but that human beings have to be studied in relation to their milieu—or, to use the technical term, to the "cultural pattern." The realization that in different societies women fulfil different social functions and accordingly display different attitudes and mental characteristics has shattered the idea of the all-powerful influence of anatomy and biological facts on character-traits. As Clara Thompson has pointed out,[36] it is possible to explain every single trait attributed by Freud to a biologically determined development of the libido (such as all the implications of "penis-envy," the repression of aggressiveness, passivity and masochism, the narcissistic need to be loved, the rigidity, i.e. prematurely arrested character development of women, the weaker super-ego, etc.) by the influence of "cultural pressures," that is by the impact of a concrete historical situation on character structures.

To suppose that human beings are born as "tabulae rasae" on which every trait is to be impressed by social and cultural influences of the surroundings would certainly be no less a mistake than to assume that "anatomy is destiny." The dangers of a one-sided stress on environmental factors, which a purely sociological point of view might entail, has been considerably reduced by the new turn which psycho-analytical theory has been taking, and no doubt, the integration of psycho-analytical with socio-

---

[35] Dr. Helene Deutsch: *Psychology of Woman* (Grune & Stratton, 1944).
[36] Clara Thompson: "Cultural Pressures in the Psychology of Women," published in *Psychiatry*, Vol. V, No. 3. Baltimore, Aug. 1942.

logical thinking which we are witnessing at present will be most fruitful in its effects both on psychological and sociological knowledge.

References

S. FREUD: "The Psychology of Women" (Chapter XXXIII, *New Introductory Lectures*, Hogarth Press, London, 1933).

"Three Contributions to the Theory of Sex" (*Imago*, London, 1942).

Taboo of Virginity, 1918.

Civilization and Its Discontent (Hogarth Press, London, 1930).

Totem and Taboo (Kegan Paul, London, 1919).

The Psychogenesis of a Case of Homosexuality in a Woman (Collected Papers, London, 1920).

"Civilized Sexual Morality and Modern Nervousness" (*Collected Papers*, Vol. 2, London, 1924).

Analysis Terminable and Unterminable (London, 1937).

"Some Psychological Consequences of the Anatomical Distinction Between the Sexes" (*Internat. Jour. of Ps.-An.*, London, 1927).

K. ABRAHAM: "Manifestations of the Female Castration Complex" (*Internat. Jour. of Ps.-An.*, Vol. III, March, 1922).

PAUL BOUSFIELD: *Sex and Civilization* (Kegan Paul, London, 1925).

C. D. DALY: "The Psychology of Man's Attitude Towards Woman" (*British Jour. of Medic. Psychology*, Vol. X, 1930).

HELENE DEUTSCH: "The Psychology of Women in Relation to the Functions of Reproduction" (*Internat. Jour. of Ps.-An.*, Vol. VI, 1925).

"The Significance of Masochism in the Mental Life of Women" (*Internat. Jour. of Ps.-An.*, 1930).

Psychology of Woman (Grune & Stratton, 1944).

J. HARNIK: "The Various Developments Undergone by Narcissism in Men and Women" (*Internat. Jour. of Ps.-An.*, Vol. V, 1925).

KAREN HORNEY: "On the Genesis of the Castration Complex in Women" (*Internat. Jour. of Ps.-An.*, Vol. V, January 1924).

"The Flight from Womanhood: The Masculinity in Women as Viewed by Men and by Women" (*Internat. Jour. of Ps.-An.*, Vol. VII, 1926).

"The Denial of the Vagina" (*Internat. Jour. of Ps.-An.*, 1933).

The Neurotic Personality of Our Time (Kegan Paul, London, 1937).

New Ways in Psycho-Analysis (Kegan Paul, London, 1939).

ERNEST JONES: "Early Development of Female Sexuality (*Internat. Jour. of Ps.-An.*, 1927).

"Phallic Phase" (*Internat. Jour. of Ps.-An.*, 1927).

J. H. W. VAN OPHUISEN: "Contributions to the Masculinity Complex in Women" (*Internat. Jour. of Ps.-An.*, Vol. V, 1924).

CLARA THOMPSON: "The Rôle of Women in this Culture" (*Psychiatry*, Vol. 4, 1941).

"Cultural Pressures in the Psychology of Women" (*Psychiatry*, Vol. 5, 1942).

" 'Penis Envy' in Women" (*Psychiatry*, Vol. 6, 1943).

ALFRED ADLER: *The Practice and Theory of Individual Psychology* (Kegan Paul, London, 1924).

ALICE RÜHLE-GERSTEL: *Freud und Adler* (Dresden, 1924).

Das Frauenproblem der Gegenwart (Leipzig, 1932).

ERWIN WEXBERG: *Individual Psychology and Sex* (Jonathan Cape, London, 1931).

GEORG SIMMEL: "Das Relative und das Absolute im Geschlechterproblem" (*Philosophische Kultur*, Leipzig, 1911).

GREGORY ZILBOORG: "Masculine and Feminine Some Biological and Cultural Aspects" (*Psychiatry*, Vol. 7, 1944).

24

CLARA THOMPSON

Some Effects of the Derogatory Attitude Towards Female Sexuality*

In an earlier paper[1] I stressed the fact that the actual envy of the penis as such is not as important in the psychology of women as their envy of the position of the male in our society. This position of privilege and alleged superiority is symbolized by the possession of a penis. The owner of this badge of power has special opportunities while those without have more limited possibilities. I questioned in that paper whether the penis in its own right as a sexual organ was necessarily an object of envy at all.

That there are innate biological differences between the sexual life of man and woman is so obvious that one must apologize for mentioning it. Yet those who stress this aspect most are too often among the first to claim knowledge of the psychic experiences and feelings of the opposite sex. Thus for many centuries male writers have been busy trying to explain the female. In recent years a few women have attempted to present the inner life of their own sex, but they themselves seem to have had difficulty in freeing their thinking from the male orientation. Psychoanalysts, female as well as male, seem for the most part still to be dominated by Freud's thinking about women.

* Read at a Symposium on Feminine Psychology, given under the auspices of the Department of Psychiatry of the New York Medical College, March 19, 1950. Reprinted by permission of The William Alanson White Psychiatric Foundation, Inc. from *Psychiatry*, 1950, 13:349-354. Copyright, 1950, by The William Alanson White Psychiatric Foundation, Inc.
[1] Clara Thompson, "Penis Envy in Women," *Psychiatry* (1943) 6:123-125.

Freud was a very perceptive thinker but he was a male, and a male quite ready to subscribe to the theory of male superiority prevalent in the culture. This must have definitely hampered his understanding of experiences in a woman's life, especially those specifically associated with her feminine role.

Of course this thinking can be carried to extreme lengths and one can say that no human being can really know what another human being actually experiences about anything. However, the presence of similar organs justifies us in thinking that we can at least approximate an understanding of another person's experiences in many cases. A headache, a cough, a pain in the heart, intestinal cramps, weeping, laughter, joy, a sense of well-being— we assume that all of these feel to other people very similar to what we ourselves experience under those titles.

In the case of sexual experiences, however, one sex has no adequate means of identifying with the experience of the other sex. A woman, for instance, cannot possibly be sure that she knows what the subjective experience of an erection and male orgasm is. Nor can a man identify with the tension and sensations of menstruation, or female genital excitation, or child birth. Since for many years most of the psychoanalysts were men this may account for the prevalence of some misconceptions about female sexuality. Horney pointed out in 1926 that Freud's theory that little girls believed they had been castrated and that they envied boys their penises is definitely a male orientation to the subject.[2] In this paper she listed several ideas which little boys have about girls' genitals. These ideas, she shows, are practically identical with the classical psychoanalytic conception of the female. The little boys' ideas are based on the assumption that girls also have penises, which results in a shock at the discovery of their absence. A boy, reasoning from his own life experience, assumes this is a mutilation, as a punishment for sexual misdemeanor. This makes more vivid to him any castration threats which have been made to him. He concludes that the girl must feel inferior and envy him because she must have come to the same conclusions about her state. In short, the little boy, incapable of imagining

---

[2] Karen Horney, "Flight from Womanhood," *Internat. J. Psycho-Analysis* (1926) 7:324-339.

that one could feel complete without a penis, assumes that the little girl must feel deprived. It is doubtless true that her lack of a penis can activate any latent anxiety the boy may have about the security of his own organ, but it does not necessarily follow that the girl feels more insecure because of it.

In the "Economic Problem of Masochism" [3] Freud assumes that masochism is a part of female sexuality, but he gives as his evidence the phantasies of passive male homosexuals. What a passive male homosexual imagines about the experience of being a woman is not necessarily similar to female sexual experience. In fact, a healthy woman's sexual life is probably not remotely similar to the phantasies and longings of a highly disturbed passive male personality.

Recently I heard to my amazement that a well-known psychiatrist had told a group of students that in the female sexual life there is no orgasm. I can only explain such a statement by assuming that this man could not conceive of orgasm in the absence of ejaculation. If he had speculated that the female orgasm must be a qualitatively different experience from that of the male because of the absence of ejaculation, one could agree that this may well be the case. I think these examples suffice to show that many current ideas about female psychosexual life may be distorted by being seen through male eyes.

In "Sex and Character" [4] Fromm has pointed out that the biological differences in the sexual experience may contribute to greater emphasis on one or the other character trends in the two sexes. Thus he notes that for the male it is necessary to be able to perform, while no achievement is required of the female. This, he believes, can have a definite effect on the general character trends. This gives the man a greater need to demonstrate, to produce, to have power, while the woman's need is more in the direction of being accepted, being desirable. Since her satisfaction is dependent on the man's ability to produce, her fear is in being abandoned, being frustrated, while his is fear of failure. Fromm points out that the woman can make herself available at any time and give satisfaction to the man, but the man's possibility of

[3] Freud, *Collected Papers* 2:255-268; London, Hogarth Press, 1925.
[4] Erich Fromm, "Sex and Character," *Psychiatry* (1943) 6:21-31.

satisfying her is not entirely within his control. He cannot always produce an erection at will.

The effect of basic sexual differences on the character structure is not pertinent to this paper. Fromm's thesis that the ability to perform is important in male sexual life, that it is especially a matter of concern to the male because it is not entirely within his control, and that the female may perform at all times if she so wishes, are points of importance in my thesis. But I should like to develop somewhat different aspects of the situation. Fromm shows that the woman can at any time satisfy the male, and he mentions the male's concern over successfully performing for the female, but he does not at any point discuss how important obtaining satisfaction for themselves is in the total reaction.

In general the male gets at least some physiological satisfaction out of his sexual performance. Some experiences are more pleasurable than others, to be sure, and there are cases of orgasm without pleasure. However, for the very reason that he cannot force himself to perform, he is less likely to find himself in the midst of a totally uncongenial situation.

The female, however, who permits herself to be used when she is not sexually interested or is at most only mildly aroused frequently finds herself in the midst of an unsatisfactory experience. At most she can have only a vicarious satisfaction in the male's pleasure. I might mention parenthetically here that some male analysts, for example Ferenczi, are inclined to think that identification with the male in his orgasm constitutes a woman's true sexual fulfillment. This I would question.

One frequently finds resentment in women who have for some reason consented to being used for the male's pleasure. This is in many cases covered by an attitude of resignation. A frequent answer from women when they are asked about marital sexual relations is: "It is all right. He doesn't bother me much." This attitude may hold even when in other respects the husband and wife like each other; that is, such an attitude may exist even when the woman has not been intimidated by threats or violence. She simply assumes that her interests are not an important consideration.

Obviously the sexual act is satisfactory to the woman only when she actively and from choice participates in her own characteristic way. If she considered herself free to choose, she would refuse the male except when she actually did desire to participate.

This being the case, it might be fruitful to examine the situations in which the woman submits with little or no interest. There are, of course, occasions when she genuinely wishes to do this for the man's sake; this does not create a problem. More frequently the cause is a feeling of insecurity in the relationship; this insecurity may arise from external factors—that is, the male concerned may insist on his satisfaction or else! The insecurity may also arise from within because of the woman's own feelings of inadequacy. These feelings may arise simply from the fact that the woman subscribes to the cultural attitude that her needs are not as insistent as the man's; but in addition she may have personal neurotic difficulties.

The question arises, How has it become socially acceptable for a man to insist on his sexual rights whenever he desires? Is this because rape is a possibility, and the woman is physically relatively defenseless? This must have had some influence in the course of society's development. However, it has often been proved that even rape is not easy without some cooperation from the woman. The neurotic condition of vaginismus illustrates that in some conditions even unconscious unwillingness on the part of the woman may effectively block male performance. So while the superior physical power of the male may be an important factor in the frequency of passive compliance, there must be other factors. These other factors are not of a biological nature, for the participation in sexual relations without accompanying excitement is most obviously possible in human females, although not definitely impossible in other animals.

One must look to cultural attitudes for the answer. There are two general concepts which are significant here, and to which both men and women subscribe in our culture. One is that the female sexual drive is not as pressing or important as the male. Therefore there is less need to be concerned in satisfying it or considering it. The other is the analytically much discussed thesis that the female sex organs are considered inferior to those of the male.

In recent years there has been a definite tendency to move away from the first idea as far as actual sexual performance is concerned. With the increasing tendency to be more open in observing facts about sex, women in many groups have become able not only to admit to themselves but also to men that their sexual needs are important. However, this is still not true of all groups. Moreover, at almost the same time another important aspect of woman's sexual life has diminished in importance; that is, the bearing of children. Woman's specific type of creativeness is no longer highly desired in many situations. This is an important subject in itself and will not be discussed here.

As we know, during the Victorian era a woman's sexual needs were supposed to be practically nonexistent. A woman was expected to be able to control her sexual desires at all times. Thus an extramarital pregnancy was allegedly entirely due to the woman's weakness or depravity. The man's participation in such an extramarital relationship was looked upon with more tolerance, and there was little or no social disgrace attached to him. The double standard of sexual morality also implied an assumption that woman's sexual drive was not as insistent as the male's.

The fact that evidence of erotic excitement could be concealed much better by a woman than by a man made the development of such thinking possible. Since she was not supposed to be erotic and since the man must have his satisfaction, a pattern was developed in which the dutiful wife offered herself to her husband without actively participating in the act herself. I am sure many women were sufficiently normal to find nonparticipation difficult, and doubtless many men did not subscribe to the feeling that they should be horrified at any evidence of passion in their wives. Nevertheless as recently as twenty years ago a woman, who consulted me about her marital difficulties, reported that her husband felt disgust, it seemed, whenever she responded sexually to him. She tried to conceal her sexual responses, including orgasm, from him, then would lie awake the rest of the night in misery and rage. Since I saw this woman only twice, I am not in a position to say how much this situation contributed to her suicide about a year later. Undoubtedly there were many other difficulties in her relation to her husband of which the sexual may have been only one expression. Certainly this extreme denial of sexual interest is seldom required of women today, but an attenuated form still remains, especially in marriage. Here it is found not only in frigid women who, realizing their inadequacy as mates, make amends as best they can by a nonparticipating offering of themselves. But one also finds the attitude even in women with adequate sexual responsiveness in many situations. They have accepted the idea that the male's needs are greater than their own and that therefore his wishes and needs are paramount.

So the feeling that woman's sexual life is not as important or insistent as the male's may produce two unfortunate situations. It may inhibit the woman's natural expressions of desire for fear of appearing unwomanly, or it may lead her to feel she must be ready to accommodate on all occasions—that is, she has no rights of her own. Both extremes mean an interference with her natural self-expression and spontaneity with resulting resentment and discontent.

Moreover, since the male has often been indoctrinated with the idea that woman's sexual life is not important, he may not exert himself much to make her interested. He fails to see the importance of the art of love.

When an important aspect of a person's life becomes undervalued, this has a negative effect on the self-esteem. What a woman actually has to offer in sexual responsiveness becomes undervalued, and this in turn affects her own evaluation of herself as a person.

The second way in which our culture has minimized woman's sexual assets is in the derogation of her genitals. This in classical terminology is connected with the idea of penis envy. I wish to approach the problem differently. As I said earlier, the idea of penis envy is a male concept. It is the male who experiences the penis as a valuable organ and he assumes that women also must feel that way about it. But a woman cannot really imagine the sexual pleasure of the penis—she can only appreciate the social advantages its possessor has.[5] What a woman needs rather is a feeling of the importance of her own organs. I believe that much more important than penis envy in the psychology of woman is

---

[5] I do not wish to leave the impression that there is never a woman who thinks she desires to possess the male genital as such, but I believe such women are found relatively rarely.

her reaction to the undervaluation of her own organs. I think we can concede that the acceptance of one's body and all its functions is a basic need in the establishment of self-respect and self-esteem.

The short plump brunette girl may feel that she would be more acceptable if she were a tall thin blond—in other words, if she were somebody else. The solution of her problem lies not in becoming a blond but in finding out why she is not accepting of what she is. The history will show either that some significant person in her early life preferred a tall blond or that being a brunette has become associated with other unacceptable characteristics. Thus in one case in which this envy of the blond type was present, being brunette meant being sexy, and being sexy was frowned upon.

Sex in general has come under the disapproval of two kinds of thinking in our culture. The puritan ideal is denial of body pleasure, and this makes sexual needs something of which to be ashamed. Traces of this attitude still remain today in the feelings of both sexes.

We also have another attitude which derogates sexuality, especially female sexuality. We are people with great emphasis on cleanliness. In many people's minds the genital organs are classed with the organs of excretion and thus become associated with the idea of being unclean. With the male some of the curse is removed because he gets rid of the objectionable product. The female, however, receives it, and when her attitude is strongly influenced by the dirty excretion concept, this increases her feeling of unacceptability. Moreover, the men who feel the sexual product is unclean reinforce the woman's feeling that her genitals are unclean.

The child's unrestrained pleasure in his body and its products begins to be curbed at an early age. This is such a fundamental part of our basic training that most of us would have difficulty imagining the effect on our psychic and emotional life of a more permissive attitude. What has happened is that this training has created a kind of moral attitude towards our body products. Sphincter morality, as Ferenczi has called it, extends to more than the control of urine and feces. To some extent genital products come also under the idea of sphincter morality. Obviously this especially has an influence on attitudes towards the female genitals where no sphincter control is possible. My attention was first called to this by a paper written in German by Bertram Lewin twenty years ago.[6] In this paper he presented, among other things, clinical data in which the menses were compared to an unwanted loss of feces and urine due to lack of sphincter control. In one case which he reported the woman had become very proficient at contracting the vaginal muscles so that she attained some semblance of control of the quantity of menstrual flow. Although in my own practice I have never encountered a patient who actually tried to produce a sphincter, I have frequent evidence that the inability not only to control menstruation but all secretions of the female genitals has contributed to a feeling of unacceptability and dirtiness. One patient on being presented by her mother with a perineal napkin on the occasion of her first menses refused to use it. To her it meant a baby's diaper, and she felt completely humiliated. Obviously she presently felt even more humiliated because of the inevitable consequences of her refusal.

Also because of the culture's overevaluation of cleanliness another attribute of the female genital can be a source of distress, that is, the fact that it has an odor. Thus one of the chief means by which the female attracts the male among animals has been labelled unpleasant, to many even disgusting. For example, a female patient whose profession requires her appearing before audiences has been greatly handicapped for many years by a feeling of being "stinking" which is greatly augmented whenever she is in a position to have her body observed. Thus she can talk over the radio but not before an audience. Another patient felt for years that she could never marry because she would not be able to keep her body clean at every moment in the presence of her husband. Whenever she had a date with a man she prepared for it by a very vigorous cleansing of the genitals especially trying to make them dry. When she finally had sexual relations she was surprised and greatly helped in her estimation of her body

---

[6] B. Lewin, "Kotschmieren, Menses und weibliches über-Ich," *Internat. Zschr. Psychoanal.* (1930) 16:43-56.

by discovering that this highly prized dryness was just the opposite of what was pleasing to the man.

In two cases the feeling of genital unacceptability had been a factor in promiscuity. In each case an experience with a man who kissed her genitals in an obviously accepting way was the final step in bringing about a complete transformation of feeling. In both cases all need to be promiscuous disappeared, and each of the women felt loved for the first time.

I am obviously oversimplifying these cases in order to make my point clear. I do not wish to leave the impression that the feeling of dirtiness connected with the genitals was the sole cause of a feeling of unacceptability in these patients. There was in each case a feeling from early childhood of not being acceptable, produced by specific attitudes in the parents. The feeling of unacceptability became focused on the genitals eventually for different reasons in each case. For example, in three cases the woman had risen above the lowly social position of her parents and with each of these three women the feeling of having dirty genitals became symbolic of her lowly origin of which she was ashamed. The parents had not placed such an emphasis on baths as they found to be the case in the new social milieu. Therefore any evidence of body secretion or odor betrayed them, and this made sex itself evidence of lower-class origin. On the other hand two other patients suffered from their own mothers' overemphasis on body cleanliness. In each of these two cases the mother was cold and puritanical as well as overclean, and the patient felt humiliated because she had a more healthy sexual drive which she felt was proclaimed to the world by her body's odors and secretions.

From these observations I hope I have emphasized the fact that the problem of a woman's sexual life is not in becoming reconciled to having no penis but in accepting her own sexuality in its own right. In this she is hampered by certain attitudes in the culture such as that her sexual drive is not important and her genitals are not clean. With these two deprecatory cultural attitudes in the background of women's lives it is to be expected that both are important points at which difficulties in interpersonal relations may be expressed.

II

THERAPY

Goals of Treatment

Psychoanalysis is primarily a method of treatment. Since this is so, it ought to be a simple matter to state its goal, namely the regaining of mental health, both in terms of symptoms and character structure. However, the goals have not been generally so stated. For Freud, they were the making conscious of the unconscious, the removal of the infantile amnesia, and the overcoming of resistances. The difficulty with such a formulation of therapeutic goals is that it makes them dependent upon the validity of the theory and removes them from the human being who is the patient.

An attempt to formulate the essential goal of treatment in terms of the patient is made in the paper by Balint. To put it simply, the goal of therapy is to regain the ability to love others, a capacity which is notably impaired in the mentally ill. It has the advantage that it does not depend on the validity of any particular theory, but on what is generally agreed to be a need and capacity of mankind. Further, it does not impel the therapist to work in the direction of a goal, such as the removal of the infantile amnesia, which adequate experience has now shown does not cause cure, but which may be a by-product of cure.

Since psychoanalysis is a process in which both the therapist and patient engage, an understanding of their relationship through its various vicissitudes is part of any formulation of goals. This process, which Alexander calls the corrective emotional experience, is one of the analyst's most useful therapeutic devices, and the technical resources at his command are described in Alexander's paper.

A view of the goals of constructive therapy is given by Rank.

25

MICHAEL BALINT

The Final Goal of
Psycho-Analytic Treatment*

One can confidently describe psycho-analytic treatment as a natural process of development in the patient. If, then, I inquire into the final goal of our therapy, I do not mean by this a prescribed final state, which, deduced from some philosophical, religious, moral, sociological, or even biological premise, requires that everyone should "get well" according to its particular model. I ask rather: is our clinical experience sufficient to define the final goal, or at least the final direction of this natural development?

There are special cases particularly suitable for this inquiry. I am thinking of those people who—like Freud's famous Wolf-man—break off the analysis with only partial results, and then, after an interval of years, continue the treatment, possibly with another analyst. The resumed work offers a very favourable opportunity for a fresh investigation of the former non-adjusted obstacles, and a cure in such a case supplies the proof that it was precisely those obstacles that had previously blocked the way to recovery.[1]

* Read before the Thirteenth International Psycho-analytical Congress, Lucerne, 1934. First published in German in *Int. Z.f. Psa.* (1935), 21, 36-45. In English: *Int. J. of PsA.* (1936), 17, 206-16. Reprinted from *Primary Love and Psycho-Analytic Technique* by Michael Balint, published by Liveright Publishing Corp.

[1] I do not believe, in fact, that smoothly running cases, which terminate without complications, can offer much for our purpose. First of all, in these

A case of this kind first set before me the problem of how our patients become cured and what is really the final goal of psycho-analytic treatment. As the case offers nothing of special interest apart from this, I will mention here only what is of importance for the formulation of our problem. The man in question, who was well on in his forties and whose illness presented a picture in which phobic and obsessional neurotic features were originally to the fore, had already undergone some four years of thorough analysis. When, after an interval of two further years, he came to me since he was not able to return to his former analyst, his neurosis had taken the form of a fairly serious conversion-hysteria. We worked some further 500 hours together. The analysis came to an end two years ago, and the result is one of the best in my practice. Now this was attained without anything new that is worth mentioning being brought to light from the unconscious. Everything had already been partly remembered, partly reconstructed, in the previous analysis, and during this second period of work, which was certainly very intensive, and also successful, no change occurred in the picture, already familiar to the patient, of his infantile and subsequent course of development. In spite of this—and I can assert it without exaggeration—the man was cured during this time.

I would remark at once that this is not an exceptional case. Ever since this case taught me to pay attention to such processes I have been able regularly to observe that in all cases where the analysis was deep enough, the final phase turns out similarly. In the last months fresh material is only rarely made conscious, and infantile incidents which were not already known or had till then remained unconscious are hardly ever brought to light. Neverthe-

---

cases one can never be quite sure whether our therapeutic work did not merely set going some mechanism which remains hidden from us, and whether the patients did not recover with the help of this—to us—unknown process. Secondly, it often happens that one can only observe the result and not the process of recovery. We can learn far more from an analysis that does not run smoothly. Firstly, one is, of necessity, bound to reflect more upon it; in a difficult case one notices a problem much sooner than in those where results are easily obtained. Secondly, an obstinate, unchanging obstacle, on which the treatment comes to grief, is more easily perceived than the very subtle changes which finally bring about recovery.

less, during this time something very important must have happened to our patients, for before it they were still ill, and during it they became well. I know that all this is already familiar; it was precisely such observations that supplied the material for the concept of "working through." But that concept, or, more correctly, the clinical factors on which that concept is based, were not adequately taken into consideration by the different investigators when they attempted to describe the goal of psycho-analytic treatment. For this reason all the descriptions proposed have fallen short.

One group of these descriptions of the final goal deals only with the structural changes in the mind; this we may call the classical group. The other lays stress on the dynamic or the emotional factor; this could be called the romantic group. All descriptions of the first group derive from Freud. According to him the goal of the treatment was *the making conscious of the unconscious,* or, *the removal of infantile amnesia,* or, *the overcoming of the resistances.* The three descriptions are almost synonymous. In my opinion they go too far. As we have seen in the case described, after a certain point in the treatment no really new material came to light, nothing worth mentioning could be added to the picture of the development in early childhood, and in spite of this the neurosis was cured. On the other hand, it is generally known that even analysed people still dream, and that dream analysis encounters resistance with them also. Consequently, even after the end of an analysis, at least so much remains unconscious in the mind as is necessary for dream formation, and enough resistance unresolved to be able to disturb a dream-analysis considerably. Others, also, have surely had the experience that after a finished analysis, months or even years later, patients suddenly remember fragments of their infantile history. Often we had already been able to reconstruct these in the analysis, so that the suddenly emerging memories are only a confirmation of the analytic work; sometimes, however, these pieces bring to light material which was never even suspected and never used in the analysis, and though these pieces fit in well with the known picture they are none the less quite new. These

three descriptions of the final goal of the treatment consist therefore of attributes which, to use mathematical terminology, are
neither necessary nor sufficient.

Now let us turn to the second group of descriptions. They
are all either paraphrases or more precise restatements of the
old description which dates from the time of catharsis. According to this the final goal of our therapeutic efforts is *"the abreacting of the strangulated affects."* This is doubtless correct but
it is stated too generally. We have as yet no means of telling
whether all the strangulated affects have in fact been dealt with,
nor whether those already dealt with suffice for a cure. Since the
theoretical clarifications of the repetition factor, not a few attempts have been made to arrive at some more precise criterion
for judging this point. Ferenczi and Rank describe the goal as
*"the complete reproduction of the Oedipus relation in analytic
experience."* [2] Since we know how complicated the early infantile
Oedipus relation is, this description, though it doubtless signifies
a notable advance, seems to say too much. Rank claims the final
goal to be *"the abreacting of the birth trauma."* [3] So much has
already been written on the merits and defects of this theory,
that further criticism is superfluous. V. Kovács's formulation,
"the unwinding of the repetition factor," [4] emphasises, in contrast
to the two previous ones, the dynamics of the curative process,
but is still too generally stated. W. Reich comes to almost the
same conclusions as I.[5] But he gives as the final goal *"the attaining of full genitality, of orgastic potency."* This is partly correct;
nobody is healthy who lacks the capacity for a regular periodic
orgasm. If I have understood him rightly, however, he seeks to
explain by means of the vague concept of "constitution" the cases
in which, in spite of a deep analysis, orgastic potency cannot be
reached. On the other hand, most of us have seen, and even observed analytically, more than one person who, in spite of perfect
orgastic potency, is decidedly neurotic.

Since the descriptions already proposed do not entirely satisfy

---

[2] *Entwicklungsziele der Psychoanalyse*, Int. PsA. Verlag, Wien, 1924, p.
54-5.
[3] *Das Trauma der Geburt*, Int. PsA. Verlag, Wien, 1924.
[4] "Wiederholungstendenz und Charakterbildung, *Int. Z. f. Psa.* (1931), 17.
[5] *Charakteranalyse*, 1933.

us, I shall venture to discuss this question on the basis of the views which I put forward at Wiesbaden.[6] I have been able regularly to observe that in the final phase of the treatment patients begin to give expression to long-forgotten, infantile, instinctual wishes, and to demand their gratification from their environment. These wishes are, at first, only faintly indicated, and their appearance often causes resistance, even extreme anxiety. It is only after many difficulties have been overcome and by very slow degrees that they are openly admitted, and it is not until even later that their gratification is experienced as pleasure. I have called this phenomenon the "New Beginning," and I believe I have established the fact that it occurs just before the end, in all sufficiently profound analyses, and that it even constitutes an essential mechanism of the process of cure.

Let us now turn to some criticisms. First, as I remarked at Wiesbaden, a single New Beginning is hardly ever enough. On the other hand, the patient need not make a New Beginning with all of the early instinctual wishes that were important for him. Moreover, after the analysis has ended, instincts may remain whose gratification brings no pleasure and even causes pain.

At this point a host of technical questions arise. Assuming that with the New Beginning we have in our hands an important criterion for the termination of the treatment, then one would like to know how many such recurrent waves of New Beginning are necessary and sufficient. Further, for which component instincts is a New Beginning obligatory, for which accidental, and finally, for which superfluous? I cannot answer any of these questions, and therefore I propose to examine the New Beginning more closely; perhaps we shall come to the opinion that these questions, however important they may appear to us now, do not arise from the actual facts of the case, and are therefore unanswerable.

Since all these phenomena appear only in the last phase of the treatment, and since, unfortunately, not a few analyses have to be broken off on practical grounds before this phase is reached, it was naturally some time before I became aware of a

---

[6] "Charakteranalyse und Neubeginn," *Int. Z f. Psa.* (1934), 20. ("Character Analysis and New Beginning.")

significant characteristic of these newly begun pleasurable activities. *They are, without exception, directed towards objects.*
This discovery rather surprised me. According to our generally
accepted theory of today, the first and most primitive phase
of the libido is auto-erotic. I tried to reconcile my findings with
the theory by arguing that the earlier phases of the development
of the libido (auto-erotism and narcissism) were dealt with in
the middle period of the treatment. Naturally, then, the carrying-
over of the libido to object-relations must remain as a task for
the final phase.

But I remained dissatisfied. The activities realised in this New
Beginning period, as well as its phantasies, were so childish, so
natural, so absolutely unproblematical, that I simply could not
regard them as the final links in a complicated chain of development. And, to go farther, we have long known that in analytic
treatment it is precisely the most deeply hidden, the most primitive layers that come to light last. Then came another constantly
repeated observation. As I pointed out at Wiesbaden, after a
first, and usually very timid, performance of the activity in
question, a passionate phase habitually follows. The patients are
seized, as it were, with an addiction. For days on end they can
simply do nothing else but continually repeat these newly begun
pleasurable actions, or, at least make phantasies about them.
This is a dangerous situation for the continuation of the treatment. The patients were mostly so happy that they were able to
deceive themselves and to begin with, I must admit, myself also.
They feel ultra-healthy, and some made use of this fact, with my
consent, to break off the treatment. This state of passionate happiness, resembling that felt by a drug addict, unfortunately does
not last. As I learnt from a psychologically perceptive patient
who came back to me, it degenerates into ever more and more
extensive demands which at last can no longer be satisfied by
any real object. The end is an intensified narcissism with overweening pride, self-importance and outstanding selfishness, veiled
by superficial politeness and insincere modesty. (Perhaps this
provides an explanation for the very similar behaviour of real
addicts.)

If, however, both patient and analyst hold out, this passionate phase passes and in its place a true object-relation, adjusted to reality, develops before our eyes. Thus, to put it shortly, there is first an unmistakably primitive-infantile object-relation, and this —if not rightly understood and treated—ends in unrealisable demands and a narcissistic state, very disagreeable for the whole environment (as is the case with a spoiled child); if rightly guided, however, it gives way to a relation without conflicts for the subject as well as for those around him. These observations do not harmonise at all with the usual doctrine of the analytical libido theory, according to which auto-erotism should be the primal state of sexuality. A solution of this discrepancy can only be offered by a theoretical picture which is able, at the same time, to explain both the former theory of libidinal development, founded on innumerable clinical data, as well as these latter observations. This solution I found not only suggested but already to a considerable extent built up by Ferenczi.

In his favourite work—*Thalassa*—he describes a process which he calls the development of the erotic sense of reality. He sets forth three stages whose goal always remains the same, and which are distinguished only in that they strive to reach this common goal by different ways, better and better adjusted to reality. This goal is the return to the mother's womb (according to Ferenczi the primal aim of all human sexuality) and the three stages are: passive object-love, the auto-plastic or masturbating phase and finally the alloplastic phase, or, as I should like to call it—active object-love.

What is important for our problem is that the child, as Ferenczi has often pointed out, lives in a libidinal object-relation from the very beginning, and without this libidinal object-relation simply cannot exist; this relation is, however, *passive*. The child does not love but *is loved*. For a time the fostering outer world can fulfill its requirements; but with advancing age these become ever greater, more numerous and more difficult of realisation, so that some time or other real frustration is bound to come. The child replies to this with well-founded hate and aggressiveness, and with a turning away from reality, i.e. with an introversion of his love. If upbringing does not work against this change of direction, i.e. does not attempt to bind the child to reality with enough love, there follows the period of auto-erotic distribution of the libido, the period of various self-gratifications, of defiant self-sufficiency. In my opinion the "anal-sadistic" and "phallic phases," i.e. the observed forms of object-relations, theoretically comprised under these concepts, are artefacts. They do not represent stages or even points in the normal development of psychosexual relations to the outer world; they are not in any respect normal phenomena, but where they can be observed they point to a considerably disturbed development. They are signs of a rather sharp deflection in the normal psychosexual relations to the outer world, occasioned by a consistently unsuitable influence on the part of the environment—above all, by a lack of understanding in upbringing.

I have already given further evidence in support of this seemingly bold assertion before the Budapest Psycho-Analytical Society, and I hope to be able to publish them shortly in a separate paper.[7] Here I will only quote two passages from Freud. He shows in his *Introductory Lectures* that many component instincts of sexuality (such as sadism, for instance) possess an object from the very beginning. He continues: "Others, more plainly connected with particular erotogenic areas in the body, only have an object in the beginning, so long as they are still dependent upon the non-sexual functions and give it up when they become detached from these latter." Oral erotism is here referred to. The other passage runs: *"The oral impulse becomes auto-erotic,* as the anal and other erotogenic impulses are from the beginning. Further development has, to put it as concisely as possible, two aims: first, to renounce auto-erotism, to give up again the object found in the child's own body in exchange *again* for an external one." (What follows does not relate to our present theme.)[8] Here it is explicitly declared that the oral instinct, which has hitherto served in theoretical discussions as the perfect example, as it were, of auto-erotism, passes through a stage of object-relationship at its very outset. What was new in my Budapest paper was the attempt to build up a theory which should take into

[7] "Critical Notes on the Theory of the Pregenital Organisations of the Libido," this vol., p. 49.

[8] *Introductory Lectures on Psycho-analysis,* G. Allen and Unwin, London, Fifth edn., 1936, pp. 276-7. (The italics are mine.)

account this fact, which is generally known but has never been fully appreciated.

According to this theory, all instincts, including those originally described as auto-erotic, are primarily bound to objects.[9] This primitive object-relation is always passive. This passive primal aim of human sexuality—the desire to be gratified, or, the desire to be loved—is preserved throughout life. Reality, unavoidable frustration from without, forces man into by-paths, and he has to be content with these. One by-path is auto-erotism, narcissism: if the world does not gratify me, does not love me enough, I must gratify and love myself. The other by-path is active object-love; this attains the original aim better, but at a sacrifice. We love and gratify our partner (this is the sacrifice) so that in the end we may be gratified and loved by him in return.

If all this is true, then it is easily intelligible that every New Beginning has to take place in an object-relation. One cause of neurosis is always real frustration. Usually the analyst underestimates the importance of this cause, because its counterpart in the aetiological complemental series, the endogenic factor, is continually pushed into the foreground by the analytic work. What we work at for months, even years, are the structural defects of the soul, the torn connections, the psychical material that was rendered incapable of becoming conscious. But one thing we should never forget is that all these defects of development, which we group under the collective name of "the repressed," were originally forced into that state by external influences. That is to say, there is no repression without reality, without an object-relation. It is to the lasting credit of Ferenczi that, in the years during which interest was centred upon what was called "ego-psychology" and upon the investigation of mental structure, he never tired of continually stressing the importance of external factors.

How necessary this was, and still is, I will show by a single example, and for this purpose I have chosen from among many

---

[9] I may refer here to a paper on "The Development of the Capacity for Love and the Sense of Reality," by Alice Balint (published in Hungarian at Budapest in 1933) in which the author anticipated me in arriving at almost the same results by a different path.

other works one that can well bear criticism, since its excellent qualities are very generally recognized. I refer to Melanie Klein's illuminating book.[10]

If we turn to the index of that work we shall look in vain for the following words: lack of understanding in upbringing, parental sadism, unkindness, harshness, spoiling, want of love, and the like. It is a remarkable fact that the word "love" is itself absent.[11] (This word is absent too in the index to Fenichel's *Hysterie und Zwangsneurose.*) This corresponds to another feature of the book: the prominence which it gives to the structural factor and the innate constitution. I will give one example. Everywhere in the book (as well as in her Lucern Congress paper) Mrs. Klein speaks of the split "good" and "bad" mother imagos which the child creates in order to have an object always at hand for his constitutionally intensified sadism. Naturally, then, he must always be afraid of the vengeance of these hated and maltreated "bad" imagos. But could it not perhaps be put in this way—that in the eyes of the child his parents are capricious beings who, quite unaccountably, are sometimes bad to him and sometimes good? And the more neurotic the behaviour of the parents the harder is the task of adjustment for the child, who, in the end, has no choice but to treat his mother, for instance, as two fundamentally different beings. Sometimes the "fairy" is there, and sometimes the "witch." The fear of vengeance would then be revealed as a fear *determined by reality,* and the "constitutionally" intense sadism as the effect of lack of understanding in upbringing. That something in my assumption is true is shown precisely by the success of child analysis. With an understanding upbringing on the part of a mother imago who does not behave neurotically—I am thinking of Mrs. Klein—the way to adjustment is opened to the child. I am of the opinion that it is a pity to stop at the structural defects of the mind; our path can lead us still farther, namely to errors of upbringing—or, as Ferenczi expressed it in his Wiesbaden paper, to the "confusion of tongues" between the adults and the child.

---

[10] *The Psycho-analysis of Children.* Int. PsA. Libr. London, 1932.

[11] Naturally all these subjects are discussed, but the fact that they are absent from the index is of symptomatic importance. (The remarks in the text apply, of course, to the index of the German edition.)

Now we can understand also why the question as to the necessary number and origin of the newly begun gratifications turned out to be unanswerable. The question arose from a way of thinking that had become schematic and not from the actual facts of the case. It is not particular component instincts that must be begun anew but object-love itself.

With the help of these reflections I believe I have been able to formulate the final goal of psycho-analytic treatment more exactly. A person becomes ill because, from his childhood, he has been treated with more or less lack of understanding by those around him. Gratifications were denied him which were necessary to him, whereas others were forced on him which were superfluous, unimportant or even harmful. His mind, moreover, had to submit to external force: it had to build up various structures and, above all, what we call a super-ego, in order to make him able automatically to avoid conflicts with his reality. He comes to us; we co-operate in a study of his biological and mental structure, and try to bring this into connection with his conscious and primal history. Finally he understands his own nature, and also the long and painful process through which he was formed into the man he now knows. Many people who were not too severely damaged in their object-relation are content with the relief which comes with consciousness, with the accompanying better control of their actions and the extended capacity for pleasure. As the work progresses they become slowly, almost imperceptibly healthy. With them the real end phase of the treatment is absent, or, at most, is merely indicated.

With the others, however, who were made to suffer severely from the "confusion of tongues," whose capacity for love was artificially wholly stunted by lack of understanding in their upbringing, quite a peculiar situation finally arises. Everything turns on one decision. Shall one regard all past suffering as over and done with, settle accounts with the past for good, and, in the last resort, try to make the best use of what possibilities there are in the life still lying ahead? This decision to begin to love really anew is far from easy. Here the analyst can help considerably. Right interpretations are important; by them he shows that he understands his ward and will not treat him with lack of understanding as was once the case. The most important thing here, however, is that one should take notice of the timid attempts, often only extremely feebly indicated, towards the New Beginning of the object-relation and not frighten them off. One should never forget that the beginnings of object-libido pursue passive aims and can only be brought to development through the tactful and, in the literal sense of the word, "lovable" behaviour of the object. And even later one must treat these newly begun relations indulgently so that they may find their way to reality and active love.

Unfortunately not everyone can achieve this decision for a New Beginning of love. There are people who cannot give up demanding ever fresh compensation from the whole world for all the wrong ever done them, who know, indeed, that such behaviour is obsessive, and at the present time quite unreal—simply a transference—but, nevertheless, cannot give it up, who want only to be loved and are not able to give love. On a few occasions, though not often, I have come to this point with patients, and have not been able to bring them farther. These isolated cases, which incidentally, showed considerable improvement, but which I was not able to cure, forced me to recognise the limits of my therapeutic powers. With my present technique I can only cure such people as, in the course of the analytic work, can acquire the ability to attempt to begin to love anew. How those few others are to be helped I do not at present see. But I do not believe that we need let ourselves be defeated by the constitutional factors. Ferenczi always used to say that as long as a patient is willing to continue the treatment, a way must be found to help him. Those who knew his way of working know that with him this was no empty phrase. He made many experiments, and he also succeeded in helping many who had already been given up by others as hopeless. Unfortunately not all. The old proverb has proved true again: *ars longa, vita brevis*. It is the duty of the pupils to carry on the work which the master began.

I am at the end of my paper. I believe I have shown that it was one-sided to base our theories and our way of thinking principally on structural considerations and on the instinctual constitution. Without wishing to detract from the great achievement of the researches made in this direction, I have endeavoured to point out that the study of loving object-relations, which has been gravely neglected in recent years, can contribute much towards the understanding of the human mind and towards the improvement of our therapeutic powers. In my opinion there is today too much talk about constitutionally determined sadism and masochism in analytical theory. Thus the motto of my paper would run: less sadism and more love.

26

FRANZ ALEXANDER

Analysis of the Therapeutic Factors in Psychoanalytic Treatment*

Observations made during the therapeutic procedure are the primary source of psychoanalytic knowledge. Most of our knowledge of psychodynamics stems from this source. Precise understanding of the therapeutic factors is significant both for improving our therapeutic techniques and also for increasing our theoretical knowledge. Between theory and therapy there is a reciprocal relationship: observations made during treatment are the main source of our theoretical knowledge, and we apply our theoretical formulations to improve our technique.

This presentation is based on the premise that much in our therapeutic procedure is still empirical, and that many of the processes which take place in patients during psychoanalysis are not yet fully understood.

In particular, there is divergence of opinion concerning 1, the relative therapeutic value of the patient's intellectual insight into the origin and nature of his neurosis; 2, the relative value of emotional discharge (abreaction); 3, the role of emotional experiences during treatment as they evolve in the transference; 4, the role of parallel experiences in life; 5, the significance of the time factor (frequency of interviews, technical interruptions, length of the treatment). The last question is practical and the answer

* Reprinted by permission from the Psychoanalytic Quarterly, Vol. 19, pp. 482-500, 1950. Copyright 1950 by The Psychoanalytic Quarterly, Inc.

to it depends both on clinical experience and on the clarification of the first four.

One of the basic observations on which Freud's theoretical structure was built was the therapeutic value of emotional abreaction in hypnosis. Emotionally charged, forgotten memories appeared with dramatic expression of the repressed emotions. Substituting barbiturates for hypnosis, this principle was widely applied to war neuroses during and after the recent war.

The second step was the recognition that abreaction alone has no permanent curative value; that the ego must face and learn to handle the repressed emotions. The emphasis was on insight. There followed then the period in which Freud's therapeutic interest was focused on reconstructing the traumatic events of the past and making the patient understand and remember them. Reconstructions and interpretations of past pertinent events had to be understood and accepted by the patients in order to be cured.

The third step was the discovery of the transference which shifted the emphasis again to emotional experience and expression. This is, of course, an oversimplification. Actually, abreaction, insight and transference have long been considered in their interrelationships, and only the emphasis has changed from time to time with different authors. One element, however, was common to all these views: the insistence upon the necessity of making repressed material conscious. In hypnosis, repressed material was mobilized by reducing the ego's defenses. During the period in which free association was used, but before the importance of the transference was clearly recognized, the therapist's intellectual understanding was imparted to the patient in the hope that this intellectual insight would enable the patient to face what he repressed. The recognition of the transference led to a better understanding of the therapeutic processes as well as a more effective therapy. In the transference, the original pathogenic conflicts of the early family relationships are repeated with lesser intensity. This is what is called the "transference neurosis." The emotional re-enactment in relation to the therapist of the crucial conflicts gradually increases the ego's capacity to face these conflicts. One may say, it increases the ego's permeability to the repressed material. Freud's formulation was that in the transference the stronger adult ego faces the same but less intensive conflicts which the weaker infantile ego had to repress. This dynamic equation represents the essence of our present views of therapy: in childhood the weak ego faces overwhelming emotions; in the transference the adult's stronger ego faces a weaker edition of the original conflict. Accordingly, the treatment ultimately aims at changing the ego to enable it to resolve conflicts with which it could not cope before. The method by which this change in the ego is achieved is a kind of gradual learning through practice—by exposing the ego, step by step, to conflicts as they emerge in the course of treatment. At the same time the defenses of the ego against repressed material are reduced by making them explicit by precise verbalization. This process—commonly termed "working through"—can be described as a kind of emotional gymnastics.

The course of most successful treatments can be visualized as a gradually increasing capacity of the patient to recognize and express repressed psychological content. The simplest example is the depressive patient who gradually becomes able to recognize and express his hostility directed toward an ambivalently loved person. This increased ability to express repressed material is achieved primarily by the analyst's recognizing and verbalizing the slightest manifestations of the patient's repressed emotions and of his defenses against these emotions. An interpretation of hostility expressed against the analyst, which is given objectively and without any resentment, encourages its freer expression by the patient. By helping the patient to verbalize without judging and evaluating what the patient could not express, the analyst encourages the patient's becoming conscious of repressed content. The original repression of hostility was a response to parental influences. The analyst assumes a role different from that of the parents. He is emotionally not involved. This difference makes possible what we have called the corrective emotional experience [1].

According to this view, the intensity of the transference should have a certain optimal level. This is supported by the common observation that if the emotional involvement of the patient is insufficient, the treatment may be greatly retarded and the analysis becomes merely an intellectual exercise. If, however, the transference neurosis becomes too intense, the patient's ego may face a situation similar to the one which it could not meet originally. It is well known and well demonstrated by Köhler's and French's contributions that the ego's integrative functions are impeded by excessive emotion [2, 3]. Violent anxiety, rage, or guilt may become so formidable that the ego's coördinating functions cannot master them. From this it must be evident that one of the aims of therapy is to keep the transference on an optimal level.

A common type of unsuccessful analysis is due to the development of a too intensive dependent transference from which the patient cannot be dislodged. The analyst's hope that further working through eventually will resolve this dependent attachment, as well as the patient's own procrastinating tendency, collaborate to produce this therapeutic impasse. The neurotic is inclined to side-step renewed attempts to cope with life, retreats into fantasy, produces symptoms. During the treatment he exchanges symptoms for a neurotic transference relationship but resists abandoning this newly acquired substitute for his neurosis for new attempts in life. Thus the situation develops to which Freud tersely referred by saying that the patient's wish to be cured gradually changes into his wish to be treated [4]. Since with certain types of chronic neurotics this development is a common one, the problem how to avoid this danger is obviously one of the important problems of psychoanalytic technique.

The question how to keep the analysis on a transference level of optimal intensity, particularly how to avoid a too intensive dependent relationship resulting in an interminable analysis, leads us to the quantitative aspects of the psychoanalytic treatment. These we shall discuss in the light of the previous formulation of the therapeutic process and of the corrective emotional experience.

We start from Freud's emphasis on the fact that in the transference the patient's adult ego is given opportunity to face those emotional situations which it could not manage in childhood when the ego was weaker. The weak ego had to repress these emotions which therefore remained excluded from the ego's integrative activity. The emphasis is on the difference between the integrative powers of the adult and the immature ego. The other important fact, according to Freud, is that the repetition of the old conflict in the transference is of lesser intensity. Its intensity is reduced because the transference emotions are reactions to previous experiences and not to the actual patient-physician relation. The only actual relationship between the patient and doctor is that the patient comes to the physician for help. It is only in the patient's mind that the therapist assumes the role of the father or mother or of an older or younger sibling. The most important consideration in this connection is that neurotic patterns do not develop in a vacuum; they are adaptive reactions to parental attitudes. In the transference the original interpersonal relationship between child and parent is re-established only so far as the patient is concerned. The crucial therapeutic factor is that the analyst's reactions are different from those of the parents. The simplest example is the repression of self-assertive and aggressive attitudes due to parental intimidation which encourages dependence and causes all kinds of inhibitions in human relations. In the transference the therapist's attitude must reverse that of the intimidating parent. The fact that the patient's aggressions are met objectively without emotional response or retaliation on the part of the analyst corrects the original intimidating influence of the parent. The parental intimidation is undone by the more tolerant and sympathetic attitude of the therapist who replaces the authoritarian parent in the patient's mind. As the patient realizes that his modest self-assertion will not be punished, he will experiment more boldly and express himself more freely toward persons in authority in his daily life. This increases the ego's capacity to deal with aggressive attitudes which anxiety had previously repressed. This is actually a much more complicated process but this simple example may serve to explain the principle of corrective emotional experience. Parental intimidation, however, is not the only form of pathogenic experience. Parental overindulgence, emotional rejection, and ambivalence are of equal importance.

As soon as we clearly recognize the specific problem of the patient, it becomes possible to work consistently toward the right kind of corrective experience. It is generally assumed that the objective and understanding attitude of the therapist alone is sufficient to produce such a corrective emotional experience. No doubt, the most important therapeutic factor in psychoanalysis is the objective and yet helpful attitude of the therapist, something which does not exist in any other relationship. Parents, friends, relatives, may be helpful but they are always emotionally involved. Their attitude may be sympathetic but never objective and never primarily understanding. To experience such a novel human relationship in itself has a tremendous therapeutic significance which cannot be overrated. The old reaction patterns do not fit into this new human relationship. This explains why the patient's behavior in the transference becomes a one-sided shadowboxing. The old patterns developed as reactions to parental attitudes and lose their sense in the transference relationship. This compels the patient gradually to change and to revise his neurotic patterns. He deals with someone who neither resents his aggressions nor feels guilty like a parent who overindulges the child because of his unconscious rejection of the child. Under the influence of his unimpaired critical judgment, which we assume in a non-psychotic individual, the patient will be gradually forced to learn new emotional patterns which fit into this new experience. The old reactions fitted and had sense only in the family. No doubt, therefore, the objective, understanding attitude of the analyst in itself is a most powerful therapeutic factor. This attitude, combined with correct interpretation of material which is about to emerge from repression, together with the analysis of the ego's defenses, is primarily responsible for the therapeutic effectiveness of psychoanalysis. This effectiveness, in comparison with all other methods in psychiatry, is so impressive that it is easy to be satisfied with all this and forget about those aspects of therapy which require further improvement. What I mean primarily is the question, how economic is this procedure? In other words, can its effectiveness still be increased and the length of treatment reduced?

My experience is that the objective and helpful attitude of

the analyst allows, without any artificial play acting, ample opportunity for modifying the patient-therapist relationship in such a way that it will facilitate and intensify the corrective emotional experience. I have described the treatment of a forty-two-year-old patient suffering from hysterical convulsions, impotence and a severe character neurosis which was about to break up his marriage [1]. The essential factor in this case was an overbearing, tyrannical father who succeeded completely in undermining this patient's self-confidence and normal self-assertion. The patient had, as a defense, developed an overbearing attitude in his home and treated his family, particularly his son, as he was treated by his own father. The treatment consisted of twenty-six interviews over a ten-week period with satisfactory results. Not only have all his symptoms disappeared including the convulsions and his impotence, but his attitude toward his son and wife has changed. The wife, who had decided to divorce him, reversed her decision. This patient's case has been followed up. After four years he is still married, his symptoms have not returned and there are only occasional relapses into irritability and impatience toward his son, an attitude which he is able to control. I do not quote this case because of the therapeutic result, unusual because of the small number of interviews. I quote it because it is a simple example of corrective emotional experience. This was achieved by creating an emotional atmosphere in the transference which was particularly suited to reverse the original intimidating influence of the patient's father. My attitude was not simply objective and helpful; it was consistently tolerant and definitely encouraging, exactly the opposite of his father's attitude. While the father was overbearing and omniscient, the analyst emphasized repeatedly the limitations of psychiatry and of his own knowledge, encouraging the patient to express his disagreement with interpretations. The father had been extremely critical of the patient; the analyst openly displayed admiration of certain of the patient's qualities. This was of course all within the limits of the usual attitude of the analyst, but I gave a definite emotional coloring to the transference, which might be criticized as not psycho-analytic but psychotherapeutic because of its openly encouraging connotation. This entirely new situation which he had never encountered was most embarrassing for the patient. He did not know how to react to it. At first he tried in his dreams to make the analyst a replica of his domineering father. In one, the analyst smashed glassware the patient had manufactured which reminded him of the time his father, a glass manufacturer, in violent rage had smashed glassware because he had not liked the design. After these distortions had been interpreted, the patient desperately tried to provoke the analyst to act as his father did. When all this failed he gradually began to change his own behavior.

In another case, the corrective emotional experience was provoked by a different departure from the conventional psychoanalytic attitude on the therapist's part. The patient was a young university student who was unable to apply himself to his studies. He idled about, spent a great part of the day in bed, masturbated excessively, read cheap detective stories and was unable to form any meaningful social relations. He had no attachments to women, frequented poolrooms and felt quite miserable about his purposeless way of living. His "laziness" was the symptom of a latent compulsion neurosis. During his first consultation he justified his idleness by stating that his father never loved him and never gave him anything of value; therefore, his father should support him. In his first analytic session he reported a dream.

> I wanted to sell my diamond ring but the jeweler after testing the stone declared it was false.

He immediately remarked that the dream was silly because he knew that his ring was genuine. In the course of further associations it transpired that the ring was a present from his father. The dream expressed transparently the patient's defensive formula that he had never received anything of value from his father; hence, the motive for proving in his dream that his father's gift was spurious. His whole neurotic structure was founded on the belief that he owed nothing to his father.

External circumstances forced him to move from the city and he was transferred to another analyst who died after a short period. He continued with another analyst, and a few months later he asked me for an interview. He complained that as his analyst disliked him continuation of the treatment was impossible. The analyst was always polite and kindly, but he felt that this was all calculated play acting. In reality, he said, the therapist hated him. I talked with his analyst who, to my surprise, substantiated the patient's story: he felt a strong aversion to the patient which he tried his best to conceal. He urged me and I agreed to continue the treatment. I soon understood my predecessor's prejudice. The patient did everything to make himself disagreeable. He usually arrived unwashed, unshaven and unkempt, bit his nails, spoke in a scarcely intelligible mumble, criticized everything, and paid a very low fee. If I kept him waiting a minute he immediately accused me of doing so because he paid less than others. He was so unpleasant in every possible way that it was difficult to tolerate him. One day I spoke to him somewhat impatiently. He jumped up from the couch and exclaimed, "You are just like your colleague. Do you deny that you dislike me and do you call it analysis being impatient with your patient?" I realized that I had better admit my dislike of him. He was extremely perturbed by this admission. I explained that his behavior was unconsciously calculated and succeeded in making him disliked. He wanted to prove that just as his father supposedly disliked him, the analyst also rejected him; this allowed him to feel hostile and continue his old neurotic pattern of life. I reminded him of the dream about the diamond ring. This session became a dramatic turning point of this analysis, which before had begun to appear a stalemate. He became well groomed, and tried to be as pleasant as possible. He started to apply himself to his studies and to organize his daily activities.

In this case the corrective emotional experience was, in a sense, opposite to the one previously described. This patient had an indulgent father to whom his son was the apple of his eye. He supported him freely without reproach, although during his schooling he did not apply himself to his studies. This paternal indulgence created intolerable feelings of guilt in the boy who, as a defense, tried to persuade himself that his father really disliked him.

In the dramatic interview in which he discovered my dislike

for him, it suddenly became clear to him that the situation with his father could not be repeated; that it was a unique relationship, and that no one but his indulgent father would love him despite all his provocations. He realized that to be loved he must make himself worthy of love; furthermore, the guilt feelings resulting from his father's goodness diminished with the analyst's open admission of his dislike. At the end of his analysis this patient was very appreciative, presenting the analyst with a photograph of his new self. Years later he called on me. He had become successful and was married happily. Every experienced analyst has had similar experiences. The case is noteworthy because of the dynamics of the patient's remarkable improvement which was induced not by the usual understanding objective attitude of the analyst but by an involuntary display of his irritation.

The analyst's reaction was not calculated to be different from that of the patient's father. He simply lost, for a moment, the type of control which we consider so important in psychoanalytic therapy. I do not want to imply that in general this control is not necessary. My point is that the knowledge of the early interpersonal attitudes which contributed to a patient's neurosis can help the analyst to assume intentionally a kind of attitude which is conducive to provoking the kind of emotional experience in the patient which is suited to undo the pathogenic effect of the original parental attitude. Such intensive revelatory emotional experiences give us the clue for those puzzling therapeutic results which are obtained in a considerably shorter time than is usual in psychoanalysis. The important question facing us is whether it is possible in many cases to manage the transference in a way to precipitate such intensive revelatory experiences. At present it is difficult to generalize about how such intensive revelatory experiences can be provoked. One thing is obvious: the corrective emotional experience is possible only after the intrapsychic conflict has been reconverted into an interpersonal relationship in the transference and the introjected parental influences are projected upon the analyst; in other words, when the original neurosis has been transformed into a transference neurosis. This aim is most difficult to achieve in severe compulsion neurotics in whom the original child-parent relationship is completely incorporated in the personality in a complex intrapsychic conflict between the different structural parts of the personality. This keeps the intensity of the transference on a relatively low level and the whole therapeutic procedure tends to become over-intellectualized. In such cases, patient, prolonged preliminary work is often required before the intrapsychic neurotic system is disrupted and transformed into a neurotic interpersonal relationship.

This whole problem is closely related to the countertransference. The proposition made here is that the analyst should attempt to replace his spontaneous countertransference reactions with attitudes which are consciously planned and adopted according to the dynamic exigencies of the therapeutic situation. This requires the analyst's awareness of his spontaneous countertransference reactions, his ability to control them and substitute for them responses which are conducive to correcting the pathogenic emotional influences in the patient's past. Occasionally, as in the case of the student, the spontaneous countertransference reaction of the analyst is accidentally the desirable attitude, but this is a rare exception. As a rule spontaneous countertransference reactions of the analyst resemble parental attitudes. The analyst, like the parents, is apt to react with positive feelings to the patient's flattery, with helpful attitude and sympathy to the patient's suffering, and with resentment to the patient's provocative behavior as the parents did. Even if he does not give overt expression to his countertransference, the patient may sense it. Since the phenomenon of countertransference has been recognized, we know that a completely objective attitude of the analyst exists only in theory no matter how painstakingly he may try to live up to this requirement. The main point is, however, that within the framework of the objective atmosphere of the psychoanalytic situation, there is sufficient opportunity for replacing the spontaneous countertransference reactions with well-defined and designed attitudes which facilitate the patient's own emotional reorientation. In this connection, it should be considered that the objective, detached attitude of the psychoanalyst itself is an adopted, studied attitude and is not a spontaneous reaction to the patient. It is not more difficult for the analyst to create a definite emotional climate, such as consistent permissiveness or a stronghand, as the patient's dynamic situation requires.

Having presented the corrective emotional experience as the dynamic axis of the treatment, let us turn to the other well-established therapeutic factors and first examine the therapeutic importance of recovered memories.

After Freud abandoned hypnosis, his main interest lay in reconstructing the early emotional development by resolving the "infantile amnesia." When he substituted free association for hypnosis, he tried to induce the patient to recall repressed traumatic memories. At this time all his interest was focused upon tracing the genesis of neurosis and of personality development in general. He had first to understand the natural history of neuroses in order to develop a sensible method of treatment. It was a lucky circumstance that this etiological study of the individual's past history coincided, partially at least, with therapeutic aims. Both required recovery of forgotten memories and this became for a time the main therapeutic device. He came only gradually to realize the therapeutic significance of transference and the importance of the patient's reliving, not merely recalling, his early conflicts. His first impression, however, was so strong that the belief in the primary therapeutic significance of genetic reconstruction was perpetuated.[1]

We know now that the recovery of memories is a sign of improvement rather than its cause. As the ego's capacity to cope with repressed emotions increases through experience in the transference, the patient is able to remember repressed events because of their similar emotional connotations. The ability to remember shows the ego's increased capacity to face certain types of psychological content. This change in the ego is achieved through the emotional experiences of the treatment, although it cannot be denied that remembering and understanding the origin of neurotic patterns have a therapeutic influence and help the reintegration of repressed psychological content into the total personality.

The therapeutic evaluation of intellectual insight is probably one of the most difficult problems of the theory of treatment.

---

[1] The importance of genetic understanding in relation to emotional experience is discussed further on.

We used to distinguish three therapeutic factors: abreaction, insight, and working through. *Abreaction* means the free expression of repressed emotions. *Insight* was considered to be effective only when it coincided with emotional abreaction. As Freud expressed it, "An enemy cannot be licked who is not seen." The patient must feel what he understands, otherwise he could be cured by a textbook. *Working through* refers to the repetitive, more and more precise verbalization of all the details of the emotional patterns, including abreaction and insight, during analysis as the ego's defensive measures are gradually reduced. It consists of experiencing and understanding each aspect of the neurosis as it is revealed under treatment and as the patient's resistance to self-expression diminishes.

In evaluating the mutual relation of these three factors in therapy, it is important to realize that often quite definite changes in the emotional pattern can be observed in patients without intellectual formulation by the analyst or patient. The corrective emotional experience in the transference alone may produce lasting therapeutic results. A purely intellectual understanding of the neurosis has seldom much therapeutic effect. On the other hand, intellectual insight based on and combined with emotional experiences stabilizes emotional gains and paves the way for new emotional experiences. The ego's basic function is mastery of impulses through integration. This is the essence of the function we call understanding. Understanding gives the patient a feeling of mastery, and this in turn encourages mobilization of repressed material which before could not be mastered by integration with the rest of the conscious personality. Through insight the ego is prepared to face emerging unconscious material and is not taken by surprise when it actually appears in consciousness. This explains the common observation that the same interpretation which was given repeatedly during treatment and which seemingly has left the patient completely unimpressed, one day provokes a revelatory emotional response. This happens when the previous, merely intellectual understanding of repressed material becomes combined with emotional experiences of the same material as it emerges from repression. The previous interpretations were, however, not without effect: they paved the way for the emotional experience. Intellectualization by interpretation of content, however, in certain cases must be avoided as much as possible. The substitution of understanding for feeling is one of the principal defenses of the compulsive personality. In such cases the corrective emotional experiences must be achieved without too much intellectual preparation. The patient must experience his basic ambivalence toward the analyst which can be facilitated if the analyst's own spontaneous emotional reactions, which the patient's ambivalence has provoked, are kept under control and are replaced by a well-planned attitude.

It is universally accepted that the central therapeutic issue consists in the mobilization of unconscious material. Only if the ego is actually confronted with those impulses which it could not handle before except by repression, can the patient learn to handle such impulses. The defenses of the ego originally developed under the influence of personal relationships: parental intimidation, overindulgence, guilt, ambivalence, rejection, and unconscious seduction are the most common etiological factors. Intellectual insight into the nature of the ego defenses alone is not sufficient to abolish their influence. The emotional content of the patient-physician relationship, the fact that the therapist's attitude is different from the original parental attitudes, is the major dynamic factor which allows repressed material to become conscious.

In the light of this discussion, certain quantitative factors in therapy—those therapeutic measures by which an optimal level of the transference neurosis may be achieved—can be evaluated.

Experience shows that the transference neurosis develops spontaneously as the result of continued contact with the therapist. The outlook for a prolonged treatment favors the patient's procrastination and disinclination to face the problems from which he escaped into neurosis. The transference neurosis soon loses many of the unpleasant features of the original neurosis because it is seen to be a necessary part of the treatment, and the conflicts provoked by the regressive tendencies are reduced by the analyst's attitude. This allows the patient to be neurotic during treatment without too much conflict. Reducing the frequency of interviews is one of the simplest means of preventing the transference from becoming too powerful an outlet for the patient's neurosis: by frustration, the dependent strivings become conscious and the patient is compelled to resist them consciously.

Whenever the patient's ego shows signs of need for emotional support, increasing the frequency of interviews may be indicated. In doing so, however, one must be aware that allowing the patient a greater dependent gratification is a tactical concession which the therapist has to make at the moment, but which will increase some time later the task of weaning. It is unwise to generalize, and experience and skill are required to estimate when and how to reduce or increase the frequency of the sessions. In many cases it is advisable to see the patient once, twice or three times a week, instead of daily, to prevent too much dependence.

Reducing the frequency of the interviews is probably the most effective application of the principle of abstinence. It prevents the unnoticed hidden gratification of dependent needs thus forcing them to become conscious. This principle was most consistently developed by Ferenczi, who pointed out that denying the patient just that satisfaction which he most intensively desires has proven most useful in producing pertinent unconscious material [5]. According to this principle, the patient's dependence upon the analyst becomes conscious through curtailing its gratification. Were a person fed every half hour, he would never become conscious of feeling hunger. The patient's dependence upon the analyst, gratified by the routine of daily interviews on which the patient can count indefinitely, may never become conscious with sufficient vividness if the sessions are not reduced in some phase of the analysis. Everyone knows the stimulating influence of an unplanned cancellation of an interview upon the production of unconscious material. Vacations which are undertaken in the therapist's and not in the patient's interest may also have such an effect. My point is that we should not leave this important therapeutic tool to chance but use it systematically whenever the patient's analytic situation requires.

Longer interruptions have a somewhat different therapeutic function. In the early twenties Eitingon made experiments with interrupted analyses in the outpatient clinic of the Berlin Psychoanalytic Institute. Since then this device has been systematically tested in the Chicago Institute for Psychoanalysis [6].

Interruptions of shorter or longer duration have the function of increasing the patient's self-confidence. During the interruptions he will have to apply independently in life what he gained during the treatment. The tendency of the neurotic is to avoid renewed attempts to cope with the life situation from which he retreated into fantasy and symptom formation. Interruptions counteract the patient's tendency to postpone indefinitely the solution of his problems. They are one of the strongest weapons against perpetuating the transference neurosis indefinitely. Interruptions must be imposed tentatively, since there is no way of telling exactly when the patient is ready to accept them without relapsing.

One must remember that the patient, while he is being analyzed, continues his ordinary life. It is true that many of his neurotic needs will be gratified in the transference. This as a rule allows the patient to behave less neurotically outside. On the other hand, the therapist must not allow the patient to withdraw his attention from his outside relationships and to escape completely into the therapeutic situation. Originally the patient came to the therapist with current problems. The transference allowed him to relieve the pressure of these current problems by retreating from life into the shadow world of the transference. There must be a constant pressure to keep the patient in contact with his actual problems in life from which he only too readily has withdrawn into the transference. It is not realistic to expect that a patient, who has postponed the solution of his real problems for months or years and withdrawn into the relatively isolated world of transference, will one day suddenly return a well-adjusted person to the world of reality. While the patient works through his resistances and becomes able to express more and more frankly in the transference his neurotic attitudes, he learns gradually to modify them at first in relation to the analyst and later also in his extra-analytic human relationships. The latter takes place to some degree automatically but the neurotic tendency is to delay the attack upon his actual problems. A steady pressure must be exerted upon the patient to apply every analytical gain to his life outside the analysis. The analytic process cannot be divided into two separate phases: first, one which encourages the development of the transference neurosis and, second, one in which the patient is induced to return with modified attitudes to the solution of his actual problems. The two must take place more or less simultaneously.

Another significance of extratherapeutic experiences was first explicitly emphasized by Edoardo Weiss [7]. The transference cannot always repeat all the neurotic patterns of a patient. Some aspects of his neurosis he will of necessity re-enact in his life; moreover, it is often advantageous to relieve too intensive positive or negative emotional attitudes within the transference by taking advantage of corresponding extra-analytic interpersonal relationships. In the Chicago Institute for Psychoanalysis, some of the members of the staff believe that in some cases most of the patient's problems can be worked out by the analysis of the extratherapeutic experiences, and that a real transference neurosis can be avoided. I personally lean toward the view that a well-defined transference neurosis is not only unavoidable but desirable in most cases.

Summary

The need for re-evaluation of the psychodynamic factors operative during treatment is emphasized. According to the view presented, the dynamic axis of psychoanalytic therapy is the corrective emotional experience which the patient obtains in the transference. The significant factor is not only that the patient relives his original conflicts in his relationship with the analyst, but that the analyst does not react as the parents did. His reactions should correct the pathogenic effects of the parental attitudes. The objective, understanding attitude of the analyst in itself is so different from that of the parents that this alone necessitates a change in the patient's original attitudes. If the analyst succeeds in reconstructing precisely the original pathogenic parental attitude, he may facilitate the occurrence of intensive corrective emotional experiences by assuming an attitude toward the patient opposite to that of the most relevant pathogenic attitude which prevailed in the past. This does not consist in artificial play acting but in creating an emotional atmosphere which is conducive to undoing the traumatic effects of early family influences. The corrective emotional experience is the most powerful factor in making the patient's original ego defenses unnecessary and thus allowing the mobilization and emergence into consciousness of repressed material. It helps the patient's ego to assume a modified attitude toward hitherto repressed or inhibited impulses. Other important technical measures serve to keep the transference on an optimal level, such as changing the frequency of interviews according to the state of the analysis, correctly timed interruptions, and encouraging the required kind of extratherapeutic experiences.

Our experience in the Chicago Institute for Psychoanalysis is that with the consistent observance of these principles and technical measures the treatment becomes more effective and economical [8]. Although the total duration of the treatment as a rule is not spectacularly shortened, the actual number of interviews can be substantially reduced in the great majority of cases. The principle which is stressed is that of flexibility in preference to routine. Briefness, in so far as the total duration of the treatment is concerned, does not characterize this approach.

Naturally the personality of the analyst and his sex are of great importance for creating the kind of emotional atmosphere and experiences in the transference which are most conducive to reversing the adverse influences in the patient's past. The selection of an analyst for each patient is an involved problem and requires special consideration.

Reasons are submitted for the urgent need for a careful reexamination of the therapeutic process.

References

[1] ALEXANDER, FRANZ; FRENCH, THOMAS M., ET AL.: The Principle of Corrective Emotional Experience. In: *Psychoanalytic Therapy, Principles and Application.* New York: The Ronald Press Co., 1946, p. 66.

[2] FRENCH, THOMAS M.: *A Clinical Study of Learning in the Course of a Psychoanalytic Treatment.* Psychoanalytic Quarterly, V, 1936, pp. 148-194.

[3] KÖHLER, WOLFGANG: The Mentality of Apes. London: Kegan Paul, Trench, Trubner & Co., 1931.

[4] FREUD: Further Recommendations in the Technique of Psychoanalysis. Coll. Papers, II, pp. 342-391.

[5] FERENCZI, SANDOR: The Further Development of an Active Therapy in Psychoanalysis. In: Further Contributions to the Theory and Technique of Psychoanalysis. London: Hogarth Press, 1926, pp. 201, 202.

[6] ALEXANDER, FRANZ; FRENCH, THOMAS M., ET AL.: The Principle of Flexibility. Interruptions and Termination of Treatment. Op. cit., p. 35.

[7] WEISS, EDOARDO: Emotional Memories and Acting Out. Psychoanalytic Quarterly, XI, 1942, pp. 477-492.

[8] ALEXANDER, FRANZ; FRENCH, THOMAS M., ET AL.: Op. cit.

27

OTTO RANK

The Basis of a Will Therapy*

"Es gibt kein Hindernis, das man nicht zerbrechen kann, denn das Hindernis ist nur des Willens wegen da, und in Wahrheit sind keine Hindernisse als nur im Geist."

"There are no obstacles that one cannot overcome, for the obstacle is only there on account of the will and in truth there are no obstacles but psychic ones."

RABBI NACHMAN

Psychoanalysis in its mingling of theory and therapy has failed to detect the actually effective therapeutic agent and psychological understanding of which alone can furnish the basis for theoretical generalization. First it was the making conscious of the unconscious (association) which we know today is not itself therapeutic. Then it was the abreaction of the affects, a kind of psychic emptying (catharsis) which at best means only a temporary relief, nothing lasting or constructively effective. Finally it was the transference relationship which forms a kind of synthesis of these two psychological factors. Transference not only contains something passive, temporary, derived, but actually represents that aspect of the relationship to the analyst. But passivity, dependence, or weakness of will in any form is just the difficulty on account of

* Reprinted from Will Therapy & Truth and Reality by Otto Rank, translated from the German by Jessie Taft, by permission of Alfred A. Knopf, Inc., and The Vision Press, Ltd. Copyright, 1936, 1945, by Alfred A. Knopf, Inc.

which the neurotic comes for treatment, therefore transference cannot be the therapy to which we attach the idea of something positive.

What is naturally and spontaneously effective in the transference situation and, rightly understood and handled, is also effective therapeutically is the same thing that is potent in every relationship between two human beings, namely the will. Two wills clash, either the one overthrows the other or both struggle with and against one another for supremacy. Adler has seen this battle for supremacy in analysis, "the will to be on top" (Obensein wollen), as he calls it, at least he has not denied it, for it is so clear that only the wish not to see it can explain its neglect by Freud. However, Adler has apparently not been able to see that the phenomena described by him represent only the form in which the will manifests itself in the analytic situation as in similar life situations. In other words, he takes this will to superiority as an ultimate psychological fact, but gives no psychology of will in general, which alone would make these phenomena intelligible. In contrast to this social pedagogical presentation of Adler, Freud's whole life work is nothing but a continued attempt to interpret what Adler naïvely takes for what it seems, and to explain it by tracing it back to primitive biological roots. The peculiarly psychological problem seems to me to lie exactly between the two. Whence comes the will, and why psychologically must we interpret this will not understood in its origin, now as will to power and again as sex drive, and more than that, why must we interpret it at all, instead of being able to recognize its true psychological nature? This problem includes in itself as we see, epistemological and ethical questions the answers to which belong to a philosophy of the psychic. It seems, therefore, to be no accident that Adler's "attempt to dominate" (Herrschsucht) represents an ultimate fact, just as the will to power does for Nietzsche, and that Freud's libido concept and death instinct show a like relation to Schopenhauer's blind will and the denial of it in the Nirvana wish.

In every case, however, they arrived at no will psychology because (with Nietzsche on the whole excepted) they brought in moral or social values which are probably justified therapeutically or pedagogically, yes, might even be necessary, but stand in the way of a purely psychological understanding. For Adler's "will to power" is at bottom exactly as "bad" as Freud's instinct, which he euphemistically calls the infantile wish, and with both, the therapy consists in freeing from, rooting out, mastering or sublimating. Where Freud met the will of the other he called it "resistance" (to his will), and where Adler came upon this counter-will he called it masculine protest in the light of his conscious psychology, or obstinacy in the pedagogical meaning. At the basis of both presentations lies a moral evaluation; it is "bad." Resistance one must overcome or break like obstinacy. Perhaps such evaluation is unavoidable in therapy and education for they must apparently be governed by some such norms. But one must know this and allow for it instead of first creating for their apparent grounding a psychology that is oriented to these very same norms. A purely scientific psychology must guard itself against including moralistic values of any kind. It must first of all be purely psychological, apart from values—in a word must describe what is, not what should be, and explain why it is so or must be so. The fact that self assertion, protest, obstinacy are pedagogically undesirable is another thing, just as will, insistence on freedom, and assertion of personality are socially frowned upon. But you will find no strong willed man and likewise no great leadership as an expression of this strong will, without its seeming to the individual who comes up against it, to be self will, obstinacy, or contrariness.[1] What Adler wishes apparently is the pedagogical ideal of the super-result without that burdensome accessory phenomenon. What such a pedagogical method can achieve is no super-result, but only an average, just as Freud's medically oriented therapy for the neurotic strives for an ideal of normality.

In relation to the problem of a constructive individual therapy then, this is to be noted, that first of all in opposition to pedagogy and pedagogically oriented psychoanalysis with its father complex, it must refrain from moral evaluation of every kind. It is important that the neurotic above all learn to will, discover that

---

[1] In this sense the clever American is right in his ironical version of the Adlerian inferiority complex, which he, with reference to the compensatory benefits, designated as the golden complex. (Lee Wilson Dodd: "The Golden Complex. A defence of Inferiority." N. Y. 1927.)

he can will without getting guilt feeling on account of willing. The danger which one might see in this does not exist in reality, for there remain always many regulating factors (repressions and ideals) which restrain him from converting this will of his into action. One can see such a danger in therapy only if like Freud he conceives of morality in general as externally determined. Purely psychological consideration would show that it is his own inner inhibitions that make the individual not only moral but even hyper-ethical. In this will psychology I shall show how the rehabilitation of will solves many problems at one stroke; in therapy, will has always played a great role, but it has lacked its own psychology which would have made it scientifically acceptable as a therapeutic agent and therefore also therapeutically effective. Instead it has been given over to fakirs, hypnotists, and charlatans of every kind. With what contempt we still look down upon all methods of strengthening and training the will, even to Coué, although they have helped many human beings. Not that I myself believe that a neurotic can be healed, because he daily declares that things are better with him, but what is manifested in all these teachings and the experiences by which they are supported, is the fact of the will, not merely the belief in its power, the feeble wish that it be so strong and mighty. The very suggestion that the will be strong, is itself an expression of the strength of the will, for which apparently we are obliged to seek a justification, or cover, as Freud did in the romantic garb of the "wish." The power of will is so great and its expressions in the individual as in humanity so notorious, that one could fill volumes and libraries with the description of human acts of will and their beneficial and destructive effects, not only could fill, but has filled, in the writing of the history of humanity history of every form and kind, especially the kind that is known under the name of Psychology.

The psychological problem par excellence makes its first appearance with this question, why must we always deny the will, call it now God, now Fate, or attribute to it an "id." In other words, the essential problem of psychology is our abolition of the fact of will, the explanation of the manifold types of abolition of will and its varying interpretation at different times. This psychological problem, actually *the* problem of psychology, as it meets us in psychoanalysis, is therefore a universal problem, which psychoanalysis did not recognize because as therapeutic, i.e. as a morally oriented psychology, it could not. We seem to have here a kind of universal guilt feeling as far as will is concerned. Human willing is the root of the peculiar guilt problem which psychoanalysis could not explain because it had fallen into it therapeutically itself. Psychotherapy must make the person not only well but also good, yet the bad, the arch evil, is the will, no matter whether one interprets it biologically like Freud as sex drive (libido), or like Adler sociologically as will to power, or pedagogically as obstinacy. For an understanding of the motives which lead universally to the necessity of an interpretation of will, of one kind or another, we have first to comprehend fully the psychological evaluation of human nature as well as the modern psychology of the individual.

After this necessary digression into will psychology, we now turn back to will therapy and shall describe how the will is denied in the analytic situation before we present the positive side, that is, how the will expresses itself in a therapeutic experience and how it can and must be constructively used. In Freud's analysis, the will apparently plays no particular part, either on the side of the patient or on the side of the analyst. The basic analytic rule of "free association" specifically states, eliminate entirely the little bit of will which your neurotic weakness has perhaps not yet undermined and resign yourself to the guidance of the unconscious, to the id, also taking pains to eliminate the ethical inhibitions of the censor, the super-ego. Likewise the analyst, according to the rule which holds for him also, must guard against forcing his will upon the patient, either by prohibitions or commands, or even by premature or enforced interpretations. We know that on both sides this is possible only to a certain degree, and that is lucky, for the impossibility of carrying through this Buddhistic will-lessness provides the therapeutic foundation of the analytic situation. With reference to later deductions, it would not be paradoxical to say that psychoanalysis, in its therapeutic consequences, is an involuntary proof of the existence and strength of the will, and this was and also is its only therapeutic value.

When I say that the mutual exclusion of will in the analytic situation is possible to a limited degree only, I describe an ideal situation whose therapeutic value however is always arrived at by its miscarriage. Actually, the analytic situation shows not merely that exclusion of will is possible only to a degree but that as a fact it is impossible and every attempt to exclude it only strengthens the will reactions. In this continuous conflict of wills which analysis presents it is then of minor importance whose will reactions are stronger, or to use the well known question, who began it. Usually it is the analyst with his fundamental rule who at once sets up a will conflict which is not concluded to the very end of the analysis and often beyond it. I say usually it is the analyst who begins, that is true only if one is not willing to understand the coming of the patient for help as a disguised challenge to a duel, in reality, however, a manifestation of his own inner conflict of will. The physician advises his patient and the patient by accepting this advice makes this his own will regardless of whether it has to do with taking a medicine, depriving of an indulgence, seeking of a watering place, or the deciding upon an operation. The analyst to whom the patient turns for help, cannot advise him, avoids carefully everything which approaches that, in order thus to find and permit the patient to find what he himself actually wants. The analyst insists only on this one strict rule, which actually dictates to the patient, what he shall do in the analysis, which is, psychologically speaking, not to will; a rule which the patient does not and cannot understand, which one cannot even explain to him, and which he accordingly cannot make his own will even if he follows it. This situation presents factually and psychologically therefore nothing other than the opening of a great duel of wills, in which this first easy victory over the apparently weak-willed patient is bitterly avenged many times. Be that as it may, always his downfall, in the true sense of the word, is only external, for the chief rule of free association the patient cannot follow even if he would. From this fact one may explain the two typical reaction patterns which always rule the analytic picture, resistance and guilt feeling. It is evident already that in the analytic situation and because of it every expression of the will of the patient can only manifest itself as resistance, even though he must react to it with guilt feeling because he ought not to have any resistance, that is, ought to abolish his will. We know that the honest assurance that resistance is unavoidable, nay is even necessary, helps not at all, because it only means that the will cannot be exterminated, while one's intention is to abolish it practically, as one has denied it theoretically. Whether this resistance manifests itself as the father complex of the man, or the masculine protest of the woman, or desire to dominate in general, is unimportant as compared to the psychological understanding of the situation. One must recognize that the individual suffers not necessarily from a father complex or a masculine protest, but from a situation in which a strange will is forced on him and makes him react with accentuation of his own will. This counter-will takes for its content at times a varying ideology, in terms of which the psychoanalyst habitually interprets it, and inevitably, as a voluntarily accepted representative of authority at the same time evaluates it morally. It is more important, however, to recognize that this negative reaction of the patient represents the actual therapeutic value, the expression of will as such, which in the analytic situation can only manifest itself as resistance, as protest,—that is, only as counter-will.

With this initial will conflict of the analytic situation, the struggle is naturally not settled. There come sooner or later strong phases of resistance or guilt reactions, which are insurmountable for the classical analytic technique and they forced Freud to the construction of new theories, which led him even further away from the will problem. Even when one knows how to avoid such dangerous obstacles by patience or guidance, every analysis necessarily comes at last to a point in which the will conflict, however neglected, breaks out openly, without one's having recognized it before, much less having made it useful therapeutically. The ending of the analysis is crucial even when one sets no definite limit, when as the classical analysis maintains, the whole analytic release depends on the acceptance of a definite content.

For the most part, this content presents itself in the reconstruction of early history, which therapeutically has no other value than that of a "bone," over which both parties struggle to the utmost. That this struggle is carried out around a spying upon coitus, in and for itself most uninteresting, or about a castration threat in childhood, lends to the patient the affective emphasis which he needs to bear it and for the analyst on his side it has value because of his interest in the confirmation of his theory. The essential point, however, is that this bone of contention is usually tied up with the problem of the ending of the analysis, which leads to that final struggle characteristic of analytic therapy, an unheard of phenomenon in the whole field of the healing art. The patient against the assertion of the analyst that the analysis is at an end, that he is cured, reacts with a protest, which can be explained not simply as transference resistance, but psychologically must be comprehended as a will protest, as a contradiction. It is well known that one cannot release these final struggles successfully, at most only increase them, if one treats them as resistances. And also even where such an analysis is ending well, it is only after the patient succeeds in putting over his own will in some way or other, whether it be in the form of a love demand or whether it be more open resistance, thus for example, when he afterwards submits to an operation, only to prove that he was right and the other wrong about his illness.

I, myself, grasped relatively early the therapeutic meaning of the will problem, but only now am able to formulate it clearly. I soon realized that all the active measures which could not be entirely avoided even by Freud and whose specific use as prohibitions by Ferenczi naturally could only lead to an increase of the resistances, at bottom mean nothing except challenges of will, and that it would make no difference therefore, whether one forbade to the patient smoking or sex activity or certain foods. So I very early limited myself to one active measure, which relates to the analytic situation itself and in its very nature is unavoidable, that is, the end setting; naturally, as I have always emphasized, not in the sense of an arbitrary act on the part of the analyst, but as it seemed certain that the ending of the analysis represents a will conflict, and as there is no doubt that it must be ended sometime (although there are endless analyses) it appeared to me logical as well as psychological to allow the patient to carry out the unavoidable will conflict in the problem of ending. When I introduced end setting into analysis, therefore, I did it with the full knowledge of the meaning of active measures in general and tried not to make it an apple of discord through force, but to let it be carried through by choice as a purely inner conflict of will. I looked also for criteria in the patient's own expressions of will even if not always obvious, in order to discover when he himself should be ripe for the definite time of termination. It was then evident that the patient, even with his own will directed to ending the analysis, reacted to the fixing of an ending with resistance. However, these reactions were so evidently contrariness that the patient could hardly deny in them his own will conflict. Specifically they moved in two extreme directions, indifferently, either of which revealed itself as an expression of counter-will. They would demand either the continuation of the analysis with the rationalization that the ending as determined could not possibly allow sufficient time or an immediate breaking off, because in so short a period nothing more was to be accomplished. These demands only mean therefore "No—otherwise!" One need not trouble to search for a particular reason for this will reaction.

The technical superiority of this ending technique is as great as its therapeutic advantage, provided, of course, it is applied in the right spirit, that is, with the understanding of the will psychology, which shows that the will under the pressure of the strange will can only manifest itself as counter-will in the analytic situation. This automatic reaction, which the therapeutic situation with its apparent disadvantage to the patient regularly produces, governs the entire analytic situation from the beginning; it only needed an exact study of the will reactions of the patient in the open struggle of the ending to recognize and understand this in its full significance. This showed that one was dealing essentially neither with father-resistance, masculine protest, nor yet with mother fixation, but purely with an inner conflict of will which manifests itself externally according to the situation. In the final struggle, this inner conflict becomes evident through the fact that the patient, as we have seen, wants two different things at the same time, both the end and the continuation of the analysis. Incidentally this throws a light on the nature of so-called ambivalence, as a conflict of will, or better said, as the human capacity for mobilizing will and counter-will at one time. The technique of end setting used by me brings into relief the whole will problem in its double-sided aspect (ambivalence), and correctly handled carries it to a solution. The analyst yields to the growing will of the patient to end the analysis, while at the same time through fixing a definite time, which is necessary for the solution of this will conflict, he contradicts the patient, inhibits his will. This situation provokes the whole ambivalent conflict of the patient, because it corresponds to it so perfectly. When one gives in, he doesn't want his own way any more and when one does not yield, he wants it again. The essential point is that one can easily show him in these final reactions that this will conflict has to do with an internal, not an external struggle, and represents the fundamental conflict of his whole psychic life.

Why and how this is so, belongs to a presentation of will psychology which I shall give elsewhere simultaneously.[2] Here we shall examine further the therapeutic aspects of such a conception of the will problem. Having pointed out how this fundamental will conflict manifests itself in the analytic final struggle, we go back to the moment in which the patient sought analysis. We said before that, with reference to the later course of the therapeutic process, one could consider the appearance (in the office) of the patient seeking help as a challenge to a battle of wills. This is doubtless correct, but the patient shows at the same time another will, that is, to yield, to submit himself, which is what brings him as a seeker for help to the therapist. Yes, we can and must go even further and say that when the patient appears he has already gone through a will conflict usually of quite long duration, which we designate as neurosis, in which at the time of his coming the will to submit has the upper hand. In other words, the help-seeking patient brings his whole neurotic conflict, which at bottom is a will conflict, to the analytic situation, to which he wishes to submit himself but which at the same time

---

[2] *Truth and Reality.* Alfred A. Knopf, 1936.

he resists. On this very conflict the inability to submit and the inability to put over his own will positively, his whole neurosis depends. In the analytic situation he seeks to solve externally this inner will conflict, since he puts a strange will over his own, but soon feels this will as forced on him. Accordingly the task of the therapist is not to act as will, which the patient would like, but only to function as counter-will in such a way that the will of the patient shall not be broken, but strengthened. If for any reason the therapist does not understand this dynamics of will, then he plays the role of "divine will" temporarily put on him by the patient while the patient acts out the counter-will, the resistance, the negative lead, but all only in the terms of the old neurotic reaction pattern. One could formulate the whole antithesis by expressing the Freudian compulsory rule in terms of the will psychology, "Say whatever you wish, for it is all one what you say." It *is* essential how you say it (or do not say it) and when. What the patient needs is the positive expression of his will without the inhibiting guilt feeling, a goal which is to be attained only by the actual overcoming of the therapist and complete ruling of the analytic moment of experience.

This conception of the will conflict and its therapeutic value in the analytic experience throws a light also upon one of the most important of its manifestations, which, without reference to the will psychology, remains unintelligible. It is the problem of the so-called will-to-health. Evidently the patient must have in addition to his neurosis something like a will-to-health also, when he gives himself over to treatment. It seems to me equally certain that this will-to-health becomes less as soon as the treatment has begun and continues to decrease, the further it advances, if one does not understand how to comprehend its psychologically and use it therapeutically. For the first thing the patient does when he begins treatment, is to project his will-to-health onto the analyst who represents it as it were, just by virtue of his profession. That is, the patient himself no longer needs to will to become well, as the analyst must and will make him sound. This is an example of the tendency of the patient just described to make the therapist represent positive will, and to keep for himself the negative role, a tendency on whose correct understanding the whole psychotherapeutic process stands or falls. Its success depends on just this, the ability to allow this will-to-health to be preserved and strengthened in the patient himself, instead of permitting it to be projected upon the analyst. This is possible only when the whole therapeutic situation in all its manifestations is evaluated constructively in terms of the will problem. The positive strengthening of the will-to-health to the level of an actual becoming well and remaining well depends completely and entirely upon the will of the patient which even for the period of this treatment must take over the capacity for becoming well and later for remaining well. The imperfect comprehension of this problem explains a typical tendency to interpretation which reveals the whole controversy between psychoanalysis and will psychology. We shall again confine ourselves to the purely therapeutic aspect of this problem, which at the same time throws a light on its general meaning. We can best illustrate it by an objection which was raised against end setting, and the criteria which I have applied to determine it. When the patient, let us say for example in dreams, betrays signs that he wants to leave the analysis and I interpret it not only as resistance but also as progress, the objection is made that it might be merely a "wish" of the patient. This objection is easy as it rests on the wish-fulfilment theory of dreams, without questioning its psychological foundation. Where, however, the patient expresses this tendency toward freeing himself, not in a dream, but in other forms of emotional reaction, then the analyst will rather tend to speak of "resistance." In both cases he overlooks, in my opinion which I will establish elsewhere theoretically, the positive expression of will appearing in these reactions, which manifests itself now as resistance, again disguises itself as wish.[3]

[3] The dream work which Freud emphasizes, is just the dynamic guided by the dreamer within himself, whose consequence the therapist can determine only after the fact. With reference to affects worked out in the dream, Freud's wish-fulfilment theory proves to be too narrow, rather one could speak of an unburdening function of the dream. As to the dreams produced in analysis and particularly in the last phase, they show clearly that they have to do with an attempt by the will to control the situation. The dream is here no wish-fulfilment, but a will accomplishment, a distinction which is meaningful as the distinction between wish and will, for it says that the patient wants to accomplish the whole task within himself and will find release only in his own

To the difficulty of recognizing the expression of will as such and also why it manifests itself in the patient now as wish and another time as resistance is added the psychology of the analyst. If, specifically, the reaction of the patient is one an analyst has in mind, then the suspicion of suggestion occurs and this leads to the interpretation of will expression as "wish"; if the reaction of the patient is not in the analyst's mind, then it must be interpreted as resistance. Here again we see how the correct understanding of the reactions of the patient depends on the general attitude of the analyst to the whole therapeutic experience, and not merely to details of the analytic situation. If the will of the patient from the beginning is systematically and purposefully made to be the bearer of the whole therapeutic process, then there can be no question practically whether his tendency toward freeing himself is only a wish or merely resistance. For in both cases it concerns one of the numerous will expressions of the patient, all of which he seeks to deny; in one case directly since he says, that is not my will but only the expression of my counter-will, my spirit of opposition, another time indirectly, when he says this is not my will but only a wish. In other words, the explanation of expressions of will on the basis of psycho-analytic theory strengthens the patient in his tendency to deny all will expressions, which is just the essence of his neurosis.

That the will in the therapeutic experience can only manifest itself as resistance or as a timid wish, lies in the pedagogic setting of the analytic situation. The difference, therefore, between the analytic therapy and the will therapy is, as has already been said, that analysis is pedagogically oriented, while will therapy works purely psychologically. The one wants to work educationally, the other constructively, that is, in a self determining way. In

---

autonomous self. This explains moreover the appearance of dreams soon after the beginning of the analysis in persons who usually do not dream at all or very seldom. That, in addition, the dream can also have during the treatment the reversed meaning of a present, a gift to the analyst, proves nothing against its autonomous tendency, which it has naturally. For the dream is not destined usually for sharing and yet certainly has an auto-therapeutic effect. In the production of dreams, especially in the end phase of treatment, the patient seizes only upon the natural function of the dream, as a psychic self-regulator in order thus to make himself independent of the analyst once more, that is of the therapeutic situation.

analysis, resistance stands in the center, the goal is to conquer it, which in my opinion can never happen either in pedagogy or in pedagogically oriented therapy. The goal of constructive therapy is not the overcoming of resistance, but the transformation of the negative will expression (counter-will) underlying them into positive and eventually creative expression.

Transference and Countertransference

The phenomenon of transference was one of Freud's major discoveries. For the first time, it provided an explanation and a method for constructively coping with a phenomenon which intruded into every therapeutic situation. The patient would experience intense emotions toward the therapist which had little to do with the realities of the situation. The emotions might be affiliative, either affectionate or sexual, or they might be hostile, but in either event they might disrupt the course of the therapy. Freud discovered that the sources of this phenomenon were emotions felt toward important figures in the patient's early life, which were now transferred to the person of the therapist, hence the name transference.

Since the transference might be expected to develop most clearly if it were not confused with the patient's reactions to the actual personality of the analyst, Freud felt that it was necessary for the analyst to remain as amorphous a figure as possible. The rationale for this is discussed in the paper by Balint. It was soon recognized by many analysts that this was not entirely feasible, since the therapist's real personality was, in fact, part of the situation and could not be ignored. Further research as described in the paper by French suggests that it may be possible to manipulate the transference in a useful manner.

Since the phenomenon of transference was discovered before the psychoanalytic understanding of character, the two entities were for a long time treated as separate though parallel streams. There is, however, as the paper by Thompson shows, cogent ground for considering the two as related, and it may well develop that as our understanding of character becomes clearer the concept of transference may be adequately included in it.

There is another recent development that is hinted at in the paper by Rioch and more fully developed in that of Rado in the *next section. Rioch draws the analogy between the automatically repetitive characteristics of transference and the phenomenon of hypnosis. Rado relates the two more explicitly, suggesting that transference may be induced by those elements of the analytic situation which foster the dependence of the patient.*

The phenomenon of countertransference, analogous to transference, but occurring in the analyst, is described in the paper by Cohen.

28

MICHAEL BALINT

On Transference of Emotions*

Psycho-analysis has been built up on two well-established facts of clinical experience. The one is *resistance*. During the flow of free associations the patient often feels an impulse not to tell the next idea (or a series of ideas) because it would be unpleasant, ridiculous, unessential, painful, etc. The analyst notices the resistance by the unequal flow of the associations, i.e. sudden deviations, accelerations, retardations or even complete interruption of speech. These experiences have been the source of the assumption of the unconscious mind, of repression, and in general of the dynamic conception of psychic processes. The facts, the basis of these ideas, are so obvious, so easily observable by everyone, so undeniable, that the above-mentioned ideas—though sometimes under different names—have already been accepted by the scientific world; nowadays a completely hostile criticism is scarcely ever heard.

The situation is entirely different with regard to the second, equally important observation: transference. This important fact of experience which led to a psycho-analytic theory of instincts, and recently to the beginnings of a psycho-analytic character-ology, has been challenged, often disapproved of, even completely rejected. This attitude has two main causes. The one is that transference, though in the same way a general phenomenon, needs a trained, unprejudiced observer; the other is that it is intimately

* Paper originally read in 1933 to the Hungarian Psychological Society. British examples substituted later. Published in Hungarian Gyógyászat (1933), 73. Reprinted from *Primary Love and Psycho-Analytic Technique*, by Michael Balint, published by Liveright Publishing Corp.

connected with the field of emotions. Let us begin therefore with some—not very dangerous—examples. In a hot dispute it may occur that one or the other disputant hits the table with his fist, as it were to give more weight to his arguments. Or it may happen that one hears things which make one angry; if one's excitement has not cooled down by the end of the talk one may bang the door when going out of the room. Or, after taking leave from his best beloved a young man may notice that she has forgotten her gloves; again it may happen that the young man feels still happier in the possession of these valuable objects, even that he kisses them.

Let us study these rather uninteresting examples more closely. We see that in each of them a very intense emotion takes hold of the person. Obviously, this emotion is caused by, and directed towards, a certain person; yet it is lived out on something else. Our man is not at all angry with the table or with the door, not at all in love with the gloves, and still they have to suffer, or to rejoice as the case may be. Described in scientific language: our man has transferred his feelings, his emotions, from the original object to something else.

My next task is to show you with what an important, general phenomenon we are dealing, a phenomenon which permeates the whole of our social life. It is not at all an exaggeration to say that there is scarcely any sphere of social, religious, political life where transference is not a very important factor. First of all there is the realm of symbols: the National Ensign, the British Lion and Unicorn, the crest of a family, owe their great importance to transference of feelings. The same holds true for the Queen's uniform, or for the officer's epaulettes. It would mean carrying coals to Newcastle should I try to prove the significance of symbols for inciting or appeasing feelings to a British audience. "British" itself is such a symbol, carefully chosen not to hurt the feelings of any nationality of the United Kingdom. Then each corner of a postage stamp bears a symbolic flower: the rose, the thistle, the daffodil and the shamrock. A criminal act is taken as having injured the sovereign, and all prosecutions are in his name, *Regina v.* N. Every official envelope bears the imprint "On Her Majesty's Service," and it cannot be left unmentioned that the vast Commonwealth of British Nations is legally held together not by institutions, treaties or laws but mainly by a symbol, the Queen's person.

Less important symbols are the colours of the universities (e.g. dark blue and light blue) or those of clubs. Of much greater importance are the religious symbols: the cross, the genuflexion, the different ways of ringing the church bells. It is quite obvious that the symbol itself is almost valueless, its immense value is due to the transferred emotions.

Social and political life often tries to make good use of transference, frequently it is intentionally provoked for certain premeditated effects, e.g. inventing a new slogan or a new way of greeting.

Another field where transference plays an outstanding rôle is tradition. Very often the usage, the institution itself, is time-worn and decrepit, often even very boring and annoying, still we stick to it, as is often said, because of our honour and love for our fathers. That means that the usage, the institution, has inherited the feelings which, by rights, belonged to our fathers. As one of the innumerable examples let me quote the wigs worn by the Speaker, Judges, Barristers, etc.

A very similar phenomenon is reverence, the basis of which is always transference. A letter, a valueless object like a glove, a cane, a dried flower, a hideous piece of furniture, are kept with the same care, with the same love, which were due to their owners. A very instructive proof is a visit to a so-called Memorial Museum. In Weimar, for instance, Goethe's wash-basin and even his chamber-pot are reverently kept, and with the same reverence the Manchester Literary and Philosophical Society exhibited the top hat and the bedroom-slippers of Dalton in a glass case.

A further inexhaustible sphere for studying transference is *love*. It is impossible to imagine or even invent an object which could not be used, and occasionally has not been used, for transference. Beginning with punched tickets, used when together, and pieces of clothing worn by her or by him, everything in the world was, is and will be taken by lovers to represent him or her, to be kept in love, honour or adoration in his or her place. Quite recently I heard of a dental surgeon who kept a girl's tooth extracted by him in high esteem for two years and married the girl afterwards.

A very frequent technique of joking is based on transference. To quote only one famous story: the dilemma of a husband who surprised his wife with his partner. If he throws out the wife, he has to give the dowry back, if he throws out the partner, his business will go bankrupt, and thus, finally, after long hesitation, he throws out the couch.

In linguistics, too, transference plays an important rôle. To prove it I have only to remind you of such phrases as: the front of a house, the leg of a table, the brow of a hill; then: the pale moon, the blushing sky, a happy day, distressful years, etc.

This enumeration could be continued endlessly. I hope this much is enough to show that transference really is a general phenomenon. It is not difficult to detect both the causes and the aims of transference. The cause is always the circumstance that (at that moment) the emotion cannot be lived out on the original person or object or even cannot be lived out on it at all. This is clearly demonstrated by our story of the couch. The same is true of reverence where the original person is either dead or remote. Sometimes the original person is present, but some other feeling, e.g. fear, compassion, love, etc., prevents us from *doing* to him what we would like to do. As you see, transference has a great economical value for the mind; it enables us to live out emotions which otherwise must be carefully controlled, and so frees us from unnecessary strain—e.g. after having banged the door or hit the table we feel easier—and in the same way it is easier to endure the loss of a beloved person if we have something to keep him or her in our memory. This economical function is one of the aims of transference.

I am afraid that for the present you may see hardly any connection with psycho-analysis. This is my fault. I have deliberately omitted something. Up till now we have studied transference from the standpoint of the transferring subject only, and we have not even asked what the object, on to which—deservedly or undeservedly—the emotions had been transferred, will say to it. To wit, we have not yet asked what the triumphantly waved dark-blue piece of cloth, the reverently preserved glove, or the angrily banged door would like to say! I know this question sounds odd or even funny. But I can confess now that I have aimed at this effect, I have intentionally selected only such examples where the object, being inanimate, cannot say anything. Only this procedure made it possible for me to demonstrate to you such clear, obvious situations. The whole picture at once becomes different when emotions are transferred on to a human being, to whom it matters considerably whether he has been caressed or hit, honoured or despised. He certainly will not remain unimpressed and will react according to his aroused emotions, hopelessly disturbing the clear psychological situation. And more than that, transference being an absolutely general tendency, he too will strive to get rid of the strain existing in him, i.e. he will strive to transfer his non-abreacted emotions to everyone within his reach. A complete mess.

You remember I said that transference, though a trivial experience, cannot be as easily observed as resistance. Here we have the explanation. I want to add one more explanation only. We all know what is needed to bring about a clear situation again. One of the two persons concerned has to undertake the by no means easy task of behaving—in the first approach—as passively as the flag, the glove or the door. This person is the analyst, and the resulting situation has been called "the psycho-analytic situation." What will happen if the analyst abandons his passive rôle? A very trivial thing, namely the same which constantly happens among men: he will be glad if he has been treated gently, if he has heard nice words; and on the other hand, he will be angry if he has been hit, bitterly reproached, told off or railed at, i.e. he too will react and transfer his emotions on to his patient. Thus the psycho-analytic relation will change into a trivial human relation of friendliness or hostility, sympathy, love or hate, or even indifference.

On the other hand, if the analyst has been able to preserve his elastic passivity, by not bringing anything from his side into the developing relationship, then the patient alone has to form it. Only under such condition is it possible to show up the effects of the patient's transference and to follow them in detail. I cannot sufficiently emphasise how difficult this task can be. Generally it

is thought that the real difficulty for the analyst is to remember
the innumerable data, events, details, reported by each of his
patients, or to keep apart the different material concerning the
different patients, or to interpret it. All these tasks are not at all
difficult compared with the preserving of this elastic passivity,
with the benevolent conducting of the transference, with the absolute mastering of his own counter-transference; these are the
touch-stones of the analyst. Analytic treatment requires something similar to surgical or bacteriological sterility; and as these
cannot be learned from books, but only by practice, so there is
only one way to learn this analytic sterility: the didactic or training analysis. As is well known, this means that the student has to
undergo the same procedure which he intends to use with his future patients. I think a lot of polypragmasy could be prevented,
should it be possible to introduce this requirement into the general
medical and especially surgical curriculum.

I would like to illustrate with a few examples the difficulties
waiting for the analyst. At the same time you will see how cunning the unconscious mind can be in inventing ingenious devices
with the single aim of forcing the analyst to abandon his passivity.
E.g. one day a man appears to consult me about his nervous complaints. He tells me his name, his family relations, really everything, a very complicated story. As usual, before asking anything,
I tell him that he would do better to refuse to answer than to
answer not quite sincerely; this makes a deep impression on him,
and he readily answers all my questions. Nevertheless I cannot get
a clear enough picture of his problems and I tell him so, when
after more than an hour I have to end the interview. We agree
that in a few days he will ring me up again. He does so, he comes
again and continues his story. After a while I interrupt him with
the confession that I am still unable to understand the situation:
the more he tells me, the less clearly I see. My man takes a deep
breath and says: "At last—a sincere man." Then he tells me that
his name is different, the whole story—family relations, nervous
symptoms, everything was invented; he wanted to test me first,
because he wants a truthful man to whom to disclose his secrets.
He has already tried several physicians in the same way, but each
of them fell into the trap, giving him advice and prescriptions for

his faked symptoms. Of course I agreed with him, really nobody ought to be trusted before being tested, but I added that it was rather an expensive and very tiresome method of testing; there are certainly ways of arriving at the same result with less cunning and at a smaller price. As you can see, this man came in a prepared attitude, entirely independent of my personality; this attitude, the transference, was—in this case—a severe obstacle to be overcome before he could establish a workable relation between his physician and himself. The attitude in this case was conscious, even well rationalised. It is true that the energy required was not in proportion with the result aimed at. With such a disproportion it is certain that the scheme of transference has—besides its conscious source—also a powerful unconscious one, but the discovery of this usually requires long and tiresome analytic work. In this case there was no time for it. Therefore it is advisable in such a situation simply to agree with the patient, but at the same time to show him how uneconomic his attitude is, and thereby to try to change his "natural" attitude into a problematic one.

The end of the analytic session is another example of such a transference, again consciously well rationalised. Usually we work an hour a day with our patients, the end of the time being signalled in rather a stereotyped form. People react to it in various ways. There are some who get up at once, say good-bye and are already gone. Another cannot go away, he would like so much to tell just this one idea then certainly he will go, he knows that the next patient is already waiting; but just this one story is so nice, etc. . . . A third feels it as a grave offence that I am ending the session and not he; during a great part, often the greater part, of our working time, he has to prepare himself to endure this unjust blow. A fourth is very matter-of-fact, no emotions at all; the time is over, he has to go; but he has to tell me that something very important came into his mind just at this moment; certainly he has to wait with it till to-morrow—if he does not forget it, which undoubtedly would be a great pity, caused by the analyst's rigidity, indifference and impatience, etc., etc., in thousands of variations.

As you see, each of them feels his attitude to be logical and natural. But to us it must appear suspicious that each thinks that his is the only understandable attitude. To us, who see the whole picture, the particular attitude is not so much natural as characteristic for that certain person. With this we have arrived at characterology. You know that there are as many character-ologies as authors investigating this problem. Each of them in-troduced a new classificatory system, supposed some new funda-mental characters or temperaments different in many respects from any previously described. The main cause of this mess is the "unsterile" way of investigation. The different authors brought their own likes and dislikes, their own character and tempera-ment, into the material and observed and described the phe-nomena through the spectacles of their own transference. The result of such work is naturally a psychology or a characterology of the psychologist himself.

Psycho-analysis has gone a different way. Instead of begin-ning by supposing some basic types, it investigated the mature character-traits by studying their actual working in the analytical situation. Each man has his more or less automatic forms, even schemes of reactions, and some of these have been assimilated to such an extent that any other form is not only impossible, but literally does not exist for the person in question. We call these forms the character-traits. How are they to be treated in an analy-sis? First of all the analyst must not react to them. That means, taking the end of a session as an example, he does not find it natural that even after an agitated hour his patient should be able simply to go away without a moment's rest to collect himself; neither does he allow the conversation to slip into a pleasant chat; nor is he frightened that something very valuable could be irrep-arably lost, etc. Thus keeping the analytic situation free of his counter-transference, the analyst can demonstrate the automa-tisms working in the patient, often without his being conscious of them. It is a big step if not only the automatism itself but also the effect which is aimed at can be made conscious. So, keeping to the examples given above, the patient who habitually runs away at once was possibly a too-well-trained child, who has be-come unable to feel and still less to express a desire. The other, who cannot stop the new ideas coming into his mind, is skilfully hiding the fact that he cannot acquiesce in simply being sent away. The third, who suffers almost from the beginning of the session from the expectation of being sent away, is often a spoilt child, with a lot of aggressiveness behind his sensitivity. The fourth, though seemingly very submissive, really wants to throw the burden of responsibility on the analyst.

A still further step is to demonstrate that though this automatism can be economic under certain conditions, it is not always so; very often it leads to unmanageable situations. The next aim of the analysis is to look for the original situation, to which this form of reaction was well adapted, often the only possible adaptation. This found, we are able to follow up the whole process which led to the establishing of this particular automatism, or, by its other name, of this character-trait. As you see, this way is thoroughly different from that hitherto used in characterology. We have no idea how many and which are the basic types of character; we are simply collecting data in the hope that the material will arrange itself with our increasing knowledge.

I want to show what is meant when I stated that every character-trait has its individual history. We may get something unexpected too, namely that quite unimportant trifles may let loose a storm of transference. Therefore I have to begin with such unimportant details. For a time my consulting-room was so arranged that the couch was quite near my writing-desk. A rather big plant used to stand on the corner of the desk, throwing its shadow on the couch. One day the plant had been taken out of my room to be washed and had not been brought back. Neither I nor the first one or two patients noticed its absence. The next one—contrary to his habit—began the session by remaining silent. It was quite obvious by his whole behaviour that he was feeling uneasy, was almost suffering. Finally, after some encouragement, he burst out violently: "Why do you do such things to me? And if it has to be done, why so brutally?" Only after further encouragement was he able to tell that until now he felt so comfortable in the shadow of the plant, it was so reassuring, so homely. But now that the plant had been taken away, he felt like one expelled, an outcast, a prey to the whole

world, defencelessly handed over to every evil. You have to
imagine that he was a physically absolutely healthy youth, an
athlete, a champion weight-lifter and a member of his university
eight. At that time I already knew that he had had to leave his
home when nine years old for a very severe boarding school, run
by Jesuits. The political situation at that time, i.e. the end of
the war, three revolutions rapidly following one another and
the Rumanian occupation of Hungary, made it impossible for
his parents for about two years to take him home, or even to
come to see him; so he had to stand on his own feet. Outwardly
he was quite successful; a "cheerful" child at school, he developed
into a sincere and frank man who was always popular with
everyone. Now we had to learn what was the price he had to
pay for it. In his childhood he had to struggle against the same
emotions of being thrown out without mercy, but as there was
no hope of finding understanding, even a big risk of being laughed
at, he had to appear as a strong, robust man, and to keep his
real, tender feelings to himself. Even today nobody knows what
he really feels; he has numerous good companions, not one
intimate friend. If possible, he sits in a corner, shielded by the
walls, speaks very little, is always on his guard and, curiously
enough, he does not like to do anything by himself, e.g. when
preparing for an examination he looks for somebody with whom
to work together, when rowing he always tries to make someone accompany him in order not to be alone in the boat, even
if he has to do the work of two. Of course his sexual life, his
love affairs, show the same picture: a strong longing for human
proximity with inability to maintain a real intimacy. The picture is in fact not simple, there are many ramifications, but two
tendencies are obvious: the fear of disclosing his affectionate
feelings and the striving not to become conspicuous. Needless to
say, the unveiling of this part of his history was an important
step in his analysis.

Let us take another case. The patient is a woman, of about
thirty-five, single; a very difficult case. I am her second analyst;
the first analysis was almost a failure. The main obstacle to the
analytical work is her peculiar behaviour. Should there be anything in her mind which is disagreeable or only inconvenient for

her to tell, she keeps silent or begins to chat about petty affairs of the day. At times I can show her that she tendentiously tries to avoid a specific subject in her associations, as often as not even then she tells lies in order to escape. Days later, when her emotions have gone, she admits her fears and insincere tricks. Of course, in this way we need an immense amount of time for the simplest matters. She knows very well that her whole life has been made a hopeless mess by just such behaviour.

In one of our last sessions she produced again the same "comedy"—which is her own word. From the beginning it was quite obvious that she was keeping something back. It cost more than half an hour of hard work—for both of us—till she could tell me that she had received a letter of recommendation from her family doctor, and that in this letter she was described as a conscientious and reliable person. On this occasion it was possible to analyse some aspects of her behaviour. Here, naturally, I can report only the main tendencies brought to light. First of all, in her opinion it is a bad thing to be a grown-up; really everyone should be afraid of it. In fact, it means to be sentenced to hard labour for the rest of your life, and moreover to be fully responsible for everything that you do. On the other hand, a child is permitted to do what he likes, he has no responsibility—if anything should happen the parents are the persons responsible; then there is no compulsion to work; everybody finds it natural and even lovely when a child spends the time playing. And really no one can demand hard work of a little girl, not even a psycho-analyst.

Consequently her behaviour means: I am a little girl, you should love me as I am, and you should not try to make me work. This attitude could be traced back to her childhood. The mother was and still is a fanatic for work; life for her, I quote her own words, is "work, sweat and duty." She is the father's second wife, and he probably married her because he wanted somebody to work for him. The father, who died some years ago, was a happy-go-lucky fellow; he did not like my patient, his only daughter, but preferred his sons.

Her whole life is but a series of similar stories. She makes an excellent start; later, when she notices that people take her seriously, begin to expect something of her—i.e. expect her to work—she gets frightened of the responsibility, she begins to "play the comedy," i.e. she demonstrates that she is a little girl, quite irresponsible. E.g. at school she was one of the best pupils, a candidate for a scholarship, was offered the position of prefect—the result was that in a couple of weeks she made herself quite impossible, and had to leave the school before her H.S.C. In several jobs she did the same trick; once she worked as a nurse to two children, everybody was entirely satisfied with her, the parents offered her a rise in salary—then in an amazingly short time she turned everything upside down and left the post. Obviously she does not want to be a grown-up because it would mean leading a life similar to that of her mother. The following day she reported that she presented herself with the letter and took up a job. Very characteristically she became the secretary of a domestic agent, i.e., in her own words, she sits by the telephone and sends the others to work. Needless to say, that almost every day she comes with new reasons as to why it would be advisable for her to quit her job.

What can we see in all these examples? The behaviour of these people is not free, is not well adapted to the actual requirements. There is a pattern working in them, and this pattern determines their attitude towards important persons in their life. This attitude, this pattern, is more or less automatic, either constantly present, as with the last-mentioned patient, or a very small stimulus is sufficient to activate it, as was the case with our athlete. The main thing is that this pattern prescribes the emotions felt towards a certain type of person; the persons themselves have very little or even no part at all in evoking these emotions. All these patterns have an individual history, and if this history—I mean the original situation, in which this emotion was first felt as a reasonable response to the real situation, and all the subsequent changes of this response—if this whole history can be brought to consciousness the pattern becomes less imperative and the way to a new, more elastic adaptation is opened.

Does this mean that all character-traits are based on transference-patterns? Certainly not exclusively. But I would not like to embark upon this endless subject of characterology, with all its fine discriminations between style, character, personality, etc., and with all its complex involvements between psychology, physiology, endocrinology, genetics, sexual-biology, etc. My only purpose was to show that transference of emotions plays a very important part in shaping our character.

I should finally like to draw your attention to an important point of detail which we have not yet discussed. All the reported cases, without exception, show that the transferred emotions, though often very intense or even stormy, are in fact somewhat childish. This clinical fact, once a most surprising discovery, led to a much deeper understanding of the so-called Oedipus situation. You know that by that term psycho-analysis denotes all those complex, often contradictory but always very intense feelings and emotions which originate in every child during his first years of existence. A great part of these emotions must remain without any outlet or with an inappropriate outlet only, many desires without proper gratification. It is general knowledge that desires, especially love and hate, can live unnoticed for very long periods and return at a favourable occasion in their old strength. Psycho-analysis was able to show that these ungratified mental tendencies are not only persistent but that they cause a considerable strain in the mind, because they have to be kept in an inactive, so-called repressed, state. One means of alleviating this strain is transference.

Now we understand better why all of us always can, and actually do, transfer emotions on to everyone who is available, why the whole of our social, cultural, religious, political life is entirely permeated with transferred emotions. All these emotions originate from the immense reservoir of the Oedipus complex. This explains too why no attention was paid to these phenomena before Freud, and how he came to discover them. The psycho-analytic situation resembles in many respects the Oedipus situation. It is understandable that under such circumstances emotions are always transferred. It is not a paradox to state first that our whole cultural life is permeated with transference, that transference plays a paramount rôle in shaping our political, religious, social life, and then to assert that the same transference is childish. There is no contradiction, because we are speaking of the psychology of transference, and not of its cultural value—which are two entirely different aspects.

These two attributes of transference, (a) the seemingly loose connection between stimulus and reaction, and (b) the child-ishness, would lead us, if followed to their origins, to infantile sexuality.

Before ending I would like to enumerate some of the important problems which I have had to leave out: the qualitative study of the transferred feelings and emotions which leads to problems of the psychology of instincts. The cultural function of trans-ference, which is no longer a purely psychological problem. Next the difference between conscious and unconscious transference, and the difference between individual and cultural (mass) trans-ference, which would lead to the problem of repression, to very interesting problems of ego-psychology and the question of the interrelations between culture and the individual. Then trans-ference as one of the main factors of psycho-analytic treatment, a purely technical problem; and last but not least transference as one form, maybe the only true form, of manifestations of the unconscious mind.

With this enumeration I wanted to demonstrate that trans-ference is a very intricate subject, not at all as simple as shown in this lecture.

Anyhow, I am at the end. We have seen that transference is a general feature of human life, everybody is always transferring his emotions to everybody within his reach. It is impossible to get a clear, understandable situation, if the object of transference is a second human being, because (a) the second person will react to the transferred feeling and (b) he too will try to transfer his un-abreacted emotions on to the first. The only way to see clearly is what I called the "sterile" way of working, namely the elastic, tactful passivity, the complete mastering of the analyst's own transference.

29

JANET MACKENZIE RIOCH

The Transference Phenomenon
in Psychoanalytic Therapy*

The significance of the transference phenomenon impressed
Freud so profoundly that he continued through the years to
develop his ideas about it. His classical observations on the
patient Dora formed the basis for his first formulations of this
concept. He says, "What are transferences? They are the new
editions or facsimiles of the tendencies and phantasies which
are aroused and made conscious during the progress of the
analysis; but they have this peculiarity, which is characteristic for
their species, that they replace some earlier person by the person of the physician. To put it another way: a whole series of
psychological experiences are revived, not as belonging to the
past, but as applying to the person of the physician at the present
moment." [1]

According to Freud's view, the process of psychoanalytic cure
depends mainly upon the patient's ability to remember that which
is forgotten and repressed, and thus to gain conviction that
the analytical conclusions arrived at are correct. However, "the
unconscious feelings strive to avoid the recognition which the

* An address presented before the Association for the Advancement of
Psychoanalysis, 23 March 1943. Reprinted by special permission of The
William Alanson White Psychiatric Foundation, Inc., and Patrick Mullahy
from A Study of Interpersonal Relations edited by Patrick Mullahy and published by Hermitage House, Inc., New York. Copyright, 1949, by Hermitage
Press, Inc. (Originally published in Psychiatry, 1943, 6:147-156.)
[1] Freud, Sigmund, Collected Papers; London, Hogarth (1933) 3:139.

cure demands"; [2] they seek instead, emotional discharge, regardless of the reality of the situation.

Freud believed that these unconscious feelings which the patient strives to hide are made up of that part of the libidinal impulse which has turned away from consciousness and reality, due to the frustration of a desired gratification. Because the attraction of reality has weakened, the libidinal energy is still maintained in a state of regression attached to the original infantile sexual objects, although the reasons for the recoil from reality have disappeared.[3]

Freud states that in the analytic treatment, the analyst pursues this part of the libido to its hiding place, "aiming always at unearthing it, making it accessible to consciousness and at last serviceable to reality." [3] The patient tries to achieve an emotional discharge of this libidinal energy under the pressure of the compulsion to repeat experiences over and over again rather than to become conscious of their origin. He uses the method of transferring to the person of the physician past psychological experiences and reacting to this, at times, with all the power of hallucination.[2] The patient vehemently insists that his impression of the analyst is true for the immediate present, in this way avoiding the recognition of his own unconscious impulses.

Thus, Freud regarded the transference-manifestations as a major problem of the resistance. However, Freud says, "It must not be forgotten that they (the transference-manifestations) and they only, render the invaluable service of making the patient's buried and forgotten love-emotions actual and manifest." [4]

Freud regards the transference-manifestations as having two general aspects—positive and negative. The negative, he at first regarded as having no value in psychoanalytic cure and only something to be "raised" [5] into consciousness to avoid interference with the progress of the analysis. He later[6] accorded it a place of importance in the therapeutic experience. The positive transference he considered to be ultimately sexual in origin, since

[2] Reference footnote 1; 2:321.
[3] Reference footnote 1; 2:316.
[4] Reference footnote 1; p. 322.
[5] Reference footnote 1; p. 319.
[6] Freud, Sigmund, *Gesammelte Werke*; London, Imago (1940) 12:223.

Freud says, "To begin with, we knew none but sexual objects." [5] However, he divides the positive transference into two components—one, the repressed erotic component, which is used in the service of resistance; the other, the friendly and affectionate component, which, although originally sexual, is the "unobjectionable" aspect of the positive transference, and is that which "brings about the successful result in psycho-analysis, as in all other remedial methods." [5] Freud refers here to the element of suggestion in psychoanalytic therapy, about which I wish to speak in detail a little later on.

At the moment, I should like to state that, although not agreeing with the view of Freud that human behavior depends ultimately on the biological sexual drives, I believe that it would be a mistake to deny the value and importance of his formulations regarding transference phenomena. As I shall indicate shortly, I differ on certain points with Freud, but I do not differ with the formulation that early impressions acquired during childhood are revived in the analytical situation, and are felt as immediate and real—that they form potentially the greatest obstacles to analysis, if unnoticed and, as Freud puts it, the greatest ally of the analysis when understood. I agree that the main work of the analysis consists in analyzing the transference phenomena, although I differ somewhat as to how this results in cure. It is my conviction that the transference is a strictly interpersonal experience. Freud gives the impression that under the stress of the repetition-compulsion the patient is bound to repeat the identical pattern, regardless of the other person. I believe that the personality of the analyst tends to determine the character of the transference illusions, and especially to determine whether the attempt at analysis will result in cure. Horney[7] has shown that there is no valid reason for assuming that the tendency to repeat past experiences again and again has an instinctual basis. The particular character structure of the person requires that he integrate with any given situation according to the necessities of his character structure.

In discussing my own views regarding the transference and

[7] Horney, Karen, *New Ways in Psychoanalysis*; New York, Norton, 1939 (313 pp.).

its use in therapy, it is necessary to begin at the beginning, and to point out in a very schematic way how a person acquires his particular orientation to himself and the world—which one might call his character structure, and the implications of this in psychoanalytic therapy.

The infant is born without a frame of reference, as far as interpersonal experience goes. He is already acquainted with the feeling of bodily movement—with sucking and swallowing— but, among other things, he has had no knowledge of the existence of another *person* in relationship to himself. Although I do not wish to draw any particular conclusions from this analogy, I want to mention a simple phenomenon, described by Sherif,[8] connected with the problem of the frame of reference. If you have a completely dark room, with no possibility of any light being seen, and you then turn on a small-pin-point of light, which is kept stationary, this light will soon appear to be moving about. I am sure a good many of you have noticed this phenomenon when gazing at a single star. The light seems to move, and it does so, apparently, because there is no reference point in relation to which one can establish it at a fixed place in space. It just wanders around. If, however, one can at the same time see some other fixed object in the room, the light immediately becomes stationary. A reference point has been established, and there is no longer any uncertainty, any vague wandering of the spot of light. It is fixed. The pin-point of light wandering in the dark room is symbolic of the original attitude of the person to himself, undetermined, unstructured, with no reference points.

The new-born infant probably perceives everything in a vague and uncertain way, including himself. Gradually, reference points are established; a connection begins to occur between hunger and breast, between a relief of bladder tension and a wet diaper, between playing with his genitals and a smack on the hand. The physical boundaries and potentialities of the self are explored. One can observe the baby investigating the extent, shape and potentialities of his own body. He finds that he can scream and mother will come, or will not come, that he can hold his breath

    [8] Sherif, Muzafer A. F., *The Psychology of Social Norms*; New York, Harper, 1936 (xii and 210 pp.).

and everyone will get excited, that he can smile and coo and people will be enchanted, or just the opposite. The nature of the emotional reference points that he determines depends upon the environment. By that still unknown quality called "empathy," he discovers the reference points which help to determine his emotional attitude toward himself. If his mother did not want him, is disgusted with him, treats him with utter disregard, he comes to look upon himself as a thing-to-be-disregarded. With the profound human drive to make this rational, he gradually builds up a system of "reasons why." Underneath all these "reasons," is a basic sense of worthlessness, undetermined and undefined, related directly to the original reference frame. Another child discovers that the state of being regarded is dependent upon specific factors—all is well as long as one does not act spontaneously, as long as one is not a separate person, as long as one is good, as the state of being good is continuously defined by the parents. Under these conditions, and these only, this child can feel a sense of self-regard.

Other people are encountered with the original reference frame in mind. The child tends to carry over into later situations the patterns he first learned to know. The rigidity with which these original patterns are retained depends upon the nature of the child's experience. If this has been of a traumatic character so that spontaneity has been blocked and further emotional development has been inhibited, the original orientation will tend to persist. Discrepancies may be rationalized or repressed. Thus, the original impression of the hostile mother may be retained, while the contact with the new person is rationalized to fit the original reference frame. The new person encountered acts differently, but probably that is just a pose. She is just being nice because she does not know me. If she really knew me, she would act differently. Or, the original impressions are so out of line with the present actuality, that they remain unconscious, but make themselves apparent in inappropriate behavior or attitudes, which remain outside the awareness of the person concerned.

The incongruity of the behavior pattern, or of the attitude, may be a source of astonishment to the other person involved.

Sullivan[9] provides insight into the process by the elucidation of
what he calls the "parataxic distortions." He points out that in
the development of the personality, certain integrative patterns
are organized in response to the important persons in the child's
past. There is a "self-in-relation-to-A" pattern, or "self-in-rela-
tion-to-B" pattern. These patterns of response become familiar
and useful. The person learns to get along as a "self-in-relation-
to A" or B, C and D, depending on the number of important
people to whom he had to adjust in the course of his early
development. For example, a young girl, who had a severely
dominating mother and a weak, kindly father, learned a pattern
of adjustment to her mother which could be briefly described as
submissive, mildly rebellious in a secret way, but mostly lacking
in spontaneity. Toward the father she developed a loving, but
contemptuous attitude. When she encountered other people, regardless of sex, she oriented herself to them partly as the real
people they were, and partly as she had learned to respond to
her mother and father in her past. She thus was feeling toward
the real person involved as if she were dealing with two people
at once. However, since it is very necessary for people to behave
as rational persons she suppressed the knowledge that some of
her reactions were inappropriate to the immediate situation, and
wove an intricate mesh of rationalizations, which permitted her
to believe that the person with whom she was dealing really was
someone either to be feared and submitted to, as her mother,
or to be contemptuous of, as her father. The more nearly the
real person fitted the original picture of the mother and father,
the easier it was for her to maintain that the original "self-in-
relation-to A or B" was the real and valid expression of herself.

It happened, however, that this girl had had a kindly nurse
who was not a weak person, although occupying an inferior
position in the household. During the many hours when she
was with this nurse, she was able to experience a great deal
of unreserved warmth, and of freedom for self-realization. No
demands for emotional conformity were made on her in this
relationship. Her own capacities for love and spontaneous ac-

---

[9] Sullivan, Harry Stack, Conceptions of Modern Psychiatry. PSYCHIATRY
(1940) 3:1-117.

tivity were able to flourish. Unfortunately, the contact with this nurse was all too brief. But there remained, despite the necessity for the rigid development of the patterns towards the mother and father, a deeply repressed, but still vital experience of self, which most closely approximated the fullest realization of her potentialities. This, which one might call her *real self*, although "snowed under" and handicapped by all the distortions incurred by her relationship to the parents, was finally able to emerge and become again active in analysis. In the course of this treatment, she learned how much her reactions to people were "transference" reactions, or as Sullivan would say, "parataxic distortions."

I have deliberately tried to schematize this illustration. For instance, when I speak of the early frame of reference and then just mention the parents, I do not overlook all the other possible reference frames. Also, one has to realize that one pattern connects with another—the whole making a tangled mass that only years of analysis can unscramble. I also have not taken the time to outline the compensatory drives that the neurotic person has to develop in order to handle his life situation. Each compensatory manœuvre causes some change in his frame of reference, since the development of a defensive trait in his personality sets off a new set of relationships to those around him. The little child who grows more and more negativistic, because of injuries and frustrations, evokes more and more hostility in his environment. However, and this is important, the basic reactions of hostility on the part of the parents, which originally induced his negativism, are still there. Thus, the pattern does not change much in character—it just gets worse in the same direction. Those persons whose later life experience perpetuate the original frames of reference, are more severely injured. A young child, who has a hostile mother, may then have a hostile teacher. If, by good luck, he got a kind teacher and if his own attitude was not already badly warped, so that he did not induce hostility in this kind teacher, he would be introduced into a startlingly new and pleasant frame of reference, and his personality might not suffer too greatly, especially if a kindly aunt or uncle happened to be around. I am sure that if the details of the life histories of healthy people were studied, it would be found that they had had some very satisfactory experiences early enough to establish in them a feeling of validity as persons. The profoundly sick people have been so early injured, in such a rigid and limited frame of reference, that they are not able to make use of kindliness, decency or regard when it does come their way. They meet the world as if it were potentially menacing. They have already developed defensive traits entirely appropriate to their original experience, and then carry them out in completely inappropriate situations, rationalizing the discrepancies, but never daring to believe that people are different to the ones they early learned to distrust and hate. By reason of bitter early experience, they learn never to let their guards down, never to permit intimacy, lest at that moment the death blow would be dealt to their already partly destroyed sense of self-regard. Despairing of real joy in living, they develop secondary neurotic goals which give a pseudo-satisfaction. The secondary gains at first glance might seem to be what the person was really striving for—revenge, power and exclusive possession. Actually, these are but the expressions of the deep injuries sustained by the person. They can not be fundamentally cured until those interpersonal relationships which caused the original injury are brought back to consciousness in the analytical situation. Step by step, each phase of the long period of emotional development is exposed, by no means chronologically; the interconnecting, overlapping reference frames are made conscious; those points at which a distortion of reality, or a repression of part of the self *had* to occur, are uncovered. The reality gradually becomes "undistorted," the self, re-found, in the personal relationship between the analyst and the patient. This personal relationship with the analyst is the situation in which the transference distortions can be analyzed.

In Freud's view, the transference was either positive or negative, and was related in a rather isolated way to a particular person in the past. In my view, the transference is the experiencing in the analytic situation the entire pattern of the original reference frames, which included at every moment the relationship of the patient to himself, to the important persons, and to others, as he experienced them at that time, in the light of his interrelationships with the important people.

The therapeutic aim in this process is not to uncover childhood memories which will then lend themselves to analytic interpretation. Here, I think, is an important difference to Freud's view. Fromm[10] has pointed this out in a recent lecture. Psychoanalytic cure is not the amassing of data, either from childhood, or from the study of the present situation. Nor does cure result from a repetition of the original injurious experience in the analytical relationship. What is curative in the process is that in tending to reconstruct with the analyst that atmosphere which obtained in childhood, the patient actually achieves something new. He discovers that part of himself which had to be repressed at the time of the original experience. He can only do this in an interpersonal relationship with the analyst, which is suitable to such a re-discovery. To illustrate this point: if a patient had a hostile parent towards whom he was required to show deference, he would have to repress certain of his own spontaneous feelings. In the analytical situation, he tends to carry over his original frame of reference and again tends to feel himself to be in a similar situation. If the analyst's personality also contains elements of a need for deference, that need will unconsciously be imparted to the patient, who will, therefore, still repress his spontaneity as he did before. True enough, he may act or try to act as if analyzed, since by definition, that is what the analyst is attempting to accomplish. But he will *never* have found his repressed self, because the analytical relationship contains for him elements actually identical with his original situation. Only if the analyst provides a genuinely *new* frame of reference—that is, if he is truly non-hostile, and truly not in need of deference— can this patient discover, and it is a real *discovery,* the repressed elements of his own personality. Thus, the transference phenomenon is used so that the patient will completely reëxperience the original frames of reference, and himself within those frames, in a truly different relationship with the analyst, to the end that

---

[10] Fromm, Erich, Lectures on *Ideas and Ideologies* presented at the New School for Social Research, N.Y.C. 1943.

he can discover the invalidity of his conclusions about himself and others.

I do not mean by this to deny the correctness of Freud's view of transference also acting as a resistance. As a matter of fact, the tendency of the patient to re-establish the original reference frame is precisely because he is afraid to experience the other person in a direct and unreserved way. He has organized his whole system of getting along in the world, bad as that system might be, on the basis of the original distortions of his personality and his subsequent vicissitudes. His capacity for spontaneous feeling and acting has gone into hiding. Now it has to be sought. If some such phrase as the "capacity for self-realization" be substituted in place of Freud's concept of the repressed libidinal impulse, much the same conclusions can be reached about the way in which the transference-manifestations appear in the analysis as resistance. It is just in the safest situation, where the spontaneous feeling might come out of hiding, that the patient develops intense feelings, sometimes of a hallucinatory character, that relate to the most dreaded experiences of the past. It is at this point that the nature and the use by the patient of the transference distortions have to be understood and correctly interpreted, by the analyst. It is also here that the personality of the analyst modifies the transference reaction. A patient cannot feel close to a detached or hostile analyst and will therefore never display the full intensity of his transference illusions. The complexity of this process, whereby the transference can be used as the therapeutic instrument and, at the same time, as a resistance may be illustrated by the following example: a patient had developed intense feelings of attachment to a father surrogate in his everyday life. The transference feelings towards this man were of great value in elucidating his original problems with his real father. As the patient became more and more aware of his own personal validity, he found this masochistic attachment to be weakening. This occasioned acute feelings of anxiety, since his sense of independence was not yet fully established. At that point, he developed very disturbing feelings regarding the analyst, believing that she was untrustworthy and hostile, although prior to this, he had succeeded in establishing a realistically positive relationship to her. The feelings of untrustworthiness precisely reproduced an ancient pattern with his mother. He experienced them at this particular point in the analysis in order to retain and to justify his attachment to the father figure, the weakening of which attachment had threatened him so profoundly. The entire pattern was elucidated when it was seen that he was reëxperiencing an ancient triangle, in which he was continuously driven to a submissive attachment to a dominating father, due to the utter untrustworthiness of his weak mother. If the transference character of this sudden feeling of untrustworthiness of the analyst had not been clarified, he would have turned again submissively to his father surrogate, which would have further postponed his development of independence. Nevertheless, the development of this transference to the analyst brought to light a new insight.

I wish to make one remark about Freud's view of the so-called narcissistic neuroses. Freud felt that personality disorders called schizophrenia or paranoia cannot be analyzed because the patient is unable to develop a transference to the analyst. It is my view that the real difficulty in treating such disorders is that the relationship is essentially nothing but transference illusions. Such persons hallucinate the original frame of reference to the exclusion of reality. Nowhere in the realm of psychoanalysis can one find more complete proof of the effect of early experience on the person than in attempting to treat these patients. Frieda Fromm-Reichmann[11] has shown in her work with schizophrenics the necessity to realize the intensity of the transference reactions, which have become almost completely real to the patient. And yet, if one knows the correct interpretations, by actually feeling the patient's needs, one can over years of time do the identical thing which is accomplished more quickly and less dramatically with patients suffering a less severe disturbance of their interpersonal relationships.

Another point which I wish to discuss for a moment is the following:

Freud takes the position that all subsequent experience in

---

[11] Fromm-Reichmann, Frieda, Transference Problems in Schizophrenics. Psychoanalytic Quart. (1939) 8:412-426.

normal life is merely a repetition of the original one.[12] Thus love is experienced for someone today *in terms of* the love felt for someone in the past. I do not believe this to be exactly true. The child who has not had to repress certain aspects of his personality enters into a new situation dynamically, not just as a repetition of what he felt, say, with his mother, but as an active continuation of it. I believe that there are constitutional differences with respect to the total capacity for emotional experience, just as there are with respect to the total capacity for intellectual experiences. Given this constitutional substrate, the child engages in personal relationships not passively as a lump of clay waiting to be molded, but most dynamically, bringing into play all his emotional potentialities. He may possibly find someone later whose capacity for response is deeper than his mother's. If *he* is capable of that greater depth, he experiences an expansion of himself. Many later in life have met a "great" person and have felt a sense of newness in the relationship which is described to others as "wonderful" and which is regarded with a certain amount of awe. This is not a "transference" experience, but represents a dynamic extension of the self to a new horizon.

In considering the process of psychoanalytic cure, Freud very seriously discussed the relationship of analysis to suggestion therapy and hypnosis. He believed as I previously mentioned that part of the positive transference could be made use of in the analysis to bring about the successful result. He says, "In so far we readily admit that the results of psychoanalysis rest upon a basis of suggestion; only by suggestion we must be understood to mean that which we, with Ferenczi, find that it consists of— influence on a person through and by means of the transference —manifestations of which he is capable. The eventual independence of the patient is our ultimate object when we use suggestion to bring him to carry out a mental operation that will necessarily result in a lasting improvement in his mental condition." [12] Freud elsewhere indicates very clearly that in hypnosis, the relationship of the patient to the hypnotist is not worked through, whereas in analysis the transference to the analyst is resolved by bringing it entirely into consciousness. He

[12] Reference footnote 1; p. 387.

also says that the patient is protected from the unwitting suggestive influence of the analysts by the awakening of his own unconscious resistances.[13]

I should like to discuss hypnosis a little more in detail and to make a few remarks about its correlation with the transference phenomenon in psychoanalytic therapy.

According to White,[14] the subject under hypnosis is a person striving to act like a hypnotized person as that state is continuously defined by the hypnotist. He also says that the state of being hypnotized is an "altered state of consciousness." However, as Maslow[15] points out, it is not an abnormal state. In everyday life transient manifestations of all the phenomena that occur in hypnosis can be seen. Such examples are cited as the trance-like state a person experiences when completely occupied with an absorbing book. Among the phenomena of the hypnotic state are the amnesia for the trance; the development of certain anæsthesias, such as insensitivity to pain; deafness to sounds other than the hypnotist's voice; greater ability to recall forgotten events; loss of capacity to spontaneously initiate activities; and a much greater suggestibility. This heightened suggestibility in the trance state is the most important phenomenon of hypnosis. Changes in behavior and feeling can be induced, such as painful or pleasant experiences, headaches, nausea, or feelings of well-being. Post-hypnotic behavior can be influenced by suggestion, this being one of the most important aspects of experimental hypnosis for the clarifying of psychopathological problems.

The hypnotic state is induced by a combination of methods which may include relaxation, visual concentration and verbal suggestion. The methods vary with the personality of the experimenter and the subject.

Maslow has pointed out the interpersonal character of hypnosis, which accounts for some of the different conclusions by different experimenters. Roughly, the types of experimenters may be divided into three groups—the dominant type, the friendly

[13] Reference footnote 6; p. 226.

[14] White, Robert W., A Preface to the Theory of Hypnotism. *J. Abnormal and Social Psychol.* (1941) 36:477-505.

[15] Maslow, A. H., and Mittelmann, Bela, *Principles of Abnormal Psychology;* New York, Harper, 1941.

or brotherly type, and the cold, detached, scientific type. According to the inner needs of the subject, he will be able to be hypnotized more readily by one type or the other. The brotherly hypnotizer cannot, for instance, hypnotize a subject whose inner need is to be dominated.

Freud [16] believed that the relationship of the subject to the hypnotist was that of an emotional, erotic attachment. He comments on the "uncanny" character of hypnosis and says that "the hypnotist awakens in the subject a portion of his archaic inheritance which had also made him compliant to his parents." What is thus awakened is the concept of "the dreaded primal father," "towards whom only a passive-masochistic attitude is possible, towards whom one's will has to be surrendered."

Ferenczi [17] considered the hypnotic state to be one in which the patient transferred onto the hypnotist his early infantile erotic attachment to the parents with the same tendency to blind belief and to uncritical obedience as obtained then. He calls attention to the paternal or frightening type of hypnosis and the maternal or gentle, stroking type. In both instances the situation tends to favour the "conscious and unconscious imaginary return to childhood."

The only point of disagreement with these views that I have is that one does not need to postulate an *erotic* attachment to the hypnotist or a "transference" of infantile sexual wishes. The sole necessity is a willingness to surrender oneself. The child whose parent wished to control it, by one way or another, is forced to do this, in order to be loved, or at least to be taken care of. The patient transfers this willingness to surrender to the hypnotist.[18] He will also transfer it to the analyst or to the leader of a group. In any one of these situations the authoritative person, be he hypnotist, analyst or leader, promises by reason of great power or knowledge the assurance of safety, cure or happiness, as the case may be. The patient, or the isolated person,

[16] Freud, Sigmund, *Group Psychology and the Analysis of the Ego*; London, The International Psycho-Analytical Press, 1922 (134 pp.).

[17] Ferenczi, Sandor, *Sex in Psycho-Analysis*; Boston, Badger, 1916 (338 pp.) —in particular, Introjection and Transference.

[18] I am indebted to Erich Fromm for suggestions in the following discussion.

regresses emotionally to a state of helplessness and lack of initiative similar to the child who has been dominated.

If it be asked how in the first place the child is brought into a state of submissiveness, it may be discovered that the original situation of the child had certain aspects which already resemble a hypnotic situation. This depends upon the parents. If they are destructive or authoritarian they can achieve long lasting results. The child is continuously subjected to being told *how* and *what* he is. Day in and day out, in the limited frame of reference of his home, he is subjected to the repetition, over and over again: "You are a naughty boy." "You are a bad girl." "You are just a nuisance." "You are always giving me trouble." "You are dumb," "you are stupid," "you are a little fool." "You always make mistakes." "You can never do anything right," or, "That's right; I love you when you are a good boy." "That's the kind of boy I like." "Now you are a nice boy." "Smile sweetly." "Pay attention to mother." "Mother loves a good boy who does what she tells him." "Mother knows best, mother always knows best." "If you would listen to mother, you would get along all right. Just listen to her." "Don't pay attention to those naughty children. Just listen to your mother."

Over and over again, with exhortations to pay attention, to listen, to be good, the child is brought under the spell. "When you get older, never forget what I told you. Always remember what mother says, then you will never get into trouble." These are like post-hypnotic suggestions. "You will never come to a good end. You will always be in trouble." "If you are not good, you will always be unhappy." "If you don't do what I say, you will regret it." "If you do not live up to the right things—again, 'right' as continuously defined by the mother—you will be sorry."

It was called to my attention that the Papago Indians deliberately make use of a certain method of suggestion to influence the child favorably. When the child is falling asleep at night the grandfather sits by him and repeats over and over—"You will be a fast runner. You will be a good hunter." [19]

---

[19] Underhill, Ruth, *Social Organization of the Papago Indians* [Columbia University Contributions to Anthropology: Vol. 30]; New York, Columbia University Press, 1939 (ix and 280 pp.).

Hypnotic experiments, according to Hull,[20] indicate that children, on the whole, are more susceptible than adults. Certainly, for many reasons, including that of learning the uses and misuses of language, there is a marked rise of verbal suggestibility up to five years, with a sharp dropping off at around the eighth year. Ferenczi refers to the subsequent effects of threats or orders given in childhood as "having much in common with the post-hypnotic command-automatisms." He points out how the neurotic patient follows out, without being able to explain the motive, a command repressed long ago, just as in hypnosis a post-hypnotic suggestion is carried out for which amnesia has been produced.

It is not my intention in this paper to try to explain the altered state of consciousness which is seen in the hypnotized subject. I have had no personal experience with hypnosis. The reason I refer to hypnosis in discussing the transference is in order to further an understanding of the analytic relationship. The child may be regarded as being in a state of "chronic hypnosis," as I have described, with all sorts of post-hypnotic suggestions thrown in during this period. This entire pattern—this entire early frame of reference—may be "transferred" to the analyst. When this has happened the patient is in a highly suggestible state. Due to a number of intrinsic and extrinsic factors, the analyst is now in the position of a sort of "chronic hypnotist." First, by reason of his position of a doctor he has a certain prestige. Second, the patient *comes* to him, even if expressedly unwillingly; still if there were not something in the patient which was coöperative he would not come at all, or at least he would not stay. The office is relatively quiet, external stimuli relatively reduced. The frame of reference is limited. Many analysts maintain an anonymity about themselves. The attention is focussed on the interpersonal relationship. In this relatively undefined and unstructured field the patient is able to discover his "transference" feelings, since he has few reference points in the analytical situation to go by. This is greatly enhanced by having the patient assume a physical position in the room whereby he does not see the analyst. Thus the ordinary reference points of facial expression and gesture are

---

[20] Hull, Clark L., *Hypnosis and Suggestibility*; New York, Appleton-Century, 1933 (xii and 416 pp.).

lacking. True enough, he can look around or get up and walk about. But for considerable periods of time he lies down—itself a symbolically submissive position. He does what is called "free association." This is again giving up—willingly, to be sure—the conscious control of his thoughts. I want to stress the willingness and coöperativeness of all these acts. That is precisely the necessary condition for hypnosis. The lack of immediate reference points permits the eruption into consciousness of the old patterns of feeling. The original frame of reference becomes more and more clearly outlined and felt. The power which the parent originally had to cast the spell is transferred to the analytical situation. Now it is the analyst who is in the position to do the same thing—placed there partly by the nature of the external situation, partly by the patient who comes to be freed from his suffering.

There is no such thing as an impersonal analyst, nor is the idea of the analyst's acting as a mirror anything more than the "neatest trick of the week." Whether intentionally or not, whether conscious of it or not, the analyst does express, day in and day out, subtle or overt evidences of his own personality in relationship to the patient.

The analyst may express explicitly his wish not to be coercive, but if he has an unconscious wish to control the patient, it is impossible for him correctly to analyze and to resolve the transference distortions. The patient is thus not able to become free from his original difficulties and for lack of something better, adopts the analyst as a new and less dangerous authority. Then the situation occurs in which it is not "my mother says" or "my father says," but now "my analyst says." The so-called chronic patients who need lifelong support may benefit by such a relationship. I am of the opinion, however, that frequently the long-continued unconscious attachment—by which I do *not* mean genuine affection or regard—is maintained because of a failure on the analyst's part to recognize and resolve the sense of being under a sort of hypnotic spell which originated in childhood.

To develop an adequate therapeutic interpersonal relationship, the analyst must be devoid of those personal traits which tend to unconsciously perpetuate the originally destructive or authoritative situation. In addition to this, he must be able, by reason of

his training, to be aware of every evidence of the transference
phenomena; and lastly, he must understand the significance of
the hypnotic-like situation which analysis helps to reproduce. If,
with the best of intentions, he unwittingly makes use of the enormous power with which he is endowed by the patient, he may
certainly achieve something that looks like change. His suggestions, exhortations and pronouncements, based on the patient's
revelation of himself, may certainly make an impression. The
analyst may say, "You must not do this just because I say so."
That is in itself a sort of post-hypnotic command. The patient
then strives to be "an analyzed person acting on his own account"
—because he was told to do so. He is still not really acting on his
own.

It is my firm conviction that analysis is terminable. A person
can continue to grow and expand all his life. The process of
analysis, however, as an interpersonal experience, has a definite
end. That end is achieved when the patient has rediscovered his
own self as an actively and independently functioning entity.

30

THOMAS M. FRENCH

The Transference Phenomenon*

Although it is agreed that the central dynamic problem in psycho-analytic therapy is the handling of transference, there is a great deal of confusion as to what "transference" really means. The term, in psychoanalytic as well as in general literature, has undergone the fate of most popular terms and is often used to refer indiscriminately to many things not included in Freud's original concept. The sense of the word has been loosely extended to include everything from the "transference neurosis" proper, to the "emotional relationship existing between patient and analyst," to the "treatment situation as a whole."

As Freud originally used the term, however, its sense was much more restricted. By "transference" Freud meant reactions to the 'analyst as though he were not himself but some person in the patient's past. According to this definition, a patient's transference to the analyst is only that part of the patient's reaction to the analyst which repeats the patient's reactions to a person who has, at some previous time, played an important role in the patient's life.

Reality Testing. It is important to distinguish between such transference reactions and reactions that are adequate to the present real situation. A patient does not react to the therapist only as though the therapist were somebody else, only as though he were some important figure in the patient's past. Sometimes he

* Reprinted by permission from *Psycho-Analytic Therapy*, by Franz Alexander and Thomas Morton French. Copyright 1946 The Ronald Press Company.

reacts quite naturally to what the therapist actually does or says, to the therapist's actual personality characteristics and behavior.

In actual therapeutic practice, this distinction is of the greatest practical importance. Especially in the later stages of a psychoanalytic treatment, one of our most important therapeutic tasks is to help the patient distinguish neurotic transference reactions (that are based upon a repetition of earlier stereotyped patterns) from normal reactions to the analyst and to the therapeutic situation as a present reality. It is a fundamental part of all psychotherapy to teach the patient that his neurotic reactions are in accord with old, outmoded patterns, that they are anachronistic, and to help him acquire new ways of reacting that conform more closely to the new situations. This is the part of the therapy we call "reality testing."

This concept of reality testing seems to imply a contrast between transference reactions and reality adjusted behavior, that these terms are mutually exclusive. On the other hand, it is clear that all behavior is patterned upon the past, is based on experience. If we based our concept of transference on this fact alone, it would have to include all of the patient's emotional reactions to the therapist, for they are all presumably based upon some pattern from the past. The only distinction left, then, is that in reality adjusted behavior the patterns from the past have been modified to take adequate account of the differences between present reality and the situations in the past upon which they are based.

When we use the word "transference" in this strict sense, we mean an irrational repetition of stereotyped reaction patterns which have not been adjusted to conform to the present situation. In the psychoanalytic literature we have another term which has always been used in this more precise sense, the "transference neurosis." In the transference neurosis we include only such repetitions of earlier reaction patterns as are neurotic, i.e., only those that are irrational or inappropriate in the present real therapeutic situation. The concepts "transference neurosis" and "reality adjusted behavior" are truly, therefore, mutually exclusive, just as the more general concept "neurosis" is quite incompatible with that of reality adjusted behavior.

Definitions. We may summarize the preceding discussion in the form of a few definitions:

In its *widest* sense, as we here use the word, transference is the exact repetition of *any* former reaction without adjusting it to fit the present situation. In a more specific sense, transference is the *neurotic* repetition *with relation to the analyst* of a stereotyped, unsuitable behavior pattern based on the patient's past. It is in this latter sense that the word is most frequently used in this book. The transference "relationship," then, is that relationship which obtains within the therapeutic situation wherein the therapist is indeed the representative of a figure of importance from out the patient's past.

When defined in this way, the transference relationship becomes identical with the transference "neurosis" except that transient neurotic transference reactions are not usually dignified with the name of "transference neurosis." Thus the transference "neurosis" may be defined as that mass of stereotyped neurotic behavior patterns (evidenced in the analytic situation) which are based on the past and do not take into account the differences between the past and the present. In contrast, we have "reality adjusted behavior," which we define as behavior in which patterns based upon past experience *have been corrected* to take adequate account of the differences between the present and the past.

If we wish to make our terminology more complete, it will be helpful to take account of still another possibility. Sometimes the real therapeutic situation is not significantly different from a situation in the past to which one of the patient's stereotyped transference patterns was adequate. For example, it is a quite adequate reaction to the therapy for the patient to turn to the therapist for help. Consequently, in the therapeutic situation, a stereotyped pattern of dependence upon parental figures may for a long time be a quite adequate reaction to the therapeutic situation. In such a case it will not be immediately evident that this reaction is a stereotyped one that cannot be modified to take adequate account of the differences between present and past.

If the therapeutic situation later changes, however, so that this reaction pattern is no longer adequate, its stereotyped character will immediately become evident. For example, if the therapeutic situation later requires that the therapist attempt to wean the patient from his dependence upon him, an energetic protest against this weaning process may reveal the fact that the patient's dependence is a stereotyped pattern that persists even after the therapeutic situation demands that he emancipate himself. Such an apparently adequate reaction to the therapeutic situation, that shows its inadequate and stereotyped character only when the situation changes, we may call a *"latent* transference reaction."

Neurosis the Result of Interrupted Learning Process.   In order to give explicit recognition to this distinction between normal and neurotic reactions, it is helpful to think of the function of therapy as one of facilitating a learning process. (This is in accord with a suggestion of Freud's who once referred to the psychoanalytic treatment as a process of reeducation.) Let us consider more in detail the nature of the difference between a neurosis and reality adjusted behavior.

We have pointed out that all behavior is based upon past experience. In normal development, however, patterns from the past undergo progressive modification. One learns from experience by correcting earlier patterns in the light of later events. When a problem becomes too disturbing to face, however, this learning process is interrupted and subsequent attempts to solve this problem must, therefore, assume the character of stereotyped repetitions of previous unsuccessful attempts to solve it. A neurosis may be defined as a series of such stereotyped reactions to problems that the patient has never solved in the past and is still unable to solve in the present. In other words, a neurosis is the result of an interrupted learning process.

This concept of a neurosis has obvious implications for our understanding of psychotherapy. It is the task of the therapy to help the patient resume and complete the learning process which was interrupted when his neurosis began.

Reactions to therapy

Let us now apply these distinctions to the methods by which therapeutic effects are achieved, first considering that rational use of therapy which is motivated by the patient's desire for help.

Rational Utilization. Sometimes a patient's symptoms disappear soon after he comes into treatment in a way which we call a "transference cure" and which we attribute to the fact that the patient gains emotional release and reassurance from having someone to whom he can talk freely—without danger of arousing the condemnation or other disturbing emotional reactions he might call forth if he told the same things to someone else. In the strictest sense, this is not "transference" but a rational and adequate reaction to the therapeutic situation.

This patient may perhaps find even permanent relief from his symptoms by such a rational use of the therapist as someone to whom he can turn for emotional support. The relief the patient derives from thus unburdening himself of his difficulties may, after a time, make possible a better adjustment to his real life situation; then, when his real situation has been improved, he may find the emotional support he has been receiving from the therapist no longer necessary. When the patient is able, after a period of such help, to achieve a better adjustment in his real life situation, we must admit that he has found a solution for his problem without developing a transference neurosis, that his use of the therapeutic situation has remained on a rational basis from beginning to end. After all, it is one of the therapist's most elementary functions to help people by listening sympathetically and without condemnation, and the patient has merely made intelligent use of the therapist in this role.

Not infrequently, however, even in supportive therapy, such a rational use of the therapy is blocked by the development of a transference neurosis. Even in purely supportive therapy where no attempt is made to give the patient insight into the motivations for his actions, the patient is likely to have neurotic reaction patterns which will cause him to react to *all* people upon whom he is dependent for help with guilt or injured pride or both.

Resistance and Transference in Insight Therapy. In insight or "uncovering" therapy, it is important to understand the dynamic relationship between transference and resistance.

To illustrate this relationship we cite the case of an attractive young woman who spent the greater part of one analytic interview talking in glowing terms of a minister with whom she was closely associated in church work. She concluded by remarking that it sounded as though she were in love with the minister. The therapist quietly agreed that she must indeed be in love with him, and the rest of the hour was spent in friendly discussion of the problem created by the fact that the minister was married. Two days later this patient had a violent temper tantrum; when she was seen by the analyst (before her anger had subsided), she was quite unaware of the cause of her outburst.

To the therapist, however, it was evident that, although disguised, this was a natural, and indeed inevitable, reaction to the interpretation that had been made in the previous session. At that time the patient had been able to discuss her feelings for the minister because she had not yet fully sensed the conflict into which they must plunge her. She had thought of her feelings for the minister in terms of her pleasure in working with him professionally. Even after it occurred to her that she was talking as if she were in love with him, she did not take the idea very seriously. She was able to agree with the therapist that she must be in love with the minister because at the time she had no sense of the intensity of her feeling for him nor of the conflict and frustration in which these feelings involved her. Such an attachment to a married man was quite incompatible with her conscience, reinforced as it was by her religious training. Her love for the minister, therefore, faced her with frustration either of her forbidden love or of her devotion to her religious standards—both of which were very strong. Anyone who attempts to intervene in a quarrel between friends is likely to draw the anger of both upon him. Similarly, a therapist who attempts to make a patient aware of a conflict between two strong but incompatible wishes must inevitably stir up the resentment of both sides of the patient's conflict against himself. It was inevitable that this patient should react with anger to an interpretation that involved so much frustration for her.

In our psychotherapeutic thinking we often do not distinguish carefully enough between neurotic transference reactions and this kind of resistance to a disturbing interpretation. Frank opposition to an unwelcome interpretation may be a normal reaction in defense of the neurosis and irrational only in the sense that the neurosis itself is irrational. The patient's reaction in the case just cited differs from such a frank protest only in that, instead of being an open refusal of the proffered insight, it is unconsciously disguised as general ill-temper so that the patient is able to avoid full awareness of the conflict exposed by the new insight. A disturbing interpretation is a present reality, an attempt upon the part of the therapist to interfere with defenses necessary to the patient's peace of mind. When a patient reacts with anger to such an interpretation, therefore, his anger is not based upon a misunderstanding of the present situation as a repetition of a memory from the past. His anger is rather a direct reaction to the therapist as a real and present threat to the patient's peace of mind. Such a reaction is obviously a manifestation of the patient's resistance to treatment, but it cannot be looked upon as a manifestation of a transference neurosis.

The importance of this distinction must become clear as soon as we reflect upon the fact that, in insight therapy, the chief real contact between patient and therapist arises directly from the therapist's efforts to free the patient of his neurosis. Very often, however, not only does the patient wish (consciously) to be free of his neurosis, but he also clings (unconsciously) to his neurosis as a defense against conflicts which he is unwilling to face. As a result of this ambivalence toward his neurosis, the patient must inevitably develop a corresponding ambivalence toward the therapist who is trying to free him of his neurosis by making him aware of the underlying conflicts. In uncovering or insight therapy, the therapist becomes the representative or advocate of the repressed conflicts that he has interpreted to the patient, and very often also of emerging conflicts that the patient unconsciously expects the therapist to interpret. As a rule, in insight therapy this role of the therapist as representative and advocate of disturbing conflicts becomes for the patient the most important real aspect of the therapeutic situation.

Undisguised resistance reactions—frank protests against particular interpretations or against the therapist in his role as advocate of repressed tendencies—have a significance intermediate between that of a rational utilization of the therapy and that of a transference neurosis. They resemble reality adjusted behavior and differ from a transference neurosis in that they are reactions to an important real aspect of the therapeutic situation. They are irrational only in the sense that they are in defense of the patient's neurosis—which is by definition irrational.

One of the most frequent causes of a transference neurosis is the need to hide or cloak such frank resistance reactions. Frank resistance to an interpretation, or frank resentment of the therapist for having made it, is often tantamount to a confession that the interpretation has hit home; and if the therapist is quick to follow up such resistance reactions, he can usually utilize them very effectively to demonstrate the correctness of the original interpretation. The defense is much more efficacious, therefore, if the patient can distort his real resistance to the therapist's interpretation by substituting in its place a misinterpretation of the therapeutic situation as a repetition of some other situation from the patient's past.

As an example of such a regressive substitution of a neurotic transference pattern for a protest against the therapist in his real role as the author of an unwelcome interpretation, we cite the following incident. The therapist had interpreted a patient's conflict between his fear of the therapy and his shame at betraying his fear; to this the patient reacted with a dream in which a small boy urinated on him. In this dream the patient was protecting himself from a humiliating insight by reacting to the therapist's interpretation as being merely an insult. The symbolism by means of which the dream characterized this insult was based upon childhood fantasies of being urinated upon by the father, against which the patient's pride had reacted by substituting fantasies of being urinated upon by one of his younger brothers. Although this dream could have been interpreted as expressive of a homosexual wish toward the analyst (based upon a similar wish in his childhood toward the younger brother and toward the father), such an interpretation would have missed entirely the fantasy's real present significance—protest against the therapist's interpretation of the preceding day.

Thus upon careful analysis we find that the reactions of the patient toward the therapist fall into three categories: (1) a rational utilization of the therapy motivated by the patient's desire for help, (2) resistance reactions against the therapist in his role as advocate of the patient's disturbing conflicts, and (3) manifestations of the transference neurosis based upon a misinterpretation of the therapeutic situation as a repetition of some other situation from the patient's past.

Should the transference neurosis be avoided or utilized?

If we now attempt a more flexible approach to the problems of therapy, several questions suggest themselves. Is a transference neurosis inevitable? Or is it within the power of the therapist to determine to what extent the patient's neurosis shall become a transference neurosis? And—granting that the therapist can exert an influence—to what extent should he permit or encourage a transference neurosis and under what circumstances should he diminish the intensity of a transference neurosis that has already developed? We shall attempt to answer some of these questions here; other aspects are considered in Chapter 3 [of *Psychoanalytic Therapy*] under the heading "Manipulation of the Transference Relationship."

The Transference Neurosis in Supportive Therapy. In a therapy based upon emotional support, a transference neurosis is always a complication and has little positive value. If, for example, the patient reacts with guilt or shame to the therapist's efforts to help him, he may become completely unable to benefit further from a permissive and supportive attitude on the part of the therapist. In such a case, then, it may be necessary for the therapist to interpret (and thus help the patient to gain insight into) the motives of guilt and pride that underlie his transference neurosis in order that the patient may become capable of accepting further help.

Aichhorn has shown, however, that this kind of transference neurosis may be held back or very much diminished by decreasing the patient's sense of dependence on and obligation toward the therapist. Inducing such a patient to perform a service for the therapist, for instance, tends to relieve the patient's excessive guilt feelings and thus makes him more comfortable. Or better still, the therapist may use his influence to encourage healthy outside interests in the patient and thus lessen the patient's too intense absorption with his emotional relationship to the therapist.

Variations in the frequency of interviews may also be utilized to regulate the intensity of a patient's dependence upon a sympathetic therapist. Since the intensity of a patient's underlying dependence tends to increase with a greater frequency of interview, less frequent interviews will usually decrease the feelings of guilt and shame that may arise out of too intense dependent cravings.[1]

The Transference Neurosis in Insight Therapy. As we know, these irrational reactions that react to the present only as a repetition of the past can be a very perplexing and disturbing complication in the therapeutic process. It is, therefore, one of Freud's most important discoveries that these reactions, disturbing as they are, can also be turned to therapeutic account. As Freud once phrased it, one cannot overcome an enemy who is absent. By acting out his neurotic patterns in the analytic situation, the patient makes it possible for the therapist to observe them directly and to demonstrate to him their motivation.

Because of this double significance of the transference neurosis in insight therapy, it is evidently a matter of very great importance to inquire how to make maximum use of it to demonstrate to the patient the motives of his irrational reaction patterns while at the same time reducing to a minimum the complications that may result from it. We shall discuss first the principles involved in such an effort to make maximum use of the transference neurosis, and shall then apply these principles to some of the more important problems of therapeutic strategy.

The principles that should guide us in our efforts to regulate and utilize the transference neurosis are well known and relatively simple. A transference neurosis of moderate intensity can be very profitably utilized to bring the patient's neurotic reaction patterns out into the open where they can be observed. To the

---

[1] While the initial result of a reduction in the frequency of interview is to bring the patient's dependence into consciousness, once this first stage has been passed the patient's dependence may then be expected to decrease.

end that the patient may gain insight into the motives for his neurotic behavior, irrational impulses inside the therapeutic situation have certain advantages over their being carried out in real life, as the patient might otherwise be impelled to do. Not only can the patient's behavior in the analytic situation be more directly and more accurately observed but, what may seem even more important to the patient, many of the practical consequences of acting out disturbing impulses in real life may be avoided by giving voice to them within the therapeutic situation where the patient is expressly permitted to say anything and the therapist is trained to react to every utterance of the patient's with sympathetic, but otherwise dispassionate and scientific, interest and without praise or blame.

If the transference neurosis is allowed to exceed a certain optimum degree of intensity, however, its value for purposes of demonstration will be very greatly impaired. For purposes of therapy it is not enough to bring the patient's neurotic reaction patterns out into the open where the therapist can observe them. In insight therapy, the object of making the patient aware of his irrational impulses is to help the patient himself understand the motives for them, to help him become aware of the differences between the past situations which first gave rise to these impulses, and the present situation with which he is now confronted, so that he may modify his behavior accordingly. In order to help the patient to such an understanding, the therapist must appeal to the patient's good judgment. The therapist must work in cooperation with the patient's own ego. As soon as the patient's neurosis begins to affect his relation to the therapist, however, the patient's judgment will be impaired and this cooperation will become much more difficult.

The advantages of facilitating the transference of the patient's unsolved conflicts into the therapeutic situation must, therefore, be balanced against the danger of making impossible the cooperation between the therapist and the patient's ego that will be necessary if the patient is to be helped to an adequate understanding of his conflict. To this end it is important that the transference neurosis not be permitted to exceed a certain degree of intensity.

Importance of the Therapist's Attitude.   With these principles in mind, it will be of interest next to inquire what means the therapist has either to facilitate or to damp down the transference neurosis, and how he can best make use of these means to help the patient to an understanding of the motives of his behavior.

To induce a repetition of the patient's emerging neurotic mechanisms in the therapeutic situation is far from difficult. The most trivial accidents often provoke neurotic transference reactions of great intensity. For example, a young woman patient found on the couch a penny that had fallen out of the pocket of the patient who had preceded her and became so angry and reproachful that she could hardly be induced to speak to her analyst (a man) for several days. Later the therapist learned that when she was a child her mother had frequently sent her out to find the father when he failed to come home, and that the father —who was very promiscuous but to whom she was deeply attached—would often give her a penny for candy as a bribe not to disturb him when he was with another woman.

If the therapist knows what kind of problem is emerging into consciousness, he will find it simple to elicit such reactions deliberately. He may, for example, praise a patient for therapeutic progress in order to bring out a latent guilt feeling about receiving the father's approval. Or he may express approval of a friend of the patient's in order to bring out latent jealousy reactions.

Therapists of experience know, however, that such devices must be used with the greatest caution and circumspection, for the reaction evoked may be one of such intensity that it is difficult to control. What is even more important, if the therapist has, in fact, deliberately provoked such a reaction, it may later be much more difficult to convince the patient that his reaction is really a repetition of an earlier pattern and not a quite natural reaction to the therapist's behavior.

To be able to control transference reactions and promote reality testing is, in most cases, much more difficult. It is for the very purpose of better understanding transference reactions that in a standard psychoanalysis the analyst strives to keep his own personality out of the picture. He sits behind the patient where the patient cannot see him, and avoids either telling the patient about his own private affairs or having social contacts with him. He tries to create, as far as possible, a controlled laboratory situation in which the individual peculiarities of the analyst shall play as little role as possible in stimulating the patient's reactions. Human behavior is complex enough in any case. The patient will be sure to react to what he discerns of the analyst's personal motivations and it simplifies the analyst's task enormously if he can reduce his own behavior, as far as possible, to a standard and well controlled pattern.

Psychotherapeutic Situation. The effect upon the patient, however, is likely to be just the opposite. Let us consider the patient's psychological situation when he first comes to the therapist for treatment.

Let us assume that the patient knows he is ill, that he is consulting the therapist as a physician, wanting to be cured of his illness. He has consulted physicians before and has some experience of being treated for physical ailments. Beyond this experience his impressions are very vague. He has little understanding of the concept that neurotic symptoms are motivated, or he may have picked up some rather bizarre notions about it; and as to psychotherapy or psychoanalysis, he either knows little or nothing or he may think of a psychoanalyst as a kind of wonderworker who does, or claims to be able to, perform strange and incomprehensible feats of insight and therapy.

With this aura of mystery surrounding him the analyst, after one or two preliminary interviews, tries to behave in accordance with his professional ideal of suppressing his own personality as much as possible. He is supposed to listen sympathetically but not say very much and, after the first few sessions, he sits out of the patient's sight. He does not respond to what the patient says in the same way other people might be expected to respond. He neither praises nor blames. He encourages the patient to tell him everything and tries not to permit himself to become angry when he is insulted or to be pleased when the patient becomes fond of him. He answers questions only after he knows their motive. If he responds at all, it is with an interpretation of the patient's motives, with an interpretation that treats the patient's behavior not as something to be reacted to but as something to be studied with an unemotional technical interest.

It is easy for an analyst who has become accustomed to trying to live up to this ideal of impersonal behavior to underestimate the impression of unreality that it tends to make—especially upon an unsophisticated patient. (It is for this reason that in the psychotherapy of children and adolescents the therapist abandons this impersonal attitude for one of warm and sympathetic interest.) The impression of unreality that the standard technique fosters is beautifully caricatured by a dream one patient brought her analyst after she had been in analysis a long time. In the dream she pictured the analyst as in the hospital, in danger of dying from pneumonia; but when she visited him out of kindness of her heart, his only response was to reprove her for acting without analyzing the motives for her coming.

The effect of the aura of mystery resulting from the analyst's strangely impersonal behavior must evidently be to make reality testing more difficult for the patient. If the patient knows almost nothing about the analyst, it will be easier for him to become conscious of unreal fantasies about him. It is in the dark that one most often sees ghosts; a world in which the outlines of all objects are unclear is very easily peopled with figures out of one's own imagination. In other words, when the analyst sits where the patient cannot see his reactions and keeps the patient in the dark about what kind of person the analyst is, he makes it easier for the patient to develop a transference neurosis.

In a psychoanalysis, one of our most important aims is to make the patient aware of his unconscious irrational and ego-alien impulses. This process may often be facilitated by introducing the patient into a situation about which he knows almost nothing and by thus making the process of immediate reality testing more difficult for him. The advantages of facilitating a transference neurosis in this way, however, are short-lived. As we have already pointed out, in order to help the patient to an understanding of the motives of his irrational behavior, the therapist must appeal to the patient's good judgment and work in cooperation with the patient's own ego. By undermining the patient's capacity for reality testing, however, we make it much more difficult for the patient's ego to participate in the effort to gain insight. On this account it is desirable to damp down the patient's tendency to develop an unwieldy transference neurosis, and to facilitate the process of reality testing instead of making it more difficult.

To this end we must strive to make the therapy understandable to the patient, to rob the psychotherapeutic situation of its mystery. As we have already pointed out, many features of the psychotherapeutic procedure will seem strange to the unsophisticated patient. The therapist should therefore explain the reasons for any procedure that differs from what the patient might normally expect in such a situation.

In one very important respect, the psychotherapeutic situation is different from the ordinary relationship between doctor and patient. Ordinarily the patient expects the doctor to tell him what to do and, in return for doing as he is told, he expects the doctor to cure him. In psychotherapy the patient must be taught to play a more responsible role. In most cases it should be explained to the patient very early that he has two roles to play in the therapeutic situation: on the one hand it is the patient's thoughts, impulses, and behavior that are being studied, but on the other hand the patient must join with the therapist in trying to understand the motives for this behavior. Thus from the very beginning the therapist aims to take the patient into his confidence and to secure just as far as possible the cooperation of the patient's ego in the therapeutic task.

The Modern Attitude. To achieve this end, we must modify somewhat the above-described ideal of impersonal behavior on the part of the analyst. The therapist should not aim to be a blank screen upon which the patient is encouraged to project pictures out of his own imagination but, whenever possible, should endeavor rather to put the patient at his ease by behaving in the way the patient would normally expect from one to whom he has come for help and counsel. For instance, since the patient has come to the therapist hoping to be cured of a disturbing illness—or perhaps merely seeking advice and help in dealing with a disturbing problem in external adjustment—it will usually be quite in accordance with his expectations if he is asked to give an account of his problem and of the circumstances leading up to it. Then, as suggested in the chapter on planning psychotherapy, it will be well at first to accept the patient's own view of his problem. If he thinks he is suffering from an organic illness, we investigate this possibility objectively; if he feels that he is being unfairly treated on the job, we inquire sympathetically into the evidence for this belief.

In other words, we not only behave in such a way as to correspond to the patient's normal expectations, but we also tentatively treat the patient as a normal and rational human being and we continue to do so except when the patient himself proves the contrary. By so doing, we make it easier for him to behave toward us as a normal human being in the therapeutic situation and thus we lay the groundwork for the cooperation of the patient's ego in the task of understanding the motives for his less rational behavior.

When we assume this attitude, we also achieve even more effectively the aim of throwing irrational motivations into sharp relief, for just because we behave in a way the patient has a normal right to expect, and just because we proceed tentatively on the assumption that in his dealings with us he is a normal and rational human being, we thereby throw into sharper contrast any irrational tendencies that may develop in this relatively normal environment. We project the patient's behavior not against a blank screen but against a background of normal behavior, and the very fact that our behavior does not encourage the patient's irrational tendencies makes them all the more conspicuous when they do occur.

Advantages of emphasizing external reality

Considerations similar to those just discussed require that in the choice and timing of interpretations our guiding principles should be to keep the patient's as well as our own interest focused upon the patient's problem in adjusting to the present external reality.

At one time the real interest of psychoanalysts was concentrated chiefly upon reconstructing the patient's past history and, in particular, his infantile neurosis. After Freud pointed out the importance of repetition and working through in the therapeutic process, this interest in the past became focused upon helping the patient to work through his infantile neurosis in the transference relationship. We do not wish to minimize the importance of this interest in the infantile neurosis from the point of view of scientific investigation or for the therapist's orientation in planning the therapy, but we do wish to point out that when we make the working through of the infantile neurosis the center of therapeutic interest, it will in many cases have the effect of encouraging to a much greater extent than is necessary the tendency for the patient to misinterpret present situations as though they were identical with traumatic situations in the past.

In other words, by focusing interest on the infantile neurosis we tend to favor the compulsive repetition of memories from the past to the detriment of the reality testing function. Accordingly, insofar as it is our purpose to strengthen the reality testing function of the ego, our policy should be just the opposite: we should center the patient's attention rather upon his real present problems and should turn his attention to disturbing events in the past only for the purpose of throwing light upon the motives for irrational reactions in the present.

With this end in view, we should also try to keep the patient's attention focused upon his problems in the external world rather than upon his reactions to the therapist. We should, first of all, encourage the patient's rational cooperation in trying to understand his reactions to problems outside the therapeutic situation; then, when emotional reactions to the therapist occur, the therapist should pay close attention to the role of his own interpretations in provoking such reactions.

Problem Is Real.   The patient has come to us with a problem of adjustment to external reality that originated outside the therapeutic situation. In response to his request for help, we attempt to help him understand the conflicting motives that have prevented his finding a satisfactory solution for this problem. The patient's neurosis, however, has arisen as a defense against having to face insight into the nature of his conflicting motives. In spite of his desire for help, therefore, he will also resent the therapist's attempt to get him to face this disturbing insight. If the intensity of his conflict is not too great, he may be able to recognize frankly his resistance to the insight that the therapist has offered him; and he will then proceed, with the help of the therapist's emotional support, to struggle frankly with the conflict that the therapist's interpretation has reopened for him, until he has found a more reality adjusted and satisfactory solution for it. In such a case the reaction of the patient's ego to the therapist will remain, throughout his struggle with the reawakened conflict, a quite open and rational one.

If the interpretation is too disturbing, however, the patient may be unable to recognize his resentment of the interpretation frankly for what it is. As we have already pointed out, frank resistance to an interpretation is tantamount to a confession that the interpretation has hit home. Consequently, if the patient is quite unable to face what it is that he is resisting, he will attempt to rationalize his resistance by distorting his understanding of the nature of the relationship between himself and the therapist.

In searching for a basis for such a rationalization, the patient may unconsciously draw upon either one or both of two possible sources. The therapist must first consider the possibility that the rationalization may be true. Therapists, like patients, are very human and it may be that the patient is right when he says, for example, that the therapist was irritated or wished to depreciate him. In such a case we must admit that the patient's reaction is based in part upon reality and must wait for less ambiguous evidence that he is protesting against an unwelcome insight.

If the patient's resistance, however, is unable to find a fact in present reality upon which to base rationalizations, then he will be compelled to draw upon memories from the past upon which to base his misinterpretation of the therapeutic situation. To cite two very familiar examples, an interpretation of a sexual or of an aggressive impulse may be reacted to as a rebuke or as a threat of punishment from the father; or an interpretation of sexual impulses may be felt to be an attempt on the part of the therapist to seduce the patient as some father- or mother-figure once did.

In the handling of such a transference reaction, it is very important for the therapist to be alert to the fact that it has been precipitated by his recent interpretation and not allow himself unwittingly to be diverted from the task of helping the patient to gain insight into his present behavior. The therapist will, of course, be interested in the memories upon which the patient has based his misinterpretation of the therapeutic situation, but will also not lose sight of the ultimate goal—to make the patient aware of the differences between the memories he is re-living and the situation provoked by the therapist's interpretation.

It is important to analyze carefully the form taken by the patient's resistance to a particular interpretation. Such a reaction is a valuable indication both of the nature and of the intensity of his resistance to that interpretation. The mere fact, for instance, that the patient distorts his understanding of the therapeutic situation by misinterpreting it in terms of the past, must be regarded as a sign that the patient is not at the moment able to assimilate the disturbing interpretation by struggling openly either with the reactivated conflict or even with his resistance against the interpretation. It is usually better, therefore, for the therapist not to persist stubbornly in reiterating his original interpretation but rather to follow closely the patient's reactions to it.

An important interpretation is usually the beginning rather than the end of a chapter in the therapy. The experienced therapist does not expect the patient to accept an important interpretation immediately, and knows that even an apparent understanding and agreement on the part of the patient is not equivalent to a real assimilation of the proffered insight. The experienced therapist expects rather that the patient, by a careful day-by-day study of his own reactions to the interpretation, will gradually gain insight into its full import for him and will finally assimilate the interpretation completely by finding a better solution for the conflict reopened by it. One of the most frequent errors of an inexperienced therapist is to fail to follow up in this way the impression he has made upon the patient by an initial, well-chosen interpretation.

One Problem at a Time. As soon as the therapist centers his therapeutic interest not upon the past but upon the patient's present problems, another very important principle becomes almost self-evident. This is the principle that it is best to choose and time interpretations in such a way as to focus the patient's attention upon only one problem at a time. Until a patient has utilized the insight contained in one interpretation by finding a better solution for the conflict that has been reopened by it, it is better to keep his attention focused upon analyzing the resistance to it and not stir up quite new and unsolved problems. If this rule is not followed, the patient's resistance tends to take on much more complex forms, since the therapist becomes the representative or advocate of not one but a number of conflicts that the patient is unable to face and that may be very difficult to disentangle. On the other hand, by concentrating the patient's attention and resistance upon one problem at a time we tend to polarize his reactions about a single conflict and thus make them much easier for both therapist and patient to understand.

Ideally each therapeutic session should either help the patient toward a solution of a problem that has been stirred up in a previous session, or else leave the patient with a clearly defined problem to work upon until the next session. In a well-conducted therapy as much or more happens in the intervals between interviews as in the interviews themselves. The patient should feel that every session brings him some gain, and each session should provide the patient with enough momentum to carry him to the next step in the treatment. This next step is, so to speak, the next lesson for which the patient does "homework" in the interval between. Here, again, keen awareness of the trend of the patient's thoughts and feelings is required so that, not only can one time interpretations and the frequency of interviews carefully, one can also know on just what note to stop a particular interview. This is especially well illustrated by Case U, in which each session brings the patient to the very brink of the next bit of insight which the patient then discovers for himself.

Correct therapeutic orientation

The more attention is focused upon the patient's present problems, the more apparent becomes the value of Freud's concept of the therapy as a process of reeducation, a resumption of an interrupted learning process. This concept of psychotherapy should be the guiding principle of every therapist in his attempts to understand and direct the therapeutic process.

The patient's neurosis is an unsuccessful attempt to solve a problem in the present by means of behavior patterns that failed to solve it in the past. We are interested in the past as the source of these stereotyped behavior patterns, but our primary interest is in helping the patient find a solution for his present problem by correcting these unsuccessful patterns, by helping him to take account of the differences between present and past.

The great advantage of this kind of orientation toward our therapeutic problem lies in the fact that it centers our attention upon the dynamic potentialities of the patient's personality for healthy development, upon the forces that must be actually utilized in the therapeutic process rather than primarily upon the pathological mechanisms that are obstacles to the treatment.

Such an orientation is important because even the most disturbing symptoms are often manifestations of the very forces most essential for the therapeutic process. An outstanding example of this is to be found in the alcoholic, traditionally one of the most difficult of all cases in which to effect a permanent cure.

The aggressive protest of an alcoholic against his dependent cravings may take such disturbing forms that we are tempted to reject him as a hopeless case. If we overcome our irritation, however, and look for the rationale behind this disturbing behavior, we discover that this aggressive protest is only an excessive (but at the same time, a futile) manifestation of the very incentive that must be utilized in helping him learn to play a more independent role. At first he is so ashamed of his intense dependent cravings that he must use all his aggressive energy in attempts to deny them. If we can satisfy some of these dependent needs in the transference relationship and help him find satisfaction in his daily life (and thus diminish the intensity of his dependent cravings), he may become less ashamed of them and therefore able to accept some insight into the universality of the need for dependent gratification. When he no longer feels the necessity of denying his cravings, he will no longer have to overcompensate for them but will eventually turn his aggressive energies away from futile protest to constructive efforts at a more independent adjustment.

In making interpretations we often set up for ourselves the ideal neither to praise nor to condemn the motives that have activated the patient's behavior. We deceive ourselves, however, if we hope thereby to keep the patient from reading praise or blame into our interpretations. We are, of course, familiar with the tendency of a patient to attribute to the therapist attitudes similar to those of his parents and to that of his own conscience toward his unconscious impulses. But it is not only as a result of such transference mechanisms that the patient may get an impression as to how the therapist evaluates the motives he interprets.

If, for example, a young man has just formed an attachment for a young woman who in many ways resembles his mother, and if his therapist decides to call attention to this resemblance, it is by no means a matter of indifference just how he shall go about it. If he tells the patient that he is attracted to the young woman because she represents his mother, the implication will be that the patient should inhibit any sexual impulse toward the young woman as he would toward his mother. On the other hand, if the therapist waits until the patient has already begun to react with guilt to his sexual impulses toward the young woman and then points out to the patient that he feels guilty because he identifies the girl with the mother, the implication of this interpretation will tend to diminish the patient's guilt feelings because the patient will feel that the therapist is reminding him that the girl is really not his mother. It is evident, therefore, that it is a matter of great importance to the advancement of the therapeutic process in which way the therapist chooses to make this interpretation.

In order to decide correctly between the two alternatives, the therapist must first orient himself by forming some concept of the problem which the patient is at this time struggling to solve. It may be, for example, that the young woman resembles the mother not so much in her own personal characteristics as in the fact that the patient is attracted to her on account of his competitive urges toward another man. In such a case the problem with which the patient is struggling regards what to do with his competitive impulses and it will be necessary for the therapist to point out that the patient's competing for the young woman is leading him into the same kind of conflict that once resulted from competition with his father for the mother.

If, on the other hand, the young woman to whom the patient is attracted resembles the mother only in her physical features and personality traits and not in some way that would necessarily involve the patient in a repetition of his oedipal conflict, then the therapist must conclude that the patient's attraction to this girl is a step toward freeing himself from the mother by turning to another woman. If this conclusion is correct, then it must become immediately evident that telling the patient that this girl represents his mother will tend to inhibit his impulse to accept the girl as a substitute for the mother and will thus tend to keep the patient fixated upon his mother. The therapeutic indication in this case is just the opposite, to make the interpretation in such a way as to call attention to the fact that the girl is not the patient's mother and thus to facilitate the patient's attempts to solve his conflict by finding an innocent alternative to take the place of the forbidden sexual impulses.

Conclusion

The more we keep our attention focused upon the patient's immediate problem in life, the more clearly do we come to realize that the patient's neurosis is an unsuccessful attempt to solve a problem in the present by means of behavior patterns that failed to solve it in the past. We are interested in the past as the source of these stereotyped behavior patterns, but our primary interest is in helping the patient find a solution for his present problems by correcting these unsuccessful patterns, helping him take account of the differences between present and past, and giving him repeated opportunity for actual efforts at readjustment within the transference situation. Then, when the patient attempts to put his new attitudes into practice in outside life, he will find they have become second-nature. Thus does psychotherapy indeed become a process of emotional reeducation.

31

CLARA THOMPSON

Transference and Character Analysis*

What is the difference between transference and character resistance? Those who have lived through thirty odd years of the evolving concepts of psychoanalysis were slow to group the two concepts together. Transference was the older theory and compared
with the concept of character resistance seems relatively simple.
As Freud first formulated it and as it was accepted for many
years, transference was the phenomenon, invariably seen in every
analysis of the patient's reliving his infantile attitudes and emotions with the analyst. Freud's first simple formulation was that
the patient relived in analysis his feelings towards his parents at
the Oedipus period. These attitudes were seen as irrational in that
they did not make sense when applied to the relationship to the
physician. Moreover, they seemed to serve as an obstacle to the
progress of the analysis. When all was going smoothly, there
would suddenly have to be time out while the patient picked a
fight or engaged in some other emotional reaction to the analyst.
However, in the course of time, it became clear that this apparent
obstacle was a valuable source of insight. By reliving the emotions
of the past the meaning of these earlier experiences became clear.
All of this made sense and for many years there was little modification of the early theory, but around 1920, Freud made some
new revolutionary discoveries, one of which was the repetition
compulsion. With this discovery transference again came under
scrutiny as a theory and Freud concluded that transference was
a typical example of the repetition compulsion. In transference

* Reprinted by permission from *Samiksa*, Vol. 7, 1953, pp. 260-270.

were repeated automatically feelings and reactions of earlier periods even when these experiences were unpleasant. Thus Freud
saw people tend to get into the same kind of difficulties over and
over again throughout life often in spite of strenuous efforts to
prevent this from happening. For example, a man who has made
a failure of one marriage makes every effort in the next marriage
to choose a different kind of woman. But in spite of all precautions the same type of difficulty seems to appear again. As this
was first formulated, it looked as if this repetition compulsion was
some stupid trend in the organism to relive earlier states. In fact,
Freud saw it as derived from the death instinct. The driving force
of the death instinct was to return to an earlier state of being—in
the last analysis organic matter seeks to return to the inorganic
state. This phantasy of its origin, however, was not particularly
helpful in elucidating the dynamics of the repetition compulsion
—I say phantasy advisedly for, as far as I know, Freud never
stated this as a scientific thesis—he spoke of it as letting his imagination play with the idea.

The next important step was the working out of theories of the
ego. Prior to about 1925, there was little interest in the ego and
its activities. In fact, compared with the interest in the libido and
its activities, the ego and its importance in the dynamics of personality were but shadowy concepts. But after Freud's formulation of the pattern of the total personality with his description of
superego, ego and id, interest became focused for the first time
on the importance of the ego in the dynamics of living.

At about the same time as the development of this new interest, another innovation was taking place, partly, no doubt, as a
result of the new interest in the ego, but partly the new changes
were due to the dissatisfaction with the results of analysis as it
was practiced around 1920. At that time, analysts were faithfully leading the patient back to his past whenever he expressed
feelings about the analyst. Any statement made would elicit the
remark, "You must have felt this about your father," or some
other figure in childhood, thus, in fact, encouraging the patient to
turn away from his present feelings and recall more of the past.
Rank was the first to point out that in doing this the patient was
led away from the living present, the area of real feeling. As he

put it, it is always easier to talk about the past because it is not present. He and Ferenczi stressed, for the first time, that not every attitude towards the analyst is transferred from the past, that there is some reaction to the analyst in his own right and it is actually anxiety relieving and, therefore, stops the progress of analysis to point out to the patient you do not really feel this way about me but about your father, etc. Thus, if the patient finally gets the courage to tell the analyst he looks like a pig the whole issue may be conveniently buried by referring it to the past, saying that must be what you thought of your father. Two things may happen as a result—the analyst does not have to face the fact that he does look like a pig and the patient feels, "I got safely out of that one," but he does not feel more secure thereby, because he knows he really meant the analyst and not his father. From that day on, he is likely to assume that the analyst's feelings have to be protected. Realizing this, Rank and Ferenczi discovered the importance in the picture of the analyst in his own right. So, transference became more precisely defined as only the irrational attitudes felt and expressed towards the analyst. At this point, Rank and Ferenczi as well as Sullivan, were beginning to define the analytic situation as an interpersonal process although this was not explicitly so stated.

All of these discoveries contributed significantly to the working out of a method of character analysis, and work around this has come to be known as ego psychology. As I understand it, this term is used to describe the largely unconscious defensive activities of the ego in carrying out its function of making the individual acceptable to his environment. Freud defined the function of the ego as the task of reconciling the impulses of the id with the harsh demands of the superego, and also making the whole behavior acceptable to the outside world. The task of the ego, therefore, was to sufficiently alter id impulses through reaction formations against them or sublimations of them so that they become acceptable ways of behavior. This process was recognized as going on outside awareness and these reaction formations and sublimations were recognized as defenses against instinctual drives. Thus, it was concluded, the character of a person is formed. This character is a fairly stable structure not easily broken down and one of its functions is to keep the individual free from anxiety.

So we come to character analysis around 1925. To recapitulate the steps leading up to it—the new formulation of the concept of transference in terms of the repetition compulsion, the new interest in the ego and its dynamic function of reconciling the personality with its environment, the new awareness of the importance of the present situation in comparison with the recall of the past. The next step was the evolution of a method of character analysis and this was first described by Wilhelm Reich, while he was training candidates in the Vienna Institute between 1925 and 1930. (These lectures have been incorporated in his present book, *Character Analysis,* which, because it contains many of his later distorted ideas, has many defects, but the practical technical contributions of his earlier years make this still one of the few helpful books on the subject.) Since his work, many analysts have contributed to knowledge of character structure and techniques for analyzing it—Franz Alexander, Anna Freud, Sullivan and Fromm—to mention a few. Reich's method in oversimplified terms was first to point out to the patient that he defends himself, secondly, the way in which he does it, and only then is the patient ready to see what he defends himself against.

Among classical analysts, the analysis of character is even considered today as something qualitatively quite different and much more difficult to achieve than the analysis of transference. Thus, it is recognized that there are two general patterns of irrational feelings—one, the old transferred attitudes from childhood and, two, habitual attitudes developed in the course of a lifetime as ways of coping with life. It was thought that entirely different techniques must be used in coping with these. I wish to show that this idea—that one is dealing with two entirely different problems is a mistake, probably growing out of the different theories of their origins and functions.

Understanding of character structure has been approached in two different ways—the classical Freudian way and the interpersonal way best described by Sullivan and Fromm. In the classical Freudian thinking, character traits are seen fundamentally as defensive armor. They defend the ego from bombardment by unacceptable impulses because they incorporate the energy of those impulses in themselves in the form of sublimation and reaction formation. By thus making the impulses acceptable, they protect the ego from the disapproval of the superego and the outside world. If we use this theoretical orientation, the relation of character structure to transference is not obvious. The only things the two have in common is that they both act as resistances in analysis and at the same time offer a source of insight into what is going on in the patient. However, according to Freudian theory, the nature of their origins is different. Transference is an emotion or attitude transferred unaltered from some earlier situation whereas a character trait is in addition a transformed instinct.

However, if we try to understand character and transference in interpersonal terms it will be seen that both have similar origins as well as performing similar functions. According to Sullivan and Fromm, the child's personality is formed as a result of his interaction with the significant people of his childhood. As Sullivan describes it, out of the mass of his potentialities the child tends to develop those aspects of himself which meet with approval and to dissociate and deny as belonging to him those aspects of himself which meet with disapproval. So in time he develops a self dynamism which he thinks of as himself. In reality it is the product of the impact upon him of other people's evaluations. Since he lacks the knowledge and experience necessary to make his own evaluation, we can say then that his self is moulded around the selves of other people and their selves in turn have been similarly formed, and eventually his self dynamism will affect the lives of still other people and so on. This self to be sure is somewhat modifiable by later impacts but it is not changed with ease, for the unconscious assumption is that all people will react as the first significant people did—that is, they will approve and disapprove of the same traits. Therefore it is anxiety-producing to try to alter the self system. Thus rigid character traits are formed. If the parents were derogatory, a derogatory attitude is expected from others and the person himself assumes he is not much good. If the parents were overprotective, the person grows up assuming he is unable to care for himself and expecting others to think the same and care for him. Thus the oral personality—to use a Freudian term but explain its origin differently—develops in an environment of overprotection. One is given things, one can expect to receive, one need only be compliant and receptive and all things will come to you. This attitude is formed from actual early experience. Oral sadistic character, on the other hand, comes from an ungiving home. One has to become clever and manipulate the environment to get what one needs. The anal character as Fromm interprets it in interpersonal terms comes from a home in which nothing is given nor can something be obtained by manipulation. It is necessary to fend for oneself and because this is precarious and difficult, it is better to hoard whatever you do get because you may never get any more. Thus, according to Sullivan and Fromm, an anal character may be formed before the period of toilet training because it is not produced by a sublimation of anal impulses, but is a reaction pattern to a certain type of parent personality. This type of parent personality is often very stern and rigid in toilet training also—but long before this the parental attitudes have had their impact on the child. These are, of course, all extreme pictures and rarely are seen in pure culture. The same statement, i.e. the fact that they are never seen in pure culture, would hold true also of the Freudian categories as defined in Freudian terms.

Now how does this cultural interpersonal orientation account for transference? One can say the whole picture, both transference and character structure, is that of transferring attitudes from the past and applying them to present situations where they are often inappropriate. The question is why do we do this? The infant learns a way of reacting to the mother for example. The child assumes because he has no other experience at the time that she is the way people are. In other words, all life is like this.

Therefore he assumes it is well to act in all situations in a similar fashion. By doing this he often manages to make people react to him the way mother did. How does he bring that about? For example, supposing mother over-protected him. Suppose in addition he came to resent this because it interfered with his freedom. If he were free from ties to the past he would certainly break loose from this situation as soon as possible and establish his independence. Consciously this is what he wishes to do, but his character pattern is otherwise. The attitude of helplessness is deeply ingrained in his personality. He does not know how to do the simplest thing, e.g. a patient of 30 had never bought a shirt for himself and had never thought about how it is done. He seemed so helpless that the women who became attached to him just naturally took over the job. Why did they not rebel? Because his helplessness appealed to motherly types. Other types of women were not attracted to him. It suited their life pattern to cater to him. And so the original pattern was maintained. This, in interpersonal terms, is the way the repetition compulsion works. But the other part of the pattern also worked. For some reason not understood by him, this man would find himself over and over again becoming annoyed at the way all the women he knew seemed to want to care for him which he felt as a wish to dominate him. One affair after another ended in the same way without his becoming aware of his contribution to the picture. According to Sullivan's thinking, therefore, the repetition compulsion is not simply a compulsive reliving of the past, but a repeated recreating of similar situations so structured that the outcome is inevitably the same. To take a little more complicated example, a woman found herself 2 or 3 times getting involved with men married to unstable domineering women whom they could not leave because they feared what would happen to the wife. This woman came to the conclusion all men are cowed and browbeaten, but on each occasion she had to try to be different from the wife by being helpful, making no demands, not making the usual fuss about neglect, etc., and always secretly hoping she would save the man and he would love her for it. This proved to be the childhood pattern of her relation to her father. A secret love existed between them but her mother continued to dominate the father. The same was true of her lovers. She was the preferred one, but none of them was free to affirm his love. Once we would have said this is simple transference. This woman relives her Oedipus situation over and over again. But to call it a simple automatic reliving is to overlook its dynamics. What function does it serve in her present life? Is she simply frustrated and unhappy? The answer is "No." She has come to find some satisfaction in her secret love life. Somehow, she has created the situation she actually wants in her present life. For her the possibility of successful marriage would produce panic. It would threaten her character structure, in other words, her defense systems. She has structured her life around being the helpful different one. But in order to become this kind of person, she had to develop a certain detachment. She had to be a kind of therapist to the men she loved. This meant subordinating her own needs with a compensatory development of neurotic independence. What do I mean by neurotic independence? I mean close relatedness to another person has become anxiety provoking. Thus, instead of a simple transference of a situation from the past, we have a kind of character development, which is not resolved by simply recalling its origin. The patient has to work out all the subsequent defensive maneuvers she developed in the course of growing in order to protect herself from being hurt. These are her character structure, but they are developed on the basis of thinking all men are like her father, and so, unwittingly, she forces them all to act the same part, and assigns the same role to herself, not realizing her contribution.

The more actively destructive interpersonal patterns are formed in a similar way. A woman tells in tears of how her husband abuses her. Almost anything she does is a pretext for a fight. He calls her the vilest names and usually leaves threatening not to return. In other words, it looks as if he were a villain. This picture can only be understood in terms of reciprocal reactions. As a child, this type of behavior went on with the father. At the age of seven, she recalls being forcibly separated from a psychotic mother who was to be taken to a hospital. She blamed her father for this separation (and we must assume that previous behavior on his part made this seem a rational possibility or perhaps her mother's interpretation of his behavior). Throughout her childhood she and her father fought on every conceivable occasion. We can see that she was hating him, but she assumed the fights were because she was a bad and worthless child. The same pattern was repeated in her marriage. This only served to emphasize to her that she really was worthless and that her husband despised her. The whole thing suddenly became clear to her when the analyst had the occasion to observe the beginning of a fight with her husband. The two had come to the analyst's office together to discuss divorce. The analyst asked the husband, "Is it true there is nothing you admire about your wife?" The husband replied with sincerity, "I think she has been a good mother to our child." Suddenly, the woman, in a fury, said, "Is that all you want of me?"—and a first class fight was started. As a result of this encounter, the patient, for the first time, became aware of her contribution to the endless fights. She said, "I was a little aware as I said it that I wanted to hurt and test him. When he got mad back, I felt good. I thought this will show you what he does to me. When you pointed out what I had done to him, I was furious with you. I felt you had deserted me and he had won again."

These examples give some indication of the type of thing one looks for in analyzing character. I hope I have made clear the ways in which character patterns develop on the basis of early experience and perpetuate themselves. Character structure we might define as the defensive reactions developed around transference and strengthened by repeated life experiences. It can not be resolved by simply referring it back to the original situation, for subsequent life experience, including neurotic goals, have become involved in its structure. Therefore, as Reich expressed it, character traits must be analyzed by removing the subsequent layers one at a time, removing the most recent first, as you would remove the layers of an onion.

Thus far, I have tried to translate interpersonal concepts into Freudian language assuming you are better acquainted with this way of thinking. In closing, however, I would like to present Sullivan's concept of parataxic distortion in his own way of thinking because I feel his thinking makes the most sense on this subject. Sullivan coined the term parataxic distortion to include the two types of clinical pictures which Freud included under transference and character structure. He said an interpersonal relation may be said to exist between two or more people, all but one of whom may be illusory to a greater or lesser extent. In other words, a person, in relating to another person, may see and react to many things which are not there in reality. Thus, he may see in the other person hostility when it is his own projected hostility. He may see in the other person all kinds of positive attributes which his dependency needs require. He may assume, because his image of the perfect love object is a tall blond female, that the particular tall blond female whom he meets is the perfect mate irrespective of her other qualities, etc. Also, he may assume that all men in authority are like his father and proceed to act accordingly. All of this goes into an interpersonal relation, but all of these illusory attributes are parataxic distortions growing out of the person's previous life experiences. As you can see, some of these distortions may be due to a relatively simple transferring of attitudes towards earlier real figures. Some of the distortions are conjured up in response to neurotic needs, e.g. hostility, the perfect mate, etc., but all are reacted to by the patient as if they were realities in the present. Thus A assumes he is communicating with B, but, instead of seeing B clearly, he sees B with a cup full of C in him, or, if A is psychotic, he may actually see nothing but C when he communicates with B, or he sees B with some projected attitudes of himself, A, clinging to him. Of course, it is to be assumed that, in most human relations, B is doing the same thing with A. Assuming now that B is the analyst, it is the ideal goal of B, the one for which he submits himself to a long analysis, to do a minimum of distorting of A, so that he will be more free to observe A's distortions. So, in Sullivanian terms, therapy consists of the gradual clarifying for the patient the kind of things he is doing to and with other people, as a result of his distortion of them. Finally, this comes out most clearly in pointing out his distorted attitudes and behavior towards the analyst. But it is not enough simply to help him understand the history of the development of his distortions—he must, in addition, see clearly what function it serves in the present and how it is meeting his needs. Thus, for example, a man complains he has no friends. This has a history which one might say, in a way, explains it. In the course of treatment, it is presently apparent that he has contempt for most people who are his equals or superiors in one way or another. Anything making it necessary to acknowledge the even temporary success of another, produced depression. It soon became apparent that his contempt appeared most frequently in sarcastic belittling remarks which undoubtedly alienated people. Soon this appeared in the analysis—there were references to my not being very bright, and sexually most unattractive. He repeatedly had to tell me how I should have phrased some question or interpretative statement. Since he was a colleague of some experience, this was calculated to have a sting. The whole thing eventually became clear. Invariably, the attacks occurred when he felt in danger of liking me or admiring me. This positive feeling was a threat to his security for he dared not trust anyone. So, the patient who came with the complaint that he had no friends not only presently became aware of what he did to keep people away, but presently he discovered the motive for his behavior in his fear of positive feelings. He came to see that having a friend was potentially more disturbing than being lonely. Thus, one layer of the onion was removed and the next step would be to investigate the fear of intimacy. One must ask how did the patient picture me? How did he explain being afraid of me? One picture was that I was a sexually starved female looking for a good lay. Therefore any description of sexual success on his part must make me envious and, if I am envious, there may be reprisals. Another picture he had of me was I am a founder of a school and, therefore, am looking for converts. I will see in him a promising man, who will be a credit to me and will, in the end, enhance my prestige, so I won't let him live his own life. Both of these charges are, at least, theoretically within the realm of possibility and I must consider whether they have any validity, that is whether any behavior on my part contributes to these evaluations. But I must also keep my mind open to why these two things, even if true, could be threatening to him. Does he simply conjure them up hoping to make me angry and thus drive me away? This is certainly one factor with this man, but there are other possibilities. Does he, for example, secretly feel he is God's gift to women, and does he secretly hope he is my white haired boy whom I will adore if he helps me become famous? All of these and many more are considerations of significance in the interpersonal situation and can be explained without recourse to considering the sublimation of instincts.

Many have questioned whether Sullivan's concept of parataxic distortion may not be identical with the Freudian concept of transference and character structure. It certainly includes the same observable phenomena, but the theory of origin is different, and this I consider Sullivan's important contribution to psychoanalysis. He sees a personality always in its aspects of intercommunication with other personalities. The fact that this makes the origin of character structure similar to the origin of transference is but one example of the implications for a new theoretical approach.

32

MABEL BLAKE COHEN

Countertransference and Anxiety*

Transference has been defined by Freud [1] as the "re-impressions and reproductions of the emotions and phantasies . . . characterized by the replacement of a former person by the physician." This definition does not make explicit the concept that such attitudes must be irrational—that is, not appropriately held in relation to the person who is the analyst—though this is generally accepted. Countertransference can be roughly defined as the converse of transference: the repetition of previously acquired attitudes toward the patient, such attitudes being irrational in the given situation. Much time and attention has been given to the study of the transference attitudes of the patient in analysis, but until recent years comparatively very little to the study of countertransference, which had been assumed to be absent, except in situations where the analyst was incompletely analyzed. This assumption has gradually given way to the recognition that countertransference attitudes are present in all analytical situations, perhaps roughly proportionate to the degree of success of the therapist's analysis, but nonetheless present in all.[2]

In the belief that the study of the countertransference can provide useful material to the analysis, just as does the study

* Reprinted by permission of The William Alanson White Psychiatric Foundation, Inc., from Psychiatry, 1952, 15:231-243. Copyright, 1952, by The William Alanson White Psychiatric Foundation, Inc.

[1] See Freud's definition [taken from Bruchstück (Fragment), as translated by Ernest Jones] in Leland E. Hinsie and Jacob Shatzky, Psychiatric Dictionary (New York, Oxford University Press, 1940).

[2] Margaret Little, "Countertransference and the Patient's Response to It," Internat. J. Psychoanal. (1951) 32:32-40.

of the transference, this paper represents an attempt to continue the analysis and dynamic understanding of the phenomenon.

The analytic situation can be looked upon as an interaction between two people, therapist and patient. Using a mathematical analogy, we have an equation which contains two variables, patient and therapist. Each main variable is itself a complex term composed of many factors, known and unknown. But of the two variables, that representing the therapist is known to a much greater degree than that representing the patient. In solving the equation, if the therapist variable can become known, the equation can be solved and the value of the patient variable determined. Many of the therapist's attitudes and reactions to the patient are utilized on a nonverbal experiential level, of course, as the result of training. The more experienced and capable the therapist, the more use he makes of such material. Yet the lack of concrete description and study of this aspect of treatment tends to keep it obscure, to hamper its use in training, and to prevent further development of theory and technique pertaining to it. Far too often the young therapist enters into his first treatment experiences with the concept that he should not have "countertransference feelings" toward the patient, that entertaining such feelings is evidence that he is incompletely analyzed or technically incompetent. This leads to an attempt to suppress such attitudes where they are conscious and to a tendency to discourage a widening of awareness to include those which are less easily available because more anxiety-connected. The contrary point of view, that of welcoming as wide an awareness as possible of all one's responses to a patient, with the hope of understanding the sources of whatever anxiety or other complex feelings and impulses the patient may inspire in one, is far more conducive to the development of the needed skills as well as the needed objectivity and friendliness in the analyst.

But the point of greatest importance is that when the treatment is in a phase of difficulty, the analyst may often obtain valuable clues as to the nature of the obstacles in the way of the patient's favorable development by careful observation of the responses elicited in himself at such times. One may assume

that such responses elicited in the therapist by the patient's behavior are similar to (though not necessarily identical with)
those elicited from some important person in the patient's previous life. Of course, one also assumes that the responses elicited
in the therapist are similar to (though not necessarily identical
with) his responses to some person of importance in his own life.
And therefore, by recognizing some particular constellation of
feelings in his response to the patient, understanding their roots
and meaning in his own life, the therapist may extrapolate from
his own experience to make a guess as to what the patient's experience has been in the past and is currently in the therapeutic
relationship. These data, being available to both participants,
may be used to document and make more convincing an interpretation of the problem of the patient.

An operational definition

Some discussion of a working definition of the term countertransference is necessary, since it is by no means agreed upon
by analysts that is can be correctly considered the converse of
transference. D. W. Winnicott, for instance, has recently written
about the importance of attitudes of hate from analyst to patient,
particularly in dealing with psychotic and antisocial patients.
He speaks mainly of "objective countertransference," meaning
"the analyst's love and hate in reaction to the actual personality
and behavior of the patient based on objective observation." [3]
However, he also mentions countertransference feelings that are
under repression in the analyst and need more analysis. His
concept of "objective countertransference" would not be included
under the term countertransference if the latter is used as the
converse of transference. Frieda Fromm-Reichmann[4] separates
the responses of the psychoanalyst to the patient into those of
a private and those of a professional person and recognizes the
possibility of countertransference distortions occurring in both

[3] D. W. Winnicott, "Hate in the Counter-transference," *Internat. J.
Psychoanal.* (1949) 30:69-74; p. 70.

[4] Frieda Fromm-Reichmann, *Principles of Intensive Psychotherapy*; Chicago,
Univ. of Chicago Press, 1950.

aspects. Franz Alexander[5] has used the term to mean all of the attitudes of the doctor toward the patient, while Sandor Ferenczi[6] used it to cover the positive, affectionate, loving, or sexual attitudes of the doctor toward the patient. Michael Balint, looking at a somewhat different aspect, calls attention to the fact that every human relation is libidinous, not only the patient's relation to his analyst, but also the analyst's relation to the patient. He says that no human being can in the long run tolerate any relation which brings only frustration and that it is as true for the one as for the other. "The question is, therefore, . . . how much and what kind of satisfaction is needed by the patient on the one hand and by the analyst on the other, to keep the tension in the psycho-analytical situation at or near the optimal level." [7]

In developing his theory of interpersonal relations, Harry Stack Sullivan has defined the psychotherapeutic effort of the analyst as being carried on by the method of participant observation. He says, "The expertness of the psychiatrist refers to his skill in participant observation of the unfortunate patterns of his own and the patient's living, in contrast to merely participating in such unfortunate patterns with the patient." [8] In the use of the term "unfortunate patterns" Sullivan includes the concept of countertransference, or in his words "parataxic distortions."

In several important recent papers, Leo Berman, Paula Heiman, Annie Reich, Margaret Little, and Maxwell Gitelson have made a beginning in the attempt to clarify the concept and to formulate some dynamic principles regarding the phenomena included in this category. Berman[9] is mainly concerned with defining the optimal attitude of the analyst to the patient, an

---

[5] Franz Alexander, *Fundamentals of Psychoanalysis*; New York, Norton, 1948.

[6] Sandor Ferenczi, *Further Contributions to the Theory and Technique of Psycho-analysis*; London, Hogarth Press, 1950.

[7] Michael Balint, "Changing Therapeutic Aims and Techniques in Psychoanalysis," *Internat. J. Psychoanal.* (1950) 31:117-124; p. 122.

[8] Harry Stack Sullivan, "The Theory of Anxiety and the Nature of Psychotherapy," PSYCHIATRY (1949) 12:3-12; p. 12.

[9] Leo Berman, "Countertransference and Attitudes of the Analyst in the Therapeutic Process," PSYCHIATRY (1949) 12:159-166.

attitude which he characterizes as "dedicated." This description is based on the assumption that the analyst's emotional responses to the patient will be quantitatively less than those of the average person and of shorter duration, as the result of being quickly worked through by self-analysis. This, then, would represent an ideal goal of minimal and easily handled countertransference responses.

Heiman[10] takes a step forward when she states that the analyst's emotional responses to his patient within the analytic situation represent one of the most important tools for his work, and that the analyst's countertransference is an instrument of research into the patient's unconscious. This important formulation is, in my opinion, the basis upon which the study of the analyst's part of the interaction with the patient should be built. Previously, the statement has frequently been made that the analyst's unconscious understands the patient's unconscious. However, it is presumed that much hitherto unconscious material becomes available to awareness after a successful analysis, so that the understanding should theoretically not be only on an unconscious level but should be formulable in words.

Reich[11] has classified a number of countertransference attitudes of the analyst. She separates them into two main types: those where the analyst acts out some unconscious need with the patient, and those where the analyst defends against some unconscious need. On the whole, countertransference responses are reflections of permanent neurotic difficulties of the analyst, in which the patient is often not a real object but rather is used as a tool by means of which some need of the analyst is gratified. In some instances, there may be sudden, acute countertransference responses which do not necessarily arise from neurotic character difficulties of the analyst. However, Reich points out that the interest in becoming an analyst is itself partially determined by unconscious motivation, such as curiosity about other people's secrets, which is evidence that countertransference

[10] Paula Heiman, "On Counter-transference," *Internat. J. Psychoanal.* (1950) 31:81-84.

[11] Annie Reich, "On Counter-transference," *Internat. J. Psychoanal.* (1951) 32:25-31.

attitudes are a necessary prerequisite for analysts. The contrast between the healthy and neurotic analyst is that in the one the curiosity is desexualized and sublimated in character, while in the other it remains a method of acting out unconscious fantasies.

Margaret Little continues the search for an adequate definition of countertransference, concluding that it should be used primarily to refer to "repressed elements, hitherto unanalysed, in the analyst himself which attach to the patient in the same way as the patient transfers to the analyst affects, etc., belonging to his parents or to the objects of his childhood: i.e., the analyst regards the patient (temporarily and varyingly) as he regarded his own parents." However, in addition, Little thinks that other aspects of the analyst's attitudes toward the patient, such as some specific attitude or mechanism with which he meets the patient's transference, or some of his conscious attitudes, should be considered countertransference responses. She confirms Heiman's statement that the use of countertransference may become an extremely valuable tool in psychoanalysis, comparing it in importance to the advances made when transference interpretations began to be used therapeutically. She sees transference and countertransference as inseparable phenomena; both should become increasingly clear to both doctor and patient as the analysis progresses. To that end, she advocates judicious use of countertransference interpretations by the analyst. Both "are essential to psycho-analysis, and counter-transference is no more to be feared or avoided than is transference; in fact it *cannot* be avoided, it can only be looked out for, controlled to some extent, and perhaps used." [12]

Gitelson,[13] in a comprehensive paper, continues to clarify the phenomena under scrutiny. He goes back to the original definition of countertransference used by Freud—the analyst's reaction to the patient's transference—and separates this set of responses from another set which he refers to as the transference attitudes of the analyst. These transference attitudes, which are the result

---

[12] Reference footnote 2; p. 40.
[13] Maxwell Gitelson, "The Emotional Position of the Analyst in the Psychoanalytic Situation," *Internat. J. Psychoanal.* (1952) 33:1-10.

of "surviving neurotic transference potential" in the analyst, involve "total" reactions to the patient—that is, over-all feelings about and toward the patient—while the countertransference attitudes are "partial" reactions to the patient—that is, emergency defense reactions elicited when the analysis touches upon unresolved problems in the analyst.

This classification, while valid enough, does not seem to forward investigation to any great extent. For example, Gitelson feels in general that the existence of "total" or transference attitudes toward a patient is a contraindication for that analyst to work with that patient, whereas the partial responses are more amenable to working through via the processes of self-analysis. I am extremely skeptical whether it is possible for one to avoid "total" reactions to a patient—that is, general feelings of liking for, dislike of, and responsiveness toward the patient, and so on, are present from the time of the first interview. These do vary in intensity; when extreme, they may indicate that a nontherapeutic relationship would result should the two persons attempt working together. On the other hand, their presence in awareness may permit the successful scrutiny and resolution of whatever problem is involved, whereas their presence outside of awareness would render this impossible. In other words, it is not so much a question whether "total" responses are present or not, but rather a question as to their amenability to recognition and resolution. For this reason, some other type of classification would, in my opinion, be more useful for investigative purposes.

This comment by no means disputes the validity of Gitelson's criticism of the rationalization of much countertransference acting-out under the heading of "corrective emotional experience." He emphasizes that motherly or fatherly attitudes in the analyst are often character defenses unrecognized as such by him. Although the analyst, according to Gitelson, cannot deny his personality nor its operation in the analytic situation as a significant factor, this does not mean that his personality is the chief instrument of the therapy. He also reports the observation that when the analyst appears as himself in the patient's dreams, it is often the herald of the development of an unmanageably intense transference neurosis, the unmanageability being the difficulties of the analyst's situation. Similarly, when the patient appears as himself in the analyst's dreams, it is often a signal of unconscious countertransference processes going on.

In summary, then, we see that the recent studies on countertransference have included in their concepts attitudes of the therapist which are both conscious and unconscious; attitudes which are responses both to real and to fantasied attributes of the patient; attitudes which are stimulated by unconscious needs of the analyst and attitudes which are stimulated by sudden outbursts of affect on the part of the patient; attitudes which arise from responding to the patient as though he were some previously important person in the analyst's life; and attitudes which do not use the patient as a real object but rather as a tool for the gratification of some unconscious need. This group of responses covers a tremendously wide territory, yet it does not include, of course, all of the analyst's responses to the patient. On what common ground are the above attitudes singled out to be called countertransference?

It seems to this writer that the common factor in the above responses is the presence of anxiety in the therapist—whether recognized in awareness or defended against and kept out of awareness. The contrast between the dedicated attitude described as the ideal attitude of the analyst—or the analyst as an expert in problems of living, as Sullivan puts it—and the so-called countertransference responses, is the presence of anxiety, arising from a variety of different sources in the whole field of patient-therapist interrelationship.

If countertransference attitudes and behavior were to be thought of as determined by the presence of anxiety in the therapist, we might have an operational definition which would be more useful than the more descriptive one based on identifying patterns in the analyst which were derived from important past relationships. The definition would, of course, have to include situations both of felt discomfort and also those where the anxiety was out of awareness and replaced by a defensive operation. Such a viewpoint of countertransference would be useful in that it would include all situations where the analyst was unable to be useful to the patient because of difficulties with his own responses.

The definition might be precisely stated as follows: *When, in the patient-analyst relationship, anxiety is aroused in the analyst with the effect that communication between the two is interfered with by some alteration in the analyst's behavior (verbal or otherwise), then contertransference is present.*

The question might be asked, If countertransference were defined in this way, would the definition hold good for transference responses also? It would seem that on a very generalized level this might be so, but on the level of practical therapeutic understanding such a statement would not be enlightening. While it could safely be said of every patient that the appearance of his anxiety or defensive behavior in the treatment situation is due to an impairment of communication with the analyst which in turn is due to his attributing to the analyst some critical or otherwise disturbing attitude which in its turn was originally derived from his experience with his parents—still this would leave out of consideration the fact that the patient's whole life pattern and his relation to all of the important authority figures in it would show a similar stereotyped defensive response. So that, certainly in the early stages of treatment and to a lesser extent in later stages, the anxiety responses of the patient are for the most part generalized and stereotyped rather than particularized with special reference to his relationship with the analyst.

This, however, is not true of the analyst. Having been analyzed himself, most of such anxiety-laden responses as he has experienced with others have entered awareness and many of them have been worked through and abandoned in favor of more mature and integrated responses. What remain, then, are not such stereotyped or universal responses. To illustrate, all patients do not automatically represent sibling rivals, while it is possible that a particular, unusually competitive patient may still represent a younger sibling to an analyst who had some difficulties in his own life with being the elder child.

To speak of the same thing from another point of view, the analyst is not working on his problems in the analysis; he is working on the patient's. Therefore, while the patient brings his anxiety responses to the analysis as his primary concern, the fact that the analyst's problems are not under scrutiny permits him a greater degree of detachment and objectivity. This is, to be sure, only a relative truth, since the analyst at times and under certain circumstances is certainly bringing his problems into the relationship, and at times, at least in some analyses, the attention of both the patient and the analyst are directed to the analyst's problems. However, it is on the whole valid to describe the analytic situation as one designed to focus attention on the anxieties of the patient and to leave in the background the anxieties of the therapist, so that when these do appear they are of particular significance in terms of the relationship itself.

Classification of countertransference responses

Using the above definition, we can attempt to classify the situations in analysis when anxiety-tinged processes are operating in the analyst. The classification suggested below is not a clear-cut separation of such situations, since the groups shade off into one another. Nor are any of the responses to be thought of as entirely free of neurotic attitudes on the part of the therapist. Even in the most extreme examples of situational stress (where ordinarily the analyst's response is thought of as being an objective response to the stress rather than a neurotic response), personal, characterological factors will color his response, as will also the nature of his relationship with the patient. Take, for instance, the situation where the analyst comes to his office in a state of acute tension as the result of a quarrel with his wife. With one patient he may remain preoccupied with his personal troubles throughout the hour, while with another he may be able shortly to bring his attention to the analytic situation. Something in each patient's personality and method of production, and in the analyst's response to each, has affected the analyst's behavior.

Anxiety-arousing situations in the patient-analyst interaction have been classified as follows: (1) Situational factors—that is, reality factors such as intercurrent events in the analyst's life;

and also, social factors such as need for success and recognition as a competent therapist. (2) Unresolved neurotic problems of the therapist. (3) Communication of the patient's anxiety to the therapist.

Situational Factors. This group of responses is, of course, very much influenced by the character make-up of the doctor. How much need for conformity to convention he retains will influence his response to the patient who shouts loudly during an analytic hour. But the response will also be affected by the degree to which his office is soundproof, whether there is another patient in the waiting room, whether a colleague in an adjoining office can overhear, and so on. So that, even leaving out the private characterological aspect of the situation for the therapist, there remains a sizable set of reality needs which, if threatened, will lead to unanalytic behavior on his part.

The greatest number of these have to do with the physician's role in our culture. There is a high value attached to the role of successful physician. This is not, of course, confined to the vague group of people known as the public; it is also actively present in the professional colleagues. There is a reality need for recognition of his competence by his colleagues, which has a dollars and cents value as well as an emotional one. While it is true that his reputation will not be made or broken by one success or failure, it does not follow that a suicide or psychotic breakdown in a patient does not represent a reality threat to him. Consequently, he cannot be expected to handle such threatening crises with complete equanimity. In addition to such a reality need to be known as competent by his colleagues and the public, there is a potent and valid need on the doctor's part for creative accomplishment. This appears in the therapeutic situation as an expectation of and a need to see favorable change in the patient. It is entirely impossible for a therapist to participate in a treatment situation where the goal is improvement or cure without suffering frustration, disappointment, and at times anxiety when his efforts result in no apparent progress. Such situations are at times handled by therapists with the attitude, "Let him stew in his own juice until he sees that he will have to change," or by the belief that he, the doctor, must be making an error which he does not understand and should redouble his efforts. Frequently, the resolution of such a difficulty can be achieved by the realization on the part of the therapist that his reality fear of failure is keeping him from recognizing an important aspect of the patient's neurosis having to do with laying the responsibility for his welfare on another's shoulders. The reality fear of failure cannot be ignored but rather has to be put up with, so to speak, since an attempt on the part of the therapist to remove it by "making" the patient get well is bound to increase the chances of failure.

Further difficulties are introduced by the traditional cultural definition of the healer's role—that is, according to the Hippocratic oath. The physician-healer is expected to play a fatherly or even godlike role with his patient, in which he both sees through him—knows mysteriously what is wrong with his insides—and also takes responsibility for him. This magic-healer role has heavy reinforcement from many of the personal motivations of the analyst for becoming a physician and a psychotherapist. These range from needs to know other people's secrets, as mentioned by Reich, to needs to cure oneself vicariously by curing others, needs for magical power to cover up one's own feelings of weakness and inadequacy, needs to do better than one's own analyst. Unfortunately, some aspects of psychoanalytical training tend to reinforce the interpretation of the therapist as a magically powerful person. The admonition, for instance, to become a "mature character," while excellent advice, still carries with it a connotation of perfect adjustment and perhaps brings pressure to bear on the trainee not to recognize his immaturities or deficiencies. Even such precepts as to be a "mirror" or a "surgeon" or "dedicated" emphasize the analyst's moral power in relation to the patient and, still worse, institutionalize it as good technique. Since the patient, too, enters the analytic situation with an inevitable belief in the analyst's power, it is regrettably easy for both persons to participate in a mutually gratifying relationship which satisfies the patient's dependency and the doctor's need for power.

The main situations in the patient-doctor relationship which undermine the therapeutic role and therefore may result in anxiety in the therapist can be listed as follows: (a) When the doctor is helpless to affect the patient's neurosis. (b) When the doctor is treated consistently as an object of fear, hatred, criticism, or contempt. (c) When the patient calls on the doctor for advice or reassurance as evidence of his professional competence or interest in the patient. (d) When the patient attempts to establish a relationship of romantic love with the doctor. (e) When the patient calls on the doctor for other intimacy.

To illustrate, I would like to use an example in which the doctor's social role of taking responsibility for a sick person came into conflict with the patient's therapeutic needs.

A young woman in analysis following a schizophrenic episode, had periodically during several years of treatment become acutely disturbed as the result of recurring conflicts in her relationship with her mother. Her lifelong pattern, developed as early as five years of age, had been to get into trouble in such a way that she was actually injured and persecuted by others. The analyst was forced to play an active role in the patient's affairs at such critical times in order to prevent realistic catastrophes. One method of preventing self-injury was to make himself available to the patient by telephone whenever her tension was such that she felt unable to carry on. He also used advice-giving about how to handle specific situations to prevent her being kicked out of college and discharged from a job. At the beginning of treatment, this activity was, or seemed to be, necessary to prevent the patient's complete failure and hospitalization. However, though she improved and more and more of her psychotic character was modified by treatment, the recurrent crises persisted with undiminished intensity and it still seemed that the therapist must use the same means to prevent the same catastrophes. Eventually, the therapist decided, though with severe misgivings about the danger of psychosis and with considerable feeling that he was refusing to take a responsibility that he had agreed to in becoming the patient's doctor in the first place, to withdraw the supportive telephone conversations and the active advice-giving in times of crisis. The patient throve, promptly took over the management of the crises herself, and eventually went on to finish her analysis with satisfactory result.

In this example there is probably some neurotic involvement on the part of the therapist in that he was unable to discern the

point at which his patient became capable of handling her own
affairs and continued to think of a neurotic transference attitude
as still being an ego deficiency of psychotic severity. However,
the severity of the patient's illness and the correspondingly great
degree of real responsibility assumed by the doctor by virtue of
his taking the case acted as a second, more realistic, pressure
in preventing him from recognizing the time when she was ready
for more mature behavior.

Unresolved Neurotic Problems of the Therapist. This is
a subject on which it is very difficult to generalize since such
problems will be different in every therapist. To be sure, there
are large general categories into which most therapists can be
classified, and hence there are certain over-all attitudes which
may be held in common, as for instance the category of the
obsessional therapist who still retains remnants of a compulsive
need to be in control, or the masochistically overcompensated
therapist who compulsively makes reparation to the patient, as
described by Little.

One may scrutinize all analysts, from the top of the ladder to
the bottom, and, as is obvious, will find characteristic types of
patients chosen and characteristic courses of analytic treatment
in each case. Gitelson seems to underweight this factor when
he says that the analyst "cannot deny his personality nor its
operation in the analytic situation as a significant factor. . . .
This is far from saying, however, that his personality is the chief
instrument of the therapy which we call psycho-analysis. There
is a great difference between the selection and playing of a role
and the awareness of the fact that one has found one's self cast
for a part. It is of primary importance for the analyst to conduct
himself so that the analytic process proceeds on the basis of
what the patient brings to it." [14]

It is not the selection and playing of a role which creates the
countertransference problem of the average, relatively healthy
analyst, but the fact that one habitually and incessantly plays a
role which is determined by one's character structure, so that

---

≠ Reference rootnote 13; p. 5.

one is at times handicapped from seeing and dealing with the role in which one is cast by the patient.

A relatively simple example of transference-countertransference distortion in a treatment situation will be used to illustrate some of the problems. It was chosen largely because of its short duration and simplicity.

A patient arrives for his hour five minutes late. He reacts with feelings of guilt and the expectation of being criticized. On arrival, he notices a certain stiffness in the facial expression of the physician, which is a hangover from a telephone conversation the physician was having just before the patient's arrival. The patient, instead of inquiring whether the doctor is offended by his tardiness, immediately plunges into an explanation of why it happened. The physician (who is certainly not very alert at the moment) wonders why the patient is responding in such a guilty manner to such a small offense, but (being a person who likes to be thought of as kindly and who is therefore inclined to become anxious when treated as a tyrant) does not inquire but merely waits in silence for the patient to "get down to business." The lack of response convinces the patient that the physician is unmollified by his explanation. He thinks (but does not say) that he had better produce some pretty good free associations this hour to make up for his lateness. The hour goes on. The patient notices that he is dismissed two minutes early. (Up to this time, the analyst is unaware that the patient is so upset, and the part played by his facial expression in the sequence of events has also escaped his notice.)

On the way home the patient begins to think that the early stopping was a retaliation on the doctor's part for his lateness and resolves to come early next time. He comes five minutes early for his next appointment and the doctor is detained by his previous patient so that he is not ready to start until five minutes after the scheduled time. The patient now believes that the doctor's lateness—which is for the same amount of time as his own—is deliberate, to continue punishing him for his tardiness the previous hour. A very tangled emotional situation is the result. The patient has, he thinks, clear proof that the doctor is malicious toward him. The doctor has a patient who is blocking, anxious, and resentful, without the ghost of a notion why. Finally, at this point when the patient's blocking and anxiety have become acute, the analyst makes an inquiry and then hears the patient's account of what happened.

It is apparent that, in order to deal with the distortions introduced by the patient, the doctor needs to be aware of the following things: (a) that he has an unamiable expression on his face when the patient arrives five minutes late for the first hour, and (b) that he is annoyed (made anxious) by the patient's imputation of malice to him. If he were aware of (a), he would, perhaps, be in a position to interrupt the fearful apologies of the patient with a question as to why the patient thinks he is angry. If he were unaware of (a) or did not think it wise to interrupt, still if he were aware of his anxiety reaction (b), he would be in a position to recognize that his annoyance at being apologized to was leading to a somewhat sulky silence on his part. Once this were within awareness, the annoyance could be expected to lift and the therapeutic needs of the situation could then be handled on their own merits.

Communication of the Patient's Anxiety to the Therapist. This is a most interesting and somewhat mysterious phenomenon which is exhibited on occasion—and perhaps more frequently than we realize—by both analysts and patients. It seems to have some relationship to the process described as empathy. It is a well-known fact that certain types of persons are literally barometers for the tension-level of other persons with whom they are in contact. Apparently cues are picked up from small shifts in muscular tension as well as changes in voice tone. Tonal changes are more widely recognized to provide such cues, as evidenced by the common expression, "It wasn't what he said but the way he said it." But there are numbers of instances where the posture of a patient while walking into the consulting room gave the cue to the analyst that anxiety was present, even though there was no gross abnormality but merely a slight stiffness or jerkiness to be observed. A somewhat similar observation can be made in supervised analyses, where the supervisee communicates to the supervisor that he is in an anxiety-arousing situation with the patient, not by the material he relates, but by some appearance of increased tension in his manner of reporting.

It is a moot point whether anxiety responses of therapists in situations where the anxiety is "caught" from the patient can be considered to be entirely free of personal conflict on the part of the analyst. It would seem probable that habitual alertness to the tension-level of others, however desirable a trait in the analyst, must have had its origins in tension-laden atmospheres of the past, and hence must have specific personal meaning to the analyst.

The contagious aspects of the patient's anxiety have been most often mentioned in connection with the treatment of psychotics. In dealing with a patient whose defenses are those of violent counter-aggression, most analysts experience both fear and anxiety. The fear is on a relatively rational basis—the danger of actually suffering physical hurt. The anxiety derives from (a) retaliatory impulses toward the attacker, (b) wounded self-esteem that one's helpful intent is so misinterpreted by the patient, and (c) a sort of primitive envy of or identification with the uncontrolled venting of violent feelings. It has been found by experience in attempting to treat such patients that the therapist can function at a more effective level if he is encouraged to be aware of and handle consciously his irrational responses to the patient's violence.

A milder variant of this response can frequently be found in office practice. It can be noted that when affect of more than usual intensity enters the treatment situation the analyst tends to interrupt the patient. This interruption may take any one of a variety of forms, such as a relevant question, an interpretative remark, a reassuring remark, a change of subject. Whatever its content, it has the effect of diluting the intensity of feeling being expressed and/or shifting the trend of the associations. This, of course, is technically desirable in some instances, but when it occurs automatically, without awareness and therefore without consideration of whether it is desirable or not, its occurrence must be attributed to uneasiness in the analyst. Ruesch and Prestwood [15] have made an extended study of the phenomenon of communication of patients' anxiety to the therapist, in which they demonstrated that the communication is much more positively correlated with the tonal and expressive qualities of speech

---

[15] Jurgen Ruesch and A. Rodney Prestwood, "Anxiety," *Arch. Neurol. and Psychiat.* (1949) 62:1-24.

than with the verbal content. Such factors as rate of speech, frequency of use of personal pronouns, frequency of expressions of feeling, and so on, showed significant variations in the anxious patient as contrasted with either the relaxed or the angry patient. In this study, the subjective responses of a number of psychiatrists while listening to sections of recorded interviews varied significantly according to the emotional tone of the material. A relaxed interview elicited a relaxed response in the listening psychiatrists; the anxious interviews were responded to with a variety of subjective feelings, from being ill-at-ease to being disturbed or angry.

These uncomfortable responses, coupled with numerous types of avoidance behavior on the part of the analyst, such as those mentioned above, appear to occur much more frequently than has been hitherto realized. It is difficult to detect them except by an "ear witness," since the therapist himself will usually be unable to report them subsequent to an hour. They were noticed to occur frequently in a study of intensive psycho-therapy by experienced analysts which was carried out by means of recorded interviews.[16]

In this particular type of anxious response on the part of the analyst, the chances seem particularly good that careful self-observation will give the therapist more information about what is going on with the patient. This would be even more useful if further classification of these responses were made and the study of recorded interviews included in the training of analysts.

A young man with a severe character neurosis entered treatment and lost no time in convincing his therapist of the urgency of his need for it. However, his attitude was also that of a person who was about to depart. He gave the doctor to understand that he was highly skeptical of the value of treatment, that the concept of free association seemed like nonsense to him, and that his interest in keeping his appointments was of the slightest. His analyst found himself involved in trying to show the patient, by his work, what was the use and meaning of psychoanalysis. He felt on trial, and as

---

[16] Alexander Halperin, Edward M. Ohaneson, Otto A. Will, Mabel B. Cohen, and Robert A. Cohen, "A Personality Study of Successful Naval Officers," unpublished report to the Office of Naval Research.

though he would have to be careful not to make the patient too anxious lest he abandon his effort to help himself and discontinue treatment. The analyst also found himself offering the patient reassurance, against his better judgment. This pattern of the doctor's being on tenterhooks and the patient's being always on the point of withdrawal first made the analyst uncomfortable and discouraged, and then eventually came to his conscious notice. Thereupon, he was able to observe that the patient was in fact intensely attached to treatment and had no remote intention of withdrawing. However, the threat of withdrawal had been since childhood the patient's chief means of eliciting sympathy, concern, and attention from the significant adults in his life. This defense had worked equally well with the analyst until the analyst noticed his apprehension and insecurity with the patient. Following this, the defensive withdrawal proved to be analyzable.

In a similar way, it seems that the patient applies great pressure to the analyst in a variety of nonverbal ways to behave like the significant adults in the patient's earlier life. It is not merely a matter of the patient's seeing the analyst as like his father, but of his actually manipulating the relationship in such a way as to elicit the same kind of behavior from the analyst. Conscious use of one's observations of how one fits in with the patient's needs can therefore be a fruitful source of information about the patient's patterns of interaction.

Methods of Handling Countertransference Responses. Provided one accepts the hypothesis that even successfully analyzed therapists are still continually involved in countertransference attitudes toward their patients, the question arises: What can be done with such reactions in the therapeutic situation? Experience indicates that the less intense anxiety responses, where the discomfort is within awareness, can be quickly handled by an experienced and not too neurotic analyst. These are probably chiefly the situational or reality stimuli to anxiety. But where awareness is interfered with by the occurrence of a wide variety of defensive operations, is there anything to be done? Is the analyst capable of identifying such anxiety-laden attitudes in himself and proceeding to work them out? Certainly there are such extreme situations that the analyst unaided cannot handle them and must seek discussion with a colleague or further analytic help for himself. However, there is a wide intermediate ground where alertness to clues or signals that all is not well may be sufficient to start the analyst on a process of self-resolution of the difficulty.

The following is a tentative and necessarily incomplete list of situations which may provide a clue to the analyst that he is involved anxiously or defensively with the patient. It includes signals that I have found useful in my own work and in supervision, but it probably could be added to by others according to their particular experience.

(1) The analyst has an unreasoning dislike for the patient.

(2) The analyst cannot identify with the patient, who seems unreal or mechanical. When the patient reports that he is upset, the analyst feels no emotional response.

(3) The analyst becomes overemotional in regard to the patient's troubles.

(4) The analyst likes the patient excessively, feels that he is his best patient.

(5) The analyst dreads the hours with a particular patient or is uncomfortable during them.

(6) The analyst is preoccupied with the patient to an unusual degree in intervals between hours and may find himself fantasying questions or remarks to be made to the patient.

(7) The analyst finds it difficult to pay attention to the patient. He goes to sleep during hours, becomes very drowsy, or is preoccupied with personal affairs.

(8) The analyst is habitually late with a particular patient or shows other disturbance in the time arrangement, such as always running over the end of the hour.

(9) The analyst gets into arguments with the patient.

(10) The analyst becomes defensive with the patient or exhibits unusual vulnerability to the patient's criticism.

(11) The patient seems to consistently misunderstand the analyst's interpretations or never agrees with them. This is, of course, quite often correctly interpreted as resistance on the part of the patient, but it may also be the result of a countertransference distortion on the part of the analyst such that his interpretations actually are wrong.

(12) The analyst tries to elicit affect from the patient—for instance, by provocative or dramatic statements.

(13) The analyst is overconcerned about the confidentiality of his work with the patient (Fromm-Reichmann, personal communication).

(14) The analyst is angrily sympathetic with the patient regarding his mistreatment by some authority figure (Fromm-Reichmann, personal communication).

(15) The analyst feels impelled to do something active (Gitelson).

(16) The analyst appears in the patient's dreams as himself, or the patient appears in the analyst's dreams (Gitelson).

In discussing this list, I would like to recapitulate briefly some of the points mentioned earlier in the paper. It becomes apparent that in order to broaden the scope of psychoanalytic therapy, to expedite and make more efficient the analytic process, and to increase our knowledge of the dynamics of interaction, ways and means of studying the transference-countertransference aspects of treatment need to be developed. It is my opinion that this can best be accomplished by setting up the hypothesis that countertransference phenomena are present in every analysis. This is in agreement with the position of Heiman and Little. These phenomena are probably frequently either ignored or repressed, partly because of a lack of knowledge of what to do with them, partly because analysts are accustomed to deal with them in various nonverbal ways, and partly because they are sufficiently provocative of anxiety in the therapist to produce one or another kind of defense reaction. However, since the successfully analyzed psychotherapist has tools at his command for recognizing and resolving defensive behavior via the development of greater insight, the necessity for suppressing or repressing countertransference responses is not urgent. Where the analyst deliberately searches for recognition and understanding of his own difficulties in the interrelationship, his first observation is likely to be that he has an attitude similar to one of those mentioned in the above list. With this as a signal, he may then, by further noticing in the analytic situation what particular aspects of the patient's behavior stimulate such responses in him, eventually find a way of bringing such behavior out into the open for scrutiny, communication, and eventual resolution. For instance, sleepiness in the analyst is very frequently an unconscious expression of resentment at the emotional barrenness of the patient's communication, perhaps springing from a feeling of helplessness on the part of the analyst. When the analyst recognizes that he is sleepy as a retaliation for his patient's uncommunicativeness, and that he is making this response because, up to now, he has been unable to find a more effective way of handling it, the precipitating factor—the uncommunicativeness—can be investigated as a problem.

In addition to this use of his responses as a clue to the meaning of the behavior of the patient, the analyst is also constantly in need of using his observations of himself as a means of further resolution of his own difficulties. For instance, an analyst who had doubts of his intellectual ability habitually overvalued and competed with his more intelligent patients. This would become particularly accentuated when he was trying to treat patients who themselves used intellectual achievement as protection against fears of being overpowered. Thus the analyst, as the result of his overestimation of such a patient's capacity, would fail to make ordinary garden-variety interpretations, believing that these must be obvious to such a bright person. Instead, he would exert himself to point out the subtler manifestations of the patient's neurosis, with the result that there would be much interesting talk but little change in the patients.

This type of error can go unnoticed while the analyst learns eventually that he is unable to treat successfully certain types of patients. However, it can also be slowly and gradually rectified as the result of further experience. In such a case, the analyst is learning on a nonverbal level. However, if some such signal as finding himself fantasying questions or remarks to put to the patient in the next hour is noted by the analyst, he then has the means of expediting and bringing into full awareness the self-scrutiny which can lead to resolution.

It will be noted that the focus of attention of these remarks is on the analyst's own self-scrutiny, both of his responses to the patient's behavior and of his defensive attitudes and actions. Much has been said by others (Heiman, Little, Gitelson) regarding the pros and cons of introducing discussion of countertransference material into the analytic situation itself. That, however, is a question which, in my opinion, it is not possible to answer in the present state of our knowledge. Rather, it is my intent here to discuss the possible ways and means of improving the analyst's awareness of his own participation in the patient-analyst interaction and of improving his ability to clearly formulate this to himself (or to an observer). It would seem more feasible to devise techniques for utilizing such material in the therapeutic situation after the area has been more precisely explored and studied—or, rather, concurrently with further study and exploration.

One further point might be added regarding the contrast between the subjective experience of the analyst when anxiety is not present and when it is. When anxiety is not present, he may experience a feeling of being at ease, of accomplishing something, of grasping what the patient is trying to communicate. Certainly in periods when progress is being made, something of the same feeling is shared by the patient, even though he may at the same time be working through troubled areas. Perhaps the loss of the feeling that communication is going on is the most commonly used signal which starts the analyst on a search for what is going wrong.

Conclusions

The study of countertransference responses provides a rich field for the further investigation of the doctor-patient relationship in psychoanalysis and intensive psychotherapy. This is made more feasible by the possibility of using recordings of interviews both as research tools and as training adjuncts. As the therapist increases his awareness of the nature of his participation with the patient—both on the basis of his own emotional needs and on the basis of the roles cast for him by the patient—his therapeutic management of the interaction can become more precise and the range of neurotic problems which he is able to tackle can be expected to increase.

The Psychoanalytic Process

The psychoanalytic process, what actually occurs in therapy, has been sparsely described in the literature. The paper by Maslow and Mittelmann is a coherent account of an analytic process. It needs to be noted, however, that no one account can be taken as a prototype, since each psychoanalysis will necessarily be different depending on the nature of the patient and on the theoretical orientation and the personal style of the analyst.

It is a challenging fact that successful therapeutic work is done by analysts using various theories. This suggests that there are factors involved which have little or nothing to do with the theoretical persuasion of the analyst. It is necessary therefore to determine which of the many operations of the analyst are truly therapeutic. An attempt to simplify and put into operational terms the processes that occur in the analytic situation is made in Rado's paper. Operational formulations of the kind proposed by Rado offer a means for retesting some of the basic propositions of psychoanalysis.

33

A. H. MASLOW AND
BELA MITTELMANN

Psychoanalytic Therapy*

Method of Procedure

The most common practice is that the patient comes five times a week on consecutive days, that he lies on the couch, and that the analyst sits at the head of the couch outside the patient's range of vision. However, the procedure has become more elastic in the last fifteen years, and the patient may come three or four times a week and may have the choice of sitting across the desk from the analyst or lying down. Some investigators maintain that with some patients equally significant material and equal therapeutic results can be obtained by spacing the interviews once a week or even less frequently (Alexander, Hahn-Kende).

The patient is instructed to tell the analyst everything that enters his mind, regardless of whether it is embarrassing or foolish, or whether it refers to his attitudes toward the analyst. These thoughts usually include events of the previous day, his complaints, his reactions, and his dreams. The analyst then interprets to the patient the meanings of and the reasons for his reaction patterns. The patient, as a rule, does most of the talking, in a spontaneous manner, during the hour. Continuity and general uniformity of procedure are important. At the same time, the setup is elastic; the analyst may, for various reasons, bring certain topics to the fore and vary different aspects of the procedure.

* Reprinted by permission from *Principles of Abnormal Psychology*, by A. H. Maslow and Bela Mittelmann. Copyright, 1941, 1951, by Harper & Brothers.

Significance of frequent interviews and of the procedure

There are important reasons for the above procedure. Only if the patient is seen frequently can the analyst obtain all the data necessary for interpretations and convey them to the patient safely and effectively. The connection between the events of the preceding day and his responses to them are still fresh in the patient's mind, and he can tell them to the analyst without difficulty. Furthermore, events can be disturbing to the patient, and he is likely to suffer if the analyst does not see him within a day or two to interpret his reactions. The problem of the frequency of visits mentioned previously is an individual one. With the majority of patients, during most of the treatment, there may be no significant difference in the information obtained and the therapeutic effect accomplished between five, four, and three visits a week. With some patients, or at some periods of any treatment, raising the number of visits from three to four may make the difference between the treatment being stalled and moving ahead constructively. Frequent visits are indispensable with (1) patients showing intense emotional reactions, particularly anxiety, with which they cannot cope without seeing the analyst daily, and (2) patients who are inclined to be detached and also have involved ways of displacement and substitution. On the other hand, daily visits become somewhat burdensome for patients who move at a somewhat slow pace, adequate for three or four hours per week but not quite for five. Any of these situations may arise at periods in the course of the analysis.

The patient lies on a couch because he can relax more completely and "let his mind go" with greater ease. Moreover, this posture may assume changing emotional implications for him at various periods of the analysis—e.g., helplessness, submission, dependence, humiliation. On the other hand, sitting up is of distinct advantage with very anxious patients who need the closeness of supportive contact represented by seeing the analyst or for whom the submissive-dependent implication of lying on the couch, together with the defenselessness, is too great a threat. Still other patients are so much inclined to go off into fantasy without the reality-testing implied by seeing the analyst as a real person that their anxiety mounts or they maintain their aloof detachment and use the analysis without ever carrying the insights of the analysis into practice. Still other patients present a combination of anxiety, depression, detachment, and inhibition; these patients give inadequate verbal material, and the revelations from changes in their facial expressions become indispensable for the analyst. Again, all the situations mentioned may arise at certain periods in the course of the analysis (Fenichel, Mittelmann). The fact that the analyst is out of sight enables the patient to talk more easily about embarrassing and humiliating thoughts and feelings.

The frequency of interpretation varies considerably in practice. Some analysts prefer not to make any comment for weeks or even months; if the patient is silent, the analyst waits until the patient takes the initiative of talking, even if this means silence during most of the hour. Other analysts make interpretative comments during most, even the first few, hours—as soon as something is clear to the analyst and, in his judgment, can be gotten across to the patient; in case of prolonged silences, they ask the patient questions to enable him to go on with the work. For many patients, these differences in the relative activity of the analysts do not matter greatly. Other patients apparently can hardly progress with their problems without active stimulus, of the type mentioned, on the part of the analyst.

Role of free association

"Letting one's mind go" is usually referred to as "free association." This is a different "set" from that which the patient has when he applies himself to a given task deliberately. The feelings and thoughts that arise during free association are determined, just as thoughts and activities are determined when the individual is bent on accomplishing a task with conscious effort. The mood of free association is similar to that of daydreaming. It is mostly the patient's wishes, needs, hopes, fears, and angers that guide the flow of thoughts and feelings.

In analysis there are certain determining factors: the patient comes to the analyst for help, but he has definite expectations as to how the help is to be extended. He has definite reactions both to everything the analyst says and to events in his daily life while he is relating them to the analyst. Because many of these thoughts and impulses are such that the patient is ashamed of them or afraid of their consequences, he would exclude them, shut them out of awareness, if he chose topics for conversation as deliberately as he would set about solving a mathematical problem. . . .

Role of dreams

Dreams are psychological products which represent a person's reactions to his daily experiences. They express psychological forces, the nature of which can be clearly determined with adequate methods of investigation. As we shall see, the dream is a source of significant information in the analysis; Freud called it "the royal road to the unconscious."

Dreams can be interpreted; that is, an analyst can state both the response they represent and the underlying event that caused them. In analyzing dreams, the analyst follows the patient's associations or asks him to tell what comes to his mind in connection with the dream. He follows this same procedure with each element of the dream. Adequate interpretation is possible only if the analyst knows the patient well, the circumstances under which the dream occurred, the events preceding it, and the patient's immediate reactions to them.

The psychological forces expressed in dreams are mostly emotional and often irrational. Frequently they are of a forbidden character; that is, in them are embodied the impulses—hostile and sexual impulses, attitudes of dependence, feelings of humiliation, fear, and guilt—for which a person fears punishment and about which he feels guilty. Even when an individual succeeds in maintaining a smooth front and convincing himself that his behavior is serene and sensible, his dreams may furnish information which reveals difficulties. Thus a man who feels perfectly calm during the day may tell the analyst that he feels well and is adequately adjusted, but he may have nightmares which indicate disturbances.

Dreams frequently represent an attitude or idea graphically and often embody the phenomenon of so-called condensation. For example, one patient who was afraid to discuss a certain topic dreamed that he was standing panic-stricken at the edge of a precipice. Near him was a person in whom were combined the features of the analyst, of a former employer who had been extremely harsh, and of a very severe teacher who by failing him in high school had caused him one of the unhappiest incidents in his life. Thus in this patient's reaction to the current analytic situation was condensed the memory of two previous experiences.

Some interesting experiments have been done on symbolization in dreams. Schrotter hypnotized a woman and discussed a homosexual incident with her. After she was awakened, she remembered dreaming that she had seen a woman carrying a traveling bag which was labeled "For women only." Betlheim and Hartmann told stories with a sexual content to patients suffering from Korsakoff syndrome (memory disturbance with confabulation). When asked to repeat the stories, the patients gave a distorted version; for example, instead of the sexual event, people jumped up and down a stairway. Similar symbolizations occur in dreams. Displacement is also frequent.

Not all dreams are analyzable; that is, the analyst is sometimes unable to construct a sound interpretation when the situation is so involved that the patient finds it difficult or is unconsciously reluctant to reveal some of his attitudes. Whether everyone dreams every night is, of course, impossible to answer because of the lack of adequate proof, although recent work with electroencephalograms gives some indication that at least some periods of sleep are dreamless. Unquestionably, however, a person may dream and not remember it. This is shown in the instances in which a sleeping individual says something which someone else hears. Often these remarks are analyzable and can be interpreted like the dream. An analyst's patient was once heard by his wife to say in his sleep, "That's nonsense. I know as much as you do." This man's attitude toward the analyst was at the time characterized by rivalry and an attempt to show that his knowledge was as great as the analyst's.

The duration of the average dream cannot be stated with certainty. Both accidental and experimental observations show, however, that, on the basis of the dreamer's recollections after he wakes, an amazing amount can happen and an exceedingly long period of time can be covered in an extremely short time from the observer's point of view. Maury's experience is a famous example. Once, while he was ill in bed, a piece of board fell and hit him on the back of his neck as he slept. His mother, who was sitting beside him, noticed that he woke immediately. As he waked up, he remembered a long dream in which he was captured in the French Revolution, brought before the tribunal, sentenced to be guillotined, and then guillotined.

Data Obtained by the Psychoanalytic Method

Certain data can be obtained through psychoanalysis that as yet cannot be obtained in full by any other method of investigation.

Conscious and unconscious types of data

Obviously, the analyst can obtain information from the patient only if the latter tells him something or behaves in a certain way. Under other circumstances he may surmise, on the basis of his general knowledge and previous experience, that certain types of information will be forthcoming from the patient even when it is not yet available and the evidence for it is not yet obvious. Such information, however, becomes definite data only after the patient can talk about it or show it in his behavior. It is clear from this that the patient has various degrees of consciousness concerning the information that he eventually imparts in the course of the analytic treatment. Sometimes, because of shame or guilt, the patient withholds information from the analyst, although he knows it is important and that he should speak about it. Several weeks or months may pass before he imparts the information.

At times the patient knows that it is important to tell of the events of the previous day, his reactions to them, and his dreams, but does not because he feels that he ought to have a full understanding of and insight into all of his reactions before he speaks about them to the analyst. In such instances the patient's feeling of worthlessness and his extreme need to establish his worth in his own eyes and in those of the analyst bar the way to his imparting significant information.

At other times the patient reveals something in his behavior but cannot account for it; even when the analyst interprets it, the patient is not at first aware of his motivations.

In still other instances the patient knows about an event that occurred the previous day, but does not speak about it at first, although he does talk about symptoms that are closely connected with it. Later in the hour, or often on direct questioning by the analyst, he relates it, and the significance of the event then becomes manifest. In such instances the patient does not impart the information because, for emotional reasons, he does not recognize the connection between his complaints and the event.

The last two situations—namely, when the patient imparts some information but cannot account for it, and when he does not mention pertinent happenings or mentions them but does not see the interrelation between them and his reactions—are common in analysis. There is still another situation which is usual and very significant: the patient agrees to "tell everything" to the analyst, but he cannot, simply because he is entirely unaware of some impulses which have a very important role in his difficulties.

The conscious and unconscious data obtained by psychoanalysis can be classified as follows:

Need for Dependence and Complete Care. There are extreme cases in which patients will want the analyst to be with them twenty-four hours a day, instruct them on how to behave, and handle by direct action every situation in business or at home.

Hostile Impulses Directed Toward Others. These include reactions of anger, rivalry, and the desire to injure, humiliate, destroy, or triumph over others to the point of deriving pleasure from cruelty.

Destructive Impulses Directed Toward Oneself. These include the impulse to injure and humiliate oneself, the attitude of self-contempt, the desire to submit, to be exploited, and to be physically injured by another.

A schoolteacher undertook analytic treatment because of dissatisfaction with his love life. He was always calm; his philosophy was one of "serenity and nonparticipation" in all significant life situations. He had dreams in which he humbly scrubbed the bathroom floor of a famous educator, but he was unaware in his daily life of the self-humiliating attitude represented by this type of dream.

Ambition, Desire for Accomplishment, Pride

This same teacher never admitted any ambition to advance himself in his work. He changed positions several times, but only, as he put it, "to be able to work less for more pay." Considerable analytic work was necessary to make him realize that his apparent lack of ambition was due to his feeling of helplessness and his unconscious fear of dismal failure if he ever strove for success. To escape the conflict between ambition and fear of failure, he adopted an exaggerated attitude of "serenity and nonparticipation."

Desire for Closeness, Affection, Love, and Warmth

This same man never allowed himself to become fully attached to anyone. He was married, but he said that he had chosen a woman who was self-supporting and would therefore not be dependent upon him. He opposed her desire to have a child because this would tie him to her. After the tenth month of analysis his emotional condition was characterized by a vague fear and general discomfort. This occurred after situations in which he felt comfortable, congenial, and emotionally close to someone. He soon realized that his feeling of fear resulted from his desire for closeness. In other words, he did not lack the desire for closeness and affection; he was really afraid of them. Of the several reasons for his fear, only one will be mentioned here. His desire was so exaggerated that if he yielded to it, he feared there would be no bounds to what he would do. He would kiss people on the street, would even submit to them sexually. He would be subject to utter humiliation and would be effaced as an individual. Rather than this, he chose (unconsciously) to be emotionally detached, serene, and nonparticipating.

Attitudes of Superiority; Self-Aggrandizing Trends. The patient who shows these trends not only wants to be respected and esteemed; he often has the need to consider himself superior to other individuals in some attribute.

A thirty-year-old man was unusually talented in music, art, and science; but he never followed through any pursuit, partly because he felt that any accomplishment, even becoming a famous concert artist, would not do justice to his potentialities. Both his self-disparaging and his self-aggrandizing trends manifested themselves strikingly in the analysis. He felt that the analyst was superior to him in every respect; but unless he could consider himself superior in some way, he would not be able to go on with the analysis. In his desperate need for help he finally hit on a solution: He was able to feel superior to the analyst because he (the patient) could trace his ancestry back six generations, whereas the analyst could not. This solution, however, was charged with serious conflict for him. Not until four months after he became conscious of this attitude did he tell the analyst about it because he was afraid that the analyst would discharge him—and this in spite of the fact that he knew very well that in analysis one talks about everything that comes to mind.

Oral, Genital, and Excretory Impulses and Fantasies. Various bodily functions constitute a natural and indispensable part of everyone's existence. Even so, many people have conflicts about the forms of bodily functions that are approved of by their society. Frequently the individual has impulses and desires that are strongly disapproved of both by his society and by himself. The conflicts over such impulses are extremely severe. They may appear as conscious desires and fantasies accompanied by strong discomfort, or they may be entirely unconscious.

Thus a woman may have unconscious impulses to behave as a prostitute or to deprive a man of his masculinity. Other such impulses are expressed in unconscious fantasies of a woman being a man, of urinating on other individuals with the intent to humiliate them, or of committing incest. Such impulses are shut out of awareness because of shame, self-condemnation, fear of disapproval, fear of consequences, or guilt feelings.

Memories and Reactions of Childhood. Childhood memories generally fall into one of two classes: (1) Incidents which the patient has forgotten so completely that even if he thought about a particular period in his life, he still would not be able to remember them, even though they disturbed him greatly at the time and had a significant influence on his development. The memory of sexual seduction by an adult is such an incident.

A successful businessman who, although he was in love with his wife, drank periodically when he visited prostitutes and who had periods of depression, finally remembered what he had "forgotten"; he had been repeatedly seduced by a maid when he was three and one-half years old, and he had greatly feared his parents' disapproval and punishment. The feelings of fear and guilt, the resentment toward the maid, and his conflicts about his parents had a strong influence on his development.

(2) Incidents which the patient remembers, but certain aspects of which are either completely blotted out at first or, if remembered, are not told to the analyst until relatively late in the treatment.

A gifted musician was being given analysis because of recent difficulties in his work. For many months he told the analyst that he had been devoted to his mother, had loved and admired her. He had felt no grief over her death, which occurred when he was nineteen. In fact, not until a certain period in the analysis was he emotionally aware of the fact that she was dead. He first said that his mother had treated the children with devotion, understanding, and care, but later he related the following incident: When he was five and one-half years old, he whipped a horse to see him jump. His mother, finding this out, took the whip out of his hand and said, "I want you to feel what you are doing to the horse." With this, she whipped him. The patient was deeply disturbed, and the analyst remarked that he must have been angry at his mother. Only after considerable work was the analyst able to make him realize that he had ever had any feelings of resentment toward her. The patient had not "forgotten" the incident of the whipping. If he thought of that period of his childhood, he could always recall it; but he wanted to isolate it and not connect it with the picture he had of his relationship with his mother. He had a need to keep this relationship free from any flaw on the part of his mother, and free from any anger on his part.

Most frequently the childhood memories which are more fully recovered in the analysis and whose significance is fully elucidated fall into the second class. Whichever type of memory it is, it usually deals with attitudes of hostility and sexual activities which have been partly or completely repressed because of guilt and the fear of punishment and a loss of love.

Emotions and Attitudes of Fear and Guilt. The patients are partly or completely unconscious of certain attitudes because they consider them dangerous. The danger that they anticipate may be that of being deprived of help and gratification, or injured or destroyed, or utterly humiliated, exploited, disgraced, and condemned by others as well as by themselves. These fears arise particularly in connection with reactions of hostility, self-destruction, forbidden sexual attitudes, and rivalry. It is important to realize that the attitudes of fear and guilt may themselves not be known to the patient. He represses them for several reasons. He wants to protect himself against the feared consequences of these impulses; he can do this even more by shutting his feelings of fear and guilt out of awareness. Further, these latter feelings are extremely distressing, sometimes actually incapacitating. The patient tries to attain a state of comfort and to maintain his ability to function by repressing them. It is extremely important in analysis to uncover such reactions and make the patient realize their significance. They form an important part of the data obtained through psychoanalysis.

A social worker, aged twenty-nine, entered upon analysis when his marriage was threatened with dissolution. His wife wanted to leave him because of his continued emotional distance. This man was usually calm and aloof in all life situations. Although he maintained in the analysis that he was undisturbed, that his calmness showed genuine strength, and that it was the right way of living, he often had frightening dreams in which he was shot at or elevators fell while he was riding in them.

Working Concepts

Working concepts are assumptions based on observations, which attempt to establish interrelations between isolated observations and which furnish the practitioner with tools that enable him to deal with the phenomena he encounters. It is convenient to group psychoanalytic working concepts in the following classes: (1) concepts which influence chiefly the practice of the analysis itself, and which are closely connected with the method of procedure; (2) concepts which are constantly used in psychoanalytic practice, but which have wide application in the study of psychology and psychopathology; (3) concepts which systematize a large body of observations and in which the element of assumption is greatest. These last will be called hypotheses.

Concepts influencing chiefly the practice of analysis

The Patient's Need for Help. The need for help is the patient's strongest reason for beginning and continuing analytic treatment. This need, the hope of fulfilling it, and the actual experience of relief make him willing to persist even when some of the analyst's comments are distressing. The patient tells the analyst particularly about his weaknesses and disabilities, and he usually expects the analyst to concentrate on them and not on his achievements. However, it does not follow that he is happy to find out the reasons for his difficulties and eager to correct them as quickly as possible. On the contrary, he has his own emotional needs and ideas of the kind of help he should be given, and he clings to them persistently. If the help offered differs from what he wants, he reacts strongly; resentment, disappointment, fear, humiliation, and self-condemnation follow. He again requests the type of help which he felt was refused him before. All these reactions are the ultimate results of his feeling of helplessness.

The analyst is constantly aware of the patient's suffering and of his need for help. In some very precarious situations, as when there is danger of suicide or of incapacity, his most immediate task is to give the patient relief by some means. More generally, however, the concept of the patient's need for help has a long-range significance for the analyst. It is on the basis of this assumption that he denies many of the patient's requests, such as a set of rules for his conduct, and that he points out reaction patterns to the patient—e.g., hostility, or the need for exclusive affection and care—although he knows that the immediate effect will be disturbing. It is obvious from this that the working assumption of the patient's need for help is quite different for the analyst than for the patient. The aims of analytic therapy and the factors operating in achieving these aims will be discussed in the section on practical application. Here we wish to show that the working concept of the patient's need for help influences every activity which occurs in the analysis.

Reaction Patterns. During the analytic interview the patient reacts to occurrences in his daily life and to experiences. These reactions can be interpreted to him, and they can be further used as a yardstick for gauging the progress of the analysis. The analyst considers the analysis as progressing satisfactorily if the patient is furnishing adequate data for such interpretations, and if he can utilize these interpretations in his further reactions. All types of reactions are of significance in the analysis, including attitudes of disparagement toward the analyst. Reactions of fear, attitudes of superiority toward the analyst, emotional withdrawal, are all significant and useful if they are clear and if they can be utilized for interpretation. If reactions are not clear, the analyst's first task is to determine what is responsible for the lack of clarity; in other words, this lack is itself considered and is dealt with as a reaction pattern.

Essential Identity of the Patient's Reactions to Daily Events and to the Analyst. The patient displays the same patterns of behavior toward the analyst as he does toward people and his work; many of these patterns are emotional and irrational. Examination and discussion of the patient's reactions to the analyst give important clues as to the needs and motivations which are responsible for the illness.

Examination of the patient's emotional reaction to the analyst is important for another reason. In spite of the latter's essentially kind, understanding, and helpful attitude, the patient often reacts to him with anger, fear, and a feeling of humiliation. The reasons for these reactions lie within the patient; the reactions are transferred by him to the analyst, a phenomenon commonly known as "transference." Because of the working concept of the transference, the analyst constantly considers what reactions the patient is displaying toward him and calls his attention to them. This is one of the most important aspects of analytic work.

The question is often raised as to how it is possible for the patient to have the same attitudes toward the analyst as he does toward other people in his daily life—his family, friends, coworkers—when he knows that his relationship with the analyst has definite limitations. The phenomenon becomes understandable, however, if we realize that the patient undergoes analysis because he feels helpless; this undertaking is of great significance for him. He feels in need of help; with this he immediately displays the reasons for his need, his needs and ideas of how help is to be given him, his conflicts about these needs and desires, and his fear of the individual from whom he wants them. Furthermore, when the analyst denies him his requests and desires, he reacts to this just as he reacts to denials in other situations. When the analyst makes interpretations which inevitably cut deep and concern vital needs, he reacts to them as he does to stresses and to threats to his vital needs in life situations. Further aspects of the patient's emotional, irrational attitudes toward the analyst will be discussed under therapy.

Resistance. When the analyst constructs a reaction from the data and interprets it to the patient, the latter is usually reluctant to accept it; he struggles against it and tries to prove the analyst wrong. The patient continues to react in this way during subsequent interviews, although he has allegedly accepted the fact that his old reaction had disadvantages. Resistance is also manifest when a patient maintains a stubborn silence, when he is unable to think of anything significant, or when he talks but omits significant facts and thoughts.

"Resistance" is a collective term for some of the most important reactions brought out by the analysis. It is prompted by the patient's struggles and his refusal to give up a vital need. The reactions which constitute resistance are just as significant as the patient's final acceptance; in fact, the largest part of the analysis deals with resistance reactions. . . .

Recent Developments in Analysis

The following shifts of focus have taken place in psychoanalytic theory and observation:

1. Greater accent on anxiety, and, as a result, emphasis on the methods by which the patient is trying to escape danger and distress—often referred to as "ego psychology."

2. Greater emphasis on problems of self-esteem, self-assertion, and the need for affection and love, these forces being viewed as total personality reactions and not as derivatives of sexual strivings.

3. Greater accent on the unconscious intricacies of current reactions.

In the following an approach will be presented which integrates, with some additions, the concepts that seem most significant and effective in the treatment of a patient.

The nature of dominant psychological forces

The following psychological forces, all of them in part or entirely unconscious, have nearly equal significance in the pathological dynamics of patients.

Self-Evaluation: Self-Esteem and Moral Worth. "Self-esteem" refers mainly to a general feeling of ability to accomplish tasks according to one's own standards and in comparison with other individuals. The most obvious disturbances of this striving are feelings of inadequacy or its opposite—namely, feeling of excess ability.

Disturbances of moral worth are manifested through self-condemnation and guilt and the feeling of being condemned by others. The opposite is the feeling of excessive moral worth, always having to do the right thing, together with the feeling of moral superiority. The two opposites of self-evaluation, as well as opposites to be discussed later, often exist side by side.

Evaluation of the Environment.   This has two aspects: evaluation of the strength and emotional attitude of the environment. The healthy attitude of the individual is that his strength equals that of the environment or that he can adjust, within reason, to a stronger environment and is able to handle a weaker one without exploitation. Disturbances of evaluation of the strength of the environment are: considering the environment as all-powerful and always ready to crush its victim (helplessness), or, on the contrary, considering the environment at one's mercy. These attitudes and many of those to be discussed overlap in part. The threat of the environment may be considered in terms not only of destruction but also of complete humiliation or condemnation. As regards evaluation of the environment in terms of affection, the healthy attitude is that there can be an adequate give and take of love between the individual and most members of his surroundings. The most obvious disturbances are: a feeling of being rejected or, on the contrary, of being loved unqualifiedly, corresponding in part to the constant need to give unlimited affection and love to the surroundings under all circumstances.

Interpersonal Orientation and Behavior.   The healthy orientation is the desire for self-assertion and the ability to accept disappointment within reason. The most obvious disturbances are: complete dependence on and complete submission to the environment or, on the contrary, the need to dominate it and overpower it. As regards affection, there may be constant resentment, feeling of rejection or detachment, and avoidance of situations of affection or, on the contrary, excessive attachment. The attitudes and orientations mentioned represent strivings in themselves or lead to strivings in the form of goals and "policies" on the part of the individual.

Organ-Functional Strivings. These can be grouped into pleasure strivings and strivings of utility and mastery (self-preservation). The most important organ functions here referred to are the oral, excretory, genital, and motor functions, as well as looking, hearing, touching (with other functions of the skin), and smelling. The pleasure aim predominates almost entirely in the genital function, although the urinary function never gets entirely separated from it because of their close anatomical relationship. In the oral, urinary, and anal functions, both are present with almost equal accent. The self-preservative aspect of these functions is of prime importance psychologically either because of the knowledge of their survival value or because of the experience of discomfort and threat to health in case of disturbance. In motility, the utilitarian and the pleasure aspect are equally great in childhood, whereas later the utilitarian predominates by far. As regards skin, both aspects are about equal, with perhaps pleasure predominating. In connection with looking and hearing, as a rule the utilitarian aspect predominates, but there can be heavy accent on the pleasure aspect also. The disturbances in these functions can be: (1) excessive intensification or excessive suppression of the function; (2) disturbance of the relative balance in the organization of these various functions—e.g., the oral function outstripping the genital function in the dominant pleasure aims of the individual; (3) disturbance in the relative balance of the pleasure function and the utilitarian function of mastery in these functions; and (4) the distortion of the pleasure function by indispensable accent on pain (masochism) or on cruelty (sadism). These strivings and disturbances also overlap with the ones mentioned previously and to be mentioned later. The suppression of function or excessive function is related to the anticipation of injury, condemnation, humiliation, and frustration by other individuals.

Emotional Reactions. Emotional reactions here include not only subjective experience but also the impulse to ask more of the situation, in the case of positive ones, and avoidance or mastery, in the case of negative ones. Under healthy circumstances the individual reacts to a situation essentially with proportional emotions of a positive and negative kind commensurate to the situation. The emotions here considered are anxiety, hostility, depression with the feeling of loss, enjoyment, sympathy, pity, friendship, etc. The obvious disturbances are: need for suppression of emotions, excessive emotions, and inappropriate reactions. The last implies, for example, the occurrence of anxiety or hostility when enjoyment ought to appear. A key position from the point of view of pathology is occupied by anxiety and hostility. Here again there is an overlap with the previous forces, as anxiety may be the fear of being crushed, frustrated, humiliated, and condemned. Aggression may have the same active implication—of humiliating, biting, etc.

Experiential Tendency (*Erlebnistyp*). This is the main quality of the individual's sound strivings, developed in the course of his life history: his special training, his intelligence, creativeness, his tendency to utilize internal experience (introversiveness) or to deal mainly with situations (extrotensiveness), his ability to exercise relatively extensive control over impulses, or, on the contrary, his need for considerable latitude to follow up impulses and have limited responsibilities. Some individuals are remarkably versatile, but the majority show clear-cut preferences. Under healthy circumstances the individual is in an occupation and a social and economic position which enable him to follow through these interests close to his needs and abilities. Under pathological circumstances energy may be largely spent on work incompatible with his main strivings; e.g., an intellectual, introversive person is in business, spending most of his time in buying and selling and being in contact with individuals whose philosophies of life and interests differ from his own. The consequences of this kind of difficulty may be varied. Apart from unhappiness, the individual may try excessively to intensify the disliked activity, or he may be inefficient, or, in the case of individuals who have difficulty in the amount of control required over their impulses, there may be recurrent breaking loose of objectionable activity or, on the contrary, excessive self-control. This problem, too, overlaps with the previous points because the disturbance may manifest itself in any of the previously discussed fields.

The relationship between the various forces; conflict, protective and coping measures

It has been mentioned repeatedly that there is an overlap between the major psychological fields and forces. There is still another integral relationship among them. Conflicts may arise within the forces listed under the same headings—e.g., between need for moral worth and need for self-esteem because of their extremeness and the prerequisites needed to satisfy them. The individual's self-esteem may demand that he be able to carry out any kind of act, regardless of any objections by himself or by the environment; the moral position may require that he must not even assert himself, let alone injure anybody. Conflicts thus arising lead to a feeling of inner disorganization, of helplessness, and of anxiety. Now, one of several things may happen. The individual may reinforce one of the strivings and solve the situation that way—e.g., carry out the act. However, after a period the guilt resulting reëstablishes the old conflict. Or the individual may try to solve the conflict by a shift to activity in another field—e.g., to obtain the unqualified love of another individual or to engage in some pleasure-seeking activity, such as genital activity—and thus obviate both the need for self-assertion and the guilt over it. These substitute activities may also solve the problem for the time being, but the excessive, self-effacing love soon leads to a lowering of self-esteem, and the sexual activity may lead to guilt. The result then is that both the feeling of inadequacy and the feeling of guilt and moral worthlessness are reinstituted.

This example has two implications for the forces under discussion: (1) the forces themselves (striving for self-evaluation, organ strivings) are the result in part of conflict, anxiety, and defensive and coping measures; (2) the pressure in any of the fields mentioned may manifest itself in any of the other fields. Thus the individual may have developed a masochistic orientation in sexual activity. Then, on the occasion of sexual urge, he may consider this activity too injurious or humiliating. The result may then be that sexual activity gets suppressed and satisfaction is sought in purely affectionate relationships. The guilt that may be present over the original striving may then add the coloring of altruistic self-sacrifice to the relationship.

The relationship between current and genetic dynamics

Psychopathology, at any given age of the individual, is the sum total of all currently related forces as they were shaped during his life history. The major link to be added now to these inter-relationships is a double one: (1) The individual reasons, in the main unconsciously, "Such events have occurred in my past; therefore my current orientation and striving are vitally necessary." (2) Certain attitudes and orientations have been preserved from the past, essentially unaltered, and form a part of the individual's current orientation. This double link again forms a vicious circle with the current strivings. The individual's reasoning, "Past experiences justify current orientation," reinforces either his feeling of helplessness or, let us say, his violent attempt to dominate the world. This violent hostility then again leads to fear of retribution. With the renewal of anxiety, he looks for further past proofs and protective and coping measures. This sequence of events then contributes to preserving the past orientation and striving intact.

The question of the relationship between current and past dynamics may be rounded out further. Events in the past narrow down and determine in part the individual's future development. Further, the memory of past events constantly influences the individual's reaction to new ones. There is, however, an equally important process in the opposite direction. When the individual meets with new reversals, the evaluation of past events also alters. His current helplessness results in reinforcing his feeling of help-lessness in the past. The evaluation of past events constantly alters and gets more complex in connection with later experiences. In fact, the same past event may be used for contradictory proof under the pressure of contradictory strivings in current situations, this being one of the reasons for the difficulties in reconstructing past events. Thus, to prove the need for extreme caution, the patient may accent in a past conflict with his father his feeling of helplessness. In order to reinforce his belief in the miraculous benevolence of the world at other times, or even simultaneously, he may accent the fact that his relationship with his father was a close one.

As regards the main traumatic situations, the most significant nodal point may be found at any period of the individual's life. The individual is constantly confronted with new problems, which he approaches with both old and new strivings and hopes, and the resultant event may lead to a new pathological constellation of forces. Thus the striving for achievement becomes considerably intensified, beginning with school attendance; it is then used to reëstablish self-esteem and the affection of other individuals, as a substitute for genital pride; in addition, it has the character of a new force. Entering an occupation or a marriage again confronts the individual with new problems and new hopes. Disappointment may lead to the final crystallization of a feeling that the world is a potentially frustrating place, that there is no way of establishing self-esteem other than to be always right, that sexual gratification is indispensably vital and at the same time leads to ultimate danger situations, that every new attempt toward satisfaction would end in failure, that therefore all extreme strivings, conscious and unconscious, are inescapable yet have to be held in check. In the treatment of, let us say, a woman of thirty-five years who has gone through this type of development, the period of failure after the early months of marriage proves to be the nodal historical period where most of the genetic threats meet. It may then be as much underplayed or forgotten by her in its various aspects and may have to be gone back to throughout the analysis against equally great resistance as any period of her childhood. . . .

Therapeutic Aims and Effects of Analysis

The general therapeutic aims of psychoanalysis are the disappearance of symptoms, increased efficiency and ability to enjoy life, increased ability to stand stress and to make the best of one's opportunities, and the like. The special therapeutic aim is an extremely thoroughgoing recasting of those reaction patterns which are responsible for the patient's difficulties. Not only are symptoms relieved, but there are also changes in some aspects of his relationship with others, his evaluation of himself and of others, his goals and the way in which he seeks to attain them. No other therapeutic method today seems able to accomplish this to the same extent as psychoanalysis.

The length of time that the treatment requires depends on the patient's difficulties and on how thorough a recasting is desired by himself and the analyst. Usually the patient shows an early improvement. If a satisfactory analysis is interrupted for any valid reason, the patient may nevertheless derive benefit from it. The lessening of symptoms is often rapid, particularly in patients who are suffering markedly when they start the analysis; but the symptoms return in varying intensity when new life stresses arise and when new disturbing topics are taken up in the analysis. Gradually the patient's behavior in situations of stress improves; and finally his behavior rises above its previous level even in situations in which he excelled. Completely satisfactory analyses may vary in length from about two to five years.

Not all patients are equally benefited by psychoanalytic treatment. There are four prerequisites for a patient to be analyzable: (1) He must desire to be treated. Often the explanatory statement that he needs treatment suffices to create a willingness to undertake analysis. Some patients at first are averse to analysis either because they are afraid of becoming completely dependent or because their need for self-esteem is so intense that they want to handle all their difficulties, no matter how great, themselves. Such patients may eventually change their outlook, however; and their treatment is often very successful. (2) The patient must have enough intelligence to realize that his suffering may have emotional causes, and to understand the analyst's explanations. Feeble-minded people, for example, are not analyzable. (3) The procedure should be adapted to the patient's illness and individuality. Border-line psychotic patients may come for treatment by their own decision; frank psychotics do not, yet many of them can be analyzed with a modified technique. One might say in general that any technical modification or measure that takes care of issues that are beyond the individual patient's coping capacity at the time not only does not interfere with the analysis but helps it; and such measures are at times indispensable. Such auxiliary measures are simultaneous analysis of husband and wife or of parent and child by the same analyst (Mittelmann, Sperling); direct contact at regular intervals with other members of the family to get their coöperation and to handle their difficulties (Mittelmann); the use of hypnotics or hypnosis in the therapeutic session when the analysis "stalls" after satisfactory progress for a long time; temporary hospitalization in severe cases, with possible auxiliary use of "shock" treatment in case of psychosis to make the patient more accessible. Analysis in a private office not only may be of no help, but may actually be dangerous because during a reaction to stress situations the patient may commit suicide or engage in some violent act. (4) The patient's life goals must be essentially good; if they need to be changed, his situation must be such that he can do so. Furthermore, he must be able to obtain from his surroundings an indispensable minimum of emotional support. For example, a patient suffers from anxiety attacks; he has spoiled his relationships with most people, and he must therefore live alone. He may be very intelligent, but he may have broken off his professional training. Because of his dissatisfaction with his station in life and because of the unbearable strain of living alone, analytic treatment may not be able to bring him even to the point where he could alter his situation.

The question whether the patient's psychological disturbance is amenable to psychoanalytic treatment, whether he can change his life goal if necessary, and whether he can obtain the minimum emotional support from his environment cannot always be easily answered at the beginning of the analysis. The analyst may begin the treatment even though he has serious doubts, and the analysis may be successful.

It must not be assumed that a patient who has been successfully analyzed is free from shortcomings. He is making the best of his opportunities and will continue to do so increasingly after the analysis is completed. Furthermore, he is able to handle his minor shortcomings successfully. Under new and very adverse life situations, he may need help again.

If an individual undergoes analysis as part of his professional training, the analysis proceeds essentially as has been described.

The reason for this is that no one is free from fears and difficulties, although he may cope with them more successfully by means of various psychological devices. His manner of functioning in life, however, can always be improved. A successful analysis will enable such a person to live his life more fully. While his psychological devices are being broken through in the analysis, he may go through considerable emotional stress, for analysis can never be a purely intellectual experience. . . .

Curative factors in analytic treatment

Now that we have presented an account of the psychoanalytic procedure and of its therapeutic effects, we shall discuss what psychological factors are operative in achieving these results. Many of the factors are the same as those discussed in connection with psychotherapy in general. These will be referred to briefly, the emphasis being placed on the features characteristic of the analytic procedure.

Support and Reassurance by the Analyst; Permissive Attitudes. Although these topics have been discussed previously, it should be mentioned here that the patient desires the analyst's *unqualified* and *unlimited* support, reassurance, and approval. He is not permitted the illusion that he is receiving this; if he is, any topic he or the analyst discusses will only serve to maintain this illusion. How much the analyst comments on this attitude depends on the immediate analytic situation and on how much deprivation the patient can stand at the moment.

Effects of Investigation of Attitudes Toward the Analyst. The fact that the patient manifests all the significant psychological attitudes in relationship to the analyst turns the analysis into a living experience for him. He must face and work out his emotional problems in this new interhuman relationship; thus he experiences his impulses under a unique set of circumstances. Comments on his reactions are made at the time they occur; he must face them. Furthermore, the impulse is not met by the analyst with moral approval or disapproval, or with counterattack or submission; nor

can the problem be settled by action as in the patient's daily life. It is met with understanding and explanation, and with the implication that the patient should change his method of dealing with problems. Therefore the "fate" of the impulse and its effect on the patient's whole personality are different from what they would be under other circumstances.

The most important irrational attitudes that the patient has toward the analyst are: the expectation that the analyst will cure him by a sort of magic act, and that the analyst is all-powerful, omniscient, and perfect; an attitude of and a desire for complete submission in order to obtain the needed help; the assumption that the analyst looks down on him, especially because of the above attitudes, and that the analyst wants to dominate or overpower him and keep him in subjection (counterpart of complete submission); anger toward the analyst for this reason and for his refusal to give the desired help; a desire to rule the analyst and to do to him everything that he thinks the analyst will do to him; fear of the analyst because of the anger toward him, chiefly fear of loss of his love and approval, and fear of injury; desire for gratifications; impulse to attack the analyst at certain parts of the body, and fear that the analyst will attack him at the same places.

The patient's various attitudes toward the analyst arise and are recognized partly spontaneously, but they are brought out particularly in response to the analyst's interpretations.

Unconscious Attitudes Becoming Conscious. The exact therapeutic effect of the becoming conscious of an unconscious impulse is a complicated question. Permissive and supportive attitudes on the part of the analyst often play an important part in the resulting relief. Another significant aspect is the following: The patient, because of his fear, shuts a distressing problem out of awareness and in that way renounces control over it; he becomes helpless to handle it. As a result of analytic work, his fear of the problem lessens, and it becomes acceptable to him for consideration. This has a further effect: He now receives a key to a problem which has distressed and perplexed him, and he acquires mastery over it. In some cases this effect of analytic work is very striking.

A patient arrived for the analytic interview in a disturbed emotional state and complaining that her feet felt numb. The complaints persisted throughout the entire interview, in spite of repeated attempts at interpretation. She finally related an incident which had occurred not long before this interview and which up to this point she had not mentioned or thought of. She had expected a telephone call from her husband at noon, which had not come. She had felt that this was inconsiderate of him, and was angry and hurt, but then she had become worried lest he might be leaving her. Soon afterward her complaint had started. As she discussed this incident with the analyst, her complaint disappeared. In this instance the patient had been afraid of the consequences of her anger toward her husband and had therefore repressed her impulse and the memory of the incident. With the aid of the analyst, she acquired enough self-confidence to see the immediate problem and acquire mastery over it.

This patient was well along in her understanding of the type of problem that this incident presented, and it was for this reason that the effect was so immediate and clear. Usually a patient is at first afraid to become conscious of attitudes which have been repressed, and he struggles against the analyst's efforts to enable him to see them. The lessening of the fear and the acquisition of mastery in such instances are achieved after some period of time.

Forcing the Patient to Change His Attitudes. As has been said, all interpretations have the unvoiced implication that, although they arise from helplessness, the patient's goals—e.g., complete dependence—have pernicious consequences and should be changed by him. The patient, however, reacts to this as if it were a threat to a vital need, and he pursues the same goal in a different form. Again this is interpreted to him, and thus the struggle goes on until he feels himself forced out of the attitude; he then, almost in desperation at first, begins to make a new effort. Thus every important change in the patient's reaction patterns is a result not only of lessening anxiety, increased self-confidence, increased feelings of mastery and approval, but also of being forced to abandon goals whose realization is refused. In this process the patient's desire to proceed further with his problems and to acquire increased self-esteem also plays a role. From this and what has been said under the two previous heads, interpreta-

tion is seen to be one of the most powerful therapeutic weapons of psychoanalysis.

Resolution of Conflicts and of Vicious Circles; Relief of Bodily Distress. As a result of the analytic work, the feeling of helplessness and worthlessness and the catastrophic expectations are gradually relieved. With this, both the intense need for dependence and the hostile reactions subside, as well as the self-condemnation, the feelings of guilt, the self-aggrandizement, and the frantic struggle to reach implacable ideals. Thus the conflicts grow less intense and are finally resolved, and compromise formations and substitute bodily gratifications are abandoned. The tense struggle to reach normal functioning abates, as does the continuous tension resulting from unsatisfiable psychological and physiological needs. Consequently the whole vicious circle of reactions is halted.

Increase in Self-Confidence and Well-Being. Almost from the beginning of the analysis there is an increase in the patient's self-confidence and in his psychological strength. This is true in spite of the fact that the patient's fears become recurrently intense. The self-confidence and strength are not to be taken here as always meaning subjective comfort. They imply that the patient takes up problems which previously he could not face at all, regardless of the fact that they frighten him. These terms further imply that many of his functions improve when he is free from intense stress. Direct encouragement and reassurance are rarely given in the analytic interview. The patient often asks: "What can I do to have more self-confidence? How can I overcome my fears? In what ways is analysis going to help me?" The analyst may answer such questions once, but his answers are invariably interpreted by the patient either as containing magic help in themselves or as falling far short of the kind of help he needs. Usually the patient repeats such questions later as if he had not asked them before and as if he had not had an answer. The reason for that is that these questions are really disguised statements and requests on the part of the patient; therefore they have to be analyzed, not answered. The remarkable fact is that the patient's self-confidence increases as a result both of the implied supportive and permissive aspects of analysis and of the resolution of conflicts and dangerous attitudes, and also because of increasing mastery. As the analysis progresses, successfully completed tasks and new gratifications increase the patient's desire for new efforts and in turn increase his self-confidence and strength, thus establishing a healthy circle of psychological and physiological reactions.

34

SANDOR RADO

Recent Advances
in Psychoanalytic Therapy[*]

Freud's motivational theory of behavior, known as classical psychodynamics, is the basis of the classical technique of psychoanalytic therapy. Adaptational psychodynamics, a consistent development of the classical theory, seeks to place the analysis of behavior on a sound biological foundation, and to depict motivation in a close-to-the-fact language that facilitates its clinical verification. This revised theory sheds new light on the therapeutic mechanisms by which the various treatment procedures operate, discloses the imperfections of the classical technique as well as its lasting achievements, and leads to the development of a new technique of psychoanalytic therapy which I call the adaptational technique.

Limiting the scope of my assignment to this line of recent development, in the present paper I shall introduce a conceptual scheme for the comparative study of diverse psychotherapeutic methods, take a fresh view of the chief therapeutic ideas evolved in the past, outline the new adaptational technique and finally glance at the problems that lie ahead.

* Reprinted by permission from *Psychiatric Treatment*—Proceedings of the Association for Research in Nervous and Mental Disease, Dec. 14 and 15, 1951, New York, N. Y. Published by The Williams & Wilkins Company, Baltimore, 1953. Copyright, 1953, Association for Research in Nervous and Mental Disease.

The Conceptual Scheme

Psychotherapy is a medical procedure; it may be defined as the use of human influence for the treatment of behavior disorders. We distinguish between the patient's *treatment behavior* and his *life performance*. The term treatment behavior refers to his co-operation with the physician; the term life performance, to the rest of his activities in daily life.

The patient's treatment behavior can be understood only in terms of his own shifting *designs for co-operation* whether he is aware of them or not. The various designs for co-operation encountered in our patients fall into a hierarchically ordered scheme of levels; this order is shown in table 1.

These designs for co-operation are subject to complications. For example, instead of co-operating the patient may wish to take the place of the physician; or he may be divided against himself and secretly prefer to stay ill. However, such complications do not affect the validity of our hierarchical scheme.

At the self-reliant and aspiring levels the patient's treatment behavior is based on common sense. In contrast, at the parentifying and magic-craving levels his treatment behavior reveals excessive emotional dependence on the physician, befitting a child more than an adult. Often unknown to himself he sees in the physician an idealized re-incarnation of his own parent, brought back to the scene by the power of his desire. Accordingly, his co-operation aims at obtaining the privileges of a favorite child, not at learning and maturation. Thus in our hierarchical scheme the sharp dividing line runs between the self-reliant and parentifying levels: above this line the patient's co-operation is adult, below it, child-like.

While the aspiring and self-reliant levels are not available in every patient, proneness of the helpless adult to regress to parentifying or magic-craving behavior is ineradicable and universal.

The fundamental clinical fact is that patients can be successfully treated at every level of treatment behavior. However, the goals and techniques of treatment are so different from level to level that it becomes an important technical task to counteract

TABLE 1 *Hierarchic order of the patient's designs for co-operation*

Aspiring Level: Available only in the adult who is capable and desirous of self-advancement by extensive learning and maturation.	"I am delighted to co-operate with the doctor. This is my opportunity to learn how to make full use of all my potential resources for adaptive growth."
Self-Reliant Level: Available in the average adult who is capable of learning the simple know-how of daily life.	"I am ready to co-operate with the doctor. I must learn how to help myself and do things for myself."

ADULT

——————————————————————

CHILD-LIKE

Parentifying Level: When the adult feels like a helpless child, he seeks parental help and therefore parentifies the therapist.	"I don't know what the doctor expects of me. I couldn't do it anyway. He should cure me by *his* effort."
Magic-Craving Level: The completely discouraged adult retreats to the hope that the parentified therapist will do miracles for him.	"The doctor must not only cure me, he must do everything for me—by magic."

↑ = ADVANCE.   ↓ = REGRESSION.

the patient's inclination to shift from one level to another, in particular, to cross the line that divides the levels of adult co-operation from the levels of child-like co-operation.

The physician must seek to stabilize the patient's co-operation at the level selected for his treatment. For this purpose he uses measures devised to regulate the patient's treatment behavior; we call these *priming measures*. In contradistinction, we call the measures devised to modify the patient's life performance *modifying measures*. Measures intended to prime and modify at the same time are called *double duty measures*.

Each particular method of psychotherapy has its own *plan for priming* and its own *plan for modifying*. Of course, its plan for modifying depends upon its plan for priming. These two plans may be conveniently used as a basis for classification of all methods of psychotherapy.

Lineage of Psychotherapeutic Methods

Comparative analysis shows that the historical development of the major psychotherapeutic methods has an inherent logical consistency. To demonstrate this instructive fact, in our re-examination of these methods we shall follow the order of their historical appearance. The lineage of psychotherapeutic methods is shown in table 2.

Hypnotherapy

Priming

Hypnotherapy's plan for priming is to put the patient into a hypnotic state by taking full advantage of his craving for magical help [7, 11, 12]. As a child the patient knew the ironclad rule that he must purchase the "magical" ministrations of his parents with his own obedience. When told by the physician that he should go to sleep though he is not sleepy at all, the patient senses that the ironclad rule is still in force. Hence, by the action of his own desire the patient lapses into a hypnotic state, a state of almost *automatic obedience* to the parentified physician. Far from resenting this necessity, the patient feels hopeful, even triumphant: his dream of magical help is coming true. Therefore he will act upon the physician's orders as if acting upon his own intentions.

Magic-craving of the distressed is craving for security through obedience. Hypnotherapy works at the magic-craving level of treatment behavior.

1. The prohibitive technique: modifying

Having thus primed the patient for automatic obedience, the physician must decide what modifying measure to employ. He may choose the most primitive modifying measure known, the exercise of disciplinary authority. In effect, the physician tells the hypnotized patient: "Stop this nonsense!

TABLE 2 *Lineage of psychotherapeutic methods*

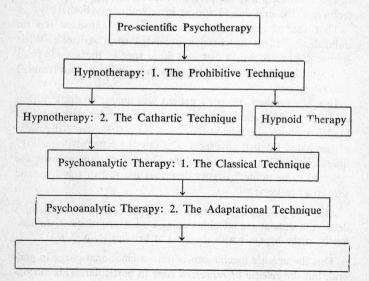

Pre-scientific Psychotherapy

Hypnotherapy: 1. The Prohibitive Technique

Hypnotherapy: 2. The Cathartic Technique

Hypnoid Therapy

Psychoanalytic Therapy: 1. The Classical Technique

Psychoanalytic Therapy: 2. The Adaptational Technique

You are not ill! You feel fine!" The proper designation of this procedure is the prohibitive technique of hypnotherapy.

This technique tries to cure the patient with parental discipline. Therapeutic results are obtained at the cost of increased inner tension; their collapse is only a question of time. Nonetheless, this technique may still be used to tide the patient over an emergency.

2. *The cathartic technique: modifying*

In 1880-82 a patient of Dr. Joseph Breuer of Vienna taught the medical profession how to make better therapeutic use of the hypnotic state. This young lady knew that hypnosis is but a means to an end: what she sought to obtain by her almost automatic obedience was *permission to disobey*. She wished to have *her* say while under hypnosis. With Breuer's consent she revived forgotten emotional experiences, and the emotional relief freed her from her symptoms. She called this procedure "chimney sweeping." In 1893, Breuer, by then in collaboration with Freud, called it the cathartic method of hypnotherapy, or hypnocatharsis [1]. In contradistinction to the prohibitive technique, it is a permissive technique, the first one to appear in scientific psychotherapy.

That the wholesale discharge of pent-up emotions has an unburdening effect has been appreciated since Aristotle. What Breuer discovered was a new and more specific therapeutic principle, but his true discovery was lost in a shuffle of unwarranted generalizations.

In a hot summer, Breuer's patient was unable to drink a drop of water because she could not touch the tumbler with her lips. Under hypnosis she related that once when she entered the room of her hated English governess, she saw the latter's "disgusting" little dog drinking out of a tumbler. She said nothing because she "wanted to be polite." Breuer describes the rest of this hypnotic session as follows:

After she gave energetic expression to her anger, she asked for a drink, and without any inhibition drank a great deal of water, awakening from the hypnosis with the glass at her lips [1, p. 23].

This therapeutic mechanism is not an emotional purge in general, but the *release of repressed rage* in particular. This mechanism can remove only symptoms that serve as a vicarious outlet for rage *recently* repressed. The inability of Breuer's patient to touch the tumbler with her lips gave pantomimic expression to her bitter resentment of the governess: "You see what your inconsiderate action did to me! For all I know this may be the same tumbler you allowed your disgusting pet to use. How can you expect me to touch it with my lips? If I die of thirst it will be your fault."

We also learn from this case that release of rage is therapeutic only if certain additional criteria are satisfied. It was with Breuer's approval that the patient released her anger at the governess. This put an end to her humiliation, restored her pride, and assuaged her guilty fear of the governess. Had Breuer reprimanded her for her disrespect of the governess, he would have destroyed the therapeutic success. Another crucial point is that the patient felt free to recall the incident responsible for her rage. Had she feared that Breuer might criticize her, she would have remained silent or vented her anger on Breuer; in either case she would have retained her symptom.

Today we may formulate the modifying measure discovered by Breuer as follows:

The release of repressed rage is a decompressive procedure comparable to the opening of a blind abscess. To release the repressed rage, one must first locate and revive it in the memory context of the life experience that provoked it. Furthermore, to be successful, the release must retrieve the patient's lost pride; this effect can be obtained only if the patient feels that the physician approves of his released rage.

Hypnoid Therapy

The hypnoid state is a wakeful counterpart of the hypnotic state. In the hypnoid state the patient displays a degree of *uncritical obedience* to the parentified physician, that makes him act upon the latter's propositions as if acting on his own intentions. The degree of uncritical obedience varies in a wide range. Uncritical obedience may result 1) from the patient's craving for magic, or 2) from his craving for a helpful ersatzparent, helpful in a more or less realistic sense. Thus hypnoid therapy may work 1) at the magic-craving level, or 2) at the parentifying level.

1. Priming and modifying at the magic-craving level

Magic-craving may be a fleeting episode evoked by distress in the healthy or the sick. Priming must sustain the patient's craving and belief that the physician is the person he needs. The means used may be crude or subtle; they amount to a reassuring display of what the patient believes to be the superior powers of the physician.

Modifying is done by disguised hypnoid orders; the vehicle used may be a placebo or a measure of true medical value. The magic-craving patient may supply himself with the desired hypnoid orders regardless of the physician's own intentions. This applies to all physicians and all medical procedures.

Hypnoid therapy at the magic-craving level is known as suggestive therapy or as the suggestive component of all medical procedures.

What enables the magic-craving patient to act upon the physician's hypnoid orders, whether these are explicit, implied or simply presumed by the patient? By parentifying the physician at the cost of uncritical obedience, the patient experiences an uplift, increased self-confidence and sense of emotional security; these changes relax his inhibitions, allay his fears and facilitate his life performance. Owing to the patient's own desire, the parentified physician may thus be able to induce him to do things he was unable to do by himself. However, the physician must first comfort the patient and help him to unburden himself by discharging his pent-up emotions. He may help the patient over the hump by sound advice and other supportive measures.

2. Priming and modifying at the parentifying level

Priming follows the same principles as above; but here the physician must be more subtle because the patient is more critical. As compared with the magic-craving level, here the physician's opportunity for modifying is greatly increased. By utilizing the patient's desire for security through obedience he may employ modifying measures that will induce in the patient true processes of emotional learning. Many of the therapeutic results thus achieved may survive even if later the patient loses his hypnoid faith in the physician. However, the patient will then have to find another ersatzparent.

We have no descriptive name for this type of treatment; the term "brief psychotherapy" has some currency.

Psychoanalytic Therapy: 1. The Classical Technique

Freud's conception of psychoanalytic treatment

Freud's discovery of free association—thinking out loud—was a fruit of the bold initiative of Breuer's patient. With the introduction of this new investigative method it has become a psychodynamic principle that the patient shall have *his* say in his treatment. Safeguarded by the Hippocratic oath of the physician and prompted by his own need for help, he may be more candid with the physician than he ever dared to be with himself. The new investigative method disclosed the patient's life history in intimate detail and enabled Freud to organize this hitherto inaccessible material in terms of motivation and development. This type of work, he said, may relieve the patient from the necessity of sustaining inner resistances; he may recall his forgotten past, his repressed desires, and handle them in the superior manner of conscious control. Since conscious desires can produce no vicarious activity (viewed at the time as the general mechanism of symptom formation) "the continuance and even the renewal of the morbid condition is impossible" [3]. As this statement shows, Freud attributed almost unlimited therapeutic power to the undoing of the patient's repressions, hence his vision of psychoanalysis as a therapy of total reconstruction that would lift the patient to a higher level of psychodynamic organization.

Freud's threefold formulation of the mode of action of psychoanalytic therapy is basic to the classical technique. He advanced it in 1904, repeating it unchanged throughout his life [3-6]:

The aim of our efforts may be expressed in various formulas—making conscious the unconscious, removing the repressions, filling in the gaps in memory; they all amount to the same thing.

We do nothing for our patients but enable this one mental change to take place in them; the extent to which it is achieved is the extent of the benefit we do them (5, p. 377).

Freud's discovery and interpretation of parentifying treatment behavior

To explain the unexpected fact that the patient turns child-like in his treatment behavior, Freud introduced a hypothesis of far-reaching consequences. The patient, he said, is subject to an inner force that compels him to *transfer* his infantile responses from his past relationship to his parents to his present relationship to the physician. He thus viewed parentifying treatment behavior as a forced repetition of the patient's past, and called it *transference*. This hypothesis made parentifying treatment behavior a phenomenon independent from and unmotivated by the patient's present situation in treatment and life.

This hypothesis enabled Freud to consider parentifying treatment behavior as but another form in which the patient reproduces his past. Recollections and repetitions complement one another, each revealing the patient's past in its own way. Freud's classification of transference and the meaning of his terms are shown in table 3.

TABLE 3   *"Transference": terms and meaning*

TERMS *Forms of transference:*	MEANING *Patient behaves the way he did when he was:*
Positive transference	An obedient child
Resistant transference	A disobedient child
1) Negative transference	1) A defiant child
2) Sensual transference	2) A child bent on sexual gratification

Priming

In Freud's view, positive transference is the force—the only force—that enables the patient to absorb and act upon the interpretations proposed to him by the physician:

The outcome in this struggle [between repression and therapeutic undoing of repression] is not decided by his [the patient's] intellectual insight—it is neither strong enough nor free enough to accomplish such a thing—but solely by his relationship to the physician. In so far as his transference bears the positive sign, it clothes the physician with authority, transforms itself into faith in his findings and in his views. Without this kind of transference or with a negative one, the physician and his arguments would never even be listened to. Faith repeats the history of its own origin; it is a derivative of love and at first it needed no arguments. Not until later does it admit them so far as to take them into critical consideration if they have been offered by someone who is loved. Without this support arguments have no weight with the patient, never do have any with most people in life [5, p. 387].

This passage is the basis of Freud's three rules for the handling of transference: 1) Positive transference must be preserved intact throughout the treatment. 2) Resistant transference must be dissolved and the patient restored to positive transference. This can be done, he said, by showing the patient that it is a now senseless repetition of his infantile behavior towards his parents. 3) At the conclusion of the treatment positive transference "must be dissolved"; Freud did not say how this could be done.

Freud's rules, translated into the language of our conceptual scheme, might read as follows: Only in a state of child-like dependence upon the physician, a state of uncritical obedience, can the patient absorb and act upon the interpretations proposed to him by the physician. Therefore his child-like dependence, his uncritical obedience, must be preserved intact throughout the treatment. His disobedience—defiance—must be broken: he must be shown that it is a repetition of his infantile behavior, now disturbingly injected into his relationship to the physician. At the conclusion of the treatment he must be induced to terminate his uncritical obedience.

To sum up: the classical technique primes the patient for un-critical co-operation with the physician. The classical technique is a technique of child-like emotional dependence; it works at the parentifying level of treatment behavior.

Modifying

An adequate plan for modifying the patient's life performance must first consider the relation of available means to desired ends. It must include an itemized list of the problems; an itemized list of the tools; a set of instructions as to how to put the latter to work.

The classical plan for modifying includes no itemized list of the problems; it merely implies that the problem is to cure the patient of his psychoneurosis. This limits the plan to an outline of the relationship of the tools to one another.

The modifying measures used by the classical technique fall into three groups:

1. Interpretation of the patient's recollections for the purpose of undoing his repressions; reinforcement of the emerging insights by repeated "working-through" of the material.

2. Interpretation, for the same purpose, of the patient's resist-ant transference, particularly his negative transference. Trans-lated into the language of our conceptual scheme: the physician must trace selected phases of the patient's parentifying treatment behavior to comparable phases of his childhood behavior; in par-ticular, he must trace the patient's present defiance to his defiance of his parents in early life. The objective is to familiarize the patient with his repertoire of defiance and incestuous desires; awareness will enable him to control these infantile impulses in his life performance.

Since interpretation of the patient's resistant transference is also used to regulate his treatment behavior, it is a double duty measure in the sense of our conceptual scheme.

3. Measures of so-called "activity" on the part of the physi-cian, such as pledging the patient to abstain from making crucial decisions while under treatment, persuading him to make an

effort to fight his phobic avoidances, setting a deadline for the treatment.

In the classical technique, interpretation is based on classical psychodynamics. The emphasis is on making the patient understand his development, that is his libidinal development, his temptations, fears and mechanisms of defense. In classical psychodynamics, neurotic and psychotic behavior are described and explained in terms of libidinal development; so is, for that matter, all behavior. In the classical technique excessive preoccupation with questions of libidinal meaning and development has completely dwarfed the basic question of all psychotherapy: the ascertaining of the adaptive value (positive or negative) of the patient's life performance. The disclosure of motivation and development is notoriously mistaken for an evaluation of performance. Let me make this clear with an example. A piece of writing may be a work of art or the senseless effusion of a deranged mind; which it is can be ascertained only by critical evaluation in the cultural context, not by disclosure of its author's motivation and development.

Critical evaluation of the classical technique

The aim of psychoanalytic therapy is to increase the patient's capacity for enjoyment and active achievement in life by lifting him to a higher level of psychodynamic organization. The preanalytic methods of psychotherapy could not even conceive the possibility of such total reconstruction. To have evolved this objective is a lasting achievement of the classical technique. How far has it advanced towards the attainment of its goal? Measuring it by its own yardstick, this is what we find:

1. The classical technique works at the parentifying level of treatment behavior. To the extent of his uncritical obedience to the physician the patient continues practicing child-like emotional dependence throughout his treatment. Therefore, this technique cannot lift him to a higher level of psychodynamic organization. By offering the patient a singular opportunity for emotional learning over a lengthy period of time, it may achieve unmatched ther-

apeutic results; but it cannot significantly reduce his proneness to inappropriate emotional dependence. If the burden of his adaptive task increases he will seek shelter with an ersatzparent.

2. Parentifying treatment behavior is a product of the patient's therapeutic situation. The transference theory views it as a product of repetition-compulsion [4], a hypothetical force exempt from the hedonic self-regulation of the organism, operating "beyond the pleasure principle." Thus parentifying treatment behavior appears on the scene like a *deus ex machina*. Attributing parentifying treatment behavior to the intervention of an almost supernatural force has rendered its true understanding impossible. Ultimately, it threatens to strip psychoanalytic therapy of its unique scientific and practical value, and to turn it into a ritual.

3. Analysis of the patient's parentifying treatment behavior in terms of negative transference, variously featured in psychoanalytic literature as erlebnistherapie, neocatharsis [2], corrective experience, and the like, is an inadequate procedure for the all-important therapeutic release of the patient's resentments. In Breuer's catharsis the released rage retains its true object; therein lies the therapeutic efficacy of Breuer's procedure. In the transference procedure whenever the patient vents his rage on the physician, there follows a penetrating search for the infantile origins of his rage resulting as a rule in the finding that he has again repeated his rage against his father. This procedure relieves neither the patient's true resentment of the physician nor his true resentment of his father; still less does it relieve the resentments of his current life-situation which are in no small measure responsible for his present suffering. In therapeutic efficacy the scapegoat principle of negative transference lags far behind the true-release principle embodied in Breuer's procedure.

4. A one-sided developmental frame of reference of whatever kind is inadequate for the purposes of psychodynamic understanding and therapeutic interpretation. It tends to concentrate all interest and effort on the patient's past, to the neglect of his present. This fact is reflected in psychoanalytic literature, which refers neatly to the entirety of the patient's present life as his "current conflict."

5. The modifying power of the undoing of repressions is over-

rated. To overcome repressions and thus be able to recall the past is one thing; to learn from it and be able to act on the new knowledge, another. It is the patient's undue inhibitions that make him unable to act and learn by acting. These undue inhibitions develop in childhood and are carried over into adult life as automatizations. Undoing the repression of thought and desire does not by itself remove the automatized inhibition of executive action.

However, such shortcomings of the classical technique are not final. Psychoanalytic therapy surges with values and therapeutic resources; in its development, the classical technique is not the end but the beginning.

Psychoanalytic Therapy: 2. The Adaptational Technique

Patients lastingly incapable of adult co-operation are not eligible for a therapy of total reconstruction. They require other treatment methods. The adaptational technique is designed to work at the self-reliant or preferably the aspiring level of treatment behavior.

In the adaptational psychodynamics of behavior disorders we encounter organized sequences of events which we have come to recognize as processes of miscarried prevention and miscarried repair [8, 13-16]. They are brought into play in early life by the child's faulty emergency responses, his over-reaction to danger, particularly to the parental threat of punishment. The early phase of behavior disorder, emergency dyscontrol, appears in the child's dependency relationship to his parents; its products are carried over into adult life. The ensemble of the patient's faulty emergency responses includes excessive or inappropriate fears, rages, guilty fears and guilty rages; most damaging are the undue inhibitions which have arrested function, growth and development in the affected areas, pre-eminently in group membership and sexual behavior. In the treatment of behavior disorders, the critical task is to bring the patient's emergency emotions under control; to remove his damaging inhibitions; to generate in him an emotional matrix dominated by welfare emotions (pleasurable desire, joy, love and pride) and controlled by adaptive insight, a matrix conducive to a healthy life performance. In the adaptational technique the plans for priming and modifying seek to fulfill this task.

Priming

The adaptational plan for priming is to hold the patient as much as possible at the adult levels of co-operation with the physician. When his treatment behavior turns or threatens to turn child-like, we seek to bring him back to the adult level without delay.

Child-like co-operation, that is, parentifying treatment behavior, must be understood in the context of the here and now. Adaptational psychodynamics views the patient's search for an ersatzparent as a process of miscarried repair, a cardinal feature of behavior disorders. Before he entered treatment, he moved in disillusion from one ersatzparent to the next. During treatment, as soon as he loses his self-confidence, he parentifies the physician. Resorting to the adaptive pattern, the goals and tactics, of a child, he then plies the parentified physician with smiles, tears and lashings, as shown schematically in table 6.

We know the patient's personal program for parentifying behavior from his life history; he performed this program time and again in his relationship to his parents and ersatzparents. The adaptational technique seeks to forestall the unnecessary repetition of this program in the patient's treatment behavior by the priming measure of *interceptive interpretation*. This is an intricate procedure; to succeed, the physician must first bolster up the patient's self-confidence on *realistic grounds*. Interpretation is a double duty measure: it is used for modifying the patient's life performance as well as regulating his treatment behavior. We shall deal with it under the next heading.

Modifying

The adaptational technique's plan for modifying is too elaborate to be presented here in detail. I shall touch only upon a few major points.

We interpret to the patient his treatment behavior and life performance in an adaptational framework of meaning. By adaptations we mean improvements in the organism's pattern of interaction with its environment; these are composed of changes undergone by the organism itself ("autoplastic" adaptations) and changes brought about by the organism in the environment ("alloplastic" adaptations).

TABLE 4   *Plying the parentified physician with smiles, tears, and lashings*

Ingratiating: "I am courting your favor, doing everything you wish, be nice to me."

Impatient: "It's time for you to cure me (by magic)."

Seductive: "Meanwhile, make love to me (the magic of your love will cure me)."

Upon feeling rejected by the physician:

Expiatory: "Your aloofness fills me with guilty fear. I should like to expiate for my disobedience and promise to be obedient—please forgive me."

Resentful: "When I was a child my parents never let me have my way. You said yourself that's how they started my intimidation and illness. It's *your* job to undo the wrong they did me. True, you urge me 'to get it off my chest,' but you hold me in your clutches just the same. You can't fool me."

Coercive: "Now I am really furious. Stop this double talk and cure me."

Vindictive: "I shall get even with you . . . I never wish to see you again."

The patient must learn to view life, himself, and others in terms of opportunities and responsibilities, successes and failures. He must learn to understand his doings in terms of motivation and control, to evaluate his doings in terms of the cultural context, and to understand his development in terms of his background and life history.

The meaning of non-reporting (unconscious) motivation can be stated only in extrapolated terms of conscious motivation [11, 15]; the strength of non-reporting motivation can be determined only in relation to the strength of conscious motivation. Therefore interpretation must always embrace the conscious as well as the non-reporting phases of motivation. Even when the biographical material on hand reaches far into the past, interpretation must always begin and end with the patient's present life performance, his present adaptive task. The significance of this rule cannot be overstated.

A mathematical interpretation may be a purely intellectual process. A therapeutic interpretation must engender in the patient an emotional process or else miss its purpose. Freud described psychoanalytic therapy as a process of re-education; I should like to stress that it is pre-eminently a process of *emotional* re-education. In behavior disorders emotions control reason; a crucial goal of treatment is to adjust emotion to reason. Insight alone has little if any therapeutic effect. This is pre-eminently true of painful insight which is at the mercy of the patient's next emotional upheaval. Using the material of his own life experience, we show the patient how brute emotions, emotional thought, and unemotional thought differ from one another in integrative action [13, 14]. He can learn to change his faulty pattern of emotional responses in one way only: by practice; he must begin to do this before the eyes of the physician. Thus, the process of emotional re-education always begins with the therapeutic release of the resentments of his current life situation. Rage glues the patient's attention to the past, to the damage he believes to have suffered; he must learn to look to the future, learn from the damage and seek repair if and when possible. If the patient arrives in the physician's office in a state of acute emotional distress, the first order of business is of course to relieve his distress.

Let me show with one example how emotional re-education works. Suppose the patient is in a state of apprehension, unable to tackle an inescapable task. Asked to give free rein to his thought, he piles up his memories of failure at comparable tasks. Emotional thought tends of course to justify and thus to feed the emotion from which it springs and by which it is controlled. We can indeed see that his apprehension grows. Suppose further that by a stroke of good luck he not only arrives at the historical origin of this particular apprehension but also discovers its connection with a latent fear of damage to his sexual anatomy. In whatever frame of reference the physician interprets this material, with whatever skill, the patient will leave the office more disheartened than he was when he came. I have seen this often enough in my patients and in patients of other analysts.

There is a silver lining in every cloud. Memories can be looked at from many angles. More often than we think, even memories of true failure, not to speak of memories of presumed failure, do contain elements of success. The therapeutic task is to neutralize the perturbing power of memories of failure by playing up the elements conducive to pleasure [10]. If this is done on a sufficiently large scale the patient advances from unwarranted despair to warranted hope. We need not fear that we will becloud his judgment and teach him how to deceive himself. On the contrary, it is only when this emotional neutralization succeeds and his fears and rages subside that he becomes capable of clear thought and realistic judgment. This procedure, the *emotional redefinition of memories,* is a powerful aid in the task of transforming the patient's emotional outlook or, as we may put it, his field of emotional expectation, and restoring his lost self-confidence. These changes are a prerequisite of all further emotional learning.

One need not fear that treatment at the adult level of co-operation deprives the patient of the requisite emotional incentive. At first the child learns only if he loves those who teach him. Later he discovers the intellectual and practical value of the subject matter to which he is exposed. He then develops the proper emotional incentives for learning by taking pleasure and pride in his growing knowledge and skills. If the patient missed out on this development he must acquire the proper emotional mechanism of learning in his treatment.

A unique instrument of emotional re-education is the therapeutic analysis of the patient's dreams; the proved value of dream analysis is considerably increased by a revised procedure. Other innovations are the preventive handling of the patient's riddance impulses [8, 13], known in the psychoanalytic literature as "acting out"; the reversal of the vicious circles of disorder into benign ones, and the dissolution of still accessible inhibitions. Here I can do no more than mention these subjects. The same applies to the development of special procedures for the treatment of the patterns of self-damaging defiance and sexual pain-dependence, other common sexual disorders, and the obsessive and depressive patterns [16].

Concluding remarks on the adaptational technique

Viewed in its entirety, treatment with the adaptational technique takes place in a different intellectual and emotional climate. As elsewhere in medicine, this change can be ascertained only through the physician's own practical experience. This of course requires thorough familiarity with all the details and finesses of the adaptational technique.

Scientific psychotherapy has undergone a process of gradual liberalization that has lifted the patient in status from subject to citizen. Breuer's patient must be recognized as the pioneer of this development. It was her good fortune and the good fortune of psychotherapy that she sought help from a physician of the scientific stature of Joseph Breuer. Breuer replaced the ancient prohibitive technique of hypnotherapy with his permissive technique. There followed the emancipation of psychotherapy from the hypnotic state, and its advance to the various forms of suggestive therapy. Freud's catharsis in the waking state led to his discovery of free association and of the patient's biography as a proper subject of medical study. This marked the beginning of a new epoch of psychotherapy based on psychodynamic principles. Freud's discovery of parentifying treatment behavior opened up the patient's emotional relationship to the physician and posed it as a crucial problem of all psychotherapy. However, under the metaphysical guise of a repetition-compulsion, the classical technique relapsed: it re-introduced the authoritarian principle in the treatment of the patient. The adaptational technique is an attempt to restore the line of development initiated by Breuer's patient.

The Task Ahead

Digging in the patient's past yields diminishing returns. This fact poses a host of unexplored problems. Our technical skill in dealing with emotions is still in its infancy. Emotional resonance, known in everyday life as the contagiousness of emotions, is a significant mechanism in the therapeutic interaction of patient and physician; it awaits experimental investigation. Work on the patient's completely automatized inhibitions has hardly begun; as yet we have only glimpsed the mechanism of reinforcement.

The adaptational technique pursues the Freudian goal of total reconstruction. However, adaptational psychodynamics and some of the new principles of the adaptational technique can be used to develop a variety of other treatment procedures that would attain lesser goals in much shorter time. The social need for what I call trouble-shooting and easing methods of treatment is pressing.

Though therapy is obviously a process of interaction of patient and physician, the psychodynamics of the physician is still a rather neglected chapter of inquiry. We have viewed the patient's designs for co-operation in terms of a four-level scheme; we shall have to view the therapeutic intentions of the physician in terms of a corresponding scheme. We shall have to explore how the physician's own emotional matrix influences his choice of method, and how the fluctuations in his own emotional state influence his conduct of the treatment.

We may look forward with confidence to the future development of psychoanalytic therapy.

References

[1] BREUER, J. AND S. FREUD: Studies in hysteria. New York, Nervous and Mental Disease Publishing Company, 1936. Published in German. 1895.

[2] FERENCZI, S.: The principle of relaxation and neocatharsis. *Int. J. Psychoanal.*, 11:428, 1930.

[3] FREUD, S.: Freud's psychoanalytic method. In *Collected papers*, 1:264, London, 1925. Published in German, 1904.

[4] FREUD, S.: Papers on technique. In *Collected papers*, 2:285. London, 1924. Published in German, 1910-1919.

[5] FREUD, S.: "Transference" and "the analytic therapy." In *A general introduction to psychoanalysis*, New York, 1935. Published in German, 1917.

[6] FREUD, S.: Analysis terminable and interminable. In *Collected papers*, 5:316, London, 1950. Published in German, 1937.

[7] RADO, S.: The economic principle in psychoanalytic technique. *Int. J. Psychoanal.*, 6:35, 1925.

[8] RADO, S.: Developments in the psychoanalytic conception and treatment of the neuroses. *Psychoanalyt. Quart.*, 8:427, 1939.

[9] RADO, S.: The relationship of patient to therapist. *Am. J. Orthopyschiat.*, 12:542, 1942.

[10] RADO, S.: Pathodynamics and treatment of traumatic war neurosis (traumatophobia). *Psychosom. Med.*, 4:362, 1942.

[11] RADO, S.: Mind, unconscious mind and brain. *Psychosom. Med.*, 11:165, 1949.

[12] RADO, S.: Between reason and magic. 105th annual meeting of the Am. Psychia. Ass., Montreal, Quebec, 1949.

[13] RADO, S.: Emergency behavior; with an introduction to the dynamics of conscience. In *Anxiety* (Eds. Hoch and Zubin), New York, Grune and Stratton, 1950.

[14] RADO, S.: On the psychoanalytic exploration of fear and other emotions. *Transact. N. Y. Acad. Sc. II*, 14:280.

[15] RADO, S.: Hedonic control, action-self and the depressive spell. In press.

[16] RADO, S.: Behavior disorders: their dynamics and classification. To be published.

GLOSSARY

Abreaction: the re-experiencing of emotion associated with a forgotten event in a psychotherapeutic situation.

Alloplastic: referring to deviant interpersonal behavior, as seen in psychopathic states; see *autoplastic*.

Ambivalence: the simultaneous occurrence of two opposing emotions, such as love and hate.

Amnesia: loss of memory.

Anal character: (see pp. 298-319).

Anxiety: a state of apprehension, with bodily signs and symptoms, in which the danger is not objective.

Autism: a more or less exclusive preoccupation with one's own inner self.

Autoerotism: sexual behavior directed toward one's own body.

Autoplastic: referring to deviant behavior based on intrapsychic forces, as distinguished from deviant behavior induced by interpersonal forces.

Castration fear: the fear of a traumatic removal of the genitalia as punishment for forbidden sexual desires.

Catharsis: the purging of the mind of repressed emotional material by verbalization or acting out in a psychotherapeutic situation.

Cathexis: investment of an object or concept with emotional energy.

Character: the relatively permanent set of attitudes and modes of behavior.

Compulsion: a compelling need to perform an act alien to the conscious wishes of the individual.

Condensation: the unconscious representation of two or more people, ideas or emotions by one symbol.

Conscious: that which is in awareness.

Consensual validation: the confirmation of the correctness of one's own attitudes, beliefs, or emotions by another.

Conversion hysteria: a type of neurosis in which somatic symptoms symbolically represent a repressed emotion.

Death instinct: (see pp. 5-8).

Displacement: the shifting of emotion from one object to another or from one part of the body to another.

Ego: in Freud's terminology, that part of the psychic apparatus which is in contact with the environment, and which mediates between the needs of the id and the demands of the superego.

Electra complex: a term formerly used to describe the erotic attachment of a female child to her father (now included in the term *Oedipus complex*).

Electroencephalogram: a record of the varying electrical potentials in the brain.

Empathy: a perception of the state of feeling of another person obtained through processes not involving verbalization or other conscious communication.

Eros: (see pp. 5-8).

Erotogenic (or Erogenous) zones: areas of the body which give rise to libidinal responses, e.g. oral, anal, genital.

Fixation: the arrest of personality development at a pregenital stage of development.

Free association: the uncensored verbalization of all that comes to mind in an analytic situation.

Genital stage: the final libidinal stage in which the genital interest is directed toward others.

Gestalt(en): the total configuration in contrast to the detailing of the parts.

Id: that part of the psychic apparatus which contains unconscious instinctual drives.

Interpretation: a statement made by the analyst to clarify or revise previously held conceptions.

Kinesthesia: the awareness of muscular movement and position.

Latency period: Freud's term for the period in childhood during which sexual activity is absent, usually extending from the fifth or sixth year until puberty.

Libido: in psychoanalytic theory the psychic energy of the sexual instincts.

Masculine protest: in Adlerian psychology, the drive for masculine supremacy (mastery) designed to compensate for a basic feeling of inferiority.

Mother fixation: excessive dependency in an adult on the mother.

Narcissism: a) primary: original self-love (normal).
b) secondary: erotic involvement with oneself resulting from interference in the development of the love impulse toward others.

Negativism: automatic opposition to the real or fancied manipulation by others.

Oedipus complex: the erotic attachment of a child to the parent of the opposite sex [based on the well-known Greek myth].

Obsession: uncontrollable repetitive desire or thought felt as being foreign to the person.

Ontogeny: the developmental history of the individual.

Parataxis: Sullivan's term used to describe distortions of the present in terms of the past; similar to transference.

Participant observation: a term used by Sullivan that makes explicit the fact that the therapist-observer is also a participant in the therapeutic process.

Phallic stage: a libidinal stage in which the genital interest is directed toward the self as contrasted with the genital stage.

Phylogeny: developmental history of a race.

Pleasure principle: the hypothesis by Freud that the libidinal instincts have but one drive, pleasure.

Polymorphous—perverse: undifferentiated sexual strivings, normal in infants.

Polypragmasy: simultaneous administration of many drugs or of an excessive quantity of drugs.

Primary process: the completely free expression of libidinal drives, as contrasted with *secondary process*.

Regression: in Freudian theory the return to an earlier phase of libidinal development.

Repetition Compulsion: a pressing need to repeat early experiences for the purpose of reliving the residual anxiety associated with them.

Repression: a process by which anxiety-laden impulses, thoughts and emotions are made unconscious.

Resistance: the unconscious defenses which thwart self-exploration.

Schizoid: a personality type characterized by excessive shyness and withdrawal; akin to but not identical with schizophrenia.

Screen memory: a vivid but in itself relatively unimportant memory-recall which replaces one laden with anxiety.

Secondary process: inhibitions or fixations of libido which modify the free expression of libidinal drives (see *primary process*).

Security operation: Sullivan's term to describe a defensive operation designed to minimize anxiety.

Self-dynamism: Sullivan's term for the organization of the self, its security operation, and its modes of securing satisfactions.

"Shock" treatment: the treatment of the psychiatric patient by chemical or physical means which produce convulsions.

Sublimation: the process of diverting unacceptable, unconscious libidinal drives into socially acceptable channels.

Substitution: a mental mechanism in which one concept is replaced by another.

Superego: in Freud's terminology that part of the psychic apparatus which has a censoring and censuring function toward the ego in relation to the demands of the id; hence related to conscience.

Transference: the distorted perception of the present in terms of the past, whereby the individual attributes to people in his current life the attitudes and emotions of those in his early family constellation.

Unconscious: that which is outside of awareness.

Vegetative: referring to that part of the nervous system which controls the involuntary activities of the organism; consists of sympathetic and parasympathetic systems.

Wolfman: the popular name given to one of Freud's early patients.